SPAIN: THE ROOT AND THE FLOWER

By the same author

THE EPIC OF LATIN AMERICA

MEXICO TODAY

SPANISH AMERICAN LIFE

FEDERICO GARCÍA LORCA

PANORAMA DE LAS AMERICAS

ITALY: A JOURNEY THROUGH TIME

GREECE: THE MAGIC SPRING

SPAIN
The Root and the Flower

An Interpretation of Spain and the Spanish People

Third Edition, Expanded and Updated

JOHN A. CROW

UNIVERSITY OF CALIFORNIA PRESS
Berkeley   Los Angeles   London

University of California Press
Berkeley and Los Angeles, California

University of California Press, Ltd.
London, England

Fourth California paperback printing 2005

Library of Congress Cataloging in Publication Data

Crow, John Armstrong.
  Spain : the root and the flower.

  Bibliography: p. 435
  Includes index.
  1. Spain—Civilization. 2. National characteristics,
Spanish. I. Title.
DP48.C8 1985   946   84-8652
ISBN 0–520–24496-6 (pbk : alk. paper)

Printed in the United States of America

10 9 8 7 6 5 4 3 2 1

This book is printed on New Leaf EcoBook 60,
containing 60% post-consumer waste, processed
chlorine free; 30% de-inked recycled fiber,
elemental chlorine free; and 10% FSC-certified
virgin fiber, totally chlorine free. EcoBook 60 is
acid-free and meets the minimum requirements of
ANSI/ASTM D5634-01 (*Permanence of Paper*).

*To the people of Spain, whose culture
has absorbed my entire professional life*

CONTENTS

Preface   xi

1 THE LAND: THE PEOPLE   1

2 THE DARK BEGINNING   23

3 THE CROSS, THE CRESCENT, AND
   THE STAR   46

4 THE CHRISTIAN KINGDOMS: CROSS
   AND SWORD   78

5 LIFE IN THE MEDIEVAL TOWNS   113

6 THE SPANISH RENAISSANCE   139

7 THE GOLDEN AGE: POLITICS AND THE
   SOCIAL ORDER   161

8 BELLES-LETTRES IN THE GOLDEN AGE   185

9 THE FINE ARTS—END OF THE GOLDEN AGE   212

10 THE BOURBONS   228

11 MAIN CURRENTS OF SPANISH THOUGHT   258
   (1870–1931)

12 THE POLITICAL AND SOCIAL BACKGROUNDS   284
OF THE SECOND REPUBLIC

13 THE SPANISH REPUBLIC (1931–1939)   304

14 COMMUNISM AND FASCISM IN SPAIN   326

15 VALLEY OF THE FALLEN   346

16 FRANCO'S LEGACY: ORDER AND PROGRESS   370

THE ECONOMIC MIRACLE   370

THE TOURIST INDUSTRY   376

THE ECONOMY   380

SALARIES, PRICES, INFLATION   383

PROBLEM AREAS   384

AGRICULTURE   384

LABOR   395

EMIGRATION   396

17 SPAIN TODAY: THE IMPOSSIBLE DREAM   399

A SOCIETY IN TRANSITION

References   435

Important Dates in Spanish History   441

Glossary of Spanish Words   445

Index   447

PREFACE

This book is a history and an interpretation of the civilization of Spain from its earliest beginnings. There are chapters on the Romans, the Jews, and the Moors in Spain, and particular attention has been paid to Spanish art, literature, architecture, and music. I have not tried to write a topical or journalistic portrait of Spain today, although the Franco regime and today's democracy are soberly presented. My primary intention has been to analyze the main currents in the ebb and flow of Spanish life. There are no long lists of all the kings, queens, and ministers of Spain, nor any detailed account of every war or political change which the country has undergone. This book is not straight history. History usually emphasizes political events. My purpose has been to emphasize the underlying feelings and *mores* which bring about these events.

My first visit to Spain was in 1928, during the Primo de Rivera dictatorship, while Alfonso XIII was still king. Since then I have returned many times, and during the republic remained for two years in order to obtain my degree of Doctor in Philosophy and Letters from the University of Madrid. While in the country I came to know personally many of Spain's leading writers: García Lorca, Antonio Machado, Juan Ramón Jiménez (winner of the Nobel Prize), Américo Castro, Menéndez Pidal, Pedro Salinas, Moreno Villa, and a great many others. All of them have contributed to the development of my own ideas concerning Spanish civilization. No one but myself, however, is in any way responsible for any statement or opinion expressed in this book.

JOHN A. CROW
University of California
Los Angeles

SPAIN: THE ROOT AND THE FLOWER

1

THE LAND: THE PEOPLE

This land is the Paradise of the Lord.
                                    Alfonso X, 1252–1284

Spain is like a great castle that rises from the sea. The entire perimeter of the country is marked by ranges of mountains. Within the ring of these soaring walls of granite lies the courtyard of the castle, the vast tableland of Castile. Some of the higher surrounding peaks are covered with snow during many months of the year, hence the name *Sierra Nevada* (snow-covered sierra), a name the Spaniards brought to the United States. The mountains of Spain have, in general, a harsh and lonely aspect. They are craggy, rough, serpentine, lofty, frequently scarped; they have surprisingly few trees and are sparsely populated. They are seen to best advantage at sunrise or at sunset when a great sweep of rose-colored or lilac shadow clothes them with a majestic serenity.

To the ancients the shape of Spain resembled a bull's hide staked out in the sun. The comparison is an apt one, but gives an insufficient idea of the gouged out and serrated character of the land. The entire nation is a vast jumble of mountains, running in almost all directions, thus effectively walling off the distinctive regions. Even the central tableland of Castile is broken into smaller segments by transverse interior ranges. Madrid, the capital, close to the geographic heart of the country, is only thirty-five miles south of the Guadarrama range whose lowest pass to the north is 4,700 feet above sea level.

The traveler in Spain is seldom out of the sight of mountains. They are the most typical feature of the physiography of "the hard land of Iberia."

The geographic unity of Spain, therefore, is an illusion. Although the country has a compact appearance on the map, her various regions were, for centuries, mutually inaccessible. The locomotive and the airplane have reduced this inaccessibility, but communications in Spain are still behind those of Italy. The country's compact land mass is geographically subdivided into smaller regions which correspond roughly to the old Roman areas of the peninsula, and reflect more precisely still the petty Spanish kingdoms of medieval times. Each of these separate regions is characterized by geographic, climatic, cultural, psychological, even linguistic differences. In many areas the children speak only the local dialect until they enter school, where they are taught Castilian. A few miles outside of metropolitan Barcelona live thousands of adult countryfolk who, sans benefit of schooling, do not know Spanish. Catalan is their language; they are proud of it, and want no other.

Pío Baroja, possibly the greatest Spanish novelist of this century (Hemingway called him "Master"), was a Basque who did not learn Castilian until he attended school. His Spanish style strikes many Castilians as having an odd and acrid quality.

My difficulty in writing Castilian, [he says in his autobiography] does not arise from any deficiency in grammar nor any want of syntax. I fail in measure, in rhythm of style, and this shocks those who open my books for the first time. They note that there is something about them that does not sound right, which is due to the fact that there is a manner of respiration in them, a system of pauses, which is not traditionally Castilian.[1]

Sometimes, in considering the language and attitudes of the inhabitants of the outlying regions of Spain, it will be noted that far more than the respiration is different. There is a considerable basis of truth in the old statement that every Spaniard's first loyalty is to his *patria chica*, his small homeland or native region. Ask him where he is from and the answer will almost invariably be: *Soy hijo de Galicia, soy hijo de Granada*, "I am a son of Galicia, I am a son of Granada," or of Asturias, León, Navarre, Aragon, Castilla, Valencia, Catalonia, or Andalusia. Perhaps, after that, he is willing to be a Spaniard. If a fair plebiscite were held today on this very issue in Catalonia, the province of which Barcelona is the capital, no one could foretell what the results might be. During the Spanish civil war (1936–1939) there still existed "the Catalan republic," and autonomy in that region has never ceased to be an explosive issue. Thus, the struggle for a stronger nationhood, carried on unceasingly for so many centuries by the Castilians, has been impeded at every step by this primary loyalty to the native region. Nevertheless, the core spirit of Spain or *España* as we know her today is Castilian; but the core of the apple is not its fruit. It bears only the protective fiber and the seeds.

To keep the record straight it must be pointed out that this longing for separatism, so strong in Catalonia and in the Basque provinces, does not express itself with such vigor in the other regions, where Castilian political hegemony is an accepted fact of life. Local intransigence asserts itself here in other ways, in the culture, in the psychology, and in the customs of the inhabitants. This excessive regionalism emerges as one of the basic weaknesses of whatever system of national government the Spaniards have devised. Symptomatic of this disunion for many centuries was the country's lack of a fixed capital. Paris and London have been the centers and capitals of their respective countries since their foundation. The capital of Spain was successively Toledo, León, Burgos, Seville, Valladolid, Segovia, and other cities. Madrid was only a sprawling country town when Philip II finally moved his capital there from Toledo in 1561. But by this time Spanish character was formed, regional loyalties were fixed, and the new capital, despite its phenomenal growth in population in recent years, has presided over the decline of Spain as a great power.

The climate of Spain is as variegated as its geography. The wet, green, cloud-filled northwest (Galicia and Asturias) differs from subtropical southern Spain (Andalusia) as much as Vermont does from Texas. The wide, blue *rías* (fjords) of Galicia are a far cry from the shrunken rivers of Castile, the Adaja of Avila, and the Manzanares at Madrid. The fertile *vega* of Granada does not faintly resemble the red-brown steppes of Segovia or the calcined sterility of certain areas around Murcia where the slight moisture that falls dries up quicker than a woman's tears. There are, nevertheless, two principal climatic zones in Spain. The northern perimeter of the country (Pyrenees and Cantabrian areas) constitutes the cool, wet belt; the much larger central and southern portion of the country is the dry and "sunny Spain" of song and story. Botanically this division may be noted by the oleander (*adelfa*) and carob trees (*algarrobos*) of the south, and their general absence in the north.

The central tableland of Castile comprises approximately 60 per cent of the total area of Spain. The elevation of this great plateau varies between two thousand and three thousand feet. This Castilian *meseta* is not only the heart but also the citadel of Spain. It is a land of dryness, of treeless mountains, and of waterless plains. The air is clear and sharp, blistering in summer, bitterly cold in winter. *Nueve meses de invierno y tres de infierno* ("Nine months of winter and three of hell"), says the proverb. The icy blasts that sweep down on Madrid from the Guadarramas in midwinter have frozen sentries at their posts. Sun and shadow in Madrid in any month of the year can be poles apart. The plateau air is like a rarefied gas responding readily to the heat or cold.

A great feeling of loftiness and space pervades the atmosphere of Castile. This is the part of Spain that has given to the country its stern character, its primitive robustness, its stoic endurance to pain and suffering, its vitality and its bareness. Castile is a stark and flinty land, emblematic of its inhabitants, formerly a land of castles (hence its name), today an area of rock-fenced fields, of stark denuded landscapes, of vast silences and great distances. A Spanish proverb states: "There is in Castile hardly a branch on which a bird may light." The thick forests of ancient times have long since disappeared. Even the houses and fences are now of stone. The few trees are mostly *encinas,* a scrubby wild oak of unimpressive proportions. Everywhere there are rocks, granitic mountains, gouged-out, eroded fields, horizons that are monkish in their austerity.

The Cid, that renowned warrior hero whose dignity and courage are made immortal in the starkly beautiful epic of Spanish literature, *The Poem of the Cid,* was a Castilian. Also Castilian were Fernando the Saint, who drove the Moors from Sevilla, and his son, Alfonso X, the Learned, the famous scholar king who gathered around himself the most brilliant minds of his day (Moors, Hebrews, and Christians). Isabella the Catholic, wife of Ferdinand, was a Castilian, and so was Miguel Cervantes, most famous of all Spanish writers. The great literature of Spain is also Castilian; even when written by persons from other regions the language is *castellano.*

Castile is likewise the key to Spain's communication systems. Madrid, in the very center of the Castilian *meseta,* is the hub or axis of all rail, highway, and air lines in the country. Like the spokes in a wheel all lines depart from Madrid. The Spanish railways were never outstanding for their comfort or for their modernity, but now, despite their rather generally outworn equipment, they do link together most of the peninsula.

The railway that goes from Madrid into Galicia or the Cantabrian area gradually leaves the Castilian plateau and climbs steadily upward to enter an area of transverse mountains through which it turns and winds like a serpent of steel slowly boring into earth and rock. There are so many tunnels that the pupils of one's eyes scarcely have time to get used to the light when suddenly the train hurls itself again into a dark and cavernous labyrinth that pierces another mountain. The inaccessibility of the outlying areas of the peninsula is made clear by these coiled strings of tunnels and the many miles of precarious ledges along which the railway must pass, as laboriously, sometimes at a snail's pace, it gnaws up the distance.

The first railway in Spain was that which ran from Barcelona to Mataró in 1848; the second was the line from Madrid to Aranjuez in 1851. The Spaniards were a few years late in getting their trains, as they have been a few years late in getting nearly every other product of industrial civilization. However, people in Spain were not completely ignorant of what a railway looked like, for as early as 1830 a Spanish book (printed in London, to be sure) carried a rude sketch of the new steam engine and its wagons. This book contained a drawing of a seaport in which there was a factory belching smoke, and in front of it a small square box of steel, also spewing smoke; this was followed by some odd-looking coaches separated from each other by at least a yard, and across these open spaces were links of chain. It was not until eighteen years later, as we have pointed out, that there was a real train on Spanish soil. This was twenty-three years later than the English had their first steam rail line, eighteen years later than the United States, and eighteen years later than neighboring France.

The idea of a rail line linking Spain with France naturally occurred to some Spaniards. But the memory of the French invasions of 1808 and 1823 was still vivid in many minds, and the reception given the suggestion was anything but enthusiastic. In 1842, as a matter of fact, the construction of an ordinary road between Pamplona and France was discussed in the Spanish senate, and one senator, a certain General Seoane, opposed it vigorously. "Lack of foresight, and a very great lack of foresight indeed," remarked the general, "was the opening of the highway through Irun. Spain weeps for this, and God forbid that we should have cause to weep anew." Another senator,

González Castejón, was even more vehement in his plea: "My constant opinion," said this gentleman, "has been that never, for any reason whatsoever, should the Pyrenees be levelled; rather, on the contrary, other Pyrenees laid on top of the mountains we now have would suit us a great deal better." General Seaone added that he would resign his position as senator before he would vote for such an iniquity. Forty years later, in 1881, a book on military matters in Spain pointed out that "anything that tends to isolate us is to our advantage. Some of the doors we already have open to France ought to be closed posthaste."[2]

The line between France and Madrid was not opened until 1860, and until very recent years (1947) there was no railway between Madrid and Valencia, the country's third largest city. It is a curious historic fact that George Stephenson himself, inventor of the first practical steam locomotive in 1814, visited Spain in the autumn of 1845. He had come to study the projected rail line between Madrid and France. Stephenson and the engineers who accompanied him were given the usual Spanish runaround by the Spanish government, and after frittering away several fruitless days in the capital the Britishers became bored and were ready to leave the country. The Spaniards invited them all to a bullfight, the eternal bullfight. Stephenson's biographer writes: "But as this was not exactly the object of their trip, they courteously refused the honor." Stephenson and his companions left Spain, and the railway was not constructed.

Spain is not only a castle, it is also, for all practical purposes, an island. The country's insularity is proverbial. She belongs neither to Europe nor to Africa, but is a way station in between with qualities of each. Spain has ceased to be European by virtue of her Moorish blood. "Africa begins at the Pyrenees," is more than an apt phrase. It expresses succinctly the exotic, half-oriental quality which gives to the people and to the culture of Spain their most distinctive features. One must be careful to specify that the Africa here referred to is not the lower part of the Dark Continent peopled by black men. It is northern Africa, the ancient homeland of the Iberians, of the Carthaginians, a Semitic race, of the Jews themselves, and of the Moors, composed of many Arabic-speaking groups. All of these ethnic and cultural groups have poured their blood and energy into the dead-end funnel that is Spain. The towering Pyrenees have sealed that funnel off from the rest of Europe more effectively than the Alps have ever sealed off Italy. Their average altitude, in fact, is higher than that of the Alps. In any case, insularity is a state of mind and a way of life; it is not merely a matter of mountains, or altitudes, or islands.

The name that a country bears will often give some insight into the attitudes and history of her people. Spain was first called Iberia, a name given to the land by its Iberian inhabitants (of African stock). The name was supposedly based on the Iberian word for river, *Iber*. When these desert folk arrived in Spain they saw the country as a land of great rivers. But any creek would probably have appeared impressive to the desert-dwelling Iberians, who reached Spain in the centuries of prehistory, possibly as early as 3000 B.C. When the Greeks arrived on Spanish soil, around 600 B.C., they referred to the peninsula as *Hesperia*, which means "land of the setting sun." When the Carthaginians came around 300 B.C. they called the country *Ispania* (from *Sphan*, "rabbit"), which means "land of the rabbits." Strangely, the long-eared, timid creature appears on the early Iberian coins. The Romans arrived a century later and simply adopted the Carthaginian name of the country, calling it *Hispania*. Later, this became the present-day Spanish name for the country, *España*. From this is derived our adjective Hispanic, and the Spanish words *español, hispano*, etc. Thus, because of the Romans and their language, the rabbits won out over the sunset and over the rivers.

The rabbit, like the Spaniard, never moves in a straight line, nor at a steady speed. It leaps about at a rapid but jerky pace, hurling itself first in one direction, then in another. Rabbits have always been numerous in Spain. Cervantes mentions them frequently in his narration of the travels of Sancho and Don Quixote. A rabbit stew is one of the main dishes of the countryfolk of Spain. The Spanish phrase for a great deception is *dar gato por liebre* ("to give one a cat instead of a hare"). As in the time of Martial, the hare is considered to be the glory of the edible quadrupeds. Anywhere one walks in the Spanish countryside the wild hare may suddenly appear. As the proverb states: *Donde menos se piensa salta la liebre*, "Where one least expects it the hare leaps up." It is the typical phrase for anything unexpected. A few months ago I visited the site of the famous Moorish Palace of Medina Azahara, a few miles from Córdoba. Above the ruins of this once marvelous creation of Moorish art rise a series of rolling hills, dotted here and there with a few scrawny live oaks and olive trees. As we stood watching the scene, and listening to two Cordobese extol the incomparable virtues and incomparable grace

of the dead idol of Córdoba, Manolete, a couple of wild hares suddenly leapt from a clump of grass and scurried across the hillside. The
Cordobese stopped talking momentarily and one of them pointed
out: "Those hills are full of rabid hares. The people dare not eat
them any more. It's an epidemic of national proportions." Then they
went back to the conversation on Manolete. The whole scene was a
symbol of the country today, rabid and hungry, but still talking
excitedly of the bullfight, or of some past victory, some ancient glory.

The landscape of Spain is everywhere impressive. The misty green
mountains and lovely wide *rías* of Galicia, the desolate rocky austerity
of Castile, the flowing fountains and irrigated *vega* of Granada, the
orange groves of Valencia and Seville, the long tortuous scar of the
Tagus as it winds around Toledo, each of these in its own way possesses an element of singular beauty. Also a bigness, a feeling of
spaciousness and of size. The only geographic element in Spain that
suggests smallness is the rivers. The rivers of Spain are puny, regardless of what the Iberians might have thought about them. During
a great part of the year most of them are but mere trickles of water
straggling along the bottoms of their dried and rocky beds. Even the
famed Guadalquivir, which made inland Seville one of the country's most important ports in ancient times and again in the sixteenth century, is an ugly, mud-colored river, unfit for navigation, and
unlovely to the sight. Alexandre Dumas, who viewed the Guadalquivir in 1846, describes it well in one of those charming letters to
the unidentified (and possibly nonexistent) French lady for whom
he recounted his adventures in Spain.

You may have quite a wrong impression of the Guadalquivir, Madame,
for Arab poets, who had never seen so much water, praised it to the
skies, and French writers, never having seen it at all, believed the Arabs.
True, Spanish writers could have revealed the less picturesque truth, but
since it is the only river in their country large enough to take a boat, why
should they decry it? When we got there we found that between the flat
and uninteresting banks rolled a mass, not of water, but of liquid mud
with the color and the consistency, if not the taste, of milk chocolate. We
stood scratching our ears for a moment in perplexity and disappointment.[3]

If Alexandre Dumas was so severely disappointed, it is easy to
imagine the feelings of the North American visitor, who has seen
the Mississippi, the Missouri, the Ohio, the Hudson, the Susque-
hanna, or the Columbia. Yet still today the poets of Spain sing the
praises of the Guadalquivir. García Lorca, whose untimely death in

1936 cut short the career of one of Spain's most promising young writers, makes a frequent refrain of its evocative waters. "Voices of death sounded on the Guadalquivir." In all fairness be it said that rivers are not only geography, they are also history, and evoke a state of mind inseparable from the experiences of the people who have lived and died along their banks throughout the centuries. Thus, in spite of their puny size and insignificant flow, the rivers of Spain call forth a telluric and nostalgic quality which ties in with the gaunt spaciousness of the Spanish landscape and the monkish severity of its colors.

Quien dice España dice todo, says the Spaniard, proud of the infinite variety of his land. ("Who says Spain, says everything.") Other Spaniards, seeking for an element of hope or of stability in their country, affirm heatedly that beneath all the regional variations Spain is one, that there is some mysterious alchemy of the land which holds it all together, some common denominator which gives the Spaniards the same character, the same aspirations, the same ideals. This wishful thinking has been going on among Spaniards for centuries, but the reality is that Spain is not a homogeneous country, with homogeneous strivings. Spain is heterogeneous at the base, and heterodoxy is her true religion. The only common denominator is that of sharing the same land and the same history which has created Spaniards out of something that was not Spanish before. But this element of Spanishness, españolismo, is a brittle thing which, with all the courage in the world, suffers inevitable fragmentation under stress. Theoretically, the majority of Spaniards do, of course, want happiness, justice, freedom, and a higher standard of living. But this is merely an illusory bond of union much like that linking the pompous preachers and politicians who strongly espouse civic virtues and lower taxes.

True, both the landscape and the peoples of Spain suggest a wild but static vitality, energies that are not canalized, promises undeveloped, an unfulfilled destiny. There is an awful tenacity to the Spanish character, and a powerful will that is proud as Lucifer. But the Spaniards have never learned to live or to work together. Strabo, the famous Greek geographer, wrote that the ancient Iberians, who were dauntless warriors, never learned to hold their shields together in battle. They fought bravely, but it was always every man for himself. Greek, Carthaginian, and Roman soldiers, in far fewer numbers, were repeatedly able to defeat the native population simply because of superior teamwork in battle. The static, primitive vitality of Spain has been repeatedly neutralized by a lack of direction, and a lack of concerted effort.

After living under the Romans for six centuries, then fighting the Moors for another eight centuries, the Spaniards did finally learn to hold their shields together, and by the fifteenth century the solid Spanish phalanx was the toughest military unit in the world. Perhaps there may be an equally long wait between learning how to fight together and learning how to live together. A modern Spanish writer, Pereda, in an essay on Spanish character, refers jocosely to the remarks of Chateaubriand, who once said that as soldiers the Spaniards were irresistible on the field of battle, but that as soon as the enemy had been dislodged from his position, they would throw themselves into it, a cigarette in the mouth and a guitar in the hands, to celebrate the victory. Pereda does not agree wholeheartedly with this estimate of Spanish temperament, but he sagely avers that if we

take a bit of the French color out of this picture, it will be true. Indeed, these remarks characterize us not only in warfare, but also in all the imaginable situations of life. Perhaps not the guitar, but national lassitude absorbs our five senses, and only when hunger pinches, or the itch to appear well-to-do and happy bites us, are we able to shake off our lethargy. We attack every problem with vigor, but indifference or violence soon overtakes us. And that's as far as we ever get. Our politics, our industry and our contemporary literature declare it well. Everyone else is ahead of us.

The words were written over half a century ago, but they characterize Spain today even better than they did the Spain of the time of Pereda. The same writer continues in these words:

We are always imitating everybody else, except when it comes to stepping ahead of the procession; we live on the castoffs of others and every rag that comes our way is greeted with mad enthusiasm, as if it were expressly cut for us. We view ourselves as *illustrious* statesmen, *invincible* warriors, *learned* economists, *distinguished* writers, *hard-working* industrialists, and *honorable* workers. We have had French codes of law, English codes of law, American codes of law; *revolutions* of every kind, *triumphs* of every caliber, *progress* of every size, manner, and form; yet at the present moment the citizen of Spain who owns his own bed considers himself well off.[4]

The Duke of Wellington once remarked that to boast of the strength of Spain was the national weakness. Today, more than a century later, no one in Spain boasts of the strength of his country. Not militarily, in any case. But almost everyone still calls to mind her past power and majesty, and General Franco himself was a puny imitator of Philip II. Every Spaniard, whatever his affiliation or region, still boasts of being Spanish. "We *might* have been a Christian Greece," wrote Ganivet, in those sad words characterizing his unhappy nation. If Spaniards praise Spain, however, and no one denies them the right, they also bitterly censure Spain, as the above sentences indicate. The criticism of Spaniards by Spaniards is indeed almost a literary genre. "If a man speaks well of France, he is French, if he speaks well of England, he is English, but if he speaks ill of Spain, then he is a Spaniard," so runs the old jingle known to every schoolchild in the land of the rabbits. Spanish criticism is frequently brilliant, but it is seldom constructive. It makes fine literature, but it rarely passes from the printed page or the fiery café speech to the arena of social action. The Spaniard will die bravely for his country or for his beliefs; he will, indeed, die at the barricades of Oviedo, Madrid, or Córdoba for universal justice and liberty, but he is unable to subordinate his personal beliefs in a collective and progressive political endeavor.

Spanish pride is legendary. Unamuno, former president of the University of Salamanca and a noted Spanish philosopher, in one of his essays points out that the Spanish John Smith (Juan López), if he has no other source of pride, will be inordinately proud that he is Juan López, because in the whole world there can be no other Juan López exactly like him. All of the qualities, good, bad, and indifferent, that have combined to form his personality will never again reunite in precisely the same proportions in any other individual. The Spaniard, thus, does not feel that he is born to realize any social end, but that he is born primarily to realize himself. His sense of personal dignity is admirable at times, exasperating at others; selfhood is the center of his gravity. His individual person has a value that is sacred and irreplaceable. In the universe he may be nothing, but to himself he is everything. This excessive personalism undoubtedly contributes to a weakened statehood; it also causes the Spaniard to see his main value in personal achievement or creativity, hence the truly great men and women of Spain have been the individual artist, architect, writer, musician, saint, conquistador, adventurer, explorer, poet. These are all fields in which peak expression may be realized without going outside of one's own person.

The Spaniards spring from an Afro-Semitic race, with a little leavening from the Romans and the northern European tribes. But their essential base is Afro-Semitic. The keynote of this primitive racial mixture is overwhelming individuality. The people of Spain are Spanish in much the same way that the Jew is Jewish. The Jew may be from any one of a number of regions or cultures, but he still has a bedrock of Jewishness which is his main source of pride and to which he will doggedly cling, often without being able to define it, and which he will defend with his whole heart and even with his life. The Spaniard, part Jewish and part Moor in blood, in psychology, and in his interpretation of reality and of destiny, possesses a quality that is analogous. This quality is not by any means a weakness; it is a strength unknown to the peoples of other nations. The only unfortunate thing is that up to now the Spaniard's tremendous energy and racial pride have not been applied in those areas of collective expression which the Western world has come to hold as its primary values: economic organization, democratic government, social cohesion, industrial development, any kind of collective enterprise. In the arts Spain has never lagged behind, except in periods of quiet desperation. Her great men, Cervantes, El Greco, Velázquez, Goya, Góngora, "are the equals or more than the equals of the great men of any other country, while our actual life is not equal to that of Morocco or of Portugal."[5]

To this root cause of exaggerated individualism, continues the philosopher Unamuno, may be attributed all that Spaniards have accomplished in history: their transient imperial greatness, their permanent tenacity, their excellence in the arts. "This feeling of individuality lies deep down in the root of the race and cunning politicians have turned it to the advantage of their ambitions."

Pío Baroja, in the prologue of one of his novels, points out that the strong individualities of Spain have usually been unquiet and tumultuous.

Spain [he says], which never had a complete social system and has unfolded her life and her art by a series of spiritual convulsions, as men of strength and action have come bursting forth, today feels herself ruined in her eruptive life, and longs to compete with other countries in their love for the commonplace and well-regulated and in their abhorrence for individuality.

In Spain, where the individual and only the individual was everything, the collectivist aspirations of other peoples are now accepted as indisputable dogmas. Today our country begins to offer a brilliant future to the man who can cry up general ideas and sentiments, even though these ideas and sentiments are at war with the genius of our race.[6]

Baroja wrote these words prior to the Franco regime. He was referring to the "democratic-bourgeois tendency of the day," not to the kind of Spanish fascism which induced Franco to attempt to revive Philip II's concept of the Spanish church-state. Baroja is wrong when he claims that the collectivist aspirations of other peoples now have common currency in Spain. General Franco's dynamics of "stepping courageously forward toward yesterday" was the final proof that such is not the case. But if the time should come when one of these collectivist aspirations turns into a religion (communism could be this religion), then watch out for the volcano!

Proud and poor, these two words fit the people of Spain like a glove. An old saying goes: "If God were not God he would be the King of Spain, and the King of France would be his cook." But the proverb which states that *altivez y pereza, llaves son de la pobreza* ("pride and lethargy are the keys of poverty") bears a closer scrutiny. The Spaniard, it is true, would prefer to be a soldier, a priest, or an adventurer rather than a laborer. But he is not lazy; he will carry out any task that is assigned to him with a diligence that is tireless. But he likes to perform it in his own way. The poverty of Spain comes from other things: a soil that has been denuded of trees and eroded by the rains, a government which has never had the people's welfare at heart, a system of latifundia or huge estates as outrageous of those of Persia or of Rome, which have left the masses of rural workers without land, a lack of decent housing, industry and technological development and, last of all, a wealthy class that will not share and a mass of workers who will not cooperate. These concrete items, not lethargy, explain the poverty of Spain. Is it any wonder that the Spaniard clings to pride, which is his only true wealth?

The proud and stoic attitude toward life of the Spaniard is, therefore, a philosophy of desperation. Seneca, a Roman born in Spain, expressed this attitude in cogent words: "Do not let yourself be conquered by anything alien to your spirit." Ganivet, a nineteenth century Spaniard, and a great admirer of Seneca, recapitulates the Roman writer's philosophy in these words:

Remember, in the midst of the accidents of life, that you have within you a vital energy, something strong and indestructible, like a diamantine axis, around which turn the petty happenings that form the fabric of your daily life; and whatever things may befall you, be they prospering, adverse, or reviling in their contact, hold yourself in such a manner firm and erect, that at least it may always be said of you that you are a man.

This is Spanish to the bone [adds Ganivet] and it is so completely Spanish that Seneca did not have to invent it, because he found it already invented. All he needed to do was to pick it up and give it a permanent form, thus operating as true men of genius always operate. The Spanish spirit, rough, without form, skeletal and naked, does not cover that primitive nakedness with artificial clothes: it clothes itself with the fig leaf of Senecquism.[7]

Then Ganivet points out that this same Senecquism has deeply touched the religious, moral, and even legal fiber of Spain, that it has penetrated Spanish art and folklore, that it is omnipresent in the proverbs, maxims, and sayings of the common people, that it even permeates many branches of cultivated learning. We might add that the very atmosphere and earth of Spain, particularly of Castile, represent a kind of stoic climate and geography. And Castile was preeminently the land of soldiers; the stoic and the soldier are necessarily one.

"Cortés is the equal of any Da Vinci," affirms another distinguished Spaniard, thus asserting Spanish equality during the Renaissance with Italy herself. In a word, Italy's contribution to the Renaissance was her universal men, her men gifted in all the arts, while the principal contribution of Spain was the conquistador. On the one hand, men who created art, and on the other, men who created nations. Whether or not the dictum is true does not really matter; what matters is that this typifies the Spanish point of view and is generally accepted by Spaniards.

"Spain was Christian perhaps before Christ"; this is another of the pithy statements of Seneca. Christianity was taken up by the Spaniards with an enthusiasm unparalleled in any other country. It is also a kind of Christianity that differs considerably from that of the other Catholic countries, and has even less in common with the cold, logical, dry, unfeeling Protestantism of northern Europe. The reason for this is that the Spaniards never gave up their paganism; they simply added Christianity to a pagan base. God is a concrete presence in the religious imagery of Spain. Later still, they took from Moor and Jew a sensuous feeling for religion which never reached the Protestant countries. Religion became both a passion and an art, and its ritual became a dazzling liturgy. Witness the brilliant pomp of Holy Week in Seville, where the Virgins are Byzantine empresses, witness the religious processions anywhere in Spain at Easter, witness the mysticism of many Spanish religious thinkers, a mysticism that is sensuality repressed by virtue and by misery.

Moor and Jew also gave to Spain that key concept of Spanish Catholicism: religion as a way to nationalism. With no other kind of unity to hold them together the petty Spanish states of medieval times made the banner of the Cross their military, and then their national standard. There have been only two successful crusades in history and Spain waged both: the crusade against the Moslem Moors, and the crusade to conquer and Christianize the pagan Indians of the New World. In Spain there never arose a single Protestant church. And throughout the Franco years, by governmental edict, no synagogue or Protestant church was allowed to put on its outside walls any kind of religious symbol, marking, letters, or identifying features of any kind whatsoever.

Spain is about twice the size of the British Isles and approximately the size of California plus about one-third of the state of Nevada. If we believe the ancient writers, it was once an Eden, a garden of splendor, of plenty and of delight. *Nihil otiosum, nihil sterile in Hispania* ("There was nothing idle, nothing barren in Spain"). This was a land of milk and honey, like the fabled Canaan of the children of Israel. It was an earthly paradise, as Alfonso X called it in his famous history. But now of all this richness and all these beauties so little is standing. The country remembers its past with a vital anguish that calls to mind some outworn god of antiquity lamenting the extinction of his cult. Ah, what this might have been, this poor, this tragic Spain! There is no region of Spain today that can compare in wealth to California. Still, her varied geography is the wonder of all travelers.

The principal regions of the country, beginning at the northwest corner, just above and bordering on Portugal, are as follows:

1. *The Cantabrian zone,* composed of Galicia, Asturias, and the Basque provinces. Of these Galicia is the most cloudy, foggy, and wet, but all three regions are green and cool, with fruitful fields, and an abundance of water. This is an area of rugged mountains, where the stone houses are perched firmly on hill and dale, and marked by a spiral of blue-gray smoke even in summer. Grains are stored in stone

or wooden chests called *hórreos*, which are raised from the ground on four legs in order to protect them from the rodents. Each bin of grain bears a cross at one end to invoke the protection of God. The country churches in these mountains are picturesque, gray and damp, of an anciency that is primitive and soul-stirring. The people of these mountains are deeply sentimental and melancholy; they have a passionate love of their homeland which in the Galician can become a real illness if he must live abroad. They call the sickness *morriña*, and celebrate it in song and story. The people in this part of Spain eat better than in the south, but they need to eat better in order to survive at all in their damp climate of eternal mists.

This region of Spain has produced many of the country's finest writers. Their descriptions of the Cantabrian mountains and its people are colored intensely with the inside view. The medieval school of Galician lyric poetry was western Spain's answer to the Provençal troubadour tradition which is much better known in European literary history. Also, some of the earliest songs preserved in Spain are those of a Galician minstrel of the thirteenth century named Martin Codax whose songs evoke the plaintive, mysterious, and nostalgic quality of this mountainous land. They were written to be sung by women whose men had gone off to war to fight the Moors; their words and melody are suffused with a sense of absence and loss. Some of these haunting songs, recently recorded, pull at the heart roots of a primitive past that lies buried within us deep in the unconscious.

Rosalía de Castro (1837–1885), illegitimate daughter of a Galician parish priest, has described her beloved province with exquisite feminine sensitivity. In her poems the beauty of the Galician landscape and the melancholy of its inhabitants are given form in simple, exquisite lines which call to mind the spontaneity and condensed emotive quality of folk couplets. Rosalía's tomb near Santiago is a regional shrine. In the prologue to one of her books Rosalía writes:

Lakes, cascades, torrents, flowering *vegas*, valleys, mountains, skies sometimes blue and serene as those of Italy, melancholy and clouded horizons, although always beautiful like those of Switzerland; tranquil and serene streams and shores, tempestuous capes that terrify and amaze by their gigantic and dull fury . . . immense seas . . . what more shall I say? There is no pen that can enumerate so many charms. The earth is covered in all seasons of the year with green grasses, herbs and flowers; the mountains are clad with pine trees, with oaks and with *salgueiros*; the gentle winds touch them lightly; the fountains and torrents gush forth to crystalline spray, summer and winter, now through the smiling field, now in the deep and shadowy glens. . . . Galicia is always a garden where sweet aromas, freshness and poetry are inhaled with every breath of air.

Another writer who remembered her native Galicia with deep nostalgia or *morriña* was Countess Emilia Pardo-Barzán, who spent her most active years in Madrid. She recalled the mountain peaks of her province, "like nests of eagles," and the magnificent chestnut trees "whose aroma fills the atmosphere and mixes its perfume with that of other sweet-scented herbs and trees," the tiny lichen "white as ermine, soft and compact as the fleece of a lamb," the rolling brooks that leap among the green fields and boulders "crowned by huge ferns," the ancient stone fountains "covered with parasitic plants and carpeted with greenish moss, over which the water glides, thread after thread, like tears on the cheeks of a person in sorrow."

A contemporary writer, Ramón María del Valle-Inclán (1866–1936), describes his native Galicia with overtones of tragedy and horror. Everywhere he finds "something alive and frightening, but which we cannot see." In the works of Valle-Inclán the atmosphere is always nebulous and mysterious; dogs howl in the night announcing some tragedy, the symbolic echo of the storms and sorrows of the world; characters are carved out of oak or solid rock; they sin fearfully and reap the awful consequences; things and figures move mysteriously or stand motionless in the pale light. Flocks of sheep return to their folds and "the repose of the fields frozen and rigid in the winter is scarcely disturbed by the tinkling of their bells." There is much rain, many somber clouds, and ancient churches and monasteries rise gauntly among the green hills, "producing an indefinable sensation of antipathy and of terror." Sometimes the sound of the sea is heard "fierce and ululating in the distance, as if it were a hungry wolf hidden among the pine groves."

2. *The Pyrenees region* lies to the east of the Cantabrian, and is made up of three provinces which begin on the Spanish side of the Pyrenees range and extend southward. The Pyrenees provinces are Navarre, Aragon, and on the east coast, Catalonia, with its great capital of Barcelona. To go eastward from Navarre to Catalonia is to move from a primitive country of stolid, hardheaded, jota-dancing peasants to a province of maritime wealth and thrifty, business-minded entrepreneurs. The Catalan is the Scotsman of Spain. He is

industrious and crafty, but he is also thrifty to a point of exaggeration, or so, at least, say the stories. I have not found it to be a fact, nor among Scotsmen either.

Pamplona, picturesque capital of Navarre, lies in a magnificent setting at the foot of the Pyrenees. Only twenty-eight miles to the north is the famous pass of Roncesvalles where Roland and Charlemagne's rear guard made their legendary stand against the Spaniards. It is Alpine scenery all the way: pine trees, wild roses, cascades of water, and lonely peaks. One remembers that in the *Song of Roland*, the French epic, Charlemagne, who was two hundred years old, could command the sun itself to stand still. Dying, Archbishop Turpin slays four hundred soldiers with his sword, and Roland with sixty men puts to flight an army of a hundred thousand. Finally, when brave Roland realizes the certainty of his death, he blows so loudly on his horn that his brain comes bursting out of his ears. No one had the power to slay this valiant knight; he had killed himself. There is nothing in Spanish literature like this. The Spaniards are realists, and the epic of the Cid is the story of a stalwart hero, rooted in the stern reality of his times.

The country of the Pyrenees is everywhere full of historic recollections, monuments. Every village recalls a battle. At Calahorra Sertorius resisted Pompey, at Tudela the French routed General Castaños, at Numantia, a few miles to the south, Scipio Africanus met a foe whose valor amazed the Romans, at Navarrete Peter the Cruel conquered Henry of Trastamare, at Saragossa, in Aragon, an entire city withstood the French army of Napoleon for nearly a year. There are Roman and Arab ruins and medieval monuments hoary with history and legend. The aspect of the country varies at every moment, but the background of the Pyrenees is a sublime fixture of the landscape. Saragossa is surrounded by its green fields, but farther on there are only undulating plains, barren and dry and bare.

The Ebro River winds in great curves along the road, now quite near, so that it seems as if the train would dive into it, now far away like a stream of silver that appears and disappears among the elevations of ground and bushes on the banks. In the distance one sees a chain of blue mountains, and beyond them the white summits of the Pyrenees. Near Tudela is a canal; after passing Castejón the country becomes verdant; and as one goes on, the arid plains alternate with olive trees, and some streaks of vivid green break here and there the dry yellowish look of the abandoned fields. On the tops of the distant hills appear the ruins of enormous castles, surmounted by broken, shattered, and corroded towers, resembling the giant torsos of prostrate giants who are still menacing.[9]

Barcelona, the great metropolis of the northeast coast, occupies a bay surrounded by mountains. A few miles outside the city is the monastery of Montserrat, legendary repository of the Holy Grail utilized in Wagner's *Parsifal*. Montserrat is a wild mountainous retreat, silent as an iceberg, banked around with crested rocks. It resembles the landscape of an uninhabited planet. Here in this secluded and mysterious place Ignatius Loyola pledged his soul to God and thus began his new life as a soldier of Christ; out of this vow arose the Society of Jesus, the Jesuit organization. They call their Virgin of Montserrat "the Rose of April, the dark one of the mountain." She is the patron saint of Catalonia, blackened by age and candle smoke. Emperor Charles V visited her nine times during his life and was at Montserrat when news of the conquest of Mexico reached him. Charles died clasping in his hand a candle from this shrine, as did his son, Philip II.

3. *The Castilian tableland*, or *meseta*, occupies the center of Spain. It is south of the Pyrenees region, and just inside and east of the Cantabrian part of Spain. To its west lies Extremadura, which is but an extension of New Castile, and after Extremadura comes Portugal. The Castilian tableland is composed of the ancient kingdoms of León, Old Castile, New Castile, and La Mancha, the southernmost part of the Castilian plateau. Don Quixote and Sancho Panza were from La Mancha. The train now roars across this flattened land of cultivated fields where in years gone by the hero of Cervantes and his stout squire tilted with windmills and scattered a herd of bawling sheep, taking them for an army of Moors. As the train or automobile hurtles along, the passenger can see against the horizon the jagged and lilac teeth of a distant range of mountains.

We have already described the area of Castile, but an inside view of this heart of Spain may add some further dimensions to our picture. The population of the Castilian *meseta* lives mostly in villages, hamlets and towns, which are separated from each other by great distances and immense naked solitudes. The people of this part of Spain zealously avoid the desolate loneliness of the plains; even the farmers live in small clusters of houses. This compactness gives them a feeling of security. Such is their heritage of fear from the many centuries of warfare against the Moors and against each other, during which of necessity they lived in towns as a measure of protection from the marauding armies. The Castilian countryside, unlike that of Galicia and Asturias, is often completely unpopulated. Clusters of farmhouses huddle around the church for warmth and as a defense against the rigors of nature and the desolation of the plateau. Oftentimes the villagers must travel great distances on muleback in order to work their fields, each field isolated from the others, each family isolated from the rest during the hours of labor.

A notable sight it is to see them at nightfall, mounted on their mules, their figures silhouetted against the pale sky, their sad, slow, monotonous songs dying away on the sharp air into the infinity of the furrowed plain.

In the long winter evenings it is usual for masters and servingfolk to assemble together, while the latter dance to the accompaniment of the sharp, dry tap of the tambourine, or sometimes to an old ballad measure.

Go into one of these villages or drowsing towns of the plain, where life flows slowly and calmly in a monotonous procession of hours, and there you will find the living soul beneath whose transitory existence lies the eternal essence out of which is woven the inner history of Castile.[5]

The Castilians are a dry and frugal breed, inured alike to sun and cold, sinewy of body, and with the stern dignity of dethroned kings. Their sobriety and endurance are legendary. They are realists by nature, sententious in their language, indefatigable. They do not take readily to a new idea. Their songs are lamentations, of long-drawn-out notes, songs of the steppes, suggesting the slow motion of the plow as it cuts through the hard, bare earth. Their vitality is sharp-edged and ascetic; their plateau has the clarity of nakedness and light. There has never been a school of landscape painters in Castile.

4. *Andalusia* is southern Spain. This is where the Moorish tradition is strongest. Granada, Córdoba and Seville are its most famous cities and its most famous provinces. The Moors called it *Al-Andalus*, land of the Vandals, hence the name Andalusia. This is the African part of Spain; its tall mountains, just behind the coastal plain, its rolling lower hills and olive groves, its fertile irrigated valleys, its Mediterranean climate—all these suggest northern Africa. The highways are rimmed by strange ancient hills and often on reaching a town the ruins of an old castle stand as mute testimony to the medieval or Moorish past. The fertile *vega* of Granada lies within the sight of mountain peaks capped with eternal snow. There are fields of sugarcane and of tobacco. There are palm trees, oleanders, myrtles, poplars, carnations, plumbago, and bougainvillaeas. Córdoba

lies breathless under a blazing sun, and in Seville one seeks the cool shadows. It is a land of warm winds and singing birds. It is a dry, parched, summer land, populated by a highly volatile, sensuous race whose African heritage is indisputable. Often, at night, the strange notes of a quavering guitar, and the eerie notes of some *cante jondo* song of southern Spain.

The songs of Andalusia, grouped under the general head of *cante jondo* or "deep song," differ radically from those of the other regions of Spain. They are wild tremulous laments of love, sadness, loss, and sometimes of religious passion, which have arisen spontaneously from the mixture of African-Moorish-Hebrew cultures of this part of Spain. Their sliding and fragmented notes, their sharp quavers which often suggest a piercing cry, their staccato accompaniment on the Spanish flamenco guitar, these qualities suggest in sound the trajectory of a gliding, wavering, and piercing arrow. When *cante jondo* songs are of a religious nature, expressing a plea for forgiveness, they are indeed called *saetas*, or "arrows" of song. The gypsies did not originate these songs, for they are mentioned by the Roman writers long before the gypsies reached Spain in the early fifteenth century. But today the gypsies do perform them with that peculiarly accurate, imitative grace which seems to be theirs in all lands.

5. *The Levant*, or East Coast, is the last of our five noteworthy regions of Spain. Its main area is the long narrow coastal province of Valencia, captured from the Moors centuries ago by Spain's national hero, the Cid. Valencia is the irrigated *huerta* or citrus- and rice-growing region of Spain. Without irrigation it would be as barren and windblown as the steppes. With irrigation it has blossomed like the rose. Water is rationed in Valencia by an ancient water tribunal which has presided over this vital and delicate task for nearly a thousand years. The area is one of the most productive on earth.

Where it touches the sea Valencia picks up the luminosity of the blue Mediterranean. The irrigated *huerta* back of the coast is a dark green mass of orange trees in endless groves. A reddish road winds among them. Scattered here and there are dwellings that are rose-colored, blue, or a gleaming white. Against the thick foliage are aromatic flowers and fruits. Thousands upon thousands of little globes of gold stand out among the leaves. The Valencian novelist, Blasco Ibáñez, describes it well:

The sky is of a brilliant blue that suggests terse silk. Near the seacoast are angular mountains, roughly scarped, with piercing towers that suggest a picture by Doré, and farther inland, floating above the emerald lakes of the groves at their feet another more distant mountain range is clad in purple mist. The sun glides among the gases formed by the evaporation of incessant irrigation.

Move away from the cultivated *vega* a few miles and the landscape changes completely, taking on suddenly the harsh and flinty aspect of the tableland of Castile.

Pío Baroja, the Basque writer, describes thus one of his journeys into this region of the East Coast:

I once rode to Valencia with two priests who were by no means unknown. We talked of our respective homes; they eulogized the Valencian plain while I replied that I preferred the mountains. As we passed some bare, treeless hills such as those that abound near Chinchilla, one of them remarked to me:
"This must remind you of your own country."
I was dumfounded. How could I identify those arid, parched, glinting rocks with the Basque landscape, with the humid, green shaded countryside of homeland? It was easy to see that the image of a landscape existing in the mind of that priest provided only the general idea of a mountain, and that he was unable to distinguish, as I was, between a green mountainside overgrown with turf and trees, and an arid hillside of dry rocks."[1]

Such is the face of Spain in all its variety, in all its mystery, in all its splendor. We cannot seek for a common denominator in geography, or in land forms, or in climate. Even the language lacks uniformity. Religion did once unify, but now divides, Spaniards. It has been said that *everybody* in Spain follows the Church, half of them with a candle, the other half with a club. This ancient unity, therefore, despite the frantic efforts of the Franco regime, is no more. There remains always the intangible bedrock of Spanish character, the element of Spanishness, of *hispanidad*. Perhaps the essence of the country can be found in its austere strength, its permanent vitality, but this too is an elusive quality. Whatever, wherever it is, the unity of Spain stands forth only as a vital structure of history, the sharing of a common destiny. Yet, harsh, primitive, bare, but rich in earth scent and spontaneous flowers, "in wild vegetation, in uncultivated grace, the Peninsula is in itself, apart from the people who inhabit it, a great power and a great presence."[10]

2

THE DARK BEGINNING

In Spain everything decays but the race.

Cánovas del Castillo

It is only about twenty miles from Santander, the port city of Old Castile, to the medieval village of Santillana del Mar and to the caves of Altamira which are just above this latter town. The road is heavy with traffic for most of the distance, and at one point it passes by a huge acid factory which spews the air with stinking fumes and smoke, dimming an otherwise brilliant sky. Santillana is a beautiful little medieval town, preserved much as it was many centuries ago, and with perhaps the same number of flies. There is an inn, run by the government, which occupies an ancient castle. The place has only eight rooms, so it is difficult to find lodging here. The narrow streets of Santillana belong to another epoch, but they are packed with the tourists of the twentieth century.

Despite the many impressive remains in Santillana (Romanesque architecture in its finest flower) the great glory of this place lies within the bowels of a hill above the town. The top of the hill is dotted with tall trees, among them the mimosa and the acacia. Standing beneath them there is always a crowd of people awaiting their turn to enter the caves. In batches of twenty or so they are allowed inside. The caves are filled with charred bones, but they are only animal bones. The human dead must have been buried elsewhere, and no one knows exactly where. The guide always carries a strong flashlight and a candle, for the pictures are best seen in the soft glow of candlelight. Compared with Carlsbad Caverns these Spanish caves are small in size, but their human history puts Carlsbad in the shade. In crossing this narrow threshold and shutting away the sun, how quickly does one shut away the whole mechanical world outside, and close the portals on man's awkward progress toward the stars.

The prehistoric inhabitants of Spain, who have left their amazing paintings on the ceiling of the cave at Altamira, are a people about whom little else is known. These paintings are at least 13,000 years old, possibly older, but are remarkably well preserved. They constitute the earliest representation of pictorial art in the peninsula, a field in which the Spaniards have excelled ever since the dark beginnings of their history. In order to see the pictures properly the viewer must lie flat on his back on a piece of canvas placed atop one of the rock "couches" inside the cave; otherwise the figures appear distorted. The prehistoric artists must originally have drawn them lying in this position, working much as Michelangelo did in the Sistine Chapel. The paintings are probably of a religious or ritualistic nature. They represent wild stags, horses, boars, in warm and rich sepia tones, and with a fine feeling for movement, rhythm, and form. They express well the telluric quality of the ancient race who drew them. The low ceiling of the room which holds the paintings is always wet from the condensation of vapor inside the cave, and it is said that this has been a preservative; whereas water penetrating the roof and dripping through would have destroyed them. So much for the dark portals of prehistory, and eight thousand years of time. After this, Spain emerges from the shadows.

The Iberians, who are responsible for giving the peninsula its name, probably began to arrive in Spain from northern Africa around 3000 B.C. They occupied mainly the southern two-thirds of the peninsula, along and below the Ebro River. The name Ebro itself is from *Iber*, which is Iberian for "river." In the valley of the Ebro and near the Valencian coast the Iberians achieved a flourishing culture. They lived in walled cities, and some of the megalithic stones used in their ramparts still remain in place, for example, at Tarragona. The Iberians were a small, wiry, dark-complexioned race, great riders of horses, and excessively clannish and tribalistic in their social organization. They created beautiful small bronze figures; they had a passion to represent bulls, other animals, and flowers. They produced a vigorous art, in its final period strongly influenced by the Greeks.

The Phoenicians, a Semitic race of the Canaanite branch, began their trade with Spain many centuries before Christ, perhaps as early as the twelfth century B.C. The language of these people clearly belongs to the same family as ancient Hebrew. The Phoenicians (originally from Tyre) came primarily as merchants, and carried on a profitable commerce with the peninsula for an extended period. They are said to have founded the cities of Cádiz and Málaga in southern Spain, the former around 1100 B.C. It was mainly the mineral wealth of this southwestern portion of the country, possibly the Tarshish of the Old Testament, which attracted the Phoenician traders. Their "ships of Tarshish" dominated the western Mediterranean for many centuries. It was reported that even the anchors of their vessels returning from Spain were of solid silver. Although trade was the primary interest of these Phoenicians, the arts of music were not foreign to them. The prophet Isaiah said of Tyre, in the days of its shame: "Take an harp, go about the city, thou harlot that hast been forgotten; make sweet melody, sing many songs, that thou mayest be remembered." (Isa. 23:16.)

The Celts, a Nordic race, began to drift into Spain from the north around 900 B.C.; three hundred years later (600 B.C.) there was a second Celtic invasion. The Celts occupied the northern portion of the country, above the Ebro River. In the central part of Spain the mixture of this northern race with the Iberians produced the Celtiberians who were encountered later by both the Greeks and the Romans. The Celts left a strong physical imprint on the population of northern Spain. In the Cantabrian and Pyrenean areas there is still today a high percentage of light-colored eyes (blue and hazel) and fair skin and hair. Galicia and Asturias are noted for their blond types, and in the Basque provinces the proportion is nearly 40 per cent. In the territory of Aragon approximately 35 per cent of the population falls into the fair-skinned, light-eyed group. As one proceeds southward both the shading of the skin and coloration of the eyes darken. The typical Andalusian is a dark-skinned, dark-eyed type, reflecting the strong Moorish admixture in this area, but blonds do exist today in Andalusia as they also do among the Arabic-speaking population of northern Africa.

It is a tenuous thing to speak of racial qualities, especially so many hundreds of years ago, but some of the qualities for which both the Iberians and Celts were noted in Strabo's time can still be recognized today: their hospitality, their grand manners, their arrogance, and above all, their love of freedom, which was shown in fierce resistance to conquerors and fanatical defense of beleaguered cities; Saguntum and Numantia begin the long list of famous sieges in Spanish history.[21]

In Grecian literature the early history of Spain is mentioned frequently. Plato in the *Timaeus* refers to the lost civilization of Atlantis, and Strabo mentions it in his famous geography. A modern writer Edwin Björkman has made out a good case for placing Atlantis at or near the site of present-day Cádiz in Spain. In Greek mythology the tenth task assigned to Hercules was to travel to a land in the west, under the rays of the setting sun, and there capture the oxen of Geryon. "The description is thought to apply to Spain, of which Geryon was King," writes Gayley in his *Classic Myths*.

After crossing various countries, Hercules at last reached the western extremity of the Mediterranean, where he raised two great columns, the mountains of Calpe and Abyla, as a monument to his progress. These legendary Pillars of Hercules are today's Gibraltar and Ceuta. The story goes on to say that the Greek hero engraved an entwined S-shaped legend around the pillars which in its Latin form was *Non plus ultra* ("Do not go beyond here"). This legend marked the westernmost limits of the Mediterranean world, and the S-shaped inscription was the origin of a widely used monetary symbol known in the United States as the dollar sign.

The eleventh labor of Hercules was to steal the golden apples of the Hesperides. These might have been nuggets of gold, or could they have been simply the golden sunsets or the wild oranges of southern Spain? Atlas was the father of the Hesperides, the nymphs who guarded the golden apples, so Hercules asked him to seek and gather them, offering to take the burden of the heavens on his own shoulders while Atlas did so. Atlas soon returned with the golden apples and wanted to take them back to Greece himself. Hercules agreed but begged the giant to hold the heavy load for a moment, while he procured a pad to ease his shoulders. Thus Atlas resumed the burden of the heavens, and Hercules absconded with the apples.

The Greeks reached Spain around 600 B.C. They came first as traders but later established several trading posts mainly along the Mediterranean coast of the country, and also possibly along the northern Cantabrian shores. Their art fused with that of the more primitive Iberians. The famous stone bust of the *Dama de Elche* ("Lady of Elche"), with its enigmatic face, revealing an almost oriental serenity, is the finest example of this Greco-Iberian art. The headdress and jewelry are Iberian. The statue was found near Alicante on the Valencian coast. The Greeks left no great stone temples in Spain comparable to those at Syracuse in Sicily or at Paestum, south of Naples, in Italy. Their Spanish structures were not enduring things.

The Greeks did bring their music and their musical instruments into Spain.

The songs of Tyre are not remembered. Yet one may fancy that some vestige of them, mingled with the melos of Greece and of Islam, lingers in the cantilena of an Iberian folksong whose beginnings are lost in the dimness of time. Certain it is that the lore of Greece was implanted in the Iberian peninsula after the Phoenician ascendancy had given way to Hellenic supremacy in the Mediterranean. . . . In Grecian temples and theatres built on Iberian soil, men worshipped Diana of Ephesus and sang their odes and dithyrambs to the accompanyment of the lyre and the aulos.[11]

In the third century B.C. Carthage, a powerful Phoenician city in northern Africa, invaded Spain after she had lost the First Punic War to Rome. Hamilcar Barca utilized the lull after the war to conquer a good part of Andalusia and the Valencian coastal area. Barcelona owes its name to Hamilcar Barca; a second Carthaginian city was Carthago Nova or New Carthage, today's Cartagena. Hamilcar Barca assembled a fine army of Spanish infantry and Numidian horsemen and laid plans for the conquest of Italy. After Hamilcar's death, his son Hannibal, one of the greatest generals of antiquity, put these plans into effect. In 218 B.C. he captured and destroyed the city of Saguntum (near today's Valencia), and almost immediately took his victorious army across the Alps and down into Italy. He met and decisively defeated a larger Roman army at Cannae in 216 B.C. It was perhaps the biggest Roman army ever put into the field. Roman casualties at Cannae were staggering, and among the dead were eighty members of the Roman senate. Hardly a family in the Imperial City escaped bereavement. But the Romans pulled themselves together, Rome itself was still strongly defended, and a second army was put into the field. This one constantly obstructed the Carthaginians but carefully avoided a head-on clash.

Hannibal at once freed all captured Roman allies and did everything in his power to persuade them and their cities to desert Rome and come over to his side. He met with only slight success, for the Roman policy of fair treatment of the subject peoples, and Carthage's well-known reputation for despoliation, now paid off handsomely for Rome, and even on the brink of defeat the loyalty of her allies did not waver.

Hannibal hung on for ten long years. He swept up and down Italy, winning many victories, but was unable to consolidate his position. The Romans dogged his path but refused to engage him in a pitched battle. Hannibal's brother Hasdrubal at last came from Spain with reinforcements, and the Carthaginians took new heart. But this army was headed off and destroyed by the Romans. Hasdrubal himself was killed, and in a gory gesture the Romans threw his head into Hannibal's camp. For four more years Hannibal remained in Italy, but his forces were now dwindling while the opposition mounted steadily. In 203 B.C. he was forced to return to Africa.

In the meantime the Roman legions, under Publius Cornelius Scipio (later called Africanus), had been engaging and beating the Carthaginians in Spain. In 209 B.C. Scipio captured their base at Cartagena, and by 205 B.C. the last Carthaginians were driven from the peninsula, which then became a Roman province under the name *Hispania*. Scipio took his victorious army to Africa and there defeated Hannibal on his own home ground in 202 B.C. It took yet another Punic War to bring about the complete destruction of Carthage, but Spain was now freed of the enemy and ready for Roman colonization. It was not until nearly two centuries later, however, under Augustus (19 B.C.), that the last of the restless and impressionable Spanish tribes were conquered and a true Pax Romana prevailed throughout the peninsula. Augustus himself was forced to come to Spain to direct the final campaign against the indomitable mountaineers of that "wild Cantabrian land which will not bow to Roman yoke" of Horace's famous ode.

For the next four hundred years Spain progressed rapidly under Roman rule. Gibbon, using Strabo as his reference, summarizes the situation of the country as follows:

Spain, the western extremity of the empire, of Europe, and of the ancient world, has, in every age, invariably preserved the same natural limits: the Pyrenees mountains, the Mediterranean, and the Atlantic Ocean. That great peninsula was distributed by Augustus into three provinces,

Lusitania, Baetica, and Tarraconensis. The kingdom of Portugal now fills the place of the warlike country of the Lusitanians. The confines of Granada and Andalusia correspond with those of ancient Baetica. The remainder of Spain, Galicia and Asturias, Biscay and Navarre, León and the two Castiles, Murcia, Valencia, Catalonia, and Aragon, all contributed to form the third and most considerable of the Roman governments, which, from the name of its capital, was styled the province of Tarragona. Of the native barbarians, the Celtiberians were the most powerful, as the Cantabrians and Asturians proved the most obstinate. Confident in the strength of their mountains, they were the last who submitted to the arms of Rome, and the first who threw off the yoke of the Arabs.[12]

Hispania soon became the granary of Rome, and the wealthiest province of the empire. Agriculture and the raising of livestock were promoted on an extensive scale. Spanish horses were much sought after for the Roman circuses because of their courage and swiftness. Olive oil, wines, and fruits were produced abundantly. As Pliny states, the Romans were extremely sensitive to the influence of language over the national manners, and it became their immediate concern "to extend, with the progress of their arms, the use of the Latin tongue." The Latin spoken by the Roman soldiers, called vulgar Latin in order to distinguish it from the erudite Latin written by Cicero, Horace, Virgil, etc., became the language of Spain. Roman law and customs were adopted throughout the land. The people gradually became Romanized, and once peace and order were established only a single legion remained in the country as a symbolic guardian of the province.

Flourishing cities sprang up in all parts of the peninsula, and a great Roman highway, the Via Augusta, stretched from the Imperial City all the way across Spain with its terminus at Gades (Cádiz), at the southwestern corner. Additional Roman roads connected the other important cities of the country. Incredible aqueducts of monolithic granite blocks were constructed to bring water to the towns of the dry tableland. The one still standing at Segovia, in a marvelous state of preservation and still carrying water, would make any traveler believe that this was once a great metropolis, not merely a provincial Spanish town. Bridges, amphitheaters, temples, circuses, arches were also constructed. Pliny, who was for a time Roman procurator in Spain, listed and described 360 different Spanish cities. The civilization of Spain became an urban thing, not urban and separate as in the days of the Iberians and Celtiberians, but urban and unified with perhaps the finest road system the country has ever had, certainly the best up to the days of Primo de Rivera.

The mineral wealth of Spain, particularly the mines of gold and silver, were zealously exploited by the Romans. Gibbon states that twenty thousand pounds of gold was received each year from three Spanish provinces. The Romans forced the natives to work the mines for the benefit of their rulers; and thus was rooted inextricably in the Spanish mind that love of precious metals which centuries later was reflected in the mining economies of colonial Mexico and Peru.

Christianity reached Spain in the first century A.D., also by way of Rome. Legend has it that St. James brought the gospel to Aragon, León, and Galicia around 40 A.D., but this is not corroborated by the early church writers. Paul probably did pass through Aragon, and Peter is reported to have sent missionaries to Andalusia. Under the Emperor Nero (54 A.D.–68 A.D.) there were several Christian martyrs in Spain. These martyrs strewed the early history of the church in Spain with tormented bodies and great memories. Santa Eulalia, still a young girl, trudged into Mérida eager for martyrdom. She burst into the presence of the city magistrates and shouted: "The old gods are worthless, the Emperor himself is nothing; the former are nothing because they are made with human hands, the latter is nothing because he worships them. All of that is worthless and nothing!" The praetor felt that he was forced to punish this daring child who thus could call into question the power of the state. They trussed her up and tore her body to pieces with hot pincers, but she continued to sing out triumphantly in her small child's voice. Her spirit, in the form of a white dove, flew out of her mouth and soared into heaven. Tertullian describes the unforgettable scene, and then pungently adds "that girl must have some great, hidden power that we do not possess."[13] He was stating a widespread view among the Romans of his day.

The same thing was happening in other parts of Spain. St. Vincent died at Saguntum; Tarragona and Gerona also had their heroic dead, and in Saragossa there were eighteen famous martyrs. Santa Engracia's torment is described graphically in a poem by Prudentius—breasts ripped off, liver cut out, limbs filled with gangrene.

These martyrs shed their benefits on the land as water flows from springs: their sacred blood keeps away all dark ghosts and envious daemons from the doors: those who have visited their tombs with tears return home smiling: on their birthdays (as the anniversaries of their deaths were called) the people hold a feast at their shrines. The poem ends with an adjuration: "Prostrate yourselves with me, noble citizens, before these holy tombs: then you will all of you follow quickly those resurgent souls and limbs."

I need not point out to anyone who knows Spain how typical this poem is of certain aspects of Spanish life. The local Saint or Madonna is still the protector of her city and a figure of patriotic pride and devotion even to those who have ceased to be practicing Catholics. Arguments as to which town has the best saints and holds the best processions are still to be heard in any café. Till recently processions of flagellants with blood-stained backs offered a milder version of the cruel scenes of the amphitheater, whilst the bull-fight represents the eternal drama of the triumph of spirit over brute force.[14]

These early martyrs gave real impetus to the new Spanish church. Indeed, the Spanish interest in martyrdom exceeded that of any other country. Many centuries later, under the Inquisition, it was to be practiced in a cruel reversal of roles. Nevertheless, it was not until the reign of Constantine (325 A.D.) that all of Spain, along with the entire Roman Empire, became dominantly Christian.

Education made great progress in Spain under the Romans, but it was limited to the ruling caste. Many of the most distinguished writers of the empire were born in Spain. The literature of the Silver Age was largely the product of these writers of the "Spanish Latinity": Seneca, Martial, Quintilian, Lucan, and many others, whose works all belong to the first century A.D. The two great emperors Trajan (98 A.D.–117 A.D.) and Hadrian (117 A.D.–138 A.D.) were also born in Spain, as were the later emperors Antonius Pius and Marcus Aurelius. Under Trajan the Roman Empire reached its greatest territorial extension. Gibbon succinctly states:

> The works of Trajan bear the stamp of his genius. The public monuments, with which Hadrian adorned every province of the empire, were executed not only by his orders, but under his immediate inspection. He was himself an artist; and he loved the arts, as they conduced to the glory of the monarch. They were encouraged by the Antonines, as they contributed to the happiness of the people. But if the emperors were the first, they were not the only architects of their dominions. Their example was universally imitated by their principal subjects, who were not afraid of declaring to the world that they had the spirit to conceive, and the wealth to accomplish, the noblest undertakings.

The Roman writer Martial retired to a small farm in Aragon after he had gotten fed up with the purple togas and the conversation of haughty widows in the great capital of the empire. In a letter to his friend Juvenal he describes his life in Spain in these words:

Here we live lazily and work pleasantly in Boterdum and Platea—these are our rough Celtiberian place names—and I enjoy a vast and shameless sleep. Often I don't wake up until after ten o'clock, and so I'm making up for all the sleep I've lost in thirty years. You'll find no togas here; if you ask for one, they'll give you the nearest rug off a broken chair. I get up in the morning to a glorious fire of great logs from the oak forest, and the land-agent's wife crowns it with her pots and pans. The strapping young hunts-man comes in, and you feel the urge to follow him into the teeming woods. The land-agent doles out the rations to the boys, and asks permis-sion to have his long hair cut. *That's how I like to live, and that's how I hope to die.*

This is the same Martial who had seen and praised the fiery and sensual dancing of the *gaditanas*, the girls of Cádiz, whose *crusmata* or castanets fascinated him as did the "gracefully raised arms, the swirling figure, the sinuous movement, the dark emotions" of these dancers.

On another day, when he was not so optimistic, Martial revealed the other side of the picture—that the nearby town is a stupid little place. There is no conversation, no theater, no literary interest or taste. The great Roman is bored with the country life.

Other Roman writers fill out the picture of Spain. Pliny praises the coastal regions of the peninsula, the lovely colors of the Spanish dyes, "the energy of its workmen, the skill of its slaves, the endurance of its people, and their vehement spirit." Cicero exclaimed that the poetry that came out of Córdoba sounded as if it had got mixed up with the olive oil. Hosius, the Bishop of Córdoba, wrote to the emperor himself forbidding him to meddle with the Spanish church. Prudentius wrote many extensive hymns to the famous Spanish Christian martyrs, and Priscillian allowed dancing to be a part of the church ritual, a practice that still survives in the Dance of the Seises in the Cathedral of Seville at the time of Corpus Christi.

The Roman propensity for thermal bathing also had its effect in Spain. Latin writers of those times refer frequently to the Roman *thermae* or hot baths in the main towns, and to the custom of the people who used them regularly. After the Second Punic War bathing became widely popular throughout Roman Spain (circa 100 B.C.). When the Visigoths, a warlike Germanic race, took over the country in the fifth century they destroyed the baths and *thermae* of the Romans, in the belief that they tended to encourage softness and effeminacy. The invasion of the Moors in 711 reversed the practice, and bathing again became the fashion. Both Moslem and Jew in Spain believed that cleanliness was next to godliness, and they also used water constantly in their religious ablutions. The rugged Castilian soldiers of medieval days, who had little opportunity or inclination for keeping their bodies clean, commenced to associate their own dirtiness with right religious thinking (their own, of course), and hence the bathing of Jew and Moor took on a heretical meaning. The ritualistic washing of the dead, practiced by both Moslem and Jew, who appeared to believe that this rite helped to wash away the sins of the deceased, was especially repugnant to the Christians. The Castilians also accused the Moors of turning their baths into notoriously sensual orgies, and regarded bathing as inseparably linked with the immoral and sinful practices of that race.

The mendicant Spanish monks, according to their practice of setting up a directly antagonistic principle, considered physical dirt as the test of moral purity and true faith; and by dining and sleeping from year's end to year's end in the same unchanged woolen frock, arrived at the height of their ambition, according to their view of the *odor of sanctity*, the *olor de santidad*. This was a euphemism for "foul smell," but it came to represent Christian godliness, and many of the saints are pictured sitting in their own excrement. Cardinal Jiménez de Cisneros, himself a Franciscan, induced Ferdinand and Isabella to close and abolish the Moorish baths after their conquest of Granada. "They forbade not only the Christians but the Moors from using anything but holy water. Fire, not water, became the grand element of inquisitorial purification."[46]

Priests were even instructed to ask their young feminine penitents if they had overwashed, and if they had, absolution was sometimes denied. The Princess Isabel, the "daughter of the eye" of King Philip II, made a solemn vow never to change her clothes until Ostend was taken. The siege lasted three years, three months, and thirteen days.

The royal garment acquired a tawny color, which was called *Isabel* by the courtiers, in compliment to the pious princess. (The word still means "dirty gray" in Belgium.) Again, Southey relates that the devout Saint Eufraxia entered a convent of 130 nuns, not one of whom had ever washed her feet, and the very mention of a bath was an abomination.[46]

These obedient sisters were referred to by one of the religious writers of those days as "a sweet garden of flowers, perfumed by the good odor and fame of sanctity." In consequence of all this history the Spaniards fell into the habit of not bathing, a habit which was continued until the nineteenth century.

Starting in the reign of Hadrian (117 A.D.–138 A.D.), and increasing among the Antonines, the Jews began to pour into Spain. According to Jewish legend the ancient Hebrews had established colonies there many hundreds of years before the time of Christ, having been introduced into the country "by the fleets of Solomon and the arms of Nebuchadnezzar," but history does not corroborate this. The Antonines, however, did restore to the Jews the ancient privileges, and they were permitted to move about freely in the empire, to acquire the freedom of Rome, and to enjoy municipal honors.

New synagogues arose in the principal cities of the empire, and the sabbaths and feast days were celebrated in the most solemn and public manner. Spain, in particular, with its Mediterranean climate, dry mountains, and groves of olive trees, so reminiscent of Israel, became a new homeland for the Jews who had left the Near East. They brought an important racial and cultural element into the population and the history of Spain. At this juncture in history, as Gibbon very accurately points out, "the Jews were a *nation*, the Christians were a *sect*." Within a few centuries this situation would be reversed, with the gravest consequences for both Christians and Jews.

During the first four centuries of the Christian Era Spain, separated on all sides from the enemies of Rome, by mountains, sea, and intermediate provinces, enjoyed a period of long and prosperous tranquillity. In the second century the Spanish cities of Augusta Emerita (Mérida), Córdoba, Seville (Hispalis), Zaragoza (Caesar Augusta), Lugo, Cádiz (Gades) and Tarragona, were among the most illustrious of the empire. This was the time when there was no idleness in Spain, and the land was fruitful beyond belief. The Spaniards did eventually become softened by the long peace, but at the hostile approach of the Germanic tribes their old military ardor was rekindled, and as long as the mountains were defended by the native militia the barbarians were repelled and defeated. But when the native troops were replaced by Honorian bands in the service of the emperor, the gates of northern Spain were treacherously opened.

In 409 A.D. three different Germanic tribes, the Suevi, the Vandals, and the Alani, poured into the peninsula. The Vandals overran the

entire country but settled mostly in southern Spain, hence the name
Andalusia (Vandalusia, or Land of the Vandals). All three barbarian
tribes ravaged the country, but the Vandals were excessively brutal,
hence the term "vandalism." A few years later, the fourth Germanic
tribe, the semi-civilized Visigoths, swept into Spain and overcame the
first three invaders. The Vandals were forced out of southern Spain
and into northern Africa. The Visigoths, partially Romanized and
largely Christian, established their own dynasty in the peninsula. The
days of Roman domination were definitely over (500 A.D.).

The heritage of the Romans, however, left an indelible imprint
on the nation and on the character of the people. This heritage
consisted of a formidable trinity: (1) the Spanish language, derived
from spoken Latin; (2) Roman law; and (3) the Christian religion.
To these must be added the contributions of Roman art, architecture, political organization, and customs. It must be made clear
that the inhabitants of Spain were not yet really "Spaniards" in their
ways of thinking, in their feelings, or in their actions. Certainly,
there were notable differences between these people and the Spaniards who conquered the Moors and discovered and colonized the
New World. Hispanic culture was still in a state of flux. The language spoken in Spain in 400 A.D. would have to undergo many radical changes before it eventually became Spanish. Roman law, too,
would be considerably altered by the Visigothic code and by the
Moors. Spanish Christianity, after many centuries of contact with
Moslems and Jews, evolved a church and a concept of religion vastly
different from those of the fourth century A.D.

Nevertheless, after the long Roman domination, Spanish culture
and psychology were polarized in two opposing tendencies: On the
one hand, the Roman feeling for union, centralization, and imperium;
and on the other, the African tendency toward disunion, tribalism,
and separatism. Throughout the following centuries the people of
Spain have expressed themselves by moving first in one of these directions, only to swing suddenly in an about-face and move in the
other. This essential dichotomy has never been resolved by democratic compromise for more than the briefest periods.

The tendency toward separatism, which can only be controlled by
the strongest repressive government, has frequently appeared at the
very moment of apparent victory for a sensible union, and arbitrary autocracy then again becomes the only means of a stable political order. The kindest name for this tendency toward separatism

is Spanish individualism; but perhaps a more accurate term would be *cantonalism* or *kabylism,* the tendency to disruption, to separate into tribes. Martin Hume, supported by the Spanish writer Unamuno, traces it back to the original Iberian inhabitants of the peninsula. In his history of Spain Hume alludes to it in these notable lines:

In any case, what is known of their (Iberian) physique seems to negate the supposition that they were of Indo-European or Aryan origin; and to find their counterpart at the present time, it is only necessary to seek the Kabyl tribes of the Atlas, the original inhabitants of the African coast opposite Spain, who were driven back into the mountains by successive waves of invasion. Not alone in physique do these tribes resemble what the early Iberian must have been, but in the more unchanging peculiarities of character and institutions the likeness is easily traceable to the Spaniard of today. The organization of the Iberians, like that of the Atlas peoples, was clannish and tribal, and their chief characteristic was their indomitable local independence. Warlike and brave, sober and light-hearted, the Kabyl tribesman has for thousands of years stubbornly refused all attempts to weld him to a uniform dominion, while the Iberian, starting probably from the same stock, was blended with Aryan races possessing other qualities, and was submitted for six centuries to the unifying organization of the greatest governing race the world ever saw—the Romans; yet, withal, even at the present day, the main characteristic of the Spanish nation, like that of the Kabyl tribes, is lack of solidarity.[15]

Hume repeats this idea throughout his book like a refrain or leitmotiv. Unamuno, the Spaniard, does not wish to attribute the kabylistic tendency to race; he claims that it arises out of the pastoral history of the Spaniard, to whom tending a flock was the natural way of life. The pure Spaniard, he says, has always been "an agriculturist by necessity, and a shepherd by choice, when he was not a soldier." On this point both Unamuno and Hume agree. In any case, whatever the history, whatever the causes, when the Roman domination of Spain came to an end with the invasion of the Germanic tribes, the opposing Spanish tendencies of despotic unification on the one hand, and of disruption on the other, joined in a bitter struggle which has continued without letup for sixteen hundred years; and it still continues. Any book on Spain, any interpretation of the Spanish culture or people, must rest upon this fact and then seek to analyze its manifestations.

The Visigoths did not get a firm hold on Spain until the end of the sixth century (around 600 A.D.). They formed a kind of nobility of warriors among the other inhabitants of the country, and probably never numbered more than two hundred thousand. They squabbled constantly among themselves, and their kings, of whom there were more than thirty during the two centuries of Visigothic rule, were often elevated and often deposed in baths of blood. One of them was enjoying a fine dinner at his palace when suddenly the lights went out and a dozen swords, held by outraged husbands and fathers, pierced the regal body.

Many Visigothic kings wore ermine mantles and purple slippers as symbols of royalty. Following the Visigothic custom they all let their hair and beards grow long. They adopted the showier Roman style of dressing, and wore jewelry in a lavish fashion.

The Visigoths, like the other barbarians who had invaded Spain before them, were Arians rather than Trinitarian Catholics. They did not believe that Christ was of one substance with the Father, but regarded him only as a great prophet, and they refused to accept the co-equality of the three figures in the Holy Trinity, the Father, the Son and the Holy Ghost. The Visigothic Arians rigorously persecuted the Spanish Roman Catholics. One of their kings, Leovigild, made this persecution the basic policy of his government. He plundered the Roman churches, extorted vast sums from the rich, sent others into exile, to the dungeon, or to the scaffold. With the wealth thus acquired he surrounded his court with unwonted splendor. He was publicly crowned with a brilliant ceremony in which no other Gothic king had indulged, for the king had hitherto been but slightly elevated above the chieftains who elected him. Leovigild raised a magnificent throne in his palace, and ruled with great pomp and circumstance. The effigy of the king was now stamped on Visigothic coins for the first time.

Leovigild's son, Hermenegild, was the Catholic martyr whose death eventually turned the Arian Visigoths into Roman Catholics. Hermenegild had married a Merovingian Catholic princess who was only thirteen. The young bride was vilely treated at the Visigothic court in Toledo; the Queen Mother, in particular, was extremely cruel to her, and incensed by her resistance to suasion, on one occasion grabbed the child's long hair, "dashed her to the ground, kicked her till she was covered with blood, and at last gave orders that she should be stripped and thrown into a fishpond."

Hermenegild was so moved when he heard of his young bride's stoic endurance of this cruel treatment that he himself became a

Roman Catholic, and rebelled against his father, seeking allies wherever he could find them. The old king, Leovigild, won the civil war which ensued and had his son executed. Hermenegild thus became the first royal martyr for the Roman Catholic cause in Spain. Many centuries after his death Hermenegild became St. Hermenegild (1586).

His brother, Recared, came to the throne when old Leovigild died (589 A.D.). He restored the treasures which had been wrested from the Catholics, adopted a policy of toleration, and convoked a council in Toledo at which seventy bishops and all the Visigothic nobles attended. Before this august gathering Recared abjured Arianism and besought all of his subjects to follow him. With only scattered opposition the conversion was carried out and Recared became "the first Catholic king of Spain," and Roman Catholicism became the state religion.

Recared could hardly be called a king of passionate religious belief. What he did was politically astute rather than religiously Messianic. He very simply wanted the church on his side, and as the king generally appointed the bishops, he could make certain of this. Recared, like his Visigothic predecessors on the shaky throne at Toledo, needed a strong ally to equalize the power of the Visigothic nobles, who had always been a thorn in the king's side. Now that the regal authority had found this ally, Visigothic Spain was on its way to becoming a Visigothic-Romanic-Hispanic nation. Had this process of history been allowed to continue, Spain would have stayed in the main current of European history and culture. The Moors prevented it; they remained in the peninsula for nearly eight centuries, altering radically the very bedrock of the beliefs, character, and psychology of the people.

The Roman Catholic Visigoths, after Recared, turned their newfound religious union upon the Jews, who constituted the only important minority within the realm. The Spanish Jews now numbered many thousands, and were among the most industrious and most intelligent inhabitants of the country. The wealth they had accumulated in commerce and finance excited the avarice of their rulers, their religion was hated and unpalatable, and they had long since lost the use, even the remembrance, of arms. Sisebut, a Gothic king who ruled in the beginning of the seventh century, delighted in the most abhorrent persecution of these unfortunate people. At his behest edicts were passed compelling the Jews to receive baptism.

It was reported that some eighty thousand submitted to this indignity rather than suffer torture or death. Obstinate Jews had their property confiscated, their bodies tortured, their families scattered.

Among the Christians the belief began to spread that many converted Jews silently blasphemed as they took the sacraments, hence the Catholic clergy attempted to soften the excessive zeal of the fanatical Sisebut. The frequent relapses of the Jews, however, caused one of Sisebut's successors to banish the entire Jewish nation from his dominions, and a council held at Toledo decreed that every Gothic king must swear to uphold this salutary edict. In spite of all this the Jews continued in Spain; they multiplied under servitude and distress; and the Visigoths could not bring themselves to expel in a body or to annihilate the Jewish victims and slaves who served so well to vent their fury and exalt their dominion. From all this it is easy to understand why the Jews welcomed the invasion of the Moors, in the year 711.

There lived in southern Spain during the rule of the Goths a learned Roman Catholic encyclopedist, theologian, bishop and saint, called Isidore of Seville (570–636). Isidore was one of the most prolific writers of his epoch, and represented Visigothic-Romanic learning at its best. He summarized all the knowledge accessible to him in the old Latin authors in a work called *Origins*, a kind of general encyclopedia which was so highly regarded that nearly a thousand medieval manuscripts of it survive. Almost every medieval monastery had a copy. Isidore's monumental labor was very definitely a *European* rather than a *Spanish* undertaking and accomplishment. It was written in Latin, which was the international language of Europe in that epoch. It was also European (and not Spanish) in point of view, and was one of the brightest beacons in the midst of the dark ages of the Continent and its culture, a beacon around which scholars of all countries could gather for study and inspiration.

Isidore became an international figure and continued to be widely read throughout the Middle Ages and on into the Renaissance. Among the subjects treated in his *Origins* (or *Etymologies*) are anthropology, cosmology, the seven liberal arts, history, law, medicine, church matters, theology, zoology, architecture, psychology, and agriculture. Most of what Isidore wrote had been extracted from Greek and Roman classics and the works of former encyclopedists, mainly the Latins. Isidore knew no Greek and his methods are anything but scientific, hence he has been derided by some modern scholars. However, his encyclopedia is a comprehensive view of the world as it was seen and felt in the seventh century.

But Isidore is the author of another, and to us more important work, *The History of the Goths*. In this work he presents a clear-cut view of Hispano-Gothic reality and feeling in the seventh century. It was a reality that was sure of itself, secure and without grief or anguish, in which the overwhelming drive of religion of a later date was lacking. Isidore's history was almost pagan in its glorification of courage and warfare. In the beginning of the work there is a *De laude Hispaniae* ("In praise of Spain") in which these characteristic views are expressed:

Of all the lands that extend from the west to India, thou art the fairest, oh sacred Hispania, ever-fecund mother of princes and peoples, rightful queen of all the provinces, from whom west and east draw their light. . . . With good reason in another time golden Rome, chief of the peoples, desired to possess thee; but even though Roman valor, victorious, might first take thee as a bride, the driving race of the Goths came later and carried thee off to love thee, after many victorious wars fought over the vastness of the earth. That race delights in thee today, secure in the happiness of its domain, with regal dignity and greatness of wealth.[16]

According to Isidore the world "can be encompassed and dominated by courage in warfare, and also through knowledge and intellectual reflection. Religious faith is not the only leading motive in this optimistic and, at times, worldly approach to life." Visigothic Spain in Isidore's time was an integral part of Europe, and would have followed a path analogous to that of the other European nations had it not been for the invasion of the Moors. Isidore's voice expressed a certitude of destiny such as the country was not to feel again until 1492, but when that year arrived it was a very different destiny indeed that the Spaniards envisioned.

The Visigoths wanted desperately to be the new Romans. They spoke Latin; they imitated the Romans in their dress and at their court; they imitated also Roman law, and they adopted the Roman Catholic religion. However, they were a race whose vacillating culture rested on no long tradition or firm achievement. They could, therefore, neither preserve their own cultural past, nor immerse themselves completely in the Roman present. They could neither organize, nor rule, nor build as had the Romans. As the years passed they lost their zeal for war, became soft and pleasure-loving, corrupt, and divisive. They formed in Spain a kind of nobility which did not endure long enough to find new strength in the emergent reality of the Spanish nation. The Visigoths were never able to conquer and subjugate the bellicose tribes who inhabited the Cantabrian and Pyrenees mountains; these were the least Romanized of all the inhabitants of the peninsula, and were the folk who later undertook the reconquest of Spain from the Moslems. In a word, when the great blow fell the Visigothic Spanish empire suddenly split apart because it had never been very firmly welded together. A dissolute, heterogeneous, arbitrary, often intolerant caste of nobles was attempting to rule a vast nation. Why, then, were these people so certain of their destiny? Because they had once shown indomitable courage in war, and as a result had won many stunning victories. Two Roman emperors had died in battles against them, their armies courageously defeated.

The Visigoths had every reason to believe that they were not *destroying* the Roman Empire, but that, on the contrary, they were *preserving* it with themselves in the seats of power. They proved to be an inept group politically, but they did preserve the Roman language and the Roman church. One of the few remaining churches of the Visigothic epoch is at Venta de Baños, not far from Burgos. It is called the Basilica of San Juan Bautista; and was constructed in the reign of King Receswinth around 661. The ruins of the Roman temple to the Goddess of the Thermae (the hot baths) were used in erecting the Visigothic church. It is a low, flat building of gray stone, almost without windows, and very much resembles a turtle with a crest on his back. Its simple and classic Romanesque interior is one of the most impressive of those early days.

But for the hazard of history the Visigothic dreams of forging a great Spanish nation might possibly have been realized, as did happen with the Normans in England.

We have arrived now at that fateful year of Spanish history when the Visigoths were defeated by the Arabs: 711 A.D. The Goths maintained a fortress in northern Africa at Ceuta, the mountain which is opposite Gibraltar. This stronghold was in the command of Count Julian, general of the Visigoths. Legend has it that Julian's daughter, who lived at the court in Toledo, had been seduced by the Gothic king, Roderick. To revenge himself Julian is said to have allied himself with the Arabs, inviting them to undertake the conquest of Spain. History does not corroborate this apocryphal story, though it has been celebrated widely in the ancient ballads and chronicles of

Spain. What probably happened was that Julian backed the wrong side in the latest of many squabbles among the Gothic factions around the throne, and, too cowardly to face the consequences or to challenge King Roderick on his own, had sought the aid of a foreign power.

The Goths were no longer the victorious barbarians, who had humbled the pride of Rome, despoiled the queen of nations, and penetrated from the Danube to the Atlantic Ocean. Secluded from the world by the Pyrenean mountains, the successors of Alaric had slumbered in a long peace: the walls of the cities were mouldered into dust: the youth had abandoned the exercise of arms; and the presumption of their ancient renown would expose them in a field of battle to the first assault of the invaders.[12]

The Moors, on the other hand, were fired with their zeal for the new religion of Mohammed. Hitherto a group of motley and heterogeneous tribes (Arabs, Berbers, Syrians, etc.), this newfound religious unity gave them a focus and an incentive for collective warfare and expansion. Islam and the Arabic language were the only unities that bound them, but this was sufficient. They were brave warriors, and all they needed was a banner. Islam gave them the banner.

Roderick was in northern Spain when he heard of the invasion of the infidels; he assembled his hosts as quickly as he could, and at the head of a large army "of almost one hundred thousand men," the king of the Romans steadied himself for the encounter. He was "wearing on his head a golden crown, encumbered with a heavy robe of silken embroidery, and reclining on a litter or car of ivory drawn by two white mules, as was the way the Gothic kings of those days went about." Thus weighted down, Roderick led his soldiers to the plains of Jerez on the banks of the Guadalete, and there engaged the Moors in battle. The Spanish *General Chronicle,* an ancient thirteenth century history, very carefully points out that the Goths were all thin and sickly "for they had just gone through two awful years of pestilence and famine." The two armies fought to a standstill for many hours, but finally there was a defection among the Christians, in that part of the army led by Count Julian; the Arabs broke the ranks of the Visigoths and routed them in dismay. After this it was every man for himself. Tradition extends the battle to cover eight bloody days, but this is almost certainly an exaggeration.

King Roderick leapt from his car, mounted his swift horse Orelia, and fled from the field of battle. He escaped a soldier's death only to drown ignobly in the waters of the blood-filled river. His diadem, robes, and charger were found on the banks, but the body of Roderick was never recovered. A meaner head was chopped off and exposed in triumph before the palace of Damascus. "And such," writes a valiant historian of the Arabs, "is the fate of those kings who withdraw themselves from a field of battle." The Moors swept on to Toledo, and in a few brief months Visigothic Spain had ceased to exist. The invaders were in complete control of the peninsula except for a very reduced area in the Cantabrian mountains. It was from these mountains that the reconquest of the country began, and was continued for the next eight hundred years.

The defeat of Roderick has excited the imagination of the Spanish ballad makers, chroniclers, and even of the English Romantics. Walter Scott wrote a long poem about it, as did Walter Savage Landor and Robert Southey, the poet laureate. They all embroidered the story of Julian's beautiful daughter, Florinda or La Cava, seduced at the hands of the Gothic king. The old Spanish ballads are an excellent source of inspiration to them, for these poems present a tantalizing picture of the young lady bathing in the river at Toledo, along with several of her maidens.

> La Cava was the first
> Who cast off her clothes.
> In the shadowy pool
> Her body shone so fair
> That like the sun
> She eclipsed all others there.[17]

King Roderick was watching the scene hidden in the dense ivy, and suddenly "love, with beating wings, inflamed him." The ancient ballad concludes that men will tell you it was La Cava who was to blame, while women will insist that it was Roderick.

Another of the old ballads describes the defeat of Roderick on the banks of the Guadalete in stirring words. Seeing the field "red with blood running off in rivers," the wretched king sobs out his words of lamentation. Katharine E. Strathdee has translated this ballad into English:

Alone upon the battle ground, beneath a dying star,
Rodrigo stood in bleak despair, his hosts were scattered far;
Eight battles had they bravely fought against the Moorish band,

No hope remained within their hearts to save their native land.
Rodrigo sadly turned away, forespent with grief and pain,
And journeyed in the trackless night across the barren plain.
The king descended from his steed, for now 'twas lame and blind,
Alone he staggered faint and sick, no shelter could he find.
His sword was stained with blood and dust, as though from darkest hell
It had been plucked, its scarlet hue a tale of gore did tell.
His coat of mail, that set with jewels, had glistened in the sun,
Now seemed to him a mourning cloth that some dark fate had spun.
At dawn he climbed a hill that towered above that harsh terrain,
Beneath him lay his banners torn, his noble soldiers slain,
And as the king in sorrow gazed upon that cheerless morn,
He heard a cry of victory: the Arab shout of scorn!
He searched for the brave captains that led the hosts of Spain,
But he beheld their lifeless forms upon that gory plain.
Rodrigo could no longer bear the burden of his woe,
These words he spoke as from his eyes the bitter tears did flow:
"Last night I was the king of Spain, today no fief command,
Last night fair castles held my train, today bereft I stand,
The sun shall set forever on my kingdom and my reign,
The dawn will find no trace of me throughout this vast domain.
Oh hapless day when first I bore my scepter and my sword!
Accursèd hour that I was named Hispania's ruling lord!
Oh fate most cruel that I should see the sun go down this night!
Oh, death, thou art victorious! Why fearest thou to smite?"[65]

According to another of the ancient ballads Roderick did not
drown in the river but betook himself to the mountains where he
found an old hermit, nearly a hundred years old, who heard his con-
fession and absolved him. But it was on condition that Roderick
should lie entombed until his soul had gone. The king placed himself
in the cold crypt which was already occupied by a huge coiled serpent. The hermit inquired of the king how he was faring, and Roderick replied:

> Now he is gnawing me, gnawing me
> In the part where I most sinned.

Shortly afterwards the king passes away, the bells of heaven resound
with joy, untouched by human hands, and the royal soul ascends into
heaven.

These ballads (called *romances* in Spanish) were not composed at
the time of the events they describe. However, the legend about King
Roderick may well go back to the eighth century, and is perhaps the

only survival of Visigothic literature in Spain. The above poems, and many others like them, probably belong to the fifteenth (possibly to the fourteenth) century, by which time Roderick and Visigothic Spain had become enveloped in an aura that was quite unrealistic. There were literally thousands of such ballads on every conceivable historic, legendary, and emotional subject. They were a kind of universal poetry, composed and sung by wandering minstrels, remembered, loved, and recited by the common people in all parts of Spain. The King Roderick ballads show how deeply the Christians of the Reconquest lamented the Arab invasion of their country. Quite unlike the Visigoths, the Moors were never able effectively to establish their dominion over Catholic Spain. By the eleventh century the lines of battle between the two religions and cultures were clearly drawn, and by the thirteenth century these lines had become a part of the national folk and literary tradition. Hence the particular and very Christian point of view which comes across to us from the ballads about Don Roderick, a feeble monarch who had been turned into a national legend, thus indicating how oral tradition faithfully caught and reflected the polarization of Spanish resistance to Islam.

3

THE CROSS, THE CRESCENT, AND THE STAR

In Spain the Cross is on the sword.

Rubén Darío

Everything has its day, and every civilization its brief moment in the sun. The Greeks and Romans dominated the ancient world. Western Europe has dominated that of modern times. The civilization of the Arabs was by all odds the dominant force of the Middle Ages. Its rise and fall, like that of Rome and of the Visigoths, teaches again that fundamental but never wholly learned lesson of history: that a sedentary and pleasure-loving people, no matter how civilized, no matter how prosperous, no matter what territories or power they may hold, are easy prey for a more primitive, more aggressive culture inspired by the urge to expand and the will to conquer.

When the Arabs invaded Spain in the year 711 their civilization was just beginning. Mohammed himself had died in 632, and at that time his followers were but simple nomads, who lived in tents, wandered about from place to place, and had little concept of architecture, literature, or the arts. The first mosque that Mohammed constructed at Medina in 622 was a plain and paltry thing, a large, unadorned "open square, surrounded by walls of brick and stone." Only a part of this enclosure "was roofed with mud and palm mats." But the spiritual fire of the prophet kindled a responding flame in the multitudes who followed him, and gradually this turned into a

46 ૐ

human conflagration which enveloped a great part of the Mediterranean world: Arabia, Asia Minor, Persia, North Africa, Sicily, and adjacent islands, and nearly all of Portugal and Spain. At its peak this huge Arabian empire was larger in extent than that of Rome.

Mohammed wisely had based his religion on the time-proved beliefs of Judaism and Christianity. To the founder of Islam both Moses and Jesus were great prophets. Islam itself is mostly a fusion of mandates and concepts taken from these two religions, but in its zeal for combining the priestly and political power Islam was much closer to ancient Judaism. One of the commandments of Mohammed was that his true believers must carry their religion by "fire and sword" into the lands of the infidel. Islam, in fact, divided the world into two parts: the regions under its control, and the lands which remained unsubjugated. Between these two areas there could be no peace.

Practical considerations may induce the Moslem leaders to conclude an armistice, but the obligation to conquer and, if possible convert never lapses. . . . Thanks to this concept, the waging of war acquires religious merit. The Moslem community is under an obligation to combat the infidel. The believer who loses his life in this struggle enters Paradise as a martyr of the faith. The faithful is told that the sword is the key to heaven and hell. One drop of blood spilled on the battlefield, one night spent under arms, will count for more than two months of fasting and prayer.[18]

Islam, thus, was not only a religion but a dynamic of action. This was the germ spark that resulted in the birth of Arabian civilization, which reached its greatest flowering in Spain in the cities of Córdoba, Seville, and Granada, and left its indelible mark in the blood and culture of emergent medieval Spanish society.

The Arabs were not great originators; they imitated readily, absorbed rapidly, fused esthetically whatever pleased them in the more civilized cultures which they encountered and conquered. They added to this fusion an element of lightness, sensuality, and elegance which contrasted notably with the massivity and dark power of medieval Christian civilization. At first, their greatest impact was that of a "vigorous conquering people," but by the tenth century, while the rest of Europe lay in the shadow of the Dark Ages, their brilliant civilization in Spain far outshone anything elsewhere on the Continent. In order to achieve it the Arabs had assimilated much of the best in Greek philosophy, Roman law and government, Byzantine and Persian art, Judaic and Christian theology.

The Arab writer Ibn Khaldun, whose historical writings Arnold Toynbee called "the greatest work of its kind by any mind in any time and place," gives this pointed interpretation of the success and failure of Arab civilization:

Generally speaking, the Arabs are incapable of founding an empire except on a religious basis such as the Revelation of a Prophet or a Saint . . . because their fierce character, pride, roughness and jealousy of one another, especially in political matters, make them the most difficult of peoples to lead . . ., and also because every Arab regards himself as worthy to rule.

These words were written at the end of the fourteenth century, as Ibn Khaldun saw the great Arab empire shrinking daily before his eyes; by a strange coincidence of fate they also apply perfectly to Christian Spain of the 1500's.[19]

Moorish rule in Spain, though in ever-diminishing territories, lasted from 711 to 1492. After their first startling victory over Roderick on the banks of the Guadalete, the Moslem hosts pushed into the north, crossed the Pyrenees, and at Poitiers in southern France met their first decisive defeat at the hands of Charles Martel (Charles the Hammer) in the year 732. This marked the limit of the advance of the crescent. From now on the Moslem empire would steadily decrease in size.

According to Spanish tradition, in 722 A.D., years before the engagement at Poitiers, the Moorish army sent to subdue the Cantabrian mountaineers was defeated by the Asturian chieftain Pelayo, who is also regarded as the first king of Asturias. The vale of Covadonga is marked as the place of this legendary Spanish victory, so widely celebrated in song and story. In all probability it was merely a local skirmish in which the Moslem advance guard was repulsed by the hardy Asturian mountaineers. Nevertheless, the Moors did not seek further penetration into these wild mountains, and it was from this primitive nest that the reconquest of Spain began. The heir apparent to the Spanish throne, in memory of Pelayo's victory, has always been called the Prince of Asturias, much as the heir apparent in Britain is called the Prince of Wales.

The ancient Arabic and Christian chronicles present the engagement at Covadonga in two entirely different lights. The *Chronicle of Alfonso III* (866–910) gives the Christian version, stating that after Pelayo had escaped from Córdoba where he was being held as hostage, the Arabs "entered Asturias with an army of 187,000 soldiers. Pelayo was now with his companions in the mountains, and the army of Alqama approached him and pitched innumerable tents in front of the cave in which the Asturians had taken refuge." The Moors used as emissary a Christian bishop in their midst. He called out to Pelayo to give himself up, for "even the powerful government of the Goths, which was more brilliant than that of any other country, had its great army defeated by the Moslems. So how can you possibly hope to defend yourself in that cave? Listen to me and come forth, and you will receive many favors and will enjoy the friendship of the Moors."

Pelayo answered the bishop with a shout: "Christ is our hope! From this mountain the defeat of the Goths will be avenged. I trust that the promise of the Lord will be fulfilled."[20] Seeing that an easy victory was h⁻ ieless, the Moors attacked in force, and the old chronicle concludes that 125,000 of them were slain in the battle that followed. These figures, of course, are preposterous.

The Moorish report of the engagement is quite different, and minimizes its importance. The history of Al-Maqqari states that "a savage ass named Pelayo rebelled in the land of Galicia, and then the Christians who still held unsubjugated territories elsewhere under the Moslems began also to defend themselves." Moorish soldiers attacked Asturias, driving the inhabitants out of this mountainous country, and finally

all that was left was the rocky cave where Pelayo and his three hundred companions had taken refuge. The Moslems kept up their pressure unceasingly and soon only thirty Asturian men and ten women were left alive. All they had to eat was the honey they could find in the rocks. The Moors finally scorned them and left saying: "Thirty savage asses, what harm can they do us?" In the year 733 Pelayo died and was succeeded by his son Fafila. The reign of Pelayo lasted 19 years, and that of his son two. After them both came Alfonso I, then many other Alfonsos who succeeded in prolonging their rule until today and they reconquered what the Moslems had taken from them.

After the engagement at Covadonga the Moors swarmed into France and were defeated there. Then they commenced to fight among themselves, much as the generals of Alexander fought over the remains of the imperial feast. Almost half a century passed before they called a halt to these intestine bickerings and settled down to the less exciting labor of government. But slowly order was restored throughout the peninsula and the new civilization began to take root and grow. It was marked at once by a gesture of tolerance such as the Christians themselves had never shown.

When General Muza's men reached the city of Córdoba the first thing they saw was the great Visigothic church of St. Vincent, which stood on the banks of the Baetis (called Guadalquivir or Great River by the Moors) on the spot formerly occupied by a Roman temple to Janus. The Moslems neither defaced, destroyed, nor took over the building. They bought half of it in order to have a place to hold their own services, but permitted the other half to be used by the Christians. Dual services continued in this church for nearly half a century. The reason for this tolerance was that the Christians, like the Arabs, had their own holy book, believed in a single God, and many Christian figures were regarded as great prophets by the Moslems. The Christians were not thought of as pagans whose religion was wholly unacceptable. Finally, in 785 the Emir Abderrahman I purchased the remaining half of the structure, tore it down, and put up the first part of the famous Mosque of Córdoba, which is one of the great Moorish monuments in the world today.

Abderrahman wanted to construct a mosque that would rival any in Arabia. With typical Moslem zeal he assembled building materials from many sources. Columns to be used as interior pillars were brought in from several Roman and Visigothic buildings of France and Spain, others came from the more ancient ruins of Carthage; and the Eastern Roman emperor, Leo IV, sent a crew of skilled workmen from Constantinople along with sixteen tons of tesserae (small stone pieces) for the mosaics. The pillars were of various materials: marble of various colors, jasper, porphyry, and breccia. As their height varied, some were buried below the floor level, while others were raised on added bases and topped with Corinthian capitals. The resultant height of them all thus came to thirteen feet. Resting on top of each row of pillars is a tier of horseshoe arches of almost the same height, and atop this second tier is still another. On looking upward one sees not the great spaciousness of a Gothic cathedral but the elegant, intertwined branches of a cool forest.

As the population of Córdoba grew it became necessary to increase the size of the mosque. The original rectangle was enlarged three times. Abderrahman II (822–852) lengthened the aisles in the direction of the river. The second enlargement was added by Alhakem II (961–976) in the same direction. The original size of the mosque was now doubled. The last enlargement was made by Almanzor, who added eight more aisles and also extended the outside courtyard of the orange trees.

The completed mosque was an immense place measuring 590 feet by 425 feet, one-third of which was the enclosed courtyard outside the building. In this stood a beautiful fountain, where the ablutions were performed before the faithful entered the building. The exterior walls were of cinnamon-colored, unadorned stucco; the doors, the slender minaret or prayer tower, and the flowering orange trees were the only signs of exterior beautification. Today the plain outside walls suggest an old fortress more than they do a place of worship.

The interior of the mosque is incredible. It is a delicate forest of pillars, originally at least twelve hundred, and no matter in which direction one looks the eye is lost in endless rows of them. There is no lofty ceiling overhead to detract from this earthy, varicolored stone paradise. In the days of the Moors the walls of the building contained as many doors as there were rows of columns and these doors always remained open when the mosque was in use. In the patio outside rows of orange trees continued the line of the interior columns, thus linking effectively the man-made interior world with the world of God outside.

One of the first things the Christians did when they conquered Córdoba in 1236 was to stone in most of these entrances, thus darkening the interior and closing out the courtyard and the orange trees. They then began to use the mosque as a church, and for three hundred years it continued to be so used without major modifications. Under Charles V an overzealous local bishop requested permission to tear out the center of the building and place there a large choir of sixteenth century design. The town council of Córdoba rose in fury and threatened with death any who dared lay a hand on their beloved building, which had been their cathedral for three centuries. The bishop finally got royal permission to proceed with the choir, which was installed despite the violent opposition of the townsfolk. It still stands, desecrating the architectural purity of the beautiful mosque, yet so large is the building that one does not even notice the intrusion on entering the precincts. When the king later saw the installation he is said to have remarked: "You have destroyed something that is unique in order to construct something that might have been constructed anywhere." There is a good chance, however, that without the insert the building might have been completely demolished.

The mosaics, tiles, and marble which originally covered the floor and interior walls are now all gone, as are the fixtures and draperies. The beautifully colored wooden ceiling of sculptured, enameled, and gilded cedar wood and larch has been stuccoed over and spoiled. The fine many-colored tiles which once covered the entire floor are also gone. In the main chapel the original mosaics remain, and gleam with a delicate and luminous splendor that is difficult to describe. The impression is of a network of embroidered arabesques, of mingled blue, green, scarlet, and gold, airy and iridescent. The *Mihrab* or prayer niche itself, an octagonal recess with seven sides of white marble, is roofed with a single great block carved underneath in the form of a shell, which is said to be the ideal shape acoustically. The pulpit on which an enormous jewel-studded Koran once lay was of ivory and precious woods, ebony, aloe, and sandal; six master workmen and their assistants labored seven years to carve and decorate this piece. In the solid marble floor just at the wall is a great hollow rubbed out by the knees of the myriads of faithful who came to this holy spot, faced Mecca, then wheeled away.

The mosque at one time had sixty attendants to take care of it. Its three hundred candelabra, in part made from the bells which Almanzor had stolen from the cathedral at Santiago in 997, held four thousand lamps filled with perfumed oil. The minaret outside, added by Abderrahman III, contained two winding staircases which did not meet until they reached the top where the muezzin stood to call the faithful to prayer. In the sixteenth century a part of this minaret toppled over and a new tower was built around it. This is the one which stands today.

This great Mosque of Córdoba indicates better than any other structure the birth, progress, and decline of Moorish architecture in Spain. The building is an extended rectangle, and with each addition only one wall was removed as the rectangle was increased in size. Nothing was altered or destroyed in the process. The original section begun by Abderrahman I in 785, less than a century after the Moorish conquest, is relatively crude and unrefined if compared with the second and third sections. Arab architecture reached its peak in the third extension made by Alhakem II in the tenth century. The final extension by Almanzor shows a very definite decline in artistic achievement. A careful examination of the eight hundred pillars which

THE CROSS, THE CRESCENT, AND THE STAR ◀§ 53

remain in the interior reveals almost every architectural style that ever existed in this portion of the Mediterranean world. There are ancient Carthaginian pillars from North Africa, Roman pillars from all over Spain and Gaul, white-topped Visigothic columns from Spain with their delicate fleur-de-lis carvings, pagan symbol of Visigothic art; still other pillars were a gift from the Byzantine emperor in Constantinople, and perhaps there are columns from the Roman temple of Janus which stood on this very same spot, just off the famous Via Augusta, before the Visigoths destroyed it and raised their Church of St. Vincent. Thus the Mosque of Córdoba recapitulates the artistic history of Spain in a way that no other structure can possibly do.

Moslem rule in Spain was never like that of Rome, with a strong centralized government whose capital stood outside the peninsula. There was a nominal link with Damascus, which was not completely broken until Abderrahman III in 929 declared himself independent and established the caliphate of Córdoba. However, Damascus was far away, and the Arabs were never as thoroughly organized or as efficient in government as the Romans. The empire in Spain, therefore, almost immediately took on divisive qualities of its own. It was also unfortunately a battleground for the successive waves of Moors who invaded the peninsula, each anxious to take over the rule from the preceding contingent. There was no long-term, unified Moslem government. Except for relatively brief periods Moorish Spain was composed of several petty kingdoms, just as was the Christian part of the country to the north.

Moorish rule was marked by many revolts and frequent internal warfare among the Moslem kingdoms, but there were also long periods of tranquillity, and the general course of Arab civilization was upward until the thirteenth century, that is, for a period of almost five hundred years. The original invaders, strengthened by Berber reinforcements and even by Slavs, maintained themselves for about three centuries. The last of these (912–1010) represents the zenith of the first period of Arab culture. With the death of Almanzor at the turn of the century this period comes to an end, the Arabs appear to have lost much of their momentum, and widespread rebellions break out in their dominions which result in the establishment of twenty-six splinter states. In 1085 the Christians captured Toledo, at the geographic center of the peninsula, and this victory is regarded as the most important event since the arrival of the Moors in 711. Confused and frightened, the Arab rulers decided to send an urgent call for help to the Berbers of Morocco. The call was answered and a large army of recent converts to Islam, the Almoravides ("those vowed to God"), crossed the Strait of Gibraltar in 1086. The Almoravides were a fanatical Berber group who forthwith imposed their will on the fragmented Moorish dominions. But their aggressiveness and even their intolerance were soon muted by the pleasant land and civilization of *Al-Andalus,* which was the Arab name for Moslem Spain. Half a century later an even more primitive group of Berbers from the Atlas mountains, the Almohades (unitarians), poured into the country (1146) and took over its government. Thousands of Jews and *Mozárabes* (Christians living in Arab territory) fled to the north and joined their coreligionists in the petty Spanish kingdoms. Moorish intolerance was beginning now to undermine the power and integrity of the state. Despite this unhappy political condition cultural progress continued unabated until the Moors suffered their disastrous defeat on the plains of Tolosa (*Las Navas de Tolosa*) at the hands of King Alfonso VIII of Castile, in 1212. From that day Arab dominion was doomed in the peninsula, although more than two centuries elapsed before the fall of Granada in 1492.

There were three main centers of Arab civilization in Spain: Córdoba, Seville, and Granada. Each of these cities and regions in turn enjoyed its period of efflorescence and dominion. The approximate dates of these periods of splendor are as follows:

Córdoba   756–1010
Seville   1010–1248
Granada   1248–1492

The tenth century caliphate of Córdoba is generally given as the high-water mark of Arab civilization in Spain. However, the two following centuries were those during which the intellectual achievements of the Moors reached their greatest flowering. It was during this latter period that the famous philosophers Averroës, a Moor, and Maimonides, a Jew, left their stamp on European culture. It was mainly through Averroës that the knowledge of Aristotle spread through medieval Europe.

A more detailed examination of each of the three periods will help to clarify the picture. First, the period of Córdoba 756–1010. When the Arab historians describe Córdoba they use nothing but superlatives, and it is an almost impossible task to sift fact from fancy. This is particularly true when it comes to a matter of statistics: population figures, numbers of houses, numbers of mosques, numbers of public baths, even numbers of women in the harem. The Arabs, like the early Spanish conquistadores, had no mind for statistical accuracy, and any figure of more than a couple of hundred often appeared to them as astronomical. In spite of all this the actual Moorish remains in Córdoba, Seville, and Granada conclusively prove that these cities were more populous, more prosperous, and artistically more brilliant than any Christian city in Spain or elsewhere in Europe at that time.

The Arabic historians all agree that Córdoba was "the jewel of the world," but when it becomes a matter of exact figures there is a wide disagreement even among them. Perhaps the only sensible thing to do is strike an average. Here is an old Arab statistical survey by Al-Maqqari:

One authority estimates that there were 490 mosques in the city during the reign of Abderrahman III, but it is true that the city continued to grow after that time. Another writer calculates them at 471. One of the natives has said that the baths inside and outside the city limits came to 3000, but others mention 700 as the total.

At any rate the figures given by Ben Said, an author who took his information from Ben Hayyan and other historians who actually lived in the prosperous times of the Caliphate of Córdoba, are as follows: 113,000 houses for the ordinary population of the town, and about half that figure, or perhaps a little more, for the state officials, the court favorites, military chieftains, and others.

The number of mosques in the period of greatest splendor never exceeded 700, nor the baths more than 900, but he mentions having read in an old history that in the days of Abderrahman III, the city contained 300,000 houses and 877 mosques. The figure given by Al-Bakri, 477 mosques, is far below this.

Another Moorish author assures us that he personally went around and *counted* more than 200,000 houses in the city. The contemporary Spanish historian, Claudio Sánchez-Albornoz, in his fundamental work *La España musulmana,* has gathered together many of these old documents. He himself assures us that Córdoba had a population of about half a million souls in the tenth century, and that it was undoubtedly the largest city in western Europe.

William C. Atkinson, an excellent contemporary British historian, refers to Córdoba's magnificent palaces, gardens, and fountains, "its 50,000 mansions of the aristocracy and governing classes, its 700 mosques and 900 public baths." The Lebanese historian Edward Atiyah believes that the 300 public baths assigned to Córdoba fall well within the realm of possibility. Nearly all historians mention the 400,000 volumes (manuscripts) in the library of Córdoba during the period of Caliph Alhakem II (961–976).

It is probable that there were two or three hundred thousand *volumes* (not separate titles) in this famous library. Many of these were only portions of complete books, and could today be printed on five to ten pages of paper. Also, there were probably several hundred *copies* of certain books, such as the Koran, for example. In regard to the population of the city of Córdoba, a figure of perhaps 250,000 would appear to be maximal. It is doubtful whether the Moslem economy could feed and supply a city of greater size than this.

The usually reliable Spanish historian Salvador de Madariaga mentions "the five thousand looms weaving all kinds of cloth from brocade and silk to wool and cotton" in one of the smaller courts of Andalusia, and then goes on to add, "and the Prime Minister of a small state (a kind of Islamic Goethe in his Spanish Weimar) had four hundred thousand books in his library, while the *great* and famous library of the monastery of Ripoll in Christian Catalonia boasted of its paltry 192 volumes."

Take all of the above figures with a grain of salt; whatever the statistics the glory of Córdoba rests securely on its being the largest, the wealthiest, and the most civilized city in western Europe in the tenth century. Its main streets were lighted and paved. It did have a very large number of public baths, which were used assiduously. Water obtained from the mountains was brought into town on a long aqueduct and distributed to different parts of the city in pipes of lead. Córdoba also had many beautiful homes, many lovely mosques, and a very large collection of manuscripts in its unique library. Only Byzantine Constantinople could compare with it.

Córdoba was also the scientific center of Europe in the Middle Ages. The Christian kings and nobles who were gravely ill or needed an operation came to the physicians of Córdoba for treatment. Their surgeons understood the use of anesthetics, and operations for cataracts and pressure on the brain were said to have been performed successfully on many occasions. Medicine, botany, chemistry, physics, mathematics, astronomy, geography, and Greek philosophy were but a few of the fields in which the savants of Córdoba excelled. Algebra was almost entirely an invention of the Moors, as was spherical trigonometry. They brought to Europe their Arabic numerals which were infinitely easier to use than the clumsy numerals of the Romans, and represented almost as great an advance in mathematics as the phonetic alphabet of the Phoenicians did in writing. They also gave digits the value of position, and were the first to use the decimal notation. The concept of zero was also an Arab contribution to European mathematics, though it is thought to be a concept that came originally from India.

The city of Córdoba was the center of a thriving economy and a well-developed agriculture. It was surrounded by several towns of considerable size and importance: Almodovar, 16 miles distant; Mored, 25 miles away; Alcozer, 19 miles; Gafek, two days' march; Ecija, 36 miles; Baena, two days' march; Estepona, 36 miles. In the vicinity of Córdoba "there were no less than 3000 villages, all of them provided with mosques." The surrounding area was filled with farms and the markets of Córdoba were supplied with foods and fruits, cloths, drugs, handmade goods of all kinds, jewelry, and importations which one of the old historians calls "curiosities from distant and unknown lands."

The Arabian historians state that Córdoba had a university long before there was any elsewhere in Europe; the city also boasted seventy libraries, many bookshops, and was rich in manuscripts from all over the world. Córdoba probably reached its zenith during the reign of Abderrahman III (912–961), often called "the Just," who established the caliphate. Jews, learned Arabs immersed in Greek scholarship, and Spanish Christians all frequented Abderrahman's court. One of the outstanding monuments of this patron of the arts was his palace called Medina Azahara, not far from Córdoba. Medina is the Arabic word for "city," and Azahara was the caliph's favorite wife. The palace was built as a tribute to her. If we are to believe those who describe this palace and its gardens, it was even more impressive than the famous mosque.

The last time I saw the ruins of this once lovely place was on a blistering day in August. The air was motionless as we passed through the narrow streets of Córdoba with their yellow churches, their white houses, their tiny cool green patios, their omnipresent Mozarabic latticework, and headed into the country. The driver who took me was an old man whose car was as ancient as he was, if one may judge from appearances. He was a typical Cordoban, proud, erect, impassioned, living on memories of the heroic past. He apologized for the car:

"I bought it in 1929," he said. "In 1936 I was about ready to replace it, but then the civil war broke out, and there has been no possibility of changing it for a newer model since that time. Automobiles cost an incredible sum in Spain, so I am stuck with this one until it breaks down completely. Until then it makes my living for me. I take good care of it."

As we left behind the last straggling whitewashed houses hugging the ground under their grayish-red tile roofs, the countryside opened like a great fan and the hills surrounding the town loomed before us. A few plane trees and poplars marked the road. There were many rocks and the fields were covered with grayish tufted grass. The hollows of dry water beds were choked with oleanders and tamarisk. A gentle breeze sprang up and rolled softly into the car, bearing the aroma of dry leaves permeated with a faint scent of animal manure. A single cloud, like a white feather, was ribbed against the sky. We turned to the right off the main road and headed toward one of the hills. There was a tractor plowing a nearby field.

"It's all like that around here," the old man said with a wide gesture of his hand, "there are tractors all the way to Seville or Granada. The farm workers can find no jobs. The land of Andalusia is divided up into huge estates, just as it was five hundred years ago. We live just as we did in the time of the Catholic kings."

The ancient jalopy wheezed to the top of the hill and came to a sudden halt. Beneath us and to our left lay the whole valley of Córdoba, which had opened in the sunlight like a flower. What a strange mixture of men and history is rooted to these rocky fields, these rounded hills, that distant city shining beside the Guadalquivir. Abderrahman III, the great poet Góngora, Maimonides, Almanzor, and Manolete—Córdoba was the home of these and many others.

We stood for a moment on the brow of the rounded hill. The air was soft and bright. We saw some crumbling walls below. Above them, on the slope of the hill, were a few live oaks, *encinas*, and some olive trees. The locusts chanted out their loud and imperturbable song, and the air was filled with tiny vibrancies.

The sole caretaker of Medina Azahara was a fifteen-year-old boy, who regarded the place as his treasure. In his hut which stood above the ruins he was patiently piecing together some fragments of marble and alabaster. We passed through the entrance hut and onto the promontory. The crumbled walls of the ancient palace spread out before us. Between them lay only uneven heaps of rubble and weeds. I stepped out along the top of one of the walls and sauntered along its length. There was no restoration here. What priceless relics might be lying beneath those mounds of stones and weeds?

Then we went down below. Here two men were working on the Hall of the Ambassadors, at a snail's pace, to be sure, attempting to restore it to something resembling its former beauty. Marble fragments replaced in their proper positions took on a new loveliness, but restored arches, pieced with new stucco where the old arches were turned to dust, had lost their ancient glory. It seemed better to leave things as they were, for a restored Medina Azahara would never recapture the appearance of the fallen palace. Untouched ruins take on a hallowed glow, undisturbed by the sharp polish of modernity. Better let them be. The mind can evoke its own memories, and history can be clothed with a personal light. Thus the individual may feel himself a part of all mankind, his roots sunk deep in the bottomless well of the past.

According to Moorish historians Abderrahman had eight thousand workers engaged in the task of constructing Medina Azahara, which occupied a space approximately fifteen hundred by seven hundred and fifty meters; and it required four hundred camels and one thousand mules to haul the heavy building materials. Although these figures are doubtless greatly exaggerated, Medina Azahara was truly a fabulous place. The entire area was walled, and within these walls rose a magnificent palace with four hundred rooms, spacious gardens, many accessory buildings, a large pool, and in the middle of the central patio stood a fountain filled with quicksilver which could be set in motion, causing an iridescent play of lights on the walls and trees. This fountain was the caliph's greatest delight. An aqueduct sixteen kilometers long brought water to the palace and then continued on into Córdoba. There were columns (Arab historians mention four hundred) and basins brought from Constantinople, and a Grecian hand appears to have had some part in the architecture.

Unfortunately, very little remains of Medina Azahara today, but even the ruins are sufficiently majestic to warrant the opinion that it was one of the great monuments of Moorish art. I spent many hours examining the ruins and letting my mind roam freely in an attempt to recapture some of the ancient splendor of the palace. Very little restoration has taken place at Medina Azahara, and the long rows of decaying walls, with occasional stretches of beautiful marble floors and interior wall coverings of exquisitely carved marble, are sufficient to set the imagination afire. The lacelike mural designs and arabesques of this palace are not of ground alabaster or marble plaster as in the palaces of Seville and Granada, but of solid blocks of marble intricately carved. There are clear evidences of their having been adorned with semiprecious stones, for lead settings still remain in the walls in dozens of places. The palace was burned to the ground in the year 1010 in the rebellion which toppled the caliphate, and the rebellious Moorish vandals made every effort to destroy the lovely building completely. There are still deep black marks from the tremendous heat seared into the beautiful white marble floors. Fortunately, some of the collapsing material enveloped the lower portion of the building, thus saving what has been preserved as a stark reminder of lost grandeur.

On one occasion when Abderrahman received a Christian embassy at this palace the road from Córdoba, about four miles distant, was covered with mats and lined with a double file of soldiers. At the palace dignitaries dressed in silk and brocade came out to receive the Christians, who greeted one of these men, thinking he was the caliph. But Abderrahman was "sitting in the middle of a courtyard covered with sand, wearing rude clothing, the symbol of his ascetic customs." This was the great ruler who had dazzled the world with his wealth and his splendor. When Abderrahman was an old man he is said to have recounted the various episodes of his long life, concluding sadly that he had enjoyed only fourteen completely happy days! *Sic transit gloria mundi!*

The Arabs studied astronomy assiduously and built excellent observatories. They brought many musical instruments into Europe including the lute, famous in medieval music, and the oval guitar. Their music gave that of Spain an exotic quality which is its greatest charm today. Paper was introduced into Europe by the Moors and made possible the development of printing. Glass is said to have been invented in Córdoba, and while its invention there may be dubious its practical and wide use in Spain is not to be denied. Moorish glassware and pottery was of the finest quality, and their textiles and tiles have never been surpassed. The Moors also brought into the peninsula cotton, sugarcane, rice, the palm tree, mulberry trees, and a whole new concept of irrigation in agriculture, including the waterwheel and carefully engineered irrigation ditches. They understood the use of fertilizer and were expert grafters, producing many new varieties of fruit and flowers. They built immense aqueducts and used water lavishly in order to make Al-Andalus blossom like the watered rose.

It was mainly on the base of a successful agriculture that they were able to raise the superstructure of their Hispanic civilization. The sound of water to these desert people must have had something mystical about it; it was a Moslem ritual to perform daily ablutions, and one has but to roam through any of their palaces or gardens today to become aware of how much flowing water meant to them esthetically. Their finest architectural gems are inseparable from large reflecting pools and fountains. Their lovely gardens are possible only because of the constant flow of water. As a consequence of their own great love of water the Moors very naturally thought that the Christians never washed at all. "They were sprinkled with water at the time they were born, and thus relieved from washing for the rest of their lives."[21]

Moslem rule in Spain was in the main progressive and tolerant. However, unbelievers had to pay a special income tax, and did not enjoy complete equality before the law. Obviously many Christians became converts to Islam in order to wipe out these inequalities. The Moors came to Spain without women. The first generation of Moorish soldiers all took Spanish wives, hence the second generation of Moslems were already half Spanish in blood. As time passed the original Moorish blood became very thin, and the children often learned to speak the language of their mothers. New waves of invaders came across the straits and race mixing altered notably the physical make-up of the population, particularly in Andalusia.

In the early years of their domination the Moslems enforced a tribute of feminine slaves for their harems; in the later years intermarriage was a common practice of peninsular life. Many of the emirs and caliphs stipulated that *gallegas*, blonde women from Galicia, be provided in their tribute, and Galician women slaves were always in great demand. This led to blue eyes among some of the later caliphs. There was also a considerable amount of intermarriage among the noble and royal families of Moors and Christians. King Roderick's widow wedded the son of General Muza. Pelayo's sister also married a Moor. Alfonso VI of Castile and León took as wife the daughter of a caliph of Seville. Two of Almanzor's wives were Christian princesses. One of these was given to Almanzor by the king of Navarre, who hoped thus to keep the victorious Moorish army from his borders. This Christian girl later became one of the most religious Moslems in Córdoba. King Vermudo of León also gave his daughter in marriage to the Moslem leader. These mixed unions in the royal and upper classes were multiplied by the hundreds of thousands among the masses. Centuries later, when the Spaniards came to the New World, their own soldiers found it perfectly natural to seek consorts or wives among the native Indian population.

The intellectual pursuits of the Arabs in Spain gave them the unquestioned leadership of the medieval world in this regard. The Jews too, who had been bitterly persecuted among the Visigoths, flourished under Moorish rule and many arrived from the east to settle in Córdoba, which became the great center of Hebrew learning of the Middle Ages, and one of the most famous Hebrew scholastic centers of all time. The Talmudic school of Córdoba was famous throughout Europe. Jews were frequently used as emissaries and ambassadors among the various Moorish kingdoms, for they were highly regarded and trusted by both sides. Numerous Jews held exalted posts in the community and in the government. Many of the caliphs of Córdoba had Jewish physicians. In the tenth century Abderrahman III's minister of finance and ambassador was the Jewish scholar, Hasday ben-Shaprut. The Jew Samuel ibn Nagrella became the vizier of the king of Granada in the following century; he was succeeded in office by his son. Another Jew was the vizier of the king of Saragossa in the eleventh century. Later Hebrew intellects in Spain even surpassed these men: there was Rabbi Abraham ben Ezra (glorified by Browning), Ben Gabirol of Malaga, Yehudah ha-Levi of Toledo, and the most famous of them all, Maimonides of Córdoba.

The invasion of the fanatical Almoravides and Almohades in the eleventh and twelfth centuries sent many Jews scampering into the northern Christian dominions, where the Spanish kings treated them with general esteem and tolerance until the time of Ferdinand and Isabella. The Spaniards followed the Arab custom of utilizing Jewish physicians, scientists, tax collectors, judges, diplomats, and public officials. Oftentimes Jews collected the tribute which Moorish rulers owed to the kings of Christendom, and vice versa. In this case, as among the Moors, the Jews were neutral emissaries whose morality was trusted implicitly. The Hebrew scholars who gathered around the famous Alfonso the Learned of Castile and León in the thirteenth century helped to give that medieval court its intellectual flavor. By this time the upper hand in Spain had passed from the Moors to the Christians.

Literature in both Hebrew and Arabic was cultivated under the Moors. By 850 many ecclesiastical writers were complaining that Latin was neglected, that even the church fathers and the Scriptures were no longer read. The Christian writer Alvaro in 854 deplored this attitude:

> My fellow Christians delight in the poems and romances of the Arabs. They study the works of Moslem theologians and philosophers, not in order to refute them, but to acquire a correct and elegant Arabic style. Where today can a layman be found who reads the Latin commentaries on Holy Scriptures? Alas! the young Christians who are most conspicuous for their talents have no knowledge of any literature or language save the Arabic.[18]

But there was also a third language widely used in Moorish Spain: the everyday primitive Spanish of the *Mozárabes*. Indeed this language was probably the most widely spoken idiom of the streets.

For many years it was thought that the first literature in the Spanish language was the epic *Poem of the Cid*, of 1140. However, in 1948, several very lovely lyric verses were discovered in Mozarabic Spanish, which antedate the *Cid* by over a century. The way in which these verses were composed is most interesting. Among both the Hebrews and the Arabs one of the most popular forms of literature was a sophisticated and rather long type of poem in which the final few lines, a sort of refrain or summing up, were in this Mozarabic Spanish. These lines were a popular outburst, a *cri de coeur* very possibly lifted bodily from already existing folk poetry. The rest of the poem was invariably either in Hebrew or in Arabic, and the alphabet used was always (even in the Spanish verses) either Hebrew or Arabic. Since Hebrew omits the vowels, the transcription of these verses has been difficult, but several dozens of them have now been satisfactorily turned into ancient Spanish. They resemble very strongly the popular Spanish *copla* which has always been the basis of Spanish folk poetry and folk songs. One such couplet reads as follows in Mozarabic Spanish:

> Vayse meu corachón de mib,
> ya rab, si se me tornarád?
> Tan mal meu doler li-l-habib!
> Enfermo yed, cuand sanarád?

My heart is going away from me,
Oh, God, when will it return?
So great is the grief for my beloved!
For he is ill, oh, when will he be well?

The Hebrew poetry of Mozarabic days was known and read in
Jewish communities outside of Spain as well as in the peninsula, and
the ancient Jews had a prohibition against throwing away any of their
waste paper for fear the name of God might be written on it. The
paper was thus buried rather than burned or discarded as garbage. It
is one of these buried lots of paper found in Egypt that has given us
our oldest examples of the Spanish language. Later, other similar
verses were discovered in the Arabic alphabet. It is entirely fitting that
these brief poems are of a popular, intense lyrical nature, and prove
that modern literatures, like ancient literatures, do not have to begin
with an epic. Quite the contrary, it now appears that in the brief
telescoped couplets of folklore, concerning the love of a man for a
woman, nearly all literature finds its point of origin. The Song of
Solomon is an example of this very ancient tradition among the
Hebrews of the Old Testament, a tradition which repeated itself in
Spain under the Moors.

In the year 976 the accession of a minor to the caliphate of
Córdoba led to the assumption of power by his minister, Almanzor
the Victorious. Almanzor was a gifted and impulsive general whose
swiftly maneuvering armies brought dread into every corner of Christian Spain. In fear of him the kings of León and Navarre gave the
general their daughters as wives. One of Almanzor's feats was to
destroy the cathedral at Santiago, the holiest shrine of the Christians,
carrying its bells and doors back to Córdoba where they were used
in the great mosque (997). He is said to have taken part in fifty
separate attacks on Christian territory. On some of these he was
accompanied "by forty poets and writers." Unfortunately, Almanzor
allowed Moslem fanatics to take over the government of the
caliphate.

Five years after the sacking of Santiago the great Moor died, and
according to the Christian chroniclers "was buried in hell." With his
death the glory that was Córdoba also passed away. The city was
looted by both rebellious Moors and Christians, and by 1010 had
entered a period of drastic decline. When Fernando el Santo captured
the place more than two centuries later it was no longer "the capital

of a flourishing, civilized state, but a decayed provincial town." Seville now became the center of Moslem culture in Spain.

The city of Seville had been a great center of the Roman Empire in Spain. Its name in those days was Hispalis, and from this was derived the Arabic Ishbiliya, which in Spanish became Sevilla. For a time the city was the capital of the Visigoths, then Toledo replaced it and Seville declined in importance. When the Moors arrived they immediately began to build it up again. According to the Arabic historian al-Idrisi the population of the surrounding area was of great density, and consisted of no less than eight thousand villages.

During the early period of the Moorish occupation of Spain Seville had to play second fiddle to Córdoba. Through all these years (711–1010), it was, nevertheless, the second city of Andalusia, and its size, influence, and opulence were growing constantly. After the decline of Córdoba, Seville moved into the limelight. In the second half of the eleventh century, under al-Mutamid, it became a rendezvous of scholars and artists. The Almoravide hordes put an end to this in 1086, but after a period of stress the city rebounded, and under the Almohades, who entered Spain in 1146, Seville again flourished, this time as never before. Its power and opulence lasted until Fernando III, the Saint, besieged and finally took it from the Moors in 1248.

The early fanaticism of the Almohades, like that of the Almoravides, soon died out. Their leaders were religious idealists, however primitive their Berber way of life. The influence of the Arabic culture in Spain quickly softened their aggressive zeal. In fact, as the English historian J. B. Trend points out, the Almohades believed not only in the unity of God, but in the complete spiritualization of the whole concept of God. "The Almohade creed showed signs of a philosophical breadth of view lacking in most of its contemporaries and perhaps tending to pantheism."

The Almohade period, which lasted barely a century, was the most intellectually fertile period of Moslem Spain. Christians and Jews were stimulated by this new and vigorous wave of intellectualism. The Jew, Maimonides, was a world-renowned philosopher, whose family, unfortunately, was forced to leave Córdoba under the first onslaught of Almohade bigotry. Moslem thinkers like Ibn Tufail, Avempace, and Averroës, were known throughout Europe. The names of the last two were Latinized, because of their widespread celebrity, and are generally remembered in that form. The Latin *Ave* takes the place of the Arabic *Ibn*, which means "the son of." Averroës believed in the supremacy of the human intellect; for him there could be no possible contradiction between science and religion. He would never have accepted the dogma of Christian Spain where the church might decide finally what kind of interpretation must be given either to written documents or religious events. It was Averroës too, who, when he referred to the fanatical destruction of the marvelous library of Córdoba by Moslem zealots, exclaimed: "There is no tyranny on earth like the tyranny of priests." It was through these men that Greek thought, particularly that of Aristotle, became known in medieval Europe. St. Thomas Aquinas knew well the works of all these men and was definitely influenced by some of their ideas. In his *Summa Contra Gentiles* he presented a refutation of their main philosophy.

The Almohades in Seville instituted an immense building and beautification program. The palaces, towers, quays, and dykes which were constructed under the rule of Emir Yusuf are the marvel of modern engineering. The old Roman aqueduct was repaired and enlarged, and brought water from the springs of Alcalá into the city. The Guadalquivir was spanned with a pontoon bridge, and the river itself was forced back into its proper channel with gigantic walls. These walls also served as quays and facilitated the loading and unloading of ships. Large warehouses were built on the riverbanks, and Seville became one of the great emporiums of the Mediterranean.

The defenses of the capital were also reconstructed. The ancient walls were repaired and new sections added; numerous towers were erected to command the river. In 1171 the Almohades began the construction of their famous palace, the Alcázar. Surrounded by spacious grounds it was one of the great wonders of the city. Unfortunately, little remains today of the original structure; the building which survives (not the shell but the interior) is the product of Moors who did a complete job of renovation under Peter the Cruel, in the mid-1300's. In 1220 the Almohades built a magnificent tower on the banks of the Guadalquivir to protect their palace. Known as the Tower of Gold, it is still intact, and is one of the marvels of Seville. Peter the Cruel's name is also connected with this structure for it was he who began to store his gold loot and tribute there, and thus called it the Tower of Gold.

The Almohades' greatest monument in Seville was their mosque,

which was built between 1170 and 1200. It followed the usual Arabic
rectangle in design, and measured 414 feet by 270 feet in size. This
building rivaled the famous Mosque of Córdoba. Its walls were
fringed

with Persian battlements and painted with many colors. Its arcades looked
upon a court supplied with ever-murmuring fountains and fragrant with
the odor of orange blossoms. Its hundreds of marble columns suggested
the spoliation of many a Pagan temple. The ceiling was formed by domes
of wood and stucco, whose geometrical patterns disclosed the correctness
of taste and inexhaustible fertility and fancy characteristic of the labors of
Arab artist and gilder. Its mosaic pavements, its alabaster lattices, its
curious arabesques presented finished types of Moorish decorative
splendor.

There was a minaret of moderate height at one corner of the building which was graceful in shape and elaborately decorated. Diagonally
opposite this minaret the Almohades constructed their greatest architectural monument, the famous Giralda, said to have been designed
by the man who invented algebra. The spires and top of this beautiful
tower as seen today were added by the Spaniards in the sixteenth
century. The original Moorish tower was flat on top, but was surmounted by four great golden spheres.

One of the ancient Moorish writers of the twelfth century, Ben
Abdun al-Tuchibi, in a document on the administration of Seville,
comments tartly on the Jews and Christians of his community. He
writes: "We should not sell to Jews or Christians books of science
except those by their own authors, because they translate these works
of science into their languages and attribute them to their people and
to their bishops, despite their being the works of Moslem writers."[20]

The Moorish population of Seville so loved their city and considered her so great, so wealthy, and so provided with everything, that
a proverb was made up which said: "If one were to ask for bird's milk
in Seville, he would be able to get it." The Arabic writers praise the
city's rich and abundant foods, her lovely women, her fine musicians,
her great number of excellent poets. In regard to the private dwellings
of the inhabitants one native writer says:

Their owners keep them in a state of perfection, for this is their great
zeal. In the majority of them running water is not lacking, nor shady trees,
such as the orange, the lemon, the citron and many others. . . . The
scholars who live in Seville specialize in every branch of knowledge, serious

or jocose; they are so numerous that they cannot be counted and so celebrated that their names need not be mentioned. . . . My only purpose in saying all these things about Seville is to give some idea of the representative excellencies of all Al-Andalus, because, while none of the cities there is lacking in any of these things, nevertheless, I have placed Seville, or rather God has placed her, as the mother of all the cities and the center of the glory and excellences of that territory, for it is the most populous and the greatest of her capitals.

This was the bright city which Ferdinand III, the Saint, surrounded with his large army of Christians in 1247. Seville did not fall easily. The siege lasted for sixteen months, and proved to be the most arduous and obstinately contested struggle of the Reconquest. In the beginning the Christians laid waste to the fertile plains surrounding the city; nothing was left standing that might aid the enemy. The houses were all burned, the harvests were trampled in the fields. The vineyards were destroyed, and the orchards of orange, almond, and pomegranate trees were cut down and set afire. The sky was filled with smoke and soot from these fires, so that Seville itself was so enveloped in darkness at times that its streets were impassable. The daylight hours often "exceeded the gloom of a starless night."

The thoroughness and severity of the Spanish attack was immediately effective in bringing several of the more defenseless towns of Andalusia into the Christian camp. Those which did not surrender were taken by storm, sacked, looted, leveled, and their inhabitants slain without mercy. Seville was finally isolated and left to its own deserts. Still, it was a formidable adversary. The ramparts were equipped with the most devastating engines of destruction known to the military science of the age. Enormous catapults hurled masses of stone and iron weighing hundreds of pounds. The Moorish bowmen could completely transfix a horse sheathed in armor. From the great walls Greek fire was dumped on the moving towers of the Christians, consuming them in flames. Nevertheless, the soldiers of Ferdinand held on with dogged determination, closing ever tighter their ring of steel. In the end hunger and despair made the inhabitants of Seville surrender. The Christian army entered the forbidding walls and passed down streets lined with gaunt and sorrowful faces. At last, the capital of Al-Andalus was in their hands.

Ferdinand the Saint had not won this victory alone; his ally was the Moorish king of Granada, whose knowledge of this kind of war had been invaluable. After the city was taken Ferdinand attempted to expel the entire Moslem population, and thousands (perhaps one hundred thousand) left Seville and followed the king of Granada back into his kingdom behind its mountain walls, which was all that remained of the once glorious Al-Andalus.

Ferdinand the Saint died four years after the capture of Seville. He was one of the greatest commanders and most famous kings of Old Castile. "A few hours before his death, on the 30th of May, 1252, in abasing humility he received the last sacrament, kneeling upon the bare earth, with a rope about his neck," in the guise and the attitude of a repentant sinner.

When the great mosque of Seville was torn down, only its minaret the Giralda remaining, a sumptuous cathedral was erected in its place. It is the third largest church in the world, after St. Peter's in Rome, and St. Paul's in London. A special chapel was built to house the remains of Ferdinand III, the Saint. He lies there now enshrined in a massive silver casket, around which candles burn constantly. On the walls are the historic escutcheons of Castile and of León. The royal sepulcher bears an epitaph in four languages: Latin, Spanish, Hebrew, and Arabic. Ferdinand the Saint would wholeheartedly have approved of thus showing his respect for the present and for the past. But his life and his victories had already moved Spain in another direction: the rugged dominance of Castile and of the Castilian language throughout Spain.

For many years after 1252, on each anniversary of the king's death, a detachment of Moors from Granada, with lighted tapers in their hands, stood motionless and in silence. Today, three times a year, the silver casket is opened and the body of St. Ferdinand is exposed to public view. He still wears the ancient robes, the crown, and holds the scepter of his authority. A long, white beard still covers his kingly breast. In the same chapel, but not occupying such a place of honor, also lies his son, Alfonso X, *el Sabio*, in his own right one of the truly great rulers of medieval times. But his story belongs to another chapter.

There is an old Andalusian saying: *Quien no ha visto Sevilla, no ha visto maravilla* ("Who has not seen Seville, has not seen a wonder.") This was certainly the impression made on the victorious Christian army which entered the city in 1248. The *General Chronicle* drawn up only a few years after the event by Alfonso X, the Learned, describes Seville as the Spaniards found it. They could not repress their amazement on beholding the splendor of the place, for in their own kingdoms there was nothing that could compare with it:

Seville was a great, and noble, and very rich city, replete with every comfort and all luxurious things . . . there were beautiful streets and wide plazas where all kinds of stores and shops abounded, each trade or business occupying its own section, and all neatly distributed and well ordered . . . no place so wealthy or so beautifully adorned had ever been seen before, nor any so populous, or so powerful, or so filled with noble and marvelous sights. The walls of the city were the greatest that had ever been seen; they are so high, and strong, and wide, with great towers guarding them at regular intervals, all constructed at tremendous effort . . . The Tower of Gold is a lovely and wonderful structure, and who could estimate how much it cost the king to build? And then that other great tower of Saint Mary (the Giralda), how noble, beautiful and tall it is: seventy-five feet in width, and three hundred feet in height; so wide and smooth and skillful and gradual was the construction of the stairway ramp by which one reaches the top of the tower, that the kings and queens and grandees who wish to go up mounted on their beasts may easily do so to the very summit. And on top of the first tower stands a second, which is almost fifty feet high, and marvelously wrought. And on top of this there are four huge metal spheres, one above the other; they are so large and so nobly cast that in the entire world there cannot be any others like them. . . .

The *Chronicle* then proceeds in some detail to describe these enormous balls or "apples," as the writer calls them, which are of graduated size, the smallest being the one on top. They are all brightly gilded and gleam in the sunlight. The ancient document continues:

But the one on the bottom is so enormous and of such rare workmanship that it is difficult to believe if one has not seen it. This sphere is ringed with graceful grooves or canals, five palms wide, and when it was taken down and they tried to get it into the city, it would not pass through the gate, so they had to tear off the doors and enlarge the entrance. And there are many, many other great and marvelous things besides these which we have mentioned.

The *Chronicle* then baldly states that no city in the world has the wonderful location of Seville,

a city into which ships from the sea come every day following the river, and even going inside the walls to anchor. They come with wonderful wares from all over the world: from Tangiers, Ceuta, Tunis, Bougie, Alexandria, Genoa, Lombardy, Portugal, England, Pisa, Bordeaux, Bayonne, Sicily, Gascony, Catalonia, Aragon, and even from northern France, and from many other places from far beyond the seas.[22]

There is almost an oriental sensuality in the description of the city, which so dazzled the Spaniards from their stark and wind-swept plains, their poorly constructed towns and homes, their neglected fields. The Castilian Cortes or parliament was constantly pointing out how "poor and sterile was the land" of their part of Spain, how bare and underpopulated it was, how lacking in cattle and foods. The juxtaposition of the two ways of life cannot be more clearly seen than in this early chronicle drawn up by the son of the king who took Seville from the Moors. Perhaps, too, Alfonso X was in this way honoring his great father, Ferdinand the Saint, who had led the victorious army into Seville in 1248 and thus sealed the sentence of death of Moslem Andalusia. Now there remained in Moorish hands only the tributary kingdom of Granada.

The city of Granada today is perhaps the most beautiful in all Spain. Its geographic setting is unique, incomparable. Surrounded by the towering peaks of the Sierra Nevada, the city itself lies in the midst of a green and fertile plain, called the *vega*. Water is still brought to the plain from the mountains, some of it still coursing along the ancient Moorish aqueducts. In the gardens of the Alhambra one can hear its sound unceasingly, as it flows from the earthen pipes. The Moors loved water, for they had come from a dry and waterless land, and wherever they set down their roots in Spain water was their first necessity. The series of buildings called the Alhambra, with flowering courtyards and gardens in between them, and the summer palace of the Moors, the Generalife, which is but a stone's throw distant, give one a fair idea of what life back in Moorish days must have been like. Not only are these places clean and green; they are artistically beautiful, and, as if not to omit any possible use of water, the Moors even had flush toilets in some of their private bedrooms. A constant, rapid stream ran below the marble seats.

The word "Alhambra" means "Red Palace." It was begun around the year 890, and was greatly amplified around 1250 by Mohammed ben Alahmar. Still other additions were made later. The ruling Moors of this region lived here until January 2, 1492, when Boabdil heaved his last sigh and gave the keys to the city to Ferdinand and Isabella. The thick walls of the palace are of a rust red color, and are massive but not beautiful. They stand out on top of Alhambra Hill from any point in the city, which lies below. As one ascends the hill the precincts suddenly become dark green and cool. There is a lovely wood of elm trees, brought here, it is said, by Wellington. Inside the gardens are trees of many other kinds, particularly the cypress. Here are all the flowers of Andalusia, and a few years ago there were red geraniums over twenty feet in height, climbing the walls of the buildings. Now these are all gone. But the water still flows on constantly, the frogs still sit on the lotus and lily pads, and at night the air is filled with the songs of nightingales.

For 250 years the Nasrite Arab dynasty ruled the mountain-ringed Moorish kingdom of Granada from this lovely palace. These Moorish kings showed great cunning in dividing their Christian adversaries, helping first Castile, then Aragon. The motto of the Nasrite dynasty, *And no conqueror but God*, is inscribed in many places on the Alhambra walls. Toward the end of their reign civil wars became rampant among the Moors, and with the union of Castile and Aragon in 1474 their defeat was inevitable. The final years of the Moorish epoch were marked by a violent rivalry within the harem. Zoraya, the sultana, was jealous lest the offspring of Aixa, the favorite, should supplant her own in the succession. She made a public issue of this, and was clapped into prison. Two factions were formed among the noble families: the Abencerrajes supporting Aixa, the Zegríes backing the claim of Zoraya. The Zegríes won out by accusing the Abencerrajes of plotting to take over the throne, and King Abul-Hassan had three dozen of the accused beheaded in the very halls of the Alhambra. Abul-Hassan was the father of Boabdil, the unfortunate, last of the Moorish line.

For many years the Moors had paid an annual tribute to Castile in order to be left in peace, but in 1476 when payment was demanded, Abul-Hassan proudly retorted: "The mints of Granada no longer coin gold, but steel!" The gantlet was down, and the embattled city prepared for war. The Moors, apparently misjudging the spirit of the enemy, continued their tourneys, feasts, cane-tilting, music, and dances in a constant round of revelry. Grown soft and pleasure-loving in their mountain Eden, they were in the long run unable to withstand the onslaught of a hardier race. When the city was captured by Ferdinand and Isabella in 1492 the Catholic sovereigns were struck by the beauty of the place, and for some time thereafter held court within the palace of the Alhambra. Isabella was fond of music and had forty musicians in her entourage, so the old songs, ballads, and *villancicos* of Spain were often played and sung in these ancient Moorish chambers where two ways of life had met and one had ended.

The interior walls of the palace, like the interior walls of all the main Moorish buildings, are sheathed in plaster paneling which is carved and colored in relief. There are delicate arches of many styles, but some version of the horseshoe arch is the most popular. The columns holding up the roofs are delicate and slender; their capitals are cushioned and covered with decoration. The ceilings drip pendants or "stalactites." Mosaics were frequently used at the bases of the columns, and the wainscoting and floors were generally covered with beautiful tiles, the secret of which has been lost. Many wall tiles are preserved but only in a few places does the original tile floor remain; one such spot is clearly visible in the floor of the Hall of Justice; this section used to lie *under* the thrones of Ferdinand and Isabella.

From each window and lookout of the palace (the *miradores*) there is a spectacular view of the surrounding *vega* of Granada. In one direction the viewer can see the Sacramonte caves where the gypsies have lived ever since the fifteenth century.

There is good historic evidence tracing the gypsies of Europe back to India. In 1398 this country was invaded and desolated by the renowned oriental conqueror Tamerlane (or Timur), and thousands of its inhabitants fled in dismay across the borders. Many of them finally reached Egypt, from which country they apparently entered Europe, thus the name "gypsy," which meant Egyptian.

By 1440 they had reached Spain. The Spanish gypsies have preserved the old songs (the *cante jondo*) and the old dances (*baile flamenco*) of Andalusia, but they did not originate them. These people are marvelous imitators, but they are not creators. However, it may well be that the survival of the old Andalusian music is largely due to them. The men, as well as the women, take part in these dances, and the male part is extremely virile. Escudero, one of the most famed of all the male gypsy dancers, once remarked: "If I thought there was the slightest suggestion of effeminacy to any movement of mine, I would prefer never to dance another step."

The Sacramonte caves, dug out in the hills on the opposite side of town from the Alhambra, are now neatly finished inside and provided with electric lights. Here the gypsies still perform their dances, but within the past few years the procedure has become so commercialized that they now just walk through the steps, ten to fifteen times a day or night, and then flop down beside the spectator to have their pictures taken, hoping in this manner to pick up an additional tip. The castanets they try to sell are made in Japan. They have little talent for dancing, but a shrewd instinct for where money is to be made. They even come to the hotels in Granada to entertain the tourists. If a good dancer or bullfighter does arise among them, he quickly disappears into one of the larger cities.

There is no point in giving here a detailed description of each of the patios of the Alhambra, but especial attention should be called to the courtyard of the myrtles (*patio de los arrayanes*) and to the courtyard of the lions (*patio de los leones*). The first contains a large reflecting pool, so frequently used in the larger Moorish palaces, and the second the famous fountain of the lions, which unfortunately no longer flows. The lions themselves may be Phoenician or possibly Norman-Saracenic, but were not sculptured by the Moors, who simply found them and incorporated them in their palace. This fountain was also a sundial, and at each hour the water would flow out of the mouth of a different lion. Today this lovely patio is beginning to sag crazily in its upper portion, and ugly iron crossbeams have been placed in several spots to reinforce the ceiling.

A Spanish friend of mine, who was a student at the University of Granada, spent many days in this patio copying down the Arabic inscriptions which appear in the almost unnoticed scrollwork of the walls. These inscriptions, exquisitely intertwined in the artistic motifs, are in fact a series of poems in Arabic. They have recently been translated into English by A. R. Nykl.

The royal baths in the Alhambra are also of especial interest, because they had three spigots from which flowed hot water, cold water, and perfumed water. Taking a bath was for the Moors not only a delight; it was also a ritual. Down in Granada city there is a large building containing Moorish baths of the eleventh century (circa 1050); it is called the *bañuelo*.

Washington Irving once occupied a room in the Alhambra, and it was here that he did some of the research for his *Tales of the Alhambra*, containing many legends, and for his *Conquest of Granada*. He was perhaps more responsible for the American interest in this particular building than any other writer. Irving loved Spain profoundly, and was able to describe certain aspects of it with a gifted pen. The word "romance," however, is too often suggested by his writings, and Spain is one of the most unromantic countries

in the entire world. Sensual and sensuous she may be, but not romantic. Only in her physical aspects, separated from their human
element, does the country suggest romance.

The city of Granada can also boast of many Moorish remains; the
gate of Elvira dates from the ninth century, and the gate of
Bibarrambla, which was taken down in pieces in the 1870's, has been
stored away and may someday be put back together again in its
original form. There are other gates and Moorish monuments in
various parts of town, but the Alhambra far surpasses them all. It is,
in reality, an entire chain of palaces, covering the main part of the
entire hill, and in its way is the most impressive Moorish monument in the world.

Some travelers have called the Alhambra effeminate, but I certainly do not agree with them. This incomparable building is delicate
and feminine in its lightness; but it does not connote effeminacy,
which holds the overtone of masculinity gone to seed. The relatively
small size of some of the rooms and hallways of the palace is a disappointment to some travelers, and it may also fail to come up to ex-
pectations if viewed in the broad daylight. The best time to see the
Alhambra is by moonlight. Under the tender glow of night its gardens are permeated with fresh orchard scents, the sound of its waters
is poetry on the ear, and the soft rays of the moon shed an aura
for its lacy chains of interlocking rooms and courtyards. When the
nightingales begin to sing the mind and heart are both overcome
with a quiet music, and one feels real regret that no venturesome
soul has ever· thought of introducing this celebrated songbird into
the Americas. With daylight the *vega* itself comes to life, and the
olive groves shimmer in the sun.

As the famous poet of Granada, Federico García Lorca, wrote:

> *El río Guadalquivir*
> *va entre naranjos y olivos.*
> *Los dos ríos de Granada*
> *bajan de la nieve al trigo.*

> The Guadalquivir river
> flows between orange and olive trees.
> The two rivers of Granada
> come down from the snow to the fields of wheat.

I kept thinking of Federico all the time that we were in Granada. He
had spent a year in John Jay Hall, on the Columbia University cam-

pus, just down the hall from me, and I came to know him well. As he spoke no English I often served as his guide around New York City, and introduced him to Negro spirituals, for which he developed a real passion. Later, in Spain I attended his *tertulia* or literary salon which met at a sidewalk café in Madrid. He was an accomplished musician and often he would go to the piano or pick up his guitar and play for his friends the plaintive songs of his beloved Andalusia.

Like most Andalusians, Lorca was proud of the Moorish heritage, proud of his Moorish blood, and often remarked on how fine he would look wearing a turban. When the civil war broke out in Spain he was shot by the Falangists. He was thirty-seven years old. To me his presence still seems to pervade the city of Granada. The Englishman Gerald Brenan, who has written so many wonderful books on Spain, has a touching essay on his search for the grave of Federico. He was never certain that he had found it. (The essay, originally published in the *New Yorker*, was later reprinted in the book, *The Face of Spain*.)

As I write these lines I am sitting on the terrace of the Hotel Alhambra Palace, high on the hill and within the grounds of the Alhambra. The dusk is sifting down, and the lights are coming on in the city below us. The colors of the sky are incomparable: lilac, rose, gray-blue, hazel, aquamarine, red, dusty gold, and many others. The lights of a Spanish city are unlike those of a city in America. They follow no straight lines, but twinkle in all directions; the great clumps of buildings which make up the town look as if they had been splashed with a handful of stars. The cocks, as always, are crowing in the city, and the bells, as always are tolling. The final light lingers, but it is now too dark to see what I am writing, and I put away my notebook, and sit back to drink in the sounds and the aroma that are Granada.

Our room in the hotel overlooks the entire *vega*. Its lamp hangs from the center of a decorative motif formed in the stucco ceiling which consists of the Star of David, with little shells of Santiago placed in between the points of the star. It is a strange mixture of the Hebrew and Christian past. I pick up the Granada telephone book, and memories crowd into my mind. Fifteen years ago I had consulted this directory and on its cover noted the words: *Franco! Franco! Franco! Up and forward, Spain! ¡Viva España!*

And I recalled having seen such words painted on the walls of buildings, and at the outskirts of many towns. The town of Loja, for example, not far from Granada, had this official greeting at its city limits: *Franco, Loja salutes, respects,and admires you!* Occasionally, also, one would see words like these: *Todo por la patria* ("All for the fatherland"). In spite of all these evidences of propaganda the Spaniards are not a patriotic race unless they are under the impulse of a strong belief, which obviously General Franco did not inspire.

As we get ready to leave the hotel I see the omnipresent maids splashing their mops all over the white marble floors and stairway, which gleam as if they belonged to a hospital. I stop to rest a few moments in the lobby, waiting for the car to be brought up, and take a quick look at the magazines lying there. Before looking one can be fairly certain that there will not be very much worth reading. How true: *British Trade Journal, Confectionery Production, Trade with Greece*, a couple of KLM timetables, a magazine published by a Spanish banking house, *Egypt Travel Magazine*, and three copies of a technical journal called *Metallurgy and Electricity*. An old gentleman sitting at the table had already cornered the three most interesting publications: Madrid's *ABC* which gives its very conservative view, the excellent Sunday edition of *El País*, and a copy of the magazine *Cambio 16*. This list is typical of the reading matter displayed in many Spanish hotels.

We left Granada through an archway of trees watered by the old Moorish aqueduct and entered an open landscape of gold-pastel wheat stubble and green olive groves. There were also fields of corn and of tobacco, and many sheds in which the tobacco was drying. Its acrid sweet odor permeated the atmosphere. All of the hills were covered with olive trees. There were occasional threshing floors of hard, packed earth, on which a horse or mule was pacing in its circle stamping the grain. The newspapers tell you that there are now many thousands of tractors in Spain, but I saw only one, and that one far away, on the drive from Granada to Córdoba. Spanish agriculture has a long way to go before it can be called mechanized. It has a long way to go before it can equal the neatness and productivity achieved under the Moors. All along the highway were mute reminders of their legacy: the old *norias* or waterwheels being pulled around by burros, stretches of ancient walls, ruined castles and fortresses, the very look of the Andalusian villages themselves, which is almost pure African.

4

THE CHRISTIAN KINGDOMS:
CROSS AND SWORD

The reconquest was a loom on which the history of Spain was warped.

Américo Castro

The period between 722, when Pelayo defeated the Moors in the mountain vale of Covadonga, and 1492, when Ferdinand and Isabella captured Granada, is called *La Reconquista*, the Reconquest. The Reconquest covered a period of eight centuries. It should be made plain that no other country in Europe went through any similar period in its history. The Reconquest was unique to Spain. Not only was it a war against foreign invaders who had occupied the land of Spain, it was also a war against an unacceptable religion, Islam. The two great driving forces of medieval times were war and religion, and in Spain these were fused in one: *religious war*. It is true that during the early centuries of the Reconquest the acquisition of land, wealth, and slaves was perhaps more important than defeating Islam, but as time passed religious supremacy became an increasing issue. The Moslems themselves contributed to this with the invasion from North Africa of the wave of fanatical Almoravides in 1086 and that of the Almohades in 1146.

Spanish historians all agree that the Reconquest gave Spanish history a singularity among the nations of Europe. They do not share a common opinion as to the degree and manner in which the Reconquest molded Spanish character and fashioned the history of Spain. Indeed, the two outstanding Spanish historians of today, Américo Castro and Claudio Sánchez Albornoz, have been carrying on a polemic in this regard for several years. Nevertheless, these two men are not as far apart as their sometimes impassioned words might lead one to assume. Castro states clearly that the Moslem was never an easy foe, and so the Reconquest had to be the way it was: "a loom on which the history of Spain was warped." And Sánchez Albornoz categorically affirms: "I consider the Reconquest the key to the history of Spain. . . . Let us remember the words of the Chronicle of Albeda: *The Christians fought every day, night and day.* For eight centuries they did the same." There were brief periods of peace, rarely more than a decade or two; there were wars among the Christians themselves; there were wars among the Moorish kingdoms and factions, and there were even wars in which Christians and Moors fought as allies against other Christians and Moors. In spite of these indisputable historic facts the dominant, unceasing monotone of the Reconquest was of Christian Spaniards against Moslem Spaniards, of Cross and Sword against Moorish Crescent.

Spanish character was fashioned anew under the long arm of this crusade. The church promised heaven for those who fell in battle, and the spoils of war always enriched the victorious soldier. Men came to die and live for this ideal of the "Christian soldier." Who would soil his hands with menial labor when marching off to war offered a greater and far nobler reward? Individual prowess and faith became keystones of the new Spanish nation which was slowly emerging behind the moving frontier. The Reconquest began in 722 at Covadonga with the "impetuous love of liberty" of the Asturian and Cantabrian mountaineers, the same indomitable mountaineers who had given Augustus Caesar such a hard time in the first century. These fighters were not Visigoths. They were of older Hispanic stock, a hardy people who in later years would pour onto the plains of León and Castile in the repopulation of these abandoned lands. They would carry their spirit with them, and this spirit would shape the character of Spain.

The frontier was not a fixed line. Nor did it move southward at a steady pace. It was always an uncertain boundary which advanced "whenever the Christians won a victory, whenever they took a city that dominated the entrance to a valley or which assured the possession of a plain, whenever there was a crisis or a war among the

Moors themselves." The frontier retreated as readily as it advanced. Hence, the southward movement was in a back and forth rhythm, but always with the greater impetus coming from the north.

In 722 the Christians were hemmed in behind the Cantabrian mountains, which were their line of defense. Their numbers steadily increased as other Christians abandoned their farms and homes to the south and moved in to join them. After Covadonga the Moors very foolishly decided to invade France, where they met a second defeat at the hands of Charles Martel. If, instead, they had pressed their initial advantage to the hilt, and pushed into these Cantabrian mountains, Spain might still today be a Moslem-Christian civilization, if not a Moslem country. After their defeat in France the Moors realized that they had overextended themselves, and began to retreat southward. This retreat took them back beyond the Duero River valley, whose inhabitants were already abandoning that territory for the more secure region behind the Cantabrian mountain wall. Thus, for many years there was a great wilderness between the two camps. This wilderness extended along the Duero River valley, and was completely uninhabited. The frontier of Spanish Christendom slowly began to advance southward into these uninhabited plains. The Moors swooped in and fell upon those who came. This was the way the frontier was made. Before long it was not only an inconclusive geographic line, it was also a very definite state of mind.

Of course, the eight centuries of Reconquest were not eight centuries of constant war. No people could possibly endure so much. These years also represented an interplay and fusion of social and cultural forces between the two sides, as well as an outright opposition of these forces. Christians and Moors lived together in the same land engaged successively in the two greatest actions of human life: war and lovemaking, two forms of conquest, two forms of intimacy. As warfare and physical intimacy often go hand in hand, the latter not needing a period of tranquillity for its expression, perhaps the making of love, and all that this implies, was of equal importance to the slaying of the enemy in the formation of Spain.

Asturias, the site of Pelayo's victory, was the first Christian kingdom of northern Spain. A capital was established at Oviedo in 791, but even before this there was a dynasty of Asturian kings. It must be emphasized that this was not a continuation of the Visigothic line, but was something very autochthonous, rooted in the Spanish earth. The next kingdoms to emerge were Galicia and León. By the year

900 the Christians had pushed out beyond their ring of mountains and had spread onto the plains of León, farther south. By 914 they no longer felt the need of a mountain barrier to protect them, and so, uniting their kingdoms, they moved their capital to León, forming the single kingdom of León. The initiative now had clearly passed into the Christian camp; the Moors would never again hold the upper hand.

Just as León had emerged from the southward expansion of Asturias and Galicia, Castile emerged from the southward expansion of León. At first only a small principality (circa 900), within a generation or two Castile became a land of warriors who would not bow before any man, Christian or Moor. The story of how Castile got its independence from León is told in the *Poem of Fernán González*, and reproduced in the *General Chronicle* of the thirteenth century. The great warrior Count Fernán González, idol of the Castilians, on one occasion presented himself at the court of the king of León with a "very fine moulting falcon and very noble horse." The king admired the beautiful animals, and asked if he might buy them. In conformity with the ritual of courtesy the count answered that the animals were not for sale but that he would "gladly give them to the king, since he liked them so much." The king refused to accept the gift unless, also according to the ritual of courtesy, he might be allowed to make some return. He promised to pay the count the sum of 1,000 marks of silver for the animals, and they set a date by which this payment was to be made; it was further agreed that the total should be doubled for each additional day that passed. Three years went by, and the total amounted to an astronomical sum which the king could not possibly pay. Instead he granted Castile its independence. The story is probably apocryphal, but the rituals of courtesy, and the consequent lack of punctuality on the part of the king, are fully in keeping with Spanish character and the events described.

Fernán González was the first great hero of Castile. He met the invincible Almanzor head on, and did not flinch before him. The soldiers of Castile were already the equals of the best the Moslems could put into the field. Castile was born in danger; it continued to exist by the strength of is own right arm. It was peopled by the most daring inhabitants of the mountains who had left the security of their homes in order to follow the path of adventure with the hope of glory. Castile was like a huge panzer column slowly gathering momentum as it probed ever deeper into the territories of the Moors. The Castilians suffered few defeats, and won many startling victories. In the end, they made the Reconquest possible. In order to protect themselves on their open and barren plains they lived in a line of castles which marked the southern Christian frontier, and from this was derived the name, *Castilla*, which means "land of castles."

The other Christian kingdoms of Spain were León, Navarre, Aragon, and Catalonia, bringing the grand total to five. In the early centuries of the Reconquest these Christian kingdoms fought almost as much among themselves as they did against the Moors. When Almanzor invaded León the Castilians were filled with glee, and when Castile in its turn suffered the same fate the Leonese were jubilant. Both were elated when Navarre was assaulted. In those days the term *España* (Spain) was used to refer to that part of the peninsula occupied by the Moors. When referring to their own country the Christians would say: León, Castilla, Asturias, etc. But as the centuries passed they finally learned their lesson, and by the year 1230 there were two principal Christian kingdoms left in Spain, made up of the following combinations: León-Castilla, and Aragon-Catalonia. Almost a century and a half more was to pass before these two states would merge into the single combination of Castilla-Aragon, which was to signify the unity of all Christian Spain. It was this final union which defeated and drove the Moors from their last stronghold of Granada.

The Moors, unknowingly, had taught the Spanish Christians how to win the struggle against them. Not only had they shown how essential was union itself, but they had even shown how this union might be achieved: *through the banner of a dynamic religion.* Themselves a heterogeneous group of Arabians, Yemenites, Berbers, and Syrians who had found their own union in the birth of Islam in the seventh century, the Moors successfully merged religion with warfare and established an immense empire. The Jews, with their philosophy of religion which embraced the entire vital structure of man and the universe, contributed further to the formation of the emerging Christian concept. This concept and faith eventually welded nationalism and religion together, establishing what was to become a *church-state*. Religion, in other words, was to become a weapon, the mightiest weapon of all, in the epic struggle between two cultures.

Spanish Catholicism found its answer to the aggressive faith of the Moors in its cult of St. James. It was this cult, carefully nurtured and intensely believed, that made the Reconquest possible. The cult was a purely Spanish invention; it existed in no other Catholic country of the world. History adduces almost no evidence in support of the miraculous events which gave rise to the cult of St. James, but in this case historic evidence is unimportant. What is important is that the story was believed, and this belief became so militant that it moved men to accomplish incredible deeds. If we choose to say that myths move men in history more strongly than actual events, that is another matter.

The legend is as follows: St. James the Greater, son of Zebedee, one of the twelve apostles, was believed to have come to Spain to preach the gospel for a period of six years. After that he returned to Jerusalem where he was beheaded by King Herod. His devotees embalmed his body and with it boarded a ship bound for Spain. They disembarked at the old Roman port of Iria Flavia on the Galician coast and proceeded inland to the site of the present city of Santiago, where the body was buried. For several years the tomb was a place of pilgrimage, but when Roman persecution of the Spanish Christians became intolerable the holy spot was neglected, and for six centuries, more or less, the memory of it was forgotten. Tradition then recounts that early in the ninth century (813) a hermit who lived in the area saw, on several successive nights, a bright star shining over a huge oak tree which stood alone on a hill. The vision was accompanied by the sound of celestial music. The local bishop was notified and, accompanied by several priests, he went to the spot to investigate. They found an altar and the graves of three persons, one of them decapitated. The inscription supposedly announced that this was the resting place of St. James.

On receiving the news Alfonso II, the Chaste, hastened to the place accompanied by several grandees of his court. The king examined the graves, corroborated the miraculous discovery, and established a church on the spot. Pope Leo III was apprised of the event and in a letter publicized the news universally. Pilgrims began to arrive to venerate the holy remains, and the town of Santiago arose around the church, which became one of the three great shrines of medieval days. The other two were Rome and Jerusalem.

There was some doubt as to which of the three disinterred skeletons was that of St. James, so the bones of all three were mingled and placed together in the same casket. Later they were transferred to the highly wrought silver urn in which they rest today. Visitors who view them are carefully told by the official guides that while there is widespread acceptance of St. James' preaching in Spain, of his burial there, and of the miraculous discovery of his grave, there is no proof that any of these beliefs is based on historic fact.

The events which gave the cult of St. James its final dramatic form was the legendary battle of Clavijo. (This was probably an invention of some scribe of the eleventh or twelfth century, but the *cult* of St. James dates from 813 A.D.) After several years of truce, the Moors of Córdoba had again demanded their tribute of one hundred virgins. The king of Galicia, Ramiro I, needled by one of the fated virgins, refused to comply, and the Moslems came in force to collect. The two armies supposedly met at Clavijo in 844, and during the first day of the battle the Christian forces were badly mauled. That night Ramiro regarded his beaten and exhausted Galician and Leonese soldiers and wondered what fate the next day held in store for them. On the following morning he assembled his troops and in a ringing voice announced that during the night St. James had appeared to him in a dream promising a Christian victory. The saint was mounted on a white charger and carried a white banner bearing a red cross. He had declared that the defense of the faith in Spain was his personal responsibility, and that he would be present to lead the Spaniards on the field of battle. He even told Ramiro how to dispose his troops in the most advantageous positions. When the battle commenced the Christians hurled themselves upon the Moslems shouting at the top of their lungs: *Santiago! Cierra España!* (St. James! Close in, Spain!"). They attacked with such fury that the Moslem forces fled leaving the field strewn with their dead. King Ramiro was credited with a miraculous victory. From this time on Santiago was regarded as the patron saint of Spain, and the special protector of Christian soldiers in the war of the Reconquest. Faith in him turned the tide in many a battle in favor of the Christians, and gave medieval Spanish Catholicism a unique flavor. In the eleventh century the apostle began to be called *Santiago, Matamores* ("St. James, Slayer of Moors").

After the epoch of the battle of Clavijo pilgrims began to arrive at the famous shrine in an ever-increasing stream. Convents, resting places, hospitals, schools, and other institutions were built. The original church erected on the spot by Alfonso the Chaste was considered too paltry a building for so famous a shrine, so at the turn of the century (circa 900), under Alfonso III, the Great, it was torn down and replaced by a much larger one. About a hundred years later (997), the fearsome Moorish general, Almanzor, assaulted the city, captured and sacked it, destroyed the new cathedral (leaving untouched the spot where the holy relics were kept), and had its bells and doors carried back to Córdoba with him by Christian prisoners. The stolen articles were used in the Mosque of Córdoba, the bells being made into lamps. In 1236 when Córdoba was recaptured by Fernando the Saint, of Castile and León, Moslem prisoners were forced to haul the articles back to Santiago again.

Between 1027 and 1137 the shrine was rebuilt. As most of the pilgrims passed through southern France on their way to Santiago, the French Benedictine order of Cluny took over the management and protection of the pilgrimages. These monks kept the road in good repair, established inns and monasteries at regular intervals, and gave protection against attacks by bandits. The road to Santiago became an international highway and began to be known as the *camino francés*, or "French road," a name it still bears. The Spanish phrase for "road to Santiago," *camino de Santiago*, refers to the Milky Way, because it resembled the road crowded with pilgrims and because by following it one would arrive at Santiago. The original road led through the pass at Roncesvalles, via Pamplona and Asturias to Galicia. In the late eleventh century, the main route was moved farther south via Burgos, thus indicating the Christian expansion. That French monks did so much to further the cause of Spanish nationalism is one of the anomalies of history.

The full name of the shrine was Santiago de Compostela; the term *Compostela* derived from the Latin words *campus stellae* ("field of the star") thus refers to the bright star that indicated the grave of St. James. Compostela had become an integral part of the name by the eleventh century.

The emblem of all those who made the pilgrimage to Santiago was a sea shell of the kind commonly known as *venera* or *vieira* along the Galician coast. No pilgrim returned from the shrine without his emblem. There are two stories as to how the local shell came to be so honored. One is that St. James himself frequently used these shells to baptize converts when he was preaching in Spain. The other story is that the friends of St. James, just before disembarking on the coast of Galicia with the body of the apostle, saw a maddened, runaway horse carry its noble rider into the sea before their eyes. They thought surely the knight would drown, but a mass of shells entwined in seaweed picked him up and floated him to safety despite his heavy armor. The Christians took this as a good sign and chose the shell as the emblem of their saint.

The pilgrims who streamed into Santiago came from all over Europe. Even Chaucer's Wife of Bath had been to "Galice at Seint Jame," as had thousands of others from Britain. They wore rude cloaks of the coarsest cloth, a short cape, a flexible hat, and sandals. They invariably carried a staff to which was attached a calabash, out of which they ate at the overnight stopping places. At their belt they sometimes carried a purse. Most of the men grew long beards. At night in the courtyards of the inns or monasteries along the way they often assembled and sang folk songs. When the pilgrims reached Santiago there was not enough lodging space for them, so they slept in the streets, in great human piles, much as the people of India are said to do. When they entered the cathedral in thick masses the stench was so unbearable that a huge censer was put up which could be pulled to and fro above them by ropes and pulleys, thus dulling the odor and fumigating the air. The censer is still there; it is called the *botafumeiro*, and is now used only on very special occasions. The pilgrims carried many European influences into Spain, particularly those of the French church and perhaps literary influences from Provence. When they returned to their homes they carried much knowledge of Spanish-Arabic culture back with them. The intellectual achievements of the Moors thus became widely known throughout Europe. The large numbers of pilgrims who came to Spain helped to focus attention on the Moorish wars and brought recruits and money for the Spanish cause.

The present cathedral in Santiago is a composite of many styles and buildings. In 1075 work was started on the great cathedral under Alfonso VI, but this was constructed above the ninth century burial church, which can still be seen down below. The richly sculptured Romanesque *Puerta de las Platerías* ("Door of the Silversmiths") dates from this period. The main west front of the cathedral, however, was constructed in the eighteenth century, and represents the late Spanish baroque style, often known as the Churrigueresque. This is the façade with two tall towers which stands out upon the main *Plaza de España*. It is behind and inside of this main façade that we find the real glory of the cathedral, the incomparable *Pórtico de la Gloria*, three beautiful Romanesque arches covered with 135 statues and figures in bold relief, which bear the date 1183. These are the work of the master Mateo, who was head of the Masons' Guild from 1168. Mateo worked on his masterpiece for twenty years. Such is the harmony, perfection, and arrangement of the figures that the viewer receives an overall impression of great serenity and beauty, with no sense of its being crowded or overwrought. The individual figures are powerfully expressive, far beyond the usual medieval statuary. Mateo, in his strength and vigor of design, compares very favorably with the great sculptors of the Renaissance. The *Pórtico de la Gloria* is beyond any doubt the finest piece of medieval sculpturing in Spain, and perhaps in the world.

The Pórtico is of obvious symbolic significance. The central and largest arch represents the Catholic church; the arch to the left represents the Jewish church, while the arch to the right symbolizes the church of the "wrong believers." In the middle of the central arch. is the magnificent statue of Christ, surrounded by the four evangelists, and on the pillar below them, a vigorous St. James, bearing his priestly staff. The enormous figure of Christ is almost ten feet high, dwarfing every other figure of the three arches. He is on a throne and is showing his wounded hands, feet, and side. In a semicircle above the huge Christ are the twenty-four ancients of the Apocalypse, all holding stringed instruments. Some of them are apparently tuning their instruments, while others appear to be playing pizzicato. This entire upper panel is a magnificent representation of the musical instruments of the twelfth century in Spain.

The arch to the left represents the church of the Jews with many prophets of the Old Testament: Abraham, Isaac, Jacob, Moses, David, Solomon, and several others. Christ himself occupies the center of the arch; he holds out his right hand in blessing, and his left holds the Book of Eternal Truth. Adam is on one side of him, Eve on the other.

The arch to the right represents the church of the Gentiles or "wrong believers." The false dogmas of antiquity appear to be represented here in the forms of various animals: Brahmanism, Islam, Confucianism, etc. They symbolize certain qualities: faith, justice, fortitude, envy, fury, lechery, pride, avarice, etc. This arch also contains the figures of some horrible, repellent-looking monsters or devils which are devouring human beings. They represent violence, cruelty, gluttony, greed.

The totality of the Pórtico is to show how the True Church arose from a bedrock of false dogmas and Old Testament Judaism to its unique position of eminence through the revelations and life of Christ. The master sculptor who created this imposing work of art has placed a small figure of himself behind the pillar which rises up to the center of the main arch. This figure crouches on the floor, facing the inside of the church, and is missed by many visitors.

The grouping of the figures of the Pórtico is extraordinary; most of them seem to be engaged in conversation or have a very natural turn to their heads and faces. While the prophets and apostles wear beards, the figure of Daniel is clean-shaven, and his lips reveal a bright young smile. This is only one of the many distinctive ways in which Mateo has achieved his effect, giving strong individuality as well as an overall harmony and power to his work.

When the Pórtico was finished in 1188 it was brightly polychromed in rich colors and gold. As late as 1651 it was repainted, but exposure to the elements and the placing of a plaster cast around the work in order to have it reproduced for the London Museum in South Kensington took nearly all of this color away. Now only the faintest tints can be perceived. Medieval Spanish sculpture was nearly always richly colored, but little of it remains in this state today. During the Spanish civil war the Pórtico barely missed being blown into bits by an anti-religious fanatic. Almost miraculously it was saved, and with it has survived a symbol of medieval beauty and power which only a Spanish artist could have conceived. Even foreign artists who came to the peninsula to live (Juan Juni of France, El Greco from Greece) were remolded spiritually by the graphic presence of Spain which soon deeply permeated their works.

In the twelfth century several military orders were organized in Spain to help carry on the fight against the Moors. These orders were all established on a religious as well as a military basis, following the indication of St. James, "Moor Slayer" himself. The church did not originally look with favor on holy men taking arms, but with the invasion of the Moorish Almoravides ("those vowed to God") in 1086, the blending of religion and war among the Moors was again brought to the attention of Spanish Christians who could not help realizing the effectiveness of the idea. Holy war, therefore, became the mission of the Church Militant. Among these orders were the Knights of Santiago, Calatrava, Alcantara, the Knights Templar, and the Hospitalers. The primary duty of the Knights of Santiago was to keep the pilgrim road free of bandits and evildoers. Later, they became a core group in the Moorish wars. At the end of the fifteenth century, under Ferdinand and Isabella, such core groups constituted the bone and sinew of the Christian army.

The national hero of early medieval Spain is the Cid. His story is told in the earliest preserved epic of Spanish literature, *The Poem of the Cid*, 1140. The Cid was a historic figure of the eleventh century; he lived from about 1043 to 1099, so the poem was written only forty years after his death, when his exploits were still fresh and clear in memory. The author of the poem, probably a Spanish monk living in the Moorish kingdom of Saragossa somewhere near the Christian frontier, had obviously read the *Song of Roland*, and several earlier Spanish epics which have been lost. Thus inspired he composed a poem which sticks very close to historic events, and gives a faithful picture of life along the frontier in those epic days. He does not emboss his story with fantastic happenings or strange miracles. The Cid emerges as a man of flesh and blood, a man who, through his own will and effort, achieves epic grandeur.

In this the Cid was symbolic of the total vital structure of Castilian life in the eleventh century. The Spanish Christians had as yet produced few great national heroes; the heroes of Spain were very often to be found among the Moorish leaders. Almanzor's incredible victories and his individual courage and fortitude as a man had elevated him to such a position in the mind of many Spanish warriors. The Cid, therefore, reflected very clearly the Moorish influence on the emerging value system of the Castilians. Spaniards as we know them today, and the elements of Spanish character and belief which mold the whole man, were in the process of being created in the eleventh century. A new nation was issuing from the hybrid Arabic-Christian cocoon. The Cid is, in a way, the epitome of this new culture in its incipient stages.

Shortly before the poem opens the Cid had been sent to collect the tribute which the kings of Córdoba and Seville owed to Alfonso VI of Castile. On reaching Seville he finds that this territory is being threatened by the king of Granada, supported by Count García Ordóñez, a favorite of Alfonso VI's. The Cid sends letters trying to prevent the attack, but to no avail. He then challenges the forces of Granada, meets them on the field of battle, defeats them disastrously, gathers much rich booty, captures Count García Ordóñez, whose beard he pulls in the ultimate insult of those days, and then returns to Burgos, the Castilian capital. As a consequence of his victory he is dubbed *el Cid Campeador*; Cid is from the Arabic *sidi*, "leader or lord," and *campeador* means "winner of battles."

At first the Cid is well received by Alfonso VI, but soon the king's ear is filled with suspicions by friends of Count García Ordóñez, and when the Cid undertakes on his own a large-scale raid against the Moorish king of Toledo, which had been expressly forbidden, Alfonso concludes that this man is out for himself, and exiles him from Castile. It is at this point in the Cid's life that the poem itself begins. Here is what takes place:

The Cid departs from his home town of Bivar and enters Burgos. Every door is shut to him, but the people are watching from the slits in the walls as the leader moves down the street on his horse followed by other horsemen carrying sixty pennants. Tears fill the eyes of the people of Burgos. As with a single voice they exclaim: "What a fine vassal he would be if only he had a good lord!" In a moment of fury the Cid charges toward one of the doors, stops suddenly before it and, taking his foot out of the stirrup, gives the door a mighty kick with his boot. The poem states: "but the door did not open, for it was tightly closed."

A little girl nine years old is then sent out and in her childish voice explains what is happening. The city had received a letter from the king, marked with a great seal and forbidding anyone to give aid or comfort to the Cid. "We do not dare, Cid, to give you any kind of aid," says the child, "because if we did we would lose not only all our belongings and our homes, but the very eyes in our heads. Cid, in doing us this harm you would be gaining nothing. Go on by, then, and may God protect you with his holy virtues." The little girl said these words and then went back into her house.

With this simple and touching start the Cid is launched on his career as a warrior. He offers his services to the Moorish king of Saragossa, and helps him to win many battles against the Christian forces of Barcelona. Then he strikes out on his own, wins several border victories which swell his ranks, and finally assaults the Moorish kingdom of Valencia, which he captures and rules for the final five years of his life. His victorious campaigns had the effect of rolling back the Almoravides, who were just then erupting into the peninsula. The king of Castile, Alfonso VI, had been unable to defeat them, hence the Cid had performed a great service for the Christian cause.

However, nowhere in the poem does it appear that religion is the main motive for these campaigns and these victories. The Cid does call on Santiago and Jesus Christ, but this is not yet an epic plea or faith. The poem states very plainly that "the Moors call on Mohammed, the Christians on St. James." Victory for its own glorious sake, and for the additive of booty, slaves, and dominion—these are the motives which impel the Cid in his campaigns. When he is preparing to attack Valencia he sends messengers all over Aragon, Castile, and Navarre calling for recruits. The alluring words used are, "Those who want to stop their toil and get rich, let them come with me to conquer and to populate this land." The poet adds a few telling lines after describing the great joy of those who captured Valencia: "Those who came on foot are now mounted; gold and silver, it's more than one can count. All are now rich—every one of them who went."

As a well-known contemporary Spanish poet has pointed out, the Cid is one of the first "self-made men in history." He achieves success with his own hands and will. Even the king is not essential to his victories. He is the heroic individual Castilian warrior, who, feeling the exaltation of the whole man, can bring about incredible results. He is indeed a pattern which any courageous Castilian can follow. He is the noble epitome of every soldier among them. His ideal of self, his will, his courage and dignity, his faith, his stout heart, and his *acts* which mold his total personality—these elements make him a true national hero, not one elevated into the stratosphere, but one who lives in his contemporary society, walking the streets with Everyman.

The poetic approach in the *Poem of the Cid* captures and preserves this stark and total reality of both man and his dwelling place. The poet does not alter reality. He merely reproduces it in lines that are direct and unadorned. There is no criticism or judgment of the exterior world, no moralizing about what is good and what is evil. Reality is pure and innocent. In some of the earlier primitive societies men observed with transcendent wonder the beauty and enormity of nature, and evolved their myths by personifying these great natural forces. In the *Song of Roland* that exalted French knight is made into an almost perfect being, far above the poor power of any man to identify or follow. The *Poem of the Cid* moves in neither of these directions; the poet's feet are always firmly on the ground.

On one occasion when day is just breaking the poem describes the scene in these few lines: "There were rays of dawn, morning was on its way, the sun was coming out . . . God, how beautiful it shone!"

These four phrases are all that the poet uses to paint the entire picture. Again, when the Cid takes leave of his wife Jimena and his two small daughters, the poet uses the stark metaphor: "they parted from each other as the fingernail parts from the flesh." The image may not be lovely, but it is precise, and poetically in keeping with the character of the hero.

The reality that is copied, therefore, is a reality made epic through condensation and selection. The individual is projected as being able to dominate this reality with the total application of his will and effort. The Cid was naturally the hero of every Castilian. The author makes neither a myth nor a noble legend of his life; his attitude throughout the poem is one of wonder and admiration that a single man can accomplish so much without having to go outside himself for supernatural support or projection.

Just as the figure of the Cid overshadows that of the legendary Pelayo, who defeated the Moors at Covadonga, so in the eleventh century does Castile overshadow the kingdom of León and the mountain provinces. It is supremely important to emphasize that during those crucial years when Spanish character was being molded Castile was the dwelling place where the great process went on. And Castilian was to become the language of all Spain. It was a language of stark directness and power. People who took the Latin word *forum* and by shouting turned its short vowel into a diphthong creating *fuero*, were not likely to be dominated by those who spoke the less vigorous dialects of the peninsula.[21]

Alfonso VI, king of Castile and León, was always regarded by the Castilians as a Leonese, an outsider, and this was undoubtedly one of the causes for the animosity which existed between the Cid and the monarch. A further cause was that the Cid had been among those who forced the king to swear he had had no part in the murder of his brother, Sancho, whom he had replaced on the throne. Sancho was slain before the walls of Zamora as he rested on his haunches relieving himself. The old ballads, with their own startling reproduction of reality in which every detail, good or ugly, must count, give a full report of the assassination. The Cid had been one of the supporters of King Sancho before his death. Alfonso probably never forgave him for this.

Nevertheless, Alfonso VI was a stalwart king. In his early life he had been forced to seek refuge at the court of the Moorish king of Toledo, but after the death of the man who had befriended him he assaulted Toledo and took it from the Moors in 1085. He then dubbed himself "king of the two religions." In the following year, however, the Almoravides began to pour into Spain from North Africa, and Alfonso suffered a series of reverses from which he never recovered. It was the Cid who was able to stem the Berber tide, and not Alfonso.

Castile was the dynamic part of Spain in the Middle Ages. León represented conservatism. It was already in the backwash of military action; it represented tradition, the old Visigothic monarchy governed by Visigothic law. Castile was always in the path of danger. Its rebellion against León and the consequent rivalry between the two kingdoms was inevitable, and led to many bitter conflicts. The Castilians detested the old Visigothic code of laws, called the *Fuero juzgo*, and tradition states that a huge bonfire was made in the streets of Burgos in which all known copies of it were burned. The Castilian was a pugnacious individual, of great dignity and grave demeanor; he was self-sufficient and resentful of authority. The law of Castile was based on custom; it was common law, the law that was ordained by public sanction, which expressed the habit and custom of the community's life. Even the king could not place himself above this law, which gave a rude but real feeling of democracy to early Castilian society. As time passed regard for the law of custom grew, and regard for the arbitrary law of kings diminished. Such an event as Alfonso VI's willful exile of the Cid, which took place in the eleventh century, would have been impossible a century later.

If León represented the backwash of tradition the Castilian frontier, just taken from the Moors, represented a kind of no man's land into which it was still risky to venture. It became necessary for the central government to encourage settlers to go into this border territory to establish homes, build towns, put down their roots. In order to achieve permanent colonization settlers were granted special rights and privileges called *fueros*. They were given a measure of personal freedom not known elsewhere in Spain during that epoch. Many of these *fueros*, embodying the rights, privileges, and duties of the citizens of the border towns, included Jews and Moslems as well as Christians. In those days one did not have to be a Christian in order to be a Spaniard.

William Atkinson, in his *History of Spain and Portugal*, points out that during the eighth, ninth, and tenth centuries only twelve *fueros* were granted; forty-five were granted in the eleventh, but in the twelfth and thirteenth there were nearly six hundred, almost equally divided between the two centuries. This is a clear statistical indication as to how the Reconquest was proceeding. The hundreds of newly established towns brought another element into the country's political life. The nobles had always been a severe aggravation to the king. They had come to hold great territories, and very naturally allied themselves with the church and with the military orders, also big landholders. They frequently disputed the succession to the throne, and their support usually decided who would wear the crown. The kings of Castile, finding themselves caught in this web, sought to ally themselves with the people of the townships. If they could not immediately risk a showdown with the nobility they could at least create a counterbalance. Achieving this they were able, little by little, to reduce the nobles to mere shadows around the throne. The ancient Spanish parliament called Cortes ("courts") brought the townsfolk into the national political body and thus balanced the power. The first Cortes was established in Aragon in 1162; that of León dates from 1188; Castile had its first Cortes in 1250. Thus the earliest Spanish parliament antedates that of England (which met in 1295) by 132 years. The democratically elected town councils of both León and Castile came into being around 1220. Unfortunately, this vigorous nascent democracy of the Middle Ages was not to endure for many years after the final conquest of the Moors and the establishment of the Inquisition, which led to a centralized monarchy.

As the thirteenth century dawned the Reconquest gained a sudden momentum. Alfonso VIII of Castile, who had suffered a disastrous defeat at the hands of the Moors in 1195, partly because the Leonese backed out on him at the last minute, now recouped his losses and prepared vigorously for the counterattack. He even persuaded the Pope to announce his "crusade" and call for international volunteers. He had the good sense to realize that Castile could not hope to win if she stood alone. So in the next battle, which took place on the plains of Tolosa (*Las Navas de Tolosa*) in 1212, he was joined by the forces of Navarre, Aragon, and Portugal. León again refused its support, but this time the Christians won a stunning victory, which was the *coup de grâce* for Moorish military dominion in the peninsula. A shepherd of the area led the combined Christian army through a pass marked by a cow's skull (*cabeza de vaca*) onto ground above the Moorish hordes. This superior position aided them materially. The man who had guided them through the pass was dubbed

Cabeza de Vaca by the king. One of his descendants later achieved great fame in the New World.

Alfonso's successor, Fernando III, el Santo, followed up this victory and took Córdoba in 1236; Valencia fell in 1238, and Seville was taken in 1248. This left only the Moorish kingdom of Granada, which was forced to pay a heavy tribute to the crown of Castile. Fernando III at first attempted to expel the Moors en masse from Seville and Córdoba, but the entire economy of the region fell apart, and he was forced to reconsider his position. This more tolerant policy led to a reinstatement of the high esteem in which talented Moors and Jews had formerly been held at the court of Castile. Fernando's son, Alfonso X, *el Sabio*, ("the Learned") (1252–1284), continued and expanded this tolerance, and his court became a notable gathering place for the outstanding scholars and scientists of his epoch regardless of their religion.

A sharp look at the social perspective in Spain in 1252, when Alfonso X came to the throne of Castile and León, reveals that the Spanish Christians were now passing through a period of crisis. Their national character, formerly so pliable, was at last being set. During one generation Spain had thrust herself forward in victorious armies and triumphant ennobled individual soldiers. Then somehow the steam gave out. Not enough power was left to finish off the Reconquest. Granada still remained in Moorish hands, and there was nobody in Castile or Aragon who was ready or willing to challenge it. The spirit of forward motion had come to a natural halt. Consolidation was now essential before the move toward expansion could be resumed.

Imagine, if you can, the French coming back to the United States today to take over Texas, or the Spaniards coming back to take over the state of Florida or California. They would meet head-on the full and durable expression of another civilization, which they could not possibly liquidate. The Christians who captured in rapid succession Córdoba, Seville, Valencia, and the great territories around them, encountered a similar situation. These cities had been in Moslem hands for five hundred and fifty years, that is, approximately three times as long as the United States of America has existed. They were no longer Christian, no longer visigothic, Roman, or Hispanic. They were Moorish. They represented a different world, a different culture, a different vital structure and feeling in history, but now they did "belong" to the Spaniards. Realizing the magnitude of the task, the

Christians stopped and considered. What to do with these great cities, these great territories, and these great peoples? *How to use them?* The economy fell apart immediately if use was not made of them, as Ferdinand the Saint found out.

The culture of the Arabs was superior to that of the Christians in a great many ways. In the first place, its technical superiority was obvious. The Moors were better agriculturists, better engineers, better architects, better tradesmen, better manufacturers of tiles, textiles, leather goods, armor, swords; they lived in better houses, they had larger cities, their lands were more fruitful and they possessed more things of all kinds than the Spanish Christians. But material wealth was not their only point of superiority. They were also more widely read, they were better philosophers, physicians, poets, musicians, and artists.

The Castilians and their allies, therefore, had pitted themselves against a civilization which was technically, economically, and intellectually superior to their own. And they had won. The reason is neither complex nor hard to find. Very simply the Spanish Christians were superior to the Arabs in the one thing which counted most, and which always counts most, when two civilizations engage in a deadly contest. They were superior in individual drive, in stubborn will, and indefatigable energy, in the resolution to prove themselves the equal of any man, Moor, Jew, or Christian. Their reservoir of inner strength was greater. They did not depend on outside things, but only on what they had inside themselves. Each individual soldier was a dynamic universe. Each man's soul was in constant heroic tension. Each man's faith was epic. The forward thrust of their collective might was irresistible. With the psychology of soldiers they were now compelled to come to grips with problems which were cultural, political, and social. They made a brave beginning.

Neither Ferdinand the Saint, nor his son Alfonso the Learned, nor any of their successors on the throne of Castile and León was able to complete this task effectively. Not until Castile and Aragon merged in union, with Ferdinand of Aragon as king and Isabella of Castile as queen, did the Christians have sufficient energies or sufficient solidarity to solve this problem. Even then, the solution was not the best one; it was merely a cutting of the Gordian knot that was Spain, sloughing off its Moslem and Jewish inhabitants.

This does not mean that nothing was done in the thirteenth and fourteenth centuries There were many things that could be done, many important things, and these the Christians attacked with intelligence and with vigor. The immediate problem was: how *to feel* about this culture which now was theirs for keeps. For cities and lands and fields and mountains are nothing in themselves. They all take on the quality of the people who inhabit them. Even the names of many of the recaptured places had changed while they were in Moorish hands. The famous Baetis River was now the Guadalquivir, Hispalis was now called Sevilla; Alhama, Jaén, and dozens of other towns had been founded by the Moors where there had been no towns before, even the fields were different, and the entire physical aspect of all cities was completely altered and strange. There was an occasional Roman ruin, and that was about all to remind the victors that their ancestors had ever lived in these lands before. The task was an immense and frightening one, and rather than criticize the Spanish Christians because they did not do better at it, the truth is that what they did do was the most that could be expected of any people.

Alfonso X did not pussyfoot or straddle the fence; he had the thrust and resolution of a good Castilian; he meant to incorporate this culture into his own. His task was to mold a *Spanish* culture out of roots that were Greco-Roman, Islamic, Hebraic, as well as Christian and Castilian, and he went about it with a strong will and a real wisdom. His sobriquet *el Sabio* should mean both "wise" and "learned." Since he could not hope to emulate the epic victories of his father, he would become the leader of his people in another sphere, the cultural. He would gather around him a group of savants unparalleled in any medieval court; he would be known as Spain's "scholar king." He would place a premium on culture, that vital aspect of a nation's life by which it is remembered. He would use every man and every tool at his disposal, and they were many. The Jews contributed in a very great measure to this rebirth of learning in the mid 1200's, and books in Arabic were widely known and considered *de rigueur* by the scholars at Alfonso's court.

Whereas in the previous century many thousands of Christians had been living in Moorish territory, now the situation was reversed and thousands of Moors and Islamized Spaniards were living in the kingdoms of Christendom. Thus the influence of Arabic culture was never more strongly felt. Wandering scholars from all over Europe came to Toledo to see and learn. The Greek classics, which had been turned into Arabic, were now translated again into Latin and in that form were made known in the rest of Europe. The Jewish savant was the key man in this process, for he was the only one who knew both Arabic and Latin. The scholar who wanted a particular Greek classic translated, therefore, had first to find a Jew who was willing to turn its Arabic text into Latin for him. Oftentimes this was done orally, one man copying down what the other read out loud. It is little wonder that some of the Latin versions which got back to the other European countries sounded a bit strange in style and content.

Although the court at Toledo was the center of this revival of learning, the establishment of universities in Spain (Palencia circa 1212, Salamanca circa 1243) encouraged still further the medieval thirst for knowledge. The university at Palencia lasted only a few years, but the institution at Salamanca became one of the great universities of the Middle Ages. Even the sons of kings were sent here for their intellectual training, and sat on the same hard benches in the same cold halls as the rest of the students.

Alfonso X himself was reputed to be a learned man, a lover of the arts, of science, and of literature. He liked to wear silken robes adorned with gold and precious stones. The king, he thought, should be recognized by his very presence. Alfonso honored all persons of culture; he freed teachers of all tributes and granted them the status of *caballeros* ("gentlemen"). He was benevolent with those of another religious belief, and besought his countrymen not to exert any pressure on the Jews in order to convert them to Christianity. During his reign the Church of Santa María la Blanca (which still stands in Toledo a bit over-restored) was used by all three religions: Moslems on Friday, Jews on Saturday, Christians on Sunday.

Alfonso X directed the translation of many famous works of antiquity into Spanish: the Bible, the Talmud, the Koran, the Cabala, the Indian fables of *Kalila and Dimna*, the *Treasure* of Brunetto Latini, the teacher of Dante, who was an ambassador at Alfonso's court. The king was also interested in astronomy and published two books in that field; he also put out a book on chess, a game the Spaniards had learned from the Moors. Alchemy was of particular fascination for him, and he delved into it assiduously. In the field of history he supervised the publication of the *First General Chronicle*, a history of Spain, and of the *Siete Partidas*, the seven branches of law, which was an accumulation of laws and customs based in part on Roman law, with long passages of moralistic interpretation of the rights and duties of citizens. During his reign Alfonso also decreed that Castilian was the official language of his realm.

In spite of this decree he himself composed, or had composed, a series of more than four hundred songs to the Virgin (*Cantigas de Santa María*) in the more lyrical dialect known as Galician-Portuguese. The pilgrims to Santiago had brought into Galicia strong influences from Provence, its minstrels, and its school of lyric poetry, and thus there had grown up in Galicia in the twelfth century a tradition of lyrical verse. The learned king decided to continue this tradition. In order to prepare his collection of *cantigas* Alfonso gathered about him a distinguished group of musicians, poets, and writers, including many Moorish instrumentalists and also jongleurs and troubadours from France.

The miniatures decorating the manuscript of the *Cantigas* which is preserved in the Escorial were drawn and illuminated by a group of artists from Seville and are among the most beautiful examples of medieval illumination in Spain. Those which accompany the text of the ancient manuscript indicate how the songs were composed. The king himself took a position in the center of the group, directing the proceedings. To his left are four scribes, whose duty it was to record the words and musical notations. There were also instrumentalists and minstrels. The picture indicates that the songs were "tried out" before they were written down in final form. Another illustration shows three persons dancing in a circle, holding hands. They are probably singing at the same time.

The instruments used were the lute, brought into Europe by the Arabs, the hurdy-gurdy, the oval-shaped Moorish guitar, the viol, the Latin guitar (with in-curved sides like that of the present-day Spanish guitar), the Arabian rebec, a tiny two-stringed fiddle, the triangular psaltery, sets of bells, transverse flutes, trumpets and horns, harps, bagpipes, castanets, and the pipe and drum. Some or all of these instruments obviously composed the accompaniment of the thirteenth century. It is likely that much of the music was based on well-known folk tunes, possibly somewhat altered in the process of recomposition.

Most of the songs refer to some miracle in the life of the Virgin or to some aspect of the history of Spain. They are written in the form of the Arabic *zejel*, and are not from the French *virelai* as some have supposed. They were all composed to be sung, and are in clearly written mensural notation. The words alone do not give a complete presentation to the text; still, many of them are extremely beautiful. One *cantiga* reads:

> Rose of roses and flower of flowers,
> Lady of ladies, Queen of all queens.
> Rose of beauty so fine and bright,
> Flower of joy and of delight;
> Beautiful Lady, in your great mercy
> You take away our cares and sorrows.
> Rose of roses and flower of flowers.

Alfonso X loved Spain with all his heart. Some of the feeling that inspired him to write the *General Chronicle*, a partly legendary history of the country up to the year 1250, comes out in his "Praise of Spain," a much quoted passage from this famous text:

This Spain that we speak of is like the Paradise of God: it is watered by five sounding rivers, the Duero, Ebro, Tajo, Guadalquivir and Guadiana. In between these rivers are mighty mountains and lands, and the valleys and plains are great and wide. From the goodness of the earth and the water of the rivers these are very fruitful and abound in food. . . . Moreover, Spain brings forth great crops of corn, delicious fruits, exquisite fishes, sweet milk, and all the things that are made from it. The deer roam far and wide, flocks and horses cover the wide earth, there are many mules, and the land is secure and well provided with castles, it is happy with its good wines, content with its abundance of bread, rich in metals, in lead, in tin, in quicksilver, in iron, and brass, and silver, in gold and precious stones, and in every kind of marble, in salt of the sea and salt of the earth. . . . And Spain above all others is ingenious, daring and mighty in war, light-hearted in toil, loyal to God, affirmed in study, courteous in word, perfect in every good thing: and there is no land in all the world that is like her in goodness, none that is her equal in strength, and few on earth are as great as she. Above them every one Spain abounds in grandeur; more than any other she is loyal and true. O Spain! there is no mind nor tongue which can praise you half enough!

But this noble kingdom, so rich, so powerful, so honored, was overthrown and brought down in an outburst of discord among those inhabiting this land who turned their swords against each other, as if they were lacking in enemies; and in that they lost everything, for all the cities of Spain were taken by the Moors and broken and destroyed by the hands of her enemies . . .

The *Chronicle* now moves into the realm of anguish and trembling. Its feeling is that of Hebrew or Arabic metaphysics, a weeping and a despair that no longer regards the world as dominated by individual courage or bravery in warfare. We have come a long way from the terse praise of St. Isidore, six centuries earlier, who saw the Visigothic hordes raping his fair country, and regarded them with a certain awe and admiration. For was this not the destiny of men and of nations? According to Isidore it was; but not according to Alfonso the Learned. His *Chronicle* continues:

Wretched Spain! her death came with such haste there were none left to mourn it; they call her the afflicted one, now more dead than alive, their voices sound as from another century and their words come forth as from beneath the earth, and they say with anguish: You men, who are hastening by, look well and take notice to see if any wound or grief can compare with mine! Sorrowful is the weeping, tearful are the shouts, for Spain mourns her sons and she can find no comfort because they are no longer alive. Her homes and her dwelling places were all destroyed and turned into a wilderness, her honor and her glory became confusion, for her sons and her servants died by the sword, her nobles and gentle folk all fell into captivity, her princes and peers have gone in shame and opprobrium. So great was her wound and her destruction that there is no whirlwind, nor deluge, nor tempest on the sea, which can be compared with it. What evil or what storm did not Spain suffer? . . . Who will give me water to bathe my head and who will give me endless fountains for my eyes that they may always shed tears and weep for the loss and death of those of Spain and for the wretchedness and cowardice of the Visigoths?[22]

There is even more to the long complaint, which takes on the quality of a prayer of atonement, but the repetition becomes monotonous. The *Chronicle* sums up its philosophy, and that of the mid-thirteenth century, with these telling words:

From this everyone must learn to place no great value upon himself; neither the rich man for his wealth, nor the powerful man for his might, nor the strong man for his strength, nor the learned man for his knowledge . . . but he who wished to place some value upon himself, let him find his value in serving God; since it is He who strikes and gives ointment, it is He who wounds and heals, for the whole earth is His; all of the peoples, and nations, and kingdoms, and languages—all these move about and change; but God, the Creator of everything, remains in a single state and endures forever.

Medieval Spain is now clearly at the crossroads of a new religious feeling, and a new system of values. Only in religion can man find his true value. Alone, no matter what his will or strength, he is nothing. The days of the Cid are past and gone, and the epoch of the Catholic sovereigns, Ferdinand and Isabella, is prophetically indicated by these solemn words. The holy war has not yet reached its physical extremity, but its metaphysics are clearly outlined in the thirteenth century.

And yet Alfonso's was a reign of enlightened tolerance. Numerous Jews were outstanding scholars, craftsmen, tradesmen, financiers, bankers, and physicians. The Arabs were also scholars, physicians, musicians, and tillers of the soil. While the Jews stuck mainly to the labor of artisans or to administering to the upper classes, the Moors often worked in the fields and seemed to have a green thumb when it came to making things grow. The kings almost always had Jewish financial advisers and helpers, and everyone with a bellyache sought to consult a Jewish physician, even during those later times when it was forbidden by law for Jews to be doctors.

By 1300 the psychology of the Spanish Christian had reached a point where many began to look down on the Moors, who worked with their hands, and on the Jews, who were always counting money and accumulating luxurious *things*. The Spanish Christian had expressed himself in quite a different manner. His recaptured dwelling place, his courage in battle, his poverty in material things, his lordly gravity and insatiate longing for seigniory and dominion, his thrust of the entire self in a pure drive forward—these were all qualities which characterized his nation. As the Spanish writer Américo Castro points out, the image of the good ruler who encourages peace, hard work, the tilling of fields, and commerce found no place in Spanish life, for it simply did not fit into the vital structure of Spanish society. Such orderly, efficient rule suggests rather a neat Dutch field, with peaceful cows and rows of tulips. But Castile had forged its soul on a bleak, raw land against every adversity; hence respect for material things, the accumulation of them, and the working for them, held no grip on Castilian character. However, who can say that envy played no part in this picture, for it is natural that any man who has nothing should look with envy on the possessions of another. Add to this the religious element, and the racial ideal (purity of blood was a Jewish concept long before it was Spanish), and we have the makings of the Inquisition and the later persecutions.

It would be a grave error of perspective to take leave of the reign of Alfonso X without making clear that despite the learned king's contribution to the world of culture, his political life was anything but successful. His years on the throne were filled with plots, rebellions, uprisings, many of them on the part of his reputed friends among the nobility and even by members of his royal family. Alfonso's wife abandoned him and took refuge in Catalonia, for political motives. His brothers Enrique, Felipe, and Fadrique all rose up against the king. Even his son Sancho, called *el Bravo*, the Fierce, opposed his father in his impatience for the throne. King Alfonso exclaimed in anguish: "I honored Sancho in every way that I could, and he struggled to dishonor me in the cruelest manner possible. I loved him devotedly, and he attempted to take from me the kingdom that God has given me, and desired my death."

The Spain of political disunion is clearly drawn in these despairing lines. Alfonso X had discovered the key to union, religion, but the time was not yet ripe to apply it. He had discovered also in the revival of learning during his reign the key to Spain's belonging to the mainstream of European culture, but his love of his native land was so great that he did not use it effectively. When he published his stirring *General Chronicle* and other works which might have been outstanding landmarks in the literature of the Middle Ages, he wrote in Spanish, and not in Latin. Alfonso X was the epitome of his insulated country, a seed of immense promise which two centuries later would blossom gloriously but briefly before the garden was gone.

Alfonso X died in 1284. His son Sancho IV came to the throne via a rebellion against his father, against the law, and against the infant son of his deceased older brother. The power of the nobility, many of whom had backed Sancho, had again reared its ugly head in the national political life. The Moorish wars were over, the king could no longer hold out the promise of new territories, so the nobility sought to maintain its power by deciding who should occupy the throne.

There is a long stretch between 1284, the date of Alfonso's death, and 1474, year of the union of Castile and Aragon under the reign of Ferdinand and Isabella. What is the importance of these two hundred years? It was certainly not a period of great cultural flowering, of political stability, or of economic progress. Alfonso's cosmopolitan court had no counterpart in the reigns that followed. Architecture became the great art of these two centuries of the late Middle Ages. The magnificent cathedrals of Toledo, Burgos, Seville, León, and scores of other public and religious buildings were constructed throughout the land. The church became the mother of architecture and the stepmother of art. Music too began to flow in a great hieratic stream. Some of the finest organs and most impressive organ music of Europe were found in Spain. The choral singing which developed could rank with the best anywhere on the Continent. This tradition has continued until today, and the Spaniards, who individually are very poor singers, still have some of the finest choral groups in the world, many of them composed of nonprofessionals who work at singing because they love to sing so much.

Primarily, however, these two centuries were a period of great cathedral building. Ferdinand the Saint himself, with the archbishop of Toledo, placed the cornerstone of the Cathedral of Toledo in the year 1226. The building was not finished until 1493, one year after the discovery of America. It is 385 feet long by 178 feet wide, with immense pillars sustaining a great, lofty ceiling. Its exterior is Gothic; its interior is a mixture of Gothic and almost every other architectural style that existed in Spain during those two hundred years, including the Arabic. Many have called it the most beautiful interior of any Spanish cathedral. Its choir stalls of carved wood are incomparable, so are its twelve El Greco apostles, its beautiful grillwork, the riot of sculptured figures above its main altar and those on the exterior of the main chapel. Its gold and silver treasures: crowns, chalices, candelabra and altarpieces are priceless, as is its collection of embroidered and embossed robes which were worn by the famous archbishops of Spanish history. Its stately tower, 295 feet high, built between 1380 and 1440, is one of the most impressive in Europe.

The Cathedral of Seville spans an even greater period; it was constructed mainly between 1402 and 1506, but its belfry, made by the Moors, dates from 1180. The building has never been finished. Its soaring columns, lovely stained glass windows and beautiful Giralda Tower, once the twelfth century minaret of the Moorish mosque which stood on this same spot, are the amazement of all who visit this immense cathedral. Here too are the tombs of Columbus, of Ferdinand III, the Saint, and his son, Alfonso X, the Learned. The history of the Reconquest, the epoch of the learned king, and the discovery of America are all linked together in this mighty monument to God.

When the local dignitaries of Seville met to plan the construction of their cathedral, one of them said: "Let us put up a building of such immense proportions that the rest of the world will think us mad." With this goal in mind construction was begun. Many times funds were exhausted and there was a period of inactivity, but always some way was found to continue the work. Although it is not complete in an architectural sense (for example, the façade is lacking), the present structure gives an impression of completeness and of formidable immensity. The dizzying height of its huge pillars and the loftiness of its ceiling, unsurpassed in Spain, are unforgettable. The Cathedral of Seville is the third largest in the world, coming after St. Peter's in Rome and St. Paul's in London. The building, like almost all of the great cathedrals of Spain, is a mixture of many styles: Gothic, Greco-Roman, Plateresque (which is a delicate mingling of Gothic, Renaissance, and Arabic), Arabic, and Germanic. The windows were made in Flanders and Germany.

The most striking tradition of this cathedral is the dance of *Los seises*, performed by young boys with castanets, on the eight days following the festival of *Corpus Domini*. This stately dance, with pagan overtones, is presented inside the church as part of the ritual before the reverent worshipers. It is generally accompanied by a chant. The total effect, in those precincts of enclosed loftiness and gloom, is one of overpowering mystery.

The Cathedral of Burgos was begun in 1221, and again Ferdinand the Saint placed the first stone. Construction was not completed until 1600. The building is Gothic, finished in Plateresque. It is reputed to have the most perfect exterior of any cathedral in Spain, in an almost flawless Gothic style. The twin 275-foot towers by Hans of Cologne, erected around 1450, are unique in Spain. There is a multitude of statues of angels, martyrs, warriors, princes, saints, and the great towers are perforated, chiseled, and embroidered with an exquisite grace and delicacy. One of the statues, the famous Christ of Burgos, is a body that appears to be made of human skin. It has real hair, eyebrows, lashes, and beard. The hair and hands are streaked with blood. In this magnificent cathedral there are also many mementos of the Cid, whose home town this was. It is easy to see why General Franco chose Burgos as the center of his government during the Spanish civil war. The cathedral here is the epitome of the Middle Ages in Christian Spain. The much less visited Cathedral of León, built between 1205 and 1400, is one of the unsung glories of Spain. Its stained-glass windows, covering an immense wall space at the northeast end of the choir, give this building a multicolored light and airy grace which has no parallel in any other religious structure of the country. It resembles a gorgeous butterfly with the sunshine on its delicate wings.

The cathedrals of Spain leave in one's mind two very strong general impressions: first, they are not seen to best advantage from the outside. They are eaten up, as it were, by the cluttered stone buildings that surround and crowd them. They do not even occupy the best topographic locations, for example, the highest point in the city. They rise like great carved rocks from the hard, harsh, rocky land that gave them being. There is no sweep or proper perspective to their exterior view, but when one steps inside the impression immediately changes. As soon as the eyes become accustomed to the gloom here is the recognition of another world, entirely different. It is the interior world of Spain, a world of darkness and height, of incredible size and of incomparable beauty. It is a world of glorious fusion of many styles and cultures. It is a world of gravity, nobility, and faith of epic proportions. Nowhere can one better observe in successive moments the exterior gravity and restraint of Spanish character out of which has blossomed the interior wealth and dignity of the Spanish spirit.

These great Spanish cathedrals, and countless other beautiful monasteries, refuges, and churches which accompanied them, symbolized the emerging religious unity of Spain, a unity which eventually would impose itself on the political and social organism. But so far this was not evident; political instability was the order of the day. The kings and princes of Spain contested the throne in repeated bloody encounters, and the nobility was ever ready to apply its weight for a good advantage. Profligacy in the royal families became the rule rather than the exception, reaching its peak in the time of Peter I, the Cruel (1350–1369). Peter inherited the throne when he was fifteen, and immediately he and his five illegitimate brothers squared off in a ruthless struggle for the succession. Peter drenched the country in blood, and is said to have murdered at least a dozen persons including an archbishop, several cousins, friends, half-brothers, and possibly his own French queen. His brother, Henry of Trastamare (known in history as *Henry the Bastard*), had sufficient support to be able to depose Peter, who then appealed to England's famous "Black Prince" for aid. The Englishman's support brought about his reinstatement on the throne, but when the Black Prince left Spain, disgusted with his ally's brutality, Henry of Trastamare again rose up against the king. The two brothers met in mortal combat, and Peter was slain, at the age of thirty-three. It was not one of those heroic fights where prince meets prince in open tourney or on the field of battle, but took place in a miserable tent in a wintry encampment. After a brief but furious hand-to-hand struggle Henry buried a dagger in his brother's breast. After that he succeeded him on the throne.

Peter left behind three illegitimate daughters, a trail of blood, and a legend of hate and immorality. He had boasted of quite a harem about the palace, but had shown a constant loyalty to one of these women, María Padilla, who encouraged his fratricide. Under duress he had married Princess Blanche of France but deserted her almost immediately. His mistress, María Padilla, was flaunted before the courtiers, who were forced to accept her. The palace became a center of intrigues, conspiracy, planned murders, and blatant profligacy.

The government of Spain had degenerated to a vile and abominable state. Gone was the heroic spirit of Ferdinand the Saint, gone was the zest for knowledge of Alfonso X. Gone was the hope of maintaining the royal succession by law and orderly process. Security from the Moors had turned the Spanish aggressive spirit in on itself, and these tantrums of self-destruction were the result.

Peter the Cruel, in a way, is the symbolic embodiment of the clash between Moorish sensuality and Castilian drive for power which was splitting the royal families of Spain down the middle. He represented the worst elements of both Moor and Castilian and became the despicable symbol of a tottering social order. Fortunately for Spain, among Peter's successors were stronger kings who guided their miserable nation out of the morass. But this was to take over a hundred years.

Peter is remembered in Spanish history mainly for his bloodthirstiness and moral turpitude, but his brief reign touched many other aspects of the national life. His fancy for the Moorish palace in Seville, the Alcázar, led to his complete renovation of the place at the hands of the finest *Mudéjar* craftsmen and artists. (*Mudéjar* is a Moor living under Christian rule.) The ancient palace of the Almohades (dating from 1171) was in a very poor state; since the capture of Seville in 1248 by Ferdinand the Saint it had been sadly neglected and parts of it were collapsing. In the 1360's Peter began the task of reconstruction, which was carried to completion within a few years. The Alcázar today is the finest *Mudéjar* palace in existence. Its style, resembling that of the Alhambra, is pure Arabic, for Peter made no attempt to alter the architecture or the interior adornment.

The halls and chambers of the Alcázar are an intricate maze of delicate arabesques, graceful interlacing horseshoe arches, gleaming tiles, carved and gilded wooden ceilings. The slender columns holding up the arches resemble a woman's arms. The stucco of the arabesques is of crushed marble and alabaster, and suggests, at times, stalactites or icicles, and at other times, heavy lace, all producing a pure white background brilliantly colored with reds, greens, blues, and gold. Some of the delicate arabesques are perforated like a veil. Before one has passed through one room he is stunned and confused by the marvelous artistry and profusion of design. The patios and inner chambers do not suggest those of a European palace at all, but bring to mind rooms imagined after a childhood reading of the *Arabian Nights*.

Peter loved this sensuous palace, and held his court here most of the time. It was here that he carried on his affair with María Padilla; it was also to this palace that he invited his brother Fadrique, Grand Master of the Order of Santiago, in order to have him slain. Don Fadrique came gladly at Peter's summons, anxious to seal the peace between them, but the moment he entered the portal Peter angrily denounced him. Don Fadrique clutched at his sword, the hilt of which got entangled in his mantle of Santiago, and so faced his accusers unarmed. He ran swiftly through the patios in a vain attempt to escape. One of the courtiers felled him with a mighty blow on the shoulders, and other courtiers finished him off where he lay, leaving him in a pool of blood.

On another occasion, after Peter had signed a treaty with Aragon, he found himself in the midst of a struggle between two claimants for the kingdom of Granada. The Red King had deposed the lawful emir, Mohammed, who was forced to flee to Africa. However, Mohammed soon returned with a large army, and allied himself with Peter the Cruel. The Red King, realizing that his realm was in jeopardy, hastened to Seville to beg for Peter's support. He was received graciously, and he and his thirty-seven courtiers were lodged in the Jewish quarter of the city, now known as Santa Cruz. The news rapidly spread that the Moors had brought some priceless jewels with them, and Peter was greedy to possess them, particularly one matchless ruby that the Red King sometimes wore in the center of his turban. He invited the Moors to the Alcázar for a banquet, and there in the Hall of the Ambassadors armed figures leaped from the corridors and draperies and seized the Red King and his thirty-seven Moors. A couple of days later Peter stripped the Red King of his clothes, forced him to don a scarlet robe, and then made him mount an ass and parade in an open field before the people of the city. After this cruel indignity Peter himself cast the first lance that pierced the Moorish emir's body:

"Take that," he shouted, "for the way you helped Aragon against me!"

The wounded emir cried: "What a vile thing you have done!"

In rapid succession all of the Moors were slain, the ruby and many other precious stones were taken, and Mohammed was easily able to regain his kingdom.

Later on in Peter's life, when his bastard brother had replaced him on the throne, Peter presented this ruby to the wife of the Black Prince in order to assure his aid in the struggle against Henry. The ruby was taken back to England; it is the same "fair ruby, great as a racket ball," which Queen Elizabeth showed to Melville, and it is the gem which now adorns the center of the Imperial Crown of England, to be seen in the Tower of London.

The greatest of the Moorish historians, Ben Jaldun, who was sent to Seville as an emissary from the North African emirs, adds a few interesting details about the regality of Peter's court. Ben Jaldun had come to help ratify a peace treaty between these emirs and Peter, and of this he writes:

With that object in mind I made the King a gift of some exquisite silks and of several fine thoroughbred horses with golden saddles. The moment I reached Seville I could observe the many monuments that attested to the power and wealth of my ancestors. The Christian King received me with honor, and assured me of his deep satisfaction in seeing me. His Jewish physician, Ibrahim ben Zarzar, had already praised me to the King and had informed him as to the illustrious names of my ancestors. The King then wished to keep me at his side, promising that everything that had once belonged to my family would be restored. I thanked him profoundly for the offer, as it merited, but begged him to excuse me from accepting it, trusting that I might still continue in his good graces. When I left Seville he provided me with beasts of burden and every provision for the journey, and also gave me a beautiful mule equipped with a bridle and saddle trimmed in gold, which I was to present to the King of Granada.

Peter the Cruel, like many other princes and courtiers of Spain, took great pride in being a Don Juan. The famous Don Juan de Mañara, on whose grave appear these words: "Here lie the ashes of the greatest sinner who ever lived," epitomized the attitude. Perhaps rooted in such histories the Don Juan legend became a part of medieval folk lore. Later, in Spain's Golden Age, it gave rise to one of the most powerful plays ever written, *The Deceiver of Seville*, by Tirso de Molina, which introduced the theme in western letters. Many critics have explained the Don Juan psychology in terms of the Spaniard's excessive ego with its powerful drive which leads toward trampling on the rights of others. The self, which is sacred, is driven relentlessly to express the blind and reckless thrust that lies within it, regardless of consequences. Other critics, Kierkegaard for example, regard the story as medieval Christianity's attempt to symbolize two irreconcilables—spiritual love and sensual love. But there is another side to the Don Juan character which is found in the fused Hebrew-Arabic-Castilian philosophy and concept of reality. This concept is very simply that exterior reality has no existence in and of itself. One reaches toward it, and it recedes, finally to disappear. The individual's life, therefore, is a kind of gliding across a shifting reality, which is not really there. Don Juan, thus, somewhat like the wandering Spanish *pícaro*, clutches again and again at a phantom. In his case it is the phantom of femininity, the ideal of love, the epitome of beauty. But as no single woman can embody this concept completely, it becomes necessary to move from one victim to another in an endless search. Peter the Cruel and his court caught this elusive quality of reality, and the violence with which Spaniards were beginning to seize at it, in an elevated arena which made it public property.

Peter the Cruel carried on the tolerant tradition of his father toward the Jews in Spain. During the reigns of Alfonso XI and Peter the Spanish Jews as a whole perhaps felt more at home in the country than in any other period. Peter's royal treasurer was a Jew named Samuel Levi, whose house can still be seen in Toledo. His court physician was also Jewish. The kings of Spain had come to depend on their Jewish subjects in medical, economic and financial matters. Not only were the Jews tax collectors (which caused the populace to hate them), but they were also financiers, bankers, artisans of many kinds, physicians, and scholars. In addition to all this the amount they themselves paid into the royal treasury was far in excess of that indicated by their numerical proportion in the general population. In some areas Jewish taxes accounted for one half of the total revenues. Hence, the economy of the country depended mainly on the Jews, although their total number probably never exceeded 300,000. The population of Spain in the fourteenth century was perhaps five million. (It is doubtful if there are more than three or four thousand Jews in Spain today.)

The Spanish Jew between the years 1000–1400 was not the persecuted Hebrew of the Visigothic monarchy. Accepted first by the Moors as an integral part of the Arabic culture of the peninsula, he was later accepted in the same manner by the kings of Spanich Christendom. Certain *fueros* granted the communities in the 1200's even protected Jewish orthodoxy, prohibiting Jews from reading any books that attacked the Jewish religion, and setting punishments for those who did not observe the Sabbath. In Aragon many Jews were royal judges, and the list of their activities as craftsmen is almost endless: tailors, book-binders, dyers, lantern makers, button manufacturers, turners, cutters, instrument makers, weavers, silversmiths, cobblers, apothecaries, embroiderers, scriveners, etcetera. The Jew, in brief, did almost everything; there were even Jewish women who acted as mourners and intoned funeral chants at Christian burials.[16] Thus the popular concept of the medieval Jew as a mere moneylender has no validity in Spain, where he took over those tasks abandoned by the Castilian whose psychology sought expression in the non-manual absolute, in the person who could impose and maintain himself through sheer drive and dominion.[16]

Sexual relations and intermarriage between Jews and Christians were frowned on by both groups, but in spite of this public and legalistic attitude there was a great amount of blood mixing. Spanish scholars who have carefully examined the old documents (Amador de los Ríos, Américo Castro, and others) conclude that almost all of the aristocracy of the late medieval days in Spain had some Jewish blood in their veins, and this includes some of the most famous kings and queens, even Ferdinand of Aragon, Isabella's husband. Many high dignitaries in the Church were converted Jews, as were several outstanding medieval and Renaissance authors.

The public attitude toward the Jews, like the public attitude toward any powerful minority in any country, in any epoch, had its strong ups and downs throughout the Middle Ages in Spain. Almost without exception everyone who was ill and could afford it sought out a Jewish physician, but resentment and envy at Jewish wealth and Jewish intelligence constantly smouldered in the popular mind. Thus it was that the very same Samuel Levi who was Peter the Cruel's treasurer had a long tunnel dug out connecting his home in

Toledo with the River Tagus, so that in case of a popular uprising against the Jews he might have this means of escape.

The royal power, sustained as it was by Jewish money and Jewish industry and intelligence, supported a position of tolerance toward the Jews. Many kings of Spain used the phrase "my Jews" in coming to the defense of their Hebrew subjects who were attacked by some outside authority. In 1215, when the Fourth Lateran Council ordered Jews to wear a distinctive badge to make them stand out from the Christians, a great hue and cry was raised among the Jewish population of Spain, and Ferdinand the Saint, backed by the archbishop of Toledo, appealed to the Pope to suspend the decision. Honorius III was forced to yield to the urgency of the royal plea. During these centuries the attitude of the kings of France toward the Jews was just the opposite. Saint Louis confiscated Jewish wealth, and Philip the Fair expelled the Jews en masse from his dominions. Many of these found refuge in Spain. Until the late Middle Ages, then, Jews and Moors were accepted as an integral and indispensable element of Castilian life. When this "Castilian" life became Spanish, it was through the fusion of all these cultures in a single alloy, the Hispanic. In this manner did Spain emerge from medieval times into modern history.

5

LIFE IN THE MEDIEVAL TOWNS

I told thee, soul, that joy and woe
Were but a gust, a passing dew.
I told thee so, I told thee so,
And, oh, my soul, the tale was true.
                    —From an old Spanish *Cancionero*

During the Middle Ages the church largely forgot or put aside St. Augustine's fourth century war on sex. In Spain the priest's *barragana* or mistress was an accepted institution. The priest had his right to enjoy sex like anyone else, provided he did it in concubinage instead of marriage. Many of these concubinages were, however, marriages in fact. Occasionally, in order to give the arrangement a cloak of dignity, the priest would pass it around that his "cousin" or his "niece" was going to keep house for him. With or without such an explanation the priest's *ama* or housekeeper, and bedmate, were widely accepted facts of life. Since priests associated closely with so many women in the routine performance of their duties the priest-hood in general was branded with the natural suspicion of lechery.

One of the ancient Moorish writers of the twelfth century, Ben Abdun al-Tuchibi, in a document on the administration of Seville, has a few salty comments to make on the mixing of Christians and Moslems in his community. He writes: "Moslem women must be prohibited from entering the shameful Christian churches, because the priests are a bunch of libertines, adulterers, and scoundrels . . .

Christian priests should be made to marry, as in the East, or at the very least they should be authorized to marry if they wish. If they refuse marriage, then there should not be allowed in the house of any priest a woman, or even an old lady of whatever age . . ."[20]

But Moors were not the only ones who spoke out candidly concerning the sexual activities of Spanish priests. One of the greatest writers of medieval days, Juan Ruiz, Archpriest of Hita, in his fascinating *Book of Good Love*, circa 1335, gives a lusty and full account of these affairs, and very proudly includes himself among the Lotharios of his epoch. Near the beginning of his book he states categorically:

> As Aristotle says, and it is true:
> The world labors for two things: first,
> To have food and shelter, the other,
> To couple with a pleasing female.

The author then goes on to relate how man and the other animals desire to have intercourse with the females of their species according to nature. Throughout the remainder of his book the archpriest describes a series of amorous episodes which are a part of the best erotic literature of the Middle Ages. The author generally has these experiences happen to other characters, but occasionally he forgets and sticks in his own name. One can hardly doubt that much of the book is autobiographical. Women of nearly every class are fair game for the archpriest's pen, and men are not always the aggressors. On occasion, a wayfarer in the mountains is practically assaulted by one of the Spanish *serranas* or "women of the mountains" who grabs the traveler, leads him to her hut, thaws him out, feeds him, and then demands that "he take off his clothes and get to work."

These country wenches seem to be a part of the folklore of medieval days. In order to save his conscience, or perhaps only his reputation among his superiors, the author intersperses frequent "songs to the Virgin" among his erotic stories, and he insists from time to time on his intention to clarify the difference between "good love," which is spiritual, and "bad love," which is physical. Nevertheless, in this book it is the pagan spirit of love that wins out. Near the end of the book the archpriest, egged on by the old lady go-between who had found him other morsels, even woos a nun. He writes:

Said she, "Friend, pay attention to a mother's admonition:
Go, love a nun; believe me, son, make that your one ambition,

For they can't marry afterward, nor dare breathe their condition—
With them you're safe to taste for years the pleasures of coition."[23]

The author then goes on to enumerate in some detail the many
foods, condiments, and aphrodisiacal sweetmeats that nuns give their
lovers in order to keep them stirred up. He also makes it clear that
nuns are noted to have had great practice in the arts of love, and
that no better mates may be found. Yet, after a vigorous suit the
archpriest's nun turns out to be pure in heart, and he is not able
to complete this episode. However, what he had said about nuns
in general was sufficient to damn any man before the Inquisitorial
Tribunal of a couple of centuries later.

The finale episode in the *Book of Good Love,* called "A Ballad on
the Holy Men of Talavera," is a plea for complete permissiveness
insofar as the sexual lives of priests are concerned. The ballad begins
at a monastery with the arrival of an order from the archbishop
of Talavera prohibiting concubinage. "And if it pleased some one or
two, two thousand thought it ill." The order read in part:

> Intelligence I have of sin, wherefore I put this stated,
> That every priest or clergyman who has been consecrated,
> Shall not have concubine or whore, nor wife already mated—
> All those who disobey, henceforth are excommunicated!

The deacon and treasurer of the Holy Men of Talavera rise to oppose the unseemly order. The treasurer states:

> Of course, dear friends, your injuries concern me more than mine,
> But Tessie is my innocent and pretty concubine—
> To hell with Talavera! I'll to usury incline
> Before I chase from bed and board a strumpet so divine.

There are other noisy objections to the order which has been received, and the archpriest closes his book with these lusty lines:

> But here it's time to close my tale—I'll haste its termination
> By saying all the clerks and clergy made an appellation
> Wherein they put unanimously this recommendation:
> That holy men should be allowed full rights to fornication.[23]

The archpriest was not overpresenting his case, for the holy men of
his day not only enjoyed but often flaunted their pleasant promiscuity. The flagrant and outrageous conduct of churchmen and their
concubines, who dressed in luxury and went about in great arrogance, so incensed the people of Valladolid that in 1351 the courts

of that city complained to Peter the Cruel. "The king ordered the dress of such women to be regulated by a sumptuary law, and required them to wear a red cloth under their wimples so that people might be able to distinguish them outwardly from honest women."

The author of this fascinating and unique manuscript, called by one well-known critic "the most powerful book ever written in the Spanish language," was a small-time priest in one of the insignificant villages of New Castile. He obviously knew a great deal about the Moors from firsthand contact, and his knowledge of Arabic music is stated in several verses. The entire book is a wonderful medieval arabesque which brings together most of the different cultural roots of the Spanish Middle Ages. The author mentions Cato, Aristotle, Ovid, the good knight Tristram; he frequently quotes from the Scriptures, his verses are full of proverbs, and the book contains many fables and apologues which came into Spain with the Moors. Juan Ruiz was not a learned man, but he was a wise man with a sort of thick and virile strength who very well epitomized the age in which he lived. His book is a disjointed series of episodes, linked together on the flimsiest kind of framework, entirely circular, without beginning and without end.

We feel the presence of wholly Castilian cities, the bustling and jostling of three races and faiths; there is mention of astrologers; go-betweens appear on the scene; there are references to learned books, to peasants and knights in the service of Spain, to ladies, monks, and nuns; there is a riot of tunes and songs, appetizing foods, liturgical feasts, mountain passes in the Guadarrama, exquisite language and plebeian improprieties—all mixed together in an orgy of sensations that is periodically interrupted by a flood of abstract moralizing.[16]

In the *Book of Good Love* sin is the product of nature expressing itself in human action. The archpriest can be one moment the sensual and sinful Lothario and the next moment the moralizer. He sees nothing strange in mingling the two points of view. Man he views as a kind of centauric fusion, half-dust half-deity, alike unfit to sink or soar. This attitude is typical of Islamic religion and literature, but it also expresses quite aptly the reality of Spanish life in the fourteenth century. After the years of epic tension, why not now enjoy the body? The kings of Castile were certainly doing so, and it was the natural rebound of the pendulum now that the Moorish wars seemed over. Hispanic integralism, the urge to express the whole person in autobiographical baring of self, is also reflected in the *Book of Good Love.* Even though the world glides by, and exterior reality slips through the fingers, one reaches out to seize and embrace it with the body part, and even with the spirit, for the reality of the spirit and the reality of the senses are one and the same; they are intertwined and inseparable. In the archpriest's book there is a constant movement back and forth between sensual impulse and moral restraint. These were, indeed, the two outstanding characteristics of Arabic literature: eroticism, on the one hand, and on the other, exemplary tales with a clear didactic purpose. But sex and conscience are also the essential characteristics of *homo sapiens*, in almost any civilized environment. While the archpriest fuses the two tendencies in his book, the other great writer of his generation in Spain, Don Juan Manuel, nephew of Alfonso *el Sabio*, left behind as his most famous contribution to medieval letters a collection of *exempla* or moral tales in the Arabic tradition, known as the *Count Lucanor*.

Juan Ruiz obviously delighted in writing his book; it was a projection of his virile personality, and he wanted his readers to enjoy it too and to take part in the merry chase. He was clapped into prison by the archbishop, perhaps merely because he was what he was. But his manuscript survived all the Inquisitorial fires of a later date, and despite a few obvious cullings on the part of an occasional censor, it still has the vigor and vitality of a man who feels every human urge, and who exerts himself to taste and preserve them all.

The Jews were among the finest writers in Spain during the Middle Ages. Sem Tob (or Santob), rabbi of Carrion de los Condes, Palencia, was a contemporary of Peter the Cruel, and his delicate lyrical verses are dedicated to that king. In fact, his book is called *Counsels to King Peter*, or *Moral Proverbs*. Sem Tob is ordinarily referred to as a gnomic or aphoristic poet, but he is also one of the first real lyric voices to cry out in Castilian. To this Jewish-Islamic-Castilian rabbi the exterior world is not only doubtful and fleeting, but the Jew's place in it gives rise to a literary despair. The rose dies and leaves behind its sweet rose water, which is its finest value; does man leave behind a wake that is as lasting? In any case, he must constantly exert himself, *as if* it were in his power to win despite the awful neutrality of the universe. The whole world is an endless play of opposites, and even the crown may turn into a worn-out shoe. The rose loses nothing by being born on the thorn, and good exempla do not lose being recited by a Jew. Sem Tob was the first in a long line of Jewish and Jewish convert poets of medieval times in Spain. In the next century, at the literary court of John II (father of Isabella), whose reign is the portico of the Renaissance, these Jewish-Castilian poets played a role similar in importance to that of the scholars who surrounded Alfonso *el Sabio*.

The earliest poems in the Spanish language, let us remember, are in Hebrew characters, and go back to the tenth century. The Jewish population of Spain continued to develop a rich and intense body of poetry in its own Spanish-Jewish dialect, including a whole corpus of wonderful ballads or *romances*. Many of these poems have a sharp and haunting lyrical quality. One of the most beautiful of them all is called "Face Like a Flower." This is the way it begins:

> —Open the door to me,
> Open it, face like a flower;
> You have been mine since you were a child,
> How much more so now.—
> She with the face like a flower
> Went down and opened the door;
> They went to the garden
> Hand in hand together.
> Under a green rose tree
> They set their table.
> Eating and drinking
> They fell asleep together.[17]

The man awakes with an agonizing pain in his side. The girl offers him a doctor for his healing, a bag of gold, a loaf of fresh bread. He concludes the ballad with: "When you have killed a man you talk of *healing!*" Another lovely old Jewish-Spanish ballad is called "There Was a Beautiful Lady." Its opening lines are:

> There was a beautiful lady,
> No one was more lovely:
> Her forehead is dazzling,
> And her hair is like brass.
> Her brow mother-of-pearl,
> Her eyes are almonds,
> Her nose fine as a feather,
> Her cheeks are roses,
> Her mouth very rounded,
> Her teeth are pearls,
> Slender her throat,
> Pomegranates her breasts,

Her waist small, her body
Drawn fine like a cypress.
When she went in to hear mass
The church danced with light . . .[17]

In the end we find out that the beautiful lady has waited seven empty years for her beloved. Now she is ready for another to take her. Even in these folk ballads the Jewish poet sings of separation and of loss, of love broken and of despair. His literary voice intensifies the tragedy of the individual in Spain. He gives expression to the anguish which is beginning to take over the body and soul of his adopted country. In this role he still feels that he is the outsider, not quite taken in, not quite belonging, not quite firmly rooted in the land that he loves so much, and which, for the past several hundred years at least, has treated him so well. But the sad mark of his difference goes with him wherever he moves, whatever his profession, whatever his art.

The Spanish ballads make up one of the greatest bodies of popular or folk poetry in the entire world. In both variety and number they exceed the ballads of England, but perhaps this is because the English turned away from their popular poetry and did not begin collecting it until the late eighteenth century, hence many of the finest ballads were undoubtedly lost. Thousands of Spanish ballads were written down in the years when balladry was at its peak. In Spain, and in Spanish America today, the *romance* or ballad is still very much alive. The Mexican *corrido*, which is the same thing transferred to the Mexican scene, sprang forth from the Revolution of 1910–1920 much as the ancient ballads of Spain did from the dramatic events of the Middle Ages. Some of the earliest ballads of the peninsula are about Henry of Trastamare's fratricidal struggle against his brother, Peter the Cruel. They give every evidence of having been composed at that time, that is, toward the middle of the fourteenth century.

From this period on, balladry in Spain was a flourishing field. No one knows who composed the immense majority of the ancient ballads; they were preserved mainly through the oral tradition, and were not collected until around 1500. They were originally meant to be sung and danced by the people. They are traditional poetry in its finest flower, telescoped, intense, dramatic, often lyrically beautiful, politically powerful, always the voice of the people. They are an *Iliad* without their Homer, which in their brevity capture a moment of life, a fragment of history. Their subject matter is extremely varied: the frontier wars against the Moors, the life of the Cid and his contemporaries, the exploits of other traditional heroes, the love stories of anonymous individuals as well as of princes and kings, the romances between Christians and Moors, even the mysterious songs of sirens who lure men into the briny deep. It is a fascinating fact of Spanish literature that when the Jews were exiled from Spain in 1492 they carried hundreds of these ancient ballads along with them, and so deep was their love for Spain that many of them have survived in Sephardic communities all over the world from Los Angeles to Albania.* Only recently has a concerted effort been made to collect and publish these ballads.

The influence of the *romances* on the Spanish literature of the Golden Age was tremendous. With the birth of the Romantic movement they again came into the limelight, and translations were made of them in nearly every European language. The philosopher Hegel compared them to "a necklace of pearls," Schopenhauer profoundly admired them, the English Romantics went wild over them. Archbishop Percy, in his monumental *Reliques of the Ancient English Poetry*, 1765, the cornerstone of English Romanticism, translated several of the old *romances*. Dozens of English poets follow in his footsteps: Lord Byron, Sir John Bowring, Robert Southey, Lockhart (Walter Scott's son-in-law), Thomas Rodd, and many, many others. My own doctoral thesis, written at the University of Madrid, had as its title *Spain as Seen by the English Romantics* (*España vista por los románticos ingleses*), and one of my conclusions was that the translation of all these *romances* into English was a primary reason for Spain's becoming that legendary "renowned, romantic land" in the British, and later in the American, consciousness.

Medieval life in Spain differed considerably from that in the other European countries. The vast numbers of Moors, Jews, Moorish-Christians, and other mixtures, plus the culture of these groups, constituted a fundamental point of difference. The eight centuries of the Reconquest, from which emerged many aspects of the social, economic, and political organism added further to this distinction. Feudalism, that is, the set contractual arrangement between lord and vassal embodying the duties of each, was never as deeply rooted nor

---

* The Hebrew name for Spain was *Sepharadh,* hence Jews from Spain are known as *Sephardim.*

as widespread in the peninsula as it was elsewhere in Europe. A civilization constantly on the move, expanding, fighting, accumulating through victory in battle, retrenching, consolidating, was not likely to settle back and accept the rigid class divisions of the feudal order.

In Spain the towns themselves, especially those which were established and given their special privileges in the new territories acquired from the Moors, were a potent force in the national life. Fernando de los Ríos points out that 12,525 towns, *villas*, and hamlets of medieval times enjoyed the benefit of the multiple form of public ownership then existing. This was a sort of cooperative or community ownership of the means of production and distribution, elements of which still survive in several of the communities of northern Spain today. The inhabitants of these towns enjoyed a measure of personal liberty greater than the people of any other country in Europe with the exception of England.

It requires little imagination to visualize what went on when a new town was to be populated by the conqueror, either a town just taken or one founded from scratch. As soon as the battle was over the colonization began. The town immediately became a beehive of activity. Every necessity and security had to be improvised without delay. Walls had to be raised or repaired and made stronger, houses must be built, temples constructed, wells dug, fields plowed and planted, livestock procured and pastured. After the initial flurry of building, came the more deliberate epoch of beautification. Houses were made more comfortable, churches more lovely. New inhabitants must be attracted, the town should be properly supplied and forcefully defended.

When a newly conquered town was occupied it was divided into quarters or districts, each given over to certain crafts whose workers were incorporated into guilds, regulated by officers of their own choosing and laws of their own making. From the tenth to the fourteenth centuries manual labor was still regarded as an honorable profession, and a few outstanding workers were elevated to knighthood. Later, the Castilian came to look on using his hands in work as losing caste. Work with the hands was done only by Moors or Jews.

In the new towns everything had to be done without repose under the constant threat of attack. Many decades would pass, perhaps more than a century, before the new townsmen could feel that the battle lines had definitely moved south, and they might at last go about the business of daily life. But even then there was no permanent security. The conflict continued, and if their town did not need defenders their country did, for the Moors must be conquered. Hence, the townsmen felt mainly and thought mainly of the necessities of soldiers. Many of them took from the enemy enough wealth to purchase a horse and arms, thus becoming mounted soldiers (*caballeros*), and so attaining a higher status. Most of these became *caballeros villanos* ("petty village noblemen") without great lands or power. Their wealth and power resided in their own strong arms. Participation in the various forms of community ownership and control in the new economy gave them a feeling of solidarity.

One of the ways in which this collective ownership expressed itself was in the *ejido*, a medieval institution which later was carried to the New World, and is very much alive in Mexico today. The word *ejido* may be translated "village commons"; the term is derived from the Latin *exitus*, meaning "on the way out," because these community lands were generally located on the outskirts of the villages. In Spain the *ejido* included only a part of the public lands, specifically a small, well-defined area used as the village pound, the public threshing and winnowing floor known as the *era*, and the community rubbish heap and slaughter pen. In addition to the publicly owned and operated *ejidos*, the Spanish villages also owned in common certain woodlands, streams and lakes, certain pasture lands and fields. The townsmen were artisans, farmers, craftsmen, merchants. In the early days the nobleman was definitely *persona non grata* in the free villages of Castile.

On the other hand, the nobles themselves and the religious orders, such as the Templars, owned great territories in their own right, and on these lands the condition of the peasants was often very miserable. This was the seignorial regime (not feudalism) in which the landowner *ruled* his lands and the inhabitants on them. There was *no* reciprocal agreement. It was in these areas that the division of Spanish society into two great classes—landlords and day-laborers— first became a reality. There was constant friction between the citizens of the free towns and the nobility. The free villages found a natural ally in the crown, which also felt the constant pinch of the more powerful nobles. In order to strengthen their position the Spanish nobility, in the thirteenth century, initiated the tradition of the *mayorazgo*, or entailed estate, which later, with certain modifications, was taken over by the other European countries. The *mayor-*

azgo meant simply that the oldest son should inherit his father's estate *in toto*. It was not to be divided among all of the children. This paternalistic nepotism favoring a single child had the effect of intensifying the already onerous *latifundia* or huge-estate system of the country.

There was great internal strife and even anarchy in Castile during portions of the fourteenth and fifteenth centuries, and the towns were forced to find some way to protect themselves, for individually they stood little chance against the more powerful nobility. They banded together and organized *Hermandades,* or Brotherhoods of towns, in order to secure the public peace. The name should be familiar to the readers of Lesage, who used it frequently in his accounts of the exploits of Gil Blas. The *Hermandad* was a confederation of towns bound together by a solemn league and covenant in order to defend themselves in periods of civil anarchy. The *Hermandad* of 1295 was composed of the representatives of thirty-four towns; that of 1315 included one hundred villages and cities. The *Hermandad* had its own police force, which enjoyed the right to chase down lawbreakers regardless of where they sought refuge, and to give the criminal a summary trial and sentence. With the *Hermandad* police as their main corps the townsmen were also able at times to wage a real war on the nobles. In this manner were the inhabitants of the Castilian villages able to thrive during the Middle Ages.

Thus while the inhabitants of the great towns in other parts of Europe were languishing in feudal servitude, the members of the Castilian corporations, living under the protection of their own laws and magistrates in time of peace, and commanded by their own officers in time of war, were in full enjoyment of all the essential rights and privileges of freemen.[24]

The king countenanced these *Hermandades,* despite their wild kind of justice which would appear to subtract somewhat from his own authority, for two reasons: first, because the force of the brotherhoods was directed mainly against the nobles, the king's worst enemies, and secondly, because the towns themselves were such a formidable force that to deny them would have meant the alienation of a powerful segment of his population.

With these immunities, the cities of Castile attained a degree of opulence and splendor unrivalled, unless in Italy, during the Middle Ages. At a very early period, indeed, their contact with the Arabs had familiarized them with a better system of agriculture. and a dexterity in the mechanic arts unknown in other parts of Christendom.²⁴

The Castilian villagers, in the first generations, were primarily warriors and shepherds; warriors because of necessity and shepherds because there were not enough hands to cultivate the soil on any extensive scale. All of them were adventurers, else they would not have abandoned their more tranquil homes in Galicia, Asturias, the Cantabrian and Basque provinces. Spain had always had the psychology of a nation of shepherds, and so fundamental was this aspect of the national economy that in ancient Asturias and nearby areas sheep were frequently used in place of money. When the inhabitants of these regions moved south they still wanted to be shepherds. The Reconquest had made available great stretches of open land, particularly after the capture of Córdoba (1236) and Seville (1248). This had encouraged a pastoral society, without great interest in the slow processes of industrial development. An excellent breed of sheep, the *merino*, gave them an important staple, which, with the produce of a well-cultivated soil and the development of the simpler manufacturers, formed the basis of a profitable commerce. The *merino* was introduced into Spain by the Moors, perhaps as early as the eleventh century. However, the great improvement of the breed dates from 1394, when Catherine of Lancaster* brought to Spain as part of her dowry to the heir to the throne, a flock of English *merinos*, reputed at that time to be superior to the sheep of any other country for the beauty and delicacy of their fleece. The word *merino*, incidentally, is derived from *benemerinos*, meaning "wandering"; it was the name of a tribe of Arabs who shifted their residence with the seasons. Sheep raising was given an additional boost by the terrible bubonic plague which hit Spain in the middle of the fourteenth century. The people died like flies, leaving great unpopulated tracts of land open to pasturage.

The Reconquest was not only a conflict between two faiths but was also in part a struggle for supremacy "between the Christian sheep and the Arabian horse." When Fernando the Saint took Córdoba and Seville, and occupied the vast lands of La Mancha, Extremadura, and Andalusia, the sheep triumphed over the horse. Alfonso the Learned recognized the importance of this victory in his *mesta* organization, which brought the support of the crown solidly behind

* Catherine was the wife of Henry III of Castile, the mother of John II, and the grandmother of Isabella the Catholic.

the development of the sheep industry. The horse came back into prominence with the conquest of the New World. The *mesta* was a cooperative organization of sheep and cattle owners which directed the breeding, pasturing, and selling of the flocks and their products for the common benefit. It was the shepherds' answer to the guilds and cooperative brotherhoods of the towns.

The capture of the southern territories not only gave the Christians great new areas for pasturage, but it also made possible the wide-scale migration of the flocks southward in winter and northward in summer. Thus the occupation of southern Spain was an immediate stimulant for the sheep and wool industry of the entire country. This migration of the flocks, which is specifically mentioned in the laws of the Visigoths, was interrupted by the Moorish invasion, and was not restored until the thirteenth century. It still takes place, on a reduced scale, and has given rise to one of the most beautiful of all Spanish folk songs, *Ya se van los pastores* ("The Shepherds Are Now Going Away"). The song is from the mountains of Castile.

> *Ya se van los pastores*
> *a la Extremadura;*
> *ya se queda la sierra*
> *triste y oscura.*

> The shepherds are going away
> to Extremadura;
> the Sierra is now left
> sad and deserted.

The history of the sheep and wool industry is, in a way, the capsule history of the Spanish economy. Britain and Spain both started out in the Middle Ages as agricultural and sheep-raising countries, but while Britain moved steadily from a pastoral to a textile and hence industrial economy, Spain remained essentially a nation of shepherds. This is not to say that there was never any Spanish textile industry. In the Moslem dominions weaving was one of the most developed aspects of the economy. And in the twelfth century, even in Christian Spain, there was cloth manufacturing in numerous cities: Palencia, Zamora, Avila, Segovia, Soria, Alcala, Madrid, Toledo, Cuenca, Córdoba, and Seville. However by the year 1438 this budding textile industry was all but dead.

Several things had happened to make this so. First of all Flanders, and then Britain, had developed their own textile industries, the latter by prohibiting the export of wool or the entry of cloths into its territories. When Flanders found its looms without a supply of British wool their buyers turned to Spain and began to purchase Spanish wool on a wide scale. The kings of Castile, who were always in desperate need of funds because of the Moorish wars, slapped taxes on the exportation of wool and thus kept themselves provided with funds. In fact, as long as their wars were actually going on, and new lands and wealth were being added to their dominions, the kings were not in as poor shape as they were when there was an extended period of truce, and their accumulated debts fell due. The economy of Castile, therefore, became the victim of the textile industries of Flanders and Britain. What in the beginning had appeared to be reaping the harvest in the long pull turned out to be reaping the whirlwind. Everyone seized the opportunity and began to sell wool. Nobles, monasteries, grandees, and even the inhabitants of the towns could sell their wools to the mills of Flanders at a great profit, and the royal treasury benefited mightily from the various taxes collected on the export of this commodity. One well-known historian writes: "Without wool the architectual treasures of many Castilian towns would be inexplicable." Wool profits paid for many of the impressive buildings which were being constructed throughout the land. Unfortunately, this made impossible the early industrialization of Castile, and accentuated the temperamental heritage of the Spanish people, who had always had the psychology of wanderers and of shepherds.

A few town councils were aware of what was taking place, and some of them called it to the attention of the king, begging protection of the Spanish textile industry, but without avail. Too many people were making money on raw wool, and the kings desperately needed funds in order to hold their own against the recalcitrant nobles and to make progress against the Moors. The cost of living went up, attempts were made at price fixing, wages too were fixed, and the export of foodstuffs and many other articles was prohibited, but in spite of all these things the inflation continued, and the economy of Castile found itself being enclosed within a vicious circle.

Among the merchants and traders of Spain who made great profits out of the export of wool were numerous foreigners. The masses of ignorant Spaniards, seeing the cost of living go up and up, while some elements of the population continued to prosper without hard labor, turned their suspicion and their venom on these elements, wrongly, of course, regarding as "foreign interests" what was in reality Castilian mercantilism encouraged by the crown. Thus in 1306 there occurred in Seville one of the first popular uprisings against the Genoese population of that city. It was the first flare of a conflagration which was later to focus itself on the Jews and break out all over the peninsula on such a vast and determined scale that even the king and queen felt that they could no longer control it.

The cities and towns of Spain during medieval days were hardly hygienic show places, nor indeed were those of any other country. Down the center of the street often ran a kind of gutter or ditch into which the refuse could be placed if it was something the pigs could eat. Liquid refuse was thrown out of the windows often catching passersby on the head until it became the law to shout *Agua va!* ("Here it comes!") before making the throw. With this warning the pedestrian was obliged to look out for himself. Little wonder that some of the early medieval paintings show even the saints walking down the streets with high boots on; it was the easiest way to keep from being covered with slop. Toilet facilities were of the most primitive kind, and the streets were invariably dotted with defecation and urine. The Spaniards who came to the New World were amazed by the cleanliness of the Indian towns as compared with their own.

When the Black Death hit Spain in 1348 the people were easy prey for an epidemic. This disease was probably brought from the East, and was essentially the same as the bubonic plague. It was called the "Black Death" because of the large, black blotches that appeared on the body. There were also swellings of the glands in the armpits, the groin, and neck, where huge painful lumps as large as eggs often appeared. The body was covered with smaller boils and carbuncles, and the sick person often vomited blood. The vast majority died within two or three days. Although statistics of those days are not very accurate, it has been estimated by many authorities that up to one-third of the population of Europe died as a result of the plague, possibly a total of twenty-five million people. Families were destroyed, trades were left without workers, fields without farmers, cities without inhabitants. Add to the Black Death the fateful rule of Peter the Cruel, king of Spain at this time, and the fratricidal struggle he and his brother Henry carried on for the Spanish throne, and it is easy to understand why it took two hundred years from the promising reign of Alfonso the Learned to the fulfillment of that potential.

Life in the medieval towns was in the main austere and without many creature comforts. The principal expression of wealth was in architecture, the great art of the Middle Ages. The early, heavy Romanesque style, with its thick walls and few rounded windows, was made for this land of burning sunlight and constant danger. As the centuries passed this crude, massive, and powerful architecture, almost fortress-like in character, became in the Gothic, lofty, light, refined, with delicate ribbed vaults, pointed ogival arches, and beautiful stained-glass windows.

The church invariably dominated the town. It was the symbol of the mass faith and its search for security, beauty, and God. In these great churches everyone was equal, and to their building was consecrated a part of nearly every man's life. French and German architects were often imported to construct the great Gothic cathedrals of Spain, but the Spanish instinct for rambling and fusing made a pure Gothic style almost impossible. The church of Spain was definitely a Church Militant. Even the priests often took part in the wars against the Moslems *a Dios rogando y con la maza dando* ("praying for God's grace, and thumping with a mace.")

The principal entertainments in the medieval towns were the religious fiestas, pilgrimages, community songs and dances, and, of course, the perennial weekly market or feria which was as much a social as an economic institution, for here all came to chat and exchange news as well as to barter, to buy and sell. These *ferias* are still an integral part of Spanish country life, and a visit to the weekly mart held outside the impressive twelfth century walls of Avila, can help one recapture much of the ancient flavor of the medieval fair. (Incidentally, our expression "a fair price" comes from the prices fixed at these medieval fairs.) Avila's weekly fair which takes place on the boulder-strewn, barren ground outside the town's huge walls, with its small groups of farmers and shepherds with their livestock, chatting and haggling over prices, has changed little with the passing centuries.

The medieval Spanish town was above everything else a work of unity, a work of art. The town was constructed of a piece, with harmony, with beauty, and with devotion. Everyone lent a hand for the labor. There was pride in the workmanship, pride in the crafts. Every man did his best, for by his works he would be remembered. In the churches even the places that did not show were finished with loving care, for God might see, if man did not. In the medieval town everyone *belonged*; there were no drones, no arm that was not needed, no hand that was not used, no soul that went untended. Taking a part in the community labor, participating also in the songs and dances and celebrations of all kinds, was a wonderful catharsis. The individual lost himself in the community. Tensions wore off, loneliness fled away. There was security even in the midst of war or threat of war.

To think of the medieval towns as dark and dingy places filled with foul odors, ugliness, and disease is less than half a truth. The odors they had were natural smells: of animals, of people, of food that had not been consumed, of construction. They did not know *our* odors of sulphuric acid, of chlorinated drinking water, of automobile exhausts, of gasoline, or gas, of great fumes of smoke in the air, of soot galore, of stifling smog. We have become so accustomed to these and many other odors that we seldom notice them. The medieval townsmen had even fewer smells to which they became accustomed. Nor were their cities dark and ugly. The walls were whitewashed frequently, and breathed out the sunlight and the air. Even the fortifications were works of art. Everywhere one turned there was some beauty to behold. Use was seldom conceived as separate from beauty. Are not the medieval towns that have survived the centuries visited today because of loveliness? The interiors of the houses, it is true, were not exactly places of freshness and of charm, but the streets and the plazas, the markets and the churches of the medieval towns shone with color, with people, and with light.

The cry of the hawker was in the streets. The ringing of the bells filled the air at all hours of the day and night. Song rose to the lips on every hand. The numbers of songs that have survived show that everyone sang, no matter what his station. There was music for everyone, and for all occasions. And at dawn, when it was time to rise, the cocks would crow by the hundreds, as they often do in the *Poem of the Cid*, and the birds would begin to sing in the trees or under the eaves. Then to work, to the market, to commingle, to talk, to unburden, to feel the spark of contact, the spark of oneness.

The buildings, so far from being quaint and musty, were as bright and clean as a medieval illumination, if only because they were usually whitewashed with lime, so that all the colors of the image makers, in glass or polychromed wood, would dance in reflection on the walls. Life flourished in a dilation of the senses. . . . Though diet was often meager in the Middle Ages, the most ascetic could not wholly close his eyes to beauty. The town itself was an ever-present work of art, and the very clothes of its citizens on festival days were like a flower garden in bloom.[25]

The arrival of a wandering minstrel in one of the medieval towns or at a castle was the signal for much merriment, for he would sing the deeds of the great Spanish heroes or play the softer, more lyric melodies of courtship and of love. Both peasants and nobles found enjoyment in hearing and singing the old ballads or *romances*. Knight errantry was widespread in medieval Spain, and jousts and tourneys were always great attractions. The later novels of chivalry (*libros de caballerías*), of which the peninsula had more than its share, give an exaggerated and idealized account of this aspect of Spanish life, and the *Quixote* itself starts off as a parody of them until Cervantes gets under full steam and identifies his knight as a symbol of the whole heroic fabric of Spanish life. Hunting too was a favorite sport of the nobility; indeed it was more than a sport, for the practice in horsemanship and in the use of weapons over a rugged terrain was rigorous training for war. Falconry was often a part of the hunt, and in Spain reached a high development. The first edition of the *Quixote*, 1605, carries on its frontispiece the engraving of a man's arm on which rests a hooded falcon. And the story of the fine moulting falcon and thoroughbred horse of Count Fernán González, which led to the independence of Castile when the king was unable to pay for them, shows how far back this ancient sport reaches in Spanish history.

All of the religious celebrations of medieval days had strong social overtones. More courtship was carried on at these affairs than anywhere else. Many a gallant awaited his lady love outside the church just in order to be able to follow her with his eyes. This was often enough to strike up a great fire in two impassioned hearts. The old ballads frequently mention such courtships, but one of them, called the *La misa de amor* ("The Mass of Love"), is particularly striking, for in it the choristers who are singing suddenly notice a beautiful lady enter the church, "and instead of saying amen, amen, they said amor, amor!"

The castles of Castile and León, of which there were many, were gray and rocky masses that seemed to lift themselves from the gray and rocky ground, above which they stood, sentinel-like, in a harsh and barren splendor. There are still many of these castles within a day's drive of Madrid: Oropesa, Segovia, Real de Manzanares, Peñafiel, Tordesillas, La Mota, Alba de Tormes, and many, many others. Segovia, with its white walls and piercing, ship-like prow, is an exception among this array of gray mammoths of the Middle Ages. Inside the castle walls there were sometimes real evidences of luxury: thick Moorish rugs, tapestries and draperies imported or native-made, enormous carved wooden furniture, beautifully wrought pieces of silver, occasional collections of lovely illuminated manuscripts.

There was a remarkable amount of democracy within the Castilian towns, which were separated from each other by vast tracts of unpopulated land, just as they are today. There were always many people pressed into a small space. Their municipal institutions gave them a sense of dignity and equality which does not exist in Spain today. In the old ballads and in the *fueros* ("municipal laws and privileges") we can see the townspeople hawking their wares in the narrow streets, haggling over prices at the fairs,

quarrelling over weights and measures, protesting if an importunate friar tried to be served first; it should be the same for all, they declare, friar or layman, or the turbaned stranger *not of our custom*, who had just come in from one of the outlying villages. They pushed and sweated, pointed and shouted; and along with their municipal institutions they developed their language and their literature. What does that early literature give us? A set of scenes, clear and unforgettable as the panels of a primitive painting. In the din and clatter of a crowded market-place a minstrel plucks a stringed instrument and bawls an endless story of the Cid, the seven princes of Lara, or Doña Urraca, the Magpie Lady of Zamora.[21]

The thin tone of the instrument the musician is playing defines its age and lack of a more resonant sound box; perhaps it is the ancient *vihuela*, or the lute, brought into Spain by the Arabs, or the Moorish guitar, or the in-curved Roman guitar, or perhaps there is only a drum or tambourine. In any case the music is thin and repetitious, a circular replica of the circular and delimited life of the medieval centuries. "A mysterious cleric, who says that he is a minstrel of the lord, tells rhymed stories of local saints and mundane miracles, adding that he thinks them well worth a glass of good wine." The gallants of the town watch the women go by with hungry and eager eyes, occasionally bursting into a spontaneous line of song to praise their charms. Old crones dressed in the omnipresent black scour the streets with their searching eyes, their withered figures clinging to a life that is already beyond all hope.

Perhaps too at a corner of the town plaza there is a drum beating up recruits for a new campaign. In no part of Europe was it as easy to move up in class as in medieval Spain. The poor hidalgo of Galicia or Asturias became a big landholder in Castile. The poor hidalgo of Castile was a big landholder in La Mancha, Extremadura, or Andalusia. The frontier spirit constantly lured men toward the south. For centuries they dreamed of lands and riches won at the point of a spear. For centuries that dream was true.

In spite of the economic ups and downs of the Middle Ages, in spite of the Black Death, and in spite of a series of profligate kings, there was relative wealth in Spain and the towns continued to grow. By the fifteenth century many towns had become cities, and the wealth of them all far exceeded that of the early days of the Reconquest when their necessities were not more than those of soldiers. A considerable part of this wealth was expended on public works. Cities, from which the nobles had formerly been so zealously excluded, now became their places of residence. Mansions began to be constructed for these well-to-do families, and a new surge in building commenced. In Andalusia, among the conquered Moors, there were thriving industries.

The historian of Seville describes that city, about the middle of the fifteenth century, as possessing a flourishing commerce, and a degree of opulence unexampled since the conquest. It was filled with an active population employed in the various mechanic arts. Its domestic fabrics, as well as natural products, of olive oil, wine, wool, etc., supplied a trade with France, Flanders, Italy, and England. The ports of Biscay, which belonged to the Castilian crown, were the marts of an extensive trade with the north, during the thirteenth and fourteenth centuries.[24]

The ruler of Spain during the first half of the fifteenth century was King John II (1406–1454), father of Isabella the Catholic. John inherited the throne when he was a baby; he took over the reins of government when he was fourteen. He was a weak and cowardly man in his political life, swayed first by one faction among his nobles, then by another. One notable favorite, Don Alvaro de Luna, played the strong man for a great part of King John's reign, but in the end he was beheaded at the instance of enemies in court.

King John, however, despite his lack of aggressiveness, or perhaps because of it, had a profound interest in literature, and surrounded himself with the best writers of his age. "The literary court of John II" has become a set phrase in the history of Spanish culture. Many of these writers were Jewish or Jewish converts, including the king's secretary, Alfonso de Baena, and the best writer of them all, Juan de Mena. Occasional verse flourished; praiseful odes to the king, to nobles, and to cities were frequent; Seville granted a hundred *doblas* of gold to the best poem celebrating that city.

The age of iron had passed, the age of gold had not yet arrived, and John II was attempting to transform the iron into gold, that is, turn the Middle Ages into the Renaissance via the process of refined letters. The wars against the Moors had ceased, the epic tensions of another day had temporarily disappeared. Hence was born the cavalier-poet, the writer who could dedicate his pen and life to courtly things and to love. This entourage of poets around John II was doing much the same thing that the minstrels of Provence had done many years before; in a way, they also parallel the more intellectually inclined scholar-writers of the court of Alfonso X, two centuries earlier. But now that Gallego-Portuguese school of lyric poetry was dead, Castilian had become the language of literature, and the Castilian lyric must have its day in court. Such was the reign of John II, which marked the transition between Spain's epic medieval past and her coming Renaissance.

Here is the way one of the ancient chroniclers of the period describes it:

The hardest and most courageous knights, those who found the greatest pleasure in jousts and combats, write, when they take up the pen, like young swains in love, without letting the slightest allusion to arms or matters of war infiltrate into their verses. . . . In vain does one seek in these poems for some reflection of the actual life of the times; and, if there were not other reliable testimonies, we might believe that those confused and turbulent days were the realization of a happy and beloved Arcadia.

The separation between literature and life was never greater. An idealized world was beginning to emerge, but it was a false world of perfect gallants and beautiful ladies elevated almost to the point of goddesses. Even the country girls, the *serranas*, who were so uncouth and so ugly in *The Book of Good Love*, now turn into lovely maidens. The very place names of their home towns become an integral part of this poetry. There is an attempt to specify and thus make real an Arcadia of the mind in the court of John II. But while the courtiers write poems and play music the people of Spain continue their hard lives, now without impetus, without glory, without heroic tension. However, they remember these things in their ballads, and are able to relive them in song and story, while the throne becomes more and more separated from the national life.

The literary apotheosis of chivalry among the courtly poets had its tragic counterpart in several bloody encounters between knights who deliberately used sharp, rather than blunted weapons, and went into jousts without shields. On one occasion at Orbigo, not far from Santiago de Compostela, a Castilian knight, who went by the name of Sueño de Quenones, and nine companions, defended a passage of arms against all comers in the presence of John II and his court. The object of the challenge was

to release the knight from the obligation, imposed on him by his mistress, of publicly wearing an iron collar round his neck every Thursday. The jousts continued for thirty days, and the doughty champions fought without shield or target, with weapons bearing points of Milan steel. Six hundred and twenty-seven encounters took place, and one hundred and sixty-six lances were broken, when the emprise was declared to be fairly achieved.

An eyewitness describes the whole affair, and one may fancy himself reading about the adventures of Sir Launcelot or the great Spanish Amadís. Needless to say, there were many deaths before the jousts were over. It was in such extravagant behavior and in sublimated courtly lyrics that the knights of Spain now sought their outlet. Despite the odious political and social debasement of John II's reign, it may be inscribed, says one writer, "with the golden pen of history." The rugged Castilians were now, like the French under Francis I, reaching toward refinement and elegance in their culture.

John II himself was said to be a fair poet and a good musician. The first collection of courtly lyrics, called *Cancioneros*, was dedicated to him and came out in 1445.* Many others followed. The popular ballads began to appear in book form a few years later. Not until the two currents met and mingled would the literature of Spain enter

---

* The compiler was Alfonso de Baena, a converted Jew. In the prologue Baena wrote that he had compiled it "for the disport and divertisement of his highness the King." Fifty poets were represented.

the mainstream of her Golden Age. The king, writes one of the old chroniclers, despite his notably weak character, had a fine appearance.

He was tall of body, long-limbed, extremely slender; his demeanor was pleasant, and he was very blond. He spoke rapidly, but in a quiet and moderate manner. He was much pleased to listen to intelligent and cultured men; he could speak and understand Latin well; he enjoyed literature and history, and liked to listen to poetry, which he was able to criticize with acumen; he understood the arts and was a good musician. But in spite of these graces he was very defective in the true virtues which are so essential to kings. Thus, in spite of all his graces, this timid and spineless king never spent a single hour in trying really to understand or exert himself in the proper governing of his realm. Although Castile was seething with rebellion and conspiracies, he paid them no mind at all, and gave himself over to more pleasant things, leaving the reins of power entirely in the hands of his Condestable.[26]

This condestable or constable of Castile and grand master of the Knights of Santiago, was Don Alvaro de Luna, who did everything possible to put the nobles in their place, and to elevate the crown to a position of undisputed headship. In fact, if we choose to believe the *Chronicle of Don Alvaro de Luna*, drawn up by an admirer after his death, the constable of Castile was close to being the perfect courtier and the perfect knight.

King John's weakness prevented the fruition of his plans, and Alvaro de Luna, accused by envious courtiers and by John's second wife (Isabella's mother), was condemned to death for "treachery." The constable of Castile did not deign to answer his accusers; on the scaffold he said calmly: "No manner of death brings shame, if it is supported with courage." He placed his head on the block and the executioner, in the savage manner of the day, plunged a knife into his throat and then deliberately cut off his head. In executing Don Alvaro de Luna the king, "it can be said with truth, was also killing himself, for he lived only one year and fifty days after his death, all of them days of suffering and remorse, and on many occasions he was seen to weep mightily for the death of his loyal Maestre." The king, on his own deathbed lamented to his faithful attendant Cibdarel that he wished "he had been born the son of a mechanic, instead of King of Castile."

Alvaro de Luna was, in many ways, symbolic of the great warrior leaders of Spain's heroic past. He was brave, intelligent, handsome in appearance, loyal to his sovereign, devoted to his country. By having him beheaded King John was attempting clumsily and pusillanimously to erase the evidence of his own weakness, and at the same time he threw away an excellent chance to assert the supremacy of the crown over an obstinate and greedy nobility. With John II Spain entered the portico of the Renaissance wearing false colors that would not have become the days of its grandeur.

The greatest Spanish poet of the fifteenth century lived and wrote after the death of King John II. This was Jorge Manrique (1440–1479), whose *Coplas on the Death of his Father* are one of the most impressive elegies in any language. Jorge Manrique wrote a great many things, but most of them were quite mediocre. It was only in this single poem that he caught, condensed, purified, and expressed an individual tragedy, turning it into the realm of the universal. Perhaps his very mediocrity as a poet in his other verses enabled him this once to be the perfect catalyst or alloy of his epoch. He followed the profession of arms, and died on the field of battle, at the age of thirty-nine, fighting for Queen Isabella of Castile. "Mariana, in his *History of Spain*, makes honorable mention of him, as being present at the siege of Uclés; and speaks of him as a 'youth of inestimable qualities, who in this war gave brilliant proofs of his valor.' "

The poet's father, whose death inspired the poem, was a well-known Spanish nobleman, Count of Paredes and master of the Order of Santiago. He was a brave warrior, a distinguished courtier, and a good poet in his own right. Jorge Manrique in his *Coplas* mourned the passing of his father (which took place in 1476) "as with a funeral hymn." Henry Wadsworth Longfellow, who was a professor of Romance languages at Harvard University as well as a poet, translated the *Coplas* into English. These brief lines conclude his introduction to the translation: "The poem is a model of its kind. Its conception is solemn and beautiful; and, in accordance with it, the style moves on—calm, dignified, and majestic."

There is little that is unique about the poem. Its value lies in its superior statement of a universal truth. The central idea has been expressed in many epochs and in many languages: Villon with his famous "where are the snows of yesteryear?", Thomas Gray with his "The boast of heraldry, the pomp of power, and all that beauty, all that wealth e'er gave . . .", and Omar Khayyám in Fitzgerald's "Yet Ah, that spring should vanish with the rose,"—all these and many more have stated the fleeting quality of life, the vanity of human

desires, the stark democracy of death. Jorge Manrique's statement is
a very Spanish one; it is sententious, stoic, Christian, solemn, serene.
It is fitting that Spain's Middle Ages should have found an epitaph
so noble. Here are a few verses in Longfellow's translation:

> Swiftly our pleasures glide away,
> Our hearts recall the distant day
> With many sighs;
> The moments that are speeding fast
> We heed not, but the past,—the past
> More highly prize.
>
> Our lives are rivers, gliding free
> To that unfathomed, boundless sea,
> The silent grave!
> Thither all earthly pomp and boast
> Roll, to be swallowed up and lost
> In one dark wave.
>
> The noble blood of Gothic name,
> Heroes emblazoned high to fame,
> In long array;
> How, in the onward course of time,
> The landmarks of that race sublime
> Were swept away!
>
> Who is the champion? who the strong?
> Pontiff and priest, and sceptered throng?
> On these shall fall
> As heavily the hand of Death,
> As when it stays the shepherd's breath
> Beside his stall.
>
> Where is the King, Don Juan? Where
> Each royal prince and noble heir
> Of Aragon?
> Where are the courtly gallantries?
> The deeds of love and high emprise,
> In battle done?
>
> Where are the high-born dames, and where
> Their gay attire, and jewelled hair,
> And odors sweet?
> Where are the gentle knights, that came

To kneel, and breathe love's ardent flame,
Low at their feet?

The noble steeds, and harness bright,
And gallant lord, and stalwart knight,
In rich array,
Where shall we seek them now? Alas!
Like the bright dewdrops on the grass,
They passed away.

O World! so few the years we live,
Would that the life which thou dost give
Were life indeed!
Alas! thy sorrows fall so fast,
Our happiest hour is when at last
The soul is freed.

The English verses, in spite of their accuracy and rhythm, fail to catch the sententious simplicity of the original. Jorge Manrique is a real Castilian who shuns embellishment like the plague. His poem is proof that Castilian lyric poetry has now matured, and is ready to flower in the great garden of Spain's Golden Age. Medieval life is coming to a close, but its heroes, the men of action, are remembered in these stirring *coplas* of Manrique and will be reborn again with renewed dynamism in the Spanish Renaissance.

6

THE SPANISH RENAISSANCE

In the nests of yesteryear there are no birds today.
Cervantes in *Don Quixote*

John II was succeeded by his son Henry IV, a personable prince who was warmly received as king. Henry immediately announced a campaign against the Moors, a move always certain to gain popular favor, but once in the field his constant retreats, avoidance of battle, tramping over planted fields, pillaging orchards, and living off the countryside made the populace complain loudly and lustily that the king seemed more at war with his own people than with the Moslems. This odious and pusillanimous behavior cost Henry many friends; the profligacy and tyranny of his court soon lost him the backing of many others and also turned powerful churchmen against him. The king's youthful debaucheries had already impaired his sexual vigor, and he was widely known as Henry the Impotent. His first queen, Blanche, was sent back to her family in Navarre after several years of marriage, "because of the impotence of both parties." His second wife, a Portuguese princess, gave birth to a daughter who was generally believed to be the illegitimate offspring of an affair between the queen and a handsome courtier, Beltrán de la Cueva, the duke of Albuquerque. This girl, named Juana, was called by the Castilians *la Beltraneja*, a term of opprobrium meaning "Beltrán's bastard girl."

Henry proclaimed the child heir to the throne, but a sizable faction of nobles and churchmen became incensed and demanded that the king's younger brother, Alfonso, be publicly acknowledged as his successor. Henry at first agreed, but backed down on his promise. The rebellious Castilians gathered on the rocky fields outside the medieval walls of Avila, and there deposed the king in effigy. A high platform was raised above the stony ground, and on this was seated the image of Henry, clad in sable robes, a sword at its side, a scepter in its hand, a crown upon its head. The multitude listened as a manifesto of complaints against the king was read. After this, the archbishop of Toledo ascended the platform and tore the crown from the head of the figure; other nobles plucked away the sword and scepter, and the image was then rolled in the dust. The eleven-year-old Alfonso was lifted on a shield and carried to the scaffold where he took his seat on the throne. The grandees all filed by, kissing the young boy's hand, and trumpets blew proclaiming the new sovereign. Alfonso lived barely three years after this ceremony, and the country was so sharply divided in its loyalties that neither he nor his brother Henry was really king during that interim. But when Alfonso died, Henry the Impotent resumed his kingship.

The rebellious Castilians next demanded that Henry's sister Isabella be proclaimed queen, but this young lady wisely refused the honor, stating that as long as her brother lived no one else had any claim to the throne. The rebels were taken aback by this magnanimous action, and were forced to negotiate the best agreement they could get out of the king. Henry was in such a weak position now that he gladly agreed to recognize Isabella as his rightful heir. The great majority of both factions were vastly pleased by this, for Isabella's conduct at court had always been exemplary, and her personality and beauty were admired by all.

This was the same Isabella the Catholic who later was to marry Ferdinand of Aragon. She was a princess with a very fair complexion, her hair was a bright auburn, and her green-blue eyes sparkled with sensibility. Her face was pleasing and rounded like that of a simple girl of some small Castilian town. She was very religious, and her morals and manners were both above reproach. Henry had several times attempted to marry her off to one of her various royal suitors in order to improve his own position, but Isabella had invariably turned a deaf ear to these proposals. The king of Portugal, encouraged by Henry, had persisted in his suit, but he fared no better than the others. Isabella had already fixed her attention on her kinsman, Ferdinand, prince of Aragon, who was distinguished for his comeliness and for his intelligence. Also, he was heir to the second largest kingdom in Christian Spain, and by marrying him Isabella would raise her country to a first-rate position in Europe.

Envoys were sent and the young prince determined to travel immediately to the Castilian court, but as there was so much opposition to this marriage it was decided that he should go incognito, accompanied by half a dozen attendants only. Ferdinand was disguised as a servant, so that no one would recognize him, and at each stop he waited on the other members of the party. In this manner he reached Valladolid and spoke personally with Isabella; the attraction between the two was immediate and mutual. The marriage documents were drawn up very carefully so that Isabella would clearly remain supreme within Castile. Ferdinand offered no strong objections, and the agreement was sealed. In 1469 the marriage itself took place. The royal motto of the young couple, *Tanto monta*, expresses succinctly the gist of their agreement; it is the shortened form of *Tanto monta, monta tanto, Isabel como Fernando* ("Isabella is the equal of Ferdinand"). The way things actually worked out in their joint rule was that Ferdinand became director of the foreign policy of the two kingdoms, while Isabella limited herself mainly to the internal affairs of Castile. Since she died (1504) several years before Ferdinand (1516), he actually became the prime molder of a unified Spain. Only after Isabella's death was the small kingdom of Navarre added to the nation, thus making this unity complete.

There were many obstacles before unification was accomplished. First, Isabella's own struggle to maintain her position in Castile. In 1474, when her brother Henry IV died, Isabella was proclaimed queen. She mounted a white horse and, accompanied by a brilliant retinue, proceeded to the plaza at Segovia, where the ceremony took place. Ferdinand was in Aragon at the time. The herald cried out in a loud voice: "Castile, Castile, for the king, Don Ferdinand, and his consort, Isabella, queen proprietress of these kingdoms!" A great shout arose from the assembled multitude, banners waved, all the city's bells began to peal, cannons fired a salute, and the queen then took the oath of office and retired to the cathedral. After a solemn chanting of the *Te Deum*, she knelt at the altar and implored the aid of God.

She was in dire need of all the aid she could get, divine and human, for almost immediately the king of Portugal, whose hand she had rejected for Ferdinand's, announced that he would marry and back the claim of the half-Portuguese princess, Juana (*la Beltraneja*), to the Castilian throne. Thus began a new war for the Spanish succession which raged for five years. Ferdinand and Isabella finally won that war in 1479, the same year that Ferdinand's eighty-three-year-old father died, leaving him the crown of Aragon. Hence, the real unity of Castile and Aragon dates from this year, which marks the birth of modern Spain, and puts an end to the checkered politics and petty kingdoms of the Middle Ages.

Manifold choices lay before the joint sovereigns of the new state, but unfortunately for Spain, in that historic moment all of them appeared to be religious. Religious unity was a medieval reality in the other Europeans states. Furthermore, during the eight centuries of the Reconquest, it had been the only unity that the Christian kingdoms of Spain had known. Now, in 1479, Ferdinand and Isabella decided it was high time to complete the religious unity of the peninsula. The two large religious minorities of Spain, the Moslems and the Jews, were the obvious obstacles in the way of this goal, hence they must be overwhelmed. In 1480 the Inquisition was set up in Seville for the express purpose of examining the sincerity of the Jewish converts. It quickly gathered momentum and eventually led to the persecution of the entire Jewish population of Spain. The following year, 1481, under pretext of a Moorish incursion in Spanish territory, war was declared on the Moslems. Before following these two tangled threads to their tragic end, much can be revealed by examining the status of the Jews and Moslems in Spain at this historic juncture.

The Jews had enjoyed many centuries of tranquillity in Moslem Andalusia and in the Christian kingdoms of Spain while their brethren were being brutally persecuted throughout the rest of Europe. The tolerance of both of these Spanish cultures was unique during the Middle Ages. Moslem friendliness toward the Jews lasted from 711 until 1146, when the fanatical Almohades entered Spain, thus covering more than four centuries. The Jews who then fled to the northern Christian kingdoms were received there with open arms, joining many of their brothers who had already risen to positions of prominence in the states of Castile, Navarre, and Aragon. There was no change in this relationship until the late fourteenth century. At the time of the great plague (1348) Germany, France, Switzerland, Austria, and other European states inflicted wholesale indignities, massacres, and expulsions on the unfortunate Jews, who were widely blamed for the epidemic. When the Black Death hit the peninsula without any similar upheaval in sentiment, the 250 Jewish communities of Spain breathed a sigh of relief, and thanked God for the tolerance of that land which for so many centuries had been their home. Their thanks were premature, for within a few years they were to receive a rude shock.

It was Peter the Cruel who, perhaps unwittingly, started the pendulum in the other direction. He surrounded himself with Jewish financial advisers, appointed only Jews as his tax collectors, and used only Moslems in his personal guard. This was not because of any real tolerance on Peter's part, but simply because he could not trust his own people. Before many years had passed Jews were regarded as the main instruments of the cruelty and tyranny of the crown. In 1366 when the king's bastard brother Henry rose against him in civil war, and temporarily took over the Castilian throne, he immediately punished the Jewish communities for their support of Peter by fining them heavily. Those who could not pay were sold as slaves. Henry's backers among the populace were eager enough to condone the persecution. In 1369 Henry killed Peter and took his place as king. As the two brothers met in their death struggle, Henry is said to have shouted: "You bastard Jew!"

Once the throne was his, however, Henry adopted a policy of tolerance, and appointed many Jewish advisers, but growing anti-Semitism among the nobles and clergy resulted in the passage of restrictive laws directed against the Jews. They were obliged to wear a distinctive Jewish badge, a law no pope had formerly been able to enforce in Spain, and were forbidden to keep Christian names. This was the first evidence of the later holocaust. In 1391, on Ash Wednesday, an anti-Jewish riot broke out in Seville, and the Jewish quarter of that city was burned to the ground. Many hundreds of Jews were killed. The upheaval spread to Córdoba, where the dead were piled in great heaps in the streets, and then into Castile, where seventy cities underwent a repetition of the brutalities of Andalusia. For three months the riots raged, first in one town, then in another. Thousands of lives were snuffed out.

With the history of what had happened to their race in the other European countries before them, tens of thousands of Spanish Jews accepted, or were forced to accept, baptism and conversion to Christianity. Many of these converts rose to high positions in the state and even in the church. Solomon Levi, for example, a gifted rabbí of

Burgos, took the name of Paul de Santa María, studied theology in Paris, became a priest and eventually an archbishop, was also keeper of the royal seal under Henry III, and was one of the regents during the minority of John II. He, and others like him, were constantly exhorting the Jews to abandon their ancient beliefs and embrace Christianity. They achieved a considerable measure of success. Whole communities accepted baptism, and the new converts, called *marranos** by the *old* Christians, entered all the forbidden professions, went to the universities, won important state positions, and studied for the priesthood.[45] They prospered both economically and socially. Intermarriages with the older Christian families became frequent, and within a couple of generations hardly a noble house of Castile was without its infiltration of Jewish blood. The new converts gained almost a century of renewed freedom, but hostility against them continued to smolder among the religious orders and among the masses. This was the status of affairs when Isabella and Ferdinand established the Spanish Inquisition.

Ferdinand and Isabella had already molded the *Hermandades de Castilla* ("the rural constabulary") into an efficient federal police force, called the "Holy Brotherhood," and with its support were able to stamp out social anarchy in the country districts and to break the power of the nobles, whom they adroitly converted into showy courtly appendages. Years later Sancho Panza recalled the rigorous methods of the Holy Brotherhood, and shuddered. The grand masterships of the three military orders, Santiago, Alcántara, and Calatrava, were in turn conferred on Ferdinand as they became vacant. This further increased the power of the crown, and brought in additional revenues, lands, and fortresses.

In the same year that the Inquisition was established (1480) there assembled the famous Cortes of Toledo. The nobles were thrown out of the assembly, their places taken by town lawyers educated in the Roman juridical tradition, who were more favorable to the interests of the crown. This move evoked a very popular response among the townspeople, and eventually it led to turning the nobles into mere shadows around the throne. Little did the townsmen realize that they would be the next element in the national life to be subordinated to the central authority.

---

* The word *marrano* has meant *swine* for many centuries, but its original meaning in the Arabic root word was apparently "prohibited thing," or "outsider" who refused to eat the prohibited thing, which was pork.

Anti-Jewish sentiment was strong in Spain when Ferdinand and Isabella came to the throne. The lower classes envied the wealth and influence of the Jews and of the Jewish converts who had achieved additional status by their marriages into the noble families. There were also many elements in the church which opposed the Jews. At first the throne appeared to be neutral in this opposition of interests, but when it became politically apparent that great advantage could be gained by establishing the Inquisition for the express purpose of persecuting Jewish converts for suspected heresies, both sovereigns gave their consent. They gained the cheap and cruel popularity that often derives from the persecution of any minority, but in so acting sacrificed the long-range interest of their people. The Inquisition was always under the control of the crown, and it was efficiently used to increase the royal power by depriving the suspected converts of their lands, their wealth, and their influence. In this manner it helped with the prosecution of the war against the Moslems, and furthered the religious and emotional unity of the many dissident elements which went into the makeup of the new Spain.

The original victims of the Inquisition were not Jews, but *marranos* suspected of having fallen from their new faith. The fact that many of these converts occupied important positions in the medical, professional, banking, tax-collecting, and industrial spheres was undoubtedly one of the reasons for their being envied and hated by the poorer classes. The general intellectual superiority of the Jewish portion of the Spanish population was certainly another reason. The influence of the French monks in Spain and the examples of the other European countries where persecution of the Jews had already brought a base popularity and a considerable wealth into the hands of the persecutors, was yet another factor. The number of Jewish converts who had risen to positions of prominence in the Catholic Church was a strange but very cogent fourth basis for this intolerance. Among these converts or their descendants was Isabella's private confessor, Talavera, the archbishop of Granada, and according to some authorities, Torquemada himself, the Grand Inquisitor. There were many others. It is deplorable but understandable that some of these persons increased the bitterness of the persecution in every effort to prove beyond any doubt their own "Christian" and thoroughly Spanish loyalties.

In spite of all these things

the popularity of the Inquisition was not universal. In Córdoba there was open revolt headed by the chief noblemen of the town, supported by the municipality. This was so far successful that the Inquisitor General and his obnoxious agent were removed. In Aragon, Valencia and Catalonia resistance was more general. In Saragossa the Inquisitor was murdered before the altar; there was scarcely a noble house in Aragon that was not concerned in the conspiracy. The nobles dreaded the Inquisition, the Bishops and lawyers were jealous of it; the lower classes usually applauded it, their blood was purer, their fortunes not so tempting, they regarded it as a scourge wherewith to chastise the nobles.[27]

Nevertheless, the dread efficiency of the Inquisition as an instrument of state policy increased apace. The crown was on its way to complete dominance of the political, religious, and social organism of the Spanish nation, and would brook no diminution of its newly won power. Ferdinand and Isabella had already begun their supremely "Machiavellian" policy, on the one hand persecuting the "Judaisers," on the other battling the Moslems, and with what energy was left thumping away at the nobility.

The presumptive proofs of an accused person's being a Judaiser were rather curious: if he wore better clothes or cleaner linen on the Jewish Sabbath than on the other days of the week; if, on the preceding evening he had no fire in his house; if he had shared a meal with Jews, or had eaten the meat of animals slaughtered by them; if he washed a corpse in warm water, or turned his face toward the wall when dying; if he gave Hebrew names to his children; "a provision most whimsically cruel, since, by a law of Henry II he was prohibited under severe penalties from giving them Christian names." The Inquisition hit the converts like a thunderbolt; many *marranos* were burned at the stake. A sizable number of Jews fled to Granada, and a temporary security, but in the end there was no way out for these unfortunate people.

In the meantime, the war against the Moslems progressed. Málaga and several other towns were assaulted first and overcome. The taking of Granada was no easy task; the city was in a state of full defense, and its powerful ramparts were well manned. This final war of the Reconquest took eleven years, and for the last several months the Christian army was encamped at Santa Fe, just outside the city of Granada, around which they placed a circle of steel. Gradually the siege had its effect; famine and exhaustion forced the Moslems to surrender, and on January 2, 1492, the victorious Christian army

entered the defeated stronghold. It was not an unconditional surrender; the Moslems had capitulated on terms. They were guaranteed
religious freedom and were to be allowed to retain their own laws,
their homes, and their possessions, and were to pay no extra taxes.
With these terms most of the Moslems decided to remain in Spain,
but several thousands of them did cross over to northern Africa.
Ferdinand and Isabella took up their residence in the beautiful
Alhambra palace, now presiding over a territorially unified country.

With the Moslems conquered and the *marranos* crushed the Inquisition now turned upon the Jews. As far back as 1480, first year of
the dread Tribunal, the cruel-lipped and sardonic Torquemada had
urged Ferdinand to expel the Jews from Andalusia, the region
where they lived in the greatest numbers. The king foresaw what
such an expulsion would do to the economy of the country, and
demurred. Torquemada, with satanic persistence, kept after him with
persuasive arguments: The Jews would always be a strong religious
minority in Spain, their wealth was great and would bail the king out
of all financial difficulties, the *marranos* had proved time and again
before the Tribunal that they were not devout Christians. The vision
of all that Jewish wealth and of a homogeneous Spain became more
and more inviting as the Moors were pushed back into their final
stronghold. When Granada fell the doom of the Jews was sealed, as
was that of the Moslems.

Three months after the capture of Granada the edict went forth
from the Alhambra ordering all Jews to leave the country within four
months, on pain of death. They were to be allowed to dispose of
their property, but could take with them neither gold, silver, nor
precious stones. No Christian could give them shelter or assistance
after that four month period, on penalty of total confiscation of his
possessions. The Jews were stunned by the blow. For more than
fifteen centuries their people had lived in Spain, giving liberally of
their blood, their labor, and their intelligence to the wealth and
culture of the country. Now they were to dispose of their property in
a falling market, and without even the possibility of receiving payment in gold or silver. Abrabanel, a distinguished Jew who was
attached to the royal household, was not included in the edict. He
was too valuable a man to lose. Abrabanel went before the king and
offered him a huge sum of money if the decree were lifted. Ferdinand
was about to relent, when Torquemada came bellowing into the room
holding aloft a crucifix and shouting that Judas had sold his Master

for thirty pieces of silver! The edict was not rescinded, and Abrabanel immediately determined to join his brethren in exile. Jewish properties suddenly flooded the market; an olive grove went for a mule, a nice home for a bolt of cloth, a well-stocked store for some bagatelle needful for the long journey.

At least 150,000 Jews left the country. The wealthy shared with the poor in order to make the ordeal more endurable. The exiles scattered to the four winds, but most of those who survived wound up in northern Africa, whence many of them migrated to Constantinople, the Near East, Albania, Greece. They made up a good part of the backbone of the industrial, the intellectual, and financial life of Spain. Many Jewish communities, aghast at the prospect of starting life over again in strange lands, decided to purchase immunity by accepting baptism. These were to furnish victims for the Holy Inquisition for many years to come. Such was the fate of the proudest and most prosperous Jewish community in Europe; the Jews never returned to Spain in any number, and today there are barely three or four thousand in the entire country.

The ax was not quite ready to fall on the Moors. After Granada was taken there was a brief period of tranquillity which lasted six or seven years. Then Archbishop Jiménez de Cisneros began to clamp down. At first he attempted, and with considerable success, to purchase baptismal converts with costly gifts distributed among the Moslem leaders. It began to be bruited about that conversion could be a profitable thing, and many of the common people followed their leaders to the baptismal font. On one occasion so many hundreds assembled that it was necessary to baptize them with water flung from an immense mop twirled above the heads of the multitude. When the campaign for conversions stalled, the fanatical and aggressive archbishop commenced to apply more rigorous methods. In 1499 he piled all the Arabic religious books that he could find in a huge mound in a public plaza and had them burned. Many beautiful and priceless manuscripts were consumed in the holocaust. This was followed by constant pressure, imprisonment of the "troublemakers," and dire threats to those who held out. Eventually practically every Moslem in Granada accepted baptism. There was a rebellion in the mountains, but this was harshly suppressed. In 1502 a royal decree proclaimed that the only alternative to baptism was exile. A few hundred Moslems left the country, but the immense majority remained, becoming at least nominal Christians. They were now called

Moriscos, or "converted Moors," and added their numbers to the *marranos*, or converted Jews, who up to this time had been the primary target of the Holy Office.

The country was now completely Christian through the most detestable expedients that sophistry could devise and fanaticism apply. Yet, even as *Moriscos* the ex-Moslems were not let alone. They were forbidden to wear their customary clothes, and were expressly prohibited from taking baths. Bathing was presumed to be prima facie evidence of apostasy. The phrase "the accused was known to take baths . . ." is a common one in the records of the Inquisition. The descendants of these *Moriscos* remained in Spain until the reign of Philip III, always on the ragged edge of expulsion. Finally between 1609 and 1611 the entire *Morisco* population of the country was either slaughtered or expelled from the country.

It must be remembered that a very great proportion of the Moslem inhabitants of Granada, when this city was taken by Ferdinand and Isabella in 1492, were of pure or almost pure Spanish blood. They were Moslems, but they were not in reality Moors or Arabs. This in part accounts for the rigors of the persecution, since the Christians, and particularly many of the churchmen, regarded them as heretical Spaniards. The slightest indication of their returning to their old Islamic customs was therefore sufficient to send the officials of the Inquisition into a rage. In Aragon and along the eastern coastal areas the Moslem population was much more Moorish in blood. These people were primarily farm laborers, and the landlords worked hard to prevent them from being expelled from Spain. Their best efforts only deferred but could not alter the final dictum. When it came, the loss of so many hundreds of thousands of *Morisco* workers, skilled laborers in Andalusia and farmers elsewhere, put a drain on the national resources from which Spain did not recover for centuries.

Ferdinand and Isabella had one son, Prince John, on whom rested the hopes of the Spanish nation for a continuation of the dynasty. This young man was sent to Salamanca to study, where he sat on the same hard benches in the same drafty halls as the rest of the students, listening to lectures delivered by the best intellects of Spain. He had an intelligent and promising mind. Prince John was also greatly interested in music, and frequently attended performances of Juan del Encina's eclogues at the palace of the dukes of Alba, near Salamanca. In his own palace he had regular afternoon gatherings at which he and five or six well-trained young singers, directed by a professional music master, sang for a couple of hours. The prince could play several instruments: the guitar, violin, clavi-organ, the organ, and the clavichord. His sudden death in 1497, at the age of twenty-one, was a terrible blow from which neither his parents nor his country ever recovered. A Spanish historian writes of his death: "He was in love with a passionate red-haired Flemish girl. Because he loved early and too much, and fell ill of a disease which today might be readily cured, the young prince died."

In spite of the persecutions of Jews and Moslems, Spain under Ferdinand and Isabella still held the possibility of intellectual ferment and increasing toleration. The same Cardinal Jiménez de Cisneros, who had used the whip hand on the Moslem population of Andalusia, in 1508 founded the famous University of Alcalá de Henares, later attended by Quevedo, Lope de Vega, and many other notable figures. This university became the center of humanistic studies in Spain, and for a brief period the friends of Erasmus held great influence in the peninsula. Cardinal Cisneros also directed and paid for the first critical edition of the Holy Bible, published in six volumes at Alcalá. Original manuscripts in Hebrew, Chaldean, Greek, and Latin were brought and studied carefully, and for fifteen years a group of scholars collated and edited before the final work was finished. It was a critical edition in several languages, hence is referred to as the "Polyglot Bible of Alcalá."

The reign of Ferdinand and Isabella, called in Spanish history *los reyes católicos*, or the Catholic sovereigns, marks the maturity of Spain as a modern nation, and the end of the Middle Ages. The title was conferred on them in 1496 by the Spanish Pope Alexander VI in recognition of the great services they had rendered Christendom. Under these sovereigns Spain found a way to blend the cultural unity of medieval days, which was religious and Catholic, with the political unity of the Renaissance, which signified centralization of power in the crown and the end of petty kingdoms. The Reconquest of the peninsula was in itself a kind of Crusade, and was, up to this point in time, the only successful crusade in history. Church and state had both participated in that long struggle, and together had won the victory. Cross was now firmly welded to sword, and in politics Spain became a church-state; religious as well as political authority rested firmly in the hands of the crown.

At first it had appeared that Ferdinand and Isabella looked with favor on the strong political representation of the Spanish towns, which was a balance to the unruly nobility. But once the latter had been stripped of power, their energies channeled into the Moorish wars, and their pride regaled with brilliant positions in a brilliant court, the Catholic sovereigns began at once to show their determination to dominate also the townships and their representative body, the national Cortes. Between 1482 and 1498, or for a period of sixteen years, the Cortes did not meet at all. When finally it did assemble this was simply because the crown needed funds and wanted them rubber stamped. The power of the Cortes was not entirely destroyed by the Catholic sovereigns, but it was clearly made subordinate to the royal authority.

One year during the reign of Ferdinand and Isabella stands out above all others. That year is 1492. It was the miraculous year of Spanish history, and embodied the culmination of events which had been many centuries in the making. First of all, the war against the Moslems was won; the Cross was planted on Alhambra Hill on January 2, 1492; and the Catholic sovereigns took up residence in the exquisite red palace of the Moorish kings. In that same year the Spanish Inquisition turned its full force against the other religious minority in Spain, the Jews, and they were expelled from the country en masse. Also in 1492 Rodrigo Borgia, a Spaniard, was made Pope in Rome, thus giving Ferdinand and Isabella a strong ally inside the church. The fourth historic event of 1492 was the discovery of America. Other sailors might have touched the shores of the New World before Columbus, but his trip was the only one which counted in history, linking America with Europe. The fifth important happening of 1492 was the publication of the *Castilian Grammar*, by Antonio the Nebrija, which was the first grammar of any modern European tongue. This book marked once for all the clear supremacy of Castile and its language in the language and literature of Spain.

When Nebrija gave the queen a copy of his *Grammar*, her greenish-blue eyes took on a puzzled look, and she asked: "What is it for?" The portentous answer that Nebrija gave must have bewildered her even more. He said: "Language, your majesty, is the ideal weapon of empire." But if Isabella failed in that moment to grasp the significance of this statement, the conquistadores who came to the New World certainly understood its import, and in the end Spain imposed her language on great territories and a vast population far exceeding those of the home country herself. The discovery of the New World in this crucial year also gave the exultant soldiers of Spain, who had just won their victory over the Moors, a vista of extensive new lands to conquer. While the spirit of expansion was at its psychological peak, this fortuitous discovery gave it new impetus and turned it immediately in another direction. And thus began the second long crusade in the history of Spain: the conquest, conversion, exploration, and colonization of the New World.*

One might add to this already imposing list of events of 1492 the birth of Luis Vives, Spain's greatest philosopher of those days, in Valencia. One might even mention that on Christmas Eve of 1492 Juan del Encina, father of the Spanish theater and father also of the art music of Spain's Renaissance, presented the first of his religious eclogues in the great palace of the dukes of Alba at Alba de Tormes, near the city of Salamanca. What nation has ever had so many crucial events take place within so restricted a period of time? What nation ever had before it at a single moment such a limitless horizon of potentials? What nation ever attacked the problems of expansion and of government with more vigor or more zeal? And what nation, we might add, ever faced problems of such immensity with such limited resources? The principal resource of Spain was then, as it had always been, the vital energy, the boundless determination, the incredible thrust and will of its people. What Spain achieved and what she failed to achieve both came to rest on this ultimate

---

* The Europeans were anxious to find a water route to India, and it was this that led to the discovery of America. Spices and silk fom the Orient had enriched the Italian city merchants and had helped to make Italy the mother of art. In England a pound of cloves was worth two cows. In 1499 pepper brought forty times its price in India by the time it reached Portugal. When Charles V of Spain married in 1526 his Portuguese wife's dowry consisted of 50,000 quintals of pepper, but by this date its value had declined to the point where it was worth only ten times as much as it cost in India. By 1530 its value was lower still, and the wharves of Lisbon were glutted with unsold spices. The lack of refrigeration was one thing that made spices so much sought after, for they helped to preserve and to flavor meats. When the first Portuguese set foot in Calicut a native indignantly asked what had brought them there, and the answer was reported to have been: "Christianity and spices!" The water route to the Orient was a way around the long and hard overland journey, which required passage through many countries. When the water route was found it meant the death of the Italian city states and the rise of Spain and Portugal as great world powers.

basis of the individual Spaniard, who was to the fullest quotient a man of his epoch.

Ferdinand of Aragon was the epitome of the modern king and the new concept of kingship that had emerged with the Renaissance. He adroitly played his enemies off against each other, both inside and outside of Spain; he persuaded, cajoled, lied when it was to his advantage; he fought when he could not avoid it, but only when he was certain that he would win, and he sacrificed every theoretical concept of justice to the supreme test of what would give him the most power and at the same time satisfy the most people. When he was once twitted about Louis XII of France, who had complained that Ferdinand had lied to him twice, the king of Spain laughed. "He lies," boasted Ferdinand, "I lied to him not twice but ten times."

With this blend of mendacity and force Ferdinand whipped the French in Italy, took over the kingdom of Naples, made the Spanish frontier secure from France, drove the Moors and Jews from Spain or converted them, sent his argosies across the great Atlantic into the unknown New World to establish new kingdoms on the other side of the ocean. The real home of Machiavellianism was not Italy or France, but Spain, and Machiavelli himself astutely points this out. The Italian writer admired above all men Cesare Borgia, who was a Spaniard, and Ferdinand of Aragon, his model of a perfect Renaissance prince. In his classic on the subject, *The Prince*, after listing the various qualities of duplicity and strength necessary in a good king, Machiavelli writes:

We have in our own day Ferdinand, King of Aragon, at present King of Spain. He may almost be termed a new prince, because from a weak king he has become for fame and glory the first king in Christendom, and if you regard his actions you will find them all very great and some of them extraordinary. At the beginning of his reign he assailed Granada, and that enterprise was the foundation of his state. At first he did it leisurely and without fear of being interfered with; he kept the minds of the barons of Castile occupied in this enterprise, so that thinking only of that war they did not think of making innovations, and he thus acquired reputation and power over them without their being aware of it. He was able with the money of the Church and the people to maintain his armies, and by that long war lay the foundation of his military power, which afterwards made him famous. Besides this, to be able to undertake greater enterprises, and always under the pretext of religion, he had recourse to a pious cruelty, driving out the Moors from his kingdom and despoiling them. No more admirable or rare example can be found. He also attacked under the same pretext Africa, undertook his Italian campaigns, and has lately attacked France; so that he has continually contrived great things, which have kept his subjects' minds uncertain and astonished, and occupied in watching their result.

And these actions have arisen one out of the other, so that they have left no time for men to settle down and act against him.

Too bad that Machiavelli did not live to see that plenitude of imperium in the days of Charles V and Philip II. This would have given him cause for admiration verging on frenzy!

The reign of the Catholic sovereigns marked the transition of Spain from the Middle Ages to the Renaissance. It was a period of tremendous upheaval, of incredible energies, and of countless choices. Spain might have taken the path of humanistic reform as easily as the path of intolerant reaction. She might have led the way into a new vision of human destiny as easily as she persisted, blindly and vigorously, in the attempt to hold, perpetuate, and project her past on the fabric of a rapidly moving present. She did not make all of the wrong choices, as her empire and the glory of her arts attest, but she made enough wrong choices to lose her lead among nations where the path of progress and change was advancing too rapidly for the rigidity of her medieval mind to grasp.

In 1499, during the very middle of this transition period, one of the truly great works of Spanish literature appeared. Most critics call it the second best work of Spanish literature, after the immortal novel of Cervantes. This book is *The Celestina*, and was written by a converted Aragonese Jew, named Fernando de Rojas. Although it is in the form of a dramatic dialogue, the book was never meant to be acted on the stage, hence it may be called the first modern novel, antedating the *Quixote* by well over a hundred years. *La Celestina* is a perfect literary symbol of the Renaissance in Spain. It blends beautifully all of the divergent elements which went into the make-up of the Spanish Renaissance. In this work tragedy and comedy are combined, as are idealism and realism. Medieval reality (represented by Celestina and her brood) is linked inseparably with the Renaissance idealism, the two romantic lovers, Calixto and Melibea. The net result is an expression of literary despair which might easily be taken as a prophetic announcement of what was later to happen to Spain herself when she fell broken and bleeding from her position of eminence in the tower of her glory.

The story of the *Celestina* is not of great importance: A young aristocrat follows his falcon into the garden of a beautiful young lady, the sight of whom sends him immediately into transports of joy and desire. He proffers love and reaches quickly for her skirts in a shocking gesture of haste. She is "his religion, his life, his God." He is a puppet in the hands of love. The girl demurs, but the young swain obtains the intercession of an old bawd go-between, the Celestina, who becomes the great character of the book. This run-down bawd still plies her trade with acumen and fills her language with pithy and proverbial phrases. She is one of the most real of all characters in Spanish literature. She was "a laundress, a perfumeress, a fixer of faces, a mender of broken maidenheads, a bawd, and had some smatch of the witch . . . At her home she made perfumes, civet, powders, musk and mosqueta, confections to clarify the skin, waters to make the face glisten, lip salves, ointments, and a thousand other slibber-slabbers."

She was a pimp par excellence who boasted of her palmy days when even the priests dropped their prayers to ask her about their mistresses. She seems at times almost the symbol of an old pagan cult of love, for she subordinates everything in life to sexual union, the supreme expression, the supreme delight. Her philosophy is that of a happy and universal promiscuity. She carries forward the feeling of the archpriest of Hita and his *Book of Good Love*, but adds to this the urgency and the tragedy of her epoch. The minor characters of the book are all differentiated and operate according to their individual psychologies. This gives to the *Celestina* a modern feeling and a universal appeal which will not be destroyed by time.

During the Middle Ages the center of the universe was God. During the Renaissance man became the center of the universe, not man in the aggregate, but individual man. Character differentiation on a broad scale was not possible in literature until this new concept had taken root. When the individual human life could become the center of epic conflict and epic tragedy (that is, the center of "the tragic sense of life"), the birth of modern drama and of the modern novel were possible, but not before this time.

The young man in the *Celestina*, Calixto, with the old bawd's help finally meets his lady and they consummate their love. But immediately they are discovered, the girl's father breaks into the room, Calixto, in his haste to escape, falls off the ladder and is killed, and in a gesture of hopeless despair the girl, Melibea, throws herself from the tower and commits suicide. Her father, at a glance taking in what has happened, breaks into a lament which expresses the depth of his tragedy, and the tragedy of all those who had died or been killed in this powerful and beautiful novel. His words are addressed in part to his wife, who has heard the commotion and run to see what had happened. But primarily they are addressed to the reader, and convey his own sense of irreparable tragedy. The old man laments:

Ay, ay, my poor, my noble wife! Our joy is at the bottom of the pit. All that we had is lost. Let us not wish to continue this life! . . . Oh, hardened father's heart! Why do you not break with grief, now that your beloved heir has gone? For what purpose did I build towers? For whom did I acquire honors? For whom did I plant trees? For whom did I construct ships? . . . Oh life filled with turmoil, and beset by misery! Oh, world, world! In my tenderest years I thought that you and your deeds were ruled by some kind of order; now, with the ebb and flow of your tides, you seem to be a labyrinth of errors, a frightful desert, a den of wild beasts, a game and grimace of circling men, a lake filled with slime, a patch of thorns, a steep mountain, a rocky field, a meadow of serpents, a garden blossoming but without fruit, a fountain of miseries, a river of tears, a sea of wretchedness, a toil without recompense, a sweet poison, a vain hope . . . But, who forced my daughter to die, but the strong force of love? So now, flattering world, what remedy are you going to give to my weary age? . . . Oh, love, oh, love! I did not think you had the strength or power to slay your subjects! Who has given you such power? Who gave you a name that does not suit you? If you were love, you would love your servants. If you loved them, you would not cause them sorrow. If they lived happily, they would not kill themselves, as did my daughter. Your sound is joyful, your treatment saddens. The tinder that your flame kindles is of souls and lives of human creatures. And these are so many, that were I to start listing them I would not know where to begin. Not only of Christians; but also of Jews and unbelievers, and all in payment for good services rendered. . . . I complain of the world, for in it I was born, because had it not given me life, I would not have fathered Melibea; she not being born, would not have loved; not loving, I would not face my disconsolate old age. . . . Oh, my broken, shattered daughter. Why did you have no pity on your poor mother? Why did you show yourself so cruel with your old father? Why did you leave me, when I was all ready to be leaving you? Why have you left me sad and alone in this valley of tears?"

The wonder of the *Celestina*, of course, does not reside in these few lines pulled out of their context. The beauty and power of this

work lie in its harmonious fusion and commingling of all the emotional currents and cultural and racial elements which went into the
makeup of Renaissance Spain: the Jewish philosophy which views
the human race as born to sorrow and its own people as caught in
the snares and meshes of an unreal reality they cannot grasp; the
Moslem sense of an overpowering physical love; the pagan spirit of
the emerging Renaissance; the crude and racy realism of the Spanish
Middle Ages, filled with quick body needs, sharp turns of language
and proverbial expressions; the nascent literary idealism which would
soon give birth to romantic, pastoral, and chivalresque idealized
fiction with its view of perfect man in a perfect state, a schematic
world of idea rather than of observation—all these things and more
enter into the tragicomedy of this converted Aragonese Jew, into
whose own life the Inquisition made its inquiry, and who, thus, like
his characters, found himself in the midst of a dancing chain of life
where his tiny individual human soul could make no great dent or
change of focus, yet where his language and his emotions, the very
essence of his life, could in art find their own immortality. This is
why the *Celestina* is a great work in Spanish literature, and thus
starts off the Golden Age with a flash of splendor.

The reign of Ferdinand and Isabella expresses the religious, cultural,
and political unity of the Spanish Renaissance, the *Celestina* embodies and blends in one harmonious whole its literary essence, but
the discovery and conquest of the New World is, in fact, the real
Spanish Renaissance, the true rebirth of Spain. When Columbus
stood on the prow of his ship that last night at two in the morning
and saw in the distance "something like a white sand cliff gleaming
in the moonlight," he was staring with dream-tossed, hazy eyes into
the portfolio of the future. Columbus thought he had found India;
he died still thinking so. The epochal meaning of his discovery
eluded him, but it did not for long elude the restive soldiers and
sailors of Spain, who soon learned that America was a treasure house
of gold and slaves. And it did not elude the wily eyes of the rapacious
Spanish kings Charles V and Philip II, for these new lands were the
"personal" patrimony of the crown and did not belong to the nation,
and from them the "royal fifth," increased by countless taxes, kept
Spain going for more than a century. The triumphant church also
turned its gaze toward America, for here were virgin souls to convert,
here was the possibility of creating on earth the millennium.

The Spanish conquistadores were not wild young blades, but older, maturer men whose character was already firmly set in the pattern of the home country. In 1492 Columbus himself was forty-one; Pizarro was fifty-six when he captured the Inca ruler Atahualpa; Cortés was thirty-four when he entered Mexico City; Valdivia was forty when he led his first expedition into Chile. But the Emperor Charles, first Hapsburg to wear the Spanish crown, was only sixteen when he came to the throne. Age and experience went to the New World, youth and inexperience took over the government of European Spain. But if the conquistadores were older men, they were certainly not, for all that, less durable either in mind or body than those who were their juniors in years. "Who does not venture forth does not cross the sea," says an old proverb that all of the conquistadores knew. Action, epic action, was the keynote of their conquest, action more dynamic even than that of the Reconquest of Spain herself from the Moslem invaders. The conquistadores also created a new kind of literature consisting of firsthand reports and impressions of the strange New World, its geography, its flora and fauna, its native inhabitants, and their own personal experiences, explorations, and battles. All this was history on an epic scale, and in many ways the best Spanish chroniclers who recorded it are equal to Thucydides.

Cortés, with a force never exceeding 1,500 Spaniards, penetrated to the heart of a hostile country and conquered the vast Aztec empire. Pizarro, with fewer than 400 soldiers, seized the Inca chieftain and subdued his nation of several millions. Quesada, with only 166 men, reached the savannah of Bogotá, five hundred miles inland across swamps and mountains, and overcame the Chibchas. Orellana crossed the Andes from Peru, constructed a few makeshift boats, and traveled 3,000 miles down the Amazon, finally reaching the Atlantic Ocean. Cabeza de Vaca, descendant of the old herder who had led the Christians over a mountain path onto higher ground at the Battle of *Las Navas de Tolosa*, tramped across 10,000 miles of what was later the United States and Mexico, and then headed for South America, where he walked another thousand miles across the Brazilian jungles to Paraguay. These men did not believe in wasting time. They did not evaluate the situation rationally. They attacked each problem by instinct, regarding nothing as impossible, and almost nothing was. "Who loses the morning loses the afternoon, who loses the afternoon, loses life," thus goes another proverb, which synthesizes the epic spirit of the conquest of the New World.

Spain was capable of deeds of epic proportions in 1492. The Spain of the year 1000 could never have discovered and colonized the New World. The Spain of 1800 would have been equally impotent. But in 1492 that nation stood at the pinnacle of her destiny; she exerted herself to create the golden moment, and she was able to follow through.

The Spanish Renaissance meant the decline of many of the deeply Hispanic values of the Middle Ages, but the discovery of America gave Spain a chance to revive these ancient values in a new world. If personal bravery and the value of *el hombre a secas* ("man standing alone") was no longer as alive as it had previously been in Spain, there was the whole other hemisphere. If the communal life of the medieval villages was slowly giving way to the inroads of an expanding national economy and geopolitics, there were the missions. America was the answer for this ineradicable desire to perpetuate the ancient ideals.

"The missions were born," wrote a distinguished Spanish historian, Fernando de los Ríos, "as a religious aspiration and as a protest against the covetousness of the conquistadores, against the exploitation of the Indians and against the *encomiendas*." When the Dominican Pedro de Córdoba expressed before the king his hostility to the Laws of Burgos (1512–1515) which modified but did not suppress the regime of the *encomenderos* ("estate holders") in America, the king answered him: "Take upon yourself then, Father, the charge of remedying them; you will do me a great service therein." Thus Pedro de Córdoba became the champion for the idea of the mission in the New World. Many other priests were won over to his ideal. Later, inspired by Thomas More's *Utopia* and by their own desire to restore the lost purity of the primitive church, these priests set out to establish communal mission settlements in many parts of America. The flowering of these missions is one of the glories of the colonial regime.

I would like here to insert what I wrote in another book about the conquest of the New World:

While the other European nations made of the Renaissance an epoch of the arts, literature, painting, sculpture, and building—all exaltations of the new pagan spirit—the Iberian peninsula made of it an epoch of religion and conquest, of prolonging the Middle Ages and of the super-heroism of the conquistador, their own highest achievement. These conquerors came from the lower classes. There was not a really noble family among them. They belonged to the people, and, representing the character of the people, they became like them: great and heroic, oftentimes zealous, cruel, greedy, bigoted, and ignorant, but always great and heroic.

It is little wonder that a well-known contemporary Spanish writer boasted that Cortés is the equal of any Da Vinci, for Cortés and not Da Vinci was the epitome of the Spanish Renaissance.

The discovery of America represents the greatest revolution ever effected in the history of mankind. It shifted completely the center of gravity of the known world, turned the eyes of civilization from the crusades of the East toward the conquest of the West, marked the end of the Middle Ages and the beginning of the modern era, and above all altered and broadened the entire nature of man's thinking. It was the end of the dark, the mystical, the inward life; the start of a forward motion which has not yet been arrested. The influx of gold and silver from the New World altered the value of money, created a new rich class, gave birth to capitalism itself. Men of action and enterprise replaced men of birth as leaders in deed and thought.

America was at first an illusion, later a hope, and when the great cities of gold did not materialize, the experience of the conquistadores (worth more than gold itself) made possible the creation of new empires beyond the sea. These men turned their gaze from the classic truths of antiquity toward the future and its promise of a fuller and richer life.[28]

7

THE GOLDEN AGE: POLITICS
AND THE SOCIAL ORDER

*Other nations have produced institutions, books. We have
left souls.*

Miguel de Unamuno

Spaniards are prone to refer to the reign of the Catholic sovereigns
(1479–1516) as the golden age in their history, because of Spain's
vast potential at that time. Foreigners generally regard the epoch
of Charles V and his son Philip II as the high-water mark of Spanish
history (1516–1598). It is a matter of viewpoint. Spaniards think
in terms of what might have been had the rule of Spaniards continued and Spain not become involved in politics all over Europe.
Foreigners view the obviously greater size and wealth of the Spanish
empire in the sixteenth century, and on this they base their judgment.

But there is yet another Golden Age whose limits do not correspond exactly with those of either of the above two periods. This is
the famous *Siglo de Oro* of Spanish literature and the fine arts, which
begins later and extends longer than Spain's great flash across the
pages of history. Many masterpieces of this Golden Age were produced in the seventeenth century under the inept rule of Philip III,
Philip IV, and Charles II, the Bewitched, who brought the Hapsburg
dynasty to its inglorious close. During these years of political decline,

while the nation's hegemony in Europe was withering away, there was a burgeoning of the arts such as Spain had never known. Cervantes, Lope de Vega, Calderón, El Greco, Velázquez, Murillo, and many others brought glory to Spanish literature and art. Their great works, in a manner of speaking, placed an exquisite wreath over a tomb. Because of them the culture of Spain has been beautifully represented and will be long remembered. This aspect of Spanish life deserves a chapter to itself; before entering the precious garden of art, we should examine the social and political soil which gave it root.

Charles I of Spain (he was Charles V of the Holy Roman Empire) was born in Flanders in the year 1500. His mother was Juana, daughter of Ferdinand and Isabella. His father was Philip the Handsome, an Austrian Hapsburg, the first Hapsburg in Spanish history. Philip was a dashing young prince who had a tremendous attraction for women. His wife, Juana, was insanely jealous of him, and the court was shocked by their lovers' quarrels.

Shortly after Queen Isabella's death (1504), Philip the Handsome grabbed the crown of Castile for himself. His wife, to whom it rightfully belonged, was beginning to lose her mind, so she was incapacitated for government. Philip (now Philip I of Castile) was supported by a considerable army of Burgundians, and at first the Castilians also supported him, for they had resented the regency of Ferdinand of Aragon. In the face of this opposition Ferdinand temporarily withdrew from the scene.

Philip the Handsome's brief reign was a riotous and reckless one, and he immediately alienated his Castilian supporters. His death, which came within a few months, was greeted with a sigh of relief. Ferdinand returned and became regent in Castile (1506). His grandson, Charles, was then only six years old.

The child's mother, Juana, was prostrated by the death of her handsome Hapsburg husband, and fell into a deep emotional depression from which she never recovered. She followed the casket on its long trip across Spain, and on more than one occasion forced her attendants to open the lid in order to assure herself that no one had touched the remains. Juana was judged insane and was referred to publicly as *Juana, la loca* ("Juana, the crazy one"). Thus the young Prince Charles was left without either father or mother at a very tender age.

Charles was educated in Flanders, and at Ferdinand's death in

1516,* when he was called to occupy the Spanish throne, he did not speak Spanish. He was greeted in Spain by anything but enthusiastic acclaim. Fortunately for him Cardinal Jiménez de Cisneros, the same man who had coerced the Moors of Granada into becoming Christians, had firmly held the regency until Charles arrived. When some of the rebellious nobles asked the regent what his authority was, Jiménez pointed to a long row of cannons below the conference chamber and said: "There's my authority!" With such backing Charles became king of Spain at the age of seventeen.

Nobody liked him. Charles, like his father before him, placed Flemings in high positions and quickly alienated the Spaniards. The new king was accustomed to considerable pomp and luxury in Flanders, and clearly showed his dislike of the austere Spanish court and even of his Spanish subjects. Several of the towns expressed open resentment of the king's actions and attitude. Charles was not in any mood to compromise, so in 1520 the townsmen prepared for rebellion. This revolt of the *comuneros*, or commoners, had strong support in the municipalities. Fifteen towns sent their representatives to Avila, where they made their formal demands on the king. When he disregarded them, the rebellion broke out. It produced several noteworthy heroes, but no strong single leader. Had the commoners won this struggle, Spain might have achieved a constitutional monarchy during the years of her glory. But the commoners, who were ineffectively organized, were crushed by the superior forces of the crown, and their leaders were executed. The nobles had backed the king in this fight, insuring the triumph of an absolutist regime.

The suppression of the commoners was the first manifestation of something that was to recur many times in the future history of Spain: the defeat of the best and noblest hopes of the Spanish people in every move they have made for a decent government. It happened again with the failure of the liberal Cortes of Cádiz in 1812; it was repeated with the failure of the First Republic in the 1870's; and the final disastrous repetition was the failure of the Second Republic in the 1930's followed by the bloody and catastrophic civil war. Moderation in government has never stood much of a chance in Spain. After the defeat of the commoners Charles

* After Isabella's death Ferdinand married an eighteen-year-old French princess, Germaine de Foix. It was widely reported that he took medications in order to increase his virility and that these hastened his death.

sent four thousand German troops through the disaffected towns, thus adding insult to injury. Later, with a more reasoned judgment, he relented and made an expansive gesture of pardoning those who had been involved in the insurrection.

Charles's reign placed Spain in the mainstream of European politics. From his mother, Queen Juana of Castile, and his grandfather, Ferdinand of Aragon, the young prince had inherited Castile, Aragon, Navarre, Sardinia, Sicily, the kingdom of Naples, the Roussillon, and the Spanish colonies in Africa and the New World; from his father, Philip the Handsome, he had inherited large territories in northern and eastern France, the Low Countries, and Luxembourg. He was also an heir of his grandfather, Maximilian I, ruler of the Hapsburg dominions in Austria and Bohemia, and emperor of the German or Holy Roman Empire. At Maximilian's death in 1519, Charles succeeded him in both positions, and thus became monarch of one of the largest empires in history, certainly the greatest in Europe since Charlemagne. It was, however, a loosely joined empire, vulnerable at every extremity, and Charles's attempt to synchronize its various interests and its various regions was doomed to almost certain failure.

The king nonetheless made a noble try, gradually strengthening his hand and centralizing his power. In Spain he replaced his Flemings with loyal Spaniards. He built up the strength of the Spanish army. He attacked with vigor the North African pirates and the Turks. He became engaged in wars all over Europe and America. In Europe the aim that guided his life was to overcome the Protestants and establish an immense Catholic empire. In America his main idea was to grasp as much land and as much wealth as possible, and for both these purposes there was the Spanish conquistador and the professional *tercio*, the best infantry contingent in Europe. Titian has left a famous canvas of the emperor dressed in his coat of mail, mounted on a fine charger, like Don Quixote ready to sally forth and attack the whole world.

Charles's crusading spirit was no mere pose. He regarded himself as the personal champion of Christendom, and on one occasion he challenged the king of France, Francis I, to meet him in single combat "man to man, and I promise to meet him armed or unarmed, in my shirt, with sword and dagger, on land or sea, on a bridge or an island, in a closed field, or in front of our armies, or wherever and however he may wish, and it be fair." Charles never met Francis in knightly combat, but he did once take the French king prisoner in battle. Francis then uttered his famous phrase, "All is lost but honor."

By far the most important event in the reign of Charles V (1516–1556) was the opening up of the New World. Under Charles the Spanish conquistador made world history: Cortés in Mexico, Pizarro in Peru, Valdivia in Chile, Mendoza in Argentina, Quesada in Colombia, De Soto in the United States, Alvarado in Guatemala, and many others. Within a few brief years Spain conquered and was governing a territory two or three dozen times the size of the mother country. Great wealth began to flow to Spain from Mexico and Peru. After the treasures of Montezuma and Atahualpa were exhausted, the mines of gold and silver continued to pour forth a torrent of riches for years to come. Many of those who went to the colonies became wealthy overnight. Even the common soldier prospered.

These people with money clamored for the manufactured products they needed, and their demand was a shot in the arm for Spanish industries. Suddenly textile mills blossomed up all over Spain. The very towns which had been smashed in the revolt of the commoners now leapt forward as centers of industry. Medina del Campo, center of the revolt, became the hub of a thriving manufacturing activity. Goods were shipped to the New World and sold at enormous profits.

Toledo, Segovia, Valladolid became busy manufacturing towns. . . . There was a rush from the country to the towns, where wages were rising by leaps and bounds. The manufacturing hands in Toledo were quintupled between 1525 and 1550; in some towns beggars and vagabonds were forced into the factories. The cloth trade spread southward to Granada; the silk manufacture spread northwards to Seville and thence to Toledo. We find the young Mary, Queen of Scots, receiving a gift of blue and red silk stockings from Valencia, as being of the finest quality in the world.[27]

Within a couple of decades Spain was well on her way to becoming an industrial power. But here too all the wrong decisions were made, and the king was responsible for most of them. He continued to spend huge sums in fruitless European wars and was always at his wits' end as to how to pay for them. The wealth of the New World was thrown away in futile military campaigns. Prices went sky-high in Spain; Between 1500 and 1600 the cost of the ordinary necessities increased by 400 per cent. The crown resorted to price fixing, heavy taxation, the establishment of royal monopolies (on salt, for example), the prohibition of certain exports, laws against luxury in dressing, complete regimentation of colonial trade, and many other senseless practices. None of these expedients worked for long. Charles was then forced to borrow wherever he could, paying interest of 30 to 40 percent. This meant, very simply, that all the gold and silver arriving from America barely touched Spain at Cádiz or Seville before it was transshipped to the international bankers and businessmen in the other European countries. Spain was no more than a funnel for the passage of this wealth into foreign coffers.

The Spanish colonial monopoly was equally disastrous. The logic behind it made sense, but did not work in practice. Spain might be compared to an enterprising prospector who has struck it rich, and then wants to keep others off his stake. Why let England, France, or Holland profit from the mines in the Spanish New World? Spain herself would rigorously control this great wealth. In 1503 she established in Seville the House of Trade, or *Casa de Contratación*, which was to direct all colonial commerce. Only Spaniards could trade with the colonies, goods must be carried in Spanish ships, and for protection these ships must travel together in convoys. The output of the mines would thus reach Spain undiminished, and Spain, in turn, would sell to the colonies the things they needed to buy. It sounded like an airtight system, profitable to both parties. England, Holland, and France later established similar monopolies, and they worked relatively well. The big difference was that while these countries had strong, productive industries which could supply the wants of their colonies at reasonable prices, Spain had a rapidly weakening industrial system, a declining navy, and a disintegrating merchant marine. She was saying to her colonies: "Take no other milk but mine," when she had no milk to give. To make matters worse the convoys sailed irregularly, and were often attacked and robbed by buccaneers or foreign enemies.

The American colonies, unable to obtain what they needed from the mother country, bought them in any way they could. A thriving contraband trade sprang up. In some years this illegitimate commerce supplied at least 75 per cent of the colonial imports. The result was that while an abundance of gold and silver was produced in the Spanish colonies, which indeed tripled the total European supply of those precious metals within a century, there was no real wealth in Spain herself, no lasting economic prosperity, no permanent progress. And in the colonies had grown a widespread disrespect for the laws of the mother country. By the end of Charles's reign Spain had slumped back into her proverbial poverty.

As early as 1535 the greatest poet of the age, and one of the greatest soldiers, Garcilaso de la Vega, saw the writing on the wall when he wrote:

> And everything is gone, even the name
> Of house and home and wife and memory.
> And what's the use of it? A little fame?
> The nation's thanks? A place in history?
> One day they'll write a book, and then we'll see.[21]

In 1535 these words were certainly more prophetic than expressive of the actual situation. But the Emperor Charles continued without abatement his exhaustive policy against all who opposed him. For forty years he was engaged in warfare with nearly every nation in Europe. He made war on the Pope, and reduced the papacy to a role of subservience to the Spanish state. In 1527 his German troops sacked Rome, and a company of them which was quartered in the Vatican built fires on the floor of the Sistine Chapel, thus irreparably damaging with smoke and soot the beautiful murals of Michelangelo. In 1545 the Pope granted Charles half the ecclesiastic revenues of Spain, and permitted him also to sell vast church lands in order to use the income. Always the wars continued, with the spilling of Spain's lifeblood in Europe, and with the draining away of her youngest and most enterprising men in the conquest and colonization of the New World.

In the early part of his reign Charles had taken an attitude of tolerance toward religious criticism. He is said to have been a great admirer of Erasmus. But the emperor's many long sojourns outside of Spain gave the religious orders their opportunity, and they began to clamp down on every semblance of religious freedom. Spain's two outstanding humanists, Luis Vives and Juan de Valdés, left the country never to return. Vives went to England, where he became a professor at Oxford University and attained international stature as a thinker. It is curious to note that both Erasmus and Vives were invited to Spain to teach university courses; still more unusual is the fact that neither of them accepted the invitation. The success of the Protestant revolt outside of Spain meant the triumph of the intolerant "Counter Reformation" inside of Spain. Spanish students were prohibited from studying in foreign universities, where it was feared they might become contaminated with heretical Protestant notions. The church began to proscribe the reading of certain books, and published its first *Index expurgatorius* in 1546. Spanish thought was circumscribed within a narrow orthodoxy which prevented the free influx of foreign ideas. In thought as in economy and government Spain began to lag behind in the procession of European nations.

Charles's son Philip was born in 1527. At his birth the infant's Portuguese mother had asked that her face be covered with a sheet so that no one might see her expression of pain. Philip's mother and father were first cousins, and the family tendency toward epilepsy ran strong in the children. Philip's two brothers died in their infancy from this disease. The future king of Spain was only one-fourth Spanish in blood and had the physical constitution of a sickly epileptic. He was a "grave and silent child, with a fair pink and white skin and silky yellow hair." The very air around him buzzed with prayers and admonitions against the wicked heretics. Philip soon developed the mind of a rigorous fanatic. He was constantly overhearing conversations in which his father, the emperor, appeared on the side of the Almighty engaged in a life-and-death struggle against the powers of evil. Everything Spanish and Catholic was good; everything that was non-Spanish and non-Catholic was evil. Charles had made a strong beginning toward a one-church state, and Philip made certain that Protestantism never took root in Spain.

Philip II came to the throne in 1556, when he was twenty-nine. His father, world-weary and exhausted from his many campaigns, abdicated and retired to the monastery in Yuste, in the sunny land of Extremadura. Here he passed the final two years of his life in meditation and prayer.* Philip did not take over the kingship without a long apprenticeship.

His father had made him regent at the age of sixteen, and Charles was so frequently out of the country that Philip was almost a coequal of the emperor in sharing the royal power. Charles's wisest and most loyal councilors aided him in governing, but the emperor warned his son to trust none of them separately. The only safe way to rule was to play them off one against the other and to make certain that

---

* In Yuste the ex-emperor also spent countless hours in a vain attempt to synchronize his many clocks. It is recorded that after repeated failures he exclaimed: "How could I possibly have hoped to unite all my dominions when I cannot make these clocks strike the hour together?"

final action was always the decision of the king. Even the duke of Alba was dissected for Philip's benefit; Charles referred to him as "ambitious, sanctimonious, and hypocritical; and perhaps he may even try to tempt you with women." But Charles also made clear that Alba was a grandee of considerable power and intelligence, and that in foreign affairs he was the best man in the kingdom. Hence, when his father abdicated, Philip was already a well-trained king, solemn, dedicated, suspicious, intransigent.

Philip's reign began with a spectacular *auto-de-fe* at Valladolid at which several "heretics" were burned at the stake. The king regarded heresy as a damnable thing, one to be punished with cruel efficiency. Philip now stood on the stage alone, the most powerful monarch in Christendom. He held slavishly to the distrustful absolutism of his father, and believed deeply in his divine inspiration as ruler. His methods of statecraft were rigid and unadaptable. He was no neophyte at the game of espionage and duplicity. He was anxious to hold all of the strings in his own hand, and thus wore himself out with the dreary routine of government.

He was pitted against opponents whose opportunism and elastic consciences gave them an enormous advantage over him, and the task which he inherited could hardly have had a more unfortunate champion than the monarch who led it to defeat. His sense of duty was overwhelmingly great. He was modest, laborious, and conscientious, almost to a fault; a good husband and a good father; and he strenuously did his best throughout his life, according to his limited lights. He accepted his great inheritance as a sacred trust, but his qualities were not equal to his task, and he was a splendid failure.[27]

Philip was personally pious, but he always viewed religion as an instrument of state policy. His father Charles had made war on the Pope, and imperial troops had mercilessly looted Rome. Several pontiffs had smarted under the Spanish yoke, and Paul IV, a Neapolitan, became infuriated at the Spanish invaders who had taken over a good part of Italy. Invoking the aid of the Sultan Solyman, Paul IV blasted forth in invectives against both Charles and Philip, and in 1556, the very year that Philip became king, the Pontiff violently excommunicated them both from the church. The bull of excommunication referred to the king as "the son of iniquity, Philip of Austria, offspring of the so-called Emperor Charles, who passes himself off as King of Spain; following in the footsteps of his father and rivalling him in iniquity."

But Philip was too astute to let this wrangle get out of hand. He asked the Doge of Venice to negotiate, and the duke of Alba "sulkily entered Rome, not as a conqueror but as a pretended penitent." But the fact of the matter was that Philip considered himself as ordained by God as "His Catholic Majesty," and also as especial paladin to defend the faith in the way that he, God-inspired, considered most appropriate. He would brook no interference by Rome in the Spanish church. If a war on the temporal power of the Pope was unavoidable, that was unfortunate. If the people of the Low Countries insisted on remaining Protestant heretics, he would clamp down the screws until they saw the true light, for Philip, in his own words, "would rather not rule at all if he had to rule over a nation of heretics." This dogmatic, single-minded intensity of belief lost Spain the Flemish provinces by driving those people toward Protestantism, which began to take on the dimensions of a symbolic crusade against the intolerable cruelty and injustice of the Spanish oppression. In his own country Philip's persecution of suspected heretics was merciless and unconditional. Even Archbishop Carranza of Toledo, primate of all Spain, was indicted and deposed by the Inquisition because of his admiration of Erasmus. Despite the protests of the Pope, Archbishop Carranza suffered eighteen years of imprisonment and woe before finally he died of despair, with a wasted body and a broken heart. Nine other bishops were also forced to suffer the indignity of humiliating penances. Gone were the days when Erasmus, once the friend of Charles V, could be admired in Spain. Gone was the right to use freely man's God-given and inquiring mind. Spain was sunken now in an ossified dogmatism from which the nation has not even yet recovered.

In the year 1561 Philip decided to move the capital of Spain to Madrid, which was then only a straggling and unimportant country town. Madrid was in the very center of the country, and would make a fine hub for the absolute rule of the nation that he envisaged. Besides, it would be a capital that the king himself would mold, and Philip always regarded himself as the great architect of Spanish destiny. The fact that Madrid was a drab town without important history or traditions made it doubly acceptable. He would give it a history. He would give it a heart, his own. No, it would be more accurate to say that he would give it a paper heart, for Philip II was *el rey papelero* ("king of official papers,") each one of which he must examine, digest, ponder, pass on, alter, cancel out, extend, amend, or simply sign. He must see them all. He was indeed "the paper king," and Madrid was capital of his endless files. If in this change of capitals he lost the appeal of tradition, he gained the advantage of ruling from a city which was not associated with Castilian supremacy, and this, he thought, would facilitate his rule over the outlying separatist provinces: Aragon, Catalonia, the Basque country, Andalusia.

The very existence of Madrid, therefore, is political. There was neither a historic, an economic, nor a military reason for constructing a great city in the midst of those gaunt and depopulated Castilian plains. The three cities which had recently been serving as capitals, Toledo, Segovia, and Valladolid, were all hallowed by age. Madrid, neither temple nor fortress, was an upstart in the list of Spanish cities. If Castile had been able to maintain its lead with the advent of the industrial revolution, Madrid would have made an excellent manufacturing town, but Barcelona and Bilbao, with a more enlightened population, quickly jumped ahead of the capital in this area. Hence Madrid became a kind of political dead weight athwart the stomach of Spain; it was neither ancient, nor beautiful, nor prosperous, nor forward-looking. Rather it was like Philip himself: severe, riddled with bureaucracy, unlovely, a place only where the laws were made and the politicos lived. When Castile lost out to Barcelona, Valencia, and Bilbao as centers of production, Madrid became emblematic of this loss and held back the progress of the entire country. It is still a great city surrounded by a wilderness. The traveler in all truth must be willing to recognize that sunshine, gushing fountains, trees and flowers, pure air and water, and lovemaking have in more recent days made it an attractive tourist center. Its tremendous bureaucracy has also made it a haven for every political parasite and every hopeless rural laborer in half of Spain. To Spaniards from other parts of the country Madrid has thus been in turn an object of distrust, of fear, of violence, sometimes of hope, but seldom of affection.

A couple of years after moving his capital to Madrid Philip began construction of the *Escorial*, the greatest architectural monument of his reign, thirty-two miles northwest of the new capital. This colossus in gray, of grim and severe Renaissance style, stands in a small valley in the midst of the bleak mountains that crisscross the Castilian plateau. It was built as a place to bury the royal families of Spain, and Philip's father, Charles V, was the first whose body came to rest in the pantheon of the kings. With its greenish and dirty reflecting pool, so unlike the clean, flowing waters of Moorish gardens, and its huge, forbidding granite walls, more like those of an immense prison than like those of a palace or cathedral, the *Escorial* is the stony epitome of Philip II. The building is as grim and unyielding as the Spanish Inquisition, as stern and somber as the paper king himself, as gray and gloomy as the royal heart in the latter half of the sixteenth century. One well-known critic of architecture has written, "In spite of its lack of imagination and its dreariness, the influence of the *Escorial* was profound. No other building ever so affected the trend of Spanish architecture."

Philip's father, the Emperor Charles, also left his monument in the unfinished circular Renaissance palace built within the precincts of the Alhambra, in Granada. This palace stands today, symbolically much like the *Escorial*, a circle of rounded columns which contrast harshly with the glorious color and light of the Moorish palace, a portion of which was destroyed in order that Charles might build his own courtly structure. It is fitting to point out that both of these buildings of the great Spanish kings symbolize destruction and death. Charles demolished a part of the Alhambra to construct his unfinished palace. Philip thought in terms of a colossal pantheon of the departed kings. Charles's palace is circular, like life in the Middle Ages. Philip's mausoleum is the frightening embodiment of a departed glory. Both monuments are cold, gray, prison-like, hard, and unlovely. Both leave the impression of unyielding rock. Perhaps they are the last castles of the grandeur that was Spain.

In the 1560's, as work on the *Escorial* progressed, Philip was head over heels in debt. The foreign wars continued, Flanders was a continuous thorn in his side, the English buccaneers were making his life miserable on the sea, and Spanish industry, unable to compete with that of other European countries, was stagnating. On several occasions the king confiscated all the bullion that arrived from America in the closely guarded fleets. It vanished quickly and he had to borrow more. But the interest he paid to foreign bankers was astronomical. His debts continued to increase alarmingly. In some years he spent five years' income. In 1575 he simply repudiated all of his foreign debts. Taxes became intolerable, and the economy began to break down completely. People were thrown out of jobs, and the streets became infested with beggars, *pícaros*, parasites, run-down petty noblemen, soldiers who had returned from the wars without money and without hope, useless derelicts and vagabonds of all descriptions. Aversion to honest labor became a national calamity. The Spanish picaresque novel, in which the protagonist is an anti-hero, a rogue, a sharper, gives a full account of what was happening in Spain. The exhausted country was gliding over reality, not coming to grips with the facts of history, asking for a handout or for some magic to suddenly change all that into a different life. They never found it.

With his usual bullheaded intensity Philip chose this time to turn his attention on the *Moriscos* of Andalusia, who were still wearing their Moorish clothes, who still spoke in Arabic, and who were probably still Moslems beneath their enforced conversion, more than half a century before. On several occasions had Charles made an attempt to apply the whip to this element of the population, but they had always been able to buy him off. Despite his desperate need of funds, Philip was unmoved by monetary offers. In 1567 he banned all Moslem practices and applied the full force of the national government to make the ban effective. The *Moriscos*

were forbidden to wear any distinctive garb, and the women were to appear with their faces uncovered. They were not allowed to have locks on their doors, their warm baths were made illegal; and above all, they might use no other language but Castilian, and acknowledge no other faith but the Christian.[27]

This edict was to be enforced with brutal penalties.

The *Moriscos* were stung into open rebellion. For two years Andalusia was the scene of bitter fighting. Don Juan de Austria, the king's illegitimate half brother, was sent to quell the revolt, which he did most efficiently. Then, in spite of Don Juan's most earnest pleas, the entire population of Granada was uprooted en masse and shipped to other parts of Spain. The south was now left without the most enterprising element of its inhabitants, while the regions to which the *Moriscos* were herded were saddled with a suspect and unassimilable minority. The fruitful, green fields of Andalusia became a vast desert.

Almost immediately after his victory over the *Moriscos* (1570) Don Juan de Austria was put in command of a powerful Spanish, Roman, and Venetian fleet of two hundred ships which met the Turkish fleet in the Bay of Lepanto, near Corinth, and destroyed it. Moslem power in the Mediterranean never recovered from this mighty blow. Today this naval engagement is remembered most often because one Miguel de Cervantes took part in it and was severely wounded in his left arm. He was ever afterward known as *el manco de Lepanto* ("the maimed fellow of Lepanto").

In the 1580's Philip felt the repeated stings of the English navy, particularly of Drake, who swooped into Cadiz Harbor and "singed the beard of the Spanish king" just as a great fleet was being readied for the invasion of England. These attacks infuriated Philip, and he redoubled his efforts to repay the British in kind. In 1588 his Invincible Armada sallied forth on this crusade. It was defeated by two elements: raging seas and the smaller, faster, more maneuverable ships under the command of Francis Drake. More than half the Spanish fleet and two-thirds of the men were lost in this memorable encounter.

After twenty-two years of labor, with three hundred men working round the clock, the *Escorial* was finally finished in 1584. Philip himself often sat in a chair cut out of mountain rock above the valley and observed the construction. In his declining years he retired to the grim monastery to live and to die. Here on these rocky fields the king had built "a cell for himself and a palace for God." He filled the great library with priceless manuscripts and paintings, and attended services in the huge-domed chapel. He occupied an unpretentious inside room, near the choir, from which he could hear the swish of vestments as mass was held. As his body weakened, he was unable to move about and sat for hours on end in a special chair with his swollen foot raised above the other. Several times he watched them rehearse his own funeral. Ulcers covered his body, and as antiseptics were unknown, he suffered the agonies of the damned as they spread and festered, often completely covered with insects. For nearly two months he lingered between life and death, a withering but breathing corpse. Thus in 1598 King Philip II, under whom Spain had soared, staggered, and fallen from the heights of her glory, finally expired.

His own poor body tormented by tragedy, what had this king done to the body of his country? There is only one way to put it. The physicians of those times, and even of centuries later, believed that when a person was ill the surest way to cure him was with a good bloodletting. Many a strong man was bled to death by a foolish doctor. Even our own George Washington was sent to a quicker demise by this stupid treatment. But unfortunately it was the universal remedy, and was applied with a vigor that gainsaid all reason. Philip

II of Spain was only the poor physician of his country. When he saw it sick and trembling, he decided to open the veins, and let the blood run out. Its flow was endless. It ran to Flanders in an ugly red stream, it ran to England and was lost in the salt sea waters, it ran in a great river to America and there mingled with the blood of Indians, it ran in the streets and gutters of Spain when there was heresy, it ran in Andalusia when the *Moriscos* were slain, it ran at Lepanto, in Italy, in France, in Africa, in Portugal, on the high seas; and the body of Spain grew weaker and weaker until there was no strength in it. This is the true recapitulation of the reign of Philip II. Spaniards who can still face their history and say almost with pride "But that is what we are, we cannot help it, at heart we are most of us like Philip," these people should pause and consider the awful implication of those portentous words.

As the nation's golden opportunity was wasted and its lifeblood spilled on battlefields far and wide, the face of Spain underwent a gradual change. The process of urbanization became more rapid, and there was feverish activity in the building trades, particularly for the government and for the church. A few wealthy families erected splendid mansions and filled them with art objects from all over the world: tapestries from Flanders and Italy, silver from the New World, Venetian glassware, richly carved Spanish and Italian furniture often encrusted with silver, gold, and ivory, leather work of the finest quality in Europe, glazed tiles (*azulejos*) of graceful blue-and-white designs for which Spain was justly noted, exotic items from the Orient brought across the Pacific on the Manila galleons.

But these things were only for the very few who had risen to the top. The population of the country as a whole was now more clearly than ever divided into two classes: the few who were rich, and the many who were poor. Between the two there yawned a great abyss. The general aspect for living in the cities and towns of Spain showed little improvement over medieval days. Garbage was still hurled into the middle of the street. Sidewalks were unknown until the latter part of the eighteenth century. Hence, slop, water, mud, and dust were thrown upon all pedestrians by those who passed down the streets mounted or in carriages. The ordinary dwellings were of bricks or adobe; only the church, the nobles, and the king were able to afford buildings of stone. Streets were lighted by oil lamps, which let off clouds of smoke. Houses were seldom aligned straight up and down the streets, but were piled and cluttered about here and there with no concern for design, hygiene, or ventilation. The cities were undoubtedly uglier and dirtier, and life in them was more complex and confined, than in medieval times. The expanded universe and fragmentation of the faith had destroyed the cohesive reality of the Middle Ages and put in its place an illusive majesty of overseas dominions. The individual reflected the national uncertainty and insecurity. He sought a gay and carefree life.

Particularly from Madrid southward, the central patio was where family and social life were carried on. The windows that faced the streets were covered with iron gratings at which stood the lovers and serenaders so often mentioned in the literature of the epoch. The phrase *comer hierro*, or "eating the iron," was the current idiom for "courting," so close did the gallant stick his face to his beloved's on the other side of those ponderous and rigid bars.

The inns of those days were infamous, as the picaresque tales all attest. In these novels it is a frequent thing for a ravenous character to gorge himself on a foul-tasting meal served under filthy conditions, only to have to bolt outside to relieve himself of its poisonous aftermath. It is popularly believed that the word *venta* for inn derives from the proverbial expression *vender gato por liebre*, which means to sell a cat for a hare, a phrase that appears with alarming frequency in the romances of roguery, as if it were almost a natural thing for the innkeeper to do.

The main Spanish dish was the *olla podrida*, or the rotten pottage, a name more often true than not, which consisted of pork, beef, or mutton, plus the omnipresent *garbanzos* ("chick peas"), popularized by the Carthaginians centuries ago, and cabbage, carrots, squash, garlic, pepper, olive oil, vinegar, and bacon, all stewed together to a thick consistency. Many proverbs attest the nationwide popularity of the *olla*; for example, *vaca y carnero, olla de caballero* ("beef and mutton together make a real gentleman's stew"), *olla sin verdura no tiene gracia ni hartura* ("stew without vegetables is neither tasty or filling"). The *olla* should unquestionably be cooked in an earthen pot, and if properly prepared must simmer for hours until it is done. It is still sold occasionally on the streets on market or fair days out of a huge three-legged pot under which a fire is kept going constantly. This custom is now more prevalent in Mexico and in the Andes than it is in Spain; in these places steaming soups and stews of many kinds are served from large cast-iron containers. Cheeses, generally made from goat or sheep's milk, were always available at the inns, as was wine in the old *botas*, or wineskins made of hides, from which one drank by holding over the head and pouring downward, catching the stream in one's gullet without ever touching mouth to the opening. Coarse bread dipped into the heavy *olla podrida* stew was the final ingredient of the limited diet day in and day out.

As a drink hot chocolate took the place of coffee or tea. Ever since Cortés had reported the remarkable qualities of this beverage, it had been popular in Spain. (The conquistador had written to the king that "a man can work all day on one cup of this marvelous drink.") It was invariably served at breakfast with a roll or a crust of bread, and was also frequently used as a refreshment in the afternoon; the women sometimes drank it at suppertime as well. Chocolate was served thick and foamy, and was cheap enough to be enjoyed by the masses as well as by the well-to-do. In 1628, when the duke of Olivares attempted to turn the sale of chocolate into a state monopoly in order to obtain funds for the bankrupt national treasury, the public raised such a hue and cry that he was forced to drop the idea.

The first Spanish cookbook appeared in the early sixteenth century; it was translated from the Catalan. By the middle of the century many such books on the culinary art had appeared. The people at court and the wealthy aristocrats began to eat a true baroque menu of varied and highly seasoned foods. One old account lists the foods which were supplied to the duke of Mayena when he arrived in Madrid in 1612 to negotiate a double marriage between the royal families of France and Spain. *On each meat day* the royal pantry supplied him and his entourage with the following items: 8 ducks, 26 capons, 70 hens, 100 pairs of pigeons, 50 partridges, 100 hares, 25 sheep, 40 pounds of lard, 12 hams, 3 pigs, 8 bushels of assorted fruits, and six different kinds of wine. On fast days the supply of seafood that went to the duke was equally impressive: 100 pounds of trout, 15 pounds of eels, 100 of mullet, 50 pounds each of four different kinds of preserved fish, 1,000 eggs, 100 pounds of butter, 100 pounds of codfish, and 100 pounds of anchovies![31]

At the inns and restaurants people all ate at a long wooden table in the middle of which was a big knife anchored to the table by a chain. This was passed along so that each diner in turn might use it if he wished. The bedrooms of the public inns were primitive common dormitories in which several men slept together on rude and lumpy quilts or just plain straw. In the *Quixote* Cervantes describes several of these bedrooms: "Don Quixote's hard, scanty, beggarly and miserable bed was the first of four in that dingy room; next to it was Sancho's kennel, which consisted of nothing but a bed-mat and a coverlet." In another place in the novel the author refers to the beds of the muleteers as "nothing but the pannels and coverings of the mules all thrown in a heap." Bedbugs, of course, were so common that the lack of them was a cause for concern. Lest it be thought that this description is unfair to Spain, we might here point out that Elizabethan England was in an almost identical state. The Elizabethan audience stank to high heaven, and it was often difficult for the actors to go on with the performance when all the vents were closed. British inns of those years were in the same category as those of Spain. ·

It is little wonder that the Spaniard liked "to take the sun" and to "enjoy life in the open air." Walking and parading in carriages or on whatever mount one could afford were the main everyday pleasures of these folk. Meeting and chatting with one's friends was an inseparable part of these strolls. Even business was transacted on the streets —anything to get away from those cold, dirty, dingy, cramped quarters that the people called home.

Madrid, Seville, and Toledo were the three main cities of the country during the Golden Age. When Philip II moved the capital from Toledo to Madrid in 1561, at least ten thousand government officials and members of their families came along with him. Toledo suddenly went into a decline, and Madrid spurted up in the scale. Although lacking in traditions it became a regular ant heap of activity, the streets teemed with people, the theater flourished, and *pícaros*, beggars, sharpers, and derelicts of all kinds poured into the capital. At first there was not nearly enough room in the new capital to take care of the huge influx of officials, so the king had a law passed granting the federal government use of the second floor of every building that went up. Like most laws in Spain this one too soon became a dead letter, for after its passage almost nobody constructed a two-story building. In 1623 there were approximately 10,000 dwellings in the capital. Of these, 5,436 were confined to a single story, obviously to elude government seizure. These were given the ugly name of *casas de malicia* ("houses of evil intent") but it made no difference. The king had to find other ways to procure housing for his minions. Madrid thus took on the flat and unimpressive appearance which still characterizes the city today. It also grew up lacking almost completely the picturesque aspects that characterize so many south European cities: Lisbon, Granada, and Valencia, for example.

Dress in the country regions of Spain was often very picturesque, but city clothes during the Golden Age were not particularly distinctive or colorful. The gentleman invariably wore a tightly fitting jacket, with a high stiff collar, short pantaloons, stockings, and the classic Spanish cape. During the reign of Philip II the cape became the *sine qua non* of every well-dressed man. The ladies wore a dress with hoops up to 1639, when this was prohibited because it had become the distinctive attire of the prostitutes. The hair was generally worn in the form of a diadem, and often there was a headdress with feathers or a ladies' hat with a hanging fringe. Gloves were required for all dress occasions. When on promenade women's faces were heavily made up with red and white powders, often absurdly overdone, as the popular dramas frequently mention. The most popular gifts among women of all classes were perfumes and perfumed articles, especially perfumed pastilles, which they invariably carried around with them in their embroidered handbags. Other common gifts, among the rich, were golden chains, plumes, rings, leather gloves, jewelry, lace handkerchiefs, and crucifixes. Among the poor, shoddy importations from France were the most popular presents: pins, strings of false pearls, fans, rosaries, and other cheap trifles which were sold by foreign hawkers on the main streets of nearly every Spanish city. So much money was spent by the wealthy on overwrought furniture, vases, gilded and silvered carriages, gold- and silver-threaded canopies, laces, draperies, and rugs that in 1611 a statute was passed limiting the purchase of these "articles of pure ostentation."

The bullfight was, during the Golden Age, as it had been for centuries past, the great fiesta for the masses. Its history goes back to ancient times: One author mentions Julius Caesar fighting a bull on horseback in the Colosseum in Rome; other authorities simply trace the spectacle back to the Roman circus with its combats between animals and men. Still others claim that the killing of the bull is a ritual that may be traced back to the Minoan culture on the island of Crete, many hundreds of years before Christ. A few authorities state categorically that the Moors of Spain popularized the bullfight in Spain. In any case, it is a fiesta that is hoary with age and tradition. Alfonso the Learned mentions it in his *Siete Partidas*, and decries it; Queen Isabella also abhorred the spectacle, as have other kings and queens of Spain. But the tradition was so deeply rooted that this made little difference. When Philip V, the first Bourbon, came to the Spanish throne in 1700, the masses shouted to him: "Give us bulls, your majesty!" In this particular regard, therefore, Spain has been a sort of continuation of the Roman tradition of "bread and circuses," and for Spaniards the word "circus" had the specific meaning of man against bull. Why the bull and not some other animal, for example, the lion or the tiger? Perhaps for the reasons of ritual suggested above, but more likely because the bull is the only animal that can be counted on always *to attack*. Without the certainty of this attack there can be no true fiesta with its display of cape, footwork, grace, and bravery, and the final moment of truth when the sword goes into the bull's heart. Without the bull's attack the show would turn into an ugly butchery. Animals and men would die, but without meaning, without glory.

Up to the late seventeenth century the bullfight was a spectacle in which the men who fought were always of the nobility. This was the way they proved their manhood to their ladies, to their peers, and to their underlings. In the late Golden Age professional *toreros* began to replace the hidalgos. These paid fighters usually came from the lower classes, and the whole feeling of the fiesta changed. So did the manner of fighting. The gentlemen had always fought the bull with lances on horseback; and horsemanship was a principal part of the spectacle, as it still is in the Portuguese rings of today. The bull was speared until he was *hors de combat*, and then was dispatched by a dozen lackeys who drove their swords into his vitals. The final death of the noble animal was an anticlimax to what had gone before.

If the bull proved to be too mean or tricky he was sometimes sent to an inglorious death. One reporter describes such an event which took place before Philip IV: A small door was opened and several bulls were invited to pass through it. Instead of freedom each animal immediately found himself sliding down a wooden chute which dropped him several feet onto the riverbank below. Ordinarily, when this happened, the bull fell dead below, but on occasion he was only mortally hurt and would roar for a long while, to the great delight of the multitude. In the ring in Valladolid a tricky or evil bull was sent down a greased slide into the water below, where the fight continued from boats. The animal was chased from the water to the land, and then back into the water, much like a harried rat. Such cruel deviations of the fiesta were, however, not by any means the norm.

Many efforts were made to stop the bullfight, but without avail. Pope Pius V in 1567 prohibited the fiesta on penalty of excommunication, but in 1575 Gregory XIII mitigated this by limiting the prohibition to members of the clergy, who were not allowed to attend the fiesta at any time, "but especially on days of religious festivals." In 1596, at the behest of King Philip II, Pope Clement VIII lifted the ban completely.

Up to the eighteenth century the bullfight was held in the main town plaza, the surrounding buildings serving as the benches. Every window, balcony, and roof top was filled with fans, and the numbers of balconies and windows were greater than in any other part of town. Additional temporary stands were put up around the edge of the plaza. Many thousands of persons were able to observe the fight from these points of vantage. The plaza in Madrid was surrounded by buildings that were four or five stories high, and the sight of all these teeming with people from roof top to bottom was something to behold. One old print of the Golden Age shows half-a-dozen bulls in the ring at the same time; four horsemen are fighting them with their lances, and several lackeys on foot are ready to attack with their swords. The bullfight under such conditions must have been more complex than a three-ring circus, with the drama of life and death at a point of crisis somewhere in the plaza at every moment.

It is worth noting that the Spanish term for bullfight is "fiesta of the bulls," or *corrida de toros*, "running of the bulls." The word "fight" is not used, nor is the spectacle ever regarded as a sport in our sense of the word. It is a deadly ritual in which man slays the animal; the bull invariably dies. The whole thing is a kind of sacrifice; not a sacrifice to God but a sacrifice of a noble and courageous animal in order to prove man's dominance over the greatest strength and bravery that the kingdom of the beasts can offer.

The children of Spain play at bullfighting much as the children of England play at leapfrog, or those of the United States at baseball. The cry of *toros* is heard in the streets of every town and city in the country, and the term *hacer novillos* ("to bullfight with calves") is the common idiom for "to play hooky" from school. Many other common phrases are based on the fiesta; *más cornadas da el hambre que los toros*, or "hunger gives more gorings than do the bulls," is one which reveals the whole sorry spectacle of poverty-stricken Spanish life. During the past few decades bullfighting has fallen into a decline, and while there are still wonderful *corridas* now and then, the Golden Age seems to have gone forever. Football, that is, football European style, or soccer, now attracts far more fans in Spain than does the ancient spectacle. Perhaps the shift is only temporary. Who knows?

The bullfight did not, of course, attract the attention of the entire Spanish public. Religious festivities, processions, and ceremonies came near to achieving such unanimous appeal. It was in these celebrations that the pomp and solemnity of the Catholic Church showed to best advantage. The causes for such celebrations were almost infinite: a fiesta in honor of the local virgin or saint, a canonization, the appointment of a bishop or cardinal, the foundation or consecration of a church or monastery, the arrival of one of the universally celebrated Christian holidays, and of course, the formidable *auto de fe*, or act of faith, at which those condemned by the Inquisition were publicly punished, many of them strangled or burned in the inquisitorial flames.

Nearly everyone who has written about the Spanish Inquisition is careful to point out that this institution was not limited to Spain, and that religious fanaticism and cruelty were not exclusively Roman Catholic qualities. Catholics, Anglicans, and Puritans were persecuted and killed in Britain, Savonarola and Bruno were slain in Italy; and France had numerous fanatical religious massacres, as did Switzerland, Holland, and nearly every other country in Europe. Hence, it is true that Spain was not a unique case when it came to religious intolerance during the Golden Age. However, Spain *is* a unique case when it comes to how long this intolerance lasted. The Inquisition itself was not abolished until 1820, and at the time the first edition of this book came out, in 1963, there was no religious freedom for non-Catholics in Spain. Spanish Catholics, therefore, cannot boast that such intolerance belongs strictly to the past. The Spanish Catholic church, which has always been at pains to point out how Protestant nations generated and nurtured "the black legend" of Spain, sat on its hands throughout most of the Franco years when the opportunity was greatest to become a symbol of tolerance. On the part of the Spanish church, and on the part of those millions of Catholics everywhere who believe in religious tolerance, this must be deplored. Unfortunately, most Catholics in the United States also failed to speak out against this denial of religious freedom in Spain, even under a Catholic president, John Kennedy.

The *auto de fe* of the epoch of the Golden Age was a public spectacle which attracted people for many miles. The ceremony was announced far in advance, thus allowing plenty of time for the curious to arrive. The autos were held in the public plaza, where stands were raised for the spectators and special chairs were placed for the Inquisitors, priests, announcers, and distinguished personages. The public crowded into the plaza and occupied every nearby roof, window, and balcony. The guilty wore a kind of Ku Klux Klan type of toga with a high, pointed hood; those condemned to die carried a green cross and had a noose about their necks. They all slowly filed down the streets and into the plaza. The ceremony began with a sermon about the faith, and then the individual judgments were announced. The penitents whose crimes were not irreparable were publicly forgiven and received back into the bosom of the Church. Those who were to be killed were turned over to the civil authorities and were executed, always in the presence of a member of the Inquisition. This strange "washing of the hands" was perhaps thought to be a substitute for Christian charity. There is nothing to be gained by dwelling further on the Inquisition; Spaniards themselves have condemned it in words far stronger than any I would be able to employ. But let it be remembered that religious intolerance is certainly not the policy of the present government of Spain.

The most popular games and diversions of the Golden Age in Spain were cane tilting, ring spearing, chess, jousting, hunting, fireworks, folk dances of all kinds, pilgrimages to religious shrines (romerías), gambling, and of course, wenching. According to the testimony of a sixteenth century German traveler, "after clothes, women, and horses, more money was spent on gambling in Spain than on anything else." Games of cards and dice, dancing, and guitar music were invariably supplied by all the brothels (burdeles), which attracted the criminal as well as the ordinary elements of the population. In the public gaming houses gambling went on twenty-four hours a day, and many of these provided food and toilets in the game room so that the gamblers would not have to leave their activities if they felt "hot."

In cane tilting two large groups mounted on fine horses fought with each other, showing off their horsemanship. In the "ring game" a horseman charged at a small ring at full speed, attempting to spear it with his lance. The fiestas of Moors and Christians re-enacted the old battles between these two groups, and the Moors, dressed in their ancient costumes, were of course invariably defeated. When the Spaniards arrived in the New World, all of these games were transplanted, and in the last the Indian made a natural substitute for the Moor. University students in Spain, particularly those at Alcalá and Salamanca, indulged in all kinds of pranks, jokes, nocturnal brawls, and philanderings, which called for a special police force of proctors to prevent mayhem. Every university ceremony was also an occasion for great festivity. Quevedo describes many of the most depraved pranks of the university students in his novel, *El Buscón*, called in English *The Life and Adventures of Don Pablos the Sharper.* At the other end of the spectrum, courtly ceremonies became more and more lavish as the nation grew poorer and poorer. A feverish and splendid activity kept mind and eyes off the canker beneath.

8

BELLES-LETTRES IN THE GOLDEN AGE

*There are two Spains, that of forms, and that of essence;
that of forms which wear out and that of essence which
endures; that of forms which die, and that of essence
which formulates itself always anew.*

León Felipe

The literature of Spain is one of the great literatures of the world,
and one of the qualities that makes it so is an exotic fragrance from
the Moors and Jews and from those ancient African Iberians who first
settled Spain. This is also the quality that keeps Spanish literature
from being as universally accepted by the peoples of other European
cultures as might otherwise be the case, for since the days of the
Visigoths Spain has never been a completely European country. The
scholar and student of literature, however, is fully aware of the depth,
beauty, quality, quantity, and variety in the literature of Spain. Her
ballads and popular *coplas* or couplets are unparalleled in any country. Her artistic poetry can bear comparison with the very best. Her
classic theater is worthy to stand side by side with that of England
and France. Her essayists and writers of poetic, philosophic, and
analytical sketches are of topflight caliber. She gave the world its
first and perhaps greatest novel in *Don Quixote*, and her picaresque
tales represent literary realism at its height. Since Cervantes, it is true,
her novelists have not kept at the head of the list, with the possible

exception of Galdós and Pío Baroja, and in the field of the short story the Spaniards have never excelled. But if Spain lacks the short story-tellers of France, let us say, she easily balances the scales with her far more imposing popular poetry, in which France is greatly lacking. Further comparisons would simply lead to needless polemics.

Every historian of the literature of Spain agrees that the great period of Spanish letters is the *Siglo de Oro* or Golden Age, which begins (so these scholars tell us) in the year 1543 with the posthumous publication of a book of poetry by two Spaniards, the Catalan, Juan Boscán and his co-author, Garcilaso de la Vega, of Castile. The poems are strongly permeated with Italian influences and thus open great new vistas to the Spanish muse. The Golden Age in literature came to an end in 1681, a century and a half later, with the death of the last great dramatist of the classic theater, Calderón de la Barca, so greatly admired by Shelley, Schopenhauer, Schiller, and many others. Personally, I should prefer to begin Spain's Golden Age with the *Celestina*, in 1499, but few scholars have moved it back that far. In any case, the Golden Age represents a beautiful flowering of the Spanish mind and heart which continues long after the decline of Spain's political supremacy. It even continued into the late seventeenth century, when the country was ruled by increasingly impotent and stupid kings who presided over a nation in ruins.

During these fateful years Spain was reaching the fulfillment of a will which had been many centuries in the making. The words *querer es poder*, "to will is to be able," express the idea proverbially. Spain's dynamic will reached out in three primary directions: first, in discovery, exploration, conquest, and colonization; second, in the multicolored art and literature of the Golden Age; third, in the Spanish Counter Reformation, which gave rise to the Society of Jesus, founded by Loyola, a Spaniard, to the missions of the New World, and to a literature of mysticism in Spain that has no counterpart elsewhere in Europe. The Spanish Golden Age is a reflection and a fusion of these three currents of the national life. They are, indeed, a kind of holy trinity on earth which indicate the main paths of Spanish genius during the sixteenth and seventeenth centuries.

The question very naturally arises: How could the country's literary expression maintain such a peak when her social organism was degenerating? The answer must be given symbolically: A garden flowers most beautifully just before it is to wither and die, and that flowering is brought to its greatest perfection by decaying matter which has been placed in the soil. Like the flowers in that symbolic garden the writers of the late Spanish Golden Age find nutriment in their nation's decay, and even though they must face and accept this decay as a social reality, with their golden pens they deny it all the way, in the same manner, and with the same zeal that man has always denied that death's victory over others could ever mean its victory over him.

Garcilaso de la Vega, whose poems initiated the Golden Age, produced a poetry in which reality was idealized. His beautiful eclogues picture a tranquil natural setting in which perfect men are living in a perfect state. It is a schematic world of idea, not a world of observation. It is the poetization of man's desire to achieve perfection, a desire which did not exist among the medieval writers. The Spanish novels of chivalry (*Amadís*) and the pastoral novels (*Diana*, and *Diana enamorada*) provide further dimensions for this idealized world. In the novels of chivalry love and valor are perfect; and in the pastoral novels love and nature are perfect. In both, man is almost a divine being, not subject to the laws of reality. Nature becomes the handmaiden of God; or, as Cervantes calls her, the "steward of the Lord." She shares with God the divine spirit of the universe; she is, in fact, a kind of Platonic demiurge, and in her tranquil face man can find reflected all the beauty and all the perfection of a good and perfect world. This nature is a creation of culture, a creation of the culture and emotions of the Renaissance. Poetry is no longer a reflection of reality, as it was in the *Poem of the Cid*, but is an idealization of reality epitomizing the dreams of man. Even flowers and brooks and trees are no longer merely flowers and brooks and trees; they must be ideas. "In Renaissance landscape, delicate breezes, like ordering powers, ideas, pass through the gently swaying branches, the running brooks, the peeping birds. And thus, natural landscape is converted into an idea of itself." Nature becomes the symbol of perfect harmony, goodness, and peace. The shepherd, or "natural man," embodies these same qualities of perfection, and his loves, too, are perfect. Poets, novelists and courtiers become shepherds in this pastoral literature in order to make the pattern complete.[29]

The Catholic Council of Trent (1545–1563), at which the Church of Rome took a good look at herself and determined to clean house, resulted in a more rigid interpretation of dogma and a more severe application of the canons of religious behavior. Perfect man living in a perfect state was no longer a permissible belief, for it was contrary to the doctrine of original sin. Thus such literature was condemned by the religious Counter Reformation, which bore down on man's fall from grace, and on the need for faith in order to save his soul.

Just at the time that the Council of Trent was in session there appeared the first and the best Spanish picaresque novel, *Lazarillo de Tormes*, 1554. The unknown author of this slender, powerful, shocking book makes a complete about-face from the pastoral and chivalric novels, and revels in giving us a photograph of Spanish society as seen through the eyes of a shrewd young *pícaro* or rogue, who goes from job to job and master to master, finding cruelty, avarice and opportunism on all sides. Even the church is rigorously satirized in two of these figures, hence an explanation of the anonymity of the book. The only character who emerges with dignity from this mélange is the poor squire, who, despite his poverty, is as proud as Lucifer, and has no heart to hurt any man. He is the epitome of a good part of the nation, the embodiment of personal dignity, poverty, and pride, the prophetic symbol of Spain's hunger and her emptiness of material things. In order to prove to others that he has eaten well the poor squire takes pains to scatter a few crumbs of bread over his garments, despite the fact that his stomach is gnawing at his vitals for want of food. He finds all kinds of excuses to get hold of the castaway foods that his boy, Lazarillo, brings in, and begins to relish in his presence. The juxtaposition of these two characters, the squire and his boy, both eyeing an old crust of bread or the knucklebone of a cow, the one with ravenous hunger and pride, the other with natural hunger and haste, constitutes one of the most moving and most suggestive pictures of Spanish Golden Age realism.

Spain was not really that bad in 1554. The author of *Lazarillo* is a prophet; he is foretelling what his country will be like in another hundred years. No matter what his purpose, he has given us a sharply delineated group of etchings of Spanish life much in the manner of Goya. Exaggerated though these are, they carry a burden of truth that is powerful enough to be devastating. After the turn of the century several other picaresque novels appeared, and the Spanish *pícaro* became one of the well-known figures of world literature. Later still, in France, Lesage, with his *Gil Blas* (taken from the Spanish picaresque tales), universalizes the type. But Le Sage is not superior to the Spanish novelists; he merely comes at the end of the tradition and gives it a final focus and a final push.

By 1600 the *pícaro*, in his various forms, was beginning to swarm on the streets of the cities of Spain: soldiers without jobs, many of them crippled, who had returned from Italy or Flanders; run-down lesser noblemen whose patrimony had been squandered; vagabonds and beggars of all descriptions who, unable to get to America, were at least determined not to make an honest living with their hands; countrymen who had poured into the cities and found no jobs; workers thrown into the streets when the national economy spluttered and then cracked; hangers-on milling about hoping to get into the government bureaucracy; sharpers and criminals who believed life owed them a living, and so on ad infinitum. The church, unintentionally, encouraged this parasitic attitude with its Jesuitic emphasis on faith rather than works as the way to salvation. Now that the conquests had ground to a halt, now that the soldier could no longer find his dream at the end of a spear or gun, now that the American mines were funneling wealth into a few pockets while the miners themselves labored for a pittance, now that the Midas dream vitiated every incentive for honest labor, now that Spain was drained of her very life's blood—it was fitting that the *pícaro* should come to symbolize the defeat of the national dream, and become the embodiment of the national hunger and the national despair.

It is worth noting that the most popular picaresque novel of them all, *Guzmán de Alfarache* (first part 1599, second part 1604), by Mateo Alemán, whose ancestry was Jewish, was in its day even more widely read and applauded than the *Quixote*. In its English version this novel is called *The Spanish Rogue*; the translation, in four long volumes, is by James Mabbe. In this and the other picaresque novels we see a completely pessimistic picture of the world, a despair that is overwhelming. Recent scholars have pointed out that such an attitude toward life was Jewish and Moorish, not Christian, in its origins. However, the Spanish Christian inevitably absorbed a considerable amount of this fatalistic philosophy from his mixed cultural and religious environment. Unconsciously the rationale was that since God predetermines human destiny, and since the world is the great deceiver, man had a right to try to even the score by being a cheat, a thief, a deceiver, in a word, a *pícaro*. The picaresque novel, therefore, was a very human protest, the expression of the Spaniard's existential anguish, a vision of the self in conflict as the world and reality went gliding by.

Is it any wonder that other writers of the Golden Age should seek an escape from this reality? In the poetry of the religious mystics they found it. Mysticism represents the martial spirit reduced to a religious struggle. The mystics were knights-errant of the soul. Like the great discoverers, they traveled uncharted seas, and went beyond the known boundaries of the human spirit. Fray Luis de León, a professor at the University of Salamanca, who was imprisoned five years by the Inquisition because of his interpretation of the Vulgate, was one of the most famous mystics. St. John of the Cross, with his luminous and impassioned poems of the inner life, was another. Santa Teresa de Jesús, although much in the world with her minute and burdensome daily chores, also found religious escape in her mystical writings. It is curious to note that both of the above men suffered imprisonment, and that Fray Luis and Santa Teresa both had Jewish ancestors. Fray Luis' grandmother was a converted Jewess, and St. Teresa's grandfather was also a convert.*

Santa Teresa (1515–1582) was an attractive young girl who read many novels of chivalry, and fancied herself the heroine of one of these tales. She thoroughly enjoyed the company of her male cousins, and was fascinated by their love affairs. In order to protect her Teresa's father sent her to a convent, and in time she became a nun, a Carmelite of the Convent of the Incarnation in Ávila. She took enthusiastically to the new life, and mortified her body with fasting, penances, extensive prayers, and a general disregard for physical well-being. She suffered from fainting spells, violent headaches, vomiting, extreme nervous tension, and finally, after a series of convulsions, she went into a cataleptic state and was pronounced dead. Her breathing and heartbeat were no longer discernible.

Her father and one of her brothers refused to accept the verdict of death and alternated at watch at her bedside. "The son fell asleep while on guard, dropped his candle on Teresa's bed and set fire to it. Even this, however, did not rouse her from her sleep. Her grave was dug, wax was put upon her eyes, and the nuns came for her body. To everyone's astonishment, however, Teresa woke up, ate and drank and told of her experiences while in the trance. She returned to the convent where she lay paralyzed and helpless for eight months. Finally she was able to stir and was soon up and about, convinced that her cure had been spiritual."[66]

Saint Teresa spoke of receiving direct communications from God

---

* In 1485 the Inquisition accused him of lapsing into his former Judaism. St. Teresa's seven brothers all went to Peru, very likely "to get themselves far away from Spain in order to escape painful gossip."

through "the ears of the soul." She wrote many books and poems, and led an exemplary life, which made her tremendously admired in Spain, where her following was (and is) widespread. The following beautiful sonnet gives a glimpse into that deeply religious soul; the translation is by Katharine Elizabeth Strathdee:

> 'Tis not the awful portent of Thy wrath
> That makes me follow where Thy footsteps tread;
> 'Tis not Thy holy frown, nor terror's dread
> That guides my lamp along Thy narrow path;
> Thy wond'rous love alone hath conquered me.
> Thy splendor, as a graceful mantle bright,
> On pure and sinful souls hath cast its light;
> Within the raging storm's dark mystery
> Enfoldest Thou the righteous and unjust;
> Thou hast unto each one some beauty given,
> Why must our hearts by envy then be driven,
> The vain mirage of worldly treasure trust?
> I fear Thee, though I dread not hell's dark thrust;
> And love Thee, though I have no hope of heaven![65]

Outside of their religious zeal the Spanish mystics led lives of action. They were hard workers and honest reformers. But their search for God was a flight from reality in which the individual soul sought to find union with the divine absolute. They sought a luminous path that leads from the dark night of the soul, from the dark and deceitful reality of the senses to the divine reality of God. Clutching at nothing, the mystic was able to embrace everything at once. He felt radiant and transfigured, and merged his own small soul with God. St. John of the Cross felt God as a deathless spring, hidden by night; he went through the darkness to drink of Him. It is easy to understand that a belief of such intensity might well bring its believers into jeopardy before the Inquisition, and such was indeed the case. Yet the luminous beauties these mystics found in the human soul far transcended those that we touch with our hands or see with our eyes. Their escape was the greatest that man has ever accomplished on this earth, their poetry some of the most impassioned. They represent a distillation of medieval faith despite the rapid but often awkward progress of the Renaissance.

A fourth type of Golden Age literature was the highly embellished baroque world of the great genius Góngora, which was an exaltation of reality. Góngora's poetry had little in common with the sentimental and lucidly bucolic quaverings of the pastoral poets, but, via the difficult metaphor, the brilliant poetic image, the accumulation of long streams of images, Góngora recreated the entire world in terms of his own acute poetic fancy. This world is "stylized and simplified in order to be reduced to well-drawn outlines, to agile foreshortenings, to harmonious sonorities and to splendid colors. By means of a continual and complicated metaphorical play the object tends to lose its individuality and to be entered in a metaphorical category. We do not look for sea-water, fresh water, water from a fountain or lagoon in the *Solitudes*, for *crystals* is the label that covers all."[30] But the beautiful limbs of a woman are also called *crystals*. Thus, the bewilderment and confusion begin the moment we undertake an examination of the poet's vocabulary.

Góngora created quite a furor in his own day, but after his death his poetry fell into disrepute. By the eighteenth century he was almost unread. The French symbolist poets were the first to undertake a return to Góngora. "A poet so obscure, they felt, must be very beautiful." Verlaine tried to dig into him, and got nowhere. He determined to learn Spanish in order to understand him, but never achieved his purpose. He did use the lovely image which represents the marriage bed at the end of Góngora's first *Solitude* as the epigraph of one of his sonnets: "A field of feathers for the strife of Love!" And that, perhaps, was about the extent of his knowledge of Góngora. Rubén Darío, the Spanish American modernist, was infected with Verlaine's enthusiasm, and carried this with him to Madrid. He celebrated Góngora in some of his own poems and brought his name back into the Spanish eye. The younger generation of Spanish poets who followed Darío, particularly García Lorca and his contemporaries, deeply immersed themselves in Góngora, and in 1927, the third centenary of the poet's death, the Spanish *Revista de Occidente* undertook a new edition of his works. Scholars studied the poet assiduously, and Dámaso Alonso, Lorca's friend, published a critical interpretation of his most abstruse poems. Since then Góngora has had a field day in Spain and Spanish America, and now he is regarded as one of the finest poets in the language.

Góngora was born in Córdoba in 1561, the son of a cultured, well-to-do family. His father was noted as a bibliophile and had a large personal library. Góngora was proud of his ancient city and of the Guadalquivir, "the king of rivers," along whose banks so many cultures had taken root. He attended the University of Salamanca, where he quickly learned Latin and Italian, and where he acquired the reputation of a gay and witty young blade. He spent money lavishly and made love to many women. His early verses were not highly involved, and among them are some of the loveliest artistic ballads in Spanish. His later poetry, written after 1600, represents the entirely different and artificial world of his own imagination. Góngora avoids commonplaces as the plague, and invents a vocabulary to suit his fancy. For example, since the words "white," "corn," "olive oil," and "feather," all have the feel of color to them, Góngora uses "snow" instead of "white," and "flying snow" instead of "feather." Thrashed ears of corn become in his vocabulary "beaten gold," and "olive oil" is "liquid gold." Water of any kind, as has already been pointed out, is invariably "crystal."

In a larger sphere Góngora uses the combined or extended image. A river that flows into the sea to die becomes for him "a crystal butterfly, not winged, but wavy. . . ." The sun entering the constellation of the bull contains an inverted image in which we see the bull passing "through sapphire fields to graze on stellar corn." Again, when the poet looks upon some poplars growing along a river bank, the reality that he wishes to capture via the process of recreation becomes an image of "fireworks on display." The poplars, which are never mentioned, are presented as "braiding their hair in the light of the fireworks before the mirror of the waves." In this image the trees are turned into mythical maidens caught beautifying themselves in the reflection of the fire-illuminated stream. In other images the poet sees islands in a river as "leafy parentheses," the Straits of Magellan as "an elusive hinge of silver," and village chimneys as "watchtowers of the sunset." A still longer stream of images is conjured up to express the very simple scene of a few peasants going over a mountain to a spot where there is to be a wedding. Góngora takes in the scene and records it as "a flock of cranes that cross seas of air, not like flying boats but like birds with sails full of wind, scattered across the blue, tracing designs that resemble the waxing or the waning moon, or perhaps like mysterious words written with feathers on the parchment of the sky." The simple, rustic scene has been converted into an exquisite Japanese print. The perishable moment has been captured imperishably, because it has been recreated by the imagination of the poet into a glorious baroque cathedral.

Góngora was of the belief that if things are called by their common names, their reality ends at that very moment. If they are given

another name which exalts, ennobles, and embellishes them, this is
their bid for immortality. The purpose of the poet is to follow this
process to its finale. Whether or not we agree with Góngora's results,
whether or not we are irritated by the abstruse complexity of his
imagery, we must admit that he has been able to create a unique
poetic world, one which has survived many centuries after the poet
himself has died, one in which sensitive spirits of many tongues will
find inspiration for generations to come. Indeed, the entire modern
generation of poets may be said to stem from the germ idea which
was Góngora's. The bard of Córdoba is one of the most brilliant
lights of the Spanish Golden Age.

The following sonnet by Góngora, translated by Sir Richard Fanshawe in the seventeenth century, shows the poet in one of his more
simple and more lyric moods. It is called "The Rose."

> Blown in the morning, thou shalt fade ere noon,
> What boots a life which in such haste forsakes thee?
> Thou'rt wondrous frolic, being to die so soon,
> And passing proud a little colour makes thee.
> If thee thy brittle beauty so deceives,
> Know then the thing that swells thee is thy bane;
> For the same beauty doth, in bloody leaves,
> The sentence of thy early death contain.
> Some clown's coarse lungs will poison thy sweet flower,
> If by the careless plough thou shalt be torn;
> And many Herods lie in wait each hour
> To murder thee as soon as thou art born—
> Nay, force thy bud to blow—their tyrant breath
> Anticipating life, to hasten death![67]

The most famous Spanish writer of all time, Cervantes, was a
contemporary of Góngora. He was not born into such an exalted
family, yet was himself one of the lesser hidalgos of his country. His
early education in Alcalá and later in Madrid placed him in contact
with the Erasmist and humanistic currents of the Spanish Renaissance, and this liberalizing influence is very apparent in his masterpiece *Don Quixote*, first part published in 1605, second part in 1615,
one year before his death. Cervantes travelled and worked in Italy,
fought at the battle of Lepanto against the Turks, where he was
severely wounded and lost the use of his left hand, as he says, "for
the greater glory of his right." On the way back to Spain he was
captured by pirates of the Barbary coast and was enslaved by them

for five years before he was ransomed for 500 ducats. Back in Spain he was given the task of food procurement for the Armada, a job which he carried out with no great distinction. He tried to make a living by writing, and produced several plays and other pieces which enjoyed a moderate success, but brought him little income. On several occasions he was put in jail, probably for debts that he could not pay, or for deficits which were blamed on him. He was in prison in Seville when he began to write the *Quixote*.

This novel in many ways parallels the author's life. When the first part of his great book appeared Cervantes was fifty-six years old. His hero is a man of approximately the same age. Cervantes himself had spent most of his life knocking about the world, writing books of literature, suffering slavery and imprisonment, undoubtedly hoping to achieve renown and to further the cause of justice. He was invariably defeated, but always rebounded with an optimism and belief in the goodness of life which was indomitable. Like his hero he had also read voluminously, and perhaps this turned his own head too far away from practical things, thus preventing his concentrating on the prosaic job of earning a living. At the mid-century mark, thus, Cervantes himself was a defeated idealist, a dreamer of great literary works, but the producer of none.

The reason he gives for writing the *Quixote* is that he wishes to laugh away the ridiculous romances of chivalry, and so he has his hero read these tales day and night until his mind is turned, and Don Quixote decides to become a knight-errant himself. The old gentleman makes an uncertain initial sally alone without achieving anything, then he returns home and takes a squire, Sancho Panza, a hardheaded and shrewd countryman of peasant stock. The author now begins to feel sure of himself, as the two figures set forth together on their errand of justice, each feeding the other, like alter egos. As the action progresses it becomes perfectly plain that these characters have grown into the heart of Cervantes, and his heart into them, so that his initial wish to ridicule the chivalric novels fades away into that greater catharsis-creation of his immortal portrait of human nature.

"Spain was the Mother; Cervantes but brought the sperm," thus wrote Unamuno, one of the best contemporary philosophers of the peninsula. In any case, Cervantes in his novel has given us a portrait of Spanish life and Spanish character raised to the level of great world literature. Sancho Panza represents the reality of the senses and

of the moment, and Don Quixote symbolizes the wider reality of
human belief. Each fights for his position, and each both wins and
loses because of interpenetration by the ideas and character of the
other. Don Quixote, at first, is clearly mad, but he is mad only in one
aspect of being, that of his belief in knight errantry. In all other
spheres he is the sanest man in the book, as his statements and actions often prove. Take, for example, his advice to Sancho just prior
to his taking over the government of his island, in which wisdom,
moderation, and common sense are judiciously blended. Don Quixote
is a man to whom thought and will are everything. What he thinks,
this is what he sees. He thinks giants, so windmills become giants. He
thinks armies, so the sheep become soldiers. He thinks castles, so the
inns become castles. Sancho, at first unwilling to believe any of these
things, slowly becomes infected with the fantasies of his master. Don
Quixote, in his turn, slowly becomes infected with the pragmatism of
his squire. From a man of perfect belief he goes the complete circle
and dies a man of complete disbelief, urging his friends and kinsmen
not to follow the mad life that he has led.

The entire novel is a treatment of human character, truth and
justice. Don Quixote himself states that it is his mission to do good.

I have redressed grievances [he says to a churchman who censures him],
and have righted the injured, chastised the insolent, and vanquished
giants. . . . I am in love, but no more than the profession of knight-
errantry obliges me to be; yet I am none of the Age's vicious lovers, but
a chaste platonic. My intentions are all directed to virtuous ends, and to
do no man wrong, but good to all the world. And now let your Graces
judge, most excellent Duke and Duchess [he concludes, turning from the
petulant churchman and addressing his final words to his aristocratic
hearers] whether a person who makes it his only study to practice all this,
deserves to be upbraided for a fool.

This is Don Quixote's answer to his critics both in and out of the
book. The above scene takes place at the palace of the Duke and
Duchess where several members of the upper crust are entertaining
the good Don with an eye to having a little fun with him. But in the
end, their jests turn out to be unhappy truths, and they, not Don
Quixote, are the fools, for while their actions are motivated by base
desires, his are always above reproach, and have besides the godlike
quality of not wishing to hurt any man. Despite his madness, therefore, he comes out of these experiences ennobled, whereas they come
forth mired and stogged in littleness, and cruelty, and self-conceit.

In another place in the novel Don Quixote tells his good squire, Sancho: "Know that though you should see me in the greatest extremity of danger, you must not offer to draw your sword in my defense unless you find me assaulted by base plebeians and vile scoundrels." His fight was against those whose conquest he considered meaningful. He must carry on the unending struggle against the defenders of reason, the men of common sense who are captives of physical reality. This was a dire statement for an idealist, but the only possible statement for the knight who not only believed but lived completely in his world of fancy. To observe the code even when threatened by death—this is the height of true sportsmanship of which the English make so much. It is also the very quintessence of Spanish honor at its highest level, not the honor of the Golden Age theater in which a man's honor must be reclaimed in blood, but honor in the deeper sense of human dignity as a method of survival, as a means of goodness, as a road to immortality.

Don Quixote saw no such thing as practical idealism. If it was practical, it was not idealism to him. To the good Don idealism meant precisely engaging in a death struggle against the stronger forces of injustice and evil, no matter what the odds or what the consequences. There could never be anything practical about such a struggle, for in it a man committed his whole soul without thought of compromise, retreat, or appeasement. In this manner Don Quixote's religion, for it is a religion, approaches that of Jesus Christ, who also died for his beliefs. If, at the end of the novel, we find a defeated hero, it must be clear to all intelligent readers that defeat of the hero means the survival of the hero's ideal. Great tragedy in literature always consists of this. When we see a noble character go down to defeat, whether it be on the dramatic stage or in a novel, the essence and reality of his struggle live on in the hearts of his observers, and this is precisely what the author, consciously or unconsciously, intended to achieve. Indeed, did it not require the death of Christ to establish the religion of Christianity?

One could go on and on giving all kinds of valid interpretations of Don Quixote, and in this lies the certain touch of a great author. One critic, commenting on the reception of the novel, pointed out that "in the seventeenth century it was received with a laugh, in the eighteenth century it was received with a smile, in the nineteenth century it was received with a tear." But regardless of the reception or aspect Cervantes' analysis and projection of character is so astute that new meanings can always be discovered with each rereading of the book. Hence, this masterpiece has been justly called by nearly all critics "the greatest novel in the world."

To the medieval mind God was transcendent. Man was but a mold on which the divine reality was stamped. Life was a passport to eternity. "Remember, man, that thou must die!" was the focal point of medieval life. Hence, the eternal didacticism of medieval fiction, with characters as types. There was no character differentiation until the fifteenth century.

Renaissance man began to take on a reality of his own. He no longer merely reflected reality; he embodied it. He was the point of departure for a knowledge of the universe. God no longer transcended the world, but was immanent. Nature shared with God the divine reality, and was indeed, "the Lord's steward." The universe unfolded according to laws of order and harmony, the keynote of which was love.

This concept of nature as a divine reality in literature gave rise to an ideal nature inhabited by man living in a perfect state. The poems of Garcilaso, the pastoral novel, and the novels of chivalry are an expression of the humanistic desire to attain this ideal world. It was a world untouched by history, a world of natural spirit goodness, of beauty, and of love.

Coetaneous with this idea, the other material world also existed. Golden Age realism, beginning with the *Celestina* in 1499, and flowering in the picaresque novels, gives a full account of it. This world was the other prong of the Absolute Reality. "The doctrine of the double truth, with its prongs of the universal poetic truth, on the one hand, and the historic particular truth, on the other, prepared the way for idealized and realistic fiction."[63]

After the Council of Trent anti-Platonic moralists began to censure this idealized world. Perfect man living in a perfect state was contrary to the doctrine of original sin. Gradually the literary position changed with the religious and the philosophical position. The relationship between the two truths became a problem.

"Cervantes found himself in the midst of this conflict. His solution was to synthesize the two truths, as demanded by Trent. With the novel of chivalry and the pastoral novel as a point of departure, via humor, he fused the two truths. He placed Don Quixote in the universal poetic ideal and Sancho in the historic particular. Each fights for his position, and two worlds clash, finally to blend."[63] A universe that is typically Spanish, heart and soul, is at the same time the universe of all mankind. Cervantes has rescued humanity from the mandarins of reason.

Contemporaneous with Cervantes was the birth and early development of the national theater in Spain. Lope de Vega (1562–1635), who knew the author of *Don Quixote* and kept up a kind of running literary duel with him, was the principal creator of this theater. Lope was undoubtedly the world's most prolific dramatist. He wrote between five hundred and six hundred full-length plays, many of them within a few tense hours. Over three hundred of these dramas have survived, besides an impressive number of novels, stories, poems and shorter dramatic pieces of various descriptions. Cervantes rightly characterized Lope as "the prodigy of Nature."

The Spanish *comedia** as delineated by Lope became a true popular theater, and Spain's dramatists were kept inordinately busy trying to satisfy the demands of the people. It was primarily a comedy of intrigue based on a few stereotyped situations and primary emotions: love, jealousy, honor, vengeance. This kind of theater has often been called "cape and sword drama," because of the constant presence and importance of the cape and the sword in the resolution of the intrigue. It was an accepted convention that with the cape wrapped about his chin the hero was never recognizable, so he was thus able to further the complications of the plot without great effort on the part of the dramatist. The sword was used for deeds of derring-do and in order to redeem dishonor in blood. Any gossip about a virtuous lady was sufficient cause for dishonor; the lady must always be above suspicion, and "what the people say" was just as important as what was really true. It is easy to see that this combination of elements could give rise to a drama which might readily become artificial, as indeed was frequently the case. On the other hand, despite the accepted conventions and the unavoidable restrictions imposed by public taste and the church, Spanish drama of the Golden Age did produce a considerable number of first-rate plays. In this regard Spain is certainly the peer of France, and occupies a second place only as compared with the Elizabethan theater of England.

Public demand and a set dramatic formula pushed Lope to use his fertile imagination and glib pen to the fullest extent, and he be-

* Golden Age drama, not merely comedy.

came the greatest improviser of literature the world has ever known. Spaniards have always been great improvisers: in government, in military matters, in economic problems, in conquest and exploration, in colonization, in practically every aspect of organized life. Their improvisation in literature is also proverbial, but no other Spaniard even came close to matching Lope's perennial fecundity. His facility in striking off verses was extraordinary, and he has left some of the best lyric poetry in the language, a considerable portion of it intercalated in his dramas as popular ballads, lyrics, dances, and songs. Lope also used a great number of folk *coplas* and proverbs, sprinkling these throughout his plays in many instances in order to give the entire production a popular flavor. Many of his plays are based on actual historic episodes or well-known legends. Lope was greatly loved by the masses of theatergoers, and with their support, and sometimes following their insistence that he move in a given direction in his dramas, he created the Spanish national theater.

A recent book, *Lope de Vega*, by Francis C. Hayes, brings us face to face with Lope the rake, the dramatist, the priest, the Spaniard par excellence, the opportunist, the Catholic, the funster, the lyrical poet, the father, the lover. Hayes indicates the wide range of Lope's sources:

> In search of raw material for his drama, he roved from skid row to market place, to hidalgo's home, to palace, to church, to heaven, to hell. He presented to his audience by the hundreds *pícaros*, the scum of the cities. He went down the social scale (and into jail as a prisoner) scraping bottom to drag up jailbirds, morons, bullies, bandits, pimps (male and female), whores, parasites, gigolos, and confidence men . . . Lope looked for material everywhere, from sources ancient and contemporary, foreign and national, sacred and profane, pastoral, hagiographical, proverbial, geographical, chivalresque. He moved across time and space. . . . He turned to Herodotus, Ovid, Horace, Boccaccio, Bandello, the *Celestina*, the Bible, and his predecessors in Spanish drama. Time and again he clothed in flesh and blood a mere proverb or a ballad character or a national hero or heroine. . . .[68]

Lope traveled all over Spain and met all kinds of people. He even put God in his writings as a character, and practically all of the famous kings of Spain. He made villains of many of the nobles, but never of the king. Lope stood always with the king and the common people against the corrupt nobility. Lope reflected his age. He drew constantly on what Hayes calls "the limitless reservoir of the masses," the fresh and endless folklore of the Spanish people. One moment he would have his audience on the edge of their seats all fired up with a surge of national pride, but the next moment some character would blurt out: "Honor and pride, what the hell are *they* good for in this world?" The Spaniards loved it all. They saw the ambivalence of their own incandescent natures in what Lope wrote, and in observing this dramatized on the stage before them felt a sense of catharsis very similar to that which Aristotle claimed for the ancient Greek drama.

What else might one expect from this deeply gifted man who lived life to the hilt, a man of boundless energies and keen perceptivity? Lope had two wives, several mistresses, numerous children, no surviving descendants. There were, in fact, thirteen identifiable members of Lope's onomastic harem, and at least sixteen children. A goodly number of his mistresses were married women. Lope's motto seemed to be "Sin and repent, then sin again." But nothing, absolutely nothing, ever stopped him from writing.

One of Lope's best plays is *Peribáñez and the Comendador of Ocaña*. The noble Comendador (Lord) is smitten with the wife of the farmer Peribáñez, and in order to consummate his desire he orders his subject off to war, much as King David did in order to seduce Bathsheba. Peribáñez immediately smells a rat but cannot refuse the order. He does, however, hasten home at the very first rest the troops are given, and even before he has reached his house he hears the workers in the fields singing little couplets telling that the worst has happened. Finally, he confronts the Comendador and slays him. The king orders that the murderer be arrested at once, but on hearing the whole story he not only forgives Peribáñez but commends him and raises his rank. In the theater of cape and sword a man is obliged to kill in order to defend his honor, even if the person who has dishonored him belongs to the nobility.

In another of Lope's plays, *Fuente Ovejuna,* a powerful Comendador of the village of that name dishonors several women and then insults their menfolk. One night the men of the town break into his house and slay him. When the king sends investigators to find out who the culprits are, he is confronted by a silent, stone wall, and despite the torturing of several suspected townsfolk not one name is disclosed. Oftentimes the tormented victim cries out that he will reveal all, but in answer to the question "Who did it?" he invariably gives the pat answer "Fuente Ovejuna, señor. It was Fuente Ovejuna, one and all." Because of its exaltation of a whole town this play has become particularly popular today; its success in Russia and France

has been notable. Lope was always the facile poet of dramatic intrigue. He lacked the depth of Shakespeare, and seldom delineated
great characters. Certainly, he created none equal to Hamlet, Mac-
beth, Falstaff, or Iago. He composed too fast and furiously to write
with Shakespeare's intensity.

The Spanish drama of the Golden Age brought into being a secondary character of tremendous importance, called the *gracioso*. This
figure is the servant, confidant, and friend of the hero, and serves as a
sounding board for his master's thoughts and actions. The *gracioso*
represents common sense, somewhat like Sancho Panza, and he may
be said at times also to represent public opinion. He has a symbolic
role similar to that of the chorus in Greek tragedy. The French and
Italian theaters took over the type and used it in many plays, but
without the same effectiveness. The figure has survived today in
opera; everyone is familiar with Leporello, the confidant of the Don
in Mozart's *Don Giovanni*, the libretto of which was based by da
Ponte on one of the best known dramas of the Spanish theater, Tirso de
Molina's *Deceiver of Seville*, the first Don Juan play in literature.

In the Golden Age theater the king is almost invariably presented
in a good light. He is always on the side of justice, and often takes
the part of the lower classes against the higher ups, particularly the
feudal lords. Psychologically, this reflected what was taking place in
Spain: The kings had sought to ally themselves with the masses and
with the church in order to overcome the disruptive power of the
nobility. Lope's theater pays repeated tribute to the just and honest
king, and thus cements that symbol in the public mind and favor.
One must remember, in appraising the popularity of the Golden Age
dramatists in Spain, that Spaniards were in that epoch a notably
illiterate people, and that this form of oral literature was the only
kind which was really available to them. For centuries they had
spontaneously and anonymously created hundreds and thousands of
ballads and *coplas*; now with these very elements a part of the national theater, which everyone could see, hear and understand, it was
natural that their appetite for drama and poetry should be insatiable.

Lope spent the last part of his life as a priest in the bosom of the
church (as later did Calderón and Tirso), but his early years were
anything but serene. His parents had died before he was of university
age; with the aid of the Grand Inquisitor he attended the University
of Alcalá, where he completed the course in philosophy. After gradu-
ation he became secretary of the duke of Alba. He had many love

affairs, and once fought a duel in which he critically wounded his opponent. Because of this he was forced to live in exile for several years, away from Madrid. He sailed on the Armada for England, and returned safely to Spain despite the disastrous Spanish defeat. Following this experience he began his most productive period as a writer. After the death of his second wife and the drowning of his favorite son off the coast of South America, he took holy orders and withdrew from public life (1614). Two years later, however, he embarked on his last violent love affair with a married woman thirty years younger than he. She was the Amarilis of his eclogues. Lope was overwhelmed when his young mistress went blind and then became insane; she died three years before Lope himself. When his only remaining daughter eloped, the great dramatist was crushed; he had loved her deeply and guarded her closely to no avail. He died embittered very shortly afterward. His life had been very much like one of his plays. In a recently discovered drama, written during these final unhappy months, he has an older male character lament: "Give me lions or tigers to guard, give me crocodiles, but do not give me a beautiful young girl!"

Lope was the most admired of all Spanish writers during his lifetime. The nobility as well as the theater-going masses knew and idolized him. Whenever he was seen on the street a great crowd immediately surrounded him, much as people now surround motion picture stars, except that in Lope's case the fans consisted mainly of older people. However, street urchins too ran madly after him shouting his name. A new play of Lope's was a great event in the humdrum life of Madrid. He mirrored and carried forward the popular taste as no other Spanish author ever has. Cervantes often twitted him about this quick response to the popular taste, a response that made him "King of the Spanish stage."

But Lope was also honored in other ways. He was chosen president of the religious College of Madrid, and was appointed as a "familiar" to the Inquisition, considered as a signal honor. Pope Urban VIII awarded him the Maltese Cross and the degree of doctor of theology, and sent him a flattering letter. When he died in 1635 at the age of seventy-three his funeral was one of princely magnificence. The obsequies lasted three days, and three bishops officiated in their pontifical robes. All the theaters in Spain held ceremonies honoring the deceased idol.

The contemporaries of Lope de Vega, and those who followed him, were so numerous and so important that it would be impossible even to mention them all within the limits of this book. Quevedo (Francisco Gómez de Quevedo y Villegas, 1580–1645) has sometimes been called "the Spanish Voltaire." His mordant pen, steeped in satire, caricature, and bitter laughter, reveals an inglorious and frustrated Spain. In his writings there are incapable and bungling kings, courtly favorites who are the worst sort of sycophants, immoral scribes and town councilmen, imbecile noblemen, ignorant and presumptuous doctors, hollow and conceited poets, greedy and spoiled women. Quevedo manipulates these human types, sending them into a sardonic dance of death, in which the skeleton of depravity whirls the body about. The repulsiveness and vapidity of Spanish society, rotten at the core, is Quevedo's main concern as an author. Quevedo does mock and laugh at these things, but his laughter is biting and ends in tears. His humor becomes a lament, his wit a devastating sword. If, as Bergson writes, laughter is like a foam left by the waves of the sea, a foam which any child can pick up from the sands and see turn into a few condensed drops of saline moisture, Quevedo's laughter appears to gather the foam of life in disillusion, and to hold before us only its residue of bitterness.

Quevedo was, in a sense, the conscience of Spain at one of the most crucial moments of her history. He was also a great poet of love, death, and the passage of time, all joined in one fleeting requiem. He has left a series of sonnets which are among the finest in the Spanish language:

> The last shadow that takes the white of day
> From me may close for good these loving eyes,
> And may release this soul from mortal clay
> Which has indulged its rapt and eager cries;
> But no, upon that unknown farther shore
> My flame will burst where frozen waters thaw;
> Its memory will brightly burn once more
> Without respect for man's most solemn law.
> Soul that was prison to a god in chains,
> Veins that have given fuel to so much fire,
> Bones nobly burned to mock the heart's endeavor:
> This body it will leave, but not its pains,
> They will be ash, but quickened with desire,
> They will be dust, but dust that loves forever.[69]

Baltasar Gracián (1601–1658) was one of the outstanding essayists of the Spanish Golden Age. Translated into English by Thomas North, many of his books became immensely popular in England. His moralistic essays, written in a pungent and lucid style, teeming with fertile ideas, may be read even today with pleasure and profit. The following paragraph from Gracián's *Art of Worldly Wisdom* is typical of this writer's language and thought:

Belie in yourself the weakness of your country. Water partakes of the qualities, good and bad, of the seams through which it flows; and man of the climate into which he is born. There is no nation, even of the most cultured, without some inborn defect which its neighbors will not at once strike upon, either for their caution, or their comfort. It is a commendable skill to eradicate such national weaknesses in yourself, or at least, to hide them: thus are you made unique among your kind, for what is least expected is esteemed most highly. There are weaknesses also of race, of rank, of profession, and of age, which, if gathered together in one individual, and not curbed, yield an intolerable monster.

A few additional epigrammatic sentences from Gracián recall the sententious phrases of the French La Rochefoucauld:

"Life is a struggle of man against man's malice."

"There is no beauty unaided, no excellence which does not sink to the barbarous, unless saved by art."

"The thing does not suffice, form as well is required. Bad form spoils everything, even justice and reason."

"Science without understanding is compounded madness."

"Mediocrity gets further with industry, than superiority without it."

"Hard luck is mostly the punishment of foolishness, and no disease is so catching for the mourners."

"When in doubt, there is safety in sticking with the intelligent and prudent, for sooner or later, they catch up with luck."

"There is much to know, and so little time to learn; one does not live who does not know. A man without knowledge is a universe in darkness."

Gracián's masterpiece is a strange and symbolic view of the world and mankind called *El Criticón*. An old man, Critilo, is shipwrecked on a small island. He encounters there a young waif who apparently has been raised alone among the wild beasts. The older man (representing the world's knowledge and judgment) teaches the young savage (representing natural man, the virgin soul of man) how to talk, and in this manner, civilization and nature are juxtaposed and contrasted. The young noble savage recounts his life and his experiences, and the old man is on the point of telling his own story when the two are picked up by a passing ship. The young man is bewildered when his mentor warns him against these men, calling them his enemies. It seemed strange that he who had always made friends with the wild beasts should not be friendly with his own kind. But the old gentleman points out that while man may be lacking the claws and strength of the lions or tigers, he possesses a tongue which is sharper still, a weapon which can cut a man to ribbons. The two men embark and finally land in Spain. From this point on the author gives a running commentary on civilization. The virgin soul of the natural man is frequently deceived, and even the old master does not seem to be sure of himself any longer. They go to Rome seeking for peace and happiness, but do not find it here either. Where, then, are to be found these ideal goals of life? The author tells us that they are not to be found anywhere on earth. Despite this conventional ending the book is vastly stimulating to read. Its pessimistic view of life appealed greatly to the German philosopher Schopenhauer. Gracián presents the struggles and conflicts of the world as omnipresent; everything is in a state of tension. Man is the cruelest of God's creatures. His only hope is to impose himself or to submit; he must thrust forward over all obstacles. He bears within himself the seeds of his survival, the venom of his destruction.

Lope de Vega had a host of followers in the Golden Age theater: Tirso de Molina, Ruiz de Alarcón, Guillén de Castro, Rojas Zorrilla, Mira de Amescua, Moreto, Pérez de Montalban, and last of all Calderón de la Barca, who brings the great epoch to a close with his death in 1681. We will select only the first and last of these dramatists, who are also the best, to examine briefly. Tirso (1571–1648), who did not begin to produce his plays until he was thirty-five, has left approximately one hundred fifty full-length dramas. Of these his play on the Don Juan theme, *The Deceiver of Seville*, 1630, is by all odds the best known. Based on a medieval legend of a great seducer of Seville, the story caught on and was imitated by authors in nearly every other European country: Molière, Corneille and Rostand in France, Shadwell, Byron and Shaw in Great Britain, Goldoni in Italy, Hoffman in Germany, and Pushkin in Russia. Mozart's opera *Don Giovanni*, with its fine libretto by da Ponte, has kept the story alive and on the stage of every world city until the present day.

In Tirso's play Don Juan is the perfect libertine. He seduces women for "kicks," abandons them immediately, revels in each successive seduction and abandonment. Centuries before Freud he represents the blind, reckless sex urge of the Id, which seeks expression in accordance with the pleasure principle. The taboos of social intercourse, civilization, or conscience do not slow him down even for one moment. He is the symbolic punisher of women. Modern psychology might seek explanation in Don Juan's hatred of his mother, or in his semi-impotence which needs increasing proof of its virility, but Tirso does not mention these possibilities. He merely presents the case, and carries it to its awful finale. Don Juan, to Tirso, is a dreadful and unrepentant sinner, and in the end he is killed and damned for it. He does not even consider the possibility of repentance. He dies, as he has lived, a boastful and swaggering libertine, ready to accept the consequences of his actions. The dramatists who follow Tirso and employ the Don Juan theme do not always carry the libertine to the same fate; as a matter of fact, in Spain's most popular Don Juan play, written by the Romantic Zorrilla in the 1840's, the hero is saved because of the pure love of one of his victims. This latter play is the one which is now produced every year in Madrid, sometimes with several companies putting it on at the same time, so that the public may go from one theater to the other comparing productions and Don Juans.

Tirso is interested in divine retribution. His protagonist is delineated along a single line, that of an overpowering sex urge, which brooks no obstacles of man or God in its consummation. The Don Juan of Tirso loves without reflection; he is no Faust meditating upon pleasure and destiny. He is pure flesh, pure sex necessity, animated matter, blind urge, irresponsible instinct. He represents man without civilization; to Tirso he also represents pure evil, a symbolic Satan, for Don Juan is demoniacally possessed. He is the life principle breaking away from the social organism, turning what should be creativity into destructiveness. He is vital energy gone amuck. When the statue of the Comendador whom he has slain invites him to supper over a tomb, Don Juan goes without hesitation. When the statue clasps his hand and drags him burning down to hell, justice has been done. It is a fitting end to the story, which Tirso tells with great verve and vigor. In the author's own words the moral of the drama is that in the divine scheme of things "there is no debt that goes unpaid." It is impossible for man to escape responsibility for his actions. He has always before him the free will of a choice. If he makes the wrong choice and does not repent, he is damned eternally. Don Juan is justly damned, but his driving energy, his thrust, his pride, his will, make him nonetheless a symbol of Spain, as well as of sin and error.

Calderón de la Barca (1600–1681), so exalted by the German romantic writers, is, of all the dramatists of the Spanish Golden Age, the one who is best known outside of Spain. Shelley admired and wrote about him in England, Fitzgerald, who made the *Rubaiyat* famous, translated eight of his plays, Schlegel and Schopenhauer regarded him as one of the world's greatest writers. Calderón is the Baroque dramatist par excellence. He brought the Golden Age to its conclusion in a contorted blaze of words and symbols. He was *the* poet of Spanish Catholicism. Besides his longer plays Calderón was the author of numerous "starry autos," to use Shelley's phrase, symbolic religious pieces of great poetic beauty. The Counter Reformation had by this time clamped down on all free thought in Spain, leaving room only for straight dogma *plus endless embellishment.* Character analysis and fundamental questioning are lacking in the dramas of the Golden Age. This is the true meaning of the Baroque in literature, which has its counterpart in the other arts as well, particularly in architecture.

For us today most of the plays of Calderón have a pallid core. Only the beauty of their language saves them. In *The Prodigious Magician,* Ciprian, a young pagan, is repulsed by a virtuous maiden for whom he feels a consuming passion. He implores the help of the Devil (disguised as a gentleman) with whom he had already had a long theological discussion. The Devil promises to teach him magic and to get for him the lady of his desire in return for his soul. The contract is made and sealed in blood. The girl in question, however, continues to resist; virtue and free will have made her invulnerable. Ciprian as a last resort uses his knowledge of magic to materialize his beloved, but when he seizes and attempts to embrace her, only a skeleton remains in his arms. "And thus," concludes the author, "are all the glories of this world."

In *The Mayor of Zalamea* Calderón uses essentially the same theme as Lope in his play about Peribáñez and the Comendador. Pedro Crespo, mayor of the town of Zalamea, who is a farmer, tries, condemns, and has executed Captain Alvaro, the man who has seduced his daughter, and who then refuses to marry her. The play also represents a conflict between military and civil authority, and the latter clearly wins. The king, in this play Philip II himself, pardons and rewards Pedro for his deed.

Calderón's most famous play is *Life is a Dream*, which takes place in Poland, not a realistic Poland, but a legendary Poland as far removed as possible from Spanish life of the seventeenth century. The king of Poland, who is an astrologer, reads in the stars that his son, who is about to be born, is destined to become a cruel and hateful man. Therefore, the king has the child shut up in a tower, away from the world, where he can do no harm. The young man grows to adulthood in this artificial and limited environment. Before finally making one of his nephews heir to the throne, however, the king decides to give his son one chance to prove himself. Under the influence of a strong narcotic the young prince is removed from the tower and placed in the king's bed. When he wakes up he believes that he is having a dream. He cannot tell which part of his life is real. He becomes violent, grabs and hurls a servant off the balcony, and even threatens his own father. The old king sadly orders that he again be put to sleep and taken back to the tower. This is a traumatic experience for the prince, who is now completely bewildered and unable to distinguish between the dream world and the world of reality. After a brief meditation, however, he makes the "leap of faith," and indicates that he will become a good Christian. He knows now that all human happiness, all pomp and power, all wealth and material things "pass like a dream." Only the soul is real.

The following sonnet by Calderón appears in almost every anthology of Spanish poetry:

> These flowers of lordly pomp and joy's sweet breath
> Which at the break of day unfold awaking,
> In the cold arms of night will soon be making
> A piteous wreath for vanity and death.
> This hue that challenges the star-hung sky,
> This iris stained with russet, gold, and snow,
> Teaches what every human heart must know:
> How much of life crowds each day passing by!
> These roses flourish at the touch of dawn,
> But bloom only to wither and grow old;
> Each bud is birth and grave's symbolic pawn,
> So has man felt his brevity foretold:
> Born one day, dead the next, his years unfold,
> And seem but hours when centuries have gone.[70]

During the epoch of Calderón there were only two theaters in Madrid, the *Cruz* and the *Príncipe*. But even in these days of the late Golden Age plays were frequently presented in one of the town plazas. Such outdoor locations had been used ever since the beginnings of the Spanish theater. During those formative years (1550–1570), Lope de Rueda's traveling players, generally regarded as the first organized theater of the Golden Age, went from town to town with their crude offerings. Cervantes saw one of their performances in the plaza at Segovia, and wrote that "their whole baggage would go into a single sack and consisted of four white sheepskins ornamented with gilt leather, four beards and wigs, and four crooks." An old blanket or two, pulled on cords, served as the curtain. Behind it unaccompanied musicians sang some old ballad. The players set up their performances in a plaza, in a dead-end street corner, or in an open space where two or three buildings formed a sheltered angle. These places were called *corrales*, or yards. The theater boxes were the windows and balconies of the nearby buildings. The stage was simply an elevated platform a couple of feet high made of planks placed on top of benches. A skimpy colored canvas at the back of the stage was the only scenery. One of the actors had to come out on the stage and describe the scene, if this was essential to the play. This very rudimentary stage improved with time, and in Calderón's day the actors even had a greenroom where they could dress. The actresses were constantly besieged by the men in the audience, and tried to lock themselves up before the performance. Almost invariably, however, they had to open the doors, lest these same men, if slighted, should decide to boo their performance and ruin their popularity. The stage itself, despite its bare appearance, came to represent the whole world, and indeed Golden Age plays took in every epoch and geographic region imaginable, particularly under Lope's fertile imagination.

The groundlings, called musketeers or *mosqueteros* in Spanish, occupied the pit in front of the stage. They kept up a constant hubbub as the play progressed, either of applause or of disdain. Sometimes they threw vegetables on the stage, and Cervantes once wrote that one of his early plays, while not a financial success, "was not greeted with turnips or other vegetables." The jeers of the musketeers could turn any play into a failure. Behind the groundlings was a section reserved for women, known as the *cazuela* or stewing pan. In later years this was latticed off for greater privacy. The women came to

the shows to be seen as well as to see, and made every effort to attract
the attention of the men in the audience.

The performance always took place in the afternoon. There were
no night performances. In the winter starting time was 2 P.M.; in the
summer it was 4 o'clock. Sometimes there was a canopy to protect the
audience from the hot sun, but if it rained heavily the performance
had to be canceled. Dramas were rarely put on more than once; a
week's run was an exceptional record. Hence, Lope's fertility was in
part the result of public pressures, which demanded something new
every day. The plays were almost invariably accompanied by dances,
and in the intermissions shorter skits were presented. The theater-
going public consisted of all classes, nobles as well as plebeians. This
was the one place where a kind of social equality existed, though the
well-to-do almost always occupied the best seats, the private boxes.
Only two subjects were prohibited absolutely: criticism of the institution of monarchy, and criticism of Catholic dogma. Within this
limitation a remarkable variety of dramatic works were produced.
Most of these have never been turned into English, and until recent
years the best Golden Age plays were so poorly translated that they
sounded ridiculous. Roy Campbell's spirited versions which appear in
Volume III of *The Classic Theatre: Six Spanish Plays*, are perhaps
the best, for Campbell, who died in 1957, was an excellent poet in
his own right.

During the Golden Age Spanish literature reached its zenith. It
was a highly colored literature of great poetic power and strong intensity of feeling. The direct contemplation of reality, so characteristic of medieval writers, gave way in the Golden Age to the tortured
laments of the human spirit elaborated in a Baroque style of exquisite and complex beauty. Alongside this the old folk elements persisted, with their sparkling flow from the magic spring. The writers
of the Golden Age molded these elements into an exalted reality
which caught imperishably the soul of Spain at her moment of crisis.
Literature was a distillation of the nation's history and of the human
spirit, which was immortal. Each great writer strove to create his own
universe with the meager tools of his mind and heart. Each was
striving for something eternal. Is not civilization itself the accumulation of such artistic remnants?

9

THE FINE ARTS—END OF THE GOLDEN AGE

Spain, which has never had a complete social system, has unfolded her life and her art by spiritual convulsions, according as men of strength and action have come bursting forth.

Pío Baroja

Spanish painting paralleled the literature of Spain's Golden Age. When the garden was dying its flowers achieved a rare loveliness that has not been surpassed before or since. The reigns of the three Philips (Philip II, 1556–1598; Philip III, 1598–1621; Philip IV, 1621–1665) mark the progress of Spanish art, and also the decline and fall of the Spanish empire, which gradually became a hollow shell. Velázquez's portraits of the hapless Hapsburg kings and their families reveal better than any words the inbred weakness of the line which by the time of the last king of that name, Charles II, had degenerated to the level of chronic disease and imbecility.

Spain clearly had been left behind by the rest of Europe. Doggedly she had clung to her dream of a Catholic Europe; sternly she had maintained a Catholic Spain; inefficiently she had governed her empire overseas, and ineptly she had wasted her last resources on stupid battles, immoral philanderings, and the building up of the most crowded priesthood on earth. Everybody in Spain was zealous in the avoidance of plain hard work. The victorious soldier, no longer victorious, turned easily into a vagabond, a gambler, a bandit, or a priest. He became a parasite, not a producer. And this was the tragedy of his nation.

A system of values was arising which would leave the nation hopelessly behind in the mainstream of European progress. Industry, economic development, technical advancement, constitutional government, intellectual freedom, education—in all of these spheres the other nations of Europe made steady headway, while Spain kept marking time at the tail end of the procession. Unable and unwilling to keep up with the times and the changed values by which men lived, Spain shut herself away from these things, decried and scoffed at them, claimed they were no good, and clung tenaciously to her medieval past. Spaniards had less and less to eat, but still they boasted of their great empire, their rich culture, their zealous faith, and their incomparable individual worth. "Did I not tell you they were only windmills," said Sancho to Don Quixote, after the good knight had been rudely tossed about on one of the giant blades. And in another episode Don Quixote said to Sancho: "This, Sancho, that I plainly perceive to be Mambrino's helmet appears to you to be a barber's basin, and to another it will seem to be something else." Sancho thought a while and answered: "Oh, well, that basin-helmet . . ." This was certainly one of the great dilemmas of Spain: She saw nothing clearly, not even what was in front of her own face.

But Spaniards continued to create great works of art, as they always have, even when fanaticism is casting its ugly shadow. Tastes in painting change as the years roll by, and the artists considered to be the very best yesterday are not always considered to be the best today. Fifty years ago most connoisseurs of Spanish art would have said that the three greatest painters of Spain were: Velázquez, Murillo, and Goya. Today the choice would more likely be: El Greco, Velázquez, and Goya. Murillo has dropped out of the top three, and El Greco, the fabulous Greek from the island of Crete, has moved into first place. I do not insist on this particular listing, but it undoubtedly reflects a very wide sampling of opinion.

El Greco's name was Doménico Theotocópuli, and he signed his paintings with this name in Greek letters. He was called El Griego or El Greco, because this shorter name was so much easier to handle; it means simply "the Greek." El Greco was born around the year 1548, on the island of Crete. He went to Venice as a young man, and studied in the studios of the great Titian. About 1577 he arrived in

Toledo, and spent the rest of his life there until his death in 1614. His first painting there was an *Assumption of the Virgin* which is now in the Art Institute in Chicago. A later, and far superior *Assumption* is in the little church of San Vicente of Toledo.

Toledo, perhaps the most fascinating city in all Spain, possibly the most interesting city in Europe because of its small size, vast history and variegated artistic remains, is inseparably welded to the life of the gifted artist. He painted most of his pictures for churches in the area, and his view of Toledo, in the Metropolitan Museum of New York, is one of the finest and most unusual scenes ever put on canvas. El Greco also tried his hand at sculpturing without much success, and he even served as architect for a couple of churches in the small village of Illescas, between Toledo and Madrid. Two of El Greco's paintings, rarely seen by the tourist, are still in Illescas. They are hung in one of these ancient churches, and are shown to the curious by a little old nun who seems as much a part of the atmosphere as do the paintings and the church itself. Illescas, now an abandoned and run-down town, with this one glory from the past, lives like a shadow in the midst of its ancient plains, almost within earshot of Spain's tumultuous and bustling capital, now a city of four millions. How often, in moving across the country, visiting the byways and small villages of the hinterland of Spain, does the traveler come unexpectedly on some ancient church in which there is a great treasure. How often, too, does one come upon a great uncompleted hull, an unfinished church, a monastery without a roof, a few hollow walls to which the ivy now sadly clings . . . somebody's unfinished dream. Like the dream of Spain herself . . . unfinished, incomplete.

El Greco was undoubtedly a great painter. His paintings "in the style of Titian" attracted much attention during his early years in Spain, and were much sought after. But El Greco was anxious to develop his own unique talents, and he bent every effort toward this end. Occasionally, the results were not so good. In the *Escorial*, for example, Philip II's somber, massive mausoleum-church-library-monastery, there is a painting by El Greco which was commissioned by the king himself. Its subject matter is the martyrdom of Saint Maurice. If El Greco had pleased Philip with this painting he might have gone on and decorated the entire building, but when the King saw what the Greek had done, he was greatly displeased. The colors were harsh and gray, the soldiers half naked, their ugly legs sticking out beneath fascinating faces, which pass almost unnoticed because the center of focus is not on them. Philip had the painting hidden away in a corner of the building; he did not consider it the kind of thing that should be put in a position of importance in a religious building. Perhaps, however, by losing this particular opportunity, El Greco went on to become himself. At least, after this he was not under any pressure from the king to paint in a stipulated manner. And what he did paint appeared to be very popular, for churchmen vied for his services and paid him well, and he lived very comfortably until the day of his death.

El Greco's twelve apostles, of which there are two sets in Toledo, one set in the so-called House of El Greco, the other in the cathedral, are among his best religious portraits. The apostles in his house (*La Casa del Greco*) are not finished; many of the hands, faces, and figures have not been completed by the artist, although this may not be apparent at first glance. Some of the fine faces of the apostles, particularly those in the cathedral, reflect a real biblical zeal. An even more stirring religiosity is evident in El Greco's sorrowing Christs, tear-brimmed eyes uplifted, hands resting white and gentle on the cross, the whole a mystical transfiguration of life, sorrow, and divinity.

One of El Greco's earliest paintings in Spain was his *El Expolio* (The Stripping of the Lord's Raiment), in the Cathedral of Toledo. The central figure of Christ, clothed in a deep red, is surrounded by those who are tearing at his clothes in order to divide them as Jesus passes helplessly down the street. The painting is still magnificent, but the color of Christ's robe appears very definitely to have been painted over by some later artist, much in the hue of a bullfighter's cape. A fine German painter who lived for years in Toledo copying El Greco's works viewed the picture with me, and pointed out why he was certain this is so. His reasons were convincing.

El Greco's most famous picture is *The Burial of the Count of Orgaz*, in the little *Mudéjar* Church of Santo Tomé, in Toledo. This painting was commissioned by the Cardinal Archbishop Quiroga, and was later presented by the prelate to the church. For centuries it hung on the wall in a bad shadow, its marvelous craftsmanship only partially revealed. Now the picture is properly lighted, and the whole church seems gathered around it. The count of Orgaz died in the 1300's, but El Greco used as models for the mourners personages of his own epoch, many of them famous cultural figures: Lope de Vega, Garcilaso, and Cervantes. His own small son also appears in

the funeral procession. The faces, coats of mail, and figures themselves are meticulously painted. The white hands and pallid features,
typical of El Greco's men, indicate clearly the softening that had
taken place in the noblest class of Spain. The upper portion of the
picture shows the count's soul being received into Heaven, and is in
an entirely different style. The whole painting contrasts the physical
and the supernatural worlds with masterly concept, colors, and design. The limp and pallid body of the count is being lowered into
his grave by St. Stephen and St. Augustine, who have come down
from Heaven for this purpose. St. Augustine, an old man wearing
a mitre and arrayed in rich pontifical vestments of golden tissue,
gently holds the shoulders of the dead count whose splendid dama-
skeened black armor contrasts vividly with his own golden robes.
The visitor to Toledo feels the urge to view again and again this
magnificent picture whenever he finds himself passing near this
little church, with its ancient *Mudéjar* belfry, on one of the city's
many rambling and narrow streets.

El Greco's Virgins and Holy Families are noteworthy for their
contorted forms, as are many of his saints. The portraits of his contemporaries are in a steadier vein. Among the latter the portrait of
the Grand Inquisitor, Niño de Guevara, in the Metropolitan Museum
in New York, is one of the finest. The figure moves out toward the
viewer, its face a study in stern and positive religious zeal. Many of
El Greco's figures are extended to an unusual length, often about a
head longer than they should actually be according to the other body
measurements. Some have said that this is the artist's way of giving
these persons the appearance of transcending reality. Others have
claimed that El Greco was merely reflecting the expanding universe
of his epoch. As the limits of the old world grew outward, so did
man's conception of it and of the divinity beyond it. Still others
have insisted that El Greco was afflicted with a certain malfunctioning
of the eyes which made him see bodies longer than they were, and at
a certain angle to the perpendicular. This latter contention appears
to have been proved by taking scientific measurements of many of his
paintings, but in my opinion it does not mean a thing. The fact may
be a curiosity, but it has nothing to do with the excellence (or lack
of excellence) of El Greco's art. Astigmatism could never give
quality to a canvas, nor talent to a dunce.

In many ways El Greco is the most typical of Spain's artists of
the Golden Age, and he was not born in Spain. However, he became

in time more Spanish than the Spaniards themselves; he was able to see and to reproduce the essence of the Counter Reformation as no Spaniard could. He was able to capture for all time the contorted spirit of his adopted countrymen, and the tortured frustration of their religious dreams. He was able to see Toledo as no Spaniard could, and to put its mystical greenery and unearthly cloud-flashes into form, pigment, and emotion in a manner that no other painter even approaches. When Sheldon Cheney wrote that El Greco achieved "the most nearly infallible handling of abstract elements known to Western painting," he was close to the truth. Popular during his own epoch, El Greco was neglected by art critics and by the public for nearly three centuries after his death. Manet and other French artists admired him greatly, but it remained for the Spanish critic M. B. Cossío to rediscover the artist for Europe, which he did in a series of five studies that appeared between 1908 and 1914. The English connoisseur and art collector, Sir William Stirling Maxwell, in his delightful *Stories of the Spanish Artists*, published in 1910, made El Greco well known in the British dominions.

El Greco was followed by Velázquez (1599–1660), who for centuries was the most highly regarded of all Spanish painters. Velázquez was born in Seville, "of gentle blood"; his father was descended from the great Portuguese house which traced its lineage back to the kings of Alba Longa. The young man was given a fine education, and showed a considerable disposition for languages and philosophy. His greatest predilection, however, was for art, and he drew feverishly from an early age. Herrera the Elder, himself a competent artist, was Velázquez's first teacher. Herrera was already well known throughout Andalusia, and at his house gathered a sizable group of disciples interested in painting. The teacher's greatest asset was his quick and dexterous ability to record living form and figure, but his violent temper tantrums and harsh language kept his disciples in a state of constant dismay. Velázquez, a shy and easy-going young man, learned all that he could from Herrera and then hurriedly drew away.

His next master, who later became also his father-in-law and biographer, was Pacheco, an artist less gifted than Herrera, but of a more even temperament. Velázquez soon learned that nature herself is the best teacher, and he spent long hours assiduously drawing objects, animals, and persons from life. Pacheco writes that he hired a peasant lad to stay with him permanently as a kind of apprentice and model, so that he might be able to record the boy's changing expressions and emotions whenever the urge hit him. He recorded these in rapid, charcoal strokes which he could elaborate later, if he so desired. In this manner Velázquez sharpened and refined his tremendous innate talent as an artist.

At the same time,

to acquire facility and brilliancy in coloring he devoted himself for a while to the study of animals and still life, painting all sorts of objects rich in tones and tints, and simple in configuration, such as pieces of plate, metal and earthen pots and pans, and other domestic utensils, and the birds, fish, and fruits which the woods and waters around Seville so lavishly supply to its markets.[32]

These pieces, painted in dark interior rooms (*bodegones*), form the main product of the artist's younger years, and many of them bear favorable comparison with the best Flemish masters. Human heads, precise still lifes, carefully painted animals and dark rooms—these things represented the early Velázquez.

In his next stage the artist becomes acquainted with El Greco and more specifically with El Greco's best disciple, Tristan, whose combination of sober Castilian tones blended with the brighter colors of the Venetian school appealed to him immensely. Velázquez openly confessed his admiration of Tristan, and from him he acquired a more brilliant coloring and more effective elements of contrast in his art.

Velázquez went to Madrid when he was twenty-three; he spent many hours studying at the Prado Museum and at the *Escorial*. One of his paintings of these days is a portrait of the balding Góngora, the Cordoban poet of rare conceits and beautiful images. Not long afterward the young artist was called to the attention of the king, Philip IV, who became his patron for the remainder of his life. Some three dozen of Velázquez's canvases are of this pallid-faced sybarite with the downturned eyes and the jutting Hapsburg jaw. Many others are of members of the royal family and of courtiers and attendants. Several contain full-length figures of one or more of the ugly dwarfs which were then so popular in the Spanish court. That all of these paintings are fine works of art no one denies, but they are portraits that can hardly be said to send the viewer into any surge of ecstasy. The artist's finest single figure is without a doubt his deeply moving crucified Christ, which gave rise to one of the finest poems in Spanish, written by Miguel de Unamuno, poet, essayist, philosopher, and rector of the University of Salamanca in our own time.

Velázquez made two visits to Italy, the first when he was thirty years old. Rubens, who was visiting the Spanish court, had advised him to go, and he spent two years in Italy. His second visit was when he was approaching fifty. He was now one of the most famous artists in Europe. On this occasion Pope Innocent X commissioned Velázquez to paint his portrait, which is an extraordinary work of art. "It is reported that when His Holiness saw the artist's sketch, revealing the shrewd, hard face, he winced and said, 'Too true.'" Sir Joshua Reynolds later stated that this was the finest painting in Rome. Shortly after this Velázquez painted the first female nude of Spanish art, the famous "Rokeby Venus." It shows a beautiful woman's reclining form from the back, perhaps a concession to the Spanish church which prohibited the painting of naked women.[33]

In his final period Velázquez painted the *Hilanderas* (Spinners) and the *Meninas* (Maids of Honor), both of which reveal a craftsmanship which has ever since been the admiration of all artists. Many have called the latter work the "finest painting in the world." From a technical standpoint this may possibly be true; from a standpoint of stirring an emotional response, it certainly is not. Velázquez, one of the most masterly technicians of all time, unfortunately was lacking in the ability to capture the essence of human character, anguish, or longing, qualities that come through so often in the best figures of El Greco, Michelangelo, or Rembrandt.

The third world-famous painter of Spain's Golden Age was Esteban Murillo (1617–1682), who, like Velázquez, was born in Seville. Unlike his compatriot, Murillo never studied abroad nor became a favorite of the court. Velázquez, however, did give Murillo every encouragement, and not only made it possible for him to visit all the royal galleries, but kept him as a guest in his own house, and introduced him personally to many foreign painters who visited Spain. He also urged Murillo to go to Italy to study, but the young man never made the trip.

Murillo is famous for two kinds of paintings: his religious pictures, mainly those of young Virgins with the fresh innocence of a girl in her teens, and his paintings of lower-class types, particularly street urchins and peddlers. He painted dozens of Immaculate Conceptions and Assumptions "with sweet blues predominating" in which the rounded pristine form of the Virgin appears to be painted "with blood and milk," as one Shavian critic wrote. Perhaps Murillo's finest picture, which is still in Seville, is a huge canvas of *Moses Striking the Rock*, from which a stream of water is seen gushing forth. This is one of eleven paintings that the artist produced for the Church of Saint George in Seville. He was paid approximately $3,000 for the lot. Several of them were taken to France during Napoleon's occupation of Spain in the early part of the nineteenth century. But the famous *Moses* and its colossal twin, *The Miracle of the Loaves and the Fishes*, still remain in Seville.

Murillo's street urchins and peasant types have a considerable appeal, and are a good cross section of lower-class Andalusian life in the seventeenth century. One well-known painting, *A Grandmother Delousing a Child*, records a scene which was widespread in Spain until very recent times. The old lady is carefully pulling the child's hair apart and looking for the little animals underneath. The child's expression is one of contentment.

Murillo's reputation has declined with the years. Once placed near the top of the great Spanish artists of all time, he was later regarded as being much too sentimental; in recent years he has regained some of his lost esteem. There were many other good painters of the Golden Age; the divine Morales, Sánchez Coello, Ribera, Zurbarán, and Alonso Cano are perhaps the best known. (The great Goya painted in the nineteenth century; he will be discussed later.)

The principal sculptors of note during these years were Alonso de Berruguete, Juan de Juni, Gregorio Hernández, Martínez Montañés, and Juan de Mena. None of these equaled Michelangelo, but Berruguete (1486–1561), disciple of that great Italian master, did indeed rival Donatello. Berruguete spent sixteen years studying in Florence, and was the main link between the two countries in this field. Although Italian influence was very strong in Spanish sculpture, there is a deep and often tortured realism in the best Spanish pieces which suggests a Semitic root.

Polychromed statues abounded in the churches of Spain, and Spanish choir stall and altar pieces (*retablos*) of beautifully carved wood are among the finest in the world. Those at Toledo, Ciudad Rodrigo, Seville and Burgos are good examples of this work at its best. Many of the Spanish sculptors also produced statues in wood which are unique. They often took the greatest pains to represent teardrops and blood with zealous accuracy. Spanish iron grillwork, which separated the interiors of religious buildings into various chambers, and served as gratings or railings for many other purposes, was another field in which the Spaniards excelled. Carried to the New World this art was born there anew and marked the path of conquest from one end of the empire to the other.

In architecture the Renaissance period brought in the Plateresque, an exquisite fusion of the old and new (Gothic, Moorish, and Italian Renaissance styles), which is said to have been suggested by the decorative art of the silversmiths or *plateros*. The *Mudéjar* or Moorish style also continued to exert its appeal. Many buildings, in characteristic Spanish fashion, mingled several architectural patterns into a single harmony. The High Renaissance style became more and more severe, and in *El Escorial* embodied the somber mood of Philip II. Later still, as a protest against the severity of the sixteenth century, the Baroque and then the ultra-Baroque threw restraint to the winds as architects went wild with flamboyant and overwrought designs, often so thick that it was difficult to locate the columns beneath the decoration. This style reached its peak in Mexico when the great silver mines poured forth their torrent of wealth, and miner vied with miner to see who could build the most beautiful temple to God. Borda's lovely Church of Santa Prisca in Taxco is an example of one of these buildings, but there are many, many others.

In music Spain produced some of the most outstanding composers of the age. Antonio de Cabezón, "the Spanish Bach," is still greatly admired for his superb organ music. Luis de Victoria, of Avila, probably a pupil of Palestrina, also composed some of the most stirring religious music to come out of Europe. His choral compositions have rarely been surpassed. Francisco de Salinas, of Salamanca, in 1577 published a long theoretical musical work in which several folk tunes are preserved. Salinas, who was a professor of music at the University of Salamanca, was completely blind. The mystic poet Fray Luis de León has immortalized him in a famous ode.

One of the most priceless collections of old Spanish music is found in the *Palace Song Book* (*Cancionero de Palacio*), thought lost until it was rediscovered in the Spanish National Library in 1870. This book contains approximately five hundred pieces of the fifteenth and sixteenth centuries, about seventy-five of them by Juan del Encina. The songs were of all kinds: amatory, pastoral, chivalresque, historical, religious, picaresque, humorous, and indecent! Several of these have been recently recorded, using the ancient instruments, and with the voices making every effort to capture the ancient flavor and tempo. During the Golden Age, folk songs of every kind and from every region continued to thrive: ballads, work songs, religious tunes, dances, love lyrics, pilgrims' songs, and many others. Their variety and abundance undoubtedly places Spain at the top of all European countries in the field of folk music. Many of these melodies are still sung today, although the phonograph, the radio, the motion picture, and now television are rapidly gnawing away at these ancient remains of bygone centuries.

The king of all musical instruments in Spain was, of course, the Spanish guitar. In the sixteenth century it was essentially the same instrument that it is today. It had an incurved body in the shape of a figure eight, a flat top and bottom, a long neck with frets, and was played directly with the fingers. Egyptian bas-reliefs of 3700 B.C. picture instruments of the same general type. The Spanish guitar, however, was probably derived from the Roman cithara, of Greco-Assyrian origin, which was brought into Spain around the time of Christ. It is definitely certain that the Latin guitar or *guitarra latina* of medieval Spain gave rise to the modern Spanish guitar. The Moorish guitar or *guitarra morisca* had the rounded shape of the lute; its popularity waned after expulsion of the Moors. The lute itself was introduced into Spain (and via Spain into Europe) by the Moors, but this instrument never became popular in the peninsula despite its wide appeal in the other European countries. The guitar was both cheaper to make and handier to play than the delicate and costly lute.[11]

In the sixteenth century guitars of several kinds were in use in Spain. They had four, five, six, or seven strings, or pairs of strings, all of gut, the largest instrument being the one with the most strings. It was customary to double all the strings except the highest at the unison. The Spanish word for the instrument was generally *vihuela* or *vihuela de mano*, meaning "fiddle played by hand." *Vihuela* was the term for any stringed instrument with a neck, but as the guitar was by far the most popular of these instruments in Spain it was often referred to by this name alone. As early as 1535 a vignette in Luis Milán's *El Maestro* shows Orpheus, surrounded by an audience of birds and beasts, playing a six-stringed Spanish guitar. The instrument has had a distinguished career since that time. Andrés Segovia has restored the classic dignity of the guitar of the Golden Age with his matchless artistry, and *flamenco* guitarists by the dozen have popularized the rapid rhythms of Andalusian deep song.

While the arts flourished, the national economy, the social organism, the national spirit and potential sputtered and stalled. In the final century of the Golden Age (1600–1700) the kings of Spain became progressively worse. Philip III was worse than his father Philip II, who had died in 1598; Philip IV was worse than Philip III, and Charles II, the Bewitched, last of the Hapsburgs, was the worst of all, a sickly effigy who presided over a nation in ruins. Miserable economic conditions and a succession of military defeats had reduced Spain to a second-rate power, but these kings made things infinitely worse with their own stupidities.

It is in the seventeenth century that the ancient dichotomy of Spain again rears its head: strong centralization or regional separatism—which will it be? During the previous several centuries Castile, the great heartland, had asserted her dominion and had succeeded in unifying Spain. Castile was a land of great warriors; her war spirit was admirable, and it had led to the enforced unification of many diverse provinces. "Castile had invented great enterprises; Castile had placed itself at the service of noble juridical, moral, and religious ideas; Castile had outlined a plan for a social order; Castile had imposed the standard that the superior man be preferred over the inferior, the active man over the inert, the astute man over the dull-witted, the noble man over the man of vileness."[34] And of course, Castile had imposed the idea of the stronger man over the weaker.

With the reign of Philip III we note that there has been a change in values. At first glance it appears that nothing has changed, but a closer scrutiny reveals that everything has turned hollow and rings with a note of falseness.

The same old words and ideals are still repeated, but they no longer stir the heart. The old stimulating ideas have become mere topics for literature. Nothing new is undertaken in the realm of politics, or science, or morality. All activity has come to rest precisely on the idea of *not doing anything new*, in upholding the past—its institutions and its dogmas—in suffocating every initiative, every innovating idea. Castile is transformed into the very opposite of her old self: she becomes suspicious, narrow, sordid, bitter. She no longer occupies herself in *leading* the other regions of Spain; jealous of them, she abandons them to themselves and begins to live oblivious of what is taking place in them.[34]

Separatism in Catalonia and in the Basque provinces awakens and begins to stir with renewed vigor. Castile knew how to conquer, but she did not know how to govern.

In 1609 Philip III, encouraged by his advisers, decided on the expulsion of the *Moriscos*. There were perhaps half a million of these people still in Spain. They were nominal Christians, but widespread reports of their following Moslem practices in secret had reached the court. Ships were brought and the *Moriscos* were loaded onto them under the eye of hundreds of Spanish troops. They were taken to North Africa and dumped there. Most of these *Moriscos* were agricultural or textile workers; the production of cotton, silk, paper, rice and many other products was mainly in their hands. So was nearly all of Spain's irrigated farm land, which reverted to a desert when the *Moriscos* left. The decadence of Spanish industry and agriculture dates from the time of their expulsion.

Spain appeared to be governed by a combination of fanaticisms: a loyalty to the kingship which eliminated constructive criticism, a superstitious credulity which attributed even the most obvious errors of agriculture, of economy, and of health to supernatural things, and an intransigence to change which kept the country inert while the rest of Europe was marching forward. Even when famines and epidemics of disease hit Spain, the Spaniards, instead of studying the situation and applying the best knowledge of science, shrugged their shoulders and murmured that the will of God must be accepted, and that they must have committed some sin in order to be thus visited with His ill favor.

Economic conditions were so bad in Spain that unemployment became a national scourge. Young men coming of work age could find nothing productive to do. The only security for them lay in entering the church, which attracted hundreds of thousands of them. By the mid-point of the seventeenth century it has been estimated that 1,141,000 persons held religious jobs of one kind or another in the Spanish empire, and another 447,000 held governments jobs. They became a dead weight which the remainder of Spain could not support.

The New World continued to drain away many of the country's most able workers. But here too economic conditions were often deplorable, and the priesthood became top-heavy. "This easy means of acquiring an honorable profession and a comfortable livelihood attracted such large numbers that in 1644 the town council of Mexico

City implored Philip IV to send no more monks, as more than six thousand were without employment, living on the fat of the land."⁶⁰

With the expulsion of the *Moriscos* went also the last hope of Spain's being a *clean* country. These Moorish descendants had always loved water, and had made it flow for them wherever they established residence. Their bodies and cities were so much cleaner than those of Castile that the poet Góngora, accustomed to the water-flushed cities and homes of his native Andalusia, made frequent and unsavory mention of the foul odors and filth of Madrid and of the other centers of central Spain.

Yet it was in Madrid that the extravagant Spanish court held forth with its lavish etiquette and opulent display. The money that came into the king's hands went through like sand. Debts were seldom paid on time, taxes were raised beyond all sensible limits. As if this were not bad enough the kings then began to debase the currency. Prices rose with alarming rapidity, and this led to even further debasement and inflation. There was no point in trying to do any serious business at all. The kings kept looking to American silver to bail them out, but this wealth reached Seville only to be forwarded at once to some foreign banker.

In all this drab picture there was only one haven outside of the church, the Spanish New World. Even in those days America was a land of promise. Thousands had gone to the New World and had found gold and slaves. Cervantes himself wrote that "the poverty of some, the greed of others, and the madness of all" caused a great exodus from the stricken peninsula to this land of the freer life. America became "the refuge and haven of all the poor devils of Spain, the sanctuary of the bankrupt, the safe-conduct of murderers, the escape of all gamblers, the promised land for women of free virtue, the lure and disillusionment of the many and the incomparable remedy of the few." Such are the feelings of one of Cervantes' characters who loses his fortune in the Old World and regains it in the New.

Back in Spain the conquistadores out of date, the gold-seekers gone to seed flooded the streets. Productive labor of all kinds was neglected under the backwash of the Midas dream. Villages and towns fell into ruin, and vast treeless wastes appeared, covered with weeds and briars, where cultivated fields and forests had been before. The poverty was so widespread that there were scarcely any marriages.

In spite of the prostration of the mother country the imperialism that Spain carried out in the New World has no parallel in the world's history. Never before had such a tremendous area and so many millions of diverse peoples been absorbed into the cultural and social consciousness of a conquering power. Never before had the problems of race confronted a nation on so vast a scale, and never before or since have they moved toward a solution with less racial bitterness.

The fundamental weakness of Spain as a colonial power, and the ascendency of British, Dutch, and French imperialism over her, lay in the backward and intransigent nature of the Spanish political and social institutions, in Spain's static economy, in her religious intolerance carried over into the political sphere, in her general unwillingness to swim with the current of social change, but most of all in the vastness of the problem which she undertook to handle. The British, for example, advanced slowly; they took over, populated and consolidated a relatively small territory until they had learned the art of colonial government. In 1776 when the thirteen colonies rebelled, British settlements in North America reached barely a hundred and fifty miles inland from the Atlantic, whereas Spain by 1600 had already occupied and was governing twenty or thirty times as much territory, including the millions of Indians who inhabited it. Had Britain undertaken this same heroic dream she too would almost inevitably have failed, perhaps even more miserably than Spain. This, however, in no wise excuses the ignorance and paralysis of the Spanish social and political system, or the imbecilities of the Spanish monarchs and their advisers.

When Charles II came to the throne in 1676 everything was lost. He had not the ghost of a chance to redeem Spain from her wretchedness. Every hope had fled. The dream was dead. Still, with that stubborn Spanish pertinacity which clings even more firmly to an idea that all others have abandoned as unworkable, the inhabitants of the peninsula held onto their outworn beliefs. Every law and governmental action seemed directed toward the greater concentration of power in the crown. The economic situation was so wretched, and the social classes were so neatly balanced one against the other that a state of national inertia resulted, followed by paralysis.

Philip IV had died in 1665 in the sixtieth year of his age, leaving his only son, Charles, a sickly child of four, as heir to the throne. For a time there was a regency, but when Charles was fifteen he took over the realm; he was in name absolute monarch of an empire of many millions of inhabitants and of vast territories. He was pushed and pulled about by his ministers and his advisers so that he rarely knew what was going on. In his final years he became a chronic invalid. He produced no heir to the throne. When he fell into his final illness in 1700 and knew that this was the end, he sought the counsel of the Pope as to the succession. The Pope stated that the French were the legitimate claimants to the crown.

Charles II was distressed. He hated the French.

Louis XIV had robbed him of territory, and treated him with contempt. Enfeebled in body and mind, and on a bed of suffering, his ecclesiastics, obedient to the will of the Holy Father, denounced upon him the terrors of eternal damnation if he did not bequeath the crown to the Bourbons of France. Thus appalled, the half-delirious king signed the decree which was awaiting his signature. Then, bursting into tears, he sank back upon his pillow, exclaiming, "I am already nothing." Soon after this he died, in the year 1700, in the fortieth year of his age.[36]

Spanish culture was always a fruit or a flower that came from a garden which promised even more, but, lacking the proper cultivation, went wild and died. For the past several hundred years the history of Spain has been that of a dying garden overgrown with weeds. Or, if we should prefer to look upon her national life in the symbolic representation of a physical body, we might say with the Englishman J. B. Trend, that for centuries past this national body has been suffering from a hardening of the arteries. Perhaps this has been Spain's disease ever since the day that Philip II, with his stern mistaken zeal, opened the veins and began to let the lifeblood out.

The great poet Góngora once wrote: "Not all these are nightingales singing among the flowers; it is music of the mind." And as Don Quixote lay on his deathbed, he turned to Sancho, who was anxious to be off on another sally, and said to him: "In the nests of yesteryear, Sancho, there are no birds today." If Spain had listened to that proverb she would probably not be where she is today. Grasping at a phantom dream, she always found it to elude her grasp; what remained in her hands was a skeleton. A fitting epitaph? "I sing in words that moan and remember a sad wind that blew through the olive trees," wrote García Lorca, contemporary Spain's most promising young poet, shot by the Franco fascists in his prime. With cruel and startling frequency Spain has time after time in her history slain, exiled or called into disrepute her most promising young men who dared fall out of step in the national dance of death.

10

THE BOURBONS

A Bourbon never learns anything, and never forgets any-thing.

An old Spanish saying

When Philip V, the first Bourbon, came to the throne of Spain in 1700, the country's political corpus had been anesthetized by two centuries of absolution. Philip V was the grandson of Louis XIV, and represented the relatively intelligent tendencies of the French monarchy of his epoch. His accession was not exactly welcomed with open arms, for powerful elements in England, Holland, Austria, Portugal, and several German principalities opposed him bitterly. It was feared that a French king in Spain would destroy the balance of power in Europe, giving undisputed hegemony to France. Hence, these countries supported the candidacy of Charles of Austria, who was considered more favorable to their interests. Catalonia and Aragon also supported Charles, as they feared Bourbon absolutism. These were the most progressive parts of Spain politically. The Castilians backed Philip, whom they felt would better preserve the hard won unity of Spain.

Thus began the War of the Spanish Succession which lasted for thirteen years, and exhausted the last pitiful resources of the Spanish nation. In the end, however, Philip V won his crown, although in the Peace of Utrecht Gibraltar was ceded to England. This was forevermore to be a thorn in the side of Spain.

With Philip V French thought crept into the peninsula, filling a few important nooks and crannies. French customs, which made a bigger and more obvious show, were still more widely imitated. The first three Spanish Bourbons (Philip V, Ferdinand VI, Charles III) made a valiant effort to catch up with the other nations of Europe which had passed Spain by, but their policy of "revolution and reform from above" met with little enthusiasm among the people.

In practically every aspect of life the dead weight of tradition held the country back, for the Spaniards cherished tradition. In the eighteenth century, perhaps more than in any other epoch, each individual Spaniard was certain that he was in possession of the truth, that his way of life was best, that his cultural environment was superior to that of any other European nation, as he was superior to every other European. Despite the fact that he had seen the famous Spanish *tercios* defeated on several occasions by the French who were supposed to quake at the sight of a Spanish soldier, despite the national bankruptcy, despite the grinding poverty and universal illiteracy of the masses, he still believed in the exaltation of the monarchy. If the Hapsburgs were all dead, then a Bourbon would have to do. Some Spaniards might object, and some indeed did, particularly in Catalonia, but after the young Bourbon king had overcome all opposition and taken a firm hand on the federal government, the people gladly embraced the new absolutism. The writer and statesman Campomanes put it this way in an essay that he wrote at the end of the century: "In our Spanish masses there is no opinion more deeply set than this: the king is the absolute lord of the lives, the possessions and the honor of us all. To put this truth in doubt is held as the kind of sacrilege."

The Bourbons brought in French ideas and strove to reinvigorate Spanish thought. They established the Spanish Academies of Language, Medicine, History, and Fine Arts; they liberalized the monarchy, instituted economic reforms, soft-pedalled the Inquisition, made slow headway against the national stagnation. The eighteenth century in general was characterized by a struggle between two opposing tendencies: the Europeanization of Spain, espoused by the intellectuals and by the crown, on the one hand, and, on the other, the attempt to recapture some of the essence of Spain's past glory simply by intensifying the use of measures utilized two centuries previously. This latter attitude was supported by the mass of the Spanish people. One example of this was the attitude toward the reactionary Jesuit order, disbanded by the liberal Charles III at the end of the eighteenth century because of its interference in the national political life. The Spanish masses sided with the Jesuits, and the liberal action of the king had the unexpected effect of winning supporters for their cause. With such a populace the best intentions of the most liberal monarchs would in the end come to a mere inching forward. The Spaniards resisted progress all the way. The motto of the Enlightenment, "all for the people without the people," had little meaning in Spain.

The Bourbon monarchs were not great lovers of merriment or festivities. "Philip V is melancholy, Charles III is severe and more fond of the chase than of courtly receptions. Only Ferdinand VI, who reigned between these two, enjoyed theatrical representations." The Bourbons had no real friends in Spain. For many decades they did not feel at home in this strange country. In order to remind him of his beloved Versailles, and because he so hated the gloomy *Escorial*, Philip V built a French-style palace surrounded by spacious gardens at La Granja in the foothills north of Madrid. And when the famous Alcázar of Madrid, residence of the Spanish kings ever since its construction by Charles V, was destroyed by fire in 1734, carrying many priceless works of art with it, the same Philip, in 1738, began the construction of a new palace which, when completed in 1764, was the amazement of European royalty. Its interior lavishness still makes it one of the most impressive royal palaces in the world. But in spite of their opulent palaces the Bourbons lived lives of quiet desperation.

The Bourbons made every effort to lighten their mood with musical events and by moving the court about with the regularity of a traveling circus. Charles III, for example, left Madrid always on the fifth of January and went to the nearby Pardo palace where he remained until Palm Sunday, when he returned to Madrid. At Easter the court moved down to the palace at Aranjuez, a few miles south of Madrid, and stayed there until July 21, when it went north to La Granja, remaining there until October 8. Finally the king went to the *Escorial* until December 10th, when he returned again to Madrid. During the month of April, while the court was officially in Aranjuez, he went hunting for wildcats in the mountains. The total time spent in Madrid turned out to be seventy days. However, as the other residences were all very near the capital, this in itself did not cause inefficiency in the government.

Two of the most famous musicians of the epoch were imported for the entertainment of the Spanish court: Domenico Scarlatti, the famous composer, and Farinelli (Carlos Broschi), the gifted *castrato* singer whose lovely golden tones were heard at the royal theater in the Buen Retiro gardens and at La Granja. Scarlatti "settled in Madrid in 1729 and spent the rest of his life in Spain." Philip V was charmed with Farinelli's voice and granted him a large annual pension in addition to giving him paintings, diamonds, gold jewelry of many kinds, and a beautiful carriage. He also named him director of all theatrical spectacles of the realm. Farinelli "sang the same four songs for his royal master every night for nine years."[33]

These things helped to make life livable for the Bourbons, but nothing made them truly happy. The rigidity of the court etiquette was such that it became a noxious and time-consuming affair; the liturgical stiffness took all the fun out of courtly living. Their wives were the only true friends these early Bourbons had, and at their death the kings sank into a deep depression. Philip V, overwhelmed by melancholy, abdicated when his wife died, and a broken heart sent Ferdinand VI to an untimely grave, barely a year after the death of his wife. For ten months of this time he lived in a dream world "going from one madness to another, often sitting on the edge of a stool for fifteen to twenty hours at a stretch staring vacantly into space."

In regard to religion a Spanish historian of the present generation writes:

For the Spaniards of the 18th century, as for those of the 17th and 16th centuries, the Catholic religion is not only the official religion, but is also the only religion in which one's soul may be saved. Many centuries of struggle against the Moslem and the Lutheran have strengthened this belief to definitive extremes. Those who enlist under the banners of the true faith are certain to be right. Those who do not, should strive not even to becloud with their breath the serenity of those who are convinced believers.[35]

The king of Spain was still "His Catholic Majesty." And it must be remembered that there never arose in Spain a single Protestant church. Indeed, this is one of the great tragedies of Spain as a nation. A few Protestant sects, even two or three, would have put the Spanish Catholics on their toes, would have prevented carrying religious totalitarianism over into the political sphere. But Spain was never a country where church and state could be thought of as separate entities. Bound together by the eight centuries of wars against the Moslems, they remained together until fairly recent times. Franco, in one of the fundamental policies of his government, also insisted on retying the old knot. The Spanish church-state did not in the eighteenth century and did not under Franco permit dissidents as a matter of course, whether they be political or religious.

It is true that the Bourbons did not support the Inquisition with much zeal, and Charles III, angered by the economic wealth and political intrigues of the Jesuits, finally ordered the disbanding of the Society of Jesus (1767) and the expulsion of all Jesuits from the Spanish dominions. However, not many years passed before the Jesuits came back again, with renewed energy. Except for brief periods of liberalism the Jesuits had a strangle hold on education in Spain up to the Second Republic (1931). A contemporary Catholic historian, referring to the Inquisition in the eighteenth century, writes defensively even on this point. He states that the prison cells of the Holy Office "were full of light and air. Breakfast was served at six, lunch at ten, and supper at four. Torture, used as the ordinary means of punishment in the prisons of the times, was not applied in those of the Inquisition when the accused was less than twenty-five years old, or more than sixty, or was a pregnant woman."[35]

Many foreign travelers were astonished at the lack of dignity that Spaniards showed in their churches despite their dogmatic formalism of belief. A French priest was aghast to note that in Cádiz the Virgin of the cathedral was gowned like a young bride of the epoch, and that her dress was changed just as frequently, according to the seasons. St. Joseph was dressed in the Spanish manner "with long trousers, jacket and black cape, high lace neckband, black shoes, wide hat under his left arm, big glasses on his nose, dagger and rosary in his right hand." Even the child Jesus was familiarly treated, sometimes being dressed as a canon, at others as a doctor or lawyer with a wig and carrying a cane with a golden hilt. As a magazine of the period complained:

In olden times our homes were churches; today our churches are homes. . . . Women come in and march down the main aisle right to the main altar attracting the attention of every male present. Others mount the Presbytery in order to be seen by everyone in the congregation. A meal lasting three hours can be a delightful affair, a dance lasting five or six hours can be a wonderful evening's entertainment; but a mass that lasts half an hour is insufferable, even if one is not kept on his knees.[35]

The Spanish state and monarchy rested on two firm columns: the church and the nobility. During the conquest and colonization of the New World thousands of new nobles had been created. The conquistadores, almost without exception, were lowborn men who attained to noble status because of their achievements for the crown. "I did not come to America to till the soil like a peasant," Hernán Cortés had said before he began the conquest of Mexico. He spoke for every Spanish soldier. True, this new breed of nobles did not exercise the strong military influence which the nobility had enjoyed before the days of Ferdinand and Isabella, but as familiars of the king they were in a position to reach the monarch's ear in a way that no commoner could hope to do. Despite the rigorous formalities of the Spanish court, the nobles enjoyed certain familiarities both in and out of the royal palace. Grandees did not have to take off their hats in the presence of the king. And they could stroll in and out of the royal chambers with an intimacy which was at times shocking. One old print shows a large group of them hanging around in the queen's bedroom waiting for her to give birth. This was one of the things which made intolerable the private life of the Bourbons. Their most intimate moments were a matter of public spectacle.

Under Charles III (1759–1788), the most enlightened of the eighteenth century Bourbons, official action was taken on the prevailing and deep-seated Spanish belief that a man lost status by working with his hands. A royal decree was issued which stated clearly that the work of a tanner, a blacksmith, tailor, shoemaker, and several other specified kinds of work with the hands "are decent and honorable; that the practice of them in no wise degrades the person or the family of the one who engages in them, nor does it prevent his obtaining government employment or the attaining of rank of nobility." This decree had become imperative because of the widespread reluctance of Spaniards to carry out the essential work of the nation. The papers of Madrid greeted the decree with warm praise, but several years passed before it had much effect. As the essayist and minister Campomanes wrote: "Laws might decree that there is no dishonor in being a shoemaker or a tailor, but as long as they do not also state that doing no work at all is a dishonor, there will always be *hidalgos* who will consider do-nothingness as the inseparable companion of nobility, and will regard all manual labor as a blot on him who performs it."

In education the eighteenth century had become at least less ridden with superstition and ignorance than the two previous centuries. At the same time it perpetuated firmly the "eternal principles of religion and country" on which all universal theories and human relationships must be based. The education of children was given a more important place in the national life than previously, for the child was considered as the tender seed who would grow into the mature fruit of tomorrow. The ideal was as follows: First of all, respect must be instilled for God, king, and parents. At eight children *should* learn to read and write, and to use the Castilian pronunciation. At nine they *should* learn arithmetic, algebra and geometry. At the age of ten they *ought* to be taught geography, "which is one of the sciences that most enlighten one's understanding." At this age "they *should* be forbidden to read any books of chivalry or profane comedies, because these are a sweet bait that the Devil employs to weaken the character of the most innocent maiden and of the boy in the hands of the most vigilant teacher." From ten to twelve they *should* learn sacred and profane history, and from twelve to fourteen foreign languages.

Note all of the "shoulds" and "oughts" in the above sentences. The Spanish schools in fact were a far cry from this educational ideal. The atmosphere of these schools was very severe. The teacher kept a sharp lookout and a laggard pupil was whacked across the shoulders or arms with a switch at the least provocation. As the proverb says: *La letra con sangre entra*, "it takes a little blood to let the learning in."

The Spanish universities were something else again. Gone were the great teachers of the Golden Age, yet medieval scholasticism, with all its verbose, theoretical arguments, was still the vogue. Theology was still considered as the master science of which all the other sciences were the servants. It was also the most honored and highest paid chair at the universities. Theoretical problems were disputed incessantly in Spain, while in the rest of Europe progress was being made in physics, anatomy, botany, geography, natural history, and in all the other fields of knowledge. The historian Ballesteros reported that classes in theology still discussed such subjects as what language the angels spoke, and whether the sky was of bell metal or of wine-like liquid. The University of Salamanca held that the study of Newton would not improve one's logic or metaphysics, and that Descartes was much farther from revealed truth than Aristotle. Universal categories, philosophical syllogisms, abstract arguments taught the young Spanish scholar a glib verbosity with little meaning behind it. Good maps were nonexistent. There were no laboratories. The texts were old and outdated. Many university students even believed that higher mathematics was all a bunch of lies and sorceries. When Torres Villarroel applied for the chair of Mathematics *and Astrology* at Salamanca it had been vacant for thirty years. In medical practice the *sangría* or bleeding was the cure-all. Spaniards were bled not in the arm but on the back of the hand or on the foot. Women were frequently bled two or three times a month. One learned traveler attributed the large number of blind people in Spain to the frequency of these bleedings, which debilitated the body.

Madrid, in the early eighteenth century, was perhaps the dirtiest city in Spain. It was a place of almost 200,000 inhabitants crowded into a relatively small area, hence the streets were narrow and dark. They were also filthy. When Charles III arrived from Naples in 1759 he remarked how dirty the place was compared to the cities of Italy. His wife commented on the ignorance, superstition, and barbarism of the people. The dwellings were poor and dingy. The panes in the windows were small and of a bluish color which hardly let the light through. Doors and window frames were always in need of paint. The fronts of the buildings were rundown and ugly. Some intelligent Spaniards considered it as a national disgrace that the monarch lived in the filthiest of all Spanish cities; slop was still being hurled from the windows, and even the air was malodorous. Seville, Toledo, and Valencia had undergone considerable expense to overcome similar problems, but Madrid, the capital, seemed bogged down in its endless bureaucracy, and nothing was done. At night the streets were dark, and no one ventured out unless he was fully armed. At a snail's pace the Bourbons slowly changed the appearance of Madrid, and by the end of the century it was beginning to have the aspect of a reasonably impressive South European city. It began to look very much like a second-rate Paris or Berlin.

In the cafés and inns of the capital it was against the law to smoke, to read the newspapers, to talk of politics, to play cards or billiards. Each tavern was allowed to have only a single exit, so that criminals might not escape through the back door. The subjects on which discussion might turn were typical: the theater, bullfighting, love, and poetry. Women were not allowed to linger on the premises, and a strange law passed at the end of the century stated that any un-married male tavern keeper was prohibited from having in his estab-lishment a woman waitress or cook "who was not at least forty years old, *more or less.*"

The two most popular items in the dress of the Spaniards of the eighteenth century were the long cape and a wide-brimmed hat. The cape had already been made famous by the plays of the Golden Age, and now everyone wore it. As a writer of that epoch said: "A Spaniard might be willing to go around without shoes, but without a cape, never!" The cape was the national symbol, and even the dead were buried in it. These huge dangling garments made it easy for pick-pockets and petty thieves to snatch things and hide them immediately without being caught. So frequent did this kind of crime become that finally Prince Esquilache, the minister of Charles III, decreed that the cape must be shortened and made smaller in size, and the hat also reduced. Precise measurements were mentioned. A criminal could easily escape detection, even when the police knew his identity, simply by pulling the cape up over his face and the big brim of his hat downward. But the minister made a tactical error, for his minions went about the task of enforcing the decree with uncommon vigor. Those who ignored it were simply backed up against a wall and their capes and hats clipped off with enormous shears to the proper size. A great hue and cry was raised, and before long a mob went on a rampage demanding the minister's skin. He was generally disliked because he was an outsider, an Italian who had accompanied the king to Spain. His Italian name, Squillaci, had become Esquilache in Spanish. After the riot the king himself had to flee from Madrid and take refuge in the palace at Aranjuez, a few miles distant. He re-mained there for nine months. The irascible mob would not settle down until the king had exonerated his minister from all blame in the wanton shearings.

Another item of pride in the eighteenth century was the Spanish coach. A person who could possibly afford a coach would rather go without food than do without this proof of status. Those who were able to own "colts from Córdoba" and "mules from La Mancha" were considered to be the cream of the cream. Promenading in fine coaches was one of the great delights of the well-to-do. The other citizens gaped in admiration as they passed by. Since the streets were so narrow, so ill paved, and so liberally sprinkled with slop it was often necessary for pedestrians to take refuge within the nearest vestibule in order to escape the flying blobs which went in all directions when a coach came down the street.

Charles III greatly improved the highways of Spain, and in 1788 he established a system of long distance coaches known as diligences. He also made every effort to wipe out the widespread banditry that infested the roads of Spain, for up to his reign it was practically impossible to travel across the country without being held up and robbed. He also initiated many economic reforms and a program of public works. Industrial experts were brought into Spain from other countries to teach the new processes, and 6000 Bavarians, knowledgeable in agriculture, were settled in thirteen new communities in the Sierra Morena. Education was secularized after the expulsion of the Jesuits, and the school system reorganized.

Among the social pastimes of the eighteenth century was one which has since become almost the distinguishing mark of Spanish life, the *tertulia*, or conversational gathering. The name itself originally referred to a restricted part of the theaters which was reserved for serious-minded men, many of them priests who enjoyed talking about Tertullian. Hence, their part of the theater was called the *tertulia*. Later, the term came to mean any session of men, or women, or of mixed company in which conversation held the floor. There were also literary *tertulias* at which the writers gathered. Later still, each individual writer of note had his own *tertulia* which was attended by his admirers and disciples. This custom still prevails today. These literary *tertulias* always gather at a certain café on a given day of the week, and the address is even better known to the author's friends than that of his home.

During the eighteenth century two hot drinks were served in Spain, chocolate and coffee. The latter drink was popular among the French and the few Spaniards who followed them, but hot chocolate was still by far the most popular beverage. It was more than just a beverage; it was an institution of the epoch. As in the Golden Age hot chocolate was drunk by all classes. Even Charles III himself, despite his French blood, enjoyed hot chocolate and seldom failed to ask for a second cup. The *chocolatera* or chocolate pot at the palace held fifty-six pounds of the beverage, and served a huge number of drinkers. Chocolate was considered almost as a necessity among the Spaniards, and when the Jesuits were expelled from the country it was stipulated that they were to be allowed to take with them "their breviary, a few clothes, *chocolate*, and other necessary things for their personal use." Writers of sketches of manners and popular poets made frequent mention of chocolate. The following quatrain from a Valencian poet is typical:

> Oh! divine chocolate,
> they grind you on their knees,
> folded hands whip you,
> and eyes lifted to heaven drink you!

The great passion of the Spaniards was for dancing. When the Bourbons first came to the throne French customs and dances almost obliterated those of the country, but this did not last for long. The Spanish *seguidillas*, of which the typical *Sevillanas* of Seville is the Andalusian variation, the *fandango*, and the *bolero* were among the most popular native dances, while the most popular importations were the minuet, the *contradanza*, the gavotte, the waltz, the polka, the rigadoon, and the galop. The *contradanza* came to Spain from France (*contredanse*), which had gotten it from the English *country dance*. The *contradanza* later gave rise to the *habanera*, and this in turn eventually produced the Argentine *tango*.

The intellectual life of Spain during the eighteenth century was strongly permeated with foreign influences. France, of course, exerted her dominion as she was doing at the time throughout Europe, and the Bourbon dynasty accentuated this inside Spain. Rousseau, Voltaire, Montesquieu and other French writers were admired by the handful of Spanish intellectuals. But influences from other countries were almost as strong. The English writers Francis Bacon, Locke, Young, Adam Smith, and Pope were also well known and were strongly influential in the rebirth of Spanish learning as the century progressed. The influence of the French encyclopedists took root in the latter part of the century, but resulted in only a relatively few works. Intellectual stagnation and scholasticism had reached such a low point in 1700 that it was many decades before the mind of Spain could pull itself out of the morass, and by the time it had done so, the enlightened Charles III had died and the throne was taken over by one of the weakest and most stupid of the Bourbons, Charles IV, whose imbecilic family is preserved in immortal degradation in the paintings of the artist Goya.

A Benedictine monk, Father Benito Jerónimo Feijóo (1676–

1764), was the most noteworthy among those whose efforts brought about some improvement in Spanish thinking. Father Feijóo wrote with a pungent pen essays against superstition, myths, ignorance, scholasticism, backwardness, narrow-mindedness and all the other ills of the intellectually effete Spaniards. He supported the direct study of nature and direct human experience as against useless abstract speculations and empty verbosity. An edict of 1771 requiring the modernization of all textbooks and curricula in Spain indicates the measure of Feijóo's success. His views were bitterly contested by those who upheld the ancient regime, but Feijóo had many followers, and it has been estimated that a total of half a million volumes of his appeared in print during the century. He was read even more widely than Cervantes. This indicates how desperately the best Spanish minds were reaching out for the progressive elements of European enlightenment as they swam about stogged in the heavy waters of tradition and ignorance. In the end these waters proved too deep, their current too strong, and at the turn of the century Spanish intellectualism again went to its defeat in the rotten court of Charles IV and his loose-moraled queen.

Ferdinand VI and Charles III were both honest and enlightened monarchs, but neither of them made much use of the Spanish Cortes, which met only three times in the eighteenth century. The new dynasty carried on the tradition of an ameliorated despotism. "The most meticulous of the Bourbons was Charles III. His daily life was one of absolute precision. He got up at exactly a quarter to six in the morning, if need be awakened by an aide who slept in the same room with him." For the next hour or so he prayed and meditated. At precisely seven o'clock he entered the royal chambers where there were awaiting him doctors, surgeons, a pharmacist and several other subordinates. There he got dressed, washed, and had his first cup of hot chocolate. As soon as he had drained the cup he called his Neapolitan butler and asked for a refill. The king next went to visit his children in their part of the palace. At eight o'clock he entered his own private study where he worked until eleven. At this hour the heir to the throne, the Prince of Asturias, came in and they chatted for a while. "The king then spoke with his confessor, and afterwards he received the Ambassadors of Naples (his former kingdom) and of France; following this, the other foreign Ambassadors were admitted to his presence."

"He lunched in public, his table generally being blessed by the

Archbishop of Toledo, and chatted with several persons while the meal was in progress. After lunch he took a siesta in summer, but not in the winter." He next received other foreign visitors, and then discussed important affairs of state in private with the indicated parties. In the afternoons he liked to go hunting, which was his principal diversion. If he bagged much game it was all divided up among his subordinates when he returned. Frequently he played a game of cards called Reversi until about nine-thirty, when he was served a protracted dinner. Shortly after finishing his supper he said his night prayers, and went to bed.[35]

When Charles III died in 1788 a similarly precise schedule of ceremonies followed him to his grave. All the bells of Madrid tolled out their knell announcing the death of the king. The nobles of the king's chambers dressed the body and adorned it properly with all the neckbands of his orders. The cadaver was then placed in a wooden casket, which was covered with a rich golden cloth and placed inside a larger lead sepulcher. The dead king was carried to the Hall of the Ambassadors, where he was placed on a catafalque over which his private corps mounted guard. The doors of the palace were then opened so that the public might file by and see for the last time the face of their monarch.

The following day the Nuncio said the prayer for the dead, the deans of the Golden Fleece and of the military orders approached the catafalque and respectfully removed from the body the various neckbands of office. The king's hat was also removed, and his casket was carried to the highest point on the stairway of the palace, where the final service was held. The coffin was then covered with a rich brocade and carried to a closed carriage, which then began its long journey to the *Escorial*. The road was lined with soldiers, and in the distance cannonades were heard. The populace crowded around in tears to see the cortege pass by. At the *Escorial* the casket was removed from the carriage and taken down to the *pudridero* or "rotting room" where it was solemnly turned over to the prior. (Five years later it would be removed to the pantheon or permanent burial room.) The captain of the king's guard then broke his staff of office, for there no longer existed the monarch who had given it to him for his defense. The guards fired three volleys, the bells tolled slowly and sadly for the dead. . . . The king rested at last among the bodies of his predecessors. The last best hope of Bourbon enlightenment and of reform was gone, and for the next one hundred years the na-

tion would sink again into the slough of depravity, of inertia, of useless words.

Spaniards in general have long regarded the eighteenth century as a
kind of unhappy hiatus in their history. They felt that just as Spain
had previously turned her back on the Renaissance and on the Reformation, in the latter years of the eighteenth century she turned her
back on the Enlightenment. The old xenophobia had reasserted itself
with a vengeance.

For over a century it was almost universally believed that during the
period of the Enlightenment (Spaniards refer to it as *La Ilustración*
or *El Siglo de las Luces*) the Masons and the Jesuits were engaged in
a mortal conflict, the Masons representing progressive French ideas,
the Jesuits defending Spanish conservatism. This prevailing belief was
supported by both Jesuits and Masons, each group creating a bogey.
Unfortunately, among most Spanish intellectuals it acquired the
validity of dogma: "The Masons came in 1727 from Gibraltar; they
spread their lodges to all the cities of Spain; they had secret ties with
Protestant England, until the Count of Aranda, friend of Voltaire
and scourge of the Jesuits, became grandmaster and transferred their
allegiance to atheistic France."[71]

As a consequence of this view there arose the second belief: that in
the eighteenth century Spain split into two camps, indeed into two
Spains, and that this dichotomy has continued until today. Spaniards
on both extremes have pointed to the eighteenth century as being
responsible for the country's later social, political, and intellectual ills.
Each side, of course, laid the blame for these ills on the other.

The Spanish scholar Menéndez Pelayo, in Volume III of his *Historia de los heterodoxos españoles*, 1881, declared that the Enlightenment brought forth "the capital heresy of modern times, the negation
of the divinity of Christ." Voltaire was "the symbol and the incarnation of the spirit of evil in the world." The French Encyclopedists were
his troops, spreading anti-Catholic ideas, preaching the doctrine of
materialism and irreligion, in a word, denaturalizing Spain. As a result
of this, Menéndez Pelayo concluded that Spain in his day (the last
decades of the nineteenth century) was "the most backward country
in Europe in all science and serious discipline," excepting only Turkey
and Greece.

Menéndez Pelayo spoke favorably of Feijóo and Jovellanos, the two
most appealing figures of the Spanish Enlightenment, but he decried

the works and beliefs of the liberal ministers of Charles III (Aranda, Floridablanca, Campomanes) and other Spanish Encyclopedists who, in his opinion, had attacked their own national genius, deeply rooted in the Catholic faith. These liberal and godless ministers and their ilk brought on the divisions of the following two centuries, made the "two Spains" inevitable, and divided the country against itself. They neglected *the true and honored Spanish values.*

The twentieth-century physician-historian Gregorio Marañón reached a similar conclusion: "The failure of Spain in the first half of the nineteenth century, of which its civil wars bear witness, was brought about almost exclusively by the continual stupidity of the majority of the progressives, who sought to make progress un-Spanish." On the other side of the spectrum, Américo Castro, who admired those enlightened liberals of the eighteenth century, unhappily refers to them as "the epidermis of Spanish life." Spain, he felt, has little capacity for sustained rational thought. Castro's dictum was immediately attacked by a contemporary of his, Sánchez Albornoz, who regarded this attitude as utterly demeaning to the genius of his people.

Another Spanish intellectual (of the 1930's), Ramiro de Maeztu, reiterates the theme of Menéndez Pelayo. "During the second half of the eighteenth century," he wrote, "we were governed by aristocratic Masons. . . . We chose to fulfill our dreams by trying to be what we were not, and for two hundred years we have been crying our hearts out trying to be what we are not instead of being ourselves with all our available strength."

The most famous Spanish scientist of modern times, Ramón y Cajal, took the opposing view. He thought that the sixteenth century had opened one window for Spain, facing Renaissance Italy, while the eighteenth century had opened another window, letting in the spirit of scientific criticism. Spain's task was to cast aside her ancient isolation and enter the universal currents of modern thought. The Generation of 1898 preached the same sermon.

In any event, an obvious cleavage did continue in Spain's intellectual and social life, and the civil war was later fought because of irreconcilable political differences. That war was won by the conservatives whose "glorious movement" attempted for some thirty-five years unsuccessfully to restore the ancient Spanish values. Strange to say, General Franco's greatest claim to success lies in the material progress which his regime effected, but he achieved little to bring the "two Spains" closer together in intellectual and emotional union.

Charles III died in 1788, one year before the bloodbath of the French Revolution began. He brought to a close Spain's hope for progressive political leadership. The excesses that took place in France were viewed with great trepidation in Spain, and following her usual course this country clamped down on liberalism in general:

The French Revolution accomplished in Spain what the American had failed to do. It provided the irritants that transformed into cancerous growths the hitherto innocuous discords brought on by the Enlightenment and economic expansion.

No Spaniard was stirred by events in France more deeply than Floridablanca, who was frightened by the challenge of the Revolution to the doctrine of royal absolutism into checking the institutions of enlightenment that his ministry had encouraged under Charles III. Floridablanca's reaction was similar to that of other enlightened authorities. Catherine II closed Russian frontiers to French publications and required local French residents to abjure allegiance to the Revolutionary regime; Joseph II on his deathbed in 1790 condemned the pusillanimity of Louis XVI and abolished freedom of the press in Austria; and his successor, Leopold II, pacified the nobility and clergy by abolishing enlightened reforms.[72]

Spain, therefore, was not the only European country which tried to preserve her institutions by stepping backward.

The next two Spanish kings, Charles IV, and his son Ferdinand VII, were among the worst that the country has ever had.

We know little about the early life of Charles IV save that it was a life of sin and shame. He was a man of weak intellect, impotent in action, and dissolute beyond all restraint in his habits. His wife, Maria Luisa, a Neapolitan princess, was a woman thoroughly abandoned to sensuality, without any apparent sense of her utter degradation. Soon after the accession of Charles IV to the throne, the throes of the approaching French Revolution began to be felt throughout all Europe, giving rise to the Republic and the Empire in France. The pollution of the Spanish court under Charles IV and Maria Luisa can not be described. It is admitted by all, denied by none. Neither the king nor the queen made any attempt to disguise their profligacy.[36]

In the king's bodyguard there was a handsome young soldier named Manuel Godoy. The queen's eye fell on him, and he became her gigolo and lover. Godoy rose rapidly in rank, and before very long had become prime minister, and the real ruler of Spain. He was hated by Ferdinand, the heir apparent, who plotted to depose his father and assume the crown. At this point (1807) the whole Spanish monarchy disintegrates: Ferdinand is jailed by his irate parents; the populace, incensed by Godoy's rule and the royal parents' debasement, rise to the prince's defense. Godoy is pursued by the mob and is forced to hide for thirty-six hours in the attic of the palace, rolled up inside some discarded old mats. Finally, he is rescued by the royal guard, but the mob then surges to the rooms of the king, who, mortally fearful of a revolution like that of France, abdicates in favor of his son.

Both Charles and Ferdinand immediately make every attempt to get Napoleon's backing, each realizing that without some outside support his cause would be hopeless. Napoleon, with his sharp eye for taking advantage of good opportunity, persuades them both to meet him in southern France at Bayonne. Here Charles IV, his queen, and Ferdinand put on a degrading scene before the French emperor, shouting the most filthy and scandalous insults at each other. Ferdinand brashly accuses his mother of adultery, and Napoleon points out to him that if this were true he would have no legal claim to the throne of Spain. Finally, convinced that neither father nor son would make a decent French ally on the Spanish throne, the French emperor decided to reserve that position for his own brother, Joseph Bonaparte, who he hoped would establish a new dynasty in the neighboring kingdom.

In the meantime, French troops with full Spanish consent had already entered the country for the purpose of conquering Portugal. They now took over the government of Spain, and Joseph was made king. Neither Charles nor Ferdinand was allowed to return to Spain. The populace was enraged at this trick of fate which unexpectedly gave them a foreign monarch. On May 2, 1808, there was a spontaneous uprising in Madrid against the French forces quartered there, and much bloody fighting took place before the revolt was quelled. (Goya has caught the drama of the uprising in two of his best canvases, and in a powerful series of etchings which bear the overall title of *Disasters of the War* he depicted the horrors of the conflict that ensued.) Joseph then attempted to occupy the rest of the country and to govern it. He had few supporters in Spain, where the people were already referring to him insultingly as Joe of the Bottles, *Pepe Botellas*, because of his fondness for alcohol.

The British, ever fearful of Napoleon, now saw a wonderful chance to attack the French emperor on his vulnerable flank, and invaded the peninsula with a considerable army offering the rebellious Spanish masses every military support. Thus began the Peninsular War, called in Spain the War of Independence, which the Spanish people and Wellington eventually carried to a victorious conclusion, forcing Joseph across the Pyrenees. Napoleon was unable to come to his brother's assistance. His disastrous retreat from Moscow with its irreparable losses of men and equipment had made this French defeat in Spain inevitable. It also made certain the final ruin of Napoleon. However, wars are seldom fought for a single purpose and with a clear-cut logic, and it is curious to point out that in this war in Spain, Wellington and the English were actually fighting to restore the tyrant Ferdinand to the throne of Spain, and thus also to restore the Spanish Inquisition and all the other iniquities that went along with the degenerate Bourbon dynasty.

As the war progressed the Spanish Cortes had fled from Madrid and taken refuge in Cádiz, where they had drawn up (1812) a liberal Spanish constitution. The representatives of this parliamentary body were mainly from the towns, and were considerably more enlightened than the majority of the populace. The constitution, therefore, had little chance of operating unless the Spanish monarch, whoever he might be, would support it wholeheartedly. Such was never the case. After the defeat of Napoleon (1814), Ferdinand made his way back to Spain, and the masses everywhere greeted him with shouts of: "Down with the Cortes! Long live our absolute king!" Those who supported the liberal constitution had not the ghost of a chance against this manifestation of public sentiment. The people of Spain had welcomed and embraced their own degradation.

Napoleon, reflecting on the whole affair, had this to say:

The unfortunate war in Spain proved a real wound; the first cause of the misfortunes of France. If I could have foreseen that that affair would have caused me so much vexation and chagrin, I would never have engaged in it. But, after the first steps were taken, it was impossible for me to recede. When I saw those *imbeciles* quarrelling and trying to dethrone each other, I thought I might as well take advantage of it to dismiss an inimical family . . . . The impolicy of my conduct in reference to Spain is irrevocably decided by the results. I ought to have given a liberal constitution to the Spanish nation, and charged Ferdinand with its execution. If he had acted in good faith, Spain must have prospered and harmonized with our new manners. The great object would have been obtained, and France would have acquired an intimate ally, and an additional power truly formidable. Had Ferdinand, on the contrary, proved faithless to his engagements, the Spaniards themselves would have dismissed him, and would have applied to me for a ruler in his place. At all events, that unfortunate war in Spain was a real affliction. . . . If the government I had established had remained, it would have been the best thing that ever happened to Spain. I would have regenerated the Spaniards. I would have made them a great nation. In place of a feeble, imbecilic, superstitious race of Bourbons, I would have given them a new dynasty, which would have no claims on the nation except by the good it would have rendered unto it. I would have destroyed superstition and priestcraft, and abolished the Inquisition and monasteries, and those lazy beasts of friars.[36]

Ferdinand VII took over the throne, and was acclaimed as the absolute king. He re-established the Inquisition, abolished in the brief flurry of liberalism, and crushed every manifestation of reform. He filled the prisons with those who opposed him, and again instituted the old seignorial privileges. Free discussion was extinguished. The liberals were severely punished by the new state, there were widespread executions, and many of them fled from Spain. The Jesuit order was invited back into the country and to it was entrusted the education of the young. The entire nation was impoverished. There was no industry. Bandits infested every highway, and travel was impossible. The king fiddled and debauched and shouted curses on all liberalism. The American colonies, which had taken over their own government during the regime of Joseph Bonaparte in Spain, saw that it was madness to negotiate with Ferdinand and determined to strike out permanently on their own. All hope of repossessing the Spanish empire overseas was doomed by the ignorance and fanaticism of the obsessed and despotic king.

The one shining light of Spanish culture during the stagnant years of the reigns of Charles IV, Joseph Bonaparte, and Ferdinand VII, was the incredible artistic output of paintings and etchings by Francisco Goya, one of the trio of great Spanish artists of all time. When the War for Independence broke out in 1808 Goya was sixty-two. For nearly a third of a century he had been the official painter of the Spanish court.

He had already painted the portraits—startling, grotesque, satirical, adorable, vengeful—of that family of degenerates, of prostitutes and monsters, which ruled over Spain and had gone in full force to Bayonne to grovel at the feet of Napoleon and to wash before the conqueror's eyes the dirty linen of the family and of the degraded political intrigues which were ravaging the unhappy country.[61]

He had also drawn a couple of dozen cartoons of typical scenes from Spanish life on which a series of lovely tapestries was made, but his genius reveals itself more characteristically in grimmer things.*

Goya saw the war at first hand, and its essence of depravity and horror never left his mind. His many paintings, drawings, and etchings, based directly or indirectly on that holocaust, constitute an indictment of warfare never before or since portrayed in art. Goya puts down exactly what he has witnessed, and he has seen the worst. Men turned to beasts have committed murder and rapine before his eyes; he has seen and etched a man held by the legs and sliced through the crotch with a sword, he has etched another man impaled on a tree, he has seen a wounded French soldier dragged to his death and uses the title *He Desrved It*, he has seen mothers raped in the presence of their horrified children, he has seen sensuality arise amidst the bestiality and it appears to give him a vicarious pleasure to bare the naked breasts of women who are about to be raped. With the famine of 1811 he saw women and children reduced to skeletons, and he drew these too. They hold out their pitiful hands to passersby, but receive nothing. Goya's titles are: "Shouting's No Good," "Nobody Could Help Them," "Do They Belong To Another Race?"

He etches a monk with talons on his feet and vampire's wings in place of ears, and calls that etching "Contrary to the General Interest." In a later etching the same priest's heart is sucked out by the vampire, and this is entitled "Consequences." In another a donkey holds an open book before him as he gives lessons to some monks, and Goya calls this etching "That Is Still Worse." In another etching there is the dead body of a woman, and Goya inscribes it: "Truth Lies Dead."

The "Disasters of the War" constitute the most terrible and truest

---

* Goya often laid his colors on with sticks, sponges, or dishcloths. His brushes were generally of the coarsest texture. A French critic states: "Smearing his canvas with paint, as a mason plasters a wall, he would add the delicate touches of sentiment with a dash of his thumb." Goya's picturesque scenes of Spanish life served the Spanish composer Enrique Granados (1867–1916) as the basis of his opera *Goyescas*, which contains some melodies of great beauty. The artist's black-and-white sketches of the bullfight, *Tauromaquia*, are the most moving representations of that spectacle in Spanish art. His *Maja* dressed, and also in the nude, both in the Prado, reveal the deep sensuality of the painter. The story about her being the duchess of Alba, his mistress, is highly dubious. Goya did, however, live a riotous and sensual life, and had many illegitimate children. It was also widely reported that he was a fair bullfighter.

document of any war ever fought. The living drag their feet through blood, and the dead assume grotesque attitudes with legs apart, hideous open mouths, curled fingers, unspeakable grimaces transformed into caricatures of human life. Goya often inscribes simply *I saw this, And this.*

The "Disasters" were first printed around 1824, when Goya, then seventy-eight years old, had crossed the Pyrenees alone and taken refuge in France (strange fate), in order to escape the despotism of Ferdinand VII and the Inquisition, which he feared might be re-established at any moment. His etchings on bullfighting and his series entitled *"Caprichos"* and *"Proverbios,"* which expose the vices of the Spaniards are powerful studies in black and white. Most of his artistic output, aside from his excellent cartoons and portraits, some of which are of adorable children, reveals man's monstrous inhumanity to man, the symbolic degradation and the incredible courage of the people of Spain. The paintings which he had hanging on the walls of his own home, all of which are now in the Prado Museum, represent unspeakable horrors and in many instances their meaning eludes the observer. A grotesque and monstrous Saturn chewing off the heads of his own children is one such example. Some critics maintain that Goya went mad before he died in 1828, at the ripe age of eighty-two.

Ferdinand's rule inside Spain so infuriated the enlightened portion of the population that in 1820 sizable elements in the military forces rebelled against the king, and took over the government. The liberal constitution of Cádiz was again put in force, the Inquisition was abolished, and for three years there was a semblance of liberal government in Spain. The leader of the revolt, General Riego, became a temporary hero, and a melody that was popular with his troops later became the National Anthem under the 1931 Spanish Republic. It was known as the Hymn of Riego. Some of the words to this song, and to others popular at the same time, indicate the nature of the hostilities that existed inside Spain:

> If the priests and friars only knew
> What a drubbing we are going to give them,
> They would all huddle in a group and shout:
> Liberty! Liberty! Liberty!

Si los curas y frailes supieran
La paliza que les vamos a dar,
Se pondrían en coro gritando:
Libertad! Libertad! Libertad!

There were also very obscene words to some of these songs, such as:

Trágala, trágala, trágala,
Cara de Morrón,
No queremos reina puta,
Ni queremos rey cabrón.

Swallow it, swallow it, swallow it,
Old horse-faced reactionary,
We want no harlot for a queen,
And no cuckold for a king!

The "swallow it" refers to the Constitution of 1812, which the op-position, particularly the king, was being forced to swallow. The government of these liberals, however, was only a brief and ineffective interlude in the history of Spain. As we have seen, the masses of Spanish people were hostile to enlightened government. They pre-ferred an absolute king, even a miserable degenerate like Ferdinand VII, to a constitutional regime. Hence, when French troops again invaded Spain in order to replace Ferdinand on the throne, they met no opposition. For the second time within a decade the back-ward, superstitious, reactionary Spanish populace greeted its chains as if they were of purest gold (1823).

By the time Ferdinand VII died in 1833, their ardor was some-what dimmed. He had led a life of debauchery and his government was openly corrupt for all to see. Around his very deathbed members of his family engaged in physical fisticuffs and verbal vituperation over who was to inherit the throne. Ferdinand had changed the law of the nation in order to allow his daughter Isabel, then three years old, to follow him. Carlos, the king's oldest brother, bitterly opposed this, and rose in rebellion, thus starting a long series of Carlist wars which found their main support in the extremely religious Basque provinces.

At the news of Ferdinand's death, many of the Spanish liberals, who had been forced into exile, returned to their native land, and slowly, painfully, laboriously, Spain again picked up the pieces and began her long and agonizing ascent from the bottom of the pit. They could see, as we can see, that their prostrate country had passed through the enlightenment without being enlightened, had passed through the peroid of the French Revolution without being reformed, and was passing now through the industrial revolution without being industrialized.

Elsewhere in Europe a set of values had taken root which the Spaniards did not understand and were unable to apply: constitutional government, social reform, the application of new discoveries and techniques to the economy, the buildup of communications and transportation, agricultural reform, the separation of church and state, freedom of speech, of assembly and of the press. But Spain held tenaciously onto her medieval dream. Gutted and prostrate she still spouted about her sacred faith, her glorious past, her splendid character, her matchless courage and unique zeal. It was like standing in a graveyard and boasting about the exploits of the deceased as if such boasts would cause the dead to arise again and take a new lease on life.

The Spaniard who caught the essence of this grotesque dream of Spain was Mariano José de Larra (1809–1837), one of the great writers of the nineteenth century. His father had backed Joseph Bonaparte during the French occupation, and when the French were defeated had fled with his family to Paris. The amnesty of 1818 permitted them to return to their native land. Larra as a child was something of a prodigy, and this contact with France gave him a glimpse of liberalism in action which made his future life in his own country a constant frustration. He decided on a career in journalism, and by the time he was twenty-four he had become the best paid journalist in Spain. Larra developed a pithy, mordant style, quite unlike that of the other Romantic writers of his generation, and in his many essays he punctured every inflated boast and pride of Spain, exposing the shrivelled corpus that lay underneath. "To write in Madrid is to weep," he said, because writing for Spaniards was a waste of ink and soul. Not one of the national defects escaped his pointed pen: the snobbism of the Frenchified dandies, the uncouth and gross nature of false patriotism, the proverbial indolence of the Spaniards, the widespread desire to live a life of trickery in the style of the old *picaros*, the backwardness of the social, economic and political institutions, the futility of any kind of idealism in Spain, etc.

Larra lived like an iconoclastic Romantic, and he died like one.

On February 13, 1837, his little daughter came into his study to say goodnight, and found her father lying in a pool of blood. He had put a bullet in his brain at the age of twenty-eight. The capital was shocked by the suicide, there was rumor of an extra marital love affair in which the author had been jilted, but the consensus was that he had been consumed by his bitterness. It was later revealed that both of these things were true. When the funeral took place there was a great ceremony, with the whole literary world of Madrid in attendance. As the body was readied to be lowered into the grave a frail, white-faced young man came forward and in an emotional voice read an elegy he had written to the deceased. The mourners were deeply touched by the words of the unknown young man, José Zorrilla, who thus initiated his career as a poet. Zorrilla later became one of the leading writers of the Romantic movement in Spain, and was also the author of the famous *Don Juan Tenorio*, 1844, a play which displaced on the Spanish stage the earlier one by Tirso on the same theme. This is the Don Juan play which is still tremendously popular in Spain today. It is widely presented around the time of All Souls' Day, an appropriate date for playing a drama the finale of which takes place in a cemetery.

Larra did not believe in half measures; as a writer he was absolutely devastating. He looked frantically for some evidence of a rebirth of culture and science in Spain, but found none. He searched for those elements of character which might have meant salvation, and they too were nonexistent. He came to regard the regeneration of Spain by Spaniards as an utterly impossible dream. He gave himself up to pessimism and despair, and wrote about his country and its people with a frankness that alarmed the conservatives but drew the intellectuals toward him like a magnet. Larra himself enters many of his essays as a principal character, giving them a personal and individual note lacking in other Romantic writers. This artistic personalism plus his terse, almost classic style and his faculties for hypercriticism have made the writers of later generations seek him out, exalt him, repeat and acclaim him as both genius and prophet.

In one of Larra's best essays he deliberately gets his servant drunk so that the latter will speak to him frankly, revealing the truth. The servant is glad to oblige, and thus becomes a sort of "voice of the author's conscience." He contrasts his own paltry but satisfactory material life (like that of Sancho) with his master's soaring intellectualism (somewhat like that of Don Quixote), which leads only to frustration and to despair. The servant speaks:

> You read day and night seeking the truth in books page after page, and you suffer when you cannot find it. You invent words and make of them feelings, sciences, arts, objects of existence. Politics, glory, knowledge, power, wealth, friendship, love! And when you discover that they are but words, you begin to blaspheme and to curse. Meanwhile, I eat, drink and sleep, and nobody deceives me, and if I am not happy, neither am I in despair. You command me, but you cannot command yourself. Have pity on me, writer. I am drunk on wine, it is true; but you are drunk on desires and impotence. . . . ![37]

Larra had a considerable following in Spain, but he realized that writing to influence Spaniards was like attempting to plow the sea. The three classes in Spain were equally deaf, each in its own way. Who was there to listen sincerely? The masses were

> indifferent, brutalized, useless for years to come, because they had no intellectual needs and lacked all stimulus. They were unable to move for themselves and were waiting until they would allow themselves to be moved. Or perhaps the middle class, gradually becoming more enlightened, was at last beginning to have intellectual needs, was beginning to realize that it had been and still was in a very bad state, and desired reform because change was the only way it could better itself. Last of all, there was the privileged class, not very numerous, brought up in, and dazzled by, foreign lands: the victim of political emigration—a class which believed that it alone was Spain, and was surprised, at every step, to find that it was only a hundred yards in front of the rest.[21]

In another even more mordant essay, *Día de difuntos de 1836* ("All Souls' Day of 1836"), he describes the exodus from Madrid to the cemeteries, and exclaims: "And for this they are leaving Madrid!" At the graveyard he envies the dead, and inquires of the living:

> You are going to visit your fathers and grandfathers, when you yourselves are the dead ones? They are alive, because they have peace; they have liberty, the only liberty possible on this earth, that given by death; they pay no taxes; they cannot be mobilized; they cannot be denounced nor imprisoned; they are the only ones who enjoy freedom of the press . . . They, in fine, recognize only one law, the imperious law of Nature which put them there, and that law they obey.
> "And what monument is that?" I exclaimed on commencing my stroll through the vast cemetery.

"Is it the immense skeleton of past centuries, or the tomb of other skeletons? *Royal Palace!* On one side it faces Madrid, that is to say, the other tombs . . ."

When the author reaches the government buildings in his deathly stroll, he reflects: "Here lies half of Spain: it died killed by the other half."

The stroller tries to take refuge in his own heart, but finds there only another sepulcher. "Let us read the inscription. Who has died there? Frightful epitaph! Here hope lies buried!"

"Silence, silence! The cemetery is in our hearts!"

Larra signed many of his pieces with the name *Fígaro*, hero of the famous trilogy of comedies by the Frenchman Beaumarchais in which the old regime is ridiculed. It is easy to understand why this name appealed to him so much. The second play of the trilogy, *The Marriage of Fígaro*, 1784, was one which had aroused the French with revolutionary fervor. In it Count Almaviva, who represents the aristocracy, plans to exercise his *derecho de pernada* or feudal right to sleep with the bride of his barber, Fígaro, on the night preceding their wedding. Fígaro is naturally incensed, and is doubly furious because he had helped the count win another lady in a previous amorous episode. With a considerable amount of horseplay and several of Beaumarchais' disguises of one person dressing up to pass for another, the barber finally outwits the count and marries his lady-love. The play scandalized the European aristocrats who, just before the deluge, were revealed for what they were: unscrupulous, immoral, degenerate upholders of the iniquitous old order. When Mozart turned the play into an opera (1786), he had to use Italian instead of German words so that the public would not be able to follow all the nuances of the story. The play itself was banned in Vienna, and the public performance of the opera was forbidden in Paris for fear it would stir up the masses. The authorities knew how dangerous this kind of writing could be, but despite all their caution private "rehearsals" of the opera became widely popular in Paris.

Larra made a good Spanish *Fígaro*; he was somewhat less humorous than Beaumarchais' character, and a great deal more barbed in his criticism of the status quo. He understood the Spanish ideals of vitalism, humanism, universalism, and faith, and saw that they were too deeply rooted and too powerful to bend before rationalism, science, political liberalism and social reform, which could have led to the Europeanization of Spain. It was this impasse which made his writings turn inward with hatred and self-destruction.

Isabel II, Ferdinand VII's daughter, had a long, unfortunate reign that lasted from 1833 to 1868, the first few years being under the regency of her mother. During these years Spanish liberalism made progress, and there were attempts to modernize the economy and educational system of the country. Primary schools were established, the universities were reorganized, and several cultural institutions were founded. In her private life, Isabel turned out to be almost as dissolute as her father, and she acquired the neurotic habit of appointing and dropping ministers without rhyme or reason. The government was paralyzed by these incessant changes which reflected every caprice of the queen. Isabel was an enormous woman physically, and at the court functions her elephantine gambolings (she loved to dance) were anything but esthetic. Before many years had passed she was widely referred to in Spain as "esa señora" or "that woman," in a tone that carried both scorn and condemnation. Isabel's king-consort was her cousin Francis of Assisi, whose high-pitched, unpleasant voice caused him to be known as *Paquita* or *Fanny*. When Isabel gave birth to a son (later Alfonso XII) Fanny had to be almost physically restrained from proclaiming that the baby was not his. Before the queen died, eight other children followed.

Isabel was generous, impractical, good-hearted, superstitious, emotionally infantile and unstable. Her private confessor, Father Claret, caused constant trouble by meddling in affairs of state, and Sister Patrocinio, the "bleeding Spanish nun," whose hands were said to bear the marks of Christ's wounds, was also a neurotic influence behind the throne. The bleeding nun's hands were covered with mittens when she was in public, and there was every reason to believe that her wounds were self-inflicted. With such intimates and such a temperament, Isabel II made a mockery of intelligent government.

Spain did make material progress in spite of her corrupt and bureaucratic administration. Rail lines were laid, five hundred miles of them between 1848 and 1858, and three thousand miles more between 1858 and 1868. For the first time in Spain's long history this brought her various regions into close communication with each other. However, the central authority was so inept and unpopular that better communications did little to diminish the strong separatist feelings which have always plagued the country. Moreover, there were gross financial and employment scandals involved in the laying of the Spanish railways, and as a result of these the Queen

Mother herself, who had a hand in the pie, was forced into permanent exile.[38]

The principal importance of the reign of Isabel II lies in the gradual growth of liberalism in Spain. The word must be defined. Spanish liberalism meant simply constitutional government with a moderate bill of rights for the private citizen. It signified no swing to the left or anything like that. Political events in France and England and contact with the German and English schools of philosophy sparked the movement, but many Spaniards were forced into the liberal camp because they hated Isabel II and her entourage of favorites. They had no knowledge of, or concern for, real parliamentary government. By 1868 the country was fed up with the Queen's administration and a *pronunciamiento* by General Prim put an end to her reign. "Spain with honor" was the burden of this *coup d'état*. The Spanish navy first rose in revolt, but was soon joined by the army, strange bedfellows for a liberal movement. Isabel II, finding herself without support, fled from the country bemoaning her fate. "I thought I had put down deeper roots than that!" she exclaimed.

The search for a suitable king began, and General Prim lamented: "Looking for a democratic king in Europe is like looking for an atheist in Heaven."[38] The crown was finally accepted by Amadeo of Savoy, who lasted barely a couple of years in Madrid. Fighting among the liberal cliques made his reign a nightmare for King Amadeo I. His brief rule was followed by the First Spanish Republic of 1873–1874. Emilio Castelar, a noted professor of history, and the most famous Spanish orator of his day, was the last of its four presidents. His predecessors had called themselves by party labels, but Castelar dubbed himself as a *posibilista*, or "Possibilist," which meant simply that he would do what he could. It was very little.

Neither the Republic nor its president had a hope of survival. As Castelar himself stated: "We republicans have many prophets and few politicians; we know much of the ideal, little of experience; we embrace the entire heaven of thought and stumble over the first hole in the road." There were many holes in the road: the revolt in Cuba, the splintering of the liberals, the hostility of the Cortes, dissatisfaction among the military, a full-blown Carlist war in northern Spain, scheming among the monarchists who still clamored for the Bourbons, economic and financial conditions that were frightful— these were only a few of the things that the First Republic had to contend with. The wonder is that it ever got established at all. Its death was a foregone conclusion.

In 1875 Alfonso XII, who was a cadet at Sandhurst, was invited to return to Spain and occupy the throne as constitutional monarch. He was sixteen years old. He knew parliamentary government, and respected it. His education on the Continent and in England, away from his mother's depraved court, equipped him well for the role of king. During his brief reign (he died ten years later) Spain appeared to be making real political progress. The liberals and conservatives alternated in power, the constitution was observed, and order was restored. But these alternations had little meaning; they represented merely a sort of truce during which both sides agreed to wear velvet gloves. In Spain the changeover from one party to the other was often referred to as a "changing of the guards."

Alfonso XII died in 1885 at the age of twenty-seven. His queen had borne him several daughters but no son. She was, however, with child at the time of her husband's death, and six months later the son who was to become Alfonso XIII was born. For the next sixteen years his widowed mother served as regent, and her period of rule contrasted honorably with that earlier regency under which Isabel II had been trained as Queen. In the year 1902, when Alfonso XIII took over the government of his country, Spain stood on the threshold of an epoch promising greatness. Her schools had been greatly improved, she had produced a generation of intellectuals who won the respect of the world, and the king himself appeared sympathetic to the growing liberal sentiment among his people. Things augured for great fruits in the garden. Would the Spaniards grasp this chance, or would they slip back into the abysmal pit of the past from which they had only just and so painfully emerged?

Unfortunately, the last of the Bourbons was not equal to his responsibilities. Alfonso had been brought up "by a doting mother in an intensely clerical atmosphere. His tutor, Father Montaña, was a violent reactionary. He was never sent to finish his education abroad." Alfonso reacted strongly against the stuffy atmosphere of the court, and made his best friends among the military attachés, whose adventurous spirits he admired greatly. In the end the army "came to stand in his eyes for everything that was manly and heroic."[39]

Again the church and the army; would they continue to keep Spain at the end of the parade? Need the historian really ask? The obvious talents of the precocious young king were neutralized by his upbringing, and the country's lack of experience in self-government soon became tragically apparent. There were sixty-six new ministers in the first two years of Alfonso's reign, and thirty-three entirely different governments before he fled from Spain twenty-nine years after assuming the crown.

11

MAIN CURRENTS OF SPANISH
THOUGHT (1870–1931)

Who loses the morning loses the afternoon; who loses the afternoon loses life.

Old Spanish proverb

Under Philip II in the sixteenth century Spain had fallen out of step with the other European countries. Under his successors this became a national calamity. Spain preferred to go it alone. She would cling to her own system of values. She would resist progress. During the eighteenth and nineteenth centuries the country fell far behind in the education of her people. Perhaps Portugal was worse, but Spain came close to bringing up the tail end of the European line. True, in a nation where the great majority were unable to read or write there existed a powerful sense of creativity and of dignity among the masses. The Spanish people continued to produce spontaneous poetry, songs, and other expressions of their naturally artistic popular sentiment. There is no country on earth with a more beautiful body of folk poetry and folk music than Spain. There is no country where the illiterate masses possess greater innate refinement and vitality.

The untutored Spanish people have always produced a great art and have always possessed a profound dignity and strength which nothing has destroyed. But, admirable as these qualities are, in the modern world they alone are not enough. Indeed, they made Spain somewhat of an anomaly among modern nations. Spontaneous folk genius cannot govern a country, however creative a force it may be in the realm of art. In the last half of the nineteenth century Spaniards came to realize this. Education was a crying need for the people of Spain. Literacy was no longer a luxury; ideas had become the coin of freedom. Schools, more and better schools, were the necessity of the hour if the country was not to be left behind permanently. In confronting this need one man stands out. His name was Francisco Giner de los Ríos, and he was born in the picturesque Andalusian town of Ronda in 1839.

The English hispanist J. B. Trend calls Giner "the first modern Spaniard," and the Spanish writer Salvador de Madariaga refers to him as "the noblest figure of the nineteenth century in Spain." Giner was a distinguished professor of law at the University of Madrid. In Spain a degree in law was the nearest thing to a degree in the humanities in the United States. Giner's interests fell into this much broader field of general culture. He was the epitome of the dedicated teacher.

In the 1870's the Spanish minister of education decided to call for a loyalty oath from all professors at the university, an oath to support the crown, the dynasty, and the Catholic religion. Giner, along with several other well-known professors, refused to take the oath and was dismissed. A group of teachers without a school, they decided to organize a university of their own, and to this they gave the name of Institución Libre de Enseñanza, or "Free Institution of Teaching." It was founded in 1876. Giner thus headed what was in reality the first school in Spain that was independent of the state and of the church.

His Institution did not participate in party politics, but its faculty did believe firmly in the renovation of Spain on liberal and nonreligious bases. The primary goal of the institution was to educate the youth of Spain in an atmosphere of freedom. Men of distinction by the dozen came forth from the portals of this new, free university. Juan Ramón Jiménez, who later won the Nobel Prize for poetry, studied here, as did Antonio Machado, the other great Spanish poet of the first part of this century. Giner's ideal was to produce a group of men with a well-rounded, liberal education, people of character and tolerance, who would be able to lead the nation forward. Such an ideal was like a breath of fresh air in Spain where tradition barred the progress of ideas, and where Ramón y Cajal, later a Nobel prizewinner in physiology, was still having to steal corpses in order to carry on his work in anatomy.

Giner was the mentor of a generation of Spaniards who never ceased to revere his name. Following the lead of his school other educational institutions were organized which extended the scope of unfettered ideas: the Center of Historic Studies, an advanced center where I myself did much of my work toward the doctor's degree in the days of the Second Republic; the *Residence of Señoritas* and the *Residence of Students*, colleges like those at Oxford and Cambridge; and the Committee for the Extension of Studies, an overall body which correlated the work of the other institutions. The *Residencia de Estudiantes*, located on a hilltop at Pinar 21, Madrid, was perhaps the best known of these cultural institutions to foreigners, for here in this lovely oasis in the heart of the Spanish capital summer schools for foreign students were held year after year in the best tradition of liberal education.

The residence was surrounded by a small moat, in which water flowed constantly, recalling the water-filled gardens of the Moors in Andalusia. This moat was a symbolic thing; it signified that the residence existed in a state of freedom, independent of and not dominated by any outside influence of government or religion. When I was a summer student here the residence counted among its more or less permanent residents the poet García Lorca, the essayist Moreno Villa, and the critic Dámaso Alonso, who also ran the place. The philosopher Unamuno, dressed like a Protestant clergyman, was also a frequenter of the Residence, as were Juan Ramón Jiménez, Pedro Salinas, and Jorge Guillén, poets and teachers. I remember too the Argentines Miguel Cordomí and Aramburu, and many others from France, Germany, and from every province of Spain. J. B. Trend, the Englishman, often came here to spend a while, as did distinguished Hispanists from every other western country, including many from the United States.

One of my most humorous recollections of the place is of the time when the Spanish students, who knew that their director Dámaso Alonso slept in the nude, one night filled his bed with salt. García Lorca enjoyed this prank tremendously. Dámaso, who went on to become the great interpreter of Góngora, had a Tweedledum shape and a bald head, which, added to his stentorian shouts, made his curses on this occasion memorable.

Giner's students, and those who followed them, were a strong part of that wonderful generation of Spaniards who brought in the Second Republic. They were brilliant and outstanding men of whom any nation on earth would have cause to be proud. The difficulty was that there were not enough of them. Spain had started too late in her education for freedom. What could a handful of fine men do in a nation where the millions were still illiterate, where there had been no training in self-government, where the disease of absolutism was endemic in the body politic?

Giner did not stand alone in his effort to regenerate Spain. Angel Ganivet (1865–1898), born in Granada, was the gadfly of his epoch, a kind of second Larra. No one ever had a more pungent pen or a more clairvoyant mind. This man loved Spain as have few Spaniards, loved it with a heart that felt its imperfections keenly and sought energetically to reveal and revive the eternal tradition of the Spanish spirit. Ganivet, unlike so many others of his epoch, did not preach the Europeanization of Spain; on the contrary, all that he said or wrote was a call to the Spanish soul to seek in the originality and uniqueness of its non-European past the bases for future growth. Ganivet attempted to interpret and evaluate the spirit and character of his country. He sought to reinvigorate Spain from within. His dictum, taken from St. Augustine, was this: "Do not go beyond yourself, for within you dwells your true soul." He saw this as true of individuals, and as true of nations.

Ganivet affirmed the aptitude of Spaniards for conquest, and their inadaptability in unifying and governing what was conquered. This vital energy must be revived and focussed in a new direction if Spain was to preserve her dignity among modern nations. Ganivet and Unamuno became great friends, and in their letters commented wisely on the fate of their country. Ganivet's own essays, which make up a very small package, are among the best in contemporary Spanish literature. His criticism, however, is mostly anti-democratic. "Considering the people as a social organism, they make me sick. . . . I am an ardent supporter of universal suffrage with one limitation: that no one vote." He believed that government should be left to the intelligent and to the strong.

Ganivet was a widely traveled man. He was sent by his government to Belgium, to Finland, and to Russia, where he one day drowned himself in the Dvina River. He was only thirty-three. From the vantage point of these northern countries he was able to see his own land in clearer focus; he spared his readers nothing. Like Larra, his own vitality and idealism consumed him; it has never been healthy to remain too much of an idealist in a generation of vipers.

The third man of this epoch who dedicated his life to the regeneration of Spain was Joaquín Costa (1844–1911), a hardheaded Aragonese. Costa's campaign to bring his country into line with the other European nations was both written and vocal, and was strewn with memorable catch phrases, many of which are still remembered. "The sepulcher of the Cid," he cried, "must be put under double lock and key." Spain needed "schools and food," *escuela y despensa*. She needed also a *cirujano de hierro*, "a surgeon of iron," one who would excise and amputate with a ruthless scalpel. Spain was a hollow reed, a dry river; her voting population was an "inactive mass." Spain must be de-Africanized. Spain must be Europeanized. We must swap glory for progress. We must swap battleships for schools. "Our country does not need the hot blood of heroes or martyrs, but the *sang-froid*, the cold blood of men of intellect who are able to dominate and to canalize their own emotions." Spain's decline was due to a lack of will, to economic backwardness, widespread illiteracy, and to a deeply rooted system of political bossism (*caciquismo*) which made all elections a farce. Spain needed liberty and "the source of liberty is in independence, and the root of independence is in the stomach." A hungry man is never truly free.

Costa spoke volubly and persuasively all over Spain in favor of his energetic, liberal ideas. He brought the problem of agrarian and social reform before the public at large; he focussed the attention of the young intellectuals on the cankers that festered in the social organism of their country. He urged the irrigation of the country's barren land. Admitting the inability of his people for purely democratic government, he advocated an elective dictatorship, much like that of Rome, which would force compliance on the ignorant and on dissident reactionaries. Costa had a tremendous effect on the youth of his generation, whom he made aware of the national problems.

The result of this growing wave of intellectualism in Spain was the birth of a whole group of writers and artists, called in Spanish "the generation of 1898." The war with the United States in that year, and the consequent rapid defeat of Spain, forced Spaniards to take stock of themselves, hence the name applied to this generation. The great glory of Spain's military might obviously was no more. She had lost her best colonies. Spain now stood alone, weak, poor,

bereft of majesty and even of honor among modern nations. Had
she not persecuted the Cubans cruelly under her rigid generals? Even
if the war was an unjust one, imposed on her by an unnecessarily aggressive United States, as nearly all Spaniards believed, nevertheless
it had proved, once for all, the hopeless incapacity of their own
country to withstand the challenges of the modern era.

Therefore arose the fundamental question: What is Spain? This is
what the members of "the generation of 1898" wanted to find out.
They delved into the nation's past history and culture in order to
reveal *the true soul of Spain*. They probed into her isolated towns
and villages in order to get the feel of her spiritual geography, for in
these places the past still existed as a living presence. They sought
to Europeanize Spain, but with an all-out effort of the will, like
Nietzsche. They exalted the value of sensibility as the primary source
of artistic creativity. They were suspicious of ideas, per se. Contra-
dictorily, these proponents of the strong will lived lives of *abulia*,
or "lack of will." These men who argued so cogently for renewed
faith believed that life itself was anguish, and on that tenet rested
their pessimism.

Antonio Machado, the poet who best caught the essence of Castile
in this generation, expressed perfectly the attitude of "spiritual
encystment" which characterized his country:

> *Castilla miserable, ayer dominadora,*
> *envuelta en sus andrajos, desprecia cuanto ignora.*
>
> Miserable Castile, yesterday lording it over everybody,
> now wrapped in her rags scorns all she does not know.

The writers of the "generation of 1898" were a varied and brilliant
group linked together only because of the epoch in which they lived.
Each one was a distinct personality, with an esthetic credo and
philosophy of his own. They certainly did not constitute a unified
literary movement but they certainly did produce the finest literature
to come out of Spain since the great days of the Golden Age. With
these men the hard flinty land of Iberia again struck fire and there
was kindled a tremendous potential of enthusiasm and of energy.
Spain was alive again after her long sleep of centuries.

The writers of the "generation of 1898" embodied the last, best
hope of modern Spain. The contradictions implicit in their lives and
works are the contradictions of their country. They exalted the use

of the human will, and had none. They extolled the power and glory of Castile, and were not Castilians. They argued for the Europeanization of Spain, but one finds tradition omnipresent in their works. They longed for a religion of faith, and were themselves skeptics. One thing they did achieve, as Spaniards have always achieved: They constructed a palace of beauty.

There is not space or time to discuss individually all of the members of the "generation of 1898" and their contemporaries. Lists of names are meaningless, especially if they are unfamiliar foreign names. However, a quick synthesis of the main ideas of the writers of this generation, and of two additional writers who do not actually belong to the group, but who did exert a strong influence in Spain, would surely not be amiss. The two outside writers are Benito Pérez Galdós (1843–1920), the best Spanish novelist since Cervantes, and Vicente Blasco Ibáñez (1867–1928), whose fiction has enjoyed a world-wide popularity.

Galdós, born in the Canary Islands, spent most of his life in Madrid, and became *the* interpreter of that sprawling capital. He arrived in Madrid in time to view the political and social upheavals of the 1870's, and immediately began to search for the fundamental movements and emotions of the national psychology. Although Galdós himself was liberal and anticlerical, he observed the inner workings of the Spanish psyche with a kind of benign neutrality. As Madariaga, former Spanish ambassador to the United States, says, Giner presents the *ethos* or intrinsic character of Spain, while Galdós presents its *epos*, or the epic flow of its life in the nineteenth century. Galdós is the only Spanish novelist whose reputation can bear favorable comparison with the great masters of fiction of the other European countries: Balzac and Zola in France, Dickens in England, Tolstoy and Dostoievsky in Russia, to mention only a few.

Galdós was a dedicated novelist who gave himself completely to his work. He wrote from seven in the morning until nine at night, day after day, week after week, with only a few breaks for meals and exercise. He wore shabby clothes, and was forced to forego the pleasures of a social or a café life. He was a genius at accumulating details, inventing plots, delineating characters, and in drawing these all toward his foregone conclusions. He had an amazing comprehension of human psychology, and an uncanny power of observation and of analysis. His deep human warmth gave his characters the pulse of life, but he lacked the great breath of poetry or prophecy which raises the Russian novelists above realism into a kind of symphonic magic which is a distillation of the human spirit.

Occasionally, Galdós' accumulation of details can become boring; one must at times drive himself through the long passages of his longest works. His masterpiece, *Fortunata y Jacinta*, 1886–1887, contains 1700 pages. But Galdós knew Spain as few Spaniards have, and he was able to give a full cross section of Spanish life in what he wrote. He never softened his pen in the presence of weakness, nor did he become burdensome with moralization. With vigorous optimism he opposed the blind, reckless, irrational drive of the unconscious human will. He was tolerant, understanding, sympathetic, liberal—like the ideal psychiatrist. As Galdós wrote most of his novels before the time of Freud, between 1870 and 1900, there are no Freudian terms in his work. But his dissection of character would make stimulating reading for anyone interested in probing the depths of both normal and abnormal psychology, most especially the psychology of Spaniards.

Galdós never married, but he had a succession of mistresses, and with them carried on a series of semi-family relationships. He knew and felt intimately the interplay of the roles of husband, wife, and children, as well as those of friends and lovers. He also knew people of every class and walk of life, and people of every religion. His Jewish characters are among the most powerful in Spanish literature. During his early years as a writer Galdós was influenced by French realism and naturalism, but finally he found his peace in a Tolstoyan love of humanity. His "best loved master," however, was the Englishman, Charles Dickens. Galdós had been educated in an English school and read English perfectly. As his contemporary Leopoldo Alas pointed out, the novels of Galdós had no yesterday in Spanish letters; they had only a day before yesterday. They derived from the realistic tradition of the Spanish Golden Age, and made Galdós unquestionably the greatest Spanish novelist since that time. He described Spanish life of the nineteenth century with "such fidelity and precision that beneath the anecdotal picture appears the fabric of permanent reality, and beneath the image of the 19th century man, the image of the eternal man."

The novelistic technique of Galdós is quite similar to that of his classic predecessors of the *Siglo de Oro*, the authors of the picaresque novels, the dramatists Tirso and Lope de Vega, and Cervantes himself.

For all these men the writing of a *comedia* or a novel consists in multiplying ad infinitum the episodes and incidental actions. Cervantes, even in his *Don Quixote*, gathers in and uses everything that he comes across: pastoral stories, stories of chivalry, sentimental tales, etc. So does Galdós. He takes one action, the central axis of his novel; but this action, as it advances, almost always with wearying slowness, and interrupted at every turn, is extended and ramified in every conceivable direction. . . .

This technique of Galdós, and of the writers of the Golden Age prose, also characterizes much of present-day Spanish and Spanish-American fiction.

Galdós is at his best in the development of character and in his presentation of the individual seeking fulfillment and social adjustment. He never fully accepted the deterministic naturalism of Zola, although he did reproduce both human and exterior reality with an almost clinical accuracy. But Galdós did not view the individual consciousness as determined by its physical surroundings. He gave his characters free will, one of the basic tenets of Catholicism, and he philosophically presented this in a manner suggesting Hegel, to whom the individual was a wave tossed up on the great sea of history. Individual personality in the novels of Galdós is shaped out of conflict between the *self*, on the one hand, and the *others* with whom that self comes in contact, on the other hand. The individual seeks self-enlargement and growth through his relationship with others; he encounters many different kinds of otherness, and with each encounter his own personality is altered. The relationship begins as a struggle of opposites but ends in a kind of fusion. The self absorbs from others, cancels out a part of its own individuality, grows, transcends its initial limits, and finally reaches self-realization. In the process Galdós uses a combination of literary realism, Christian idealism, and the Hegelian concept of personality.

Galdós never wrote a world masterpiece probably for two reasons: He was a very rapid and careless writer, and he was not as good a storyteller as, for example, Balzac, Tolstoy, or Dickens. In spite of this his work is a real monument in European and world literature, and he was himself the giant of nineteenth century Spanish letters. His masterpiece, *Fortunata y Jacinta*, is a broad canvas of many characters in Madrid which gives the illusion of life itself. His two principal women, wife and mistress, are delineated with a sensitivity shown by no other Spanish author. One of the male characters, Maxi Rubén, is an extreme neurotic who escapes reality in hallucinatory dreams. The telling and analysis of dreams is a basic part of Galdós' novelistic technique. The intertwining of human relationships in the novel is carried out with a masterly skill. It is a great pity that this fine work has received little recognition in English.

Galdós wrote a total of seventy-seven novels, a tremendous output. He saw, better than any other Spanish novelist,

the gravitation of the past on the present of Spain as the knot of the insoluble conflict: because a people can neither abandon its past, the basis of its essential character, nor can it live on the margin of history, for to adapt itself means constant renovation. The present, which is life, is composed of both past and future. Hence, the nation that stops, as the traditionalists wished Spain to stop, is destined to failure or to death."[62]

Galdós was anticlerical without being anti-Catholic, and in this viewpoint represented millions of enlightened Spaniards. That is, he opposed bigotry, fanaticism, and superstitions, which in Spain naturally had a Catholic face. He did not oppose religious dogma. In Spain the poor parish priests and nuns who live in poverty and dedicate their lives to service without fanaticism have never aroused the opposition of the people, but let a religious group or religious order become wealthy and powerful, like the Jesuits, and public animosity is eventually stirred. In the novel *Doña Perfecta* Galdós presents the problem of anticlericalism as it appears in a small cathedral town of Old Castile. Doña Perfecta symbolizes tradition, faith; for her, science and learning threaten to destroy the life of the spirit. Pepe Rey, the young engineer of liberal ideas, who comes to the town anxious to marry his cousin, Doña Perfecta's daughter, represents science as enlightenment. The two points of view meet in deadly conflict. The town priest, with his ironic humility, sides of course with Doña Perfecta. The entire town personifies intolerance, and comes to regard Pepe as a heretic. In the end when the young man attempts to elope with his sweetheart, he is killed by a Carlist partisan, and the girl, who has already shown signs of instability, is sent off to an asylum. The atmosphere of the place returns to its cold and riftless gray.

Galdós also wrote many dramas, which, although they are not as fine as his novels, were extremely popular in their day. *Electra,* 1901, was the most widely known. This play repeats the tragedy of *Doña Perfecta* with variations. The young liberal hero wishes to marry a girl who personifies tradition. The girl is forced into a convent by conniving clerics in an attempt to balk the marriage. In this play the forces of liberalism win out. The play was greeted with tremendous applause when it was performed, and even gave rise to disturbances of several sorts: demonstrations, strikes, attacks on convents, which ultimately caused the fall of the cabinet. The new cabinet, under Sagasta, was called "Electra."[40]

Galdós, despite his painting of the sorrows of Spanish life, is a confirmed optimist. A friend of the novelist wrote: "Is Nature pessimistic because she is sad at nightfall when it seems that day is dying forever? The sadness of art, like that of Nature, is a form of hope. Why is Christianity so artistic? Because it is the religion of sadness."

The other Spanish novelist who falls outside the "generation of 1898," but whose work parallels that of the writers of this group, was Vicente Blasco Ibáñez of Valencia, who died in 1928. Ibáñez* was the stormy petrel of his epoch, and some have claimed that he was excluded from the famous generation simply because of his phenomenal popularity. His success in the United States was meteoric, and many critics hailed him as a worthy successor of the great Russian and French novelists. William Dean Howells wrote of him: "The Russians have ceased to be actively the masters, and there is no Frenchman, Englishman, or Scandinavian who counts with Ibáñez, and of course no Italian, American, and unspeakably, no German."

The fact is that Blasco Ibáñez was merely the loudest player in the Spanish band. He had a primitive vitality and a gift for telling a good story. He enjoyed the dubious distinction of appearing on the world literary scene when it was in a temporary vacuum. His best novels deal with the region of Spain that he knew best, Valencia, and his masterpiece is *The Cabin*, which appeared in 1898. As he drew away from Valencia his work weakened. His melodramatic *Four Horsemen, Blood and Sand, Mare Nostrum,* and many others, which were his most successful novels abroad, belong to this latter period, and this has made many intelligent Spaniards somewhat ashamed of Blasco as a writer. They do not enjoy having their literature admired for its poorer works. Blasco himself was very unsure of his later efforts, and once remarked that after he had finished a novel he had no idea whether it was a masterpiece or a piece of junk.

In the United States it took H. L. Mencken to debunk the eulogy

---

* He should be called Blasco, and in Spanish is so called, but he is known as Ibáñez in English. Blasco was the surname of his father's family, Ibáñez the name of his mother's family, placed at the end according to Spanish custom.

of William Dean Howells. To Mencken, Blasco was "almost the typical Socialist—iconoclastic, oratorical, sentimental, theatrical—a fervent advocate of all sorts of lofty causes, eagerly responsive to the shibboleths of the hour." Whenever Blasco was asked what he was doing, he would answer vigorously, "Fighting!," but in truth he was travelling all over the world and writing. Mencken brought forward the name of Pío Baroja, who was one of the "generation of 1898," to replace that of Blasco in critical esteem, but the novels of Baroja (despite Hemingway's admiration of him) never took root in world literature. None the less, Baroja, Unamuno, Valle-Inclán, Azorín, Ortega, Juan Ramón Jiménez, Antonio Machado, and Benavente make up a generation which came near to sloughing off the onus that had burdened the soul of Spain since the Golden Age. But there was no Balzac, no Tolstoy, among them, and, of course, no Cervantes. They left Spain much as they found her, in a state of vital anguish, with one foot in the past, the other in the air awaiting the future; and she is still straddling the unfathomable abyss.

Miguel de Unamuno (1864–1937) was the grand old man of the "generation of 1898." He was a professor of Greek at the University of Salamanca, and later was made permanent rector or chancellor of that ancient institution. Although he was a Basque, Unamuno lived and wrote in Castile, and he saw in Castile the agonizing soul of his country. García Lorca once told me that his dearest and closest associate was an idiot son with whom he spent long hours walking along the age-old and winding streets and lanes of Spain while he, the father, discoursed on the problems of life and death. Was the whole mad world a sounding box for this unorthodox philosopher who sought to make the leap of faith in the presence of eternal doubt?

But Unamuno liked to talk to anyone who would listen intelligently. His *tertulias* were fascinating because of his conversation, or we should say monologues, for Unamuno seldom gave anyone else a chance to speak. "Ideas come with talking," he would say, and it is true that his essays vibrate with the passion of the spoken word. They are animated conversation carried to the level of first-rate literature. He addresses himself to the individual reader, and is never the orator speaking for a great public.

Unamuno was always a political dissident. Early in the century he opposed King Alfonso XIII; he opposed even more vigorously the dictatorship of Primo de Rivera, which came in 1923, and for this he was sent into exile. The authorities might possibly have connived at his escaping across the Portuguese frontier, but Unamuno was unwilling to relieve them of any embarrassment so he put a few things together, stuck a Greek New Testament and the poems of Leopardi in his pocket, and took ship to the tiny island of Fuerteventura. The people in Spain raised a tremendous howl. Thus, by both words and actions Unamuno helped to bring about the Second Spanish Republic in 1931. When it came he returned to Spain and was given a huge ovation.

He greeted the Republic with joy but issued a chary reminder that there was an "eternal Spain" which must never be forgotten, a tap root of tradition from which the national life juice sprang. Soon he was attacking the Republicans for their inept government; he hated socialism because he feared it would destroy individuality. He was always the gadfly of every political party. When finally the Nationalist revolt under General Franco came, with its strong church support, Unamuno greeted this too with a certain enthusiasm, for in it he hoped to find the regeneration of his mystical, eternal Spain. But when he saw German troops mingling with Spanish fascists in his beloved Salamanca, he cried out in mortal anguish, abominating Spanish fascism. It was too late. Shortly afterwards, the old philosopher died. They said he died with a broken body and a broken heart. Perhaps he had forgotten one of his earlier convictions: "The alliance between the Throne and the Altar is," he had said, "in the long run, fatal to both."

Once Unamuno met Blasco Ibáñez in Paris, and the fiery Valencian tried to convince him that Paris and the rest of the world were what really mattered in the twentieth century. Unamuno said pointedly: "No, give me the plaza in Salamanca. It's worth more than all of that." Strangely enough, Blasco really agreed with him subconsciously, for he was at his best when treating the problems of his own country. The Americans had made his inferior Four Horsemen a best-seller and Blasco was caught in a net of slick fiction from which he could not extricate himself.

Unamuno would never have won any popularity contest as a writer; he was much too demanding of his reader. His intensity is profoundly Spanish:

not only our own souls, the souls of those living today, are alive and operative in the soul of Spain, but in addition to these, the souls of our forefathers. Our own souls, those of the living, are those that are least alive in it, for our soul does not enter into the soul of our country until it is no longer a detached entity, until after our temporal death.

What is the use of our wanting to make our thought modern and European when our language is neither European nor modern? While we are endeavoring to make it say one thing, it is endeavoring to make us say something different, and thus we do not say the thought that we pretend we are saying, but we say the thought that we do not wish to say.

We endeavor—that is to say, many of us endeavor—to deform our spirit conformably with an external standard, and we succeed neither in making ourselves like those whom we pretend to copy nor in being ourselves. Whence results a horrible half-breed, a kind of barren hybrid.

And the most curious thing about it all is this—something that will be understood one day, if the day ever comes when anyone will occupy himself in investigating the spiritual condition of Spain at the transition from the nineteenth to the twentieth centuries—the most curious and surprising thing is that those who are held to be most Spanish, most true-blooded and of the old stock, most authentically Spanish, are those who are the most Europeanizing, the most exotic, those whose soul contains the most alien strains; and on the other hand, those whom many simple-minded folk regard as exotic spirits, anglicized, gallicized, Germanized, Norwegianized, are the ones whose roots intermingle the most closely with the roots of those who created the Spanish soul.[5]

Unamuno undoubtedly includes himself in this last category, for he was a great admirer of certain spirits in the above-mentioned cultures. Kierkegaard was his particular mentor.

"Our defects," Unamuno goes on, "or what others call our defects, are usually the root of our excellencies; the qualities that are censured as our vices are the foundation of our virtues." Unamuno sincerely believed that the *élan vital* of Spain was a kind of anciency that went clear back to the African origins of the Spanish people. He held, therefore, that the words Spanish and European were incompatible. He disliked intensely all the various schemes that had been suggested for the regeneration of his country.

The term *European* [he says] expresses a vague idea, very vague, excessively vague; but much vaguer is the idea that is expressed by the term *modern*. If we combine the two together it would seem that they ought to limit one another and result in something concrete, and that the expression *modern European* ought to be clearer than either of its two component terms; but perhaps it is vaguer still.

It will be apparent that I am proceeding by way of what some will call arbitrary statement, without documentation, without verification, independent of modern European logic and disdainful of its methods. I seek no other method than that of passion; and when I am moved with disgust, with repugnance, with pity or with contempt, I let the mouth speak from the fullness of the heart and the words come forth as they will.

We Spaniards, so they say, are arbitrary charlatans, we fill up the broken links of logic with rhetoric, we subtilize skillfully but uselessly, we lack the sense of consecutiveness and induction, we have scholastic minds, we are casuists . . . etc., etc.

I have heard similar things said of St. Augustine, the great African, the fiery soul that overflowed in waves of rhetoric, in phraseological contortions, in antitheses, in paradoxes and conceits. St. Augustine was at once a Gongorist and Conceptist. Which leads me to believe that Gongorism and Conceptism are the natural forms of passion and vehemence.

The great African, the great ancient African! Here you have an expression, *ancient African,* which can be opposed to *modern European,* and which is at least of equal value. St. Augustine was African and he was of the ancient world; so was Tertullian. And why should we not say: "We must Africanize ourselves ancientwise," or "We must ancientize ourselves Africanwise?"[5]

Unamuno is distrustful of science and of rationalism. Education, for him, should strive to lead to wisdom rather than to knowledge.

Wisdom is to science what death is to life, or, if you prefer it, wisdom is to death what science is to life. The object of science is life, and the object of wisdom is death. Science says: "We must live," and seeks the means of prolonging, increasing, facilitating and amplifying life, of making it tolerable and acceptable. Wisdom says: "We must die," and seeks how to make us die well.

Unamuno believed that there is no truer liberty than the liberty of death, and those who so avidly pursued science and life, turning their backs on wisdom and death, were seeking above all else happiness. This was the philosophy and the religion of modern Europe, but not of Spain. Unamuno then posed an arbitrary dilemma—

arbitrary, because I cannot prove it logically, because it is imposed on me by the feeling of my heart, not by the reasoning of my head: either happiness or love. If you want the one, you must renounce the other. Love kills happiness, happiness kills love.

And here it would be very apposite to adduce all that our mystics, our admirable mystics, our only classic philosophers, the creators of our Spanish wisdom, not our Spanish science—perhaps the terms *science* and *Spanish* are, happily, mutually repellent—have felt, felt rather than thought, about love and happiness—the *I die because I do not die (muero porque no muero*) and the sweet pain and all the rest that emanates from the same depths of feeling.

The individual to Unamuno was everything, the species was nothing. "Other peoples have left institutions, books—we have left souls." The individual human soul is the only true value in this universe. It is precious because it is unique and irreplaceable. When the great German poet Goethe died, his last words are said to have been: "Light, more light." The words are symbolic of the Germanic quest for knowledge. Unamuno voices a different cry. He cries out: "Warmth, more warmth, Lord, for we die of the cold and not the darkness." And in this he distinguishes the Spanish from the Nordic temperament. Then the philosopher proceeds to state the categorical imperative of his own individual soul:

I need the immortality of my soul, the indefinite persistence of my individual consciousness—I need it. Without it, without faith in it, I cannot live, and doubt; the inability to believe that I shall attain it, torments me. And since I need it, my passion leads me to affirm it, and to affirm it arbitrarily, and when I attempt to make others believe, to make myself believe, I do violence to logic and make use of arguments which are called ingenious and paradoxical by those unfortunate people who have no passion and who contemplate their ultimate dissolution with resignation. The man of passion, the arbitrary man, is the only real rebel. . . .[5]

Unamuno's Christianity was a state of anguish; he wanted to be a good Catholic, and he wanted to survive death. Philosophically his real religion was the religion of Quixotism; he wanted desperately "to rescue the sepulcher of Don Quixote from the mandarins of reason." If his words were lost in the wilderness, some day the wilderness would hear, and would become transformed into a sounding forest singing a hosanna to the eternal Lord of life and death. "If after death it is only annihilation that awaits us," he wrote, *"let us so act that it shall be an injustice."*

Ortega y Gasset (1883–1955) was the other towering mind of this generation of Spaniards. He was openly antagonistic to Unamuno, and frankly on the side of Europe. Unamuno believed firmly in the substance of Spanishness, and his philosophy was permeated with the Spanish Catholic tradition. He wanted to regenerate, to reinvigorate, and to resuscitate his country, by revealing and revitalizing its best values. Ortega y Gasset, who was a professor of philosophy at the University of Madrid, and later an influential member of the Republican parliament, stood at the opposite pole. He not only believed in the necessity of Europeanizing Spain, but was himself distrustful of pure Spanish values. He feared the masses, particularly the Spanish masses with their semi-education, and upheld the rule of a select minority. Ortega, like several other promising young Spaniards of his day, was sent to Germany for advanced education, and he came back from that country with a deep-seated admiration for Germanic thoughts and things. Sending these young men of Spain to Germany was a fundamental error. Spain could never utilize the concept of Germanic order, or power, or Germanic *kultur*. What these young Spaniards needed was a liberal education and an abiding faith in justice and parliamentary government, and Germany could not give that. The country was already infected with the power virus which led to two world wars and to the eventual rise of Hitlerism.

Ortega extolled science, order, organization, intellectualization. He feared the Spaniard's unruly anarchy; he cried out for civic order, impersonal method, and social discipline. Although he has been called a philosopher, he was not a philosopher at all but rather a well-educated and oftentimes sensational journalist whose writings and influential position in Spain gave him a unique importance. In 1923 he founded what was to become the best Spanish journal of this century, the *Revista de Occidente*. He had come of a wealthy family of journalists, and was himself "born on a printing press," as he put it. In contrast to Unamuno's deep religious sincerity and lifelong quest for God, Ortega took a more skeptical and scientific view of the universe. As his colleague and friend Madariaga wrote of him, he was the kind of man who would plaster a big headline across the first page of his paper proclaiming that GOD IS IN SIGHT!

Ortega, however, could be a rigorous critic of his country, and in his book *Invertebrate Spain*, which appeared in 1921, he pulls out all the stops. His most telling sentence from that book is: "Spain today, rather than a nation, is a cloud of dust remaining after a great people have galloped down the highway of history." Little wonder that Ortega refused to allow this work to be translated into any foreign language for a good many years, for fear it would expose too starkly the weaknesses of his own nation. But Ortega did not really believe that Spain was as bad as that. Elsewhere in the same book he makes it clear that in his opinion Spain was never as high up on the ladder of European history as many have made out, and that she was not then (in 1921) as far down on the ladder in her decay as others affirmed. Her sickness was that she was not a real society, she had no cohesiveness, no harmony of oneness. She was a conglomerate mixture, without leadership. She was an amorphous body without a head. Castile had made Spain, and Castile had unmade Spain. Her unity, an illusory unity, was Castilian in origin, but so also were her strong urges toward separatism and regionalism, felt most ardently in Catalonia and the Basque provinces. The main reason for this, says Ortega, was that Castile in her epoch of dominance had shut herself up in an impregnable tower, taking little heed of what was going on in the other provinces upon which she had enforced unification. This resulted in a permanent cantonalism. Furthermore, the classes in Spain were so far apart that people living within a stone's throw of each other were actually separated by immeasurable distances. They knew as little of each other's needs as Spaniards did of Abyssinians. How could such a people produce a harmonious society, a harmonious government, a harmonious culture? Individual Spaniards were superior human beings, but Spain in the aggregate was an unruly and incongruous mass in continual dissonance. The Spanish people refused to follow their intellectual leadership; thus the national life was disjointed and "invertebrate."

In 1930, on the very eve of the establishment of the Second Spanish Republic, Ortega published what was to become his best known work, *The Revolt of the Masses*, which was quickly translated and widely popular in the United States, then in the midst of its terrible economic depression. This book was meant to be a general interpretation of movements in European history, with its stress on the rise and revolt of the masses (by which Ortega means the middle classes, not the workers). However, the main burden of the author's thesis pertains to Spain, with her unique historic background, for here a small intellectual group was striving with all its energy and spirit to guide the reactionary masses in the direction of social liberalism. And as Ortega pointedly remarks, the masses balked and refused to move ahead. This was a fundamental error, for to Ortega the mass "is that part of society which does not act upon itself. Such is its mission. It has come into the world in order to be directed, influenced, represented, organized. . . ." When the mass acts on its own, it lynches. Thus violence has become almost the normal social action in many parts of the world today. Whenever some difficulty, conflict, or problem arises in a nation today, "the mass-man will tend to demand that the State intervene immediately and undertake a solution directly with its immense and unassailable resources. This is the gravest danger that today threatens civilization: State intervention." Ortega then points out that fascism is just such a movement of the mass. Hitler, who came later, further represented the same idea. And would not Franco, who followed them all, be the final embodiment of the ideal?

To Ortega the mass had already begun to believe that *it was the state*, and hence would "tend more and more to set its machinery working on whatever pretext, to crush beneath it any creative minority which disturbs it—disturbs it in any order of things: in politics, in ideas, in industry." He traces the origins of the idea back to the days of the Caesars of Rome, where already in the epoch of the Antonines (second century) the state had become an overbearing centralized force. Everything existed *for* the State. "The whole of life is bureaucratized. What results? The bureaucratization of life brings about its absolute decay in all orders." Then comes that urgent need of the state, its army. "The Severi, of African origin, militarize the world. . . . Recall the last words of Septimus Severus to his sons: *Remain united, pay the soldiers, and take no heed of the rest.*"

The social organism and the body politic of Roman Spain fell apart under the attack of the German hordes from the north. Later, in the eighteenth century, when the state (according to Ortega) was still quite a small affair, early capitalism and industrialization brought into being a new social class, the middle class, possessed of energy and political talent. It also had a great conceit, and invented the term "ship of state," regarding itself as "oceanic, omnipotent, pregnant with storms." This state had been built in the Middle Ages by a class of men very different from the bourgeois—"the nobles, a class admirable for their courage, their gifts of leadership, their sense of responsibility. Without them the nations of Europe would not now be in existence." But with all those virtues of the heart, the nobles lacked the virtues of the head. They were unable to develop any technique, such was their sentimental, irrational, and limited intelligence. They did not invent gunpowder. The masses got gunpowder from the East, and then proceeded to depose them. How could the warrior noble, the *caballero* stupidly covered with heavy iron, so encumbered that he could hardly move about in battle, win the struggle against the gun?

Thus it came about that the masses took over their own government. The French Revolution is symbolic of this. Ortega was always fearful of mass rule. He wrote that he believed in the rule of philosophy, and for philosophy (i.e., a great new ideal) to rule it was not necessary that the philosophers themselves be the rulers, as Plato had hoped, or even that the rulers become philosophers. "Both these things are, strictly speaking, most fatal. For philosophy to rule it is sufficient for it to exist; that is to say, for the philosophers to be philosophers. For nearly a century past, philosophers have been everything but that—politicians, pedagogues, men of letters, and men of science." Unfortunately, and perhaps unknowingly, Ortega himself and his great Spanish contemporary, Unamuno, both fall into this latter category.

When General Franco rose in rebellion against the Second Spanish Republic in 1936, Ortega was a member of the national Cortes. When Madrid fell at last, after more than two years of siege, Ortega took off for Argentina, and exile. Five years later, however, Franco's government, anxious to appear more democratic now that the Axis powers were obviously losing the war, made a grand gesture and invited him and other intellectuals back to Spain. There were to be no reprisals. Ortega accepted the invitation. The price: that he keep his mouth shut. Ortega paid the price and died ten years later, his lips now sealed in the silence that is unbreakable.

Unamuno and Ortega were undoubtedly the most influential thinkers and leaders of Spain up to the time of the Spanish civil war. Their kind of thinking had little in common. One was a traditionalist and an existentialist, while the other was an admirer of Germanic order and the myth of select minorities. Both received what might be termed a cosmopolitan education, and both misunderstood the necessity of their hour on the human stage. Spaniards in general misunderstood that necessity, so no especial blame attaches to these two men except that they were reputed to be superior men, and somehow should have known better. With hindsight it is easy to see that they should have remained inside the framework of Spanish liberalism, Unamuno by bending every effort to improve the ineptitude of the Republicans for a just government, and Ortega by remaining in exile so that his voice might still be raised in favor of justice, civil rights, and tolerance. The final years of these two brilliant leaders are an ironic comment on the political infertility of contemporary Spanish intelligence, which has been brilliant theoretically but sterile in fact.

The great novelist of the "generation of 1898" was Pío Baroja (1872–1956) who, like Unamuno, was a Basque who lived all of his adult life in Castile. Ernest Hemingway admired Baroja sincerely and called him "Master," and the American's straightforward, pungent style often suggests that of Baroja. H. L. Mencken also praised Baroja and wrote the introduction to the English translation of his spiritual autobiography, *Youth and Egolatry*, 1920. Mencken wrote:

A novelist undoubtedly as skillful as Blasco Ibáñez and a good deal more profound, he lacks the quality of enthusiasm and thus makes a more restricted appeal. In place of gaudy certainties he offers disconcerting questionings; in place of a neat and well-rounded body of doctrine he puts forward a sort of generalized contra-doctrine. . . . Baroja is the analyst, the critic, almost the cynic. If he leans toward any definite doctrine at all, it is toward the doctrine that the essential ills of man are incurable, that all the remedies proposed are as bad as the disease, that it is almost a waste of time to bother about humanity in general."[1]

Baroja's novels are primarily "novels of ideas." In plot and character delineation the Spaniard is not on a par with the other great contemporary novelists of Western letters. Yet, at a time when Blasco Ibáñez was widely popular in the United States, and the motion picture industry was making extremely successful films of his more melodramatic novels, Baroja was the most popular novelist in Spain. And this despite the fact that the clerical elements in the country, which were very considerable, disliked him intensely.

In *Youth and Egolatry*, Baroja tells of an experience he had on a train shortly after the revolutionary elements in Spain had, according to press reports, "engaged in disorders" as a protest against the inept government of Alfonso XIII. This was the general strike of August 1917 when the Spanish labor unions called for a republic. Baroja writes:

Returning from San Sebastian, I happened on a family from Madrid in the same car. The father was weak, jaundiced and sour-visaged; the mother was a fat brunette, with black eyes, who was loaded down with jewels, while her face was made up until it was brilliant white, in color like a wax candle. A rather good-looking daughter of between fifteen and twenty was escorted by a lieutenant who apparently was engaged to her. Finally, there was another girl, between twelve and fourteen, flaccid and lively as a still-life on a dinner table. Suddenly the father, who was reading a newspaper, exclaimed:

"Nothing is going to be done, I can see that; they are already applying to have the revolutionists pardoned. The Government will do nothing."

"I wish they would kill every one of them," broke in the girl who was engaged to the lieutenant. "Think of it! Firing on soldiers! They are bandits."

"Yes, and with such a king as we have!" exclaimed the fat lady with the paraffin hue, in a mournful tone. "It has ruined our summer. I wish they would shoot every one of them."

"And they are not the only ones," interrupted the father. "The men who are behind them, the writers and the leaders, hide themselves, and then they throw the first stones."

Upon entering the house, I found that the final proofs of my book had just arrived from the printer, and sat down to read them.

The words of that family from Madrid still rang in my ears: "I wish they would kill every one of them!"

However one may feel, I thought to myself, it is impossible not to hate such people. Such people are natural enemies. It is inevitable.

Now, reading over the proofs of my book, it seems to me that it is not strident enough. I could wish it were more violent, more anti-middle class.

I no longer hear the voice of prudence seducing me, as it did a few days since, to a palinode in complicity with a romantic morning of white mist.

The zest of combat, of adventure stirs in me again. The sheltered harbor seems a poor refuge in my eyes—tranquillity and serenity appear contemptible.

Here, boy, up, and throw out the sail! Run the red flag of revolution to the masthead of our frail craft, and forth to sea![1]

But let us make no bones about it, Baroja was not a real revolutionary. He was a parlor pink in his politics, but in his private and in his public life he was simply antipolitical, or unpolitical. He did run from General Franco when the time came, but he was hardly one of the intellectual leaders of his opposition. He died in a hospital in Madrid, where Hemingway visited him, in 1956.

Baroja is against everything, so he naturally pokes fun at both political extremes in Spain. He claims that the Spanish parliament is like a menagerie, and that the liberals and the conservatives both observe the same morality, but merely use a different style. "The only distinction is that the Conservatives make off with a great deal at once, while the Liberals take less, but do it more often." The so-called sternness of the law also comes in for a punch: "It was pointed out a long time ago that laws are like cobwebs; they catch the little flies, and let the big ones pass through."

But Baroja's attitude is not entirely pessimistic. In one of his novels he has a character describe the ideal state. The character says very simply: "No cops, no priests, no flies!" This is what Baroja really believed in: a country where force was not needed in order to rule, a society where clericalism did not hold back the path of progress, a place where things were clean.

Baroja's novels, like those of Galdós, present a wide cross section of Spanish life in all its ramifications. In his liking for the lower classes and their "struggle for life," which is symbolic of their country's struggle for life, he calls to mind the old picaresque tales of the Golden Age, with which his work has much in common. His characters struggle and fight for survival; in true existential fashion they act, and are responsible for their actions. They are condemned to a perfect freedom. They are, nonetheless, like shadows that flit to and fro on a dingy sheet.

One of the strangest friendships among the members of the "generation of 1898" was that between Pío Baroja, the novelist of the group, and Azorín, who, after Unamuno, was its best known interpreter and spiritual essayist. Baroja might be compared with raw cotton while Azorín was finished silk, yet these two men were devoted and loyal friends for many years. Azorín is the pen-name of José Martínez Ruiz. He was born in the southeast province of Alicante in 1874, yet like Unamuno he became a great interpreter and champion of Castile. In his essays we find a marked absence of action and a preponderance of description, thought, emotion, lyricism and symbolism. Azorín, in typical Spanish fashion, is always the personal essayist, never the objective analyst. He carries acute observation to the exalted level of the universal poetic. The poet Pedro Salinas once told an anecdote about Azorín which exemplifies his character well: Salinas, Juan Ramón Jiménez and Azorín were standing one day on a busy corner in Madrid waiting for the congested traffic to die down sufficiently for them to cross the street. While the first two querulously commented on the noise and rush, Azorín discovered a tiny escape of gas in the lamp on the corner, and was listening to its faint sibilant sound, fascinated. He takes a similar attitude in his works, for in the smallest things he finds a symbol of the great and large, and in the great and large things he sees a projection and extension of the insignificant and small.

In works like *Los pueblos*, 1905, and *Castilla*, 1912, he catches the air and spirit of the past in some vestige of the present which reveals the oneness and eternity of all time. Or, as he puts it, after the flower is dead and the vessel emptied there still hovers in the air a certain "fragrance of the glass." This feeling gives Azorín a spiritual kinship with the American novelist Thomas Wolfe, to whom "the minute-winning days, like flies, buzz home to death, and every moment is a window on all time."

One of Azorín's finest sketches is entitled simply *Sarrió*. Although it was written in 1905, it still catches the spirit of Spain today, and thus shows how little the true core of the people has changed. "In Spain it is only the surface that changes, not what lies underneath," is the way a recent prime minister, Cánovas, put it. *Sarrió*, in fact, is the name of a small and insignificant village in Asturias, but Azorín uses it as the name of one of those old decaying hidalgos found so frequently in Castile. By extension the name also readily applies, in a symbolic sense, to the town in which this old Don lives, to the province of Castile itself, and finally, to all of Spain, reduced herein to this one Castilian soul. Here is the way Azorín begins his description of the town in which this old *caballero* lives:

The friends and admirers of the illustrious man will feel consternation when they pass their gaze over these lines. Sarrió is ill; Sarrió is disappearing. . . . I have arrived in the middle of the morning in this small, tranquil and bright village; the sun was illuminating the wide plaza; a few fresh, blue shadows were falling on the angle of the eaves of the houses and bathed the doors; the church, with its two flat towers of stone, old towers, golden towers, rose in the background, standing out against the clear, luminous sky. And in the middle, the fountain flows softly from its four spouts, with a gentle sound, into the carved stone basin. I have stopped an instant, enjoying the blue shadows, the closed windows, the profound silence, the tame sound of the water, the towers, the fluttering of a swallow in the sky, the long and rhythmic bell-strokes of the ancient clock. And then I knocked on the door of the great man's house: *tan, tan!* The door was ajar; it was not an indiscretion to enter. The vestibule was deserted; on a table there was a candlestick with a half-used candle, an empty glass—perhaps of some medication—and a pile of provincial papers with their wrapping bands intact. A profound silence reigns throughout the house; the furniture is covered with dust; one or two chairs have their bottoms missing. And there floats in the air and may be seen in all the details of the place something like a profound abandonment, something like a deep lassitude, something like an irresistible despair. . . .[41]

Azorín claps his hands and after a few moments a servant appears. The look on his face suggests that he is waiting and fearing something at the same time. It is a look that is typical of these servants who live in these strange houses. Azorín asks for his friend. He is still in bed, at eleven in the morning. No, he is not ill, but he got up at three, and then went back to bed. Azorín is amazed. This is unheard of, this is absurd. Then what about his three attractive daughters: Carmen, Lola, Pepita? Carmen had married long ago; so had Lola.

Pepita, who played the piano with her long, fine, white, pointed and silken fingers, was dead.

Now, all the mystery of this atmosphere that floats in this abandoned house appears clear to me. How can the beings that we have loved so much disappear in this rapid and brutal way? Is there nothing fixed, changeless, in the world, of our loves and of our predilections?

At this moment there is a dull footstep overhead, followed by a cough, and finally by the dim voice of Sarrió. A few moments pass. Sarrió appears on the landing of the stairs. Is it he? Is it not he? He is dragging his feet. Before he used to be neatly groomed; now he has a stubble of several days' beard. His shirt is no longer starched and clean. Do you want a detail that will reveal better all of his lamentable decay? I felt in his presence a deep sadness which has come to merge with the sadness already felt. And now he is coming down the stairs, leaning heavily on the bannister. I look at him absorbed.

There are, in these small towns, ordinary, nondescript, insignificant men and women who have charmed you with their affability, with their simple words, and whose disappearance causes you as much grief as that of a hero or that of a great artist. Where are Don Pedro, Don Antonio, Don Luis, Don Rafael, Don Alberto, Don Leandro, whom we used to know in our early childhood or in our adolescence? Perhaps all of them have died while you were absent, forgetful of their friendly memories; perhaps some of them, like this Sarrió, has outlived the ruin of his house, the death of his friends, the disappearance of everything that constituted the atmosphere of his epoch. And then you realize that these tragic, sorrowful, solitary existences in the ancient houses of the villages of Spain oscillate for two, three, six years, between life and death. [Great efforts are made to save them, but all is futile.] The years have gone by; the energies of youth have been wasted; the atmosphere that is to swallow us is already formed, and every effort we make to escape from it is sterile and vain. Do you understand now the tragedy of Sarrió?

"Sarrió!" I shouted to him.

Then he stood for a moment transfixed, bewildered, looking at me with his dimmed, bland eyes; afterwards, he opened his mouth as if to say something that he was unable to say, and finally he exclaimed in an opaque, cold voice:

"Ah, yes! Azorín. . . ."

And again there fell that terrible, dense silence in the vestibule. We could not say anything to each other. What were we going to say? There was no need for us to speak. There are instants in life—when you find yourself, for example, after many years, before a person whom you have loved—there are instants in life when you believe you are going to say many things, that you are going to express a host of tumultuous sentiments, and in which, nevertheless, you find that not even the most ordinary words come to your mind. . . .

I remained silent, sad, and overwhelmed, before the great man. And when I left the house, I again saw in the tranquil village plaza the pleasant, blue shadows, the flattened towers of the church, the closed balconies; and I again heard the murmur of the water, the cries of the swallows as they swiftly crossed the sky, the bell-strokes of the ancient clock that marks its hours, rhythmic, eternal, indifferent to the sorrows of men. . . .

Sarrió is the essential spirit of Spain, old as the hills, impervious to change, living out its life clinging to an outworn and ancient memory. Spain has passed through the Renaissance and the Reformation without altering its soul. It has passed through the liberal and industrial revolutions without really taking them to heart. It has stood rooted to its history, unwilling to adopt the new, unable to reform the old, unmoved in its vaster aspect by the great human impulses which have carried other nations forward, uncompromising in its austerity and unshakable in its inertia. Let someone grow a new shoot and it is lopped away. Let a flower be grown, and it is trimmed from the vine. Let sweet music ring out, and its player must die. Spain, like Sarrió, still lives in the decaying mansion of its past, its mind unwakened and unfocussed, its garments unkempt and in disarray, its step unsteady on the stair, its very sight dimmed by the obsession to look always within. The fountains still flow, and the swallows cry out as the ancient blue shadows fall on the village plaza and its church of flattened rock, while the clock reminds us that time is passing in its eternal measurement of the human spirit which, surely, was placed in this universe for its perfectibility.

12

THE POLITICAL AND SOCIAL
BACKGROUNDS OF THE
SECOND REPUBLIC

*In Spain there is a great deal to see, but not very much
to eat.*

Ortega y Gasset

Spain entered the twentieth century with all of her old values still
alive and strong: on the extreme right, a yearning for absolutism,
linked with the church; a vigorous liberalism among the intellectuals
and many middle-class and working groups which carried forward the
best traditions of the nineteenth century; a military establishment
which was greatly overstaffed because of the wars with Cuba and with
the United States; a church that was more cautious now in its political
activities, but which was still a very potent force in the national
political life; and a rebellious sentiment in favor of separatism in
Catalonia and in the Basque provinces. Of all these elements only the
second, which supported a democratic liberalism, bore the real
burden of transforming Spain into a modern state with a true parliamentary government and a sincere program of social and economic
reform. All the rest either dragged their feet, or, directly or indirectly,
opposed most of the measures that would lead to national unity,
harmony, and progress.

But one new element had entered the national life, which was not in existence before: *the extreme left*. The radical revolutionary ideas of the nineteenth century, the ideological and financial aid received in Spain from foreign radicals, the appalling working conditions inside Spain itself, and finally, the stimulus of the Russian Revolution —these things brought about the emergence of a real extremist group of the far left. They originally called themselves anarchists and syndicalists; later, left-wing socialism and communism also made their inroads. These extreme radicals exerted their influence mainly among the labor unions. The extremists of the left, like the extremists of the right, bear a tremendous responsibility for the downfall of decent government in Spain in this century. Both groups were so egocentric that they did not see, or were unwilling to work for, the common good. Both groups, which were very well organized, threw their weight about, irresponsibly obstructing compromise, shouting rebellion, disrupting tranquillity, destroying parliamentary government. It is a great pity that these relatively small groups, consisting of perhaps not more than 5 to 10 per cent of the population on the extreme left, and of not more than twice that percentage on the extreme right, should have been able to ruin every sincere effort of the great majority of the Spanish people for an honest and just government.

The political history of Spain in this century is one of successive bright hopes and bitter frustrations. The king, Alfonso XIII, during the first ten years of his reign, showed a real inclination to identify himself with the more liberal elements of his country. But as time passed he became more and more irritated with constitutional government, and more and more friendly to the conservative interests in Spain: the big landowners, the army, the church. He spent most of his time in political maneuvers rather than dedicating himself to finding out what was really going on in Spain, and then assuming a role of vigorous leadership, above politics, and in favor of the national welfare. Perhaps this was too much to expect of any man who had been born a king of Spain; perhaps it was far too much to expect of any Bourbon. In any case, Alfonso XIII failed to meet the demands of his epoch, and that is why he was deposed. Like a typical Bourbon he never learned anything. He could not read the writing on the wall.

After Spain had lost Cuba, Puerto Rico and the Philippines as a result of the Spanish-American War, she turned her attention to that last outpost of the Spanish empire, Morocco. France and Spain jockeyed for positions in this general north African area, and Spain wound up with a relatively small colony which was to become a very big headache. Only an unrealistic stubbornness and pride made her hold onto this territory which brought the country far more trouble than it was worth, and cost far more than it ever returned, both in money and blood. But Spanish honor was involved. This was the region where the Moors and *Moriscos* who had been thrown out of Spain had gone to settle. It was fitting that modern Spain should want to assert her dominance over her ancient enemies, particularly now that she had lost all of her overseas possessions. Once the greatest colonial empire of them all, how could she deny herself this symbolic portion of the world in which colonialism was still a mark of distinction?

But if the Spanish government felt this final urge to imperium, the poor Spanish workers and peasants who had to go to Morocco as soldiers certainly did not. Gone was the day when at the beat of a drum every poor devil of Spain would rush for the nearest enlistment booth. The deception of that charade had been repeated so often that even the most ignorant countryman no longer felt any desire to seek glory on the field of battle. And against the Moors? The government must be crazy! But crazy or not, the government of Alfonso XIII had already committed itself. France had long since bitten off the choicer slice of this part of Africa, and was eager for more. In fact, it was once reliably reported that had the Spanish soldiers delayed a few hours longer in reaching their sector, they would have found that the French had preceded them there.

In 1909, because of senseless mismanagement, the Spanish army in Morocco met with a serious military reverse, and the government decided to call up the Catalan reserves. This was like a slap in the face to Catalonia for her separatist leanings. It was a stupid mistake for the central government. The workers of Barcelona called a general strike, there were riots, churches and convents were attacked, and it took several days of street fighting to put down the revolt. This was the *semana trágica*, or tragic week, which presaged the bloodier conflicts that were yet to come. Things became so tense that all of Spain was placed under martial law.

When the whole sorry mess was over, the central government made an even greater political blunder by seizing Francisco Ferrer, a fanatical but probably blameless intellectual anarchist, and charging him with having master-minded the affair. Ferrer headed a school called the *Escuela Moderna* in which one was taught to believe in social

equality and to hate the church which upheld false doctrines. There
was also a night school and a press that turned out anarchist pamphlets by the score. Ferrer, therefore, was a natural scapegoat, despite
his technical, and probably his moral, innocence. Ferrer was tried,
and though a strong case was made out for him by his counsel, he
was found guilty and shot. He immediately became a great martyr,
and a violent wave of liberal sympathy swept over Spain. There were
demonstrations against the government, and the cabinet fell. Who
wanted to die in Morocco?

The liberals now had their chance, and their leader Canalejas
proved that he was a man of strength and integrity. He was also a
politician who knew the art of compromise, a rare commodity in
Spain. But in 1912 Canalejas was assassinated by an anarchist, and
this marked the end of the liberal dream for some time to come.
Count Romanones, who was "the prototype of the Spanish politician," became Prime Minister. Had Canalejas lived, the military and
the church might have been restrained and pulled into line with a
firm democratic hand. Canalejas was that *rara avis* in Spanish history,
a good Catholic and a good liberal. But without its head the liberal
party floundered.

One afternoon in the month of March 1914 a youthful man with a
heavy forehead, expressive eyes and an attractive, if self-conscious smile,
came forward on the stage of the theatre of La Comedia in Madrid and
began to speak with quiet assurance, elegant gesture and finely modulated
voice to a crowded house which listened eagerly, and now and then interrupted with vigorous ovations.[10]

This was the famous writer and professor of philosophy at the
University of Madrid, Ortega y Gasset. His speech was a call for
progress: When our generation hears the word Spain, he said, it does
not think of the Golden Age, "it does not remember the victories of
the Cross, it does not call forth the vision of a blue sky, and under
it a splendor—it merely feels, and what it feels is grief." Ortega went
on to tear apart the "official Spain" of the Bourbon restoration. The
old Spain of abuses and privileges was dying. The restoration itself
must be ended, "for the dead must be thoroughly killed." Ortega then
waxed eloquent and voiced his call to arms, intellectual arms: everything in Spain must be liberalized, democratized, nationalized—the
army, the crown, the clergy, the workers, the aristocrats.

The liberals now had their intellectual leadership. The tree planted by Francisco Giner a generation previously in the *Institución Libre* had come to fruit. The professors and writers of Spain trained in Giner's school were alive to the national problems. The ancient spring had begun to flow. Education was finally paying off. But four months later the Austrian archduke was assassinated in Serbia, and the First World War broke out.

A shudder went through the continent and Spain braced herself for the new crisis. Her people were sharply divided in their sympathies. The upper middle class, the reactionary and clerical right, and most of the army were pro-German; the big industrialists, the intellectuals, and many of the workers were pro-Ally; the masses of peasants were indifferent. With such a sharp cleavage the country sought refuge in neutrality. The king was super-cautious in not favoring openly one side over the other. He was married to an English princess, but the Queen Mother was Austrian. Alfonso XIII walked the tightrope with his country for the four years of the holocaust.

Spain could not remain idle while the war went on. Orders for Spanish commodities poured into the country, and with them foreign influences grew apace. There was a considerable amount of industrial development with foreign capital. Gold deposits in the Bank of Spain quadrupled in four years. The national currency rose in value, and Spain's economy began to pick up. Madariaga, historian and former Spanish ambassador to the United States, writes: "The war drove a powerful current of foreign vitality right into the inmost recesses of the nation." Radicalism from France and Germany also made inroads in Spain, and the theory of uniting the workers into a consolidated political force began to become a practical reality. The king continued to play politics and his repeated coalition governments accelerated the disintegration of the political parties and the death of the party system. The Spanish electorate, which had never known a truly honest election, for all elections were "made" by the government, commenced now to penetrate this deception, and slowly became more emancipated.

In spite of all the bad things about the war for Spain, the country at last felt itself again an integral part of Europe. Madrid cast aside its provincialism and became the most important neutral city of Europe; many matters of international policy and finance were handled there. A bureau of missing soldiers from both sides was set up and worked with great efficiency. Spain took over many foreign embassies and legations in other European countries. Spanish doctors travelled in Allied hospital ships "to guarantee their *bona fide* character to the irate commanders of German submarines," and Spanish officers made frequent inspections of war prisoners' camps. Spain felt a considerable pride at this rebirth of her importance as a European nation. She lived again "an international life such as she had not known since the days of the sixteenth and seventeenth centuries when her generals, churchmen and ambassadors were paramount in the affairs of Europe."[10]

The spirit of "renovation" was in the air all over Spain. The newspaper *El Sol*, which was to become the great paper of the Second Republic, led the move to liberalize the country. In 1917 came the crisis. Backed by the big industrialists, the parties of the left, and with strong popular support, a large segment of the Cortes assembled (seventy-one deputies) and demanded thoroughgoing political reforms. What might have been a crucial switch to a real parliamentary democracy, had there been proper leadership, turned out to be nearly a national disaster when the extremists of both sides took control. The extreme right, led by the king who appointed a conservative minister and cabinet officers, met the movement with a blast of ice water. The whole country felt cheated, and the labor unions howled bloody murder. The Socialist Union in Madrid, a moderate group, took the lead in calling for a general strike. The far left Syndicalist Union of Barcelona followed suit, and soon the strike had spread to all the main cities; Madrid, Barcelona, Seville, Bilbao, Oviedo, Valencia, etc.

The Spanish economy was paralyzed; transportation and construction came to a standstill. The unions demanded a socialist democratic republic, and took to the barricades. Their hotheaded leaders had gone much too far, and delivered the country straight into the hands of the group they hated most: the military. Army units assaulted the barricaded workers, several hundreds were killed or wounded, two thousand were imprisoned, and the strike was ruthlessly suppressed. The army had "saved the country from anarchism," and now stood supreme. Extremes on the right and on the left had produced this crisis, and the right, which was the stronger of the two, had handled it with summary effectiveness.

Four years later, in 1921, there was a second disaster in Morocco. A certain General Silvestre, who commanded a large body of Spanish troops, felt the urge to finish off the Moroccan war quickly. He approached the king, who gave his personal blessings to the scheme.

Silvestre then led his troops forward, but instead of winning the victory he had hoped for they walked straight into the trap set for them by the Moroccan leader Abdel-Krim. The Spanish army was surrounded in a small valley and slaughtered. It was an inglorious disaster. Every effort was made to dissociate the king from what had happened, but the facts spoke for themselves. Anger and disappointment mounted. All kinds of investigations were made, and a new army of 140,000 soldiers was readied for the Moroccan campaign. But it was too late; nothing could save the government now.

The generals in Spain decided that it was time to take over, and General Primo de Rivera was selected for the job. "The ambition of every Spanish general," writes Madariaga, "is to save his country by becoming her ruler." Madariaga then goes on to say that this ambition is not limited to generals, but is that of every individual citizen. While the Englishman or North American is generally content to work within the party or group, the Spaniard is passionately anxious to take things into his own hands. Primo de Rivera, an Andalusian, was just such a man. He was in the true Spanish tradition, and in the true tradition of the most popular Latin-American dictators. In him the masses could see themselves and their own passionate patriotism; he was the epitome and symbol of their zeal. Like them he would cut the Gordian knot of constitutional complexity and the red tape of governmental incompetence and would set the country back on the right path with a few well-chosen decrees.

The king knew very well what was going on all the time this military plot was being hatched, but he was so perturbed at his own loss of popularity because of the Moroccan fiasco that he approved everything. On several occasions the king had denounced parliament, and during the twenty-one years of his reign he had had thirty-three ministries, an average of a change of government every seven or eight months. Under such conditions stable government was impossible. In 1923, when the *coup* came, Alfonso XIII breathed a sigh of relief. The army had taken over but was not the king commander in chief of the army? The Spanish constitution was now dead. In the passion of the moment this looked to many like a good thing, but in actuality it was a throwback to the nineteenth century habit of military rule by *pronunciamiento*. Primo de Rivera was but a newer model of Generals Riego, Prim, and the other nineteenth century military leaders who had led similar *coups*. The king, instead of ruling through the army, as he had hoped, became a prisoner of the military clique.

The dictatorship would in fact push Spain forward in a material way. Has not the catch phrase "order and progress" been the panacea of every dictatorship? But in the end it would be clear that this move resulted in enthroning the very forces which had held back real progress for a century: militarism, clericalism, the rule of the oligarchy. The new government astutely neutralized labor; it favored socialism as opposed to the far more radical syndicalism, and thus brought worker opposition to a stalemate. The socialists collaborated with the government for the first several years of the dictatorship.

Let us give the Devil his due. Primo de Rivera personally took over the command of the Moroccan war and led it to a victorious conclusion. He modernized the Spanish transportation system, and like Mussolini "he made the trains run on time." He also embarked on a large-scale highway construction program, and before his government fell Spain had the best roads since Roman times, but they soon fell into disrepair and remained so for more than a generation. Large-scale enterprises were invited to establish branches in Spain, and many did so. The army saw to it that the country enjoyed a period of order.

What was the price? First, there was a rigorous censorship of the press. The Ateneo of Madrid, the country's most famous literary, scientific, and artistic club, was put under lock and key. The president of the Supreme Court was removed. Even the textbooks were revamped in order to make them safe from a clerical point of view. Pressure was put on teachers to force them to attend mass, regardless of their wishes. In these measures Primo de Rivera was supported by the army, by the church, by business, and by the big landowners. At first, as is unfortunately the case with nearly every popular dictatorship, he had also been favored by a considerable proportion of the workers as well.

But Primo de Rivera did not long hold the support of the majority. The intellectuals were the first to oppose him. Unamuno, who was already a man of tremendous stature, became violent in his opposition. He wrote a letter to a friend in Argentina in which he lambasted the dictatorship, and without his permission the letter was published. The Spanish government countered by depriving Unamuno of his chair of Greek at Salamanca and by exiling him to a small island in the Canary Archipelago. Later, he went to France, refusing to return to Spain (despite an amnesty) as long as Primo de Rivera was in power.

Another even more unpopular blunder of the dictatorship was its handling of the shooting of two civil guards. It was not known who the culprits were. Several persons were booked, tried, and pronounced "not guilty" by the military court. The Civil Guard Corps became incensed and demanded that the decision be reversed, and the accused found guilty. Under threat this was done and the executions were carried out. The entire country seethed with anger. Unamuno and Ortega, who were in exile in France, led the opposition to this despotic action and published proof that the whole affair had been rammed through by the Spanish police without any basis in fact. Scapegoats were needed, and scapegoats were found. Innocent Spanish citizens had been sacrificed to the senseless demands of the government. Unfortunately, these reports never appeared in the strictly censored newspapers of Spain, but by word of mouth they did reach many thousands of people.

In the final years of his rule Primo de Rivera made an attempt to establish a civil government under his leadership, but popular feeling was now strongly against a dictatorship of any kind. Liberalism had grown. rapidly among all sectors of the population excepting only those of the extreme right. There were many priests in the church who were also convinced liberals. They opposed the dictatorship and supported the forces working toward the Republic. The world depression of 1930 caused a worsening of economic conditions inside Spain, and opposition to the dictatorship mounted steadily. In that same year the government closed all Spanish universities, which had become a source of overt rebellion. Disorders among the workers multiplied; in 1930 there were five hundred and four strikes, and in 1931 a proportionately even greater number. People began to sign Republican manifestos regardless of whether or not they faced imprisonment. Crowds assembled and shouted: "Down with the king!", who had been linked irretrievably with the dictatorship. They did not even mention the name of the general. In 1930 Primo de Rivera stepped down, and his place was taken by General Berenguer, who strove to re-establish a constitutional regime. But when the elections of 1931 were held in April of that year, they indicated how wide the opposition was to any military or monarchical regime, and King Alfonso XIII fled from Spain. It was time for the Republic.

The men who founded and governed the Spanish Republic were as heterogeneous a mixture as has ever appeared in the pages of Euro-

pean history. First were the intellectuals, the men of ideas, whom we
have already treated. Then came the other liberals of various shades
and colorings, some of whom were good Catholics but most of whom
were not. Next were the Catalan and Basque separatists to whom the
Republic meant local autonomy. Finally there was the Spanish Left
composed of the anarchists, the socialists, and the communists. All
of these people called themselves Republicans, and a large majority of
them were anticlerical.

This opposition to the church as a political influence had become
one of the marked characteristics of Spanish liberalism in general.
Under the Republic it turned into a violent church-state conflict.
This was not the first time that such a conflict had appeared in Spain.
Charles III had expelled the Jesuits from the country in 1767, and in
1812 and again in 1820 the Spanish liberals, temporarily in control
of the government, took a strong anticlerical stand. In all three cases
the government had stood for reform, while the church opposed it.

Things had not always been this way in Spain. In medieval times
the village priests had supported the local communities against the
central power, the poor against the wealthy, and the weak against the
strong. Then, gradually, by encouraging the persecution of the Jews,
the Moriscos, and other dissidents in Spain, by allowing the Inquisition to become so powerful and to last so long, by aligning itself
generally with reactionary social sentiments and with absolutist government, the church reversed its earlier role as the protector of the
masses. At first, the people themselves clung to their reactionary
church and opposed all political liberalism, but as the years passed
and the Spanish economy and government remained backward while
the rest of Europe surged ahead, the feeling grew among the Spanish
people that their church had somehow let them down. Considerable
numbers of them began to regard it as having deceived them. They
commenced to align themselves with the anticlerical intellectuals, and
began to turn the zeal which they had formerly felt *for* their church
against it. This accounts for the fanatical violence of the anticlerical
riots of the twentieth century, and in part for the anticlerical position
taken by the Second Republic. The rapid growth of the Spanish
parties of the left in this century was the natural outgrowth of these
historic developments. Anarchism, which envisioned a society without
government, was the first such political philosophy to make its appeal
in Spain where all government had been traditionally bad.

Michael Bakunin, a Russian aristocrat, and a man of gigantic size and energy, was the creator of Spanish (and European) anarchism as a political movement. It was the first organized expression of leftist sentiment in the country. Bakunin was at first a follower of Marx, but later broke with him. The two were in bitter conflict between 1868 and 1872. Bakunin wanted to destroy the state, to destroy God, and to destroy the wicked and powerful rich who symbolized both. He believed that if these forces were made to disappear society would spontaneously reform itself into smaller local segments which would give rise to the happy life. Bakunin based his creed on what he had seen of life in the small peasant communities of Russia in his youth, and this is why his ideas took root in Spain, where the medieval municipalities had a similar history. Bakunin, in a word, became the prophet of the age-old tradition of the Spanish masses for separatism, local government, fragmentation of the central power.

In Córdoba in 1872 an anarchistic congress, inspired by Bakunin's wild idealism and fierce hatred of the church, assembled and proceeded to draft a manifesto in which it was stated that their members (perhaps fifty to sixty thousand) proposed "to build on the ruins of national unity free and independent municipalities bound only by federal pacts." Actually, what Spanish anarchism stood for was a revived Middle Ages without the clergy and without the kings.

In the following year, 1873, in the small town of Alcoy, a few miles south of Valencia, an anarchist schoolteacher led the workers of the local paper factories in a general strike, the country's first example of this weapon of political action. There were demonstrations and discussions, the municipal authorities sided with the owners, the workers paraded in the streets and then began to shoot. There was a violent fight which lasted for several hours, leaving several dead in its wake. The workers emerged victorious. They then burned the paper factories, shot the mayor of the town, cut off his head and carried it up and down the street. A Spanish general was sent to the town with a strong military force which quickly liquidated the main culprits and suppressed the anarchist movement with deadly efficiency.

But this was only one of several times that anarchism was driven underground to come back later with renewed force and vigor. In 1891 several thousand workers marched into Jerez shouting "Long live anarchy!", murdering two shopkeepers before they were dispersed by the police. Several other violent episodes took place in the following two decades, bombs were thrown, anarchists were imprisoned and tortured, the Prime Minister himself, Cánovas del Castillo, was shot and killed in revenge (1897). This violence culminated in the general strike of 1909, with a subsequent upsurge of liberalism all over Spain.

"The source of everything Spanish is inside Spain" is one of the basic truisms of the country's problems since the beginning. The anarchists were able to make such headway in Spain because they were in step with a Spanish tradition which had never died. Not only had there been village cooperatives in medieval times, but there were still many similar cooperatives in the nineteenth and twentieth centuries. Joaquín Costa, John Langdon Davies, and Gerald Brenan (in his excellent book *The Spanish Labyrinth*) all give an account of them. The medieval communal land system led naturally to other community activities. The village of Llánabes in León, and the other villages around it, still followed this pattern of life in 1898 when Joaquín Costa wrote about it. An account of how these communal activities functioned in Llánabes in earlier days is given in Brenan, who quotes a local priest of the town:

The policy is admirable. The surgeon, the shepherds, the blacksmith, the apothecary's shop, the papal indulgences, litanies, etc., are all provided free by the municipality. Salt, seed-corn, as well as what remains over from renting the common domain, are divided up in the village fairly and justly. All the lands are common lands and are shared out every ten years in equal portions and by lot among all the neighbors. . . . There is only one *mayorazgo* (entailed estate) in the village.

There were many other examples of village communes which had survived up to the present epoch. The pasture lands of most of the valleys of the Pyrenees were communal, and there were also communal townships in Cáceres and in the Asturian mountains. In these villages all essential services, often including those of a veterinary surgeon, were provided by the municipality, as were seeds for the crops. There was frequently a cooperative store as well. The village of Caso in Asturias, which had a population of nearly fifteen thousand, owned twenty thousand head of cattle in common. In Catalonia also there were, and still are, many similar villages. In Bagur, a net manufacturing town, the net industry was owned in common. In Port de la Selva (in 1936) the village ran a fisherman's cooperative, and owned and ran in common the boats, curing factory, storehouse, refrigerating plant, shops, trucks, café, theater and assembly rooms. They even coined their own money and had a system of insurance against death, accident and loss of boats. The community provided theatrical entertainment, dances, and a series of educational and cultural lectures. Like a great many villages in Spain they had a municipal credit fund on which the villagers might draw. There were many other fisherman's communes in Catalonia.[39]

The anarchists had nothing to do with the establishment of this cooperative pattern of village life. They did, however, take great advantage of the communal spirit which had pervaded these villages from time immemorial. What is still more to the point is that in 1936, when the Nationalist revolt took place under General Franco, "every village in the anarchist districts of Spain threw off its municipality and began to govern itself through its syndicate." In townhall meetings the workers discussed their problems and decided upon the course of action that was to be taken. This meant very simply that even when the central government lost its active control these smaller communities continued to function without any diminution of their effectiveness.

In the early 1900's another movement of the far left made its entry into Spain: syndicalism. Syndicalism was a variation of anarchism and soon merged with it. Its philosopher was a Frenchman named Georges Sorel, who published a book on the subject in 1908. It is worth pointing out that while anarchism had a Russian background and syndicalism a French origin, the ideas of both movements were most widely and successfully carried out in Spain. The medieval history of the country and the ineradicable local feelings of the Spaniard account for this in part, but the deplorable religious, economic, and political conditions inside Spain must also bear their large share of the responsibility. *Syndicalisme* is the French word for trade unionism. In Spanish the word *sindicato* means "trade union."

The Spanish syndicalists took over when the anarchist unions began to lose strength. The two ideas were very close: Syndicalism was considered simply to be a means to an end, which was to establish an anarchist society. Hence, the new movement soon began to be called anarcho-syndicalism. The "tragic week" of 1909 in Barcelona, with the martyrdom of Ferrer, aroused the workers of the far left to the necessity for a stronger labor organization, one which would embrace the entire country. In the following year, 1910, such a syndicalist union was organized with the name of *Confederación Nacional del Trabajo*, in brief, the C.N.T., or National Confederation of Work. This is the union that had approximately one million members in 1936 when the Spanish civil war broke out.

Syndicalism was superior in organization and direction to the previous disjointed methods of the anarchists. The syndicalist unions were organized on a strictly local basis; there were no national craft unions. Each local union had almost complete autonomy to decide what action it would take in any given situation. This freed the workers from the hard core of centralized leadership of which Spaniards have always been so distrustful. Furthermore, the leaders and staff workers of the syndicalist organization received no pay for their work; in 1936 there was only a single secretary with a salary. Membership fees were a pittance. This gave the movement a moral superiority over the other unions, and also provided a dedicated corps of workers for the cause.

The principal weapon of the syndicalist unions was the general strike, and the first attempt in this direction took place only a few months after the C.N.T. had been organized, in 1911. The strike had not been properly prepared for, and the government, under the vigorous leadership of the Prime Minister, Canalejas, suppressed it quickly, suspended the C.N.T. itself, and put its offices under lock and key. The syndicalist movement collapsed temporarily, but it was far from dead. Then for the second time within fifteen years an anarchist shot and killed the prime minister (1912). The *mystique* of violence, which so fascinated the far left, thus resulted in the death of two of Spain's most honored statesmen, Cánovas and Canalejas. In both instances this caused a reactionary swing in the government.

The World War put a crimp in the anarcho-syndicalist movement, for it caused a deep split in the membership, some favoring neutrality, others favoring the Allies. The general strike of 1917, led by the Socialist Union, was given only halfhearted support by the anarcho-syndicalists, but in 1919, two years later, a series of strikes took place under the leadership of the latter group. They started in Barcelona and quickly spread to other parts of the country. Recruits were attracted to the movement by the hundreds.

In December of 1919 the C.N.T. held a congress in Madrid; it was attended by 450 delegates claiming to represent 700,000 worker members. The delegates met in the same La Comedia theater in which, five years previously, Ortega y Gasset had spoken so persuasively in favor of the renovation of Spain. But while Ortega had urged his countrymen to follow the path of liberal reform, the anarcho-syndicalist delegates went on record as favoring what they called "anarchist or libertarian communism." By a large majority they voted not to merge with the smaller socialist trade union, known as the U.G.T. (*Unión General de Trabajadores*). Not long after this came the disaster in Morocco, and the fall of the government, with General Primo de Rivera taking control (1923) under a dictatorship. His regime strongly favored the more moderate socialist union, and anarcho-syndicalism again went underground.

Many writers have commented that Spanish anarchism is un-adultered Iberianism. It represents the magnificent independence of the Spaniard set loose in the arena of political action. The anarchist ideal is absolute liberty, an absurd concept, of course. But in Spain there has always been a fascination for the absurd. It is essentially the religion of Quixotism. The real meaning of "libertarian communism" was reorganization of the economy and government on a collective community basis, without centralized state control. The small autonomous villages or syndicates themselves would be the bases of this new collectivism.

The anarcho-syndicalists believed passionately in one final great outbreak of violence which would end all violence. After this the new society would emerge. But first the powerful and the wicked must be killed. They were the ones who had held humanity back from the natural realization of its social ideal, liberty. The anarchists did not wish just to confiscate the luxuries of the rich, but to exterminate them. They were moved by an almost ascetic morality which reminds one of the early Christians and Jews. In many of their collectives they strove to eliminate all alcoholic beverages, tobacco, and even coffee. They suppressed the brothels in their areas with an efficiency never achieved either by the state or the church, which often winked at this social "escape valve." The anarchists never made an ideal of a "higher standard of living," as did the socialists. Thus, the anarchist movement was Spanish idealism carried to a wild extreme, but that it was truly and essentially Hispanic in nature no one should doubt, regardless of its point of origin. There is no doubt either that if the anarcho-syndicalists had come out on top after the civil war they would have in-stituted the worst conceivable kind of tyranny. To the anarchist liberty meant freedom from state, church, and capitalist control, but it did not mean freedom of conscience. If perchance some good Spaniard wished to attend mass, or send his children to a religious school, or have a drink of whisky, or live in a luxurious style, or eat something besides the local produce, or give his support to the idea of a stronger state, then he was automatically one of the evil ones who would have to be liquidated in order that the others might remain free. So stand him against the wall, give him a cigarette, and fire!

The man who possesses nothing comes naturally to have a deep hatred for material things. The Spaniard's scorn of luxury is almost innate after so many centuries of doing without. He is a natural-born stoic who exalts the stern virtues of his ancestors. In the small villages of the country today, even in the cities, many Spaniards disapprove of the most elemental luxuries and will even boast that they do not need heating in their houses, such is their physical stamina. Only soft peoples like the English and the Americans have to depend on artificial heat. A Spartan character and absolute liberty—this is the ideal of many Spaniards.

The Spanish anarchists appealed to this primitive pride and strength of the race, and in this lay a great part of their success. Furthermore, by concentrating on the autonomy of the local syndicates they appealed to the tap root of Spanish character, which was to act alone and by instinct. During the war against Joseph Bonaparte and the French, as during the Spanish civil war, this instinctive action or "organized indiscipline" resulted in guerilla warfare of the most obstinate and enduring kind. Defeating these people was like cutting down weeds only to have them grow back again as soon as the machine moved on. These instinctive guerilla tactics won against Napoleon and came near to winning against Franco, despite his Italian and his German allies. But that story we cover later.

Spanish socialism has a much more distinguished record than anarchism or anarcho-syndicalism, despite the appeal of the latter movements to the stern virtues and local pride of the working class. "The Socialism of Madrid," wrote Madariaga, "is the only true historical entity in modern Spanish politics, i.e., the only feature endowed with an inner life which gives it a permanent, growing and formative value in the life of the country." During the early days of the Second Republic it appeared to many observers that Spain was moving toward becoming a mild, socialist state. Had this move been successful Russian communism would now have a vigorous socialist opponent in western Europe, and the entire complexion of world politics might now be different. There were many things in Spain which led these observers to believe that socialism was the natural modern form for the Spanish economy and government to take. These factors were: a tradition of local collectivism, an all-embracing church, a strong centralized government, and, last but not least, a group of highly educated and highly intelligent socialist leaders. Put these factors all together, and theoretically the mixture might produce an effective socialist state. Practically, the attempt was made to do just that, but it failed miserably and ended in the civil war.

Socialism began in Spain in the 1870's at about the same time as anarchism, but its growth was much slower, for socialism required more training and more control. It was not until 1888, with the organization of the *Unión General de Trabajadores*, the U.G.T., or General Union of Workers, that the socialist movement really got under way. There were barely three thousand members of this new union, which was a moderate and well-disciplined organization with no harebrained revolutionary projects. The socialists believed in parliamentary processes, in a disciplined nation-wide union, in a national state, and in raising the standard of living. All of these beliefs separated them from the anarchists, as did also their relatively high union dues.

Just after the turn of the century the socialists (now numbering about 26,000) began to establish and to develop their *Casas del Pueblo* ("houses of the people") which gave their party a cultural as well as a political appeal. The *Casa del Pueblo* was not only the town's party center, but also provided a lending library, committee and social rooms, often a café, and frequently a program of cultural and educational extension. The *Casa del Pueblo* in Madrid was a former ducal palace; as Gerald Brenan says, "The Socialist party had a strong sense of its own dignity and felt itself the heir to the glories of the past." Had not the Spanish missions in the New World often been referred to as socialist societies? The anarchists, of course, berated these trappings of culture as proof that the socialists had sold themselves out to capitalism.

The Spanish socialists fought energetically for honest elections, in the firm belief that this would further their chances of assuming power. They also campaigned vigorously against governmental corruption, nepotism, political bossism, and illiteracy. Their participation in the general strikes of 1909 and 1917 indicated that they also exerted a considerable weight in the field of economic and political action. Hence, above all the large political parties in Spain, the socialists came to represent best the fight for honesty and decency in government, justice in the courts, education of the masses, and a fair control and distribution of the national wealth. The strike of 1917 was put down by the army, but shortly afterward several socialists were elected to the national Cortes, with some help from the anarchist voters. The party now claimed 220,000 members, and had become a political force to be reckoned with. Unfortunately, conflicts within the party weakened its effectiveness. Indalecio Prieto of Bilbao led the liberal and more flexible wing, while Largo Caballero of Madrid represented the authoritarian Castilian spirit. During the Primo de Rivera dictatorship the socialist party continued to grow, and by 1931 it had well over a million members; the anarcho-syndicalists claimed about the same number. The socialist party had many distinguished intellectuals among its members: Fernando de los Ríos, historian and professor of law, Julián Besteiro, professor of logic, and Luis Araquistain, a well-known writer.*

All of the Spanish parties of the left were composed in the main of urban workers, led by a handful of zealous revolutionaries. These urban workers, however, were mostly peasants who had poured into the cities because it was impossible for them to make a living on the land. Uprooted, they were particularly vulnerable to the new extremist ideas which had come into Spain from the other European countries.

Thus, we might say that at the very heart of Spanish leftism in general lies the basic problem of land, its unequal distribution and improper use. Originally the Spaniard was a shepherd, not a farmer. Then the Romans introduced the *latifundia*, or big estates, and agriculture got under way. Under the Visigoths agriculture deteriorated, as did everything else that the Romans had brought into Spain, except the church. When the Moors invaded Spain they went even farther than the Romans in irrigating and cultivating the land. Under them Andalusia and Valencia were crisscrossed with irrigation ditches, aqueducts, waterwheels, and other engineering projects which made the desert fruitful and green.

---

* The Spanish communist party was founded in 1920 by a few dissident socialists and anarcho-syndicalists. It was so unimportant during the Primo de Rivera' dictatorship that nothing was done either to control or to suppress it.

Castile, the heart of Spain, was not a rich agricultural land. But the Castilians were fine warriors, and they eventually overcame the Moors, occupied their smiling fields, divided them up among the great nobles, turned their sheep loose to graze, and let the vast system of irrigation fall into ruin. Thus, for the second time in Spanish history the *latifundia* became a way of life. When the *Moriscos* were expelled from Spain under Philip III the last vestiges of Moorish agriculture disappeared.

The only good sign was the establishment of numerous communal villages in Andalusia, and in these the peasants were able to wrest a passable living from the common lands. The church also owned large territories in this part of Spain. The liberal Cortes of 1812 took the fatal step of confiscating these common and church-owned lands and selling them in the open market in order to pay off the national debt. Estates were purchased for a pittance, and a whole new group of absentee landlords was created.

In 1929, just prior to the establishment of the Republic, out of 1,026,412 landowners or tenants who had been assessed in Spain, 847,548 were earning less than one peseta a day, in purchasing power perhaps about as much as a quarter in the U.S. currency of that epoch. In Andalusia today approximately 4,000 big landlords, who constitute only 2 per cent of the total number of proprietors, receive in income over twice as much as all of the 200,000 small landowners put together. The average big landowner's income is about 50 times that of the average small farmer. One half of the working population are *braceros* or landless laborers, whose daily wages are the lowest in Spain, and to make matters still worse, they are unemployed for approximately six months out of every year. Gerald Brenan, who has studied the situation with a careful eye, gives the following quotation from Campomanes, minister of Charles III in 1780, and then adds that it is "an exact description of the state of affairs today."

In Andalusia the inhabitants are nearly all simple laborers who have only temporary and precarious occupation and live the rest of the year in poverty, plunged in inaction, for lack of remunerative work. Their wives and children are without work and all, piled up in towns and large villages, live on charity . . . in a wretched starvation—which does not correspond to the fertility of the soil, and certainly is not caused by their idleness.[39]

The towns of Andalusia are mainly sizable places, of between eight thousand and twenty-five thousand inhabitants. But unlike the towns of that size in the United States or Great Britain they do not give the impression of being busy or productive centers. On the contrary, their houses and buildings suggest piles of ancient rock thrown together under a burning sun, and their inhabitants, who crowd the narrow streets, remind one of weathered lizards who have crawled out from beneath the rocks to go about their daily quest for food. The industries of these towns are of the most primitive kinds: pottery making, weaving, the manufacture of candy, tobacco processing, soap making, leather work, etc. And yet the incredible vitality of these undernourished people impresses every observer. They have practically learned to survive on the very air they breathe. But inside, there is dynamite. Let the fuse be lit and an explosion will follow as sure as night follows day.

As one travels toward the north it is obvious that conditions improve gradually, reaching their highest level in the Cantabrian area and in the foothills of the Pyrenees that extend all the way across northern Spain. But the Spanish farmer still lives at a level lower than that of the farmer of any other European country, with the possible exception of Portugal. Irrigation and mechanization could increase the productivity of vast areas of Spain's agricultural land by at least six times and, in many instances, by thirty times. The big landlords showed little interest in such improvement, for this would mean a considerable initial outlay in order to carry out the necessary projects.

It was the interplay and union of all these social forces which brought about the Second Republic, and it was the inevitable conflicts among these same forces which caused its disintegration. While the intellectuals spoke persuasively and with moderation, the labor union leaders and workers grabbed at the reins and wanted to turn the coach down their own byway. Socialists, anarchists, liberals, peasants, intellectuals, extreme leftists and moderate republicans, a good many enlightened Catholics, the Basques and the Catalans, with their longing for self-rule—such were the human bases of the Spanish Republic. Was it reasonable to hope that these utterly diverse elements, suffering from bitter conflicts among themselves and even within each individual group, could remain united long enough to transform Spain into a modern, parliamentary democracy? Such was the expectation and the dream of the great majority of the Spanish people.

13

THE SPANISH REPUBLIC
(1931–1939)

Bliss was it in that dawn to be alive,
but to be young was very heaven . . .

When William Wordsworth wrote the above lines of his famous sonnet the French Revolution was just getting under way. Everything augured for a future that might fulfill the dream of centuries. But when the revolutionists began to run amuck in their frenzy of blood, and the guillotines severed head after head until the very streets were scarlet, the English poet turned away in revulsion. The Second Spanish Republic with its bright promise, followed by the civil war with its vicious reprisals, aroused similar feelings in the hearts of many objective observers.

The Spaniards had long dreamed of their Republic, and since the nineteenth century had referred to it as *La Niña Bonita*, the "Pretty Girl." The "Pretty Girl" finally arrived only to die; she never had a real chance of becoming a matron. It is so easy to see these things with the superficial wisdom of hindsight, but in the year 1931 there were few indeed who would have voiced such a prophecy. When I reached Madrid in the summer of 1932 everyone was still exclaiming with pride: "We did it all without shedding any blood! The dictatorship fell, the king fled, and the new regime came to power, all in a matter of hours, *because the people wanted it!* And without our shedding a single drop of blood!" The professors at the university repeated these or similar words, the students echoed them, the shopkeepers said much the same thing, so did the doctors, the lawyers, the socialists, the workers; even many who had formerly been royalists were carried away by the enthusiasm of this beautiful intellectual dream.

On April 12, 1931, the country held elections for its municipal councilors; the vote was heavy, reaching 90 per cent in many places; there were no disorders of any kind, and when the final count was made it caught both sides by surprise. The vote revealed that every capital city of the fifty provinces of Spain, with four minor exceptions, had voted for an antimonarchy slate. In Madrid and Barcelona the Republican landslide was overwhelming. Royalists had carried the country districts, but as political bossism and habitual manipulations were known to prevail in these areas they did not carry great weight. The king was told that his reign was over, and was advised to leave Spain, which he promptly did, without, however, abdicating his throne. The Civil Guard Corps came over to the Republicans, and on April 14 the Republic was declared.

Madariaga gives a vivid account of what took place in Madrid. Huge crowds gathered in front of the royal palace, but were informed that the king had fled. It was not a crowd that wanted blood; they merely shouted "Viva! Viva! Long live this! Long live that!" Nevertheless, the men in charge of the palace became worried and called for more police. A "force" was promised and was sent, but it consisted only of a number of unarmed citizens. These formed a loose ring around the palace and asked the crowd to move back. The people obeyed immediately, and soon afterward they melted away.

The Republic was greeted with exultation. Here is what Ortega said: "The magnificent and momentous hour has come when fate imposes upon Spaniards the duty of thinking grandly. It is the great moment that will not return for centuries!" Unamuno, the grand old rector of the University of Salamanca, entered Madrid in triumph. He received an unprecedented ovation from hundreds of thousands. Cannons were fired and the whole city rang with enthusiasm.

A joy like that of nature in spring—such was the mood of Spain in those glorious first days of the Republic. The revolution had been so clean, so untainted by any excesses which usually soil the dramatic moments of history, so free from military interference for or against, so clearly the outcome of an orderly expression of public opinion, that the first emotion aroused by their triumph in the breast of all Republicans was one of proud joy.

So writes Madariaga, who was one of the founders and greatest leaders of the new regime.

For the first time in the history of Spain the intellectuals and the masses were standing together. Contrary to Ortega's view of an invertebrate Spain, a Spain of tremendous popular vitality but with no backbone or head, the whole nation now appeared welded into a new alloy in which the masses would be the brawn and body, as they should, while the intellectuals and educated people would be the brains and would direct, as was their mission. It was an alloy too quickly made. The intellectuals were too quixotic in their idealism, the deputies were too personal and excessively recalcitrant in their differences of opinion, the workers were too unthinking in their demands, the church, chastened and frightened by recent events, retreated temporarily but only to consolidate its strength, and the army observed the government's antimilitary policy with growing dismay. The monarchists, who formed the obvious opposition, were aghast.

The Republicans would have done well to remember that they were repeating history. Theirs was the fourth "liberal" government in a little more than a century, and the second Republic. In 1812, in 1820, in 1873, and again in 1931 the chips had rolled their way. Unfortunately, they had not learned the lessons of history, or perhaps they did not remember the ill-fated words of Alcalá Galiano, who in 1820 had exclaimed: "The French took three years of struggle and shed oceans of blood to win their liberty. All we have needed in Spain has been two days of explanation and one of rejoicing." The historian might unkindly add: "And how many years for weeping?"

The actual tally of all votes cast in the municipal elections of April 1931 indicated that the monarchists were far from dead. The numbers of municipal councilors (*concejales*) elected were: Republicans, 34,368; socialists, 4,813; communists, 67; total anti-monarchists, 39,248. On the other side, monarchists, 41,224. The country vote, frequently falsified, gave the monarchists a slim overall margin, but this should be discounted by at least 15 to 20 per cent. The result still indicates a monarchist strength of about 40 per cent of the electorate, and this was the way things actually stood at the birth of the Second Republic.

The attitude of the Catholic Church had been anything but exemplary during the epochal struggle between the two political groups. As late as 1927 an official catechism had stated that to vote liberal was a sin. In the campaign of 1931 many churchmen had referred to the Republicans as "communists," hoping thus to bring about their defeat at the polls. And barely four weeks after the municipal elections and the declaration of the Republic, the archbishop of Toledo issued a pastoral letter casting suspicion on the new regime, and assuming a truculent attitude. Without waiting to see what kind of government the Republic really would bring, he overflowed with praise for Alfonso XIII, and referred to the Republican victory at the polls as a triumph of "the enemies of the Kingdom of Jesus Christ." Other bishops were more moderate in their views, and hundreds of parish priests had voted Republican in the elections, but the primate of the Spanish church thus loudly and publicly aligned himself with the forces of reaction. Three days later mobs began to attack the churches.

It was a disgusting spectacle. Churches began to burn and red flags suddenly appeared. The riots started in Madrid and spread like wildfire throughout Spain, becoming particularly violent in Andalusia, the region of greatest poverty. Who were the vandals and arsonists? Obviously many of them were from the atheistic far left, but others were almost undoubtedly paid agents of the royalists. Over one hundred churches were gutted by flames. Communism now became a much used word, and the blissful enthusiasm of the first days of the Republic began to settle into a feeling of serious concern. The ease with which these outrages had been carried out indicated to the opposition an intrinsic weakness of the new regime: its inability to preserve order. However, the minister in charge of the home office, i.e., internal police, was Miguel Maura, a Catholic and a conservative. Apparently he had been caught completely by surprise by the suddenness and the violence of these assaults. In any case, the die was cast, red flags had identified the assailants, the outrages aroused public indignation, and the chasm between the monarchists and clericals on the one hand, and the heterogeneous parties of Republicans, on the other, was now more deeply dug.

The Catalans, with their overweening desire for separatism, had very pompously declared their region to be the Republic of Catalonia, but they were finally talked out of it, and merged with the central government on the promise of semi-autonomy. Manuel Azaña, Minister of War, drastically reduced the Spanish army, disbanding thirty-seven infantry and seventeen cavalry regiments. The supernumerary officers were retired on full pay, and at first this seemed an admirable move, but it created a large and powerful group of men who felt that they had been unjustly deprived of status.

In June elections were held in order to set up the first Republican parliament or Cortes. The vote revealed that Republican zeal had grown in spite of everything. The people of Spain were still full of hope; they were fuller still of emotion and in a great and generous gesture wanted to give their representatives carte blanche to transform their country into a modern state. The socialists elected 115 deputies, the largest single group. The total left-wing groups came to 282 deputies, as compared with only 172 for the extreme right and center. The number of men of intellectual or professional status in the Cortes was amazing: 65 professors, 41 doctors, 123 lawyers. There were only 24 workingmen.

The Republic was certainly the product of intellectuals. The Cortes proceeded to draw up a new and idealistic constitution. "Spain is a Republic of workers of all classes," this document proudly proclaimed. And then it went on to renounce war as an instrument of national policy, thus making Spain the first country to take this humanitarian stand. The constitution provided for universal suffrage, a one-chambered parliament, separation of church and state, freedom of worship, withdrawal of financial support of the clergy, the secularization of education, agrarian reform to be made possible by the expropriation of private property, and many other items of progressive legislation.

Idealistically inspired, quixotically stated, the new constitution was a beautiful paper dream. It promised more than the government could possibly deliver. It promised more than any Spanish government could possibly deliver, unless the people were thinking in terms of decades of hard work and patience instead of mere fretful weeks of waiting before their deliverance. For example, the Spanish constitution stated categorically: "The Republic will guarantee to every worker the necessary conditions for a dignified existence. Its social legislation will regulate: cases of sickness, accident, unemployment, old age, infirmity and life insurance; the labor of women and children, and in particular, the protection of motherhood; the working day and minimum and family wages; yearly paid vacations; the conditions of Spanish workers abroad; cooperative institutions" . . . etc., etc. Need we quote further?

As one of its founders states, the Republican demagogues "were determined to put all their wares in the window from the first date of the fair." The emotional hunger of the people for a transformation of their country was fed a rich dessert, but this lay heavy on an empty stomach. Spanish idealism, as always, had overshot its mark. The intellectual leaders of the Republic were men of undoubted integrity but they were very poor practical politicians, and as for real statesmanship, this was lacking almost completely. Don Quixote had returned again to Spain, and was riding his undernourished nag across the desolate wasteland, shouting his redemption of the nation. There were many indications of this quixotism besides the few lines of the constitution just quoted. For example, the drafters of the constitution sincerely believed that in order to outlaw war it would suffice to put that idea into the constitution, and then to go about reducing the army. Whereas, the essential thing was to reduce the internal tensions which might lead to war. The essential thing was to seek for a common ground on which dissidents might find an escape valve for at least a considerable part of their grievances. The essential thing was to preach toleration and patience, and to set that example before the nation in the sessions of the national Cortes. The essential thing was to follow the will of the immense majority of the Spanish people who, in every single election of these fatal years, indicated clearly their wholehearted opposition to a violent resolution of national problems. The tragedy was that while the Spanish people were moderate, the Cortes itself soon split into truculent factions. This fragmentation led to an increase of tensions, to accusations, to violence, to reprisals, to a growth of extremism at both ends of the political spectrum, and, finally, to the bloodiest war that Spain has ever known, the Spanish civil war.

Despite all encumbrances the Republic, during its first two years, struggled courageously with the task of transforming an almost medieval country long accustomed to absolutism into a modern nation with a progressive parliamentary government. The problem of education was attacked with messianic zeal. The first Minister of Education created three thousand new schools; the second, Fernando de los Ríos, who later was the Republic's ambassador in Washington, added seven thousand schools to this already startling total. The new constitution proclaimed "compulsory education," but as there were barely enough schools for one-fourth of the school population, these were idle words. Nevertheless, when the Republic fell apart in 1936 it could point with pride to the ten thousand new schools which had been added to the country's educational system. It must be made plain that not all of these new schools were properly manned. Yet the widespread public desire to be educated had become almost an obsession; this was perhaps the Republic's greatest achievement. When the civil war came the Republic continued to stress education. Even at the battle front learning went on. Books were passed around, teachers moved from point to point, pamphlets were printed, lessons were studied. People learned to read and write who had never before considered this possible. But a backward nation is not educated in five years, no matter how tremendous the effort. And to take the fanaticism out of an inflamed and dogmatic man requires an even longer period.

This brings us to the religious problem, the crux of the most violent hatred aroused in Spain by the liberal Republic. The church had always officially opposed liberalism, and Spanish liberals had almost invariably opposed the church. History should have taught the liberals to move more slowly, but the pressures of the human boiler can rise only so high without exploding. The frustrations of years of planning and waiting, the setback of the military dictatorship of Primo de Rivera, and now their triumphant mandate from the Spanish people which suddenly and unexpectedly gave their pent-up zeal an outlet—all this was too much to resist, and the Republicans steered their ship of state "full steam ahead against the immutable rocks of Spanish obduracy." Madariaga, assessing the move years later, calls this the fundamental and fatal error of the Republic. Manuel Azaña, the most respected leader of the Republicans, proclaimed at the time that the most vigorous anticlerical action was inevitable.

Azaña was no radical leftist; he had been educated by the Augustinian monks, and later took a degree in law from the University of Madrid. He was a man of wide culture and intellectual distinction, who for years had been a writer and a public servant. His literary and critical works were not widely popular, but were well written. He had the reputation of being a moderate but dynamic liberal. Unamuno said of him: "Beware of Azaña. He is an author without readers. He would be capable of starting a revolution in order to be read." The taunt was not true, of course, but the frontal assault that Azaña made on the church must have caused the old philosopher to mutter: "You see? I told you so."

The anticlerical campaign resulted in the following items being embodied in the new Spanish constitution or in special statutes enacted shortly afterward: separation of church and state, divorce to be permitted after two years of marriage by mutual consent, secularization of education, disbanding of the Jesuit order and confiscation of Jesuit property, secularization of all cemeteries and *prohibition of religious burial* unless the deceased had specifically requested it in his will, absolute freedom of worship for all cults, withdrawal of all state financial support of the clergy within two years.

This passionate frontal attack on the institutions of the church aroused immediate and passionate resistance. Had the Republicans followed a more moderate course in this regard the political dogmatism of the church would very likely have ebbed away, just as it had in many other predominantly Catholic countries: France, Italy, Belgium, Holland. More tolerant and yet vigorously progressive social legislation on the part of the Republicans would have made this almost a certainty, for there were thousands of good Catholics in Spain who would have supported such a program. But for a country which formerly had allowed no divorce at all to swing suddenly to the extreme of divorce by mutual consent after two years of marriage was much too violent, and the law prohibiting religious burial unless it was stipulated in the will of the deceased was just plain stupid intolerance, for nine out of ten Spaniards died without making a will. This revolutionary change was doubtless generated by the long-standing policy of the church to force religious burials on deceased Spaniards who held a certain importance in their communities, even when these persons had left specific instructions to the contrary.

The psychological reasons back of this intolerance on the part of the "Holy Anticlerical Church" of the liberals call for some explanation. First, the disbanding of the Jesuits was nothing new in Spain. The order had been suppressed or expelled from the country *five times* before the new statute against it was approved by the Republic. After the first expulsion of the order from all Spanish dominions by Charles III in the eighteenth century the Pope himself had dissolved the Jesuit order throughout Catholic Christendom. This conflict against religious orders within a Catholic country had nothing to do with religious dogma; it was caused by the opposition of two strong economic, political and moral forces: the powerful Jesuit organization, on the one hand, and on the other, the upcoming but heterogeneous liberalism of the Spanish state. It was inevitable that these two forces should collide, but there was no necessity for them to collide head-on, and this collision merely weakened the authority of the Republican government.

Manuel Azaña defended the disbanding of the Jesuit order by stating that this organization indoctrinated the young people in their schools with anti-democratic philosophy, thus obstructing the emergence of a modern state.

Alcalá Zamora, who was president of the provisional government of Spain, protested vigorously but in vain against these stringent anti-clerical measures. In the heat of long pent-up passion they were all passed by a considerable majority. Alcalá Zamora, who was a good Catholic, resigned his position and was succeeded by Azaña. The die was cast. A more moderate and slower course on the part of the liberals might have saved the Spanish Republic, but in the flush of victory they pushed their advantage to the breaking point.

While the dogmatic resolution of the religious question in Spain was probably the strongest cause of the downfall of the Republic, the manner in which the land problem was handled was also a great disappointment. The Spanish civil service was notably lacking in trained personnel to carry out the far-reaching agrarian reform program, or any other kind of social or political reform. Besides this, the person put in charge of the agrarian reform was totally incompetent to direct it. He was "a lighthearted and irresponsible journalist with no experience whatever in either land or administrative questions." The confiscation of the vast estates and their subsequent more equitable redistribution had barely begun when war broke out, yet such agrarian reform was then, and is still today, the *sine qua non* of social and economic progress in Spain.

The labor policy of the Republican government was somewhat more enlightened. Collective bargaining was given a fair chance; there was accident and unemployment insurance, and a program of public works to stabilize and keep unemployment at a minimum. The socialists under Largo Caballero, who was Minister of Labor, did a respectable job of liberalizing and giving dignity to the position of labor in the national economy. The syndicalists, who opposed the socialists on general principles, continued to snipe at the latter in an effort to prove that a real democratic nationalism could not possibly succeed.

In view of all the mistakes and impediments it is a wonder that the Second Republic endured as long as it did, yet in those early years of 1931–32 the faith of the liberals in their democratic vision was almost mystical. Any visitor to Spain in those dramatic years immediately noticed it. An excellent government tourist bureau, with branches in nearly every town in the country, showed what the Spaniards could do when they set their minds to it. The work of this *Patronato Nacional del Turismo* has never been equalled in Spain either before or since. Multilingual guides were provided, as were excellent free publications in all of the main European languages which described the background and significance of the various artistic monuments and geographic regions of Spain. Wherever one traveled the Spanish people seemed filled with pride and hope. There was a dream in the air in those early Republican days, particularly noticable among the students and intellectuals and among the city workers. The well-to-do and the conservative elements in the national life went about their opposition with moderation.

Workers expounded their hopes for the future of their country without cant or bias, and with a deep belief in the survival of the Spanish democracy. Writers and teachers were of the same opinion. Perhaps Spain would swing into a mild form of socialism, like Sweden. Did not the cooperative communities of her medieval past prove that this way of life was not only profoundly Spanish but also profoundly practical for Spain? Had not the bloodless revolution proved that Spain was already beyond the threat of violence as a means of government? Had not the Spanish people chosen their most distinguished men to lead them forward? Spain's golden years were yet to come. And while they dreamed, the Republican parliament was compounding its mistakes, and the conservative opposition was consolidating and compounding its resistance.

One name which appeared in the headlines with almost daily frequency in those days was that of Alejandro Lerroux, the old-time professional leader of the Spanish radical party, which had 90 representatives in the national Cortes, making it the second largest group. (The socialists had 115 deputies.) Azaña's party, Republican Action, had only 30 representatives, but because of the man's stature and integrity he had become one of the main leaders of the government. Lerroux was a typical fiery demagogue gone somewhat soft. He had begun as a blatantly anticlerical leader, but his extremism was now abated, and his large contingent of deputies gave him every right to expect deferential treatment in the parliament. Azaña did not trust or like Lerroux, whom he regarded as a coarse and vulgar politician. He discounted completely Lerroux's uncanny political sensitivity. Azaña's party, on the other hand, counted among its members the most distinguished intellectuals in the nation. The rift between these two men led to political chaos within the Cortes. This was Azaña's fatal error. Lerroux would have cooperated with him, but Azaña considered this beneath his dignity. Consequently, Lerroux, feeling himself and his deputies rejected by the liberals, began to swing toward the right.

At this conservative end of the political spectrum stood Gil Robles, a prominent and astute Roman Catholic professor and first-rate parliamentarian who was amply provided with funds. Right and left now stood with battle lines clearly drawn, after two years of "liberal" government. When the elections of 1933 took place the Spanish Republic moved abruptly toward the right. The votes of approximately six million women, enjoying suffrage for the first time, perhaps helped to account for the change in sentiment. The socialists, who in 1931 had won 115 seats in the Cortes, now held only 59. Azaña's party decreased from 30 to 5 representatives, and the total number of deputies of the left decreased from 282 to 99. On the other hand, Lerroux's party of the center increased from 90 to 104 deputies, and the total rightist vote went from 60 to 207. The socialist leader Largo Caballero, with his revolutionary tactics, had alienated great numbers of his supporters, while Gil Robles had become a political leader of national importance. Almost at once all of the liberal legislation of the first two years of the Republic was either repealed or became a dead letter. The suddenness of the swing proved beyond a doubt that the single chamber of the Spanish Cortes was a serious political error. Had there been an upper senatorial chamber to counterbalance the rapid change in sentiments of the electorate the situation would have been vastly more stable. Lacking this stabilizing force the government ran headlong into difficulties which it could not properly handle.

Lerroux, the resentful old firebrand, was asked to form a cabinet. The new premier attempted to woo back the army and the church. He appointed as head of the General Military College a general named Francisco Franco. Reaction set in almost overnight. The national economy began to sputter. Farm wages dropped disastrously, and landlords again became vindictive. Labor disputes in general were decided now in favor of the employer. On the other hand, books on Russia began to flood the country, and communism began to gain a real grip on the voters of the left. Largo Caballero's revolutionary zeal led him closer and closer to the communist philosophy. The son of Primo de Rivera, José Antonio, organized his Falange (Phalanx) party, a Spanish fascist group, and Gil Robles, the Catholic leader, after a visit to Vienna, adopted some of the manners of the Nazis. The two extremes had betrayed the center, where the real hopes of the Republic were bound to lie, and Spain began to move inevitably toward civil war.

The Spanish extreme left made the first move. Largo Caballero, head of the radical wing of the socialist party, stumped up and down the country preaching rebellion. One of his favorite phrases was that there might have to be "a dictatorship of the proletariat" if the right continued to push Spain toward fascism. When Gil Robles, the conservative Catholic leader who headed the largest coalition in the parliament, was given three portfolios: Justice, Agriculture, and Labor, the left answered with a general strike. The most important cities of the country were paralyzed. In Madrid, where it was realized what was taking place, the revolt collapsed quickly, and Largo Caballero was put in jail. But in Oviedo and in Barcelona there was much bloodshed, particularly in Oviedo, in the northwest province of Asturias, where the Asturian miners marched on the city, occupied it for a month, and established there temporarily a kind of rough-and-ready communism. The central government rallied and finally suppressed the revolt, but not before more than a thousand people had been killed, and several thousands wounded. Large parts of the city of Oviedo were demolished by the combatants. Horrible atrocity stories were told by both sides.

Just for the record let us give the leftist version of this widespread revolt. It appears in the book *Spain in Revolt*, by Harry Gannes and Theodore Repard, which appeared in 1936. These writers state:

October 1934 will always live in the memory of Spain as the period of the workers' heroic answer to the initial attempt to inaugurate a fascist dictatorship. Deliberately, on October 1, the fascist cliques, headed by the C.E.D.A. [this was the coalition of Gil Robles], aimed at provoking civil war by putting their men in the new Lerroux cabinet. Faced with a point-blank threat of a fascist dictatorship on the Italian and German model, the Spanish workers decided to wage a desperate battle.[43]

But was the threat of a fascist *coup* real? Or was it merely trumped up to suit the fancies of the left-wingers who wanted to establish themselves in power in a dictatorship of the proletariat? Salvador de

Madariaga, who is certainly no rightist, holds the latter opinion.* He points out that Gil Robles, despite the fact that he headed the largest group in the Cortes, was not asked to form the government, but that this task was given to Lerroux. Then what happened? The violent revolt took place almost immediately, not in those parts of Spain where there existed the direst poverty, but in those parts of the country where wages were highest and conditions best, but where also the workers were better organized in radical leftist unions. The central Republican government, using General Francisco Franco and other military leaders, put down the revolt, and in doing so called on Moorish troops from Morocco. The appearance of these troops in Asturias had a terrible effect on the populace, for this seemed to be a deliberate affront to their honor and to their legendary history. In any case, the revolt was suppressed with considerable violence, and Gil Robles, who could then have moved toward fascism had he wished to do so, made no such move. Instead, the country dragged along for three more years, under a faltering parliamentary regime. In 1935 Gil Robles was put in charge of the War Office, but even here he did not attempt to upset the republican form of government. Conditions went from bad to worse. The national economy began to fall apart. Strikes broke out all over the country. The agrarian reform made almost no headway. Tempers flared in the Cortes, and both sides became impassioned, fanatical, and obdurate.

Finally, in 1936, new elections were held, and these were considered a great victory for the coalition of the left, who had consolidated their ranks in what was known as the Popular Front. This heterogeneous leftist coalition received 4,206,156 votes, if the Basque nationalists are included. The center received 681,047 votes. The total for the right was 3,783,601 votes. This gave the Popular Front 256 deputies, the center 54 deputies, and the right 143 deputies. The communist party, which had not previously elected a representative to the national Cortes, on this occasion won 14 seats in that body. They gained two additional seats later. The far right won a comparable representation. The left claimed a smashing victory, but when the figures are examined closely this is obviously not the case. If the center votes were switched to the right, they would give the popular vote advantage to that side. Out of the total of 256 leftist deputies, only 110 were Marxists; of these 110 not more

* Madariaga was the ambassador of the Spanish Republic in Washington during the early months of the new government.

than one-half were extremists preaching violence and proletarian dictatorship. The people of Spain had clearly voted in favor of moderation, and in favor of a continuation of the Republic. But at this
point in the country's history the two extremes took over completely,
and moderation or compromise no longer seemed possible. The very
popular Manuel Azaña became President, but even he was powerless
to stop the avalanche. Unfortunately, as president he had less power
than as Prime Minister. The presidency was a decorative position,
and the real governing was left to others. The loss of Azaña's steady-
ing hand was a great blow to the Republic. On the far left Largo
Caballero and his extremist companions plotted a revolt, and on the
far right Francisco Franco and his colleagues made their plans for a
military uprising to take over the government. The latter broke out
before the former could get under way, and thus began the Spanish
civil war.

As the two extremes consolidated their positions the country
suffered a series of riots, assassinations, reprisals, strikes, attacks on
religious buildings and personnel, and general bedlam. The central
government, now in the hands of the Popular Front, was unable
to keep order. In June 1936 Gil Robles presented the following
tragic statistics in the Cortes, and even if they be cut by half, the
situation would still remain intolerable: 160 churches destroyed, 251
set on fire or otherwise attacked, 269 persons assassinated, 1287 persons injured, 69 political premises destroyed, 113 general strikes. The
deputies did not pay much attention to what he said. The assassinations continued, even including the murder of members of parliament. On July 17, 1936, the rightist revolt started, and the army of
Morocco was brought into Spain to spearhead the attack. The uprising broke out on the mainland the following day.

The mistakes of the Republic are not difficult to point out with
the advantage of hindsight. In the first place, the constitution was
far too idealistic, and was not flexible enough to adapt to the necessities of the epoch. The workers and labor unions, especially the
anarchists and the left-wing socialists, and of course, the communists,
provoked numerous needless strikes and fomented numerous stupid
killings and disorders, thus frightening a large segment of the population and stirring up sentiment against the Republic. The extreme
right, especially José Antonio de Rivera's Falange having imbibed
fascist ideas from Italy and Germany, was equally violent and law-
less. The entire right was undoubtedly anxious to control the Cortes,

but its political leaders were not willing to initiate a fascist revolt. This task was undertaken by the generals.

The Spaniard is willing to give his life at the barricades of Madrid or Barcelona for the freedom of Spain, or for the freedom of man, but when it comes to giving something less than his life, perhaps like a good part of his income, or his land, or his power as a labor leader, or his power as a general, or his strength and time to defend those who do not agree with him politically—the situation is quite different. He draws up an idealistic political document—Latin America and Spain are full of them—and then heaves a sigh of relief. His sacrifice is over But a parliamentary government requires much give and take. It requires, above all else, moderation and tolerance in the initial stages, until public confidence is established in its stability and integrity as a form of government. True, the majority of the people of Spain voted for moderation, but about one tenth of them supported the *extreme* left, and at least another tenth of them, supported the *extreme* right. Their leaders at both of these extremes, fired to a great pitch of passion by such evidence of popular support, charged blindly ahead without so much as a good look to see who was following them, or what was happening to their country.

The Spanish people were clearly sacrificed on the altar of this struggle for power. No middle ground was ever built up. There was never a real conservative party of integrity. The constitution established a unicameral parliament, with many operational problems, in a country and at a time when an upper house was desperately needed to give an element of stability to parliamentary government. The constitution went too far in its anticlerical program, and its labor articles aroused passion on the left and vituperation on the right. Above all, the state did not have at its disposal a properly trained civil service, above politics, which might efficiently and without bias carry out the mandates of the government. But in spite of all these things the Republic might have survived had the deputies who were chosen to lead it been men of less passion and more common sense, men who were willing to place the common good above the welfare of the party.

The forces of General Franco irrupted from the south, as had the Moors in centuries gone by, and quickly swept across the southern plains and mountains toward Castile. There were fierce pockets of resistance in the cities of Andalusia, but these were eventually wiped out. The invading army was soon within gunshot of Madrid, the

Republican capital. Here it met the main force of the Republican army, and was slowed to a walk. Finally, the decision was made to besiege the city, and for the following three years the two armies faced each other at the outskirts of the capital, in the vicinity of the present University City campus. Here many a bloody battle ensued, but the besieging forces were unable to enter Madrid, which they bombarded unceasingly. For some inexplicable reason they never cut off the city's water supply, which might have ended the siege within a few days. The aqueducts, which came from the north, were absolutely indefensible. The old University City buildings were completely destroyed in the fight, and many shells penetrated the thick walls and roof of the Royal Palace, which also stands in this part of town.

Other sectors of strong Republican resistance were in the Basque and Asturian provinces, in Valencia, and in Catalonia, especially in Barcelona. The Basques and Catalans were fighting for self-government, as much as for the Republic. The Basque group constituted the religious and conservative element on the Republican side. Not by any stretch of the imagination could these Basques, who had struggled so long against the central government in their Carlist wars, be called liberals or leftists. In Barcelona, on the other hand, thousands of Republicans were out-and-out anarchists, who were much more interested in imposing their syndicate-style local governments than they were in winning the war against General Franco. They were eager to take full advantage of the chaotic conditions of the country in order to swing themselves into power. The communists, on the other hand, were all for winning the war first, and discussing a division of the spoils later. The masses of the Republican forces, who belonged to neither of these camps, were struggling simply to defend the Republic.

The Spanish civil war was one of the cruelest struggles in history. Any civil war is bound to be divisive, but one which is fought along ideological lines divides the country right down the middle, family from family, brother from brother, father from son, friend from friend; it causes splits and hatreds in the basic fabric of family and community life which are not healed for many generations. Add to this the passionate and quickly stirred nature of the Spanish temperament, and you have the makings of a full-fledged blood bath of the most horrible kind. This is exactly what happened in Spain. The Loyalists, so called because they supported the Republic, went on a rampage killing priests, nuns, and all others thought to be Franco sympathizers. The Nationalists, so called because they imagined that their revolt reflected a strong national sentiment against the Republic, as they advanced picked out those who had supported the Republic in each of the regions and towns which fell into their hands, stood them against the walls, and shot them. About 100,000 Spaniards were killed in these brutal reprisals. The residue of brutality which still lives on in Spain today is a deep-seated and awful presence.

The military uprising, wrongly termed "nationalist uprising" by Franco and his supporters, for it was certainly far from being national, was mainly inspired by the old-line conservative tradition of absolutism. The generals who were Franco's companions-in-arms all hated the Republic because it was liberal and *because it was weak*, too weak to prevent disorder. These generals had no political or social program to offer. Everything they stood for was purely negative: They were against the Republic, against the widespread attacks on religious persons and buildings, against strikes, against liberalism in general, against giving any power to labor, against any kind of parliamentary or democratic government, against civil and religious liberties, and most vociferously against the assassination of their own sympathizers. This one central fact of the original rebels' negativism marked the character of Franco's government from its beginning.

The generals did not claim that they were revolting in order to save Spain from communism. This was a cry raised later, mainly for purposes of propaganda. In his initial manifesto General Franco did not even mention communism. What he hated was the Republic. The Republic, for its part, did not at first regard the military rebellion as a full-fledged fascist revolt, which indeed it was not, for the majority of the Spanish rightists did not favor any such uprising. In fact, the Republic took the whole thing rather lackadaisically in those first few hours when immediate action might possibly have prevented the rebellion. By the time the Republic started to move, it was too late. Most likely it would have been too late in any case, for almost the entire army, navy, and air force joined the generals. The Civil Guard Corps also threw its considerable weight over to their side. The Republic was left almost without soldiers to defend it. A few assault guards and some small military groups were loyal, but these could not compare in number with those under General

Franco. The general also almost immediately received numerous German and Italian planes to transport his troops, and these were soon joined by large contingents from the Italian and German armies. The Italians sent four full and heavily armed divisions to fight in Spain, and the Germans a sizable air force and several thousand ground troops.

The Republic, therefore, had to improvise an army, and, considering the almost insuperable obstacles, it did a remarkable job. This army, however, was mainly made up of raw recruits, improperly trained and poorly equipped. When told that they were to fight the fascists, many of them said they had never heard that word. Without adequate supplies from foreign sources this army could hardly expect to come out victorious over the more numerous and better equipped rightist forces. Those supplies were denied the Republic by almost all foreign countries, including the United States. Russia sent military and propaganda specialists and a few planes to the Republic; planes were also bought from France, but these were a mere drop in the bucket. Later in the war brigades of foreign volunteers arrived, about 80 per cent of them communist, to fight on the Republican side, but these troops were no match for the tens of thousands of Italians and Germans fighting with Franco. The main body of the Republican army was composed of Spaniards who fought with the tenacity and the bravery for which the race has always been noted.

What was the possibility of Spain becoming a communist state if the Republicans had won the civil war? There were 16 communist deputies out of a total of 473, and perhaps 50 to 60 socialists who would at least partially go along with them. The anarchists were fighting their own war, and were in a way counter-revolutionaries, for they did not wish either to preserve the Republic or to give much aid to the communists and their sympathizers. Thus we have approximately one-eighth of the deputies who might possibly be considered as communists or followers of the communist line. These did not represent one-eighth of the voters, by any means. The Englishman Arnold J. Toynbee edited a journal called *Survey of International Affairs* which gave the estimate, probably fairly accurate, that at the start of the war there were no more than 50,000 communists in Spain. At the end of the first year of fighting this number had grown to about 300,000. These zealots made every effort to penetrate and control the government, and there is no doubt that their weight far exceeded their numbers. They threw this weight around in their usual bludgeoning, bullying way. Even so, the Spanish Republic was never in the hands of the communists until those final useless months of the fight when everything was lost. These people then held on doggedly because for them defeat was equivalent to death.

It does not seem likely that communists could have dominated the government had the Republicans won the war, for they were opposed by a very large and a very powerful majority of the Spanish people. And if the United States, France, and Great Britain had shipped arms and equipment to the Republican government from the beginning, as they had every right to do, for it was the duly constituted government of Spain, these countries would have been able to apply sufficient pressure to make absolutely certain that the Republic remain in non-communist hands. But at that time everyone was deathly afraid of Hitler, and sincere but misguided people all over the world were unwilling to send arms to any country lest their own nation become inadvertently embroiled in a war. The war, of course, came anyway, when Hitler was ready for it. Again with hindsight let it be pointed out that, had war come in 1936, when Hitler was far from ready, the Allies would have had a much easier time with him, and many millions of lives would have been saved.

We have learned the hard way that a defeat for democracy anywhere in the world weakens the United States. We now follow a policy of global commitment when it is felt that we are protecting our own interests. The civil war in Spain certainly presented us with a rare opportunity, had we aided the Republic. In fact, the war was far more than a mere struggle between two factions within Spain. It was an international war in which Germany, Italy, and Russia all participated in greater or less degrees, using Spain as the battlefield and testing ground for their arms and for their propaganda. The Spanish civil war was the rehearsal for World War II. The most tragic thing of all is that for more than thirty years after Hitler and Mussolini were gone, Franco continued their demagogy and their philosophy as head of his own Spanish fascist state. His survival was a gross reminder that we did not completely win the war against fascism. This was the same General Franco, of course, who sent many thousands of Spanish soldiers to fight alongside the storm troops of Hitler in that war which cost so many American lives.

Not all Americans favored a hands-off policy in regard to the

Spanish civil war. Mrs. Roosevelt indicated very clearly that her husband, the President, wanted to ship supplies to the Republic, but was prevented from doing so by well-organized political pressure. Most of this was from the Catholics in the United States, a majority of whom favored General Franco. Henry L. Stimson, a noted Republican who served as Secretary of War in President Roosevelt's cabinet in those years, declared categorically in a letter to the editor of *The New York Times:* "The Republican Government of Spain has been recognized as the true Government of Spain by our Government." The Republic thus had every right to be allowed "to purchase the necessary supplies and munitions for the purpose of putting down the rebellion."

Mr. Stimson then commented rather caustically on the policy of "non-intervention" which the United States was being pressured into following, but which Germany, Italy, and Russia were not following:

The first thing to be said about this agreement was that it was a complete abandonment of a code of practice which the international world had adopted through the preceding ages. . . . The non-intervention agreement at once became a mockery and a failure. . . . The results have shown how futile as well as dangerous novel experiments in international law can be. The United States, on its part, has abandoned a traditional policy to which for a century and a half it had carefully adhered as a means of protecting the peace and stability of nations, which like itself, preferred to live not armed to the teeth. It is likely sorely to rue the day when that principle was abandoned and when it consented to a new precedent which may hereafter weight the scale in favor of a militaristic and thoroughly armed nation. . . .

If this Loyalist Government is overthrown, it is evident now that its defeat will be solely due to the fact that it has been deprived of its right to buy from us and from other friendly nations the munitions necessary for its defense.[44]

Herbert L. Matthews, who reproduces this quotation in his book *The Yoke and the Arrows*, adds this personal comment: "This was the voice of a true and wise American and it will be the judgment of history."

The Spanish Republicans called themselves "Loyalists," because they were "loyal" to the Republic, but General Franco's side invariably called them "Reds." On the other hand, the Republicans referred to Franco supporters as "Fascists," or as "Rebels," while they called themselves "Nationalists." The Spanish civil war was a war of words, as well as a war of ideas, of gunpowder and of steel.

In regard to public opinion in the United States while the Spanish civil war was in progress, the Gallup Poll indicated that at one time 76 per cent of the Americans who expressed an opinion on the subject favored the Loyalists. This poll must have included many American Roman Catholics. However, the Catholic lobby in Washington, more responsive to the hierarchy than to the rank and file, applied its pressure in favor of General Franco.

The Spanish civil war devastated Spain, and cost the country several hundred thousand lives. Some observers have placed the total dead at one million. The figure is probably somewhat less than that. The war left in its wake a feeling of revulsion and of terror, as both sides went berserk, with their firing squads shooting all those who were suspected of aiding the opposing faction.

This merciless butchery is still a horrible nightmare to all those who can remember it. The Franco government collected the names of 54,594 of their sympathizers who were executed by the Republicans. The number of people executed by Franco probably exceeds the above total, for Franco continued shooting "Republicans" long after the war had ended. Day after day and week after week those who lived in Madrid and Barcelona heard the volleys ring out in the early hours of dawn as the firing squads did their work. Oftentimes on a single day the toll would be two or three hundred. The jails were flooded with political prisoners, and more than two years after the war was over there were still 241,000 political prisoners in General Franco's cells. A goodly number of Spain's Protestants were among them, because to be a Protestant in those days automatically made one a suspect in the eyes of the Nationalists.

The Spanish Loyalists may have lost the war because friendly nations refused to sell their government the necessary munitions, but the Republic itself had already fallen apart because its national parliament was unable to govern. The Republican leaders were nearly all well-meaning men, sincere, idealistic, honest, dedicated, impassioned. But they did not know how to govern. They were unwilling to compromise. They allowed personal animus to disrupt the procedures of the Cortes. Azaña, Lerroux, Gil Robles, Largo Caballero, and all the others were educated men who should have learned that successful government consists mainly of the art of the possible. But these leaders were Spanish to the core. They came at the end of a tradition of absolutism in government, of inquisition in religion, of military supremacy over the civil authorities. Their failure proved again that in Spain the country must go one of two ways: either split up into regional fragments, or submit to a powerful central government, for in Spain only the strongest possible central authority can successfully impose itself over the age-old yearning for fragmentation. There is no doubt that the Spanish people themselves, as their history for centuries past bears witness, have continued to reflect these same tendencies in all that has taken place in Spain since the advent of the Second Republic.

14

COMMUNISM AND FASCISM IN SPAIN

> *In my opinion the saddest thing about our decadence is not the decadence itself, but the refined stupidity so frequently shown by the men placed in charge of our public affairs.*
>
> Angel Ganivet

During the early years of the Spanish Republic the communist party in Spain had only a few thousand members. It was an insignificant political force. Spanish fascism, or Falangism, was equally unimportant on the national scene. But both groups carried a loaded pistol. When the shooting began, the Spanish people, who were caught in the middle, were forced into taking a position at one of the two extremes. The generals eventually won a hard victory, and fascism emerged triumphant. Franco Spain became very clearly a fascist state, which for many years used all the tactics of violence, arbitrary decree, and terror that were so well known in Germany and Italy. The fact that the final Franco years revealed a softening of the dictatorship (but not, let it be here recorded, until after the defeat of the Axis powers) shows only that the generalissimo was a practical politician, not that he was democratically minded. Spain, after all, was the sole surviving fascist regime in Europe, and was completely overshadowed by the Western democracies.

The matter of communist influence on the Loyalist side is not so easily disposed of, for the experts do not agree. There is no doubt, however, that the military aid sent by Russia increased this influence tremendously after the civil war had begun. The professed position of the communist party throughout the conflict was to *win the war against fascism* and to soft-pedal all talk of a proletarian revolution, which might alarm the Western democracies. It would be helpful to review what the experts who were in Spain during these fateful years have said on the subject.

First, what were the opinions of Claude G. Bowers, who was the American ambassador in Madrid for six years, from 1933 to 1939? Mr. Bowers was not only a distinguished ambassador and public servant, but was also a first-rate historian, and the author of many well-known books. He knew personally and saw frequently all of the leaders of the Republic: Azaña, Lerroux, Gil Robles, General Miaja, Juan Negrín, Prieto, and all the others. He has never shown any particular sympathy for Russia or for communism. Mr. Bowers *was* deeply sympathetic with the Republican regime both before and throughout the civil war. He regarded the "non-intervention" agreement of the United States, Great Britain, and France as playing directly into the hands of Hitler, Mussolini, and Franco. On July 20, 1937, he predicted that "with every surrender, beginning long ago with China, followed by Abyssinia and then Spain, the Fascist powers, with vanity inflamed, will turn without delay to some other country —such as Czechoslovakia—and that with every surrender the prospects of a European war grow darker."[47]

What did Mr. Bowers think of the situation inside Spain? He arrived in 1933, the year of the rightist victory at the polls. While admitting the anti-reform bias of the new rightist government, he strongly condemns the "left-wing socialist" Largo Caballero for going about the country in 1933 and 1934 making his almost daily threats of revolution. When the revolt of 1934 did come, mainly in the mining area of Asturias and in Barcelona, Bowers reports that it was an uprising of organized labor under the left wing of the Socialist Union. He is also at pains to point out how ruthlessly the uprising was crushed by the Moorish troops and the Spanish Foreign Legion. Following this there were many months of rightist government without any constructive legislation or achievement. The reform measures of the first two years of the Republic were reversed or canceled. Dissatisfaction with the government became general. Mr. Bowers reports that ten months before the elections of 1936 Fernando de los Ríos (distinguished Republican ambassador to the United States) assured him that there would be a great defeat of the Right at the polls. When Bowers answered that this was not the opinion of the people to whom he had talked, Don Fernando explained that in a diplomatic post he would naturally hear only the reactions of the higher-ups, the industrialists, the financiers, who would not hold this view. But Fernando de los Ríos went on to say that in all the small towns and villages the people were bitter against the rightist government, and that they were infuriated by the savagery of the Moors and the Foreign Legion in Asturias, which, despite its suppression in the censored press, had been passed along by word of mouth until now it was a matter of common knowledge. When the elections of 1936 did come, the prophecy of Don Fernando was to be fulfilled to the letter.[48]

After their victory at the polls the liberals, under Azaña, formed their new government, and Mr. Bowers states that there was not one communist in it, not one socialist, not one extremist.

There was nothing in the Government of Azaña that had the slightest relation to Communism. He was a great statesman, a great thinker and political philosopher, and a militant democrat, known to everyone in Spain as an enemy of both Communism and Fascism. His Ministers were drawn exclusively from the conservative Republican and democratic parties with not even a pale pink Socialist among them, and certainly no Communists in any post. . . . No one whose brains would not rattle in a mustard seed would think of describing as Communistic the Government against which the Axis powers began to wage war. At that very time there were a hundred Communist members of the French Congress, but the French Government was not called a Communist Government; there are far more Communists in the Italian Congress today (1953), but no one calls the Italian Republic Communistic.[47]

In Spain there were 16 communist deputies out of a total of 473, and none of these held any position in the government.

This Republican government of Azaña was the one against which Franco rebelled. It is the government that Hitler and Mussolini referred to as "Red." This was given as the reason for their intervention in Spain. Both fascist leaders were anxious to make Spain become "the tomb of Bolshevism." General Franco's habit of calling all the Republicans "Reds" assured him of aid in quantity from Germany and Italy.

The reason for his rebellion, however, was the alleged inability of the Republican government to maintain order. The rightist deputy Gil Robles, who had shied away from Hitler and Mussolini, in 1936 indicted the Cortes with a long list of murders, crimes and disorders which the government appeared unable to control. Mr. Bowers does not go along with this list of grievances of Gil Robles. By this time he had been in Spain for three years and knew the country well. He made it his business to drive into the regions where the worst of these depredations were supposed to have taken place. In his long drive of several hundred miles across the country he found one church which had been gutted with flames. Obviously, he did not visit every spot where an alleged crime had occurred, but his tour of inspection was a serious one and his conclusion was categorical:

While the rebel generals, by prearrangements with Hitler and Mussolini for their military aid, plunged a peaceful people into a welter of blood, the purpose was to end the reforms of the Republic aimed at wiping out the lingering feudalism in the land and the raising of the status of the workers to that of human dignity. Since world opinion could not be mobilized for that purpose another explanation had to be found. Thus for months before the generals turned traitors to their trust, and Hitler and Mussolini poured their infantry, artillery and planes into a peaceful land, a cynically dishonest propaganda campaign began to persuade the world that Spain was in a state of anarchy and that its government, headed by Manuel Azaña, was a Communist set-up.

There was no "anarchy," as I know, since I personally went to the seat of the alleged troubles and found nothing.[47]

Mr. Bowers does not state that the figures given by Gil Robles are inaccurate, but he does state, in no uncertain terms, that every common brawl, every fight in a bar, every ordinary crime and murder, every robbery of a church, every local strike and case of vandalism was listed and headlined for propaganda purposes. He suggests that if *The New York Times* were to list and highlight similar incidents of daily occurrence in the United States, under the headline SOCIAL DISORDERS IN THE UNITED STATES, we would have somewhat the same situation, thus placing our government in a completely wrong perspective. Mr. Bowers gives numerous instances of the Republican government's going to great lengths to protect the country's churches and their personnel. He also states his certainty that many of the most widely publicized disorders and crimes were perpetrated by fascist *agents provocateurs*, many of them disguised as German "tourists" who were swarming all over Spain at that time. He states further that many incidents reported to him had, according to his first-hand knowledge, never taken place at all.

What did Ambassador Bowers think of the struggle for power among the Republicans themselves during these crucial years? Did he continue to stand back of his initial strong statement endorsing the non-communist government of Azaña formed in 1936? Did he continue to believe that the Republican government was able to maintain order in its territory after the war began? Mr. Bowers did wholeheartedly support the Republic, and he never ceased hoping that it would win the civil war, but he states very clearly that the communists infiltrated deeply into that government before the war's end. He also states that there was uncontrollable widespread violence, thousands of brutal killings, and much destruction of property in Republican territory during the war.

There had always been a split among the Republicans. Largo Caballero, leader of the 1934 revolt, was the leader of the extreme faction which was anxious to get on with the socialization of Spain. Mr. Bowers points out that Largo Caballero led the poll among the Republicans (the Popular Front candidates) in the elections of 1936. This is a strong indication as to how the wind was blowing, buttressed by the fact that Julián Besteiro, the most respected of the evolutionary socialists, failed to place at all in the initial balloting of the party. Besteiro was a cultured and dignified public servant, a man noted for his probity and for his moderation. The Republican government had asked him to quit the quiet life of his academy in order to become president of the Constituent Assembly, in which capacity he was able to maintain a posture of tolerance, fairness, gentleness, and gentility for over two years. Ambassador Bowers states that the eclipse of this distinguished man, and the elevation of Largo Caballero over him in 1936, was a great shock to the moderate Republicans of Madrid.[48]

Largo Caballero, on the other hand, a plasterer by trade, was a well-trained, rough-and-ready politician. He was "one of the boys," and it was his fashion to address his audiences as "Workers . . ." He was the leader of the Socialist Union, the radical wing of the party. He believed in the proletarian revolution, and did not want to wait too long for it. He was impatient with parliamentary processes, and regarded himself as a great proletarian savior. But Largo Caballero was also a completely honest and a completely incorruptible man; he lived a Spartan existence and had become the idol of the working class. Ambassador Bowers expressed the strong opinion that the overwhelming victory of Largo Caballero, and the initial defeat of Besteiro, was perhaps the most important single thing that made the rightists regard the leftist victory at the polls as tantamount to endorsing the social revolution. The fact that Besteiro was later nominated anyhow did little to allay these fears. Largo Caballero himself did absolutely nothing to mollify those who were so afraid of him. Puffed up by his victory, and smarting under his recent imprisonment by the rightist government after the unsuccessful revolt of 1934, he was like a match ready to light the powder keg. There were still 30,000 leftist prisoners in Spanish jails as an aftermath of that unfortunate revolt. Largo Caballero demanded that they be released at once. His demand was met. Ambassador Bowers did not note any increase in violence after their release, but Madariaga states that disorders jumped tenfold as soon as these thirty thousand extremists were set free. This was in the fatal summer of 1936.

The rightists struck on July 17, with the revolt of the army of Morocco. Ambassador Bowers reported to Secretary of State Cordell Hull that the elements supporting the military rebellion were: the monarchists; the big landowners, who wished to continue feudalistic agriculture; the industrialists and financiers; the hierarchy of the church; the fascists, headed by José Antonio Primo de Rivera, son of the former dictator of Spain; and the military.

It was after this, states Mr. Bowers, that uncontrollable disorders and violence broke out in Republican territory. These were not brought under control until the Republican government got a firm grip on the forces of public order. The old forces had abandoned the Republic: the Civil Guard Corps, many police, the soldiers, nearly all of the officers. It took a long time to establish an effective substitute.

Communism has always thrived on social disorder and political violence. Spain was no exception. On the Republican side the communists and left-wing socialists were a closely knit, well-organized group, and they immediately proceeded to make hay. They were able to occupy many positions of importance. After a few months, Largo Caballero, who had headed the original cabinet, was not sufficiently amenable to communist discipline, so the party used all its weight to oust him, replacing him on May 17, 1937 with a man more to its liking, Dr. Juan Negrín, Minister of Finance in the previous cabinet. Negrín was a professor of physiology at the University of Madrid, and in the field of politics was a relatively unknown socialist. He was an ideal man behind whom to mask the communist efforts to control

Republican policy. Ambassador Bowers states that the communists pressured the Republican government into making this change by taking every advantage of the war material which was arriving from Russia. Physical condition was given publicly as the reason for Largo Caballero's resignation, but Bowers states "there is no doubt that his loss of power was due to the insistence of the communists."[48]

Bowers admired Dr. Negrín's culture and linguistic ability; he was able to converse in five languages. He had been a favorite pupil of the Nobel prize winner Ramón y Cajal, in the field of physiology. In politics Negrín was impulsive, overconfident, positive that he could handle anything or anybody. But he could not handle the communists; they handled him. Mr. Bowers does not make note of this, and apparently to him Negrín continued to the end as a hard-working, dedicated and liberal socialist, which was indeed the label that he wore.

After May 1937, Largo Caballero had to take a back seat. He continued to make fiery speeches, and anyone who doubts his demagogic endorsement of the proletarian revolution need only read his words to become absolutely convinced. Later, he escaped to France, and when the Nazis occupied a good part of that country, he was imprisoned in a concentration camp. Bowers states that he emerged from it at the end of the war a complete physical wreck. He died in Paris in 1946, following the amputation of a leg.

Negrín was a courageous man, and fought a brave holding action during the last tragic months of the civil war in the hope that a general European war would break out and save the Spanish Republic. Toward the end of the Spanish conflict the Republicans in Madrid ousted him, considering his leadership too leftist, and Negrín had to flee. Much has been written about his political beliefs and his political action. Ambassador Bowers does not view him as the servant of the communists, nor does Hugh Thomas in his classic work *The Spanish Civil War*, nor does Herbert Matthews, who was a correspondent of *The New York Times* in Spain during the Civil War. In his book *The Yoke and the Arrows*, Matthews writes:

Don Juan Negrín, the Republican Premier in the last half of the Civil War, was no more Communist than you or I. He was nominally a Socialist, but the Spanish Socialists were not Marxists any more than the British Laborites. Dr. Negrín's problem was to win the war, or at least to hold on until the outbreak of the European war, which he and all of us saw coming. He could not continue the war or hold Republican Spain together without the Spanish Communists or without help from Russia, the only country willing to sell him arms and one of the few standing up for Spain in the League of Nations.

To argue from this that Dr. Negrín was a "Red" or even a fellow-traveler is nonsense. The Negrín government was never dominated by the Reds. To argue, as many people did and do, that Spain would have gone Communist later if the Republicans had won, is, in my opinion, just as far from the mark. . . . Personally, I am convinced that Spain would not have gone Communist, and I think the best evidence of this is what happened in Europe after the Second World War. . . . Even in Italy and France, with their large Communist movements, it proved impossible to establish Communist regimes.[44]

Ambassador Bowers, while he does not accuse Negrín and Largo Caballero personally of being fellow-travelers, states very clearly that Moscow "resorted to blackmail" in order to wring political concessions from the Republicans. Moscow said bluntly: "Give us what we ask for, or we shall stop sending you arms." Bowers also mentions that there were too many communists among the officers of the Republican army, but that "at the side of each of these there was a non-communist army officer to check on his actions." However, Bowers concludes: "If the world has learned one thing more than any other since 1945 it is that *the inclusion of Communists in political combinations for election purposes in Popular Fronts is fatal.*" The italics are mine.[48]

The attitudes of Hitler and Mussolini toward the Spanish civil war were not identical. Mussolini was anxious to dominate the Mediterranean area, and thought that an ally in Spain would aid him in that ambition. A fascist Spain would also cause France considerable worry, and draw French troops from the Italian frontier. Mussolini's great dreams of conquest and triumphant military parades also inspired him, as did his belief that the Italian soldiers must be kept well trained by fighting. Count Ciano was also an enthusiastic supporter of aid to General Franco. Both Italian leaders were desperately afraid of the possibility of a "Red" government in Spain, and made the most of it in all their public announcements.

Hitler was led to intervene in Spain by Goering, chief of the Nazi Air Force, or so, at least, the German marshal testified at the Nuremberg trials. Goering was anxious to test his young Luftwaffe under actual combat conditions. Both men were hysterically afraid of the

Red Peril. Hitler stated that had it not been for that fear he would have left Spain to the Republicans, and "the Church would have been destroyed," he added with obvious relish. Both Italy and Germany were eager to take a crack at the "decadent democracies" by helping Franco overcome the weak Spanish Republic. Furthermore, a long war in Spain would focus the attention of the Western European democracies and the United States on the peninsula while Germany proceeded with her rearmament. Both Italy and Germany viewed the civil war as a golden opportunity to rehearse their armed forces for the forthcoming greater European conflict in which they hoped to dominate all Europe.

The amount of foreign aid reaching Spain has never been precisely recorded, but from the various reports and files available, Hugh Thomas, in his excellent and exhaustive book *The Spanish Civil War*, has listed figures which must be very close to the truth. German aid to Franco totalled over half a billion reichsmarks, and at its peak, there were about 10,000 German soldiers and airmen in Spain. These included 30 artillery and antitank companies and an undisclosed number of air squadrons. Italy sent a total of 100,000 men to help Franco, but not more than half that number were in Spain at any given moment.

The war cost 6,000 Italian dead. Count Ciano stated that over 1,000 Italian planes were sent to aid General Franco, but this figure may be slightly high. The official Stefani News Agency listed 763 Italian aircraft and 141 airplane motors. The same news agency lists 7,663 motor vehicles, 10,135 automatic guns, and 1,672 tons of bombs.[49]

Aid reaching the Republicans was considerably less, and the main part of it came into Spain from the Soviet Union. The German military attaché reported that the Soviets sent 242 aircraft, 731 tanks, 1,386 trucks, and 920 officers and men. Many thousands of tons of fuel, clothing, medical stores, and smaller arms also arrived from Russia. France officially sent the Republicans 200 planes, and perhaps that many more were purchased privately from France and other countries. The total number of foreigners of all nationalities fighting on the Republican side in the International Brigades never amounted to more than 20,000 at any one time. They came from nearly every country, and a tremendous proportion of them were killed in action.

In the matter of tanks, artillery, and planes, the Republicans were outnumbered perhaps ten to one. Thus, despite their army of close to a million men, their defeat in time was a foregone conclusion unless the democracies, Great Britain, France, and the United States, sent them substantial heavy equipment. Such aid was not forthcoming.

The Republicans received token supplies from France, but Britain and the United States observed a complete "hands-off" policy. An arms embargo was placed on Spain and was accepted by both governments. When the embargo came up for a vote in the Congress of the United States it was approved with only a single dissenting vote in the House; in the Senate only Senator Nye opposed it. The Nazi government promptly praised this action, and General Franco stated that over the embargo act President Roosevelt had behaved like "a true gentleman."

No one can justifiably blame this policy of "non-intervention" or "isolationism" of the United States on the administration in Washington. The government of the United States is very responsive to public opinion, and could not possibly engage in shipping war equipment to the Spanish Republic unless there were a strong sentiment, at least a fifty per cent sentiment in this country, in favor of such a policy. There never was anything like that. The majority of the American people rather weakly hoped that the Republic would win over Franco, but few of these people were willing to risk war by extending material aid. All one can do in retrospect is to point out those of our leaders who were right in their interpretation of the situation, and those who were wrong. Ambassador Bowers, who should know better than anyone else in the government, appears to me to have been right.

Hugh Thomas in *The Spanish Civil War* reports that there was one moment when the United States was on the verge of lifting its arms embargo. This was in May 1938, after Negrín had proclaimed his thirteen points for a settlement for the conflict, the gist of which was the withdrawal of all foreign forces and the holding of a plebiscite to decide what kind of government Spain would have. Leading members of the administration in Washington and other noted citizens were at last seeing that the embargo had worked strongly in favor of the Axis powers. This was the moment when H. L. Stimson, Secretary of State under Hoover and Secretary of War under Roosevelt, made his strong statement favoring the lifting of the embargo. William Dodd, U.S. ambassador to Germany, expressed a similar view. Professor Einstein and other distinguished Americans signed a petition urging this action. Senator Nye and Representative Scott introduced resolutions in the Congress requesting that the embargo be lifted. Apparently, at this point Secretary of State Hull momentarily changed his opinion and decided to throw his weight behind these resolutions. Then "a no doubt carefully planned leak about this decision appeared in *The New York Times*." The government was anxious to find out what the public reaction would be. Ambassador Kennedy, who had just been sent to London, wired his alarm that such action might lead to a general European war. Catholics in the United States by the thousands sent in similar protests against sending aid to the Spanish Reds, and President Roosevelt, under this pressure, asked Hull to reverse his position, which he promptly did.[49]

Thomas J. Hamilton, who was sent to Spain by *The New York Times* in 1939, immediately after the civil war had ended, summarizes the fascist victory very effectively in his book *Appeasement's Child*. After pointing out that the policy of "non-intervention" on the part of the democracies assured the defeat of the Republic by denying it the right to purchase military equipment, he goes on to say:

The Axis, on the other hand, had determined to give Franco enough help to win, and it proceeded to furnish it without regard to the Committee [the Non-Intervention Committee]. If Hitler and Mussolini had desired to do so, in fact, they could have won the war for Franco at least a year earlier. The fact that they rationed their aid so carefully . . . seems to confirm the supposition that they were deliberately using the civil war to produce disunion in the democracies. Certainly it was more important to them to keep London and Paris divided than to install a fascist regime in Spain; that, to be sure, was a useful secondary achievement, but here, too, the longer the war lasted, the more firmly would fascism be saddled upon Spain and the easier it would be to keep Franco under their control.[50]

What additional role did Russia play in the Spanish civil war? The Republic had not established diplomatic relations with Russia until the war began. Then ambassadors were exchanged, and Marcel Rosenberg was sent to Madrid by the Soviet Union. He became very influential because of the Russian war material that was reaching the Republicans. One of the first mistakes the Republic made was to ship a large part of its treasure of gold, which totaled approximately half a billion dollars, to Russia for safekeeping. The left-wing socialists Juan Negrín, Minister of Finance, Prime Minister Largo Caballero, and Indalecio Prieto were responsible for this decision. General Franco's side had started the war with no gold reserves available, and this move on the part of the Republic was a grievous error. About 70 per cent of the treasure was in gold sovereigns, which the Russians promptly proceeded to melt down into bullion, charging the Republic heavily for the transformation. As bullion is worth less than coined gold they were certainly not doing the Spaniards any favor. When Soviet equipment was sent to Spain the Russian government charged a very high price for it, and this amount was supposed to be subtracted from the total on deposit. The gold in Russia was also used to purchase supplies for the Loyalists in other countries.

The upshot of the whole affair was that when a final account was published by the Soviets in 1956, they claimed that not only was all of the Spanish gold exhausted, but that the Republicans owed them fifty million dollars above and beyond this amount. The Republicans themselves never received any accounting of their treasure. Their government-in-exile made every attempt to regain control over the wealth which they still believed was in Soviet hands, but without success. The Soviet government simply denied that there was anything left. In passing, it might be pointed out that it took the Franco government, with its absolute control of the Spanish economy, *twenty years* to accumulate dollar reserves valued at half a billion dollars.

Russian help began to arrive in Spain soon after the war started, and the international brigades, whose soldiers were about 80 per cent communists or followers of the communist party line, were assembled largely by communist evangelical zeal. In New York City, there was constant communist drumming for "volunteers to fight for Spanish democracy." At these "anti-fascist" rallies, where donations were collected and impassioned speeches were made for the bleeding Spanish democracy, the communist clenched fist was raised in salute as the favorite songs of the party rang out. It is only fair to recall that when the bleeding British democracy suffered the catastrophe of Dunkirk, and the bleeding French democracy underwent the occupation of its territory by the Nazi army, the Russians raised no such hue and cry about defending democracy. In the Spanish civil war, as elsewhere, they were—as they are now—out to defend their own national interests.

There is every reason to believe that the Russians rationed their military aid in much the same manner that the Axis powers did. Once they had gotten a foothold inside the Republic they never let go, but squeezed harder and harder as the war went on. As long as things went their way, Soviet supplies flowed into Spain, but whenever the Spaniards became too independent, these supplies slowed to a trickle. Further still, this Russian equipment was constantly used to intimidate those who opposed carrying on the war as the Russians wanted it carried on.

What was the secret of communism's appeal as a political philosophy? Hugh Thomas states it clearly:

The Communists' air of possessing the future, their dynamism, their political attitude of no-nonsense, and, of course, the prestige of Russian arms made them the obvious party for ambitious people to join. Their numbers had increased to probably 300,000 by the end of 1936. But had it not been for the *propaganda by sight* (Russian aircraft and tanks), as González Peña put it, they would have been far less successful. The Communists of Barcelona, thanks additionally to their championship of individual ownership and opposition to revolution, were everywhere gaining ground.[49]

They bitterly opposed the anarchists of that region.

The communists invariably supported those who most closely adhered to their views. Largo Caballero, Juan Negrín, and Alvarez del Vayo were perhaps the three men who most abetted their efforts. The roles of the first two have already been mentioned. The third man of the group, Alvarez del Vayo, served as Foreign Secretary in the cabinet of Largo Caballero, and also in that of Negrín. Alvarez del Vayo had visited Russia in 1930, and although he too never wore the communist party label, like Negrín he vigorously followed the party line on nearly every issue. Through these men, and others appointed by them, the Soviets strove in every manner possible to gain complete control of the Republican government. Manuel Azaña, who was the president of the Republic, was little by little squeezed off into an insignificant corner.

In April 1938 Dr. Negrín applied with full force the arbitrary methods for which he was to become known. He himself took over the Ministry of National Defense without relinquishing the premiership, and the Departments of War, Navy, and Air were all put in the hands of communist under-secretaries. The Foreign Office was given to Alvarez del Vayo, who also appointed a communist under-secretary. President Manuel Azaña was not much more than a prisoner of the communists or communist followers. I shall let Alvarez del Vayo speak for himself. His book, called *Freedom's Battle*, which came out in 1940 just as World War II was getting under way, hardly reveals him as the freedom lover that he proclaims himself to be. There is no anti-communist statement in the book, and the author apparently believes that everything Russia did was worthy of his approval. But on page 219 he states exactly what his feelings are in regard to democratic government:

During Largo Caballero's premiership a Cabinet vote on important decisions was the general procedure. Whenever energetic measures were required for the defense of the Republic it usually happened that, while the majority of the votes were cast in support of the Premier's position, the Prieto group in the Cabinet inclined to vote with the moderate Republicans whose policies were more hesitant than Caballero's. When Dr. Negrín became Premier he introduced a different practice. Votes were taken only on death sentences. On no other matters was a division of Cabinet opinion allowed to coalesce. Each minister was free to express his point of view and the final decision was made by the Premier on the basis of the discussion, but no vote was taken. This assured a more vigorous leadership.[51]

I have never read a more accurate description of, or a better turned apology for, the operation of the Soviet Politburo.

In August 1938, seven months before the war came to an end, Dr. Negrín paraded all the tanks and airplanes that he could muster in and over Barcelona, and after this show of strength asked President Azaña to approve the new cabinet that he wished to install. From this moment to the end of the war, Negrín was virtual dictator of Spain. President Azaña stuck it out for another five months, and then left the country. Negrín visited him in Paris and attempted to persuade him to return, but Azaña was not willing to play the role of puppet any longer, and remained in France. Negrín returned to Spain to carry on a last-ditch fight. He was hoping that a European war would break out, which might save the Spanish Republic. He missed it by only a few weeks.

The Russians very plainly wanted Republican Spain to establish a dictatorship of the proletariat which would result in placing the communists or near-communists in power. In order to achieve this it was first necessary to win the civil war, but in fighting the war every possible effort was made to push communists or, better still, communist sympathizers, into positions of power. The communist leaders did not hesitate to use the most ruthless methods against those who opposed them, and under the Negrín government they even framed an ex-Minister of Justice, Andrés Nin, with forged documents, then arrested and murdered him. This ruthless communist campaign became successful toward the end of the war in spite of the opposition of the majority of the Republicans. But whereas the Republicans were of many minds and parties, the communists and their friends had but a single mind, hence their superior political effectiveness.

However, the communists eventually overshot their mark. The Republicans needed all the help they could get, and were willing to endure many indignities in order to receive it. The Soviet Union was the only nation which offered help, so was the only nation which was in a position to exert any strong pressure on the Spanish Republic. Had the democracies sent large-scale military aid to the Loyalists there is no doubt that they could have exerted a much stronger influence, and could have prevented communist infiltration into the Republican government. This is presupposing that they would have set out clearly and forcefully with such an end in view. Even without this opposition the Russians and their Spanish sympathizers bit off more than they could chew in Spain. Everyone knew who they were, what they were up to, and how they were going about it. While their help was essential, and there was still a chance for victory, they demanded and received great power. But during the final days of the war, the non-communist Republicans broke away from them and established a government completely free of communist influence. There was a brisk battle between the two groups, and after three days of bitter fighting, the insurgent Republicans won. They were led by Julián Besteiro,* the most respected man in Madrid, General Miaja, commander of the Loyalist armies, and Colonel Casado, in command at the capital. After the defeat of his faction Dr. Negrín took a plane for France. A couple of weeks later, on March 26, 1939, the war was ended and the Republican army was allowed to disband.

Salvador de Madariaga, old-line Republican liberal and also an ardent and militant opponent of the Franco regime, is not nearly as charitable toward his Republican colleagues as Ambassador Bowers and *New York Times* correspondents Thomas Hamilton and Herbert Matthews. Madariaga thoroughly detested the communists' appearing to make common cause with the Republican government, only to

---

* Besteiro was imprisoned when Franco entered Madrid. He died of tuberculosis in prison a few months later.

catch it in their net. He pointedly accuses the Spanish leftists under Largo Caballero of planning to revolt in 1936, and states that it was their intention to "rush Spain on to the dictatorship of the proletariat." According to Madariaga the rightists under General Franco simply revolted first. Then he goes on to add:

The Communists all over the world took up the cudgels for the Left, for the Spanish Republic, for the Loyalists, in whose government, they and their liberal friends protested, there was not a single Communist. Not a word about the thoroughgoing social revolution which was driving a coach and four through the Constitution of 1931.[10]

Madariaga's opinion of Juan Negrín and Alvarez del Vayo is that they were followers of the communist line who were willing to sacrifice almost anything for their Marxist ideals. In commenting on Negrín's thirteen points for a possible peaceful settlement of the war, which were proclaimed in May 1938, Madariaga is bitter and indignant. "They were unimpeachable so far as they went," he writes, "but as far removed from the facts and practices of his government as words have ever been, and therefore could inspire no confidence whatever in those who knew whence they came."[10]

Madariaga even denies that the aid General Franco received from the Axis powers was crucial in determining the final outcome of the civil war.

Why had the Rebels won? The lazy answer, and the passionate, is: *Because they had the help of Germany and Italy*. This answer will not do. Important though it was, this help was not crucial, and no honest and well-informed student of Spanish affairs would dare be dogmatic as to what would have happened if no foreign help whatsoever had accrued to either side. The chief reason for the failure of the Revolutionaries was the Revolution itself. When the Rebels rose, the Revolutionaries found that most of the springs of public force had gone over to the Rebel side. This in itself was due to the weakness which the Government had evinced for some time in matters of public order.[10]

These statements do not entirely coincide with those of Ambassador Bowers. Both men are sincere and honest interpreters of the Spanish Republic and the civil war; both are noted for their probity and objectivity. Bowers had the advantage of remaining in Spain throughout the war, but Madariaga had the advantage of personal friendship with many of the leaders of the Republic. The truth must lie in some middle ground, somewhere between what these two men have written.

In any case, it now seems clear that what the United States *should* have done, for its own self-interest, was to support the Republican government, to sell it arms, to start pushing early and to keep on pushing very hard right on through the civil war in order to make sure that neither communism nor fascism won a victory in Spain. We did just that in France, Italy, and Western Germany during and following the Second World War, where our actions were highly effective. Spain might not have been as immediately responsive to the call of democracy as these other Western European nations, but she would have responded, for such was the expressed will of the majority of her people, and in any case there would have been no alternative.

The physical and moral destruction caused in Spain by the civil war was tremendous. Hugh Thomas estimates that about 320,000 men died in action, perhaps 220,000 people died of disease or malnutrition, and at least 100,000 were executed or murdered. This makes a total of approximately 640,000 dead. After the war a total of at least two million persons were imprisoned for varying periods of time in the Franco jails. The war itself caused great destruction of property: 250,000 houses destroyed, another 250,000 damaged, 183 towns devastated, 2,000 churches largely ruined. The industries of Barcelona and Bilbao fortunately emerged from the war having suffered very little, but a third of the country's livestock was killed, and much of her farm machinery destroyed. The rail lines lost 61 per cent of their passenger cars, 22 per cent of their freight cars, 27 per cent of their locomotives. Approximately two billion dollars' worth of damage was done to real property by the war, but the *total cost* of the conflict to the country was at least six times that amount.[49]

One of the most sorrowful outcomes of the civil war was the abandonment of liberal principles by many of the intellectuals and the exile of hundreds of others. When war broke out most of these men were caught in Madrid, and nearly all of these signed a statement supporting the Republic. The signatures included the names of Dr. Marañón, distinguished physician, the novelist Pérez de Ayala, the literary critic Menéndez Pidal, the writer Ortega y Gasset, and many others. Republican atrocities and the increasing pressure of communists in the government soon caused these men to flee from Spain, and once safe abroad all of them repudiated the Republic.

The poet García Lorca returned to his home in Granada at the outbreak of violence, for as he said he was considered as a "small glory" there, and therefore should be safe. In the middle of the night he was picked up by the fascists and shot, because he had been a loyal supporter of the Republic.[109] Ramiro de Maeztu, well-known essayist, was shot in Madrid by the Republicans. Ramón Sender, the most prominent novelist of the younger group, enlisted in the Republican army and fought throughout the war. His wife and brothers were shot, simply because Sender was on the other side. There was a mass exodus of the best intellects of Spain, and they left a tremendous void behind them.

Pío Baroja fled from Republican territory into Nationalist territory, but he found this area also unpalatable and then escaped abroad. Soon after the war, however, he returned to Spain and was able to continue living there until he died several years later. Azorín fled to Paris, but also later returned to Spain. Antonio Machado, the great old poet of Castile, a man who had never interested himself much in political events, continued to support the Republic. He was eventually forced to flee as a refugee, and died in France in a box car; he is buried in French soil.

Unamuno was in Salamanca when the war broke out, and during the early weeks of the conflict he supported the Nationalists under General Franco. But by October he had changed his mind. German troops had profaned Spanish soil, and Spanish Falangists were screaming out fanaticisms in his beloved Salamanca. On October 12, 1936, there was a great ceremony at the University of Salamanca, celebrating what the Spaniards call the *día de la raza* ("day of the race"). It is the anniversary, of course, of the day that Spain discovered the New World and became with that event a great world power. Attending the ceremony were Señora Franco, a fascist general named Millán Astray, many professors of the university, many townsfolk, a number of Spanish Falangists, and Unamuno himself. The ceremony got off to a violent start. General Millán Astray gave an impassioned rabble-rousing speech in which he ranted against the Republic and especially against the Basque provinces and Catalonia, where many of its supporters lived. The audience was all stirred up. Several Falangists, in their blue shirts, gave the fascist salute and shouted *Long live death! Spain one and free!*

Unamuno, rector of the university, finally rose to speak. Everyone was hanging on his words. The old man did not falter; immediately he called the cry *Long live death!* a "necrophilous and senseless one." Then indignantly he defended the Basque provinces and Catalonia, and finally launched into a personal attack on General Millán Astray. There had never been any speech like this in Nationalist territory before. The general, unable to restrain himself, shouted at the top of his lungs: *Down with intelligence! Long live death!* Unamuno answered him saying:

"This is the temple of the intellect. And I am its high priest. It is you who profane its sacred precincts. You will win, because you have more than enough brute force. But you will not convince. For to convince you need to persuade. And in order to persuade you would need what you lack: Reason and Right in the struggle. I consider it futile to exhort you to think of Spain. I have spoken."

The audience was aghast. "There was a long pause. Then, with a brave gesture, the professor of canon law went out with Unamuno on one arm, and Señora Franco on the other. But this was Unamuno's last lecture. Thereafter, the rector remained under house arrest. He might have been imprisoned had not the Nationalist authorities feared the international consequences of such an action." On the last day of the year 1936, at the age of seventy-two, the old man died.[49]

Thousands of liberals fled from Spain in order to escape from Franco's new church-state. Almost the entire publishing industry left, along with the best writers, university professors, artists, and scientists. The two foremost Spanish historians, Rafael Altamira and Claudio Sánchez Albornoz, both went into exile. So did Alejandro Casona, the country's most popular dramatist, and Américo Castro, Spain's best literary and social critic, along with Madariaga, Ramón Sender, Pablo Casals, Pedro Salinas, Luis Cernuda, José Bergamín, Fernando de los Ríos, and hundreds of others too numerous to mention.

These men simply could not stomach General Franco. Not one of them is an extremist; they are all honorable liberals, who believe in justice and freedom. The loss of these men to Spain has been irreparable. In addition to the tragic dead, the voluntary exile of her most honored leaders has meant the loss of the country's very lifeblood. A total of at least three to four hundred thousand crossed the border into France; about half of these have remained in that country, while the other half have scattered widely. Many thousands eventually returned to Spain. Ten to twenty thousand entered Mexico, and a sizable number wound up in the United States. The Latin-

American nations generally, with the notable exception of Mexico, kept their doors tightly closed. The Spanish masses were left headless and invertebrate for a generation; without intellectual leadership the popular will is a chaotic mess or a submissive lamb. It has been both under the regime of General Franco.

The Spanish civil war stirred deep fires in the hearts of many world-famous intellectuals. Ernest Hemingway, André Malraux, Arthur Koestler, and George Orwell all actively supported the Republican cause, and the war shaped their lives forevermore. Camus explained why: "It was in Spain that men learned that we can be right and yet be beaten, that force can vanquish spirit, that there are times when courage is not its own reward. It is this, doubtless, which explains why so many men, the world over, regarded the Spanish drama as a personal tragedy."[73] Or as the Englishman J. B. Trend so cogently put it: "What was lost in the war was not merely a government, but a whole modern culture.[21]

15

VALLEY OF THE FALLEN

Throughout her history Spain has shown a kind of absurd compulsion to rid herself of her most promising intellects.

Salvador de Madariaga

About twenty-five miles northwest of Madrid, high in the Guadarrama range, is General Franco's bid for immortality, the famous Valley of the Fallen, or *Valle de los Caídos*, which was completed in 1959 after several years of work. The general, who in this as in many other things, liked to think of himself as a kind of modern-day Philip II, built this monument with the hope that it would be as impressive in its own way as is the *Escorial*, Philip's huge, austere mausoleum of the Spanish kings.

The monument consists of two principal items: the gigantic concrete cross that towers 450 feet above the mountain, and the famous basilica that was tunneled out of solid granite inside the mountain itself. It is 900 feet in length, but is neither as wide nor as lofty as the interior dimensions of the larger Spanish cathedrals, and certainly far less beautiful. In places the cold, rough granitic rock is left in its original state, so one gets the impression of an immense cave-basilica, part of it carefully walled in marble, part of it left in bare granite. The floor of the basilica is of marble, and the walls are partly covered with costly tapestries. At the end of the basilica is the altar, and above this rises an immense dome, 200 feet high, the ceiling of which is covered with an enormous mosaic. The central figure in the mosaic is Christ; he is surrounded by various saints. The altar and choir are unimpressive. As in everything that the general has done in Spain, they represent nothing new in creative thinking, but merely hark back to the Spanish past, whose artistic spirit far transcends that of this colossal monument.

Beneath the well-lighted dome and under a marble slab in the floor lies the body of José Antonio Primo de Rivera, the Falangist martyr, whose body was removed from the *Escorial* and placed here. The general converted him into a symbol of his victory and his regime. On the grave one sees perhaps a wreath of flowers, and just beyond it is a crude log cross, the beams of which were cut down by General Franco himself. The cross contrasts grotesquely with the highly finished surroundings.

As one walks up and down the great central aisle, piped-in religious music, flowing from the loudpeakers, fills the air. There is a dank, cold smell to the place, perhaps from the mountain rock, but possibly heightened by the fifteen to twenty thousand bodies (or skeletons) which lie buried behind the walls and tapestries. Here, the fallen on both sides of the bloody civil war "now lie in peace together," according to the general's statement. His precise reason for having built the monument was "to perpetuate the memory of the Fallen in the Crusade of Liberation, to honor those who gave their lives for God and the Fatherland, and as an example for future generations." But Franco magnanimously decided to let the dead Republicans share the cemetery, hence the more general name now given to the place, Valley of the Fallen.

Franco employed many prisoners for the task of construction. They worked around the clock to complete the monument in record time. Many Spaniards were and still are incensed that so much money and so much labor went into this tomb while the country was suffering dire poverty and stood on the verge of bankruptcy. Why not food? Why not roads? Why not shelter instead? These people ridicule the general's attempt to imitate Philip II, and refer to the mausoleum as "Franco's Folly." But there are others who regard the whole thing as an imperishable creation of the Nationalist regime, in which church and state were always united.

The Valley of the Fallen is only a few miles from the *Escorial*, and one can easily see the two monuments in a single day. The Benedictines are the caretakers of the new sanctuary and occupy a large monastery on the spot. It was originally planned to have the Franciscans take charge, but this order, dedicated to service and poverty, refused to have its monks live in a place of such luxury. Thousands of Spaniards have refused to visit the sanctuary altogether, regarding it as a sort of permanent stigma commemorating their civil war.

Many writers have characterized the monument as one of the most colossal undertakings of history, one that will almost certainly give the general his measure of immortality. Personally, I doubt this very much. When this generation passes away, and the Franco regime is forgotten, all the old hatreds will be focused on this spot, and it will either be destroyed or altered so that it no longer represents what it does today. I do not see how the future generation can act otherwise. Perhaps the monument will come to symbolize where a whole Spanish epoch lies buried. In the meantime, the sanctuary is primarily the tomb of General Franco, and of the leaders of the Nationalist "Uprising of Liberation." It is, even more, the tomb of José Antonio Primo de Rivera, the young aristocrat and playboy, son of the once-popular dictator of the 1920s, who was executed by the Republicans in the early days of the war. Just who was this José Antonio? What did he do to bring him so prominently to public view? What did he believe in, and why was he killed?

Although the failure of the Spanish Republic was due fundamentally to its disintegration from within, the military rebellion against it might have crumbled had it not been for the amazing ability of General Franco to weld the heterogeneous elements of the right into a strong, common mold. This was an ability that the Republicans did not possess. Of course, the general had tradition and history on his side, while the Republic did not.

In the beginning the military rebellion had no political policy except to overthrow the Republic and implant a dictatorship of the Spanish right composed of the army, the church, and the aristocrats. General Franco immediately saw that such an attitude was not enough. The people needed a political program. Therefore, he took over *in toto* the Spanish fascist party, the Falange, incorporated it within the frame of his struggle against the Republic, made it his own official party, and in the end wound up by rendering it completely submissive to his will. This was one of the general's striking abilities: to appropriate and utilize for his own ends the diverse elements within the rightist coalition which otherwise might have become a disrupting influence within his ranks. The moment the general became the head of the Falange its independence of action was doomed.

The Falange's motto for Spain, *One, great, and free,* suited the general admirably. Its strong Catholic sentiment added to its appeal. Therefore, General Franco began at once to refer to the military revolt that he headed as a "Christian Crusade" to save Spain from the atheists and the communists. This idea caught on fast, for had not the same essential faith inspired the ancient Castilians in their struggle against the Moslems?

The founder of the Falange party was José Antonio Primo de Rivera, son of the man who had been dictator of Spain just prior to the Republic. During the years of Franco's government half the main streets in the cities of Spain were named after this man. Even in Madrid the famous *Gran Vía* was renamed José Antonio Avenue, and so it was throughout the rest of the country. Those main arteries that did not bear the name of this young fascist were renamed the Street of the Generalissimo, or the Street of the Caudillo, which means Street of the Chief. Fortunately, when Franco died all this was changed again and the traditional names were restored.

The name *Falange* means Phalanx and was taken from the Macedonian army unit that was largely responsible for the overthrow of the Greek Republic in the fourth century B.C. The party itself was founded by José Antonio in 1933, and it quickly incorporated the other older Spanish fascist groups within its organization. In 1934 José Antonio was elected to the national Cortes as the lone fascist deputy. Gil Robles, the Catholic rightist leader, spurned the young man's political ambitions and referred to him as a *señorito* or "playboy." Robles declared that Spanish politics was not for señoritos. But José Antonio, playboy or not, was a young man of great daring and of considerable personal charm. He was zealously anxious to vindicate the name of his father, and was adamantly opposed to the Spanish Republic. He also admired both Mussolini and Hitler, and imitated them by adopting a colored shirt as the party uniform; in his case the color was blue. The party emblem was the famous "yoke and arrows" which had been the emblem of Ferdinand and Isabella, the Catholic sovereigns. The Falange flag was colored black and red. The political ideal of the Falange party was Catholic, authoritarian, fascist. During the war it built up its own militia.

Hugh Thomas writes of José Antonio: "His speeches and writings leave the impression of a talented undergraduate who has read, but not quite digested, an overlong course of political theory." Thomas then quotes a few of the young man's words: "The country is a historical totality . . . superior to each of us and to our groups. The State is founded on two principles . . . service to the united nation and the cooperation of classes." Later on, José Antonio added: "Fascism is a European inquietude. It is a way of knowing everything . . . history, the State, the achievement of the proletarianism of public life, a new way of knowing the phenomena of our epoch. Fascism has already triumphed in many countries, and in some, as in Germany, by the most irreproachable democratic means."[49]

In those terrible weeks just prior to the civil war the Spanish Falange party was doing much the same thing in Spain that Hitler's Brown Shirts did in Germany; its members were organizing riots and disorders, shouting provocative insults against the government, and engaging in all the methods of terror against those who opposed them most effectively. It was the party of violence and of assassination, despite the fact that José Antonio personally was strongly opposed to such tactics. In a period of about three months, forty Falangists and fifty Republicans were slain. A few weeks before the outbreak of the war José Antonio himself was arrested by the Republic and imprisoned first in Madrid, then in Alicante, near Valencia, where he was held as a hostage for the good behavior of his followers. He was still in prison when the military rebellion broke out on July 17, 1936. In the fall of that same year he was tried before a Republican court and condemned to death. The formal charge against him was that he had helped to prepare the revolt against the Republic.

José Antonio defended himself well, but the sentence was almost a foregone conclusion. After it was delivered he appealed to the Republican cabinet in Madrid as a court of last resort, and this group, which was not of a single mind, was still reviewing the case when the local authorities took the law into their own hands and executed José Antonio. Stanley G. Payne in his book on the Spanish Falange writes of the trial and last days of José Antonio in some detail, and concludes that the young man was probably not guilty of the crimes attributed to him.[52] He was simply a scapegoat, and of course he became, after his death, a martyr for all those who opposed the Republic. When the news of José Antonio's death reached the other side, they promptly tried and executed the son of Largo Caballero, the Republican prime minister, in reprisal.

With the death of José Antonio, the Falange became merely a pawn in the hands of General Franco. After the war the young man's body was reburied in the place of honor in front of the main altar in General Franco's Valley of the Fallen. He is still regarded by some Spaniards as the great martyr of the Franco "Crusade." Many of his old followers, however, eventually opposed the General. The Falange's political and economic philosophy, embodied largely in the concept of a national syndicalist corporate state with vertical trade unions (including management), was taken over by General Franco and subverted to his purposes. Falangists also created several persuasive slogans which General Franco later used with great psychological effectiveness. The party itself was split into a right and a left wing; those on the right thought more or less as did General Franco, while those on the left believed strongly in social reform. It was this group that the general was particularly anxious to swallow up for fear its activities and promises might get out of hand.

General Franco's full name is Francisco Paulino Hermenegildo Teodulo Franco Bahamonde. He was born in the city of El Ferrol, in the province of Galicia, in 1892. The family was noted for its longevity. His father lived to be 93, and his grandfather reached 102. Franco entered the military academy in Toledo in 1907, and the army became his career. When the Nationalist revolt broke out in 1936 he was Chief of Staff in the army of the Spanish Republic. He was instrumental in bringing about the revolt, and he immediately became leader of the rebellious forces.

Franco formerly had served for many years with the Spanish army in Morocco, where he was regarded as a strong leader who never lost his temper. He was a good administrator, and an officer of great courage. The Moroccan troops, both the Moorish contingent and the soldiers of the Spanish Foreign Legion, formed the core of his most steadfast supporters from the very beginning of his "glorious movement," as he called the rebellion. The general had nerves of steel, and possessed a cold and calculating quality untypical of most Spaniards. Sometimes he mustered a wan smile, and he received the acclamations of the crowd with very little emotional response. He never fed on applause as did Hitler and Mussolini, but always regarded it as one of the natural outcomes of his victory.

A story told of him during the days of his Moroccan service reveals much of the man's character. There was great unrest in the Foreign Legion because of the poor food, and one day the reluctant soldiers had to be summoned by several bugle calls before they finally straggled out for inspection. Franco passed down the lines without any sign of irritation. As he stopped for a moment in front of one huge soldier, the man suddenly threw the contents of his mess kit in the general's face. "You like filth!" he spat out. "Well, take this!" Franco, still without changing his expression, calmly took out his handkerchief, wiped the slop off his uniform, and completed the inspection. Afterward, he first ordered that the rations be improved immediately, then said calmly: "Take that man out and execute him."

Franco was never *simpático*, and he never enjoyed real popularity in Spain. He had cliques that would always shout for him, if this was deemed to be essential, but when he traveled to the various cities of Spain he was generally greeted with only perfunctory applause. He always rode in a bulletproof Rolls Royce, surrounded by secret service men, and on certain state occasions by a group of Moorish guards mounted on horseback and wearing turbans. Tommy guns were much in evidence when he was exposed to an assembled multitude.

I was in Madrid on the twenty-fifth anniversary of the Nationalist uprising, and a great "victory" celebration was planned. The army was going to parade along the beautiful Castellana, and huge crowds were expected. Bleachers were set up all along the length of the boulevard, but these were completely separated from the line of march by very thick barricades of barbed wire, symbolic after all those years of the ugliness and insecurity of the Franco dictatorship.

During his thirty-six years of rule, one of the longest in the history of Spain, the general and his regime were one and inseparable. He was commander-in-chief of all armed forces, the chief of the government, and the leader of the party, the only party. His parliament, the Cortes, boasted only one right: to approve his decrees, that is, if Franco submitted them for approval. He generally did so out of that peculiar feeling that Spanish and Latin American dictators have for giving a mask of legality to everything that they do.

The generalissimo's first years in power were hardly an outstanding success. The national economy sputtered, lunged, tottered, almost halted. As soon as the Spanish civil war ended World War II broke out, and Spain had no way to replace her broken-down transportation equipment and her destroyed or worn-out machinery. After that World War ended Spain found herself isolated from both the democratic and communist camps. She was excluded from the Marshall Plan, from the United Nations, and from NATO. But in June 1950 the Korean War started, and the United States, upset and frightened, became anxious to strengthen its security by building a ring of bases around the communist bloc. General Franco, who up until this moment had been very solicitous about the possibility of U.S. bases in Spain, suddenly became aloof and waited for this country to approach him. In 1953 an agreement was concluded, and then for the first time since the civil war foreign aid began to pour into Spain, undoubtedly bolstering, and perhaps saving, her economy and her government. In 1955 the country was admitted to the United Nations.

General Franco regarded his part in the civil war as a holy crusade, and most of the Spanish hierarchy agreed with him. In 1937 all but three of the bishops of Spain signed a pastoral letter endorsing the Nationalist cause. However, in this document they also pointed out that "this war was not begun in order to give birth to an autocratic state." After the war was won the generalissimo doggedly held all power in his hand, and it was not until 1953 (the date of the agreement on bases with the United States) that an agreement was reached between Franco and the Holy See concerning the Spanish church. Proceeding on his own, the general had already restored the Jesuits to their former position of influence and had canceled all the anticlerical laws of the Republic. But he needed very much to show the world that he was in respectable standing with Rome, hence the concordat of 1953.

This agreement between the Spanish head of state and the Pontiff was a definite move toward Rome, hence it was a move away from Spanish religious separatism. In the long run, it proved to be a very definite move toward religious liberalism, and away from Spanish fanaticism. In the concordat of 1953 the church was guaranteed state financial support, education was placed in its hands, Roman Catholicism was recognized as the sole religion of Spain, the clergy were given certain privileges in the courts which almost made them an independent community within the state, church property was free from taxation, the appointment of prelates was to be made by joint agreement between the Pontiff and the chief of state.

Franco partially achieved his international respectability as a result of this concordat, but many people inside Spain were irritated by it. The Falange right was hostile because the Spanish government did not retain enough power in its own hands, and the Franco opposition was hostile because the church was officially given too much power. Leaders within the church, feeling more secure in their new position, made no bones about their desire for more social justice, freedom of the press, more civil liberties, and an institutionalization of the regime which would provide for some kind of logical succession of power.

All rationally thinking citizens of Spain believed in these same things, but the church had a special interest in them as an insurance against the brutal anticlerical riots of the 1930s.

The New York Times commented: "Some experienced observers believe that the Catholic Church in Spain, long accused of being reactionary, is seeking to solidify its position in any future regime by cautiously dissociating itself in the workers' eyes from the more repressive aspects of General Franco's dictatorship."

The more conservative side of the religious picture in Spain was represented by an organization known as the Opus Dei (God's Work), which came to exert a very strong influence on the government. Critics of the left called this organization Octopus Dei (God's Octopus), or the Holy Mafia. Spaniards of the far right, on the contrary, referred to it as "a new White Masonry," that some of them regarded as too liberal. Opus Dei was founded in 1928 in Madrid by a wealthy ex-lawyer turned priest. It slowly acquired stature, money, influence, respectability. In 1950 Pope Pius XII granted the organization definitive official Catholic status as a secular institute.

Opus Dei was never numerically large. Its membership in Spain did not exceed 22,000 while its worldwide membership in some 65 countries, including the United States, was about 60,000. Only in Spain, however, did the Opus Dei become a powerful political and social force. Many cabinet ministers and other important government officials were Opus members.

The ideological goal of Opus Dei was to revitalize the traditional values: make Spain more Spanish, return to the old Spanish and Christian ethics, re-establish the old virtues, restore the ancient dignity and the glory of Spain, combat the evils of liberalism, rationalism, immorality. Opus Dei members took a vow of chastity, poverty, and obedience, but this vow could be revoked at will. Many members of the group were wealthy, and all members were expected to give any surplus personal income to the organization. Hence, Opus Dei accumulated considerable wealth and came to control many financial institutions, including one of the largest banks in Spain, the Banco Popular. It also controlled several newspapers in Madrid, Barcelona, Valladolid, and Leon, and issued several magazines.

In the field of education its influence was strong and very oppressive. Opus Dei took a clear stand in opposition to the ideals of the Free Institution of Teaching established in 1876 by Giner de los Ríos and a group of liberal professors. Its members regarded this admirable institution as the seedbed of liberalism, leftism, and irresponsibility in Spain. Many Opus members held positions of importance in several of the Spanish universities, and the organization also had its own quasi-university in Pamplona. Students and professors at several other Spanish institutions of higher learning protested against the Pamplona school, but without avail. They disliked both its academic standards and its emphasis on theology.

Opus Dei also exercised great economic influence on the Franco regime, and in this regard its policies were not as traditional or as rigid as its religious and social ideas. Big business, especially international finance, does not speak a single language, and the Opus Dei men were anxious to get into the international swim. One might say that they were almost liberal, economically speaking. They were eager for Spain to participate in the Common Market, and saw great benefits in such participation. Thus, under Opus leadership Spanish capitalists began to emerge from their semi-isolation, and entered the arena where the big money is made. The plain fact was that Spain was caught in the midst of powerful economic and political currents flowing in from all over Europe, and without realizing it one of the things that Opus Dei achieved was to prepare Spain for the post-Franco period that was sure to come. The Opus itself would then just fade away, but the economic bases that it had established would firmly remain.

Spain formally requested admission to the European Common Market on February 9, 1962, with the hope of thus becoming a part of the mainstream of European development, but as one of the officials of that group commented to a reporter in Paris: "It is all very well for Spain to decide that she is ready for us, but do we need Spain?" After all, what assets would she offer? Her main exports of olives, olive oil, citrus fruits, and wine conflict with those of Italy and France. In 1984, many years later, Spain was still trying to join the Common Market, and by this time most of the opposition to her admission had softened. In the interim Spain had become an industrial power to be reckoned with, and her continued cooperation in NATO was needed more than ever.

Many Spaniards are willing to admit that they have always had one of the worst administrations in the world, present government not excepted. The manner in which this statement is made sometimes perplexes the foreign observer, for the gesture and tone of voice are such that one is led to believe that the Spaniard is actually boasting of his poor government throughout history. In a way he seems to believe that there is nothing quite like it anywhere else in the world; therefore, bad government is a unique Spanish tradition. This may appear amusing on the surface, but it is one of the saddest facts of the national life.

It is also a reality with which any foreign country, no matter how well disposed, will have to cope.

The Franco government, of course, was an attempt to resurrect in modern times Spain's church-state past. No political double talk or impassioned chain of adjectives can conceal this basic fact. Franco and his regime epitomized intellectual backwardness. They were dead from the beginning, only they did not know it. Substantial material progress was achieved, but intellectual progress was close to zero. Their tomb is that colossal and expensive and hateful Valley of the Fallen—this century's *Escorial*.

Spain today is a composite of all that has gone before. Her taproot reaches deep into the bottomless past. On several successive occasions in history she has flowered in beauty, shedding her glory over the civilization of Europe. On many other occasions she has grimly closed her door on the outside world, and retired into the gloom of fixed memories. In spite of her perennially poor government, her vitality is ever present, and appears inexhaustible. The Spanish people are among the most generous, the most noble human beings on earth. Their spontaneous art places them in a unique category among the nations of Europe, both for its quantity and for its incomparable beauty. With one foot in the present and the other in the past, Spain today stands straddling the unfathomable abyss.

I made my last trip to Spain only a few short months ago. As the plane came in over the peninsula from the north we saw a sudden rise of mountains, then the industrial city of Bilbao, pride of the Basque country, whose smokestacks had thoroughly blackened the air. All the way from the coast to Madrid there were mountains, mountains, more mountains. There was very little level land, very little farmland; there were few towns. When the plane neared Madrid the mountains suddenly receded in the distance, and we were flying low over an open plain. The earth was now almost crystalline in the clear light. We went still lower and prepared to land. Down beneath us we could plainly see a man winnowing wheat by throwing it into the air, and letting the golden stream fall back to earth. In another nearby field another man was plowing with a mule. The countryside near Madrid was serrated and deeply eroded. There was little greenery to relieve the dry red aspect of the land. The airport was drab, crowded, functional. That is, they somehow got you in and out. It was an unpleasant entrance into an ugly city. The taxi driver tried his best to overcharge us, and he kept talking about how all prices had soared.

Finally we reached the Castellana, Madrid's famous promenade, and turned down toward the center of the city. We drove by the grim-looking National Library where I had spent so many hours reading and studying for my doctor's degree, which I obtained from the University of Madrid many years ago. Inside, as was the case when I studied there, the card cataloging was still abominable, and many of the books were still impossible to find. Every day the small group of foreign Hispanists in the country gathers on the steps of the library to discuss the personalities and latest subjects of interest in the field of Spanish culture.

The Castellana has become longer and noisier with each passing year, and there are many blocks of new buildings at the outer end of the boulevard. The older portion of this famous street, however, has not changed its appearance greatly in the past fifty years. The trees still shade its length, the fountains still flow, the crowds still promenade. There is more traffic than in the older days, and the way people dress reminds one of any big city in the United States. Blue jeans are seen everywhere, and haircuts are whatever length or configuration that the wearer might feel the urge to display.

The center of Madrid shows no signs of the civil war, despite the fact that the city was besieged and heavily bombarded for a couple of years. The huge Royal Palace, at the western edge of the metropolis, does show that it was cannonaded, but the nearby University City is new. The old university campus was completely destroyed, and the earth in this part of town was deeply gouged out with trenches running in all directions where the defenders resisted the siege. After the capture of Madrid, General Franco had the entire area scraped clean, and then set about raising a new University City. It consists of a goodly number of large buildings in an unimpressive modern style. At the entrance to the campus stands a huge chapel, and a towering arch commemorates the Nationalist victory. The arch is impressive in size, but with no claim to beauty. Its pompous inscriptions ring hollow now that Franco's fantasy is dead.

The Royal Palace, not particularly imposing on the outside, on the inside is one of the most beautiful and most luxurious palaces in Europe. It is filled with an almost endless collection of ancient and modern clocks of every size, style, and vintage of clockmaking. In this palace

Franco used to receive foreign dignitaries, and here it was that he welcomed President Eisenhower. The sight of the president of the United States driving around the city with the general gave many Spaniards a heavy feeling in the pit of the stomach. The president's verbal reference to Franco as a fine ally against communism did not improve matters, and a picture of Eisenhower embracing Franco, reproduced repeatedly in the Spanish press, further diminished the ideal of American democracy.

When the Kennedy administration took over in Washington many of its supporters hoped that this open embracing of the dictators of the world would cease, but in December of 1961, Dean Rusk, Kennedy's secretary of state, also visited General Franco, following previous visits of the secretaries of the Army, Navy, and Commerce. Rusk too praised Franco as an ally of the United States against communist aggression. The Spanish press, completely government dominated, hailed Rusk's visit. This same policy of our highest officials embracing the dictators of Latin America has resulted in a very poor impression in those countries. But the appearance of Dean Rusk with Franco in Spain, at a time when the United States was trying to present itself before the Latin American nations as a champion of the democracies of the world, was a particularly bitter pill for our neighbors to swallow. Uncle Sam, they muttered, says one thing but does another. Presidents Johnson and Nixon made no effort to disprove this suspicion.

In Toledo one sees more signs of the civil war. The Alcazar, built by Charles V, in which 1,200 civil guards and their families resisted a Loyalist siege for over two months before they were finally freed by the advancing Nationalist army, was half destroyed and had to be rebuilt. Even the beautiful convent of San Juan de los Reyes, constructed by Ferdinand and Isabella, was heavily damaged in the war. For a time in Toledo the streets ran red with human blood. But this ancient city had withstood many onslaughts before, and it survived the recent war as well. Surrounded by barren fields, and the deeply etched bed of the Tagus River which almost circles the town, bordered by white-trunked poplars and giant tamarisks, this old capital of Spain blends within its small area the remains of every invading culture that Spain has known. The waters of the Tagus are blue and yellow and catch in their net the changing light. When the evening falls, and the sky turns a ghostly rose and violet, and the *vencejos* fly in semicircles over the Tagus with their eerie cries, the entire precincts are clothed in lilac shadows and the visitor can no longer tell where one world ends and the other begins. The hour of twilight in Toledo is one of the great experiences of the traveler in Spain. I went to Toledo to stay a few days and remained for several weeks.

On the drive back to Madrid over waterless land, the view in every direction was of a great expanse of withering fields. There had been no rain for over a month. The wheat lay in stacks in row after row, and the yellow stubble marked the open fields. There were a few farms growing corn. On the low rounded hills some olive trees. Here and there that omnipresent tree of Spain, the *chopo*, or Spanish poplar, with its dancing leaves. The mountains seemed far away to the north; they were like gray-indigo mounds of wool. There were many cars and motorcycles on the road, which was lined with new industries. In the fields were the grass field huts of the laborers who at midday sought refuge in them from the burning rays of the sun. All the trees were dusty green. The only darker green was from an occasional cornfield, or from a clump of chopos waving their leaves in the wind.

Madrid at night is a fantastic city with its play of lights and its flow of water from inexhaustible fountains. The Castellana by moonlight is one of the most beautiful boulevards in the world; by day it is rather gray and cheerless looking. The same thing is true in Toledo, Granada, Seville, Cordoba, Valencia—any town of Spain. When the hour of twilight arrives the cities and towns begin to breathe and live. They become young and beautiful again, and filled with hope; even the voices of those who have slaved all day sound alert and melodious. The indefinable charm of Spain lies in these towns at night. With softness of air and the sounds of flowing water, they steal the heart completely. The shining spire of the Giralda in Seville by moonlight is an incomparable sight. The view of the city of Granada from the veranda of the Alhambra Palace Hotel, on top of Alhambra Hill, is unforgettably impressive. So too are the cries of the cocks which ring out their song day and night in this fascinating Andalusian town. The bells ring everywhere, and reverberate in waves on the *vega* and mountains. Down below Alhambra Hill, in a small park, children's voices float on the air like faraway bird songs, as they wait their turn to ride on the merry-go-round, called *tío vivo*, or "gay uncle" in Spanish. Every town of Spain has its sounds, its odors, its architecture, its history, its enchantment, and they are all different.

We took the night train out of Madrid to Santiago. Only the very poor or the very stupid traveler in Spain would attempt to go to the station or ticket office for his ticket. The hotel *conserje* or a travel agent will gladly take care of the transaction for you. Indeed it is almost imperative that he do so. The hierarchy of workers immediately begins to appear when one asks for a ticket. The head man passes the request on to a second in command, and often this one will try to pass it on to yet another. In any case at the end of the line some poor girl clerk has to call on the phone, and some poor boy in his teens has to run down to the office on a streetcar or bus to pick up the ticket. The whole transaction may well take two or three hours, and even if the traveler had that much time he might not be able to get through to the right people.

The *conserje* in the better Spanish hotels will do almost anything for you. He can buy tickets to the bullfight, rent you a car and driver, get tickets to the theater or to the concert, find you a temporary secretary or typist, make a plane or train reservation for you and pick up the necessary tickets, call long distance and make hotel reservations ahead for whatever days you wish. I have not seen such efficiency in any American hotel. The old saw about Spanish inefficiency being a national trait does not apply here. The Spaniards can be as efficient as any people on earth, when they are of a mind to be so.

Our railway sleeper to Santiago was old but comfortable, and cheap for a ride of almost 400 miles. The train slowly ascends the grade with its electric engine pulling a long string of cars. It passes in turn the *Escorial*, which stands out impressively on one side of the tracks, and then the medieval walled town of Avila, which stands out on the other. After that, the dark. The train reaches Santiago at about eight in the morning.

I was awake early watching the landscape from the car window. The earth was greener now, obviously more fertile. There were cornfields, grapevines, long rows of hops for beer. Every field was fenced in with gray stones. Galicia lacks the brilliant whiteness of Castile. Even the houses and churches are gray. There was smoke coming out of the chimneys, and the air was cool. A light mist was hanging over the landscape. There were frequent rectangular storage bins, called *hórreos*, raised off the ground to keep the grain away from the rats, some of stone and others of wood; all had a cross at one end. In the meadows cows were grazing placidly; they were strangely hobbled by a rope tied to the horns and to one leg. The green rolling mountains unfolded in successive waves on both sides of the track. We passed through tunnel after tunnel in order to avoid too steep a grade. The track was lined with purple and yellow flowers. It was obvious that we were no longer in a barren, unfruitful land.

Santiago is a glory of ancient architecture and the entire city has been declared a national monument. Its famous hotel, the Hostal de los Reyes Católicos, in a remodeled ancient building where the pilgrims used to rest, is perhaps the most interesting in Europe. The cathedral is Baroque and somber on the exterior; inside is the wonderful portico of the medieval cathedral. Santiago, like all of Spain, was filled with tourists. The last time I had visited the city it was flooded with priests, but not now. The Spanish church is putting on a low profile under the present socialist government.

A couple of days later we drove with some Spanish friends to Betanzos, the old capital of Galicia, and visited the ancient Romanesque churches there. One of these was in the hands of an old man, Father Francisco, approaching eighty, who treated us to his sacramental wine, for the wine of the country was not good enough. He had four or five bright young helpers. During the civil war the workers came to burn his church, and he stood there before it imploring them to go away. They apologized, for they knew him well, but proceeded with the burning. They had to follow orders, they said. Fortunately, he was able to put out the flames before the building was destroyed. No one had anything against this man; everyone in the neighborhood knew him and loved him. It was not that way in all the other parts of Spain.

Father Francisco, an ancient symbol of the old regime, and his young priests, symbolic of the new, were educated, tolerant, lovable human beings. Their lives were unquestionably lives of complete dedication, not to an abstract ideal but to human beings, as well as to God. It was obvious, too, that they were leading lives of poverty. The nobility of the country was plain to see in the character of these simple men. Spain has such a tremendous potential if only her people could pull together.

Spanish individualism is still anarchic and inorganic. The race is not cohesive except when it is unified "against someone or some thing." If Spaniards could only work as hard for as they do against things, their country would be one of the most dynamic and most progressive in Western Europe, perhaps in the world. Ganivet put it very well many years ago when he wrote:

In the Middle Ages our various regions wanted their own kings, not in order to be better governed, but to destroy the royal power; the cities wanted municipal privileges which would exempt them from the authority of those already diminished kings, and every social class wanted special laws, exemptions, and privileges by the dozens. At that time our country was only a couple of steps from realizing its juridicial ideal: that all Spaniards should carry in their pockets a legal document stating in clear, brief, and cogent terms: *This Spaniard is authorized to do whatever he damn well pleases.*[7]

An irritated Englishman whom I met in a hotel in Ronda said the same thing another way: "In this country every blessed beggar acts like a king!" The Spanish historian Rafael Altamira harshly criticizes this destructive individualism of his people. "The lack of solidarity in our national efforts," he says, "is due to two things: first, the fact that every Spanish government takes as its primary concern the undoing of every single thing that its predecessor supported; second, Spanish political parties have never been able to put aside doctrinal differences in order to cooperate and to collaborate for the national welfare."[55] The result of all this has been to produce a race which is politically inept and inorganic, despite its impressive artistic creativity.

Spanish humor merits a long chapter all to itself. It has a grotesque biting quality which often evokes no laughter in the American or Englishman. Jokes about death are common, and even in some of the common foods one encounters strange names like *huesos de santo* ("saint's bones"), which is a kind of sweet. The most popular drink in Spain today is called the *sangría*, or bloodletting, which looks exactly like its name. This is a reddish wine that is served at meals mixed with a bit of lemon juice, some ice, and perhaps a few other ingredients. Everyone who eats at the typical Spanish *tasca* or small café orders the sangría with his food.

One of the things about Spaniards that has always been amusing to me, and is not at all so to them, I feel certain, is the way they close in on you when you get into a warm conversation. The very moment the topic becomes hot your Spanish friend will either bombard you with head and voice or leap to his feet to get closer still until you begin to feel as if any minute he will be right on top of you. This is particularly unnerving if the two of you are standing. It is simply impossible for the Spaniard to carry on a real conversation unless his face is right beside or in front of yours, practically within a nose's reach. And if you have ever noticed two Spaniards walking down the street talking, they will almost invariably come to an abrupt halt when the subject becomes interesting; then they will turn and face each other squarely, and stand there waving their hands and shouting loud enough to be heard a block away. When the matter at hand has been disposed of they will calmly continue their stroll. Such strolls are one of the principal pastimes of Spanish life. The streets and plazas of Spain are filled with people, unless it is the hour of the siesta. There are innumerable tourists. The crowds of Andalusia are noisy and gay; in the north they are more restrained. Even the timbre of the voice changes from region to region, as does the intonation.

From the terrace of the beautiful Hostal in Santiago I see a busload of students strolling along the Plaza de España on their way to the cathedral, the Baroque façade of which is the most impressive example of its style in Spain. Half a dozen Galician women are walking along the streets carrying heavy loads on their heads, precariously balanced. They never touch these burdens with their hands, but their erect and graceful gait gives them a constant equilibrium. This accounts for the queenly grace of their manner of walking. The people are clean, but their clothes and especially their shoes are poor. An odor of olive oil and garlic cooking, a misty smell of mountain air, an acrid smoky fragrance, a faint aroma of distant incense from the cathedral, a scent of ancient, moldering wood—all these odors blend into one that is the aroma of Galicia. One can almost imagine that a smell of the sea is mingled with the rest for its salty scent does permeate so much of the province. The tiled roofs of the buildings are gray with age and smoke. Everywhere, in the tiles, on the rooftops, in the walls, in every tiny nook and cranny of the balconies are those little purple flowers, a fragile, waving bit of lace, the Galician heather.

One night in the chapel of the Hostal we heard a magnificent choral group of 110 voices composed of workers from El Ferrol. The concert did not begin, according to good Spanish custom, until eleven at night. They sang Handel, Mascagni, and North American spirituals equally well. I have never heard anywhere a finer choral group. The following night we heard another group from Pontevedra, and this time the men all wore dinner clothes while the women were dressed in white satin. These too sang beautifully. With its ancient religious musical tradition choral singing in Spain is certainly among the finest in Europe.

We walked down to the Cathedral of Santiago. Its exterior stones are crumbling from some strange disease, and in spots they have sprayed on a thick coat of paraffin in order to make the water slide off. Inside the cathedral is the magnificent *Pórtico de la Gloria*, one of the finest examples of Romanesque art in Europe. It was a part of the older cathedral, and dates from the twelfth century. The interior of the cathedral itself is somber, clammy, ornate, gray, filled with incense odors and trumpetlike organ sounds; to me it was almost terrifying. Certainly it was not lovely. At one spot in the interior walls is a heavy steel doorway behind which is the treasure of the cathedral. Once in every six years these doors are opened and the great wealth is displayed.

In another spot in the cathedral is a picture of *Santiago Matamoros, St. James, Killer of Moors.* The head of one of these unfortunate Moslems is rolling on the earth, in gory ugliness. When the king of Jordan recently visited the cathedral, this portion of the painting was carefully covered so as not to affront his majesty. In one of the smaller chapels there are figures of the Virgin and the Child Jesus, of Melchior and Gaspar, but Balthasar is missing, indicating hatred of the Moors. In yet a third place Balthasar is shown wearing dirty, ragged clothes, and his feet are bare.

The most famous item in the cathedral, of course, is a small silver casket in which are supposed to be mingled the bones of Saint James and two of his friends who were buried beside him. Not being certain as to which bones were the saint's someone placed all of them in the casket together. The actual skeletons are most probably those of some heretics of the early Visigothic era; the story about the vision of a star in the sky, and of voices telling that this was where Saint James himself was buried, was in the tradition of early Spanish religious beliefs, and the entire cult of Saint James, ardently fanned by the French monks of the order of Cluny, who were active in Spain in the crusade against the Moors, was a logical response to the earlier Christian heresies and to the fanatical Moslem blending of war and religion.

Outside on the narrow streets of Santiago again one hears the familiar noises. There is a clanking as of a blacksmith shop, but inside a man is beating out small silver-colored shells, emblems of Saint James, which are eagerly purchased by those who visit Santiago. The sound of sharp, staccato voices fills the air; one hears only the vowels, the clear perfect vowels of melodious Spanish. A mother shouts to her little son on his tricycle: "Don't go in the street, or the *coco* (the bogeyman) will get you!" A seller passing down the street cries out his wares. There is a sudden wild snatch of song from a maid scouring the tile floor in one of the houses. From an open doorway comes the sharp, sweet sound of the ever-present *gaita* or bagpipe, while the rhythm is being marked by someone else on the tambourine.

Another day we drove along the *rías bajas,* picturesque inlets from the sea, to Vigo. The roads were almost deserted. On the way we passed through a tiny village called Cesures, and there came back to my mind the refrain of an old Spanish folk tune which I had heard before in this area: *Viva la flor de Cesures . . .* Spanish folk songs are among the most beautiful in the world. Only Russia can possibly compare with Spain in the variety and beauty of her folk music. Oftentimes, the words too are of exceptional poetic loveliness:

> *De rosas y claveles*
> *y de alelíes,*
> *se te llena la boca*
> *cuando te ríes.*

> *La iglesia se ilumina*
> *cuando tú entras,*
> *y se llena de flores*
> *donde te sientas.*

As it would be impossible for me to translate these verses into acceptable poetic English, they must stand in the original. At the opposite pole of premeditated art, Spain also has flowered in the work of Picasso, Dali, Joan Miró, Juan Gris, and many other noteworthy artists of the twentieth century, whose towering individuality has literally overwhelmed modern painting.

From La Coruña we drove with some Galician friends to a fiesta in an old village near the port of El Ferrol. These friends could not do enough for us. Their generosity was overwhelming. The people in the city of El Ferrol were becoming a little impatient with the Americans at the naval depot there. These young fellows, far away from home, and untutored in the ways of Spanish life, made many a boorish mistake. One of the most unforgivable was for the visitor to stick his feet out against or upon some table or chair rung. Awkward lounging postures are not acceptable in a Spanish home. One American, however, had done yeoman duty to redeem the honor of his country. One day when there was a celebration in the city and the speakers had warmed up to their task, he asked if he might say a few words. He rose and announced dramatically that he loved Spain so much that he would gladly give his life in the public plaza for the people of Spain, if that were ever needed. The audience went wild with applause. After the event this particular American was a great hero in El Ferrol. The story was told to us with considerable admiration, many months later. It goes to show to what degree such a gesture will impress the Spanish mind. In the United States, I rather believe, such a man would be regarded as a huge show-off or as an arrant fool.

Galicia, Asturias, and the Basque provinces are mountainous, misty lands. We were told that there had not been a completely sunny day all summer, but the sun was generally out for a portion of the day. There was much rain, much overcast, and this accounts for the deep green color of the countryside. The Galicians characterize their four main towns with this saying: *Coruña se diverte, Pontevedra duerme, Vigo trabaja, Santiago reza.* ("Coruña has a good time, Pontevedra sleeps, Vigo works, and Santiago prays.") The Galician who leaves his homeland is always homesick with a nostalgia which he calls *morriña*, the love of his native province. In very few places on earth can be duplicated the greenery, the rounded mountains, the antiquity, the legendary Celtic quality that he finds in Galicia.

From Coruña we drove to Oviedo via Ribadeo, across the lovely bay from Castropol. Oviedo was clearly marked by the civil war, perhaps more than any other large town in Spain. Even the cathedral had been heavily bombarded. In Oviedo too the anomalies of Spain hit us in the face, the strange paradoxes according to which Spanish custom has evolved. For example, the waiters in the hotel were dressed in dinner clothes, and served the rolls with tongs, never touching them with their hands. But these same rolls we saw in the bakery windows unwrapped, and covered with flies. Spanish table manners are also odd; the Spaniard will daintily cut up his fruit and eat it piece by piece, and he regards the American who picks up his fruit as very uncouth. But he will stuff his mouth with bread so that he can hardly chew, carrying on a hearty conversation all the while. The waiters, despite their fine clothes, also had dirty fingernails, but every glass on the table shone like a diamond. The waste of labor is something frightful. One morning in the hotel I saw five maids all down on their knees scrubbing the marble floor with big hand mops. This was sometimes done twice a day.

The Spanish philosophy is to enjoy the present moment and shut out tomorrow. *Cojamos la flor del instante.* Let us gather rosebuds while we may. But the civil war has left its legacy of insecurity and fear that is sharpened by the whole uncertain fabric of Spanish history. As in Russia, the civil war was followed by a period of repression, but unlike Russia the period of repression in Spain was followed by another chance for freedom. The war itself is seldom mentioned today, partly because of that typical Spanish belief that if a thing is not mentioned it does not exist. It is interesting to note that Spain and Russia do have several basic features in common. They are the two Continental countries that are marginal to Europe. Their geographic position on the periphery places them in that position, but more important still is their social makeup, which for centuries has consisted mainly of large masses of backward, uneducated peasants under the domination of the big land-owners, who constitute a small aristocracy. In recent years millions of these peasants have become impoverished city workers. Such a society is ready-made for a communist (or a fascist) takeover in any time of great stress, for it lacks cohesion and is impatient and unready before the demands of self-government.

The foreigner who enters Spain with heart and mind open begins immediately to enjoy the Spanish sun and the Spanish joy of living that transcends economic insecurity. The foreigner can accept these things freely because he feels no sense of responsibility about his en-joyment. This feeling may last for several months, but at last he begins to sense the tremendous price that Spaniards have paid for their deli-cious anarchy, and then the visitor is saddened. He feels the gnaw of frustration, the sharp threat of despair. Then he too begins to realize that the Spanish *alegría* is always permeated with a deep sadness, the natural outgrowth of *la lucha por la vida*, the struggle for life. The traveler may repeat to himself that it is not his responsibility, that it is not his country, that these are not his people, and that he had nothing to do with bringing into being the restless enigma that is Spain. Yet all the while he will feel sad down deep inside, and he will realize at last that even the songs and dances of Spain are all sad songs. There is nothing really gay or picturesque about Spain when one sees it long enough to penetrate the mask. There is no such thing as "romantic" Spain, which is the superficial reaction of a few visitors who never get to know either the land or its people.

The finest Spanish dancers are not young slips of girls exposing their sexy bodies; they are ripe and full matrons in the deep grip of sorrow. The body is carefully hidden; the emotion alone is enough. Spain is a tragic land, its songs are sad songs, and its dances are tragic dances. They are all suffused with a sense of loss and separation, a sense of tragedy and of imminent doom. One moment man is alive, the next he is several scattered fragments of the universe. His being is but a temporary union of these fragments. It is the flight of a bird through a room.

Let the Spaniards take care of their own country, the traveler says, but inside he does feel, I must admit, somewhat like that odd American in Galicia who said that he was willing to give his life in the public plaza for the people of Spain. Perhaps he would never have done so in reality, but the fact that he did at one moment in time *feel* like making such a sacrifice—this was sufficient.

The Spaniard tries zealously to avoid it, but he is a true existentialist. Life begins with existence. Man is responsible for his actions. Through these actions he molds his life and his destiny as an architect forms a building. Little by little he creates his own universe. It has its own laws, its own system of beauty, its own ideals. No other man lives in a private universe which is exactly like his own. Personal values are the only values. The person is final, absolute, invulnerable, except to death. On a slab in the floor of the Cathedral of Toledo which marks the grave of an ancient archbishop of the church are these sobering words: *Aquí yace polvo, ceniza, nada.* ("Here lie dust, ashes, nothing.") But before that final day comes may we not savor the flight of that bird on the wing?

The Spaniard longs to create and to capture his own immortality in imperishable art. The archpriest of Hita put himself into his famous *Book of Good Love*, so that he would never wholly die. The sculptor Mateo made a statue of himself and placed it behind his beautiful *Pórtico de la Gloria* in the old cathedral in Santiago for the same reason. El Greco and Velázquez painted their own faces and figures in their canvasses so that they too might live on in art. Unamuno and Azorín and many other contemporary writers have made themselves characters in their own literary works in search of this same survival. Spain has never given up its belief in the resurrection of the body.

The Spanish poet, Gabriel Celaya, referring to the last Franco years, wrote: "There is little joy left in Spain, but as you see, we hope." The Spaniard has always created a kind of philosophy out of the things that he lacks. The Golden Age philosopher Gracián, echoes the words of Celaya: "The first lesson of experience is to keep hope alive but never satisfied. Find consolation in everything. For even the worthless is everlasting. . . . Leave hunger unsated. It is desire that is the measure of value." Each man bears within himself the entire cosmos of the human condition. He is a true child of the universe, no less than the trees and the stars.

Not long ago as I was walking along one of the narrowest and poorest streets of Toledo with a group from that city, a bright young man with us, uneasy at the drab surroundings, exclaimed: "Our forefathers did not leave us much wealth or a good government, but they left us an abundance of proverbs!" Then he quoted one of these proverbs that covered the case in point, *Paciencia y barajar*, "Patience, and shuffle the cards!" Poor Spain will have to do a lot of reshuffling before this unpredictable game is finished.

16

FRANCO'S LEGACY: ORDER AND PROGRESS

Let the anvils ring, and the bells be silent.

Antonio Machado

THE ECONOMIC MIRACLE

Since 1960 Spain has been catapulted into the twentieth century. Spaniards have gotten off the donkey and onto wheels. A tremendous building boom has given the country a new face, industry and business have expanded at a rapid rate, there is a new network of highways linking the major cities and bringing countless smaller communities into the orbit of the national life, medical care for the masses has taken a great leap forward, and income has risen to the highest point in the nation's history. This material progress is Franco's one solid achievement.

Only a few years ago hundreds of Spanish villages were isolated without roads, power, or water. Large-scale industry did not exist. Labor was largely unskilled and productivity per man-hour was incredibly low. Exploitation by employers, low salaries, no accident protection, abuse of child labor, and the apprentice system of training were the rule. There was a huge rural class dependent on agriculture with almost no benefits or protection against unemployment, illness, or old age. Maids in the south worked twelve to fourteen hours a day in exchange for meager food, hand-me-down clothing, and no salary, while their husbands and children worked three months out of the year as migrant laborers, for twenty to thirty pesetas per day, less than half a dollar in U.S. currency of that time.

The church had a complete monopoly on education; less than 2 percent of the population went to college, where the curricula were antiquated, classist, and oriented toward the traditional professions. The tax system was indirect, oppressive, and, like everything else in the country, was structured to favor the upper class. Politically, people on the losing side in the civil war did not exist, could not get jobs, and their widows had no legal status. Applicants for job openings were required to present baptismal certificates, and civil marriage licenses had to be accompanied by proof of marriage in the church. Blue Falangist shirts and right-wing lapel pins were worn proudly. These abject conditions drove hundreds of thousands of young Spanish workers out of the rural areas into the cities and out of Spain into the more prosperous northern European countries where labor was in short supply.

This is a far cry from the situation at the end of the Franco period. Per capita income, which was a mere $317 in 1960, exceeded $1,500 in 1975. In Spain today, because of this progress under Franco, people are enjoying the greatest material prosperity the country has ever known; television sets and home appliances, electric refrigerators, washing machines, and the like, far beyond the reach of the average Spanish family a few years ago, are now commonplace. Nearly all middle-class and many working-class families own a car, have a telephone; and social security benefits are available to a large segment of the population. The Spaniards themselves refer to this impressive economic turnabout as "the miracle." But it is no miracle at all. While the government did much to prepare the ground for the recent expansion, the hard work and sacrifice of the people themselves deserve even greater credit. This alone, however, would not have been enough to turn the tide. Without tourism (the country's number one industry), without the large sums of money sent home by Spaniards working in other European countries, and without billions in foreign aid, the so-called miracle could never have happened.

The price for turning an almost medieval economy and political setup into a twentieth-century consumer society is still being paid by *pluriempleo* (moonlighting), many hours of overtime at the factories, and humiliating treatment of "guest" Spanish workers in their host countries in northern Europe. Yet, in contrast to 1960, the average Spaniard now lives, dresses, and eats better than ever before; he receives good medical care; and he enjoys a month's vacation with pay at some overcrowded seashore resort.

Under Franco, government and business cooperated to improve productivity. Foreign experts were called in to work with teams of Spaniards in industry, business, and education, and thousands of intelligent young Spaniards went abroad to pursue advanced studies in economics, sociology, science, and education. The net result of this produced a teamwork attitude and mentality hitherto unknown in Spain.

Because of its late start Spanish industry benefited from the experience of other countries, and introduced up-to-date techniques of production and modern machinery. Courses in marketing, advertising, and public relations were organized to accelerate sales and distribution, and dollar reserves began to pile up as trade expanded and preferential agreements were reached with Common Market countries. The government guided investment by foreign companies into key areas and industries, enticing them with low taxes and cheap labor. These companies also introduced management and executive training programs, thus greatly increasing the efficiency in the top echelons of business.

Dams were built at dozens of strategic points, so both hydroelectric power and irrigation were spectacularly increased. Thermonuclear projects were also set up. The Prince (heir apparent) and the Minister of Public Works were always inaugurating some new dam or reservoir. Conservation and reforestation measures helped to reclaim land destroyed by sheep-grazing or the civil war, and the greening of the countryside was widely evident. General Franco's preoccupation with bringing water to formerly sterile and arid lands caused many Spaniards to refer to him jocularly as "Froggy Franco."

Air transportation was expanded and modernized; passenger transportation and comfort on the railways were also improved. Hundreds of miles of track were electrified. The slow, third-class wooden-chaired coaches where peasants once kindly shared their conversation and tortillas with you have been replaced by sleek express trains known as *Tafs* and *Talgos*.

The Franco government undeniably did a great deal for the worker, particularly in social legislation and higher salaries. Social security was extended to cover most areas of labor, in addition to old age, accident and health insurance, retirement, maternity and family benefits, free medical care and discounts on medicines—all of which brought Spain closer to a socialized state than anyone in the government (and many conservative Spanish citizens) would be willing to admit. The state also subsidized low-cost housing, set up technical schools, organized co-operatives, encouraged crafts, built vacation centers in the mountains and at the seashore, organized sports, recreation, and cultural progr.·ms. Government *sindicatos* (labor unions) were in control of most of these educational and cultural activities.

People poured from the countryside into the cities where salaries were higher. Madrid's population grew to over three million, and Barcelona, Valencia, Bilbao, and Seville also expanded rapidly. Modern luxury chalets were put up in many elegant suburbs. Spain also built some of the most luxurious sport complexes and yacht harbors on the Mediterranean. Spanish industry became more competitive in the European market, and tourists arrived by the millions. The old image of Spain as an exotic combination of the picturesque, flamenco, bullfights, and tertulias, and an economy based on wine, olives, oranges, and cheap labor exports began to disappear, although it still probably attracts many tourists, in combination with the Spanish sun and supposedly cheaper prices, which, alas, are not so much cheaper any longer.

Madrid, hub of this new economic ongoing wheel, changed from a traditionally bureaucratic capital to an industrialized one. This also brought several transformations in city planning and building. The "building boom" was a phenomenon parallel to the commercial and tourist industries. Everywhere in Spain construction changed the appearance of the countryside, from the seashore of Alicante and Valencia, where everyone from Madrid who could afford it bought an apartment for use one month out of every year, to the high-rise, monotonous buildings with a few pots of geraniums on the road to the Madrid airport, to the changing skylines of provincial capitals like Plasencia, Cáceres, and Orense.

After the civil war Madrid had plenty of room to expand and plan one of the most modern cities in Europe, but nothing was done to bring this about. Madrid is now near the saturation point, thanks to gross errors in city planning, flagrant abuse of zoning laws, rampant speculation in real estate, few green belts, and pollution of every type. Much of this is due to a lack of building codes and to the endless rows of ugly apartment houses built in the last few years. In Madrid today apartment hunting is probably the next most popular sport after filling out the soccer combinations. Furthermore, Madrid proper has not actually increased in area, although it has tripled in population. *Madrileños* simply changed their *barrios* (areas) of residence or moved to newer apartments.

The tremendous immigration from rural areas due to industry was absorbed by the surrounding dormitory towns and so-called industrial parks of satellite cities. Some of these towns were incorporated into Madrid proper, but a few statistics will indicate how the outlying towns have grown: Alcorcón, 400 percent in the last few years; Alcobendas and Getafe, 500 percent; and Laganés, 700 percent. Many other "decongestion points," like the sleepy university town of Alcalá de Henares, have tripled their populations because of the government plan to relocate industry. In the same area, Torrejón and Guadalajara got assembly plants and chemical factories. Many new apartments were built, and Alcalá acquired an efficient train service.

On the other side of Madrid, on the road to Toledo, a similar growth took place in Mostoles and Alcorcón, where they have tried to relocate the growing furniture industry. A comparable move outside the city to the north was made by wealthy and upper-middle-class families who created American-style suburbs with private homes, swimming pools, and tennis courts. This also necessitated the building of three additional campuses of the University of Madrid in these areas.

Traffic jams, of course, became common, but no worse than in other European cities. There was a lack of parks for children to play in. Pollution had a disastrous effect on valuable paintings in the Prado, including *Las Meninas* (maids in waiting), the masterpiece of Velázquez, as the museum is in one of the areas with the highest smog concentration in the city. Work was completed on a filtering and air purification plant to try to prevent some of the erosion and mold of canvases. One of the few bright spots is that Madrid (following the lead of Paris and London) had its face washed. The façades of important public buildings and plazas, such as the Puerta de Sol and the Puerta de Alcalá, were cleaned and restored.

Important social changes accompanied the industrial revolution, some of which began to break down the rigid class barriers. With the population shift from rural to urban areas the large proletariat became more aware of its potential, and the government made every effort to appease these workers in order to avoid a political confrontation. A large number of the old proletariat moved over into the rapidly growing middle class.

Class distinctions could not withstand these rapid changes. The key factors for success became education and affluence rather than pedigree, profession, or hereditary factors. People could rise from humble birth to influential positions in politics, education, or industry through the army, the church, Opus Dei, political loyalty, good recommendations, *oposiciones* (government board examinations) and, on increasing occasions, simply through their own will and talents.

Like the proletariat, the middle class also moved up the economic ladder. It became more fluid with more capital and more investments. The liberal professional, intellectual, and artistic elements of the Franco years tended to come from this sector, but they were still very much in the minority compared with the northern European countries. Spanish society remained traditional in its social patterns, although among the young people attitudes began to change in regard to women, marriage, themselves, familial authority, dating. Spaniards eagerly adopted the outward manifestations of progress and sophistication such as fads in dress, music, and hairstyles, albeit with a time lag, but they remained conservative in family relationships and religion no matter what their class status until after Franco's death in 1975.

There emerged a very powerful upper middle class, which included executives, managers, and technocrats, The oligarchy of the new technocracy largely merged with or replaced the old aristocracy. These technocrats, together with the industrialists and bank executives, formed the new oligarchy characterized by a conservative ideology and a neoliberal economic policy. They tended to invest in "solid" sectors such as real estate and art speculation, causing disproportionate economic reactions in these areas. Then they began to play the stock market the same way the rest of the Spaniards play the soccer pool.

A curious parenthesis to the rise of the middle class was the rise in another area—dogs. The Dalmatian and German Shepherd populations increased in proportion to affluence, replacing the mangy greyhound and lowly parakeet in a society not known for humane animal treatment. A "Curb Your Dog" campaign is desperately needed in Spain today.

Visitors from the United States frequently remarked that Spanish cities were safer than those back home while Franco was in control. One could walk down Spanish streets at any hour of the day or night without fear of being mugged, robbed, raped, threatened, or knifed. Probably the greatest nuisance at night in Spain was not being able to find the local *sereno* to let you into your apartment house. The sereno was the neighborhood night watchman with the keys to the ponderous front doors of the surrounding residences. He is the survival of an old Spanish custom that still prevails long after its necessity has passed.

More subtle changes took place at the deeper psychological level. Spaniards slowly but surely altered the way they perceived themselves in relation to the outside world as the result of education, foreign travel, the emigration of workers, tourism, radio, television. There were also changes of view in relation to Spain's own traditional institutions. Class mobility, emigration to the city, and more education all slowly affected standards of morality and the entire Spanish value system.

Spain is still an undeveloped country, but Spaniards prefer to view themselves as "in rapid process of development." They are proud of "having opened the country up" to outside influences, to joining the rest of Europe in the twentieth century. The old xenophobia is dying a natural death. Many of the problems of Spain such as inflation and industrial, labor, and agricultural difficulties are also common to the "developed countries." But under Franco, Spain's different political structure did not allow for the usual mechanisms and escape hatches of the more advanced industrial countries.

In every major institution—politics, church, military, education, labor, society—there were signs of mobility, change, and splits in attitude. In many of these areas there was a generation gap between the dominating conservative caste of men over sixty who had fought in the civil war, and the younger, more liberal factions of postwar vintage, who now control the country. One of the most important tasks for the future is to complete this transition from one generation to another in a peaceful manner.

The Tourist Industry

Although it involves several sectors, tourism may be discussed as Spain's major industry since it has long accounted for more than 10 percent of the national income and is probably the most important single influence on the country's economic policy. Franco realized the crucial importance of tourism for Spain and made every effort to encourage it. The second development plan begun in 1968 (somewhat later than expected because of the dollar devaluation in 1967) concentrated on attracting and catering to tourists. The third development plan emphasized "quality rather than quantity" in tourism, and attempted to remedy the problems that arose out of the huge influx of tourists.

The importance of this industry in Spain's balance of payments is crucial. Tourism has also had an effect on the geographic distribution of the national income. Areas of traditional migration, such as the southern Mediterranean and Balearic Islands, absorbed some 400,000 workers from agriculture into jobs created by the industry between 1960 and 1975. The Canary Islands were practically "rediscovered" through tourism.

Between 1960 and the end of the Franco regime in 1975 the number of foreign tourists entering Spain rose from 4 million to 32 million annually. They poured billions of dollars into the Spanish economy. In addition to foreign tourism, another positive aspect was that Spaniards with longer, paid vacations began to explore their own country. Increased air traffic created the need for more and better located airports to handle this type of tourism. Broad new highways along the Mediterranean, the Basque coast, and from Irún through Madrid to Málaga helped ease the influx of tourism from the rest of Europe. The number of *paradores* and *albergues* tripled within a few years. Madrid put up several new moderate and first-class hotels, and off-season tourism in the form of conventions (Madrid, Torremolinos, Barcelona) made Spain Europe's most popular convention center.

But there were a few holes in this attractive superstructure. The increase to 32 million tourists was beyond all past estimates. There was an obvious decline in the quality of hotel service, but viewed in the light of the huge influx, it became impossible to control the quality. According to the Minister of Information and Tourism, that is the next stage to work on. Until a few years ago the Ministerio used to inspect hotels quite thoroughly and control the categories, but with the increase in the number of hotels (and probably bribes) it soon became impossible to make a careful check.

The average tourist actually spends very little in Spain, something like $200 per person. Most tourists are what Spaniards call *turistas de pan y uvas* (bread and grapes tourists), meaning they spend money on the barest essentials in return for a place in the sun. The French and most students are of this type; they are the smallest spenders and the biggest invaders. In addition, Spaniards themselves have flocked to the beaches. Some beaches are as crowded as Coney Island. Half the population of Madrid goes to Benidorm for the summer to satisfy a masochistic sense of claustrophobia.

Tourism on the northern and Galician coasts is primarily Spanish, but except for sections of the Basque coast and Santander, people do not go to the north because of the uncertainty of the weather. Tourism in the Canaries, however, is practically a year-round business, and to a certain extent this is true of Mallorca. Americans who have been to the Canaries or Mallorca remark that they never hear Spanish there. Some good-humored cafe owners on the Mediterranean have signs saying *SE HABLA ESPAÑOL*. In places like Tenerife, the hotel owners, clerks, and waiters are mostly foreigners, particularly Germans, and only the maids are Spanish. This is ironic in an area of very high unemployment.

It is doubtful how much the Spanish working class has benefited from the increase in tourism. Even the famous *paradores* and *albergues* are financed through concessions from food to furniture through private concerns. Approximately 98 percent of tourism is financed by private initiative. In this respect, it is the powerful construction and real estate complexes that have profited.

The biggest offenders in this category are the tour operators, Spanish and foreign. This is the "if-it's-Tuesday-this-must-be-Belgium" category. Package tours, charter flights, particularly from America, tend to benefit the tour operator and the hotel owner. Some Madrid hotels reserve all their rooms for these tours, and when one goes to make a reservation for a single, without meals, they say they have nothing, even though half the hotel may be empty. Often it is easier to get a reservation from the United States than from Madrid. Besides, tour groups assume that everything, including tips, is included, and tend to leave little for the hotel employees themselves.

The tour operator tends to cut corners. There are, for example, tours of Toledo that last two hours. Some say "a half day tour of Madrid" and no longer include the Prado or the Royal Palace. Tourists are promised "de luxe hotels" but are not told that there are several categories of de luxe hotels that vary widely in quality. First-class hotels in Spain were authorized to increase prices, supposedly to improve the quality of service, but what really happened was that the prices became sky high and the service remained mediocre.

The Hungarian, Rumanian, and Polish airlines opened offices in Madrid and there were soon weekly flights to these countries, which Spaniards can visit with few restrictions. I have seen many groups of Russians, Hungarians, and Yugoslavs in Andalusia and Toledo. Besides this new element of tourism there is a small, very wealthy group that is also attracted to Spain, without benefiting the average Spaniard. These people are found at places like the Sotogrande real estate development near Marbella, on the southern coast, the most luxurious residential complex and golf course in Europe. It is owned by an American. Spiro Agnew, former vice-president of the United States, stayed here for two days on his three-day tour of Spain; his first day was spent at the annual *18 de julio* victory banquet at La Granja.

Spain has much more to offer than its beaches and sun. Until now these other aspects have not been exploited because "cultural tourism" is not practiced by most foreigners or Spaniards. They do not explore the variety and beauty of Spain's scenery or architecture. The country's folklore and traditional fiestas have been corrupted by the promotion of *fiestas de interés turístico* which turn simple, authentic celebrations into spectacles worthy of Cecil B. de Mille. One wonders if all the preparation of the natives is worth a couple of days of tourist invasion, with the exception of the Semana Santa, the Feria, and Pamplona.

Another form of exploitation that made great headway in the final Franco years was real estate speculation and irresponsible and unaesthetic planning, both Spanish and foreign. Ugly cement towers began to obscure the coastline because there were no building codes or somebody had bribed the local mayor in order to build a twenty-story apartment building. A recent sad example of this are the massive buildings in the beautiful Peñiscola area. The architect here designed and built a complex of high-rise apartments right on the beach, reminiscent of the medieval walls of Avila. He completely ignored the two-story apartments and small farms back of this complex. Another powerful construction company put up massive complexes of apartments in Torremolinos, hoping to sell them, in violation of building codes forbidding apartments in that area. But there was no law forbidding hotels there, so the company simply rented these unsightly buildings to foreign tours as hotels in order to get around the law.

Labor became an important controversial area prior to Franco's death. Many people migrated to the coasts and the islands as electricians, plumbers, and skilled laborers, causing a severe shortage in the rest of Spain. However, the building boom eventually slackened and this put many people out of work. Others migrated from agriculture to the coast to escape exploitation and low salaries, but their situation was not greatly improved by this. For them tourism is also seasonal, and thus a form of migrant labor. They work for long hours, have to sign "blank contracts," and receive few tips from tour groups. They get little support from the hotel syndicates, which are allied with the hotel owners.

Finally, there was the tragic consequence of pollution of almost 50 percent of Spain's beaches and the disruption of the ecosystem in the Coto de Donana. American oil company exploration off the coast of

Tarragona blackened nearby beaches, and the submarine base at Rota ruined beaches in that area because of oil spills, causing luxury hotels to be deserted.

Tourism is probably now close to its peak capacity, but the conditions described cannot persist if Spain is to continue to derive sizable benefit from this source of income.

The Economy

Industry (general). The Franco government channeled investment and foreign capital into several key areas such as auto-assembly plants, electronics, petrochemical complexes, steel, utilities, metallurgy, construction, air transport, and tourism. Spain soon ranked fourth in shipbuilding in the world, sixteenth in steel production, tenth in fishing, undoubtedly first in tourism. In agriculture, the country ranks in the top four in wine, oranges, olive oil, and cork. Spain is also in the first ten in the world in automobile export and high in the lesser industries of shoe manufacturing, textiles, and furniture.

Dollar reserves. Tourism, returns from emigrants, and foreign investment built up Spain's dollar reserves and helped the balance of payments. These three sources of income turned Spain's trade deficit of $400 million into a surplus of nearly $1 billion. Economists advised that these reserves be put to use in creating new jobs, new industries, and eliminating unemployment, but this was not done.

Liberalization. As a part of her policy to the world, Spain eased up on protective policies and restrictions on imports. Tariffs were lowered, and the government authorized more investment of Spanish companies abroad, particularly Africa and Latin America. Spain began to export much of its automobile production to Latin America, as well as thousands of technical publications. Hispanoil got a contract for exploration in the Algerian Sahara and gave technical assistance to oil companies in Saudi Arabia in exchange for a few barrels to combat gasoline prices that are among the highest in Europe. Private companies invested in a luxury hotel complex in Mauritania, which provoked loud protests from people in the waning fishing and tourist industries in Tenerife. Spanish companies financed irrigation projects in Morocco and in Paraguay, which also brought protest from sectors who feel that this sort of investment should be made within the country.

The stock market. Another sign of change in the Spanish economy was the spurt in stock market speculation, previously reserved for a select circle of *entendidos* (those in the know). Until near the end of the Franco regime, a lack of certainty about the government inhibited investment and speculation; people tended to invest in real estate rather than industry, but in the 1970s more middle-class people began to play the stock market, in addition to investing in more solid forms of returns such as property. The radio regularly gave stock market reports in daily newscasts right after the sports commentaries. Franco's economists took the stock market as a sign of middle-class confidence in the stability, peace, and prosperity of the regime.

Investment-Finance

Investment is of three types in Spain: (1) government, (2) foreign, (3) private (mainly banking). Under Franco about 60 percent of the capital in industry was controlled by government investment by way of the INI (Instituto Nacional de Industria). Much of the capital in steel, shipbuilding, and power (hydroelectric) was controlled by this state organism. Many Spaniards felt that the government should take over the financing of more public services such as electricity and gas, gasoline, and highway construction, which in Spain were in the hands of private banks and Opus capital. But this goes back to fiscal reform. In many European countries these sectors are nationalized. Iberia, Spain's airline, was nationalized in this respect. The Spanish railway network, RENFE, was also nationalized, but it lost money continually and its commercial transport section still needs to be modernized. New highways were built and planned in an effort to break Spain's traditional radial-hub system, but what the public did not realize was that many of them were toll roads which would benefit the private companies who built them and not the country as a whole.

Foreign investment accounted for about 15 percent of the total, but again it is a question of proportion. Of the twenty-five major industrial complexes in Spain in 1975, only two were completely Spanish-owned (Seat and Altos Hornos de Vizcaya). The rest, particularly automotive and petrochemical industries, were almost entirely foreign-controlled (Firestone, General Electric, Renault, Chrysler, Nestlé, Michelin, Pirelli, for example). Industries like the pharmaceutical and cosmetic sectors were entirely foreign. Ford constructed a plant at Sagunto, Valencia, among the orange groves and in the shadow of the ancient Roman theater. This caused pollution of one of the prettiest stretches of Spanish coastline, but it is near the port of Valencia and provided work for those unemployed in the waning citrus industry. General

Motors reacted soon after Ford announced its plans, and built a plant in Seville. Another area of investment controlled for years only by IBM was computers. But Dutch, French, and Japanese companies were fighting one another for rights to expand their activities in this area, since they recognized the tremendous potential of computers as an important factor in Spain's economic development.

So far the Japanese have cracked the barrier of European and American companies only in watches, cameras, transistors, and television, but they now are widening their offensive. The head of Mitsubishi in Madrid recently declared that Spain "could be our springboard for the whole Mediterranean area, including Africa." The Japanese, incidentally, have cut into Spain's guitar-making monopoly and are fascinated by flamenco. Young Japanese have invaded the taverns of Andalusia eager to master the mysteries of flamenco accompaniment. One Japanese *bailaor* (flamenco dancer) was the sensation of Málaga in the 1970s.

Private investment was a great incognito as the Franco period neared its end. Much of the capital invested in industry was in the hands of private banks, some controlled by the Opus. These people were backed by wealthy industrialists, the aristocracy, and large landowners, and together they formed an oligarchy supported by the state and the government labor unions. Their policies were economic "liberalism" and conservative, if not reactionary ideology, which caused growing tensions among other sectors of society. These groups invested in construction and real estate (*inmobiliarias*), causing uncontrolled speculation in these areas.

Since 1940, for example, all the major construction contracts, state or otherwise, were controlled by four companies: Huarte, Agroman, Dyc, Entrecanales. They got away with flagrant zoning violations by bribing local officials, and hindered rational city planning in Madrid. Often they combined to control several interests of monopolies. There were few opportunities for independent investment or "middle-sized" companies. There were either very large corporations with combined interests or very small "cottage" industries such as shoe manufacturing and furniture making.

In conclusion, the demographic shift and change from agriculture to industry caused the concentration of population and capital in three main areas of Spain: Madrid, Barcelona, Bilbao. There was also a fantastic building boom along the eastern and southern coasts to attract tourists. All of these things served to reinforce the ruling oligarchy of the upper classes while they created friction and potential political and social unrest among the lower classes. Future development plans, legal reforms, labor legislation, and tax reforms—all have been promised by the government—should help to alleviate some of the problems in this sector of the economy.

Salaries, Prices, Inflation

The situation of the average worker was improved by increased social security benefits for all classes, a higher minimum daily wage including farm workers, a plan for free education up to the age of fourteen, bonus payments, incentives, loans, and other advantages. But there were three problems: (1) Where was all the money coming from to support this move toward socialization? (2) the rise in salaries brought a corresponding rise in prices, making Spain's inflation rate one of the highest in Europe (examples: the Seat automobile works gave its workers a substantial increase in salary and promptly raised the prices on all models of its cars); (3) this apparent prosperity of the average worker was not owing to a mere raise in the basic salary but was won at the cost of moonlighting, overtime, and sacrifices within the family.

Figures on salaries in Spain seldom represent actual earnings because there is almost always a discrepancy between the base salary for the job and the amount of money received. Social security and income taxes are calculated on the base salary, but the total or real salary must be calculated by taking into account fourteen or fifteen paychecks (not just twelve), bonuses, incentives of various kinds, profit sharing, size of family, overtime, and other items. In some kinds of work this additional income represents a 50 percent addition to the base salary, and this sum is not subject to the social security tax, which is 38 percent of the base salary. The employer usually pays 30 percent of that social security tax, the worker 8 percent, but in some cases the employer pays the entire 38 percent. Social security is an unrenounceable right in Spanish labor law and is now being enforced more strictly than in the past, when there was widespread use of the surreptitious "envelope" that workers often received containing unreported extra cash, thus constituting a portion of their salary on which social security was not paid. There is now a heavy fine for this sort of thing.

It is in the area of building that Spain went mad during the final decade of Franco's regime. Not only was the industrial triangle of Madrid, Barcelona, and Bilbao sprouting and mushrooming both upward and in all directions with new buildings, but the southern and eastern coasts became congested with overbuilding and hordes of foreigners. Speculation was rampant, and little was done to collect taxes from the huge real estate developers who capitalized on the tourist boom. Spain did, however, construct three million new dwellings within a twelve-year period, and crowded living conditions were greatly relieved.

Twenty years ago on the third-class trains in Spain people talked mostly about food. Even when the civil war was mentioned they recalled the terrible hunger during and after the war rather than the atrocities. Housewives are still preoccupied with the prices of food, but hunger is no longer an obsession. On today's trains the conversation revolves around the prices of apartments, where to spend the next vacation (or where the last one was spent), how to pay for one's children's education, a larger car, and soccer. The bullfight is being displaced by the soccer pool, and the proverbial Spanish courtesy toward the foreigner has taken on an overtone of resentment, especially if the foreigner cannot speak Spanish.

Material progress is at best a tenuous thing. When it becomes most evident, and stands most in the public eye, is precisely when the people must be on guard and try to look beyond it. Nietzsche once remarked that what has not happened is, in the long run, more influential than what has happened. There is at least a modicum of truth in this statement. Franco's economic miracle solved some problems for Spain, but ignored many others, that were passed on to the government that followed him. They will not be an easy burden to bear, and it takes no genius to see that their resolution will require the patience of Job and the wisdom of Solomon. In addition to inflation, unemployment, and the rise in terrorism, outward and visible signs of weakening in Franco's tightly "structured state," there were serious basic flaws in the economy itself. All of these still remain.

PROBLEM AREAS

Agriculture

Most pressing agricultural needs

1. Train more young people, educate more specialists to introduce new techniques.

2. Raise salaries, shorten work days, extend social security, guarantee vacations.
3. Improve communications, modernize techniques and machinery.
4. Conservation, reforestation, protection of wildlife, creation of more national parks, reserves.
5. Land reform of both mini- and latifundios, controlled disappearance of small plots and redistribution of large cooperatively worked land areas.
6. Increase in amount of arable land through hydroelectric developments, dams, channeling.
7. Update organization of markets from grower to consumer.
8. Establish industrial infrastructures to balance agricultural sectors.

Given the nature of Spanish agriculture—land distribution in very large or small plots; irregular rainfall; insufficient irrigation; dry farming crops like wheat, cereals that have low returns; seasonal produce such as olives, grapes, oranges, cotton, cork, which are dependent on migrant labor; lack of mechanization; and cheap labor—the exodus to the city is logical. This exodus in itself is not harmful to the Spanish economy; in fact, it is beneficial if accompanied by intelligent land reform, modern technology, higher salaries and benefits for farm workers, and conservation techniques—in short, if the above-mentioned problems are solved. Agriculture has most certainly improved in the past two decades, but it is still at the tail end of the economic procession. The above-mentioned reforms are being accomplished slowly, but here, too, it is a problem of old structures versus new techniques. Agriculture is badly in need of trained, competent young people to transform this sector of Spanish life.

The total area of Spain is 123,400,000 acres, 8 percent totally unproductive; 51 percent forests and pastureland; 41 percent (62.6 million acres) arable land. This figure is comparable to other European countries but the results and yield are very different; 60 percent is taken up by dry farming. Only 6.3 million acres or 12.6 percent is irrigated land (mostly Ebro, Levante, Andalusia, Extremadura; to a lesser extent, Castilla). It is possible to double this figure with a good irrigation program.

Land reform: faces problems of large areas of land, not exploited by owners, left fallow, used for grazing, rented to sharecroppers, or worked by seasonal, migrant workers. In 1971 a land reform law (*Ley de Fincas y Comarcas Mejorables*) obligated large landowners to begin to cultivate some part of their estates or suffer expropriation. This law was not strictly enforced because the upper classes still had too much power, but there were a few bright spots. In Malpica del Tajo (in the province of Toledo near Talavera) the local duke and his marqués brother-in-law have turned their extensive lands into a model farm. They introduced new irrigation techniques, although they had to pull up some of the olive trees to do so, and have developed one of the largest experimental sheep ranches in Europe. At first, the local inhabitants of the moribund town were skeptical, but now they are enthusiastic and more prosperous. The increased water supply, green areas, and good hunting have in turn attracted people to build weekend homes in the town, so everyone profited.

In contrast, there are provinces like Cáceres, where 40 percent of the entire arable land is owned by 10 percent of the inhabitants. Those 10 percent are the people who own the elegant empty mansions in the picturesque old quarter of Cáceres, which is like a ghost town. They return to their homes only for weddings and baptisms. The descendants of the swineherd Pizarro are exploiting the class they originally came from, hence emigration to the cities and to foreign countries continues. This is now the land of conquistadores of what? Madrid? Germany?

The sociological and political consequences of this type of "latifundismo" are important, but the breaking up of these large areas into "minifundios" is not the solution. Those who still stay on the land want higher salaries, better living conditions, social security, better medical care, more schools, and a better future for their children. Those who emigrate seek the same benefits in the city. Absentee landowners are not only those who own latifundios but also those who have abandoned their own small plots into the hands of relatives or sharecroppers.

Another important land reform has taken place in the sector of minifundios in the north and in the south under the Institute of Agrarian Reform and Development. This program was carried out in conjunction with hydroelectric projects to increase the area and yield of arable land, and the government also encouraged more efficient farming, cooperatives, soil conservation, and attacks on plagues. This type of land reform has been successful in introducing more mechanization (2,000,000 tractors in 15 years) and in increasing the yield of crops with new fertilizers. Both of these factors are dependent on the type of terrain, rainfall, the extent of irrigation. Each year one sees more tractors and threshing machines in the fields, but in some areas, like parts of Avila, there are just too many stones and boulders, making this kind of machinery impractical.

Vast irrigation projects were undertaken and reservoirs and dams built. Noteworthy are the broad irrigated lands of Badajoz and Jaén, which were the first provinces to receive preferential treatment. Mérida is now the center of the special meat-packing industry, as the traditional end of *trashumancia* (southward migration of flocks in winter). Thanks to the channeling of the Tagus and the Guadiana, Badajoz was finally irrigated, but as yet Cáceres has done little about improving its lot (except in the section of La Vera and Plasencia). Other major hydroelectric systems such as the channeling of the Ebro through the dry Monegros in Aragon, and the Duero to irrigate the Tierra de Campos, have been effective, as well as the projects of the Sil and Mino in the north. Another important project is the so-called transvase Segura-Tajo, which involved changing a section of the course of the Tagus to flow toward the Mediterranean. This will irrigate much of the Levante region and, it is hoped, bring life to the desert areas of Murcia and Almería. This last province, by the way, has become the center of the "spaghetti western" movie industry, of a multilingual nature. This has partially taken care of a big labor problem, what to do with the gypsies. They now make more money than the locals by doubling as Indians in these films.

The minimum wage of agriculture and migrant workers has been raised several times and social security, medical care, and retirement benefits have all been extended to this area. Although the small farmer and produce grower are still exploited by the distributor, the network of regional produce markets, set up in connection with new cooperatives and supermarkets, may help them. The lobby of cattlemen and wholesalers, however, is very strong in government and keeps this aid at a bare minimum.

Another innovation in agriculture is the variation in crops, which in turn has had repercussions in exports. Spain was formerly known as an exporter of aperitifs, dessert wines, and oranges. Now Spaniards grow and process many more varieties of fruit, vegetables, olive oil, and grain, with a view toward acceptance into the Common Market.

Returning to more positive aspects of agricultural reform: in general, even in small towns, people now have more conveniences, better living conditions; television aerials proliferate; and the young people dress much better and all have transistor radios or record players which they play loudly for their *novias* (sweethearts) on the Sunday afternoon *paseo* (promenade). This year I revisited villages in hitherto backward areas such as Las Hurdes (Salamanca) and Las Alpujarras (Granada). Before, these regions were almost inaccessible; now they have paved roads built by the lumber companies or mining interests and enjoy many modern conveniences. Tourism, on one hand, has helped by promoting precisely those picturesque and backward aspects that the villagers would like to get rid of. On the other hand, there are places in the section called Las Hurdes of Leon, Zamora, and Orense which are still incredibly primitive and are the victims of mass emigration. If they had better roads and facilities, they, too, could offer tourist attractions in the area of skiing and mountain climbing.

Some of these villages located near the capitals of provinces have actually prospered. There is also a reverse phenomenon comparable to migration to the cities. Spaniards (middle-class) have longer weekends and cars to get out of the city. Everybody tries to escape at least on Sunday. The result in Madrid on Sunday night is a massive traffic jam worthy of the Los Angeles freeways. This increase of leisure time and affluence has led Spaniards to buy houses or new apartments, or fix up old farmhouses, in villages surrounding the capitals, thus putting new life into hitherto dormant villages away from the noise and maddening crowds of the city.

The government has also instituted conservation projects, particularly in reforestation and fish and game preserves. Sections of Soria, Segovia, and Jaén have been replanted with pine trees and eucalyptus. But some of these projects, particularly near the coast, were destroyed by forest fires. There were also fires in some of the most beautiful places in the provinces of Gerona, Málaga, and the mountain towns of Cádiz. This is a high price to pay for increased numbers of tourists. Conservation has also run into conflict with the most powerful sectors of real estate and touristic development, causing serious disruptions in the ecosystem.

In one area of agriculture there has been a social transformation, probably where it was least expected—in the Andalusian middle class. Although there is still traditional exploitation or disdain for the worker, the old image of the cacique and the Andalusian feudal oligarchy is changing. Technical and management schools have been created in Cordoba and there are agriculturally-based firms in Seville, Jerez, and Antequera. In contrast with the passive nobility, economically speaking, the new upper middle class with a more modern outlook has encouraged investment and introduced profitable forms of capitalism. The new Sevillian *burguesía*, the agricultural enterprises of Jerez, and the associations of workers in Cordoba are becoming more powerful politically and economically.

Tradition versus Innovation

Few Spaniards actually go back to their villages permanently once they have left. The atmosphere is too stifling. Many young people view their hometown as a place to return to for a few days for the local fiestas "of announced tourist interest," or for a family reunion or wedding, but not to live. This is the other side of the idealistic *patria chica* (small homeland) and regionalistic feeling that is still very strong in Spain. Also, the industrialization process has tended to erase barriers in the cities by forcing people from many regions into a situation of living together in unity in the face of labor conflicts. Few students actually want to go back to their villages to help improve the standard of living and initiate reforms directly. They are idealistic about instituting broad, Marxist-type revolutions, generally blaming the government (with some justification) for agrarian evils, but when it comes to helping in a specific way, they rarely put aside selfish interests.

No matter how many government reforms are introduced, it is difficult to erase the *señorito-campesino* (city boy-farmer boy) mentality. In this area it is hard for the educated city government representatives to help the pueblos without looking down on them, yet there have been some notable accomplishments. Ironically, they are from the "conservative" sectors of society: (1) the literacy campaign organized by Acción Católica, using students or other young people as volunteers to teach others to read and write in the villages during their summer vacations; (2) the army teaches boys from the villages to read and write, as well as giving instruction in vocational training; this is obligatory during the compulsory military service, and is usually carried out by army chaplains; (3) the *cátedras ambulantes* (traveling teachers) of the Sección Femenina (government subsidized) go into the remote villages in places like Soria to teach hygiene, child care, and give elementary lessons to villagers, both men and women. Despite the political ideals behind this, the young and middle-aged women who perform these tasks work heroically under adverse conditions, for little or no pay, and with a spirit of sacrifice unfortunately lacking in some of the more "liberal" sectors.

Undoubtedly the greatest problem in the field of agriculture is the lack of young people with sufficient training and ambition to transform the whole system and introduce radical changes in the structure. There are few incentives for young people to stay in their villages, although recent graduates in the teaching and medical professions are supposed to spend at least a year in a rural environment before they apply for positions in the city (students of the School of Medicine in Madrid went on strike because of this ruling).

Often boys who have completed their military service will not return to their villages. In village after village of Castile only old people are left. These people have worked their land the same way for centuries and find it difficult to understand the explanations given by the agricultural advisers sent to help them, to introduce new techniques, crop rotation, modern machinery, fertilizers, and so on. Television, of course, has done much to open the narrow world, relieve the sheer boredom of the villages, and provide incentives to go to the city.

More professional training centers are needed to give the towns new life. So far the Ministry of Agriculture has sent out a few special advisers to train farmers, but these people must also have the cooperation of traditional rural associations. This, in turn, will involve a redistribution of land which will make better use of the latifundios and combine the minifundios. It is hard to convince these people that larger areas of arable land are more profitable and can yield more and produce several crops per year.

Allied to this is the problem of "model towns," much touted by the government a few years ago. One reason for the apparent failure of these towns is that most of the young working population has migrated to the cities. Those who inhabit these towns are older people, attached to their own little plots of land which they have worked for centuries. These older folks were reluctant to be resettled. Furthermore, it is a question of aesthetics. In the older villages each house, no matter how poor, had its own individuality, while the model towns are neat, white, sterile, and lacking in personality. They are comparable to some of those beehive workers' housing developments in the city. They do, however, have more comforts and modern facilities.

There is a great number of these new model towns in La Mancha, Andalusia, and Extremadura. Most of them are located in flat areas with a large area for cultivation, irrigation, poultry, and livestock, and the most prominent building right in the middle of everything is the church with its bell tower. One such new town in La Mancha near

Valdepeñas was for a time a kind of showcase village, and tourists were encouraged to go there.

I passed several model towns in Extremadura that appeared run-down, perhaps because the inhabitants really didn't consider them their own. Many others have been abandoned, because nobody wants to live in them. One brand-new model town in the province of Zamora is largely uninhabited because the style of architecture was Andalusian and ill suited to the climate and temperament of the *zamoranos*.

In contrast to the new model towns, many older villages have also been completely abandoned, particularly in the provinces of Guadalajara, Teruel, and Soria. These ghost villages are almost empty today because their medieval reason for being, to act as defense outposts against the Moors, no longer exists, and few people can withstand the harsh climate. Other villages have been abandoned to make way for dams and reservoirs. The inhabitants migrate to that "neuralgic triangle" of three crowded cities, or to the coastal areas where they find jobs in construction or in the tourist industry. In some villages I saw only old people, who would ask me to take their picture to send to their children in Germany. In others, they threw stones at the camera, justifiably indignant that a foreigner would want to photograph their miserable conditions to exhibit abroad. At the same time, the government declares many of these villages "national monuments," but does nothing or little to improve lighting or sanitation, in the interests of preserving the picturesqueness. Some towns have simply torn down their "typical old dwellings" to make way for monotonous apartment houses, but others are trying to preserve them and at the same time construct new buildings in the same style in order to keep an architectural unity.

One inevitable literary loss in the change from a rural to industrial environment is the decreasing number of people who can recite the traditional *romances* or ballads. The old folk songs are also disappearing. Seldom does the visitor now hear singing as he walks the streets of the larger towns and cities. Spanish children, like Americans, recite television jingles rather than the old nursery rhymes. But a short walk through the main street of any village in Andalusia or the south in general will produce several varieties of fandangos, *fandanguillos, soleares*, and *flamencadas*. There is a revival of interest in all types of flamenco and even a *cátedra de flamenco* in the city of Jerez. There are numerous competitions, probably to attract the tourist trade. Unfortunately (or fortunately for the neighbors), signs in bars and taverns reading *Se prohibe cantar* (singing prohibited) are more frequent. I have never seen signs prohibiting television going full blast, or explosive motorcycles on quiet village streets, or the banging of the incredible number of pinball machines which Spaniards play incessantly.

The most serious problems in this general picture of agriculture are (1) a lack of industrial infrastructures to balance the agricultural sector and stop emigration to the cities, and (2) the lack of young trained people to introduce new techniques. For all its hectares of olives and wheat, Jaén has only a television assembly factory and one that makes zippers, while 7,000 people are out of work. The long-promised, badly needed highway from Gijón to Seville was finally approved, but the radial system of communications still predominates. In order to get from Badajoz to Alicante, one still has to go up to Madrid and then over to Alicante. What about material to build new roads and factories? A fine new Ashland Cement factory could have provided the material, but the factory owners simply closed the doors, shut down the factory, and fired the workers because of a labor dispute. A group of enterprising exploiters decided to set up a cellulose factory in Badajoz, but people protested loudly because of contamination—in July hundreds of dead fish were found floating in the Guadiana.

An attempt has been made by the government to train young people in agricultural sectors through the establishment of *Institutos laborales*, now called *Universidades laborales*. They were intended to educate lower- and lower-middle-class students, combining high school education with practical training in agriculture, animal husbandry, industry, mining, fishing, and administration. The seven-year course led to a diploma and entrance into the university at an engineering level. Although the enrollment and number of schools have increased, these schools have been criticized for several reasons: at first, they were badly located in Cordoba, Gijón, Tarragona, and Seville; many are costly (the new *Universidades laborales femeninas* in Cáceres and Zaragoza look like modern college campuses); because of the low ratio of graduates to total enrollment; and some of them ran into conflict with the Ministry of Education because of curricula and other interests. But perhaps the overriding reason that they have not been so successful is the traditional belief that real education with prestige is contained in the more humanistic *bachillerato*, not in courses that have to do with agriculture, which is considered to be a "low-class" subject. However, the technical schools similar to industrial high schools have fared better and have more popular appeal. Their function is to produce skilled workers for industry at a journeyman's and master's level. Their popularity lies partly in the fact that the skills they teach are useful in the city rather than in the country.

In sum, the lack of young skilled workers both in agriculture and industry is one of Spain's most urgent problems, as is education of all types in general. Add to that the present sad state of the university and you have a whole generation of "future leaders" who will not be properly prepared to assume their roles politically, socially, or economically.

One astute anthropologist who made a recent study of Spanish agriculture concluded as followed: "The civil war ended plans for extensive land reform as well as government and workers' movements toward collective land use. Tourist development, rather than land reform, is the prime concern of the government."[79]

The same observer then adds:

Rather than practice internal reform and work the lands, the government and the landowners have found it more expedient to sell portions of their patrimony to outsiders—to foreign investors and to tourists. The coast of Spain is owned by German, French, Swedish, Dutch, Belgian, and American companies and individuals. An advertisement in the *International Herald Tribune* advises its readers that the last land available on the Atlantic coast is for sale: the address to inquire for information is in Germany. To avoid the problem of social reconstruction or even imposing an income tax, Spain has found it more expedient simply to swap populations. The landless unemployed Spanish workers and peasants for the cash-carrying investors and tourists.

Throughout the thirty-six years of the Franco regime the large estates remained large (with few exceptions), and the old tradition that ownership of land brings status is still very much alive. This is especially true in Andalusia, where 50 percent of the productive land is still owned by 2 percent of the families.[105]

All but a very few of the great estates are haphazardly managed with little expenditure of capital or time. As in the past, the great landowners customarily live far from their estates, perhaps in Madrid, and make infrequent, or at most, weekend visits. Some never appear more than once a year; others come only to look over their land once and are never seen again. Their income is derived from other sources to which they pay more heed. If the rains come late, the absentee landlords do not know that the cattle lack feed. Some do not know or care that their cattle perish. Few, if any, hectares are sown with crops, even grass. This would require organization and investment and an increased laboring force. Some estates, reserved or rented as hunting preserves, are stocked with deer or more exotic game. During the year the estate is protected by armed guards to prevent the local people from poaching. Then, on a festive occasion, a party of men and their attendants will journey to the estate and shoot 200 deer in a single day.[79]

If they don't shoot deer they will try to raise fighting bulls for the bullrings. This, too, brings status, and is widespread. Agrarian reform, therefore, is one of the most critical problems of Spain today. The Franco government skirted around this basic issue without coming to grips with it. Mechanization and irrigation are not enough; a drastic redistribution of land is sorely needed.

Transition from Agriculture to Industry

Demographic Shift. The most obvious and most drastic characteristic of the transition from a traditionally agricultural economy to an industrial one is a profound demographic shakeup. Migration from the country to the city and from Spain to the more industrialized European countries or to the Americas has had important economic, social, and political consequences. To remedy this, the government set up a series of four-year development plans for the poorest regions, industrial parks to decongest heavy industrial concentration, and land redistribution and resettlement plans for agriculture. Some of these measures have been very successful, others have simply intensified the original problems, and the waves of migration are still continuing. A few statistics will illustrate:

1. According to the 1984 census estimate, Spain's population was 39,100,000. This represents an increase of 11 percent over the 1970 census. Both birth and death rates have declined. The average life span is now sixty-seven years.

2. Since 1900 the movement away from agriculture has increased steadily, particularly in the 1960s, when approximately two million people left the country for the city. From 1900 to 1968 the population living in the country dropped from 67.8 percent to 43.2 percent. In the same period, the population actively engaged in agriculture dropped from 69 percent to 43.2 percent. The figure of those engaged in agriculture in 1984 is less than 30 percent.

3. In the last twenty years (1964-1984) twenty-five provinces have experienced a decline in population. These same twenty-five provinces also figure below the national average in per capita income. Andalusia has lost 34 percent of its population and Extremadura 50 percent.

4. Except for Madrid, most of the population is concentrated on the coasts (Tarragona has grown 81 percent in the last fifteen years). The movement is from the inland to the coast, and from the mountains to the valleys (the meseta, the Ebro and Duero basins).

5. The industrialization process has dangerously concentrated the population and all the economic and financial power within the Madrid-Barcelona-Bilbao triangle. This represents only about 4.5 percent of the total area of Spain, but it contains over 28 percent of the population, 39 percent of the national income, and 49 percent of savings and investment. The stock market, financial oligarchy, and middle-class industrialists are also in these three key centers.

6. According to 1975 figures, three million Spaniards, or about 10 percent of the total population, were outside the country. The two million in the Americas, mostly in Venezuela, Argentina, Mexico, and Cuba, will probably not return. Many of the over one million in Europe (mostly Germany, France and Switzerland) have already returned to Spain. Together, they represent about 8 percent of Spain's active working population.

Labor

Problems

1. Concentration of industry in three major areas.
2. Lack of skilled workers.
3. Inadequate labor legislation.
4. High unemployment.
5. Little participation of worker in management and organization.
6. Inadequate salaries to combat growing inflation.
7. Emphasis on increasing production levels without taking into account the human factors of assembly line production.
8. Inadequate social services to cope with problems caused by migration to the cities.

One of the most acute areas of tension between old structures and new circumstances lies in the relationship between the working class, the industrial oligarchy, and the government. Probably one of the most important consequences of the industrialization process in Spain, on the one hand, is the increasing awareness of class-consciousness by the workers. On the other hand, the worker is regarded as a producer, a tool, but not as a consumer by his superiors.

The industrialization process has, however, caused changes in three traditional areas: (1) a breakdown of regionalistic feelings through migration to cities, and substitution of a feeling of class-consciousness and solidarity; (2) a closer relationship between the liberal members of the church and the working class, in defiance of the centuries-old church-hierarchy-state relationship; (3) the transformation of Madrid from a primarily bureaucratic capital into an industrial one.

Through the creation of *Polos de Desarrollo y Descongestión* (Points of Development and Decongestion) the government tried to relocate or redistribute industry to alleviate the problem of heavy concentration in Madrid-Bilbao-Barcelona. Besides the problems of pollution, slums and inadequate housing, and the delinquency common to any industrialization process, this concentration also presents political problems and creates an atmosphere propitious for labor agitation.

One sector in which decongestion has been accomplished is in the automotive industry. Plants in Pamplona, Valladolid, Zaragoza, and other provincial capitals have absorbed much of the labor supply from the surrounding countryside, and at the same time have tended to stabilize the traditional imbalance between agriculture and industry in these areas. The Ford plant at Sagunto and the General Motors plant at Seville have a similar aim. The industrial complex known as Campo de Gibraltar tried to absorb workers from the "Rock" after the government cut off access to Gibraltar. A major development was planned to absorb workers in Andalusia by concentrating industry in Seville. This has been only moderately successful because the waves of migration still keep going north to the three major industrial cities. Galicia, a traditionally agricultural area, will soon become an important industrial region, according to the development plan currently in effect.

Emigration

Spain has exported cheap labor to the highly industrialized countries of Europe, particularly Germany, France, and Switzerland. Over one million were working abroad during the late Franco period; the number is much less now. The majority of those who seek such work are young men: 53.3 percent are between 15 and 25 years old; 46.7 percent are 25 to 39. They come from both the country (40 percent are agricultural workers) and the city (55 percent are unskilled *peones*). In any case, it is obvious that they do not constitute the skilled workers of Spain, although they may pick up a more specialized trade in the factories.

There was a great deal of criticism about the lack of concern of the government to try to prevent the need for emigration abroad. It is possible that emigration was even encouraged, since the government, through the Ministerio de Trabajo (which works out the contracts for Spaniards who want to work abroad) got a cut (10 percent of the wages) from each worker sent. The government revenue from this source was for many years second only to that from tourism.

These workers represented 8 percent of Spain's potential labor force. The government constantly played this emigration down in the news. On one occasion at the train station in Madrid, I saw a large number of rope-tied pieces of luggage and their owners on a side track waiting to leave and saying good-bye to relatives. It was one of the saddest sights I have ever seen. They were emigrants from Orense going to work in Germany.

The life of such workers has usually been as hard in the foreign country as in Spain, yet they save to send almost everything back to the pueblo. Recently there has been much criticism of the treatment these "guest workers" receive in their "host countries." Spanish girls sometimes try to go on their own and work as maids in Paris or London or in hospitals, but they seldom are happy in a foreign environment and the Spanish government provides few services or social clubs for them.

One of the enigmas of Spain's future is the role this mass of people will play in Spanish society after they are permanently repatriated. Although they are exploited by their employers, they are having a taste of political freedom and are gaining an awareness of the workings of labor unions. They go to meetings of the communist, socialist, anarchist, and Catholic workers' parties and participate in strikes. A few return with some sort of technical skill, but they will not go back to their pueblos; instead, they will swell the growing proletariat in the cities.

Spain also accepts "guest workers" as a curious counterpart to the emigration of its workers. There are many North Africans and Cubans in Spain, for different reasons, of course. The rest of Europe is saturated with North Africans, particularly Algerians and Moroccans, who are considered the lowest category among the emigrants. Apparently the overflow has come into Spain and, as in other countries, is a source of friction. This source of labor adds to the unemployment problem in Spain.

Another minor but sad problem which does not help the labor situation is the presence of 25,000 Cuban refugees in Madrid alone. Some of these people are taken care of by Catholic charities and checks from relatives in the United States. Those who know English are hired by the largest department stores, Galerías Preciados and Corte Inglés, as a favor to their owners who had emigrated to Cuba and come back rich. Others have found jobs in advertising or publicity sectors or as secretary-translators. This has not worked out well because the Cubans cannot adapt American advertising copy or campaigns to a Spanish environment. Some found jobs dubbing or translating American television series until the public got so outraged at their translations and their accents that the project was discontinued. There are other rather pitiable cases of families which just seem to be floating around Madrid. Some enterprising capitalist set up a number of hotdog and popcorn stands manned by Cubans. Many of these people simply wait for checks from the United States or invade the American embassy for visas to get to the States. Franco's government was on good terms officially with Castro and regularly sent cultural and economic missions to Havana. It also exported farm machinery and buses. In return, Castro allowed Iberia to fly a certain number of refugees out per month.

In summary, although Franco's legacy to Spain was clearly a mixed bag, the "Order and Progress" that he achieved was a new experience in the nation's life. Such a combination is the panacea of every dictatorship. It is also, ironically, the slogan of the Positivists, who do not believe in God. Franco was only a flicker in history, but his success in providing an atmosphere of peace and material development pushed Spain into the mainstream of Western European civilization, putting an end to the quixotic dream of the 1931 Republic and to the General's own mania to restore the autocratic Spanish state of the sixteenth century. Was the price too high? A bloody and shameful civil war, three decades of repression, a blackout of the press, a loss of every dignity and freedom, an entire generation reared in intellectual stagnation, and a legacy of hatred that will endure for centuries. The Englishman, Lord Acton, once pointed out that history is made by energetic men, following ideas, mostly wrong, which determine the course of events. And the Spanish philosopher, George Santayana, wisely commented: "Those who are ignorant of history are doomed to repeat it." Now that Franco is gone only time will tell whether the Spaniards have learned that painful lesson.

17

SPAIN TODAY
THE IMPOSSIBLE DREAM

I envy the bird in the sky, his Heaven, I envy the fish in his ocean, I even envy the wild beast crouching in the undergrowth, for all of these are untroubled by memory.

Camilo José Cela

The Franco years left many painful scars that Spaniards would like to forget, yet the General's plan for a peaceful succession did work out, in large part because of the intelligence and moderation of those who succeeded him. It was not, however, with the political coloration which *el caudillo* would have liked. The chronology was as follows: on July 6, 1947, in a national referendum, Spaniards approved a Franco-drafted law declaring Spain to be a monarchy, but with no specific king as yet anointed. In 1969, twelve years later, the Cortes designated Juan Carlos de Borbon, then aged thirty-one, to become king of Spain when the General's "provisional" government came to an end. Juan Carlos had married Princess Sophia of Greece in 1962. He is the grandson of Alfonso XIII, last king of Spain, the great-great-grandson of Queen Victoria, and the son of Don Juan, the logical pretender, who was too liberal for Franco's appetite.

In June 1973 Franco resigned as "President of the Government," and appointed Admiral Carrero Blanco to head what was hoped would become the king's cabinet. The admiral was an old Franco crony, aged seventy-one, who had been running the government for several years under the General's watchful eye. This appointment was a tribute to Franco's instinct for choosing efficient, anonymous, and loyal followers, in the manner of the old Spanish kings. The admiral was assassinated a few months later by Basque terrorists.

This was the first political assassination in Spain in thirty-four years, and it sent a shudder of apprehension through the top echelons of the governing bureaucracy. For the first time since the civil war the vulnerability of high government officials was demonstrated. The Prime Minister's regular habits killed him. The assassins knew in advance exactly when he would be at a certain spot after morning mass, since he was a creature of rigid habits like a true military man.

Spaniards expressed admiration for the way the whole thing was carried out by the trained demolition crew, and pointed out ironically that the custodian of the building was a policeman. He swallowed the assassins' story that they were "artists" and "sculptors" who had to make a great deal of noise at their work, while what they did in fact was to drill a tunnel out under the street precisely where Carrero Blanco's car was to be parked. The night before the explosion they even painted a red line on the Jesuit church on the opposite side of the street to guide the detonation. When the Prime Minister entered his car he was blown clear over a five-story building, and was killed instantly. The assassination upset General Franco's plans for a succession and he clamped down a little harder. Carrero Blanco was replaced by Arias Navarro, the hard-liner former mayor of Madrid, and many Spaniards, now sensing that things were coming to a head, began to refer to the heir to the throne as Juan Carlos, the Brief.

Franco himself, during the final months of his life, had become a senile, quaking octogenarian. He was a small man in stature, only five feet three inches tall, and a jingle that once went the rounds of Spain said that he had "the restlessness of El Cid, the will to power of Charles V, the absolutism of Philip II, and the voice and backside of Isabella the Catholic."[56] Franco's mind and body were both deteriorating rapidly. According to one magazine description of him at this stage of his life, "his flesh was hanging on an aged frame, his mouth sagged, and his palsied right hand sometimes shook so noticeably that he had to grip it in his left. His voice, always shrill, had become strained and thin."[73] His infrequent pronunciamentos on national television gave increasing evidence of his senility.

Arias Navarro, the new Prime Minister, who was also a political opportunist of the first magnitude, acutely sensed the restive, increasingly explosive feeling among the people, and embarked on a cautious program of political reform. In the next two years, 1974 and 1975, cries for a change became even louder and more orchestrated. The reform measures proposed by the government now began to look toward the development of democratic liberties and more popular representation. Only 17 percent of the members of the Cortes could claim to be elected, but it was promised that henceforth the voters would make their own choices. There was even talk of allowing a rebirth of political parties, anathema to Franco in his earlier years. Euphemistic terms were used, however, to designate these, such as "contrasting opinions" (*el contraste de pareceres*), or "political associations" (*asociaciones políticas*).

Conversations in the cafés and on the streets polarized around a couple of other terms that indicated the direction Spain might take: *democratic reform*, or *democratic breakaway*. In the eyes of the people *reforma democrática* meant a gradual process, whereas *ruptura democrática* meant a clean break with the past. In February 1975 the Prime Minister announced publicly that Spaniards should begin to relieve the General of his burden and work toward making their own future. The die was cast. The facelifting prospect of gradual political reforms was rejected by most Spaniards and clamor for a clean break became more and more vociferous.[84]

Franco's five-week decline into death began in the middle of October 1975, and all sides recognized that some kind of succession was now inevitable. The General's physicians used various heroic measures to keep the caudillo alive during his final days, and there were many black jokes about this and about violent disputes around the dying man's bed. On November 20, 1975, Franco died, and on November 22, Juan Carlos was proclaimed king. The king lost no time in coming to grips with the political reality facing him. Although he had been especially groomed by Franco to carry on the old regime, the new king, from the very first day of his enthronement, made it clear that this was not his intention.

On November 25, only five days after Franco's death, the king announced a royal pardon for many political prisoners, and on December 13, a new cabinet was appointed to guide Spain through her transition period. The "National Movement," which symbolized the Franco government, was abolished on April 1, 1977, and on April 28, free trade unions were approved. On June 15, 1977, the first general elections since 1936 were held amid high feelings of both joy and fear among the electorate. In 1976, Spain gave up its last large colony, the 102,707 sq. mile Spanish Sahara on Africa's west coast. In 1977 Spain reestablished its relations with the Soviet Union.

The driving force behind these changes at governmental level was the King himself. When he came to the throne he met with a certain degree of cold courtesy on the one hand, and open hostility on the other, a common opinion being that a monarch was hardly relevant to either *ruptura* or *reforma*. And yet it is probably true to say that without the quiet determination of Juan Carlos, the emergence of the new Spain would have been far harder, much bloodier, and perhaps even impossible. Apart from holding clear views as to how things should proceed (which included changing the Prime Minister in July 1976 and choosing a man who was virtually an unknown quantity) his strong links with the military greatly reduced the possibility of direct intervention in the affairs of state by the armed forces.[84]

The king and queen quickly won the respect of the people of Spain. They had already made themselves well known by visiting all the regions of the country during the years of Franco's rule. Known then as "the prince and princess" (*los príncipes*), they went about inaugurating the opening of dams, the dedication of all kinds of public and private works, and often making a royal presence at various celebrations and commemorations. These visits were mostly perfunctory in nature, but they served the purpose of introducing the amiable personalities of the royal pair to the people at large. After Franco's death the king and queen continued these visits, and they were now received with real warmth and admiration. They also made many trips abroad with the same signal success, visiting China, Latin America, the United States, and various European countries. They brought the message that Spain was no longer an anomaly among the nations of Europe. In 1983 the king spoke vigorously in Venezuela, Brazil, and Uruguay expressing his strong support of human rights, democratic government, and any measure that would lead to political liberalization and economic progress. Indeed, Juan Carlos had by then become the symbol of democracy in the entire Spanish and Portuguese-speaking world.[87]

Spain's transition toward democratic government went much faster than most observers had considered possible. In July 1976 the Prime Minister Arias Navarro, last vestige of the Franco government, resigned his position at the request of the king, who then appointed a middle-of-the-roader, Adolfo Suárez González, to take his place. In December 1976 the Political Reform Laws drawn up by the government were overwhelmingly approved by the voters. All political parties except the Communists were now given a free rein. The Secretary General of the

Communist party, Santiago Carrillo, still under legal exile, returned to Madrid and announced that his party would present candidates in the forthcoming elections, regardless of its legal status. The government, under great pressure from rightist groups, arrested him, but the citizens at large loudly objected to this response. It was the overwhelming consensus that *ruptura democrática*, a clean break with the old regime, must be complete, and if this meant legalizing the Communists, so be it. Consequently, on April 9, 1977, the Communist party was given legal status.

The first general elections in forty-one years were held on June 15, 1977, and there was an 80 percent turnout of voters. While the Centrist Democratic party won a majority of the seats in both houses, the Socialists came out a surprisingly strong second. The new Cortes consisted of 248 senators, 4 from each mainland province, 3 from each island province, and 41 appointed by the king. The House of Deputies consisted of 350 members, all elected by popular vote. The results of the elections were as follows: the Centrist Democratic party won 165 deputies and 105 senators, while the Socialists got 118 deputies and 35 senators. The moderate temper of the electorate was clearly indicated by the small number of votes received by parties of the extreme right and extreme left. It was a real democratic victory. The Communists won only 20 deputies and 12 senators, less than 10 percent, and the far right was even less successful.[110]

The king addressed this representative assemblage at its first session, and all Spain was on tenterhooks. Would all the years of suffering really mean anything? The monarch stood at a lectern and surveyed the circle of delegates—Suárez, Prime Minister, the pragmatist, dapper, artful, handsome; Fraga Iribarne, pompous Francoist who gives out books filled with colored pictures of himself in various fancy dress; Santiago Carrillo, who had lived a lifetime during forty years of exile and had come home to lead the Communists; *La Pasionaria*, back after thirty-eight years in the Soviet Union; Felipe González, the boyish Socialist; editor José Ortega, son of the philosopher-intellectual José Ortega y Gasset, at sixty once again a motivating journalistic force as originator of *El País* and legislator as well.

"Your presence here," Juan Carlos told them, "the will of the citizens who elected you to sit in this chamber, the plurality of opinions that you represent . . . all demonstrate our desire for national harmony and the recognition of the sovereignty of the Spanish people."

And then, finally, the phrase came. In his splendid uniform with the solitary row of gold buttons running down the dark tunic, and a modest array of ribbons on his chest, the king surveyed the chamber, all the remnants of Franco, the Communists who had survived the exile, the reactionaries who had become democrats, the youthful Socialists—and to this polyglot group, this young man, ordained by a repressive, archly conservative army commander to be king of all Spain, uttered the absolute words: "Democracy has begun."[85]

He was not presiding over a nation in healthy economic or political shape. The worldwide oil embargo, the energy crisis, the drop in tourism, and the galloping inflation of 1973–74 had led to the depression of Franco's final years and Spain was still in a state of economic crisis. The hope was strong, but the facts were not auspicious. In any event, this marked a new beginning.

The first important order of business for the parliament was to draw up a new constitution. Spain adopted its first constitution in 1812, and since then there have been eight others. The constitution of 1931, which reflected the liberal intellectual flavor of Spain's educated élite who had made the new Republic, was way before its time. It granted rights that most Spaniards did not want; for example, divorce by mutual consent, and it made other commitments that could not be delivered. The constitution of 1978 was much more realistic and less doctrinaire than that of 1931, for it was drawn up with the fratricide of the civil war still ominous in memory. Work began on the document in August 1977, and in January 1978 the first draft was put before the Cortes. An all-party committee was directed to prepare a statement of general principles on which they could agree, then the more difficult items were taken up one by one. An admirable moderation was shown by those working on this assignment, and in the process of redacting a final draft, 1,133 amendments were tabled. The final text was approved in October 1978, and this document was submitted to a popular vote on December 6, 1978. With a 68 percent turnout the new constitution was approved by 87 percent of the voters. Spain was declared to be a parliamentary monarchy. The civil and legal rights of all persons were guaranteed, as was freedom of speech, freedom of the press, collective bargaining, the right to strike, and legal equality for women. The death penalty was outlawed. A considerable amount of autonomy was given to the Basques, Catalonians, and other Spanish regional minorities who had been clamoring for self rule.

Contrary to what many foreigners think, Spain is not a homogeneous country linguistically or culturally. Despite the centuries-long dominance of Castile and the Castilian language, regional differences have continued to be very strong, and the desire for autonomy in a few of the outlying regions has resulted in continuous political disruptions and frequent acts of terrorism within the framework of the nationhood. Very much aware of this the Spanish Republic granted what amounted to almost total regional autonomy to those regions that wanted it, mainly the Basque provinces and Catalonia. The new Spanish government has not gone quite that far, but regional parliaments and extensive local control were approved. The three principal regional languages of Spain are Basque, which is not a romance tongue in any sense, Catalan, and Galician. Catalan bears some kinship with old Provençal of southern France, and Galician is akin to Portuguese.

The language of the Basque provinces is an ancient Bronze Age tongue that goes back some 4,000 years to remote pre-Roman days. It is not an Indo-European language. A total of about 600,000 people speak this language inside Spain, and these people have always felt themselves to be quite different from the Spaniards. Their desire for independence goes far back in time. The Catalonians are much more numerous than the Basques, reaching a total of about twelve millions. The Galicians fall somewhere in between.

In 1936 there were twenty newspapers published regularly in Catalan, and over one thousand other publications. The language was spoken freely everywhere in the area surrounding Barcelona, and within the city itself. Many rural inhabitants of the region did not even speak Spanish. When Franco first took over the government of Spain one of his aims was to stamp out regional separation. Speaking Catalan was strongly discouraged, and publications in that language were for a time absolutely forbidden. In spite of this legal repression the language remained very much alive, although many children grew away from it. During the school year 1983–84, under the new laws, approximately half the schools in Catalonia taught most of their classes in Catalan, and less than 5 percent taught *all classes* in Spanish. The region's educational policy is, however, that all children must know the two languages.[86]

One of the factors that has kept Catalan so alive is the large number of people speaking the language. Also, in the last century and continuing today, there has been a revival of academic interest in Catalan because of its literary tradition. Galician, however, is today primarily a rural language despite its noble history, and while there has been a recent revival of interest in this language too, there does not exist in Galicia the strong feeling for separatism that impassions the Basques and Catalans. All of Spain's regional languages may now be taught in the schools, and in the Basque provinces there is a special campaign for people of all ages to attend night classes in order to perfect their knowledge of the language.

Not all Basques seek complete independence, but there is a well-organized group of extremists, the ETA (*Basque Nation and Liberty*), that has long fought for a separate Basque nation.* Much like the IRA of Ireland this group resorts to frequent acts of terrorism to state its case. The ETA was probably responsible for the assassination of Premier Carrero Blanco, Franco's friend, but when five men associated with political terrorism were executed in Spain in 1975, there was a strong wave of protest all over Europe.

In this ongoing confrontation between terrorists and the national government, Spain's *Guardia Civil* (Civil Guard) has borne the brunt of the violence. The Civil Guard was established in the nineteenth century in order to police the rural areas of the country, and it has always been regarded as an élite corps. Its officers are selected from the army, and its political alignment has always been conservative. Most of the Civil Guard went over to Franco at the outbreak of the civil war, and 1,200 of them heroically withstood the siege of the Republican army when they holed up in the basement of the Alcázar in Toledo. The Civil Guard suffered the highest casualties of any unit on Franco's side, and since the General's death in 1975 more than 300 Civil Guards have been killed and more than 3,000 wounded while trying to maintain order. The guardsmen always travel in pairs, and any traveler in Spain will meet them frequently at some unexpected turn in the road. They also patrol the Spanish railways and may be seen in many public places where there are large gatherings of people.

The Civil Guard today consists of some 58,000 well-trained men, which adds up to one guard for every 678 Spaniards. Their distinctive green uniforms and tricornered patent leather caps make them easily visible on the highways and byways of Spain. They are trained to remain aloof from the villagers, and they never serve in the part of Spain from which they come. Spaniards at large have a divided opinion

---

* Indicative of Basque sentiment for separation was the 1978 vote on the Spanish constitution. In the Basque provinces 54.5 percent of the potential voters did not vote, and 5.8 percent of the ballots were turned in blank, i.e., over 60 percent of the Basque adults were against or indifferent to a national constitution. *Blanco y Negro*, number 3476, 13/12/78.

about the Civil Guards. They are respected for their courage and for the protection they give the countryside, but their political conservatism is widely distrusted and disliked. Some villagers regard them as an occupying spy force and hate them bitterly.[84] In the 1980s the Civil Guard is again suffering heavy casualties from extremist groups within Spain. Terrorism has not yet been allowed to get out of control, but acts of violence on the part of Spanish terrorist groups have become an increasingly disruptive force in undermining the authority of the state.[111]

On February 23, 1981, a well-organized group of Civil Guards seized the Chamber of Deputies in the Spanish Cortes and held most of the nation's elected representatives as hostages. Some of the guards fired bursts from automatic weapons as they rushed into the Chamber ordering the 347 deputies and a handful of senators who were present to lie on the floor. At the same time as this seizure was in progress army tanks and troops took control of the state run television station in Madrid. On the following day, February 24, other military units began to join the revolt, but troops loyal to the government liberated the television station, and in a national telecast the king made an impassioned speech denouncing the revolt and ordering the military forces to uphold the constitution and support the democratically elected government. After this the coup quickly collapsed, only eighteen hours after it had begun. Fortunately no one was hurt in the melee.

The Civil Guards and some military officers involved in the coup were arrested and imprisoned, but none of these was vigorously prosecuted or stiffly sentenced, as it was considered too risky to proceed along this path. On February 27 more than one million people marched in the streets of Madrid in support of the king and the duly elected government. The editor-in-chief of *Le Monde* in Paris, André Fontaine, in the issue of March 11, commented that the Spanish military "had suspended a sword of Damocles over Spain. . . . There is far more sympathy than is at first apparent for the return to *strong man* rule to deal with terrorism and social and economic problems."[88]

Felipe González, leader of the Spanish Socialist party, in an interview in *Cambio 16* on March 23, agreed that the danger of a military takeover was a continuing problem that any elected Spanish government would have to face. "The objective interests of the extreme Right and extreme Left coincide," he said. He also questioned the equivocal attitude of the United States toward the attempted coup: "There was no clear statement by the American government of its attitude toward the peaceful development of democracy in Spain. . . . For about twenty-four hours the Reagan administration displayed such a lukewarm attitude toward the coup that relations between Washington and Madrid may be affected." González and millions of Spaniards had hoped that the United States would issue a forthright denunciation of the coup and an immediate statement of support for Spain's freely elected democratic regime. This was one time when a few well-chosen words would have gone a long way toward winning new friends in Europe for the United States. Ironically, only eight months later, Felipe González and his Socialists overwhelmingly won the second national elections since Franco's death and a Socialist government was established in Spain.

In the immediate post-Franco years great attention was focused on political change, but the economic crisis soon took center stage. Building activity had slowed down, there was growing unemployment, rampant inflation, an increasing national debt, the one *billion* dollars in reserves of 1973 was quickly wiped out, and by 1977 there was a serious deficit in foreign exchange. In October 1977 representatives of all political parties met at the Moncloa Palace and drew up the "Moncloa Pact," which was an all-out effort to meet this crisis. Far-sweeping changes were made in the country's economic policy; public spending was severely restricted, the money supply reduced, inflation curbed, taxation reformed, and aid to smaller business firms made available. Social security benefits were also increased, newly adopted labor regulations gave the worker a fairer break, means were sought to improve rural conditions, modernize agriculture, and ease unemployment.[84] All these measures had positive results, but they were not enough to pull Spain out of her economic crisis. Perhaps the biggest success was in reducing inflation, which was cut by 10 percent, but in 1982 it still stood at approximately 15 percent annually.

Poor economic conditions resulted in the rapid growth of the Socialist party which was promising to create 800,000 new jobs in four years. When the second post-Franco national elections were held on October 28, 1982, the Socialists, under the leadership of charismatic Felipe González, won an absolute majority in both houses of parliament. They took 201 seats out of a total of 350 in the lower house, and 134 out of 208 in the senate. In her political alignment Spain was back where she had been in the days of the liberal Republic (1931–1936).

During the Franco years (1939–1975) a rigorous censorship had made a mockery of news reporting in Spain. Only items favorable to the regime could appear in the press and frequently in an attempt to make things look good, outright lies were printed. If a headline reported that there had been NO STRIKE IN BILBAO, the reader would know at once that a strike was then in progress in Bilbao. Newspapers and magazines shrank to a few scraggly pages of sports and society news with occasional business and construction reports. Unquestionably, during those repressive years, Spain had the worst press of any European country, perhaps of any country in the civilized world.

After Franco's death restrictions were lifted and the press immediately had a field day. New newspapers and magazines sprang up like mushrooms, but many of these suffered a quick demise. Among the new dailies only *El País* of Madrid, which first appeared in 1976, became a newspaper of note. It is an independent paper which has been reporting the news fairly and objectively since its birth. Among the magazines *Cambio 16*, something like our *Time* or *Newsweek*, began to report in depth items of general interest and caught the fancy of the reading public. During the final Franco years *Cambio 16* had been the gadfly of the regime, but it was then strictly controlled. It blossomed under the new free press of the democratic monarchy.

Because of the prolonged Franco repression, Spaniards at large had ceased to be readers. In 1936 when Madrid was a city of only one million inhabitants, it had 18 newspapers, six of these with over 200,000 copies printed every day. At present, with more than four million inhabitants, the city has only seven dailies, with a single one reaching the 200,000 figure. During the period of the Republic there was a total of 2,000 daily newspapers in Spain; today there are a bare 130. Spaniards simply stopped reading when they could not get the truth, and they still have a deeply ingrained distrust of the press. The growth of radio and television newscasts has also had its effect. In the 1980s only 80 out of 1,000 Spaniards buy a newspaper.

A quick rundown of Madrid's newspapers today will give a good general perspective of the main currents in the thinking of the city's four million people:[89]

ABC is a conservative monarchist newspaper that was founded in 1905 by one of the great patriarchs of the Spanish press, D. Torcuato Luca de Tena. It is an aristocratic tabloid with several striking photogravure pages and a list of contributors of considerable literary note. Its appeal is to the old-line, well-heeled families, and it was widely popular during the Franco years. Since 1975 it has had a much more limited circulation. *ABC*'s elder companion journal, *Blanco y Negro*, ceased publication in 1981, because of economic reasons, after nearly a century of distinguished journalism. Once a magazine of the highest quality, with articles by some of Spain's best writers, *Blanco y Negro*'s final issues were skimpy pamphlets of little interest or value.

El Alcázar is also a conservative paper, and was founded in 1936 at the time of the siege of Toledo's Alcázar by the Republican forces. It has actually gained in circulation since 1975, as it represents traditional conservative opposition to the democratic, constitutional policies of the present government.

Diario 16 began publication in 1975 and is a spinoff of the more highly respected biweekly *Cambio 16*. It has been much less successful than its counterpart, is poorly written, and presents a less objective view of the news.

Marca, which is dedicated exclusively to sports news, was established early in the Franco period by Manuel Fernández Cuesta, brother of one of the founders of the Falange. It enjoyed a great vogue between 1940 and 1970, primarily because sports news was really the only news that was given a free hand by the government. Also, it was allowed to come out on Monday, when the publication of other dailies was prohibited.

El País, which has already been mentioned, is a paper whose appeal is mainly to the well-educated Spaniard: intellectuals, members of the professions, students. Its founder was José Ortega, son of the famous writer Ortega y Gasset. Its vigorous, young editorial staff has made *El País* one of the best newspapers in Europe today. It maintains a liberal but factually objective point of view. In the fall of 1983, in an all-out effort to expand circulation, *El País* opened a vigorous campaign to attract readers in the United States, mainly among the teachers of Spanish. Thousands of free copies were distributed over a five-week period with this end in mind. *El País* reminds me of *El Sol*, perhaps the most respected paper of the Republican period.

Pueblo, founded in 1940 by the government structured unions, is Madrid's only evening paper. In the past it defended Franco's social and political ideology. Its future orientation is uncertain.

Ya, dating from 1935, is a Catholic news sheet that upholds the role of the church and the principles of Christian morality. Among its contributors are found many first-rate literary figures. *Ya* strongly defends the church in its anti-abortion and antidivorce stance, and in its struggle with the Department of Education that is striving to separate the Spanish school system completely from all evidence of Catholic ideology. This battle is now heating up, and will produce firewood for years to come.

The Barcelona newspaper, *Vanguardia*, founded in 1881, is the oldest continuously published paper in the country. It was probably the best paper in Spain during the final Franco years, but has now lost some of its prestige. However, it still has the second largest circulation of any Spanish newspaper, somewhere around the 200,000 mark. *El País* of Madrid now has the largest circulation of any newspaper in Spain, an honor that it richly deserves. Its first-rate Sunday magazine section is one of the most attractive and most informative publications in Spain today, and its daily represents top-flight journalism. Spanish newspapers and magazines today give full and objective coverage of what is going on in the United States. Our cultural life is amply presented, along with our economic, political, and foreign activities. Too bad that we do not reciprocate.

The removal of censorship not only gave birth to serious journalism but also spawned the pornographic press. After forty years of repression Spaniards suddenly went wild with pornography. Photographs of nude women began to appear in all kinds of papers and magazines whose sole purpose was to excite their readers and to sell copies. Formerly sober kiosks were festooned with such displays. In the social sphere nudity became synonymous with freedom. Spanish imitations of *Playboy* and *Penthouse* now frequently lie on the living room tables of many a middle-class Spanish family in full view of the children. Cabarets advertise nude entertainers, and pornographic movies abound. Long gone are the days when Spaniards drove across the French border just in order to be able to see *Last Tango in Paris*.

Along the so-called tourist row, nightclubs bill dancers nude, except for shoes. A Madrid version of *Equus* included a nude scene that had brought gasps on Broadway. Nudity has also taken its place in advertising. A simple advertisement for bathing suits shows a couple swimming in the nude in clear water. Each is holding aloft a bathing suit. Says the copy, "It is a beautiful thing to swim without a suit, but if you have to have one, buy ours."[85]

One magazine, *Interviú*, mixed political reports with *Enquirer*-type exposés salted with sexy photographs, and circulation jumped to one million copies. For a time the pornographic mills outside of Spain could not keep up with the demand. However, once satiated, interest in this new sport began to decline, and within a few months after its appearance *Interviú* has lost 80 percent of its sales.

In the area of social and political mores, Spain has also undergone a dramatic change since Franco's death in 1975. In many ways it does not even appear to be the same country that it so recently was. The younger generation, characteristically, has embraced the new freedoms with unwonted zeal. This is especially to be noted in the sphere of moral values. Premarital sex has become widely accepted, many young people live together without being married, kissing and embracing in public is now a common sight, the newly freed gays parade in Barcelona just as they do in San Francisco and Los Angeles, pornographic magazines and motion pictures abound, and the socialists are now more popular than Franco's partisans ever were. It is a new Spain that immediately confronts the traveler's eye, and the old returned traveler is almost bound to say to himself "This is not the Spain that I once knew."

The magazine *Cambio 16* recently took some polls in order to sample its readers' opinions concerning some of the most important subjects of Spanish life. One poll back in 1977 showed that 76 percent of those responding thought divorce was acceptable, and 74 percent said that premarital sex was O.K. The same poll indicated that 60 percent of the young people who responded had abandoned the church almost completely. The number of religious deserters increased after age twenty, which coincides with the time that most young people break away from their families. A later poll taken in Barcelona in 1983 showed that 90 percent favored divorce, 86 percent thought premarital sex was all right, but 54 percent rejected prostitution. Only 4 percent had ever tried drugs, and a bare 3 percent were anxious to get married.[90]

Civil divorce has been legal in Spain since July 1981 but, of course, the church opposes it. The Franco government had made civil marriages invalid for all Catholics, and by 1975 there were nearly 100,000 separation cases waiting to be heard by the ecclesiastical tribunals. The verdict was seldom favorable unless one of the parties had plenty of money and/or influence. This was even more essential if there was a plea for annulment. The law itself supported a double standard. A male committing adultery was not guilty of anything unless he brought his mistress to his home to live with him, or established another home with her where they lived together *notoriamente* (notoriously). A woman, in contrast, could be put in jail for a term of between six months to six years if found guilty of adultery. She was also obliged to pay a heavy fine, and the loss of her children was a foregone conclusion. Things have now changed considerably but this does not mean that the old male-dominated society has disappeared. It does mean that women in Spain are on the move demanding equality. They are fighting an uphill battle, but so are women everywhere, even in the United States. Spanish women have already won 100 percent equality with their husbands in the areas of property and authority over children.

Feminist groups in Spain demonstrate openly to defend feminist causes of all kinds, and this includes demonstrations protesting the treatment of women who have engaged in adultery, especially if there are extenuating circumstances. For example, barely a year after Franco's death, 10,000 women paraded in Barcelona when a woman whose husband had abandoned her had a child from an "adulterous affair" and was hauled into court when she refused to give her child up to the ex-husband's parents.[84] Some of the women in this demonstration carried placards stating, *Jo també soc adúltera* (I too am an adultress). Partly because of demonstrations like this, and because of a widespread and growing sentiment in favor of divorce, the laws pertaining to these matters were liberalized. A new law now allows abortions for certain exceptional reasons and, in fact, such reasons can usually be stretched to cover almost any case. Gone are the days when entire planeloads of women flew to London almost weekly to have an abortion or purchase an intrauterine device. As recently as 1977 this was the only way out, "For abortions women call a number in London. The respondent answers in Spanish and advises the date of the next abortion flight. The cost, less than in Paris, includes pickup at the airport."[85]

Yet so ingrained is the Catholic attitude toward abortion in Spain that even among young people only 21 percent said in a recent poll that they favored it upon demand. In "exceptional cases" 53 percent accepted abortion, but 14 percent were against it for whatever reason. The same poll showed that 37 percent of the respondents favored abortion if the mother in a poor family with many children wanted it. If the child to be born was shown to be abnormal, 62 percent accepted abortion, and if childbirth meant the loss of the mother's life 70 percent voted for abortion, totally contrary to the Catholic teaching on the subject.[108] The vast majority of Spaniards, men and women, favor birth control. A large headline in *El País* recently stated that THE POPE'S

CONDEMNATION OF THE USE OF ALL CONTRACEPTIVE DEVICES AS A SIN IS A STEP BACKWARD. It is a step that Spaniards are unwilling to take.[91]

In summarizing the results of these polls, *Cambio 16* concluded that "the young people of Spain are now thoroughly European, and have adopted more liberal, more advanced and more progressive attitudes than the youth of France, Great Britain or Scandinavia." "In a nutshell," the magazine went on to say, "our young people are realistic, rational and reasonable, and very open and tolerant in sexual and social relations. There is one singular difference: Spanish youth is considerably more pessimistic than is the case in the rest of Europe, but our young people do still believe in the possibility of establishing in Spain a real progressive democracy."

The conclusion that the youth of Spain is more liberal in its thinking than are the young people of France, Great Britain, or Scandinavia is inaccurate. *Cambio 16*'s polls were all taken in the big urban centers and do not reflect the attitudes of the country as a whole. All they indicate is a current trend. Furthermore, their suddenly won freedom gave to the young folks of Spain a chance to throw off the reins and kick up their heels, which is exactly what they have done. At this stage of the game, at least, their thinking and their actions represent a rebound from repression, a swing of the pendulum not firmly rooted in reality. Let us see what the next twenty or thirty years may bring. Spain may never be the same again, the old Spain may be dead, but one cannot be sure. Gyrations in style, even in sexual mores, take more than a few years to become characteristic of a country. When the onus of guilt hits this new generation, there may well be a swing in the opposite direction. After all, only ten to fifteen years ago young Spaniards were saying of Franco, *Es necesario para España* (He is necessary for Spain).

The future of Spain rests in the hands of its youth, but there are some serious misgivings here, as this generation has not received an education rooted in democracy. In the middle and upper classes one can find nearly all the developments that have taken place in the United States, but the proportions are different. There are young people who live together without being married, and some married couples who go to England and France so that it will be less difficult to separate if the marriage doesn't work. There are young people with a profound antipathy toward the older generation. There are drug addicts, hippies, and the like, in spite of the stiff consequences for using or pushing hard drugs. However, in 1983 Spain legalized the smoking of "pot," and a "joint" or *porro*, as it is called, is becoming quite fashionable, much to the horror of the older generation. One is not legally allowed to grow it, sell it, "manufacture" it, or distribute it, but smoking pot carries no legal penalty.[92]

Many young people live off papa or the American girls they date. Because the majority of university students cannot work until they finish their education, they must be supported by their parents for a long time. There is no widespread program of loans, scholarships, grants, fellowships, or endowments like those in the United States. An increasing number of young couples either live together or get married while they are still studying, but the percentage of those who are able to attend the university is still relatively small.

The young people of the working class have other problems, although they have one thing in common with their more prosperous peers. They are avid consumers. Specialists in public relations and advertising techniques are well aware of this. Young people form a large part of the consumer society that spends a great deal on clothes, records, cassettes, motor scooters, and discotheques. Juvenile delinquency is still not as high as it is in the States, but it is rising rapidly. Many children must work at an early age in order to help support their families. Minors (under fourteen) work at all sorts of odd jobs from bellhops, delivery boys, dishwashers, to selling candy, newspapers, or soft drinks. The legal age for schooling is not rigidly enforced because there are not enough places or schools for these children. There is a shortage of technical schools to train them. In factories or workshops they are thrust into situations that are difficult for young people to cope with. They do not read because they have not been stimulated or trained to do so, and because books are expensive. Also, they work long hours and often have to travel great distances, so after work they are exhausted and are more interested in relaxing with a comic book or heading for the local billiard parlor. Many of these young people want to escape from the oppressiveness of their family life and their routine work, but this is difficult. Once the boy has his steady *novia*, he begins to save toward buying an apartment, and this is the end of free spending.

There is a class gap. Young workers do not like their university counterparts, whom they regard as *señoritos*. There is mutual antipathy because the university students tend to be disdainful or paternalistic, and do not care to understand the problems of the workers. Of course, very few young people of the working class ever go to the university, although the opening of several new universities in the provinces is changing this. Spanish higher education tends to divorce research and teaching, and the unfair system of *oposiciones* (board examinations) produces rote graduates who have no training or experience in a classroom situation.

There is a lack of cooperation among the different branches of the university, students and professors are hampered by bureaucracy, and the university continues to be monolithic in the face of a changing society. There is a great lack of good libraries, research equipment, and seminar-type studies at the graduate level. At present the university fulfills only one of its three traditional functions: it is occupied with turning out professionals, whereas there should be a balance between cultural and professional studies and research. But here, too, there is a paradox. Many graduates with adequate professional training, such as engineers, architects, chemists, and physicists, are working in other fields or have left the country. These people cannot find jobs in their field of specialization, because they all want to live in the big cities, and the older professionals have formed a closed circle and have a monopoly on all the contracts. At the university generally there is little basis for dialogue, political education, the learning of responsibility, the give and take required in a stable democratic society.

Despite this weakness at the top, Spanish education is making a bold effort to catch up with the rest of the world. *Cambio 16* in a recent editorial commented that "Spain has inherited from the Franco years standards of mediocrity in education that are hard to imagine, the giant thousand-headed octopus of that regime attempted to regulate even the color of the chalk and the blackboards in our schools, while the universities of our country sank into an unbelievable state of prostration."[93] Now in the early 1980s Spain is spending more on education than on any other item in the national budget except for Work and Social Security and for defense. The total Spanish budget for the year 1984 is approximately $35 billions of U.S. dollars, of which more than three billions are earmarked for education. The schools are packed everywhere. Not since the years of the Republic has there been such a zeal for education. In Madrid alone more than one million children are now enrolled, and teachers are asking for higher salaries and fewer students. National illiteracy now stands at approximately 8 percent.

Reminiscent of the old days the church and the Ministry of Education are again engaged in a battle of ideas. The church wanted to distribute a booklet called *The Path of God* to students at the fifth and sixth grade levels; in the book there is a summary of Catholic moral beliefs. One of the statements clearly equates abortion with murder, war and terrorism, all ways of destroying life. The Ministry of Education objected to this statement, and refused to approve the text, so the fight was on. Meanwhile, the federal government, without taking any moral stand, is pushing hard to *depenalize* abortion. The Catholic hierarchy, on its part, called the government's posture "socialism against the church."[91] As the old saying goes, "In Spain everybody follows the church, half of them with a candle, the other half with a club."

Young people have taken on a major importance in the voting booth. In 1931 the voting age was 23, but for the 1977 elections it was 21, and by 1979 the age had been lowered to 18. This increased the number of voters by one-and-a-half millions. Because of the death of so many men in the civil war, 52 percent of the electorate are women. The gays constitute another potentially influential political group, and the unionized workers, of course, are the strongest political force of all. Feminists and gays have not yet managed to present any kind of united front for their two groups.

Spanish workers are still the lowest paid in Europe outside of Portugal, and per capita productivity is at the same low level. Per capita income has soared in recent years, but is still below that of France or Italy. In spite of her relative underdevelopment Spain has become the ninth industrial power in the world. During the past six or seven years more than a million new cars annually have been registered in Spain, most of these manufactured in the country. General Motors, Chrysler, and Ford all have large plants operating in Spain.

The xenophobia characteristic of Spain in the past has been cast aside, and Spaniards are now eager to become accepted as *Europeans*. On May 30, 1982, Spain became a member of NATO, thus putting an end to its political isolation. There is an even stronger current of opinion seeking admission to the European Common Market, but so far this has not been forthcoming. French opposition to letting Spain in is still very strong. Spanish products are too competitive for French farmers.

During the final Franco years getting into the Common Market, renewing the Vatican Concordat, and the return of Gibraltar were the three main points of Spain's foreign policy. Now that Franco is dead two of these issues still remain: the return of Gibraltar—soft-pedaled by the present government—and entry into the Common Market—of more urgent concern. As long as Franco was in power Spain never had any real chance for admission, because the politically liberal members of the Market simply would not accept a fascist state that had aligned itself with Hitler and Mussolini. But Franco did try one line that the present government is still pursuing, "Mediterranean unity." Since France is losing its supremacy in the CM to Britain and Germany, it could use some extra support, which Spain could give, to balance the Mediterranean countries against the northern countries.

But France has exacted its own terms. Although Spain now receives preferential treatment from the CM along with its principal competitors, Morocco and Israel, who are better organized, demands imposed by the Market members are considered discriminatory and show partiality. In addition, while Morocco does have some ties to Spain, culturally and linguistically it is in the orbit of France, and has received special treatment from that country. Morocco, Spain's major competitor in the export of citrus fruit, has been allowed by the Spanish government to use Spain's railroads to ship its perishable produce to France, instead of using the longer sea route. Besides this, Morocco receives a higher price for this produce in France than Spain does.

Furthermore, the citrus industry in Valencia has been in crisis for some time now, precisely because of that foreign competition and some very unfavorable weather. Does Spain have to "bargain" this way in order to enter the European sphere at the price of deceiving her own people, or is this a concession to Morocco to build up more support for the annexation of Gibraltar? The actual picture is even more Byzantine. A few years ago Morocco extended its territorial waters into areas traditionally worked by Spanish fishermen and confiscated Spain's boats. This has directly affected Andalusia's fishing industry, already in a state of crisis, and the issue still has not been effectively resolved.

Another fly in the ointment is the fact that Spain has always been more closely associated with the Arab Moslem states than with Israel, which Franco never recognized. One reason for this is historic: Spain's North African Moslem colonies and the long residence of the Moors in Spain. The other is economic necessity, for Spain produces no oil and is dependent on Arab sources without which her industries and automobiles would all come to a halt.

The rapid industrialization process, Franco's "economic miracle," pulled women out of the home and into the job market, and the present government has helped even more to encourage and protect women who work. In 1940 women represented only 14 percent of the total working population of Spain, but by 1984 this had risen to nearly 35 percent. Women constitute a tremendous potential labor supply of about five million, or a possible 40 percent of the active working population. This has led to a legal, sociological, and professional transformation, more child-care centers, and a change in the traditional *la mujer en casa y la pata quebrada* attitude, the Spanish way of saying "a woman's place is in the home." The literal translation sheds some light on the old line male dominated society: "A woman should stay at home, even if it takes a broken leg to keep her there."

Lower-class women who have always worked—as maids and cleaning women—have tended to move toward jobs in cafeterias and department stores, not so much because this implies greater earnings (salaries for live-in maids are high, board and room provided, and conditions excellent because good maids are getting scarce), but because television has given them a different idea of life and because they want freedom of movement. Ironically, at a moment when domestic service is disappearing, protection is appearing; cleaning women who work in homes or institutions must be put on social security.

Middle-class women can still count on some domestic service, on their mothers, and on well-organized child-care centers to help them with their family obligations if they choose to work. Many of them do work part time. As in the United States, they are generally paid less and given positions of less prestige than men.

Spanish women are great wives and mothers; they have been the cement for the Spanish tribal system which, given the ruthlessness of its institutions, needs this strong core to keep it from crumbling. Many Spanish women are incredibly tough and resourceful. They are accustomed to their own name and never lose it or modify it in any way when they get married. They can be very ambitious professionally and work in a difficult career like that of lawyer or doctor while carrying on with their family responsibilities. Their mothers stand by to help. Also, the long Spanish school day and the possibility of working a "short" day in government jobs (9 to 3) helps the middle-class woman in a profession. This traditional way of life, however, is being eroded. Spanish women are influenced by women's lib to a limited degree, but at present they are more interested in achieving the basic legal foundation they need to be able to function as individuals in the face of marital difficulties.

There is another "unofficial" reason why so many women began to work, which is seldom mentioned. It dates back to a preindustrial and post civil war period and is not related to the industrialization process.

This is the number of women, particularly of the middle class, who were widowed by the war. If they were on the losing side, they had no legal status and had to resort to taking in boarders or doing menial jobs. Often the oldest daugher had to work to help remaining sons pay for their education, and she often made the most sacrifices and became the typical maiden aunt. These women worked at inferior office jobs or as shop girls. Widows on the winning side were given the tobacco stamp store concessions.

There are an impressive number of competent women lawyers who at present defend liberal causes, women's legal rights in matrimonial disputes, and the injured parties in social abuses. These lawyers are extremely effective in spite of the odds. (The word *abogada* is not accepted by the Spanish Academy; it is *una abogado;* the same applies to *médica* for doctor, but *doctora* is accepted.) In 1971 the first woman judge in juvenile court was appointed. Women doctors and psychologists have a very impressive record. A number of women are directors of small businesses and there is an Asociación de Mujeres de Empresa (Association of Business Women). There are several women in the local and national government.

Women, of course, have always played a prominent role in education, but the number of those with an education beyond the secondary level is small, and the rate of illiteracy for women is twice that of men. Until recently coeducation was frowned on, but it is widely in vogue now. Women's education was for many years in the hands of nuns dedicated to their religion. At present more women are attending the universities every year. At this level most of them now study the humanities (*filosofía y letras*) or pharmacy, in order to go into the traditional professions for women, but an increasing number are entering medicine, chemistry, the social sciences, architecture, engineering, law. Another area into which women have made great inroads is communications: journalism, radio, and television. There are university schools or departments now giving instruction in this field.

Women also work in top positions as museum curators and librarians (such as the head of the Archivo de Indias in Seville). Many women with doctoral degrees do research at the Consejo de Investigaciones Superiores, but they are rarely accepted as head professors at the university level. Of the 12,000 university professors only a handful are women, but even this is changing with the creation of new universities throughout Spain.

A number of middle-class women in their forties are going back to school at the university level to finish their education. These women married very young and their children are now of university age so that they are free of domestic responsibilities. Being in school also relieves their boredom and distracts them from marital difficulties.

An increasing number of women work in banks, which was not the case a generation ago. Many others work in publishing, as radio announcers, in marketing, in social work and health care, and as writers. Women also serve as policewomen in Madrid and in other Spanish cities in areas of heavy traffic congestion. These women have been very successful in their jobs; not even cabdrivers can argue their way out of a ticket.

Young girls with only a primary school education tend to study at academies for typing, sewing, or hair dressing, and then work in offices where they are copying papers, or in shops as seamstresses or as beauty operators. Such work brings in extra income for large families and gives the girls money for clothes, records, and other consumer items, in addition to social security benefits.

Although middle-class women can find good day-care centers, there is a drastic need for more centers for working-class women in the cities and in the small towns of Andalusia where the husband is a migrant worker and the wife herself has to work. There is also a lack of trained women in industry, and women who do work with dangerous chemicals or in metalworking plants have a high rate of accidents. Ironically, the middle-class woman has dreams of emancipation from home through work, while the lower-class girls dream of emancipation from work through marriage and a home. The fear of remaining single (the maiden-aunt complex) is still strong, but the solution is no longer the convent.

In regard to married women at home, everything is calculated to keep them in the kitchen, particularly women with large families. Franco encouraged such large families (*familias numerosas*) by giving the mothers medals, cash benefits, and the families reduced rates on railway tickets, entrance fees, and tuition. They could not be evicted from their place of residence, and their husbands received higher salaries. Many traditional, conservative, upper-middle-class families are also large, the majority of them having from four to six children.

In the area of women's legal rights great progress has been made. Formerly women were not allowed to sign a contract, to work, or to receive any kind of salary without the husband's permission. A married women could not accept an inheritance or be the executor of a will, nor could she legally dictate how the family earnings were to be spent, even though she contributed toward the income. A father was not obligated to "recognize" an illegitimate child, but women were penalized severely for adultery or abortion. The old Spanish saying, *Con la madre, la esposa y la hija no se gastan bromas* (No levity with one's own mother, wife, or daughter), was the male attitude, but with someone else's mother, wife, or daughter it was another matter. Today things are very different. All these older laws or customs have now been changed, or are in process of being changed. However, the element of *machismo* in a male dominated society is dying a very slow death.

In their dress Spanish women do not differ greatly from the women of other European countries or the United States. The widespread wearing of black has all but disappeared, except in remote areas. In the cities blue jeans are omnipresent. The dresses are just as casual and the shoes just as uncomfortable and stylized as in New York or Paris. The only difference is that not as many Spanish women can afford to (or know how to) dress quite as stylishly, but they are learning fast. There is no doubt that the fashionably appareled Spanish lady is a world beater and Spanish styles take a back seat to no other. Balenciaga's designs are an example of the extent to which Spain has come of age in the realm of fashion.

Spaniards are eating better today than ever in their history. More bread and potatoes are consumed per person than in the 1960s, and also more meat, particularly pork and chicken. Beef is still relatively expensive, and a good steak is very hard to find in Spain. Spaniards spend a higher percentage of their income on food than do the inhabitants of any other European country, but this does not mean that the Spanish diet is superior. There is the ever-present problem of an excess of fats with a consequently low vitamin intake. Despite this deficiency Spaniards have gained measurably in stature within the last twenty years, approximately two centimeters in height, in fact. But the average Spaniard is still shorter than most other Europeans, and also more overweight.[84]

The Spanish cuisine is not as highly regarded as that of France or Italy, but Spain has produced a few dishes that are truly incomparable. The one that tops them all is the *paella valenciana*, which consists of rice, colored and flavored with saffron, the rice grains separable and not sticky. Into this are added all the varieties of shellfish available, especially shrimp, clams, oysters, lobster tails, crayfish, some diced tomatoes, small pieces of pork, chicken, and a couple of kinds of Spanish sausage, *chorizo* and *longaniza*, cut into small pieces. Flavor it all with garlic, onions, herbs to suit. Steam slowly.

Although I have made many trips to Spain in my life, and have seen many wonders there and met many fine people, I still seem to remember most clearly and with deepest affection those places where I was served the best paellas. My first outstanding paella was in San Sebastián, in the Basque provinces, my second was in Segovia, of all places, for this provincial city is not near the coast. I have never been able to get a first-class paella in Madrid, despite innumerable orders in the best hotels and restaurants of the capital city.

The paella I remember most fondly of all was served in Valencia, in the old Hotel Nacional, just opposite the railway station. I arrived on the train from Seville accompanied by a large trunk, because I was embarking on a Mediterranean journey. The porter, a gnarled old man of more than sixty, grabbed the trunk, wrapped a strap around it, hoisted it on his back and said:"¿Adónde?" Where to? When I said, "Just across the street," he beamed. "It has the best food in town," he said. "Be sure to try their paella." Well, I did try their paella, and it was perfect.

I have been looking for another paella as succulent as that one ever since, without success. I am afraid that most Spanish cooks have forgotten how to make a good paella; it does take time, lots of shopping, and a good palate for taste. There are other Spanish dishes of course, that are excellent, and some unique basic food products. The Spanish fish, *merluza*, for example, cooked almost any way, is one of the best fishes in the world. The *caldo gallego* and the *fabada asturiana* are both catchall soups containing meats and potatoes, and they can have a superlatively satisfying effect on the stomach. The *gazpacho andaluz*, a cold tomato based soup, is also incomparable. It is the Andalusian counterpart of the French vichyssoise, but tastes better to many gourmets.

One of the most talked about subjects in Spain today is the presence of the United States military bases on Spanish soil. In September of 1953 General Franco signed an agreement with this country permitting the construction of these bases. Theoretically each base is presumed to be under the Spanish flag and Spanish command, and in the case of actual war the bases may not be used except by mutual (which, of course, means Spanish) consent. The total cost of the bases was over half a billion dollars.

There are four major bases: three of them are Strategic Air Command bomber bases located at Morón, near Seville; at Torrejón, near Madrid; and at Sanjurjo-Valenzuela, near Zaragoza. There is also a huge combined naval-and-air base at Rota, near Cádiz, which unhappily has been referred to as "America's answer to Gibraltar." It is our mightiest bastion in Europe, and cost well over $100 million. A 485-mile-long oil pipeline runs from the base at Rota, on up through Morón and Torrejón, and then to the base at Zaragoza. In addition to the above there are two minor air bases: at San Pablo, near Seville, and a fighter center at Reus, ninety miles southwest of Barcelona. All the bases, with the exception of Rota, were constructed at places where there were existent airfields. At other sites in Spain the United States also has the use of certain Spanish military facilities, for example, at El Ferrol, in Galicia, and at Cartagena on the Valencian coast, both of which are naval depots. The Spanish bases put U.S. bombers within 3,000 miles of the industrial heart of the Soviet Union. The naval base at Rota houses the Polaris submarines, and doubles the effectiveness of this thrust toward Russia. Unfortunately, oil leakage from this area blackened and ruined for years to come several beautiful nearby beaches.

American military men in Spain number around 10,000, perhaps less, with about the same number of dependents accompanying them. These men wear civilian clothes when they visit the Spanish towns, but of course it is as easy to spot an American in Spain as it would be to spot a kangaroo in New York. Personal relationships between the Spaniards and Americans have run the gamut from good, to bad, to indifferent. Spaniards seldom make a public issue of this, but the vast majority would certainly prefer to see the Americans go home. There are frequent manifestations and parades in the Spanish cities near the bases making this perfectly clear.

The Sixteenth Air Force, which controls the Spanish bases, is the largest of the Strategic Air Command's overseas forces. It administers all the joint bases in Spain. The Spanish base agreement has been renewed several times since it was first made, each time with more misgivings on the Spanish side. With the development of the ICBM missiles, the strategic value of the Spanish bases has declined, and may soon be approaching the vanishing point. Felipe González, the Socialist Prime Minister of Spain, in Bonn in May 1983, added his approval to the deployment of 572 new U.S. nuclear missiles in Europe. These are to be placed in Britain, West Germany, Italy, Belgium, and Holland. Spain officially joined NATO on May 30, 1982, becoming that group's sixteenth member nation, and the first new member since 1965. The Spanish people have been restive ever since, especially the Socialists.

Spain is working hard to modernize her own military forces. The defense budget for 1984 was approximately $4 billion, with more than half of this earmarked for specific areas of modernization. This was an increase of nearly 16 percent over the military budget for 1983, and represents an enormous sacrifice in view of how desperate is the need for this money in other areas.[104] During the summer of 1983 German parachutists took part in military maneuvers in Spain, and Spanish military units took part in similar maneuvers with the R.A.F. Spaniards are no longer isolationists. They realize fully that their country, behind the Pyrenees, and surrounded by water on three sides, is a well-protected bastion from which the defense of Europe might logically be directed. What they do want is to be treated as equals.

How is this expansion of the military budget being handled by the Spanish government? The military is still the key to the immediate future of Spain, as it has been for more than a century. There is no easy solution to this problem, but at least it is now being squarely faced. In February 1983 Felipe González put before the Cortes a military reform program that would require the retirement of superfluous generals (most of whom are in their 70s), institute merit promotion to replace seniority, limit the military's privilege of trying civilians and of trying its own personnel when charged with sedition or subversion, cut the size of the army but modernize and professionalize it, substantially increase the pay for all military personnel, thus making the armed forces an attractive career to a broader range of young men. Essentially the same measures were proposed, without success, in the 1880s, again by Primo de Rivera in the 1920s, and even more recently by Manuel Azaña in 1933 in the days of the Republic.[94]

The Socialists believe that this time the program may work. Recent attempts by the military to intervene politically have not gone well, the king seems committed to democracy, and the people at large are sick of military domination after nearly forty years of it. The Socialist government is playing its cards very carefully. NATO has become a crucial factor in this high-stakes game. When Spain joined NATO in 1982, the Socialists, then the opposition party, voted against membership. After winning the last elections in a landslide, Felipe González promised to hold a referendum on whether or not to continue in this alliance, but as a matter of fact the government has recently soft-pedaled the referendum and approved a huge $4 billion budget for the military.

Obviously the idea is to interest the younger officers, as a matter of pride, in bringing their commands up to NATO standards, thus keeping their minds off politics. The fervent hope is that this may remove the threat of a military intervention in the government. In taking these steps the Socialists are treading on dangerous ground, with no certainty as to the outcome, but at least it is true that there will never be a better time to change the army.

The other side of the picture is that terrorism might provoke a military coup. There is a strong feeling in the army that if the government cannot stop terrorism the army will. This is the crucial problem in Spain today. The principal source of this terrorism is the Basque ETA, the extremist group among the Basque separatists. The ETA is killing more victims than it ever did during the Franco dictatorship. "From 1968 until 1975, when Franco died, ETA terrorists killed 43 persons in Spain. In the three-year transition between dictatorship and democracy, 94 persons were killed. From 1979, when the democratic government began, until the end of 1983, the ETA killed 282 persons. The overwhelming majority of the victims were police and soldiers on duty in the Basque region. It is obvious that ETA believes that it can achieve its goal of a leftist, independent Basque homeland by provoking a coup that would somehow break up the Spanish state."[114]

Spain's delayed entrance into the Common Market is another factor that weighs heavily on which turn Spain may take. Spanish pride has been sorely hurt by the continuing rejections of her admission to the CM, and this may swing public opinion away from the desire for European cooperation and toward self-containment.[95] By chance or by necessity Spaniards are used to going it alone, and the old xenophobia is always just under the surface. The four decades of alienation from the rest of Europe under General Franco has left its indelible mark. Spain is now at the point where she could add great strength to the Western European community, of which the United States is also a partner, and if this should be lost because of a wound to Spanish pride it would be a needless waste and a political disaster.

The tourist "boom" again picked up in Spain during the 1980s, and in the choice areas hotel reservations had to be made many weeks, even months, in advance. Barcelona's *Vanguardia*, one of the most widely sold newspapers in Spain, in its issue of August 18, 1983, reproduced a large photograph of tourists sleeping on the steps of a "full" hotel in

Palma. There were similar scenes in many other parts of the country. The number of tourists entering Spain in 1983 was around 35 million and they spent over five-and-a-half billion dollars, 20 percent more than in the preceding year. U.S. tourists increased by nearly 50 percent over 1982, mainly because of the more favorable rate of exchange. A few years ago the dollar was worth 56 pesetas, in 1983 it bought 150 pesetas. Had it not been for the influx of these tourist revenues, the country's economy, which was on the ropes, might easily have collapsed. Intelligent Spaniards realize this, but the deteriorating service in many hotels certainly does not reflect any such realization.[102]

The Madrid paper, *El País*, in its issue of August 12, 1983, editorialized as follows: "Tourism has perhaps been the most important single activity in the recent economic history of Spain. The 'takeoff' of the 1960s was generated largely by tourism. Tourism stimulated construction, modified the demand for food products, provided employment for great numbers of workers, and contributed significantly toward keeping our foreign exchange in balance."[96] Tourism is just as important for Spain in the 1980s as it was in the 1960s, but rising prices and poor service may in the long run kill the goose that laid the golden egg. Unstable political conditions, increased terrorism, and mugging on the streets would definitely have that result.

In the mid-1980s Spain was again walking the tightrope, but indications appeared favorable because the majority of the people were patient, forbearing, not expecting miracles, willing to tighten their belts and give the government a chance. An editorial in *Cambio 16* in the fall of 1983 stated the case well: "Except for two frenetic minorities which have repeatedly tried to destroy our country, Spanish public opinion reveals such serenity and equilibrium that it could be said Spain is one of the most intelligent countries in Europe politically."[97]

There are points of crisis. Unemployment topped 18 percent in May 1984, the highest in Europe, and Spain's Socialist government called on workers to accept further sacrifices as a six-and-a-half billion dollar industry modernization program got under way. For decades General Franco kept obsolete and unprofitable businesses alive because of political expediency, and since the dictator's death more than two million jobs have been lost because of the new government's laissez-faire economy. Restructuring and modernization of industries is now an imperative, particularly in the areas of steel production, shipbuilding, and consumer appliances. Labor unrest is growing and is rapidly becoming a critical national problem. Inflation is 12 percent a year, the national economic growth rate is a bare 2 percent annually, terrorism is a frequent menace, and the danger of a military takeover is not past.[103] There is still considerable discontent among the higher military officers. In Andalusia, the most deprived region of the country, 40 percent of the working population under age twenty-five is unemployed, and that area was recently hit by the worst drought in history.[106] At the other end of the peninsula, in the summer of 1983 the Basque provinces suffered devastating floods. Spain was still trying to get into the European Common Market, but admission has been opposed by France.* The Spanish Minister of the Treasury, Miguel Boyer, stated: "Self-discipline is the *only* solution to our economic problems."

In a poll taken in October 1983 concerning the public's opinion of the government, results indicated that the highest dissatisfaction was with what was being done about unemployment and terrorism. The percentages given below indicate whether or not the people thought the government was doing a good job concerning certain crucial issues:[98]

	A Good Job	A Bad Job
Terrorism	24%	76%
Unemployment	26%	74%
Urban Crime	32%	68%
Economic Measures	34%	66%

At the same time 60% thought that the socialist government *on the whole* was "efficacious," and 64% felt that its measure of success would improve in the future. In November 1983 the editors of *Cambio 16* went into more detail regarding the positive and the negative aspects of the government's accomplishments. Among the positive achievements listed were: devaluation of the peseta; expropriation of the big holding company Rumasa; opening of the barrier at Gibraltar; revision of social security; reduction of inflation; unemployment at least held steady; pensions raised 13 percent to 16 percent, mandatory forty-hour work week; mandatory thirty-days vacation; high government salaries cut; abortion depenalized; penal code reformed; exports increased; reforms made in the military along with modernization of the military defense; expressways financed to improve communications.

---

* *El País*, in the issue of February 13, 1984, reported that Mitterrand had asked the Common Market countries "to accept the entrance of Spain and Portugal without delay."

Among the negative aspects of the government's policies were: government does not keep people properly informed; lack of realism in foreign policy; Spain still not in Common Market; fight against terrorism and crime ineffectual; vacillation in regard to Spain's membership in NATO; high government deficit; agricultural reforms indecisive; widespread parliamentary arrogance in relations with opposition groups.[107] The amazing thing about these lists is not how different we are from Spain, but on the contrary how similar in both the United States and Spain are the accomplishments, the problems, and the complaints of our two countries in this decade of the 1980s.

The most acute problem in Spanish industry today is the lack of skilled workers and trained personnel. This is true at the management level and even more so on a lower technical level. Spain has a large economic potential in natural and human resources, but not enough has been done to educate the worker. This also involves a change in attitude toward education and in the traditional antipathy between the lower classes and the educated *señorito*.

The vast majority of people who migrate to the cities or to Germany have no training whatsoever, except in agriculture. They try to get jobs as *peones* (the lowest unskilled construction workers) or as *serenos* or *porteros* (night watchmen or janitors). Most of these people are not reliable steady workers. Often a peon works for only a few months on a construction job and then leaves because he has found something more profitable. The turnover is particularly great in the construction industry. This does not improve the slipshod quality of Spanish construction. It is hard to get a good electrician, plumber, or even carpenter in Madrid because these artisans are vastly overworked and, like their American counterparts, charge absurd prices when they do come. Many of these skilled workers migrated to the coast to areas of hotel construction or to Mallorca, where they receive higher pay.

The *albañil* (mason) category is difficult to explain; he is more of a general handyman in construction than a simple bricklayer. This sort of situation leads to a kind of *chapuza* mentality. A chapuza is a temporary, often imaginative, but slipshod solution to a problem, implying poor quality in both material and workmanship. Spaniards are ingenious at finding solutions of this sort to utilize old material, but sometimes they do not know how to install new material. A friend of mine living in Spain was fit to be tied after battling with every type of worker for three months during major repairs on his apartment. Incidentally, the contractors who supervised the job were called *el sereno* and *el portero* by the workmen, as a reference to their former professions.

There seems to be a general lack of professionalism or what we might call "professional pride" in these sectors, perhaps because people are not really interested in the work they are doing, or the industrialization process is still too new to create that feeling. Yet, many parents of children in working-class and rural sectors can't wait until their children are old enough to get jobs. They are always looking for an *enchufe*, a personal recommendation to get their children "placed" (*colocados*). They do not want their children to go on to higher education because they have the opinion that college students are *vagos*, lazy, live off their parents, and do nothing to support the family. Nevertheless, the government has established a number of very good technical training schools which are much more successful than their agricultural counterparts. Many more are needed, however, if Spanish industrialization is to continue to grow and at the same time improve the quality of its output.

Absenteeism is an increasing problem in Spain as a protest against the tedium of assembly-line production. The managerial class and capitalistic interests are so intent on increasing production by modern methods that they forget the human consequences for the worker forced to repeat the same task time after time on monotonous shifts. This also has begun to result in shoddy workmanship. There are many courses in scientific techniques in managerial training, marketing, and production at the executive level, but there is very little help for the worker. Furthermore, foreign or multinational companies in Spain often resort to practices they would not dare to use in their own countries.

There are other consequences of the industrialization process. One of the most important has been to dilute the strong regional feelings through migration to the big cities. Andalusians and Murcianos work in Barcelona, those from Extremadura come to Madrid, people from the Castilian plateau gravitate to Bilbao, forming a heterogeneous population whose only form of cohesion is a common interest in labor rights. They have trouble with the new social milieu, even with the language, and feel at odds with the people around them.

The move to industrial centers has also produced the usual social problems: *chabolismo*, shacks and shantytowns on the outskirts of the large cities; lack of adequate housing, sanitation, lighting, water, child-care centers, inadequate social services, juvenile delinquency. Until very recently the state and the industries involved seemed to be more interested in increasing production and the GNP than in benefiting those who were making this possible. There are probably more sociologists than social workers in this country. At present there is a tenuous truce between the workers, the capitalists, and the state, but one glaring inequity remains: *the rich man does not pay his share of the way in taxes.* Until this is remedied there cannot be a real peace among these three components in Spain.

Sometimes a lack of planning or lack of foresight has caused serious problems. Franco was so obsessed with the return of Gibraltar to Spain that in an effort to strangle the territory he cut off the labor supply and land access and placed a huge iron barrier across the entranceway. Hundreds of Spanish workers who had been receiving good pay in Gibraltar were thrown out of work. To find them jobs some families were shipped to places as far away as Barcelona, while others had to be given unemployment compensation, which placed a tremendous burden on the economy.

The present government, realizing that this approach was a disaster, has removed the barrier and labor restrictions so that now these Spanish workers are again receiving good pay in English currency. However, the desire to get Gibraltar back is still very strong in Spain, and the issue is always under discussion. Whenever British warships anchor at the Rock a hue and cry is raised in Spain. For others to point out that the population of Gibraltar does not wish to live under Spanish rule cuts no ice inside Spain. All Spaniards know that this territory is historically and geographically a part of Spain, was taken from her in a war, then repopulated with British subjects, as the Spanish inhabitants who lived there were gradually pushed out. So Gibraltar is still a very sore point in Spain, and one can hardly pick up a newspaper without finding some mention of it. There exists a widespread hope that some accommodation with Great Britain might be reached. As with the Falklands, Great Britain will occasionally hold out a carrot, but there appears to be no sincere desire to come to any kind of compromise on this issue.

The building boom in Spain has now slackened off and left thousands of workers without a job. Another lamentable result of the "boom" was pointed out in a recent issue of *El País* under the heading "THE DISASTERS OF PEACE." This article stated that in the past twenty years of rebuilding Spain has suffered more destruction in her small towns and cities than in any of her wars. "Until recently Spain was a poor country, but it was beautiful," said the article. But in the fever to build, build, build, hundreds of beautiful old buildings, streets, and plazas have been destroyed or disfigured beyond repair. Perhaps this is the price of progress, but it is a very high price to pay when one considers that what has been torn down can never be replaced.

Another evidence of this same progress is the expansion of the "fast food" business in Spain. They use the English words. One advertisement points out that there are now more than ten thousand *hamburgueserías* (hamburger stands and restaurants) in the world, and the European chain is growing rapidly every year. There are already fourteen *hamburgueserías* functioning in Spain, and franchises are for sale for the enterprising entrepreneur. Along with these kinds of business ventures, of course, comes the necessity to learn English and to acquire the proper "know-how." This term is also well known in Spain. English courses are advertised in all the newspapers, and although some of them cost the student four to five hundred dollars, they are well attended.

In her eagerness to modernize and industrialize, Spain has not neglected her cultural development. The country's musical tradition has always been outstanding, and Spain has produced today's best tenor in Plácido Domingo, who sings regularly in the Metropolitan Opera of New York; one of the world's great sopranos, Montserrat Caballé, who also frequently performs at the Met; certainly one of the finest pianists in the world in Alicia de Larrocha; and before his recent death, the best cellist of this century in Pablo Casals. This is not to mention the most famous twentieth-century painter, Pablo Picasso; the eminent guitarist, Andrés Segovia; the fine musical composer, Joaquín Rodrigo; the motion picture director, Luis Buñuel; and two Nobel Laureates in literature, Juan Ramón Jiménez and Vicente Aleixandre.

A long article in a recent Sunday issue of *El País* traced Plácido Domingo's career, and pointed out that another Spanish tenor, Manuel García (1775–1832), introduced opera into the United States. Many fine Spanish singers come from the *zarzuelas*, a kind of light opera with a long and popular tradition in Spain. Plácido's parents sang in zarzuelas, and he himself got his start there. Hearing Mario Lanza sing some operatic selections in a film was what interested him in Grand Opera. The rest is history. Grand Opera has always been popular in Spain, especially in Barcelona. In this city's famous and huge opera house, known as the Liceo, are given some of the finest performances in the world.[100]

Today most Spaniards do not like to be reminded of Franco, just as most Germans prefer not to remember Hitler. In Spain most of the streets that had been renamed for the General or for José Antonio have now had their old names restored, and it cost the government a pretty penny to remake and replace hundreds of these street signs all over Spain. In Valencia recently when a statue of General Franco on horseback was torn down, the police turned out in case there was opposition. There was no need for it. Franco reminds the Spaniards of their civil war, and this is an ignominy that they profoundly wish had never taken place. In a poll recorded by *Cambio 16* the majority of those responding called the war "a brutality without precedent," and 73 percent regarded it as "a shameful episode in the history of our country that it is best to forget."[101]

Easier said than done. Spaniards can no more forget their bloody civil war than we in America can forget our own, which took place more than one hundred years ago. They can, however, refuse to talk about it, and often do, but in the subconscious mind this awful bloodletting still has its roots. It is perhaps the one most important event necessary for the understanding of Spain today.

Unamuno, the Spanish philosopher, tells the story of a South American friend of his who, on viewing a bloody statue of Christ in one of the Spanish cathedrals, exclaimed "But these Christs!—Good God! this thing repels, revolts. . . ." Unamuno answered him by saying that it revolts those who are unacquainted with the cult of suffering, but since suffering is the essence of being Spanish, these tortured, bloody, agonizing Christs do certainly have their place in the churches of Spain. "This harsh, raw manner of ours," Unamuno went on, "not everyone can stand it. It has been said that hate is rife in Spain. Perhaps it is. Perhaps we begin by hating ourselves."[5] This hatred is like a subterranean stream of lava. It explains Spanish violence. The Spaniard likes violent spectacles, which beget the emotion of tragedy. That is why the bullfight has been so popular in Spain for so many centuries. That is why Spain has had so many bloody wars. The Spaniard, above everything else, feels that to be a whole man he must know how to face death with dignity.

We always come back to the land, which is man's true umbilical cord. The Spanish earth is as varied as it is beautiful. Overall it is a hard and flinty land, but so is a diamond in the rough. The wide shining *rías* of Galicia, the green mountains of Asturias, the rock-strewn plains and hills of Castile, the olive groves of Andalusia under a blazing sun, the fertile *huerta* of Valencia, the Costa Brava north of Barcelona—they all make up what is called Spain, "the treasure house of the Lord."

The vast tableland of Castile is obviously the heart and sinew of this rather dubious organic whole. Castile knew how to conquer, but Castile has never learned how to govern. Madrid, made the capital by Philip II, will never give way in this role to any other Spanish city, for its mighty bureaucracy has multiplied so plentifully that, were it to die overnight, half of Spain would be without work. Barcelona would make a better capital in many ways, because it is a more progressive city. Its population is more energetic and less quixotic; even Valencia might be an improvement on Madrid. These are the nation's most populous regions, the one industrial, the other agricultural. But this is only daydreaming, for it will never be. The history of Spain will never change that much. Spain has to hang on until Castile and Madrid have learned the art of government, which means restricting political action to the realm of what is possible. Until that day comes all Spain must hope, wait, and suffer, while in the country's heart still lives the impossible dream.

References

Quotations have been taken from the following works, identified by the numbers as they appear in the text:

1. Pío Baroja y Nessi, *Juventud, egolatría,* called in English, *Youth and Egolatry,* Knopf, New York, 1920.
2. Azorín, *El paisaje de España visto por los españoles,* Madrid, 1917.
3. Alexandre Dumas, *Adventures in Spain* (written 1846), Doubleday, New York, 1960.
4. *España y españoles pintados por sí mismos,* ed. by Edouard Barry, Paris, n.d.
5. Miguel de Unamuno, *Essays and Soliloquies,* Knopf, New York, 1925.
6. Pío Baroja y Nessi, *Caesar or Nothing,* Knopf, New York, 1919.
7. Ángel Ganivet, *Idearium español,* Buenos Aires, 1946.
8. José Rubia Barcia, *Iconografía de Valle-Inclán,* Univ. of Cal. Press, 1960.
9. Edmondo de Amicis, *Spain and the Spaniards,* Putnam, New York, 1881.
10. Salvador de Madariaga, *Spain, a Modern History,* Praeger, New York, 1960.
11. Gilbert Chase, *The Music of Spain,* Norton, New York, 1941.
12. Edward Gibbon, *The Decline and Fall of the Roman Empire,* Modern Library, Random House, New York, n.d.
13. Gerald Brenan, *The Face of Spain,* Farrar, Straus and Cudahy, New York, 1956.
14. Gerald Brenan, *The Literature of the Spanish People,* Meridian, New York, 1957.

15. Martin A. S. Hume, *History of the Spanish People*, Cambridge Univ. Press, London, 1901.
16. Américo Castro, *The Structure of Spanish History*, Princeton Univ. Press, 1954. (See also his *The Spaniards*, University of California Press, 1971.)
17. W. S. Merwin, *Spanish Ballads*, Doubleday, New York, 1961.
18. Gustave E. von Grunebaum, *Medieval Islam*, Univ. of Chicago Press, 1961.
19. Edward Atiyah, *The Arabs*, Penguin, Edinburgh, 1958.
20. Claudio Sánchez-Albornoz, *La España musulmana, según los autores islamitas y cristianos*, 2 vols., Buenos Aires, 1946.
21. J. B. Trend, *The Civilization of Spain*, Oxford Univ. Press, London, 1958.
22. *La crónica general*, ed. by R. Menéndez Pidal, vol. 5, N.B.A.E., Madrid, 1916.
23. Elisha K. Kane, *The Book of Good Love*, a privately printed translation, William Rudge, New York, 1933.
24. William A. Prescott, *Ferdinand and Isabella*, Lippincott, Philadelphia, 1873.
25. Louis Mumford, "The Medieval Town," an article in *Horizon* magazine, July, 1961.
26. César Barja, *Libros y autores clásicos*, New York, 1941.
27. Martin A. S. Hume, *Spain, Its Greatness and Decay* (1479–1788), Cambridge Univ. Press, London, 1940.
28. John A. Crow, *The Epic of Latin America*, Doubleday, New York, 1952.
29. Pedro Salinas, *Reality and the Poet in Spanish Poetry*, Johns Hopkins Univ. Press, Baltimore, 1940.
30. Edward M. Wilson, *The Solitudes of Don Luis de Góngora*, Cambridge Univ. Press, London, 1931.
31. Ludwig Pfandl, *Introducción al siglo de oro*, Barcelona, 1929.
32. William Stirling Maxwell and Luis Carreño, *Stories of the Spanish Artists*, Chatto & Windus, London, 1910.
33. N. B. Adams, *The Heritage of Spain*, Henry Holt, New York, 1959.
34. José Ortega y Gasset, *España invertebrada*, Madrid, 1921.
35. Fernando Díaz-Plaja, *La vida española en el siglo 18*, Barcelona, 1946.
36. John S. C. Abbott, *The Romance of Spanish History*, Harper, New York, 1869.
37. Mariano José de Larra, *Artículos de costumbres*, ed. by Hespelt, Crofts, New York, 1941.
38. William C. Atkinson, *A History of Spain and Portugal*, Penguin, London, 1960.
39. Gerald Brenan, *The Spanish Labyrinth*, Cambridge Univ. Press, London, 1940.

40. John T. Reid, *Modern Spain and Liberalism*, Stanford Univ. Press, 1937.
41. Azorín, *Los pueblos*, Madrid, 1905.
42. Paul Blanshard, *Freedom and Catholic Power in Spain and Portugal*, Beacon, Boston, 1962.
43. Harry Gannes and Theodore Repard, *Spain in Revolt*, Knopf, New York, 1937.
44. Herbert L. Matthews, *The Yoke and the Arrows*, Braziller, New York, 1961.
45. Abram Leon Sachar, *A History of the Jews*, Knopf, New York, 1960.
46. Richard Ford, *Gatherings from Spain* (first published in 1846), Everyman, London, 1906.
47. F. Jay Taylor, *The United States and the Spanish Civil War*, New York, 1956.
48. Claude G. Bowers, *My Mission to Spain*, Simon and Schuster, New York, 1954.
49. Hugh Thomas, *The Spanish Civil War*, Harper, New York, 1961.
50. Thomas J. Hamilton, *Appeasement's Child, the Franco Regime in Spain*, Knopf, New York, 1943.
51. Alvarez del Vayo, *Freedom's Battle*, Knopf, New York, 1940.
52. Stanley G. Payne, *Falange*, Stanford Univ. Press, 1961.
53. Emmet John Hughes, *Report from Spain*, Henry Holt, New York, 1947.
54. Arthur P. Whitaker, *Spain and Defense of the West*, Harper, New York, 1961.
55. Rafael Altamira, *Los elementos de la civilización y del carácter españoles*, Buenos Aires, 1956.
56. "Letter from Barcelona," in *The New Yorker* magazine, Dec. 2, 1961.
57. *Noticias de actualidad*, pub. by U.S. Embassy, Madrid, several issues.
58. *Iberia* magazine, June 15, 1961, New York City.
59. *Iberia* magazine, May 15, 1962, New York City.
60. Helen Phipps, *Some Aspects of the Agrarian Question in Mexico*, Univ. of Texas Press, Austin, 1925.
61. Elie Faure, introd. to Francisco de Goya, *The Disasters of the War*, Allen & Unwin, London, 1937.
62. Angel del Río, *Historia de la literatura española*, vol. II, Dryden, New York, 1953.
63. Jeanette Campiglia, unpublished doctoral study on Lope de Vega, U.C.L.A., Los Angeles.
64. *The New York Times*, August 24, 1962.
65. Translation by Katharine Elizabeth Strathdee. Reprinted with permission of author.

66. Richard E. Chandler and Kessel Schwartz, *A New History of Spanish Literature*, Louisiana State Univ. Press, 1961.
67. Translation by Sir Richard Fanshawe, *Shorter Poems and Translations*, London, 1648.
68. Francis C. Hayes, *Lope de Vega*, Twayne Publishers, New York, 1967.
69. Translation by John A. Crow.
70. Translation by John A. Crow.
71. Richard Herr, "The Twentieth Century Spaniard Views the Spanish Enlightenment," *Hispania*, XLV, May 1962.
72. Richard Herr, *The Eighteenth Century Rebellion in Spain*, Princeton Univ. Press, 1958.
73. *Time*, December 11, 1972.
74. *Los Angeles Times*, June 24, 1973.
75. Stanley G. Payne, *A History of Spain and Portugal*, Vol. 2, Univ. of Wisconsin Press, 1973.
76. *España Hoy*, issues of January and February, 1974. This is a periodical published by the Spanish government, Madrid.
77. Jean Anderson, "Castles in Spain," in *Diversion* magazine, New York, February 1974, reports on the *paradores* and *albergues* of Spain, and lists several recommendations.
78. *España Hoy*, October 1972.
79. Jerome R. Mintz, "Trouble in Andalusia," in *Natural History Magazine*, May 1972.
80. Benjamin Welles, *Spain: The Gentle Anarchy*, New York, 1965.
81. *Los Angeles Times*, July 8, 1973.
82. *International Herald Tribune*, Paris, December 21, 1973.
83. *Los Angeles Times*, February 15, 1974.
84. Juan Kattán-Ibarra and Tim Connell, *Spain After Franco*, National Textbook Co., Skokie, Illinois, 1981.
85. Horace Sutton, "Democracy in Spain," in *Saturday Review*, October 29, 1977.
86. *El País*, Madrid, September 19, 1983.
87. *El País*, Madrid, May 22, 1983.
88. Robert G. Mead, "The Hispanic and Luso-Brazilian World," in *Hispania*, Vol. 65, May 1982.
89. David Ross Gerling, "Los diarios de Madrid," in *Hispania*, Vol. 64, September 1981.
90. *Cambio 16*, Madrid, September 12–19, 1983.
91. *El País*, Madrid, September 24, 1983.
92. *Cambio 16*, Madrid, October 3–10, 1983. Also *Newsweek*, August 1, 1983.
93. *Cambio 16*, Madrid, October 10, 1983.
94. Willliam Pfaff, "Army is the Key in Socialist Spain," in *The Los Angeles Times*, March 13, 1983.

95. *El País* (International Edition), Madrid, October 17, 1983.
96. *El País*, Madrid, August 12, 1983.
97. *Cambio 16*, Madrid, October–November, 1983.
98. *Cambio 16*, Madrid, October 3–10, 1983.
99. *Cambio 16*, Madrid, September 12–19, 1983.
100. *El País* (dominical), Madrid, May 15, 1983.
101. *Cambio 16*, Madrid, September 19–26, 1983.
102. *Vanguardia*, Barcelona, August 23, 1983.
103. *Vanguardia*, Barcelona, August 20, 1983.
104. *El País*, Madrid, September 24, 1983.
105. *El País* (International Edition), Madrid, September 12, 1983.
106. *Vanguardia*, Barcelona, August 18, 1983.
107. *Cambio 16*, Madrid, October–November, 1983.
108. *Cambio 16*, Madrid, September 1983.
109. Ian Gibson, *El asesinato de Federico García Lorca*, Editorial Bruguera, Barcelona, 1981.
110. "Spain: Democracy Wins," in *Time*, June 27, 1977.
111. "Democracy Under Siege," in *Newsweek*, May 18, 1981.
112. José Yglesias, *The Franco Years*, Bobbs-Merrill, New York, 1977.
113. Fernando Díaz-Plaja, *The Spaniard and the Seven Deadly Sins*, Charles Scribners, New York, 1967.
114. Stanley Meisler, "Basques—A Dilemma for Spain," *The Los Angeles Times*, March 2, 1984.
115. *Le Monde*, Paris, December 29, 1983. (The new no-nonsense antiterrorist laws are now being applied.)

IMPORTANT DATES IN SPANISH HISTORY

206 B.C.–409 A.D.–Roman Spain.

409 A.D.–Vandals and other barbarous tribes invade Spain.

414–Visigoths invade Spain.

711–Roderick, last Visigothic king, defeated by Moors.

722–Pelayo, the Visigoth, defeats Moors at Covadonga, Asturias.

778–Charlemagne invades Spain.

785–Abderrahman I begins the great mosque of Córdoba.

912–961–Abderrahman III: golden age of caliphate of Córdoba.

950–Castile wins independence from León.

997–Almanzor sacks Santiago de Compostela.

1010–Christians capture Córdoba temporarily and loot city.

1012–1058–The Jewish scholar, Ben Gabirol, introduces neoplatonic thought into the peninsula.

1068–1091–Reign of al-Mutamid in Seville.

1085–Alfonso VI of Castile and León captures Toledo from Moors.

1092–1167–Rabbi Ben Ezra, famous Jewish scholar.

1094–1099–The Cid takes Valencia from the Moors and rules there.

1130–Alfonso VII establishes a school of scholars at Toledo and thus spreads Arabic, Jewish, and Greek learning throughout western Europe.

1126–1198–Averroës, famous Arab scholar.

1135–1204–Moses Maimonides, famous Jewish philosopher.

1146–Almohades invade Spain from North Africa.

1188–Municipalities of León are given representation in Cortes.

1212–Christians under Alfonso VIII of Castile defeat Moors on plains of Navas de Tolosa in southern Spain.

1230–Castile and León definitively united by Ferdinand III, the Saint.

1236–Ferdinand III, the Saint, captures Córdoba.

1243–Founding of University of Salamanca.

1248—Ferdinand III, the Saint, captures Seville.

1252–1284—Reign of Alfonso X, *el Sabio,* the scholar king.

1348—The Black Death enters Spain.

1350–1369—Reign of Peter the Cruel.

1406–1454—Reign of John II, father of Isabella.

1474—Isabella becomes queen of Castile which unites with Aragon, kingdom of her husband, Ferdinand. Isabella dies in 1504; Ferdinand in 1516.

1480—The Inquisition is established.

1492—Ferdinand and Isabella capture Granada. Jews are expelled from Spain. America is discovered.

1499—*La Celestina,* by Fernando de Rojas, second most famous work of Spanish literature.

1502—Moslems remaining in Spain are given choice of conversion or expulsion. There is a mass conversion. The converted Moslems are called *Moriscos.*

1504–1506—Brief reign of the first Hapsburg, Philip the Handsome, who is married to Juana *la Loca,* daughter of Ferdinand and Isabella.

1516–1555—Reign of Charles I (Charles V of Holy Roman Empire).

1519–1522—Hernán Cortés conquers the Aztecs of Mexico.

1531–1534—Francisco Pizarro conquers Incas of Peru.

1539—Ignatius Loyola founds Society of Jesus.

1542—Book of poetry by Juan Boscán and Garcilaso de la Vega initiates the Golden Age in Spanish letters.

1545—The silver mountain at Potosí, Bolivia, discovered. By 1600 mines in the Spanish colonies have produced three times as much gold and silver as all Europe had in 1500.

1545–1563—Councils of Trent reform Catholic church and initiate the Counter Reformation.

1555–1598—Reign of Philip II.

1561—Philip II moves the capital of Spain to Madrid.

1588—Invincible Armada defeated by the English.

1605—First part of *Don Quixote* appears.

1609–1611—*Moriscos* expelled from Spain by Philip III.

1700–1746—Reign of first Bourbon, Philip V.

1704—British get Gibraltar.

1759–1788—Reign of Charles III.

1767—Charles III expels Jesuits from Spanish dominions.

1808—The French invade Spain. Napoleon places his brother Joseph on the Spanish throne.

1810—The Spanish colonies in the New World begin to establish their own governments. By 1826 independence is achieved.

1812—The Cortes of Cádiz proclaims a liberal, anticlerical constitution.

1820—Riego, with army backing, decrees constitutional government. Ferdinand VII gives in temporarily. This is the first case of military *pronunciamiento* in politics.

1820—The Inquisition is abolished.

1873–1874—The First Spanish Republic.

1923–1930—Dictatorship of General Primo de Rivera.

1931—Alfonso XIII flees from Spain. Establishment of Second Republic.

1936–1939—The Spanish civil war.

1939–1975—Rule of Caudillo, General Francisco Franco.

1953—Spain signs deal on military bases with United States in return for economic aid.

1955—Spain is admitted to United Nations.

1961—Wave of strikes spreads over Spain.

1962—Spain requests admission to European Common Market.

1969—The Spanish Cortes designates Prince Juan Carlos, grandson of Alfonso XIII, to become next king of Spain.

1970—U.S. Bases Agreement renewed.

1973—New cabinet appointed, Franco resigns as President of the Government (Prime Minister), and Admiral Carrero Blanco takes his place.

1973—Carrero Blanco is assassinated in December. Rightist cabinet appointed with Arias Navarro as Prime Minister.

1974—New cabinet begins policy of repression. Opus Dei gives way to Falange in importance in the new government.

1975—Francisco Franco dies on November 20, and on November 22 Juan Carlos is proclaimed king of Spain.

1977—First free elections in 41 years held on June 15. Moderate center parties win heavily.

1978—New constitution approved by 87 percent of the voters on December 6.

1981—Attempted coup by Civil Guard and some military units on February 23. The king denounces the coup and it fails.

1982—On May 30 Spain becomes the sixteenth member nation of the NATO alliance.

1982—The second national elections since Franco's death are held on October 28. The Socialists win a majority in both houses of the Cortes and establish a Socialist government.

1984—Felipe González, the Socialist leader, clamps down on terrorism, and approves a huge federal budget with billions of dollars earmarked for modernizing the armed forces and for education.

Glossary of Spanish Words

AUTO DE FE—act of faith, the trial and punishment of those convicted by the Inquisition

BAILE—dance

CABALLERÍA—chivalry

CABALLERO—mounted man, knight, gentleman

CANTE JONDO—deep song, flamenco song of Andalusia

CANTIGA—medieval poem and song

CAPA—Spanish cape

CHOPO—poplar tree

COMEDIA—Spanish drama of the Golden Age

COMENDADOR—lord

COMUNERO—commoner

CONQUISTADOR—conqueror

COPLA—popular verse or couplet

CORRIDA DE TOROS—running of the bulls, bullfight

CORRIDO—Mexican word for ballad

CORTES—Spanish parliament

ENCINA—live oak tree

FERIA—market, fair

FIESTA—celebration, often very solemn and of religious nature

FLAMENCO—Andalusian music, also called *cante jondo*

FUERO—medieval town's royal charter of privilege

GOBERNACIÓN—Interior Dept.

GRACIOSO—character in Golden Age drama who is companion, joker, advice-giver to the hero

GUITARRA—guitar (—LATINA, Latin guitar;—MORISCA, Moorish guitar)

HACIENDA—Dept. of Finance, Treasury

HERMANDAD–brotherhood

HOSTAL–inn, hostelry, refuge

MAJA–a person "all dressed up," a sport or flashy person

MARRANO–converted Jew; Arabic root words meant "prohibited thing" and "outsider," but derivation *marrano* later came to refer specifically to the converted Jew, and also to take on the offensive meaning of "swine"

MESETA–tableland, plateau

MESTA–medieval organization of sheep raisers

MORISCO–a converted Moor

MOZÁRABE–a Christian living in Moorish territory; his culture, art

MUDÉJAR–a Moslem Moor living in Christian territory; his culture, art

NIÑA BONITA–pretty girl, name given to the Spanish Republic

ORO–gold

PÍCARO–sharper, rogue, boy who lives by his wits

PLATERO–silversmith, hence Plateresque style in architecture

PRONUNCIAMIENTO–rebellion, decree

PUDRIDERO–rotting room in the *Escorial* where bodies of dead kings are left for five years before being entombed

REJA–grille, grating of ironwork

RETABLO–altarpiece, carved work usually back of the altar

REY–king; LOS REYES–the king and queen

ROMANCE–ballad

ROMERÍA–pilgrimage to a religious shrine accompanied by revelry

SABIO–learned, wise

SAETA–arrow (of song) in the *cante flamenco*

SIGLO DE ORO–golden century, Golden Age

SINDICATO–labor union

TASCA–restaurant

TERCIO–Spanish infantry regiment

TERTULIA–gathering for purpose of conversation, specifically a gathering at a café of some literary figure and his admirers

TORERO–bullfighter

TORO–bull

INDEX

Abderrahman III, 55, 57, 58, 60
Abortion, 413, 417
Africa, 6–7, 35, 36
Agriculture, 77, 301–303; and
  Franco, 349, 386; land reform,
  312, 385, 386; *latifundia*, 13, 123,
  301, 386, 393; and Moors, 57,
  224; resettlement, 390, 391
Al-Andalus, 20, 61, 68–89
Alba, Duke of, 169, 170; palace,
  149, 152
Albornoz, Sánchez, 242
Alcalá de Henares, University of,
  150, 184
Alcalá Zamora, 312
Alcázar, 66, 107–108, 230, 358
Alexander VI, Pope, 150, 151
Alfonso VI, 61, 89–90, 92
Alfonso VIII, 94
Alfonso X, the learned, 4, 95, 96,
  97–104; quoted, 70–71, 100–101
Alfonso XI, 140
Alfonso XII, 254–256
Alfonso XIII, 256–257, 285–286,
  288, 292, 399

Alhambra, 71–76, 147, 172, 359
Almanzor, 52, 61–62, 64, 81, 82, 89
Almohades, 54, 65, 66
Almoravides, 54, 65, 88, 90, 93
Alonso, Dámaso, 192
Altamira, caves of, 23–24
Alvarez del Vayo, 338–339, 341
Amadeo I, 255
America, 151, 152, 157–160, 166–
  167; and Ferdinand VII, 246. *See
  also* Cuba; Mexico; South
  America; United States
Anarchists, 294–299; in civil war,
  319; Ferrer, 286–287
Andalusia, 20–21, 35, 61, 359;
  Moriscos, 173, 224; poverty, 302–
  303, 393, 428
Anticlericalism, 267, 361; and
  Second Republic, 293, 307, 310–312
Arabs, 41–44, 55–57, 59–63, 96,
  148. *See also* Moors; *Moriscos;* and
  Mudéjar
Aragon, 17, 25, 82, 94. *See also*
  Ferdinand
Architecture, 59–60, 61, 126;

Architecture (*continued*)
cathedrals, 86–88, 103–106;
Escorial, 171–172; Golden Age,
221; Gothic, 128; Modern, 373,
379; Moorish, 51–53; Mudéjar,
107–108
Armada, 174, 203
Army: and Franco, 317–322; after
Franco, 425; strike of 1917, 289
Asturias, 15, 25, 48–49, 80, 366;
Prince of, 48, 239; revolt of 1934,
315–316, 327
Atlantis, 26
Auto de fe, 169, 182, 183
Automobiles, 374, 381, 388, 396
Averroës, 65–66
Avila, 128, 140, 163
Azaña, Manuel, 307, 313–314;
anticlericalism, 310–312;
president, 312, 317, 338, 339
Azorín, 274, 280, 343; quoted, 280–
283

Bakunin, Michael, 293–294
Ballads, 43–45, 118–120, 130, 131.
See also Songs
Barcelona, 2, 5, 17, 19, 171, 411,
413; and strikes, 286, 315
Baroja, Pío, 2, 186, 269, 343;
quoted, 12–13, 22, 212, 277–280
Basques, 2, 15, 25; in civil war, 319;
separatism, 405, 406
Bathing, 32–34, 61, 149, 411
Berenguer, General, 292
Besteiro, Julián, 301, 330, 331, 340
Bible of Alcalá, Polyglot, 150
Bilbao, 17, 356
Blanco y Negro, 406, 410
Blasco Ibáñez, Vicente, 21–22, 268–
269, 270
Bloodletting, 227, 235
Bonaparte, Joseph, 244, 246, 250
Bonaparte, Napoleon, 240, 244–246
Book of Good Love, 114–117
Borja, Rodrigo, 151
Boscán, Juan, 186
Bourbons, 228–233, 238, 239, 240,
245, 246, 254–257, 399

Bowers, Ambassador Claude G.,
327–332, 333, 341
Brigades, volunteer, 321, 334, 337
Building boom, 373
Bullfights, 31, 179–182, 384
Burgos, 89, 90, 105; Laws of, 159

Caballero, Largo, 301, 312, 317,
320, 327, 330–331, 332, 336, 350;
and Communists, 314–315, 338,
339
Cabezón, Antonio de, 221
Cádiz, 25, 26, 29, 34, 232;
constitution of, 248
Cajal, Ramón y, 242
Calderón de la Barca, 186, 202, 206,
208–210
Cambio 16, 412, 414
Camus, Albert, quoted, 345
Canalejas, 287, 297
Cánovas del Castillo, 294–295
Cante jondo, 21, 73, 382, 391
Carrero Blanco, Luis, 400
Cartagena, 27, 28
Carthaginians, 7, 27–28
Castelar, Emilio, 255
Castile, 4, 19, 72, 81–82, 93, 102,
123, 143, 356, 434; and Cid, 89,
90, 91; and Ferdinand III, 68–69;
influence of, 223–224, 263–264;
and Isabella, 140–142
Castilian Grammar, 151
Castilians, 19–20; bathing, 33;
language, 2, 4, 92, 405; and work,
102, 121
Castro, Américo, 79, 102, 242, 344
Catalans, 2, 17–18, 286, 319, 405
Catalonia, 2, 3, 18, 82, 295–296,
307, 405
Cathedrals, building, 103–106
Catholicism, 14–15, 22, 150; and
Franco, 344; state church, 38, 82,
150, 232, 344
Catholics: and Romans, 30–31, 35;
U.S., 323, 336
Cela, Camilo José, 399
Celestina, The, 154–157, 186
Celts, 25–26

Censorship, 168, 285, 408
Center of Historic Studies, 260
Cervantes, Miguel, 4, 7, 19, 173–174, 203, 210; quoted, 187, 225. *See also* Don Quixote; Quixotism
Charlemagne, 18
Charles II, 226–227
Charles III, 233, 237, 242, 243
Charles IV, 238, 239–240, 242, 243–244
Charles V, 19, 152n, 162–169; domain, 164
Church, Catholic; founding, 30–31; and Franco, 344; *Index expurgatorius*, 168; intolerance, 182; New World, 157, 159; and Second Republic, 293, 306–307, 310–311; and unemployment, 224. *See also* Catholicism; Catholics; Inquisition
Churches: Basilica of San Juan Bautista, 41; behavior in, 232; carved wood in, 220; Cathedral of Burgos, 105; Cathedral of León, 105; Cathedral of Santiago, 52, 86–88, 363–364; Cathedral of Seville, 69, 104–105; Cathedral of Toledo, 104; St. Vincent, 50, 53; Santa María la Blanca, 98; Santo Tomé, 215; San Vicente of Toledo, 214; Valley of the Fallen, 346–351
Church-state, 82, 150–151, 232, 344–345
Cid, the, 4, 18, 21, 92, 93, 105
Cid, Poem of the, 89–91
Cisneros, Cardinal Jiménez de, 33, 148, 150, 163
Civil Guard, 406
Civilization, Arab, 55–57, 59–63, 97
Civil War, 317–345, 433; destruction, 319, 324, 342; and intellectuals, 342–345, 433
Colonies, 166–167, 285–286
Columbus, 151, 157, 158
Common Market, 355, 417, 418, 426
Communes, 295–296
Communism: influence, 314, 371,

403; judged by Bowers, 327–333; and Republican victory, 320–322
Communists: and civil war, 319, 321, 322, 326, 331–332; in Cortes, 316; under Franco, 371; after Franco, 403
Concordat of 1953, 353, 417
Confederación Nacional del Trabajo (C.N.T.), 296–297
Conquistadores, 152, 157–160, 165, 177; as nobles, 233
Constitution: of 1812, 243; of 1931, 303, 306; of 1978, 404
Conversion: to Islam, 61; of Jews, 38–39, 143–146, 147–149; and Moors, 148–149; Visigoths, 38
Cooperatives, 295–296
Córdoba: and anarchists, 294; and Jews, 143; and Moors, 54–62, 64–65, 89; Mosque of, 50–53; and Romans, 32, 34
Córdoba, Pedro de, 159
Cortes (parliament), 94, 151, 236, 314, 403, 408; of Toledo, 144; of 1812, 302; of today, 408
Cortés, Hernán, 158, 233
Costa, Joaquín, 262
Coup of 1981, 407
Cuba, 255, 263, 284, 398

Dance of the Seises, 32, 105
Dancing, 32, 73–74, 238, 367
Dictatorship: Franco, 351 ff.; Primo de Rivera, 290
Divorce, 404, 412
Dollar: reserves, 408; value of, 408
Domingo, Plácido, 432
Drama, 207–211; Golden Age, 199–202
Dress, 179, 236, 357, 422
Drought, 428
Drugs, 414, 415

Ebro River, 18, 24, 25
Economic growth, 370
Economy: and foreign investments, 381; and Franco, 370, 380; and government investments, 381;

Economy (*continued*)
since 1960, 380; and stock market, 375, 380; and tourists, 377, 426
Education: in the 18th century, 234, 237, 239; and Franco, 354, 371, 389; since 1960, 392, 405; in the 1980s, 405, 416; under the Republic, 309; under the Romans, 31; and universities, 416; and women, 392, 420
Eisenhower, Dwight, 358
Elections: of 1931, 305–306; of 1933, 314; of 1977, 403; of 1982, 408
El Greco, 213–218
El País, 410, 411
El Sol, 289, 410
Embargo, arms, 335
Emigration, 396
Empire: Charles V, 164; Moslem, 46–48; Roman, 31, 32
Encina, Juan del, 149, 152, 221
Encyclopedia, Isidor's, 39–40
Erasmus, 167, 170
Escorial, 214, 218, 356; construction, 171–172, 174
Estates, 13, 122–123, 301, 386, 393
Exiles under Franco, 344–345

Falange, 317, 349; and Franco, 350
Fascism: and Azaña government, 328; and civil war, 336; and Franco, 322
Feijóo, Father Benito Jerónimo, 238–239
Ferdinand of Aragon, 72–73, 111, 153–154
Ferdinand and Isabella, 33, 140–154, 162; Inquisition, 144–149; and nobles, 144, 146, 151
Ferdinand VI, 230, 231, 239
Ferdinand VII, 243–246, 248, 249
Feria, 128
Fernando el Santo, 4, 64, 65, 68–69, 95, 96, 104, 105; and Jews, 112; and sheep, 124–125
Ferrer, Francisco, 286–287
Floods, 428

Food, 176–177, 422, 432
France, 5–6, 85, 238, 334, 335, 418; and Bourbons, 227–229; and Republic, 321
Franco, General Francisco, 105, 242, 314–316, 322–324, 351–353; and army revolt, 317, 321; and Basques, 356, 400; and church-state, 232, 344; criticisms of, 400; death of, 401; and economy, 370, 380; executions, 324; and Fascists, 320, 334–335; government, since 1973, 399 ff.; and industry, 372, 374; and intellectuals, 271, 342–345, 356; and literature, 77; and Morocco, 351; and negativism, 320; and Philip II, 11, 13, 346, 347; resignation as Prime Minister, 399; and U.S. Catholics, 324; and Valley of the Fallen, 346–351
Fueros, 93–94, 111

Galdós, Benito Pérez, 186, 264–268
Galicia, 15–17, 80–81, 366 ff.; poetry, 99
Ganivet, Angel, 261–262; quoted, 11, 13–14, 326, 361
Garcilaso, 198
Gay groups, 412
General Chronicle, 100–101
"Generation of 1898," 262–263, 264, 269
Geography, 1–2, 8, 15–22, 366, 433
Germany, 321, 322, 333–334
Gibbon, Edward, 28–29, 30, 31, 34
Gibraltar, 26, 228, 417, 418, 431
Gil Robles, José María, 314–317, 329
Giner de los Ríos, Francisco, 259–260, 288, 354
Giralda Tower, 67, 69, 70, 104, 359
Gold, 30, 157, 165; of Republic, 336–337
Góngora, 191–194, 225, 227
González, Felipe, 407, 408
Goths. *See* Visigoths
Goya, Francisco, 246–248; etchings, 244, 247–248; and Charles IV, 238
Gracián, Baltasar, 205–206, 368

Granada, 20, 72, 89, 95, 359; fall, 146–147, 149; and Ferdinand III, 68–69; under Franco, 76–77; manufacturing, 165; and Moriscos, 149, 173
Great Britain, 322, 335, 431
Greco, El, 213–218
Greeks, 7, 26–27
Guadalete River, 42, 43
Guadalquivir, 8–9, 43, 50
Guitar, 222–223, 382
Gypsies, 21, 73

Hadrian, 31
Hamilton, Thomas L., 336
Hannibal, 27–28
Hapsburgs, 162–175, 223–227
Hayes, Francis C., quoted, 200
Henry IV, 139–140, 141
Henry of Trastamare, 106–107, 109, 143
Hercules, 26
Hermandades de Castilla, 123, 144
Hispania, 28–29, 40
Hitler, Adolf, 322, 328, 329, 333–334
Hume, Martin, 36

Ibáñez, Vicente Blasco, 21–22, 268–270
Iberians, 6–7, 9, 24–27, 36
Ibn Khaldun, 48
Income, per capita, 371, 383, 417
Index expurgatorius, 168
Individualism, destructive, 11–12, 361
Industrial boom, 370 ff.
Industrialization process, 372
Industry: in Andalusia, 132, 396; foreign-controlled, 381
Inflation, 408, 428
Inns, 176–178, 235–236, 377
Inquisition, 170, 182–183, 190, 191, 202; established, 142, 144, 145; and Jews, 142, 144–148; and Moslems, 142, 145, 146, 147, 149; re-established, 246, 248
Institución Libre de Enseñanza, 259, 288, 354
Instituto Nacional de Industria, 381

Intellectualism, modern, 241–242, 259–264, 409
Intellectuals: and censorship, 408–411; and Franco, 342–345
Intermarriage, 61, 111
International Brigades, 321, 334, 337
Irrigation, 20, 21, 224, 301, 372, 387
Isabel II, 254–255
Isabella the Catholic, 4, 72–73, 124, 132–136, 140–141, 162. See also Ferdinand and Isabella
Isidor of Seville, 39–40
Islam, 42, 46–47. See also Moors
Italy, 321, 322, 328, 329, 333–334

James, Saint, 30, 83–85, 87, 88, 91, 364
Jerez, 42, 391
Jesuits, 19, 186, 241, 246; disbanded, 230, 232, 311, 312
Jews, 33, 34, 93, 112, 120, 133; and Alfonso X, 97, 98, 102; banished, 39; in Cordoba, 62–64; and Inquisition, 142, 144–148; and Moors, 142; and Peter the Cruel, 110–111, 143; work of, 110–111
Jiménez de Cisneros, Cardinal, 33, 148, 150, 163
Jiménez, Juan Ramón, 259, 260, 432
John of the Cross, 190, 191
John II, 132–136
Juana la Beltraneja, 139, 142
Juana of Castile, 162
Juan, Don, 109–110; Tirso play, 202, 207–208; Zorrilla play, 207, 251
Juan of Austria, Don, 173
Juan Carlos de Borbon, King, 399, 401–403

Labor, 233, 312, 379, 417
Land reform, 301, 385; and Republic, 312
Language: Castilian, 92, 99, 151, 405; Latin, 29, 35, 39
Largo Caballero, 301, 312, 314, 315, 317, 330, 336, 350; and Communists, 314, 315, 338, 341

Larra, Mariano José de, 250–254
Latifundia, 13, 123, 301, 386, 393
Latin, 29, 35, 39
Law: and Alfonso X, 98–99; Roman, 35; Visigothic, 93, 125
Leftists, 285, 301, 314–316
León, 19, 80–82, 94, 105
León, Fray Luis de, 190, 221
Lerroux, Alejandro, 313–316
Liberalism: and Franco, 342–345; and Isabel II, 254–256; and religion, 413, 417
Literature: and Alfonso X, 97–102, 103; Arab, 48, 63–64, 117; awards, 432; ballads, 43–44; *Book of Good Love*, 114–117; Castilian, 4, 92, 93, 105, 136; *Celestina*, 154–157, 186; and conquistadores, 158; and Franco, 77; Golden Age, 161–162, 211; Isidor, 39–40; and John II, 133–135; modern, 262–264, 269; novels (*see* Novel); poetry (*see* Poetry); Roman, 31
Longfellow, Henry W., 136–138
Lope de Vega, 150, 199–204, 211
Lorca, García, 8–9, 191, 227, 260, 269, 342–343; quoted, 75–76
Loyalists, defined, 319
Loyola, Ignatius, 19
Luna, Don Alvaro de, 132, 135–136

Machado, Antonio, 259, 343; quoted, 263, 370
Machiavelli, 153–154
Madariaga, Salvador de, 290, 299, 305, 310, 316, 331, 344; and Communists, 340–341; quoted, 56, 259, 264, 346
Madrid, 1, 5, 318–319, 357, 373; capital, 3, 170–171, 178, 434; and Charles III, 230, 235; University City, 319, 357
Maeztu, Ramiro de, 242, 343
Maimonides of Córdoba, 62, 65
Málaga, 25, 146
Mancha, La, 19
Manrique, Jorge, 136–138
Marañón, Gregorio, quoted, 242

Marranos, 144–147, 149
Martial, 31–32
Martyrs, Christian, 30–31, 37–38
Masons, 241
Matesa case, 389
Matthews, Herbert L., 323, 332–333
Mayorazgo, 122–123
Medievalism and anarchism, 294
Medina Azahara, 7, 57–60
Medina del Campo, 165
Mérida, 30, 34
Mexico, 158
Military, 407, 425
Missions, 159, 186
Model towns, 390
Moncloa Pact, 408
Monopolies, colonial, 166
Moors, 25, 33, 41–44, 61–62; civilization, 55–57, 59–63, 97–98; and Fernando el Santo, 68–69; government, 53–57, 59–62, 64–68, 71–72; and Jews, 142. *See also* Arabs
Moriscos, 148–149, 173, 224
Morocco, 285–287, 316, 317; in 1921, 289–290; U.S. bases, 423 ff.
Moslems. *See* Moors
Mosque of Córdoba, 50–53
Mozárabes, 54, 63
Mudéjar, 107–108, 221
Murillo, 219–220
Music, 103–104, 131, 258, and Bourbons, 231; Golden Age, 221–223; Greek, 27; instruments, 60, 87, 99, 131, 222; and Isabella, 72–73
Mussolini, 333
Mysticism, 189–190

Napoleon, 244–246, 250
NATO, 417, 425
Navarre, 17–18, 82, 141, 416
Navarrete, 18
Navarro, Arias, 401
Negrín, Dr. Juan, 331–333, 336–341
Newspapers, 77, 409–411
New World, 152, 157–160, 165–166, 224, 225
Niña Bonita, La, 304
Nobel Prize, 432

Nobility, 122–123, 144
Novel: first, 154–157; Galdós, 264–268; Golden Age, 187; picaresque, 173, 176, 188

Olla podrida, 176
Opera, 432
Opus Dei, 354–355
Orders, military, 88–89, 144
Ortega y Gasset, 273–277, 278; quoted, 274–277
Oviedo, 80, 315, 366

Paella, 422
Painting, 212–220; cave, 23–24; El Greco, 213–218; Goya, 246–248; Picasso, 432; Velázquez, 217–219
Palace Song Book, 221–222
Pamplona, 18, 379, 396
Parliament. *See* Cortes
Pelayo, 48–49, 61
Pelayo, Menéndez, 241–242
Pereda, José María de, 10
Peter I, the Cruel, 106–110, 111, 127, 143
Philip the Handsome, 162
Philip II, 19, 168, 214–215; and bloodletting, 174–175
Philip III, 222–224
Philip IV, 218, 226
Philip V, 228–230
Phoenicians, 25
Pícaros, 172, 188–189, 250
Picasso, 432
Pizarro, 158, 165
Plague, 124, 127, 142–143
Plateresque, defined, 105
Plays, 199–202, 207–211
Pliny, 29, 32
Poetry, 43–44; Calderón, 208–210; Castilian, 133, 136–138; folk, 258; Galician, 16, 99; Garcilaso de la Vega, 187; Hebrew, 63–64, 118–119; and John II, 133–134; Lope de Vega, 199; modern, 432; Mozarabic, 63–64; Sem Tob, 117
Polls, public opinion, 412, 413, 428
Pollution, 374; beaches, 379

Pope, 150, 151, 167, 169–170
Pornography, 411
Portugal, king of, 140, 141–142
Poverty, 302–303, 347, 393, 428
Prado Museum, 218, 248, 374, 378
Priests: and Franco, 353, 354; and sex, 113–116
Prieto, Indalecio, 301, 337
Prim, General, 255
Primo de Rivera, General, 269, 290–292, 317
Primo de Rivera, José Antonio, 348–351
Protestants, 14, 15, 231–232; and Franco, 324; and Hapsburgs, 167–168, 170
Pyrenees, 6, 17–19

Quevedo, 150, 184; quoted, 204
Quixote, Don, 130, 185, 194–197
Quixote, Don, and Sancho, 7, 19, 195–197, 213, 227
Quixotism, 298, 309

Railways, 4–5, 254–255, 291, 372
Ramón y Cajal, 259–260
Rebellion: and Charles V, 163–165; of 1820, 248
Reconquest, 78–82, 88–90, 94–95, 106–110, 146, 150; and ballads, 44–45; and sheep, 124
Reform: and church, 293; land, 301, 312, 386
Religion: and Franco, 353–356; since 1960, 354; and Republic, 267, 293, 307, 311; and Romans, 30–31, 35, 37–39, 41. *See also* Jews; Moors
Renaissance, 152–157, 187; and Ferdinand, 153–154; literature, 154–157
Republic, First, 255
Republic, Second, 305; and Ambassador Bowers, 327–333; and anticlericalism, 293, 307, 310–312; army, 321, 337; and Communists, 331–333, 336–343; errors of, 309–311, 312–314, 317–318, 337; and labor, 312; and land reform, 312–313; and Russia, 321, 323, 326–327,

Republic, Second (*continued*)
334; and tourist bureau, 313; and
Unamuno, 270
Residence of Students, 260
Riego, Hymn of, 248–249
Ríos, Fernando de los, 121, 159, 301,
309, 344
Rivera, José Antonio (Primo de Ri-
vera), 317, 331, 347, 348–351
Roads, 291
Roderick, King, 41–45, 61
Rojas, Ferdinand de, 154
Romances, 118–120, 130
Romans, 7, 27–32, 35–36
Romantics, 250–251
Roosevelt, President Franklin Delano,
323, 335, 336
Rosalía de Castro, 16–17
Ruiz, José Martínez, 280. *See also*
Azorín
Ruiz, Juan, 114–117
Ruiz de Alarcón, 206
Rumasa, 428
Russia, 321, 323, 326–327, 334, 367

Sacramonte caves, 73
Saguntum, 26, 27, 30
Saints, 30–31
Salamanca, university at, 98, 149, 183,
234; and Unamuno, 270
Salaries, modern day, 383, 417
Sánchez Albornoz, Claudio, 55, 79
Sancho IV, 103
Sanctity, odor of, 33–34
San Juan de los Reyes, 358
Santander, 23, 377
Santiago, 76, 83, 84, 85, 86, 360, 361;
bells, 52, 64; cathedral, 86–88;
Hostal, 361, 363
Santiago de Compostela, 76, 84–86
Santillana del Mar, 23
Saragossa, 18, 89, 90
Schools: of Giner, 259–261; modern
day, 405, 416; and Republic, 309–
310
Science: and Christians, 67; and
Moors, 56–57

Segovia, 29, 141, 165
Segovia, Andrés, 222–223, 432
Sender, Ramón, 343, 344
Separatism, 3, 35–36, 405–406
Sephardim, 120n
Seville, 20–21, 34, 68, 81, 165, 359;
and Alfonso X, 69–70, 71; cathe-
dral, 32, 69, 104–105, 359; Inquis-
ition, 142; and Jews, 143; under
Moors, 65–71; mosque, 66–67
Sex: in Middle Ages, 109–110, 113–
117; today, 412
Sheep, 124–127
Shells of Santiago, 76, 85–86
Siglo de Oro, 161–224
Silver, 165, 166
Singing, 104, 363, 382, 391
Socialists, 300, 305, 308, 313, 315, 317,
327, 330, 331, 408
Socialized state, 408
Social security, 383
Songs, 221–222, 365; *cante jondo*, 21,
382; protest, 248; to the Virgin, 99–
100
South America, 158
Soviet Union, 334, 367
Spain: and Celts, 25, 26; church, 30–
31, 353–355, 417; climate, 3; as co-
lonial power, 166, 226; economy (*see*
Economy); and French Revolution,
243; geography, 1–2, 8, 15–22, 366,
433; and Greeks, 26–27; and Iberians, 24–25, 26; isolation of, 352,
426; and Jews (*see* Jews); medievalism, 250; and Moors (*see* Moors); and
New World, 152, 157–160; and
Phoenicians, 25; Romans, 7, 27–32,
35–36; and Sarrió, 281–283; self-
criticism, 10–11; social changes since
1960, 370 ff.; state church, 38, 352;
unifying (*see* Reconquest)
Spain in Revolt, 315
Spanish: and Africa, 6–7; Mozarabic,
63–64; and pride, 11–14. *See also*
Castilians
Spanish Civil War, The, 332, 334, 335,
433

Stimson, Henry L., 323, 335
Stock market, 380, 381
Strikes: in 1873, 294; in 1909, 286; in 1911, 297; in 1917, 289; and Primo de Rivera, 292; and Republic, 315, 317; and socialists, 300–301
Syndicalism, 296–297

Teresa de Jesús, Santa, 189–191
Terrorism, 426
Tertullian, 30, 237
Textiles, 165
Theaters, 210–211
Thomas, Hugh, 332, 334, 335, 338, 342
Tirso de Molina, 110, 202, 206–208
Toledo, 37–39, 41, 90, 165, 358; and Alfonso X, 97–98; archbishop, 307; cathedral, 104; and El Greco, 214, 215–216
Tolerance: Alfonso X, 102; in Middle Ages, 93, 95; Moslem, 50; Peter the Cruel, 110–111; for Protestants, 167–168
Tolosa, Las Navas de, 94
Tombs: Escorial, 171, 347; Seville, 104; Valley of the Fallen, 346 ff.
Torquemada, 145, 147
Tourist bureau, 313
Tourist industry, 376, 426–427
Tower of Gold, 66, 70
Towns in Golden Age, 175–184; and medieval, 120–123, 126–132
Transportation, 372
Trend, J. B., 65, 227, 259, 260, 345
Trent, Council of, 187–188

Unamuno, 11, 12, 36, 260, 261, 269, 270; in civil war, 343–344; exiled, 291, 292; quoted, 195, 270–273, 433

Unemployment, 379, 427, 428
United States: embargo, 335–336; military bases, 423, 424; and Republic, 322, 323, 324. See also America
Universities in 18th century, 234–235; since 1960, 416
University City, 319, 357

Valencia, 21–22, 90, 165, 171
Valladolid, 115, 141, 169
Valle-Inclán, Ramón María del, 17
Valley of the Fallen, 346–351
Vandals, 20, 34–35
Vanguardia, 417
Vega, Garcilaso de la, 167, 186, 187
Velázquez, 217–219
Venta de Baños, 41
Vincent, Saint, 50, 53
Visigoths, 35, 37, 40–44; and bathing, 32–33
Vives, Luis, 152

Warfare: Charles V, 165–167; Philip II, 169–170, 172–174. See also Civil War
Women, modern day, 419–422
Wool, 125–127
Work: and Castilians, 102, 121; and pícaros, 189
World War I, 288–289
World War II, 322, 352

Yoke and the Arrows, The, 323, 332–333
Youth, modern day, 417 ff.

Zarzuela, 432
Zorrilla, José, 207, 251